KB093691

영어능력 시험 대비 필수어휘 학습서

ACTIVATOR
VOCA

각종 영어능력 시험 대비 필수어휘 학습서

ACTIVATOR VOCA

영어 어휘는 영어를 듣고, 말하고, 읽고, 쓰는 능력에 가장
기본이 되며, 영어를 쉽고 빠르게 익히는 데 중요한 역할을 합니다.
그렇다면 영어 어휘 학습은 어떻게 해야 할까요?

무엇보다, 영어 어휘는 무작정 암기하는 것이 아니라
실제 문맥 안에서의 정확한 뜻과 쓰임을 익혀야 합니다.
또한, 모르는 어휘는 전후 문맥을 따져 그 뜻을
유추해 내는 연습을 하는 것도 중요합니다.
영어 어휘 학습에 대한 Master Key,
바로 Activator VOCA에 모두 제시되어 있습니다.

Activator VOCA는 표제어를 주제별로 제시하여, 중요
어휘들을 전문적이고 체계적으로 학습할 수 있게 했습니다.
각 표제어마다 영영 정의와 예문이 제시되어, 명확하게
이해하고 암기할 수 있습니다.

TOEFL, TOEIC, TEPS, SAT, IELTS, G-TELP, 공무원, 편입,
특목고 시험 등 각종 영어능력 시험의 최신 경향을 분석하여,
다양한 시험 문제 유형에 대비할 수 있게 했습니다.

엄선된 표제어들과 함께 제시된 유의어, 반의어, 파생어,
그리고 Useful Tips를 통해 어휘 암기 및 학습 효과를
극대화할 수 있습니다.

각 Lesson 학습 후 제공되는 Exercises, 그리고 다섯 개의
Lesson 학습 후 제공되는 Review Test를 통해 학습한
어휘에 대한 이해도를 측정하고 다시 점검할 수 있습니다.

ACTIVATOR VOCA
Features & Format

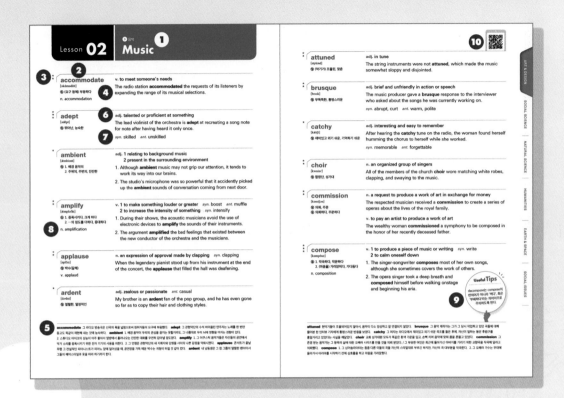

LESSON PAGES

❶ 분야별로 선별된 Lesson 주제
각종 영어능력 시험에서 빈도 높게 출제되는 선별된 주제들을 확인할 수 있습니다.

❷ 각종 시험 분석 후 엄선된 표제어
엄선된 표제어와 우리말 뜻을 암기하고, 발음을 익힐 수 있습니다.

❸ 한 눈에 보이는 단어 중요도
표제어의 중요도를 별 한 개부터 세 개까지로 표시했습니다. (★★★ 가장 중요)

❹ 아카데믹하고 전문적인 예문
각 Lesson의 주제와 관련된 아카데믹하고 전문적인 예문들이 제공되어 독해 실력 향상에 도움을 줍니다.

❺ 정확하고 자연스러운 우리말 옮김
표제어의 예문에 대한 자연스러운 우리말 해석을 보며, 어휘와 문장에 대한 이해도를 높일 수 있습니다.

❻ 품사 품사와 함께 표제어의 의미가 영문으로 제공되어, 정확한 이해를 돕습니다.
【표기】 n. 명사   v. 동사   adj. 형용사   adv. 부사   prep. 전치사

❼ 유의어·반의어 제시된 유의어와 반의어를 통해, 표제어를 더 명확하게 이해하고 어휘력을 기를 수 있습니다.
【표기】 syn. 유의어   ant. 반의어

❽ 파생어 표제어와 연관된 파생어를 함께 학습하며, 어휘를 확장할 수 있습니다.

❾ Useful Tips 단어의 실질적인 활용에 도움이 되는 정보를 얻을 수 있습니다.

❿ QR 코드 Lesson별로 QR 코드가 제공되며, 원어민의 정확한 발음으로 표제어를 들을 수 있습니다.

EXERCISES

각 Lesson의 학습을 마친 후, 문제를 풀며 학습한
표제어들을 점검해 볼 수 있습니다. Exercises 문제에
사용되는 문장들은 그 Lesson이 속한 Chapter
전체에서 주제를 선정해, 해당 표제어들이 다양한
상황에서 어떻게 활용되는지 알아볼 수 있습니다.

REVIEW TEST

다섯 개의 Lesson마다 Review Test가 제공됩니다.
각종 시험에서 가장 많이 나오는 문제 유형들을
분석하여 출제했습니다. 빠른 문제 풀이 시간을
요하는 문장 형태의 문제와 독해력을 요하는 지문
형태의 문제들을 골고루 접할 수 있어, 다양한 영어
시험에 효율적으로 대비할 수 있습니다.

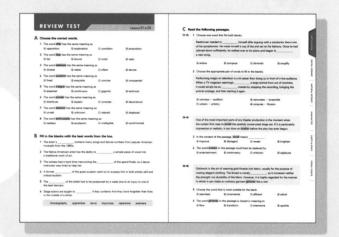

EXPANDING VOCABULARY

각 Chapter 학습을 마친 후, Expanding Vocabulary 섹션을 통해
다양한 접두사, 어근, 접미사를 접하며 영단어에 대한 이해도를
높이고 어휘 지식을 확장할 수 있습니다.

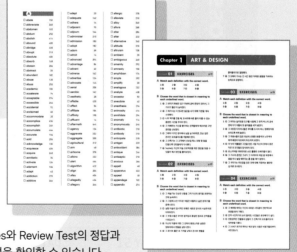

INDEX & FINAL CHECKUP

학습한 표제어를 최종적으로 점검해 볼 수 있습니다.
아는 표제어는 체크하고, 모르는 표제어는 해당
페이지로 돌아가 다시 한 번 암기할 수 있습니다.

ANSWER KEYS

Exercises와 Review Test의 정답과
문장 해석을 확인할 수 있습니다.

www.ybmbooksam.com 에서는 표제어의 정확한 발음과 우리말 뜻이 담긴 MP3파일을
다운로드 할 수 있으며, 어휘 문제를 만들고 풀어볼 수 있습니다.

Lesson Plan

학습 플랜

1 개월

단기간 최대한 많은
단어들을 암기해야
할 때 권장

학습 목표 하루에 2개의 Lesson을 학습하여 한 달 만에 완성

1일 분량 1일 60~84개의 표제어와 그에 해당하는 예문, 유의어와 반의어, 파생어

각 Lesson 학습 전, 이전 Lesson의 표제어를 살펴보고 우리말 뜻과 단어의
쓰임을 머리 속에 빠르게 떠올리며 복습

↓

해당 Lesson의 표제어와 예문, 유의어와 반의어, 파생어를 읽고 표제어 암기

Daily Lesson Plan에서 하루 2개의 Day 분량을 체크하여 진도를 확인하세요!

Daily Lesson Plan

DAY 01	DAY 02	DAY 03	DAY 04	DAY 05
☐ 어휘 학습법 숙지	☐ L1 복습	☐ L2 복습	☐ L3 복습	☐ L4 복습
☐ L1 학습	☐ L2 학습	☐ L3 학습	☐ L4 학습	☐ L5 학습
				☐ Review Test

DAY 11	DAY 12	DAY 13	DAY 14	DAY 15
☐ L10 복습	☐ L11 복습	☐ L12 복습	☐ L13 복습	☐ L14 복습
☐ L11 학습	☐ L12 학습	☐ L13 학습	☐ L14 학습	☐ L15 학습
				☐ Review Test

DAY 21	DAY 22	DAY 23	DAY 24	DAY 25
☐ L20 복습	☐ L21 복습	☐ L22 복습	☐ L23 복습	☐ L24 복습
☐ L21 학습	☐ L22 학습	☐ L23 학습	☐ L24 학습	☐ L25 학습
				☐ Review Test

DAY 31	DAY 32	DAY 33	DAY 34	DAY 35
☐ L30 복습	☐ L31 복습	☐ L32 복습	☐ L33 복습	☐ L34 복습
☐ L31 학습	☐ L32 학습	☐ L33 학습	☐ L34 학습	☐ L35 학습
				☐ Review Test

DAY 41	DAY 42	DAY 43	DAY 44	DAY 45
☐ L40 복습	☐ L41 복습	☐ L42 복습	☐ L43 복습	☐ L44 복습
☐ L41 학습	☐ L42 학습	☐ L43 학습	☐ L44 학습	☐ L45 학습
				☐ Review Test

DAY 51	DAY 52	DAY 53	DAY 54	DAY 55
☐ L50 복습	☐ L51 복습	☐ L52 복습	☐ L53 복습	☐ L54 복습
☐ L51 학습	☐ L52 학습	☐ L53 학습	☐ L54 학습	☐ L55 학습
				☐ Review Test

학습 플랜

2개월

ACTIVATOR VOCA
사용에 최적화된
학습 플랜

학습 목표 하루에 1개의 Lesson을 학습하여 두 달 만에 완성

1일 분량 1일 30~42개의 표제어와 그에 해당하는 예문, 유의어와 반의어, 파생어

각 Lesson 학습 전, 이전 Lesson의 표제어뿐 아니라 유의어, 반의어, 파생어도 함께 복습하여 많은 단어들을 심도 있게 암기

⬇

해당 Lesson의 표제어와 예문, 유의어와 반의어를 읽고 표제어 암기

⬇

유의어와 반의어, 파생어까지 암기하여 표제어에 대한 이해력 높이고 어휘력 확장

Daily Lesson Plan에서 Day별로 학습 완료한 부분을 체크하여 진도를 확인하세요!

DAY 06	**DAY 07**	**DAY 08**	**DAY 09**	**DAY 10**
☐ L5 복습	☐ L6 복습	☐ L7 복습	☐ L8 복습	☐ L9 복습
☐ L6 학습	☐ L7 학습	☐ L8 학습	☐ L9 학습	☐ L10 학습
				☐ Review Test
DAY 16	**DAY 17**	**DAY 18**	**DAY 19**	**DAY 20**
☐ L15 복습	☐ L16 복습	☐ L17 복습	☐ L18 복습	☐ L19 복습
☐ L16 학습	☐ L17 학습	☐ L18 학습	☐ L19 학습	☐ L20 학습
				☐ Review Test
DAY 26	**DAY 27**	**DAY 28**	**DAY 29**	**DAY 30**
☐ L25 복습	☐ L26 복습	☐ L27 복습	☐ L28 복습	☐ L29 복습
☐ L26 학습	☐ L27 학습	☐ L28 학습	☐ L29 학습	☐ L30 학습
				☐ Review Test
DAY 36	**DAY 37**	**DAY 38**	**DAY 39**	**DAY 40**
☐ L35 복습	☐ L36 복습	☐ L37 복습	☐ L38 복습	☐ L39 복습
☐ L36 학습	☐ L37 학습	☐ L38 학습	☐ L39 학습	☐ L40 학습
				☐ Review Test
DAY 46	**DAY 47**	**DAY 48**	**DAY 49**	**DAY 50**
☐ L45 복습	☐ L46 복습	☐ L47 복습	☐ L48 복습	☐ L49 복습
☐ L46 학습	☐ L47 학습	☐ L48 학습	☐ L49 학습	☐ L50 학습
				☐ Review Test
DAY 56	**DAY 57**	**DAY 58**	**DAY 59**	**DAY 60**
☐ L55 복습	☐ L56 복습	☐ L57 복습	☐ L58 복습	☐ L59 복습
☐ L56 학습	☐ L57 학습	☐ L58 학습	☐ L59 학습	☐ L60 학습 & 복습
				☐ Review Test

➔ Final Checkup으로 아는 단어와 모르는 단어를 체크하며 최종 점검

> 영어 어휘를 학습하고 암기하는 것은 영어 실력을 키우는 데 필수적입니다. 더 많은 어휘를 알고 있을수록 영어를 읽고, 말하고, 쓰고, 듣는 것이 수월해 집니다. 하지만 현존하는 수많은 영어 단어를 모두 외우는 것은 불가능하며, 매년 새로운 단어들도 추가되고 있습니다. 무조건 외우는 것 대신, 효율적으로 영어 어휘력을 향상시킬 수 있는 방법들을 알아봅시다. 🌙🌙

⏻ 글의 주제나 문맥을 통한 어휘 학습

방대한 양의 어휘를 효율적으로 이해하고 습득하기 위해서는 먼저 글의 주제나 문맥을 통해 어휘의 의미를 유추할 수 있어야 합니다. 글의 흐름이나 글 속에 함께 쓰인 다른 어휘 단서들을 통해 어휘의 의미를 파악하면, 그 어휘를 더 효과적으로 암기할 수 있고 추후 적절한 상황에서 사용할 수 있습니다.

> The **cacophonous** sounds of the construction work taking place on a nearby street made it impossible for the students in the library to concentrate.

이 문장에서 cacophonous라는 단어의 의미를 모른다 해도, 문장의 주제와 문장 속의 다른 어휘 단서들을 통해 cacophonous가 '귀에 거슬리는'이라는 뜻을 지닌다는 것을 유추할 수 있습니다. 이렇게 어휘의 의미를 파악한 후에는 사전을 통해 사전적 의미를 학습하고, 새로운 문장을 만들어봄으로써 어휘를 온전히 이해하고 암기하는 것이 좋습니다. Activator VOCA는 모든 표제어에 대한 주제별 예문을 제공하여, 문장 속에서 어떤 의미로 쓰이는지 확인하고 숙지할 수 있습니다.

> During the Middle Ages, **plague** was one of the greatest threats to humanity. The "Black Death," for example, is believed to have killed approximately one third of Europe's population in the 14th century. Medical and scientific advances have now given us many tools with which to protect ourselves. Despite this, viruses and other infectious diseases continue to **plague** our society, causing death and disruption.

이 문단에서 plague는 동음이의어로, 처음에는 '전염병'이라는 의미로 쓰였고, 뒤에서는 '괴롭게 하다'라는 의미로 쓰였습니다. 더 보편적으로 쓰이는 의미인 '전염병'으로만 알고 그대로 해석한다면, 글의 의미를 온전히 이해하기 어렵습니다. 글의 전체적인 흐름과 주변 어휘들을 분석하여 효과적으로 어휘의 의미를 파악하고 암기하는 것이 좋습니다. Activator VOCA의 Review Test에서 이러한 동음이의어를 활용한 문제들을 직접 풀며 연습해 볼 수 있습니다.

구성 단위를 활용한 어휘 학습

영어 어휘는 접두사, 어근, 접미사의 구성 단위로 나누어지고, 주로 라틴어, 그리스어, 앵글로색슨어에서 유래했습니다. 이러한 구성 단위들은 고유의 의미를 지니고 있어서, 낯선 어휘의 대략적인 의미를 파악하는 데 큰 도움이 됩니다.

접두사 Prefixes

접두사는 어근이나 다른 단어의 앞에 붙어서 그 뜻을 확장하거나 특정한 뜻을 더해 새로운 단어를 만듭니다. 접두사의 의미를 알면 단어의 뜻을 유추하는 데 큰 단서가 됩니다. 예를 들어, over-는 앵글로색슨어에서 나온 접두사로, '너무, 과도하게, 넘은'이라는 의미를 가지고 있습니다. 이를 통해, overdose(과다 복용), overstock(과다 공급), overwhelm(압도하다) 등의 단어를 몰라도, 그 의미를 유추할 수 있습니다.

어근 Roots

어근은 단어 형성 요소의 하나로, 단어의 중심적이고 실질적인 의미를 가진 최소의 단위입니다. 어근의 앞뒤로 접두사나 접미사가 붙어 그 의미가 확장되거나 바뀔 수 있습니다. 예를 들어, serv는 라틴어에서 나온 어근으로, 'save, keep(가지고 있다, 간직하다)'이라는 의미입니다. 이것을 알아두면, conserve(보존하다), preserve(지키다, 보호하다), reservation(예약) 등의 단어를 접했을 때 그 의미를 훨씬 더 쉽게 파악하고 잘 기억할 수 있습니다.

접미사 Suffixes

접미사는 단어의 끝부분에 위치해 특정한 뜻을 나타냅니다. 접미사인 -en은 '…하게 하다'라는 의미가 있어, fresh(신선한), sharp(날카로운), threat(위협) 등과 같은 형용사나 명사 뒤에 붙어 freshen(신선하게 하다), sharpen(날카롭게 하다), threaten(위협하다)으로 바꿉니다. 또한 접미사는 품사를 바꿔 주는 역할도 하는데, 예를 들어 -ment, -ness는 단어의 끝에 붙어 명사로 바꾸어 주고(ex. movement, sadness), -ish, -al 등은 형용사로 바꿔 주는 역할을 하며(ex. foolish, political), -ly는 형용사 끝에 붙어 부사로 만들어 줍니다(ex. softly). Activator VOCA 학습 시, 각 Lesson에 수록된 표제어들 아래에 주요 파생어가 제시되어 함께 익힐 수 있습니다.

Activator VOCA의 Expanding Vocabulary 섹션에서 다양한 접두사, 어근, 접미사 종류를 익혀, 어휘에 대한 이해도와 습득력을 확장시키세요!

CONTENTS

CHAPTER 3

Natural Science 자연 과학

CHAPTER 4

Humanities 인문학

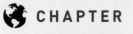

CHAPTER

Earth & Space 지구와 우주

CHAPTER

Social Issues 사회 문제

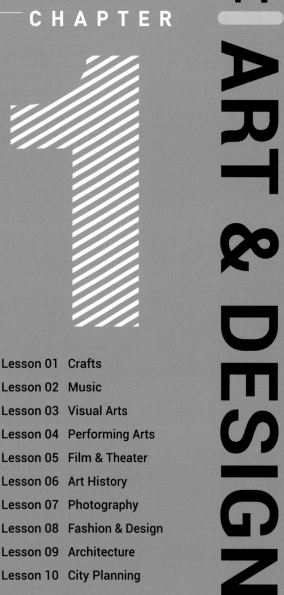

CHAPTER

1

ART & DESIGN

> 공예

Crafts

---

adhere
[ædhíər]

ⓥ 1. 붙다, 부착시키다
2. (주의·신념 등을) 고수하다

n. adhesion

v. 1 to stick firmly   2 to believe or follow the practices of

1. Epoxy is one of the most useful glues for household design projects because it will **adhere** to plastic, metal, or wood.

2. The announcer explained that any artists who failed to **adhere** to the craft competition guidelines would be excluded.

---

adroit
[ədrɔ́it]

ⓐ 솜씨 있는, 능숙한

adj. clever and skillful in using one's hands or mind

The **adroit** knitter impressed everyone with his talent by completing a whole sweater in a short time.

syn. nimble   *ant.* clumsy

---

affluent
[æfluənt]

ⓐ 부유한

adj. having a great amount of money or possessions

In late-15th-century Florence, **affluent** noblemen used to give financial assistance to metalworkers, jewelry makers, and woodcarvers.

syn. wealthy

---

apprentice
[əpréntis]

ⓝ 견습생, 도제

n. a person who learns a trade from a highly skilled individual for a fixed amount of time

The stained-glass artist was looking for an **apprentice** to whom he could pass on tricks of the trade.

---

artisan
[ɑ́ːrtəzən]

ⓝ 장인, 숙련공

n. a person who is very skilled at making artistic objects by hand

Artisans across the world have been producing beautiful items that highlight their unique culture, such as the rugs of Turkey.

---

assiduous
[əsídʒuəs]

ⓐ 근면한, 부지런한

adj. hardworking and tireless

In 3500 BC, **assiduous** workers in China took silk from cocoons and dyed it to make colorful fabric.

syn. diligent

---

adhere 1. 에폭시 수지는 플라스틱이나 금속, 또는 목재에 붙기 때문에 가정 디자인 프로젝트에 가장 유용한 접착제 중 하나이다. 2. 그 아나운서는 공예전 지침을 지키지 않은 예술가들은 누구든 탈락될 것이라고 설명했다.   **adroit** 그 솜씨 있는 편물공은 짧은 시간 안에 스웨터 한 벌을 완성하는 재능을 보여 모두에게 깊은 인상을 주었다.   **affluent** 15세기 말 피렌체에서는 부유한 귀족들이 금속 세공인, 보석 제조인, 목각사들을 재정적으로 후원하곤 했다.   **apprentice** 그 스테인드글라스 장인은 업계의 비결을 전수해 줄 도제를 찾고 있었다.   **artisan** 전 세계 장인들은 터키의 양탄자처럼 그들의 독특한 문화를 돋보이게 해 주는 아름다운 물건들을 제작해 왔다.   **assiduous** 기원전 3500년에, 중국의 근면한 노동자들이 누에고치에서 명주실을 뽑아 그것을 염색해 화려한 직물을 만들었다.

ART & DESIGN

SOCIAL SCIENCE

NATURAL SCIENCE

HUMANITIES

EARTH & SPACE

SOCIAL ISSUES

★★★ **assist**
[əsíst]
ⓥ 돕다

v. to help someone or something

The man **assisted** the shop owner by melting wax and preparing dyes in order to make batik scarves.

ant. hinder

★★★ **concern**
[kənsə́ːrn]
ⓥ 1. 우려하게 만들다
2. 관련되다

v. 1 to make someone feel worried or troubled
2 to be about; to have to do with

1. The designer was **concerned** that the matchstick structure would fall apart.

2. The requirement of wearing a mask when handling pottery glaze did not **concern** Alex because he worked only with cloth.

★★ **critic**
[krítik]
ⓝ 비평가, 평론가
adj. critical

n. a professional commentator who gives opinions on films, books, or artistic works

Some **critics** felt the leather used in the handcrafted objects on display was not attractive enough.

Useful **Tips**
critic과 철자가 유사한 단어 critique는 '평론, 비평한 글'이라는 뜻으로 사용되므로 혼동하지 않도록 유의한다.

★★★ **decorate**
[dékərèit]
ⓥ 장식하다, 꾸미다

v. to make something look more appealing by adding items to it

The students **decorated** the classroom with origami and knitted lace for the open house.

syn. embellish

★★ **defect**
[díːfekt]
ⓝ 결함, 단점

n. a fault, flaw, or imperfection

The man asked for a refund when he found a **defect** in the wooden chair he had purchased the week before.

★★★ **delicate**
[délikət]
ⓐ 1. 섬세한, 우아한
2. 부서지기 쉬운, 연약한

adj. 1 very fine and attractive in structure or quality
2 easily broken or damaged *ant.* sturdy

1. The potter used his fingers to shape the clay into **delicate** twists and curves.

2. You must be extremely careful when handling glass, as it is far more **delicate** than wooden panels or plastic frames.

assist 그 남자는 밀랍 염색 스카프를 만들기 위해 왁스를 녹이고 염색제를 준비해 그 상점 주인을 도왔다.   **concern** 1. 그 디자이너는 성냥개비로 만든 그 구조물이 무너질까 우려했다. 2. Alex는 천만 가지고 작업했기 때문에 도예용 유약을 다룰 때 마스크를 착용해야 하는 규정은 그와 상관이 없었다.   **critic** 일부 비평가들은 전시된 수공예품에 사용된 가죽이 그다지 아름답지는 않다고 느꼈다.   **decorate** 그 학생들은 학급 공개일을 위해 종이 접기 작품과 편물 레이스로 교실을 장식했다.   **defect** 그 남자는 그 전주에 구입한 나무 의자에서 결함을 발견하자 환불을 요청했다.   **delicate** 1. 그 도공은 손가락으로 점토를 주물러 섬세한 꼬임과 곡선을 만들었다. 2. 유리는 목판이나 플라스틱 틀보다 훨씬 더 약하기 때문에 다룰 때 극히 조심해야 한다.

★

excel
[iksél]
ⓥ 탁월하다, 남을 능가하다

v. to be outstanding or highly skilled in something

To **excel** in knitting, one must memorize various patterns and practice on a daily basis.

ant. underperform

★
★
★

exquisite
[ikskwízit]
ⓐ 매우 아름다운, 정교한

adj. extremely beautiful; finely made

The bright colors, careful details, and unique patterns made the vase even more **exquisite**.

★

gilded
[gíldid]
ⓐ 금박을 입힌, 도금을 한

adj. covered with a thin layer of gold or gold paint

The **gilded** wooden box shone brighter than all of the plain wooden boxes around it.

syn. golden

★
★

glance
[glæns]
ⓝ 힐끗 봄
ⓥ 힐끗[얼핏] 보다, 곁눈질하다

n. a brief look   *syn.* peek

The flowers seemed real at first **glance**, but they were actually made of sugar.

v. to look at something briefly   *syn.* peek

As she worked on her paper lantern, the girl frequently **glanced** at the reference photo to make sure the details were correct.

★

glimmer
[glímər]
ⓥ (희미하게) 빛나다, 반짝거리다

v. to give off a dim or unsteady light

The stained glass **glimmered** in the sunlight and cast unsteady reflections across the floor.

syn. sparkle

★
★

intent
[intént]
ⓝ 계획, 목적
ⓐ 몰두[열중]하는

n. conscious plan; aim

The girl quilted with the **intent** of telling a story through the images of the design.

adj. showing great concentration and attention

The artist had an **intent** gaze on his face as he started to plan out the glass lamp.

---

excel 편물을 뛰어나게 잘 하려면, 다양한 패턴을 외우고 매일 연습해야 한다.   **exquisite** 밝은 색과 세심한 세부 사항, 독특한 문양이 그 꽃병을 훨씬 더 아름답게 만들었다.   **gilded** 금박을 입힌 그 나무 상자는 그 주변의 금박을 입히지 않은 모든 나무 상자들보다 더 밝게 빛났다.   **glance** 얼핏 보아 그 꽃들은 생화처럼 보였지만, 사실은 설탕으로 만들어진 것이었다. / 그 소녀는 종이 등을 만들면서 모든 세부 사항이 정확한지 확인하려고 참조용 사진을 자주 곁눈질했다.
glimmer 그 스테인드글라스가 햇빛을 받아 반짝이며 바닥 전체에 일렁이는 반사광을 드리웠다.   **intent** 그 소녀는 디자인의 이미지들을 통해 어떤 이야기를 전달하려는 목적으로 누비이불을 만들었다. / 그 유리 램프를 기획하기 시작할 때, 그 예술가의 얼굴에는 몰두한 표정이 떠올랐다.

★★ **intertwine**
[ìntərtwáin]
[동] 꼬아 짜다, 엮다

v. to twist two or more things together

After the willow is completely dry, it is soaked in water again before its strands are **intertwined** to form a basket.

syn. interlace

★★ **loom**
[lu:m]
[명] 베틀
[동] 불안하게 다가오다

n. a machine that weaves thread or yarn to form a cloth

The woman used a **loom** to create a beautiful tapestry that showed the story of her happy childhood.

v. to come into sight in an uncertain, grand, or frightening way

After the professor announced the final art assignment, the deadline **loomed** over the students.

★★ **luxurious**
[lʌgʒúəriəs]
[형] 호화로운, 화려한

adj. very expensive, elegant, or self-indulgent

After the students saw the **luxurious** jewelry and ceramics, they were inspired to create their own.

ant. modest

★★★ **material**
[mətíəriəl]
[명] 물질, 재료

n. matter; stuff

When creating a paper fan, the craftsman needs to find **materials** of the right size and weight to get the best results.

★★ **miniature**
[míniətʃər]
[명] 축소 모형
[형] 소형의

n. something (especially a replica) that is smaller than normal

The merchant produces **miniatures** that are modeled after sports stars, singers, and movie characters.

adj. small-scale, tiny *ant.* huge

To complete the dollhouse, **miniature** carpets, furniture, and figures are necessary.

★★ **ornamental**
[ɔ̀:rnəméntl]
[형] 장식의, 장식적인

adj. decorative; for show and not for functionality

The Easter eggs in the living room are purely **ornamental**, so they cannot be eaten.

ant. functional

intertwine 버드나무가 완전히 마른 후, 그 가닥을 꼬아 바구니를 만들기 전에 다시 물 속에 담가 둔다. **loom** 그 여자는 베틀을 이용해 자신의 행복했던 어린 시절 이야기를 보여 주는 아름다운 직물을 만들었다. / 그 교수가 기말 미술 과제를 발표한 후, 제출 기한이 학생들에게 불안하게 다가왔다. **luxurious** 그 학생들은 화려한 보석과 도자기를 보고, 자신의 것을 창작할 영감을 얻었다. **material** 그 공예가가 종이 부채를 만들 때, 최상의 결과물을 얻기 위해 알맞은 크기와 무게의 재료를 찾아야 한다. **miniature** 그 상인은 스포츠 스타와 가수, 영화 주인공을 모델로 한 축소 모형을 제작한다. / 그 인형의 집을 완성하려면 소형 카펫과 가구, 그리고 인물 모형들이 필요하다. **ornamental** 거실에 있는 부활절 달걀은 순전히 장식용이라 먹을 수 없다.

★★
refined
[rifáind]
[형] 정제된, 세련된

adj. improved or enhanced

With each brushstroke, the potter continued to add layers to the picture on the jar, giving it a more **refined** look.

ant. rough

★★
seamless
[sí:mlis]
[형] 틈새 없는, 매끄러운

adj. continuous, with no apparent gaps between one thing and the next

The Russian doll looked **seamless** until the man opened it to reveal what was inside.

syn. smooth *ant.* inconsistent

★★
succinct
[səksíŋkt]
[형] 간명한, 간결한

adj. short and clear

The ice carver gave a **succinct** explanation of her sculpture while touching on a few essential points.

syn. concise

★★★
sufficient
[səfíʃənt]
[형] 충분한

adj. enough; adequate

When making a rug, one must have **sufficient** yarn or fabric to cover the entire netting to prevent it from looking sparse.

ant. insufficient

★
sweep
[swi:p]
[동] (방 등을 빗자루로) 쓸다, 청소하다

v. to remove dirt from a surface with a brush or broom

It is important to **sweep** the floor in order to keep the studio tidy for the next person.

syn. wipe

Useful Tips
청소와는 관련 없이 sweep to victory는 '낙승을 거두다'라는 뜻으로, sweep the board는 '모든 상을 독차지하다'라는 뜻으로 사용된다.

★★
textile
[tékstail]
[명] 섬유, 직물

n. cloth or fabric made by weaving thread or yarn

Textiles can be used to make a variety of things, including clothing and small personal items such as handkerchiefs.

---

refined 그 도공은 붓질을 할 때마다 그 항아리 표면의 그림에 계속 덧칠을 해, 좀 더 세련되게 보이도록 했다. **seamless** 그 러시아 인형은 그 남자가 그것을 열어 내부를 보여 주기 전까지 틈새가 없어 보였다. **succinct** 그 얼음 조각가는 몇 가지 필수 사항들을 언급하면서 자신의 조각상에 대해 간명히 설명했다. **sufficient** 양탄자를 만들 때, 성글게 보이지 않도록 골대 전체를 감싸기에 충분한 실이나 천이 있어야 한다. **sweep** 다음 사람을 위해 작업실을 깔끔하게 유지하려면 바닥을 청소하는 것이 중요하다. **textile** 의복과 손수건 같이 작은 개인 용품을 포함해 다양한 것들을 만드는 데 직물이 사용될 수 있다.

EXERCISES

ART & DESIGN

SOCIAL SCIENCE

NATURAL SCIENCE

HUMANITIES

EARTH & SPACE

SOCIAL ISSUES

A Match each definition with the correct word.

1 clever and skillful in using one's hands or mind   ⓐ intertwine

2 short and clear   ⓑ assiduous

3 having a great amount of money or possessions   ⓒ affluent

4 to twist two or more things together   ⓓ glimmer

5 hardworking and tireless   ⓔ adroit

6 extremely beautiful; finely made   ⓕ defect

7 a fault, flaw, or imperfection   ⓖ succinct

8 to give off a dim or unsteady light   ⓗ exquisite

B Choose the word that is closest in meaning to each underlined word.

1 The vintage vase had <u>gilded</u> patterns around the opening, which made it even more valuable.
   ⓐ polished   ⓑ golden   ⓒ graceful   ⓓ exact

2 The woodcarver continued making changes to the mask to give it a more <u>refined</u> texture.
   ⓐ vibrant   ⓑ shallow   ⓒ rough   ⓓ improved

3 When making a wooden frame, you must give the glue on the corners <u>sufficient</u> time to dry.
   ⓐ invaluable   ⓑ distilled   ⓒ adequate   ⓓ suitable

4 The actress gave a <u>seamless</u> storytelling performance to her adoring audience.
   ⓐ smooth   ⓑ devastating   ⓒ enchanting   ⓓ sequential

5 To <u>excel</u> in the graphic design field, you must develop an impressive online portfolio.
   ⓐ lag behind   ⓑ be reliable   ⓒ be outstanding   ⓓ get noticed

6 The architect ordered the interns to create several <u>miniature</u> models to present to the client.
   ⓐ revised   ⓑ detailed   ⓒ representative   ⓓ tiny

7 Sophie <u>glanced</u> around the room to see if she could find inspiration for her art project.
   ⓐ stared   ⓑ peeked   ⓒ squinted   ⓓ gawked

Lesson 02

음악

Music

★★

accommodate

[əkάmədèit]

[동] (요구 등에) 부응하다

n. accommodation

v. to meet someone's needs

The radio station **accommodated** the requests of its listeners by expanding the range of its musical selections.

★★★

adept

[ədépt]

[형] 뛰어난, 능숙한

adj. talented or proficient at something

The lead violinist of the orchestra is **adept** at recreating a song note for note after having heard it only once.

syn. skilled *ant.* unskilled

★

ambient

[ǽmbiənt]

[형] 1. 배경 음악의
2. 주위의, 주변의, 잔잔한

adj. 1 relating to background music
2 present in the surrounding environment

1. Although **ambient** music may not grip our attention, it tends to work its way into our brains.
2. The studio's microphone was so powerful that it accidently picked up the **ambient** sounds of conversation coming from next door.

★★

amplify

[ǽmpləfài]

[동] 1. 증폭시키다, 크게 하다
2. …의 정도를 더하다, 증대하다

n. amplification

v. 1 to make something louder or greater *syn.* boost *ant.* muffle
2 to increase the intensity of something *syn.* intensify

1. During their shows, the acoustic musicians avoid the use of electronic devices to **amplify** the sounds of their instruments.
2. The argument **amplified** the bad feelings that existed between the new conductor of the orchestra and the musicians.

★★

applause

[əplɔ́:z]

[명] 박수(갈채)

v. applaud

n. an expression of approval made by clapping *syn.* clapping

When the legendary pianist stood up from his instrument at the end of the concert, the **applause** that filled the hall was deafening.

★

ardent

[ά:rdnt]

[형] 열렬한, 열정적인

adj. zealous or passionate *ant.* casual

My brother is an **ardent** fan of the pop group, and he has even gone so far as to copy their hair and clothing styles.

accommodate 그 라디오 방송국은 선곡의 폭을 넓힘으로써 청취자들의 요구에 부응했다. **adept** 그 관현악단의 수석 바이올린 연주자는 노래를 한 번만 듣고도 똑같이 재현해 내는 것에 능숙하다. **ambient** 1. 배경 음악이 우리의 관심을 끌지는 못할지라도, 그 나름대로 우리 뇌에 영향을 미치는 경향이 있다. 2. 스튜디오 마이크의 성능이 아주 좋아서 옆방에서 흘러나오는 잔잔한 대화를 우연히 잡아낼 정도였다. **amplify** 1. 그 어쿠스틱 음악가들은 자신들의 공연에서 악기 소리를 증폭시키기 위한 전자 기기의 사용을 피한다. 2. 그 언쟁은 관현악단의 새 지휘자와 단원들 사이의 나쁜 감정을 악화시켰다. **applause** 콘서트가 끝날 무렵 그 전설적인 피아니스트가 피아노 앞에 일어섰을 때, 공연장을 가득 메운 박수는 귀청이 터질 것 같이 컸다. **ardent** 내 남동생은 그 팝 그룹의 열렬한 팬이어서 그들의 헤어스타일과 옷을 따라 하기까지 한다.

★★

attuned

[ətjúːnd]

[형] (악기가) 조율된, 맞춘

adj. in tune

The string instruments were not **attuned**, which made the music somewhat sloppy and disjointed.

★★

brusque

[brʌsk]

[형] 무뚝뚝한, 퉁명스러운

adj. brief and unfriendly in action or speech

The music producer gave a **brusque** response to the interviewer who asked about the songs he was currently working on.

syn. abrupt, curt *ant.* warm, polite

★

catchy

[kǽtʃi]

[형] 재미있고 외기 쉬운, 기억하기 쉬운

adj. interesting and easy to remember

After hearing the **catchy** tune on the radio, the woman found herself humming the chorus to herself while she worked.

syn. memorable *ant.* forgettable

★★

choir

[kwaiə*r*]

[명] 합창단, 성가대

n. an organized group of singers

All of the members of the church **choir** wore matching white robes, clapping, and swaying to the music.

★★

commission

[kəmíʃən]

[명] 의뢰, 주문
[동] 의뢰하다, 주문하다

n. a request to produce a work of art in exchange for money

The respected musician received a **commission** to create a series of operas about the lives of the royal family.

v. to pay an artist to produce a work of art

The wealthy woman **commissioned** a symphony to be composed in the honor of her recently deceased father.

★★★

compose

[kəmpóuz]

[동] 1. 작곡하다, 작문하다
2. (마음을) 가라앉히다, 가다듬다

n. composition

v. 1 to produce a piece of music or writing *syn.* write
2 to calm oneself down

1. The singer-songwriter **composes** most of her own songs, although she sometimes covers the work of others.
2. The opera singer took a deep breath and **composed** himself before walking onstage and beginning his aria.

Useful Tips

decompose는 compose의 반의어가 아니라 '썩다', 혹은 '부패하다'라는 의미이므로 주의하도록 한다.

attuned 현악기들이 조율되어있지 않아서, 음악이 다소 엉성하고 잘 연결되지 않았다. **brusque** 그 음악 제작자는 그가 그 당시 작업하고 있던 곡들에 대해 물어본 한 인터뷰 기자에게 퉁명스러운 반응을 보였다. **catchy** 그 여자는 라디오에서 재미있고 외기 쉬운 곡조를 들은 후에, 자신이 일하는 동안 후렴구를 흥얼거리고 있었다는 사실을 깨달았다. **choir** 교회 성가대원 모두가 똑같은 흰색 가운을 입고, 손뼉 치며 음악에 맞춰 몸을 흔들고 있었다. **commission** 그 존경 받는 음악가는 그 왕족의 삶에 대한 오페라 시리즈를 만들 것을 의뢰 받았다. / 그 부유한 여인은 최근에 돌아가신 아버지를 기리기 위한 교향곡을 작곡해 달라고 의뢰했다. **compose** 1. 그 싱어송라이터는 종종 다른 이들의 곡을 자신의 스타일대로 부르긴 하지만, 자신의 곡 대부분을 작곡한다. 2. 그 오페라 가수는 무대에 올라가서 아리아를 시작하기 전에 심호흡을 하고 마음을 가라앉혔다.

Useful Tips

conservatory는 천장과 벽이 유리로 둘러싸인 실내 온실을 의미하기도 한다.

---

conservatory
[kənsə́ːrvətɔ̀ːri]

⊛ 음악 학교

n. a school where music is taught

The students at the local **conservatory** can often be seen lugging their heavy instruments onto city buses.

---

dedicate
[dédikèit]

⊛ 1. (책·음악·작품 등을) 바치다, 헌정하다
2. (시간·노력을) 바치다, 전념하다

n. dedication

v. 1 to state that a work was created in someone's honor
2 to put a lot of time or effort into something *syn.* devote

1. Stevie Wonder **dedicated** the song *Sir Duke* to Duke Ellington, the great jazz musician who had a strong influence on his career.

2. The woman has **dedicated** her life to researching the usage and development of music among primitive humans.

---

diminish
[dimíniʃ]

⊛ 줄어들다, 줄이다

v. to become or make smaller in degree or amount

The band's trumpet players sometimes use a device called a "mute" to **diminish** the volume of their instruments.

syn. reduce, decrease *ant.* expand, increase

---

embellish
[imbéliʃ]

⊛ 장식하다, 꾸미다

n. embellishment

v. to make something more attractive by adding things

The pop band's live concert was **embellished** by energetic dancing and singing.

---

entice
[intáis]

⊛ …을 유도[유혹]하다

n. enticement

v. to persuade someone by offering something desirable

The conductor **enticed** musicians to join his orchestra by offering large salaries to them.

syn. tempt, lure *ant.* dissuade

---

harmonious
[haːrmóuniəs]

⊛ 1. (소리가) 듣기 좋은
2. 사이 좋은, 조화로운

v. harmonize

adj. 1 creating a pleasant sound
2 existing together peacefully *syn.* cordial *ant.* discordant

1. The **harmonious** voices of the singing children filled the night air, bringing joy and comfort to the people passing by.

2. Until they suddenly broke up in 2015, the members of the rock band had enjoyed a **harmonious** coexistence.

---

conservatory 그 지역 음악 학교 학생들이 무거운 악기를 시내버스에 싣는 모습이 종종 목격된다.　**dedicate** 1. Stevie Wonder는 그의 경력에 강한 영향을 끼친 위대한 재즈 음악가인 Duke Ellington에게 *Sir Duke*라는 곡을 헌정했다.　2. 그 여성은 원시시대 사람들 간의 음악의 사용과 발전을 연구하는 데 일생을 바쳤다.
diminish 그 악단의 트럼펫 연주자들은 그들의 악기 소리를 줄이기 위해 때때로 '약음기'라고 불리는 장치를 사용한다.　**embellish** 그 대중음악 그룹의 라이브 콘서트는 격렬한 춤과 노래로 꾸며졌다.　**entice** 그 지휘자는 음악가들에게 높은 급여를 제안하여 자신의 관현악단에 들어오도록 유도했다.
harmonious 1. 노래하는 아이들의 듣기 좋은 목소리가 밤공기를 가득 채워, 지나가는 사람들에게 기쁨과 위로를 주었다.　2. 2015년에 갑자기 해체할 때까지, 그 록 밴드의 멤버들은 사이좋게 공존했다.

★★★ improvise
[ímprəvàiz]

ⓥ 1. (연주·연설 등을) 즉흥적으로 하다
2. 뭐든 있는 것으로 처리하다, 임시변통으로 만들다

n. improvisation

v. 1 to perform without a script or sheet music
2 to make something out of available material

1. The musicians lost the bag containing their sheet music, so they were forced to **improvise**.

2. The guitarist couldn't afford to have his broken instrument properly repaired, so he had to **improvise** with tape and glue.

★ intermission
[ìntərmíʃən]

ⓝ (연극·영화 등의) 중간 휴식 시간

n. a break between parts of a show or performance

This evening's program will include two **intermissions**, during which audience members may get up and stretch their legs.

syn. interlude, interval

★ lyric
[lírik]

ⓝ (노래의) 가사
ⓐ 서정의, 서정적인

n. the words that accompany a song

The song was originally an instrumental piece, but **lyrics** were added to it by an unknown songwriter in the 1930s.

adj. using words to express emotions

Lyric poetry is sometimes accompanied by music, which changes it into a kind of song.

★★ mesmerize
[mézməràiz]

ⓥ (최면을 걸 듯) 마음을 사로잡다, 매료시키다

v. to completely hold someone's attention, as if with a magic spell

The rhythmic repetition of the song **mesmerized** the child, and she listened silently with her eyes closed.

syn. enchant, fascinate

★ nocturne
[náktəːrn]

ⓝ 야상곡, 녹턴

n. a gentle, dreamy piece of music for the piano

This piece of music is a famous **nocturne** that was composed by Chopin.

★★ obtain
[əbtéin]

ⓥ (노력 끝에) 얻다, 획득하다

v. to gain something by making an effort

After searching through the collections of several used-record stores, the man managed to **obtain** a number of rare albums.

syn. procure

---

improvise 1. 그 음악가들은 악보가 든 가방을 잃어버려서, 어쩔 수 없이 즉흥적으로 연주해야만 했다. 2. 그 기타리스트는 파손된 기타를 제대로 고칠 돈이 없어서 테이프와 접착제를 사용해 임시변통으로 고쳐야만 했다. **intermission** 오늘 저녁 프로그램은 두 번의 중간 휴식 시간이 있는데, 그 동안에 관객들은 일어나서 다리를 펼 수 있다. **lyric** 그 노래는 원래 기악곡이었으나, 1930년대에 어떤 무명 작곡가에 의해 가사가 붙여졌다. / 서정시는 종종 음악을 동반하는데, 이는 그 시를 일종의 노래로 바꾼다. **mesmerize** 그 아이는 그 노래의 반복된 리듬에 매료되어서, 눈을 감고 조용히 들었다. **nocturne** 이 곡은 Chopin이 작곡한 유명한 야상곡이다. **obtain** 여러 중고 레코드 가게들을 샅샅이 뒤진 후에, 그 남자는 많은 희귀 음반들을 구할 수 있었다.

pastoral
[pǽstərəl]

명 전원곡, 목가
형 전원(생활)의, 목가적인

n. a piece of music or writing relating to rural life

The piece can be considered a **pastoral**, as it puts one in the mind of a herd of sheep tranquilly grazing atop a hill.

adj. relating to rural life   *ant.* urban

The guitarist's **pastoral** songs were written during a period of his life when he was living in a farming community in the highlands.

ponder
[pándər]

통 곰곰이 생각하다, 숙고하다

v. to think deeply about something that requires a decision or conclusion

After **pondering** the best career path to follow, the young man decided to become a professional musician.

syn. consider

precise
[prisáis]

형 정확한, 정밀한

adj. highly exact

This song requires **precise** piano playing; a single false note will cause the entire composition to fall apart.

syn. accurate   *ant.* inaccurate

precocious
[prikóuʃəs]

형 (성격·지식 등의) 발달이 빠른, 조숙한

adj. having exceptional talent at an unusually early age

Mozart was a **precocious** musician, having begun to write and publicly perform his own songs by the age of five.

prelude
[prélju:d]

명 1. 서곡, 전주곡
2. (중요한 행동·사건 등의) 전조, 서막

n. 1 a short piece of music that precedes the main work   *ant.* coda
2 something that occurs before a more important event

1. Once the orchestra has finished playing the **prelude**, the opening act of the opera will begin.

2. The album's opening track, which is a sweet and simple song, is merely a **prelude** to greater things.

quartet
[kwɔːrtét]

명 사중주단, 사중창단

n. a group of four musicians or singers

The school's string **quartet**, consisting of two violinists, a cellist, and a viola player, will be playing in the auditorium tomorrow night.

---

pastoral 그 작품은 양떼가 언덕 위에서 평화롭게 풀을 뜯는 모습을 생각나게 하므로 전원곡이라고 할 수 있다. / 그 기타 연주자의 목가적인 노래들은 그가 산악지대의 농촌 사회에서 살고 있을 때 쓰여졌다.   **ponder** 그 젊은이는 앞으로 따를 최상의 진로를 곰곰이 생각한 후, 전문 음악가가 되기로 결심했다.
precise 이 곡은 매우 정교한 피아노 연주가 필요한데, 잘못된 음 하나가 작품 전체를 망쳐버리기 때문이다.   **precocious** Mozart는 5세에 자신의 곡을 직접 작곡하고, 대중들 앞에서 연주하기 시작한 음악적으로 발달이 빠른 음악가였다.   **prelude** 1. 그 관현악단이 전주곡 연주를 마치면, 그 오페라의 서막이 시작된다.
2. 그 음반의 첫 곡은 감미롭고 단순한 노래인데, 이는 단지 더 훌륭한 곡들의 서막에 불과하다.   **quartet** 바이올리니스트 두 명, 첼리스트 한 명, 그리고 비올라 연주자 한 명으로 구성된 교내 현악 사중주단은 내일 밤 강당에서 연주할 예정이다.

recital
[risáitl]
ⓝ 발표회, 연주회, 낭독회
v. recite

n. the performance of music or poetry by an individual or a small group

During the children's piano **recital**, proud parents gathered in the school's auditorium to take photos and cheer for their kids.

refrain
[rifréin]
ⓝ 후렴
ⓥ (특히 하고 싶을 것을) 삼가다

n. a short, simple part of a poem or song that is repeated

Although most of the song is dark and gloomy, it has an upbeat **refrain** that will remain in your head.

v. to stop oneself from doing something   *syn.* abstain

Since his fans seemed to prefer cheerful songs, the singer **refrained** from writing about social issues.

release
[rilíːs]
ⓥ (대중들에게) 공개하다, 발표하다
ⓝ 발매 음반, 발매물

v. to make a work available to the public
syn. publish   *ant.* hold back

For over a decade the band **released** a new album every year, but they decided to take an extended break in 2008.

n. something that has recently been made available to the public

In the interview, the singer refused to talk about her previous albums; instead, she wanted to discuss her latest **release**.

renowned
[rináund]
ⓐ 유명한, 명성 있는

adj. well known and highly admired

Although the drummer is **renowned** in her native land, her popularity has not yet spread to America or Europe.

syn. celebrated, distinguished   *ant.* obscure

requiem
[rékwièm]
ⓝ 진혼곡, 레퀴엠

n. a song written for a religious mass for the dead

There have been some musicians who, at the end of their lives, turned their efforts toward composing their own **requiems**.

resonate
[rézənèit]
ⓥ (깊게·낭랑하게) 울려 퍼지다

v. to create a deep, shaking sound

The powerful sound of the tuba **resonated** throughout the concert hall, echoing in the chests of the audience.

---

recital 그 아이들의 피아노 연주회 동안, 자랑스러워하는 부모들이 학교 강당에 모여 사진을 찍고 아이들을 응원했다.   **refrain** 그 곡의 대부분이 어둡고 우울하지만, 당신의 머릿속에 남을 경쾌한 후렴구가 있다. / 그 가수는 자신의 팬들이 쾌활한 음악을 선호하는 것처럼 보여서, 사회 문제에 대한 곡을 쓰는 것을 삼가다. **release** 그 밴드는 10년 넘게 매년 새 앨범을 발표했지만, 2008년에는 휴식 기간을 연장하기로 결정했다. / 그 가수는 인터뷰에서 그녀의 이전 앨범들에 대해 말하는 것을 거절하고, 대신 그녀의 최신 발매 음반에 대해 이야기하고 싶어 했다.   **renowned** 그 드럼 연주자는 그녀의 고국에서는 유명했지만, 그녀의 인기가 미국이나 유럽에까지는 아직 퍼지지 않았다.   **requiem** 말년에 자기 자신을 위한 진혼곡을 작곡하는 데 노력을 기울인 몇몇 작곡가들이 있었다.   **resonate** 튜바의 강렬한 소리가 공연장 전체에 울려 퍼지면서, 관객들의 가슴에 메아리쳤다.

scribble
[skríbl]

ⓥ …을 휘갈겨 쓰다

v. to write quickly and carelessly

As the man began to **scribble** musical notes onto the blank pages of sheet music, I realized he was creating a new song.

syn. scrawl

sequence
[síːkwəns]

ⓝ 1. 순서, 차례
2. 연속(물)

n. 1 the order in which things occur
2 a group of things that occur in a set order

1. Although the same chords are repeated over and over, the **sequence** in which they occur changes slightly.

2. The vocalist sang a **sequence** of musical notes that sounded both original and strangely familiar.

sonic
[sánik]

ⓐ 소리의, 음(파)의

adj. produced by or relating to sound waves

The musician considers her new collection of songs to be the **sonic** version of a Dali painting.

syn. aural

transient
[trǽnziənt]

ⓐ 일시적인, 순간적인

adj. existing or remaining for a short time

The **transient** nature of modern musical trends means that musicians must constantly reinvent themselves for their audiences.

syn. fleeting, temporary   *ant.* permanent

vibrate
[váibreit]

ⓥ (가늘게) 떨다[흔들리다], 진동하다

n. vibration

v. to shake or move back and forth quickly

Each time my next-door neighbor plays his stereo loudly, everything in my apartment begins to **vibrate**.

virtuoso
[vəˋːrtʃuóusou]

ⓝ 거장, 명연주자

n. someone who is extremely skilled at playing a musical instrument

People stood in line outside the concert hall for hours, waiting to see the **virtuoso** violinist.

syn. master

---

scribble 그 남자가 악보의 빈 페이지에 음표들을 휘갈겨 쓰기 시작했을 때, 나는 그가 새로운 곡을 작곡하고 있음을 깨달았다. **sequence** 1. 같은 화음들이 계속 반복됨에도 불구하고, 그 화음의 순서는 조금씩 바뀐다. 2. 그 가수는 독창적이면서도 묘하게 친숙한 음들을 연속해서 불렀다. **sonic** 그 음악가는 그녀의 새로운 노래 모음집을 Dali 작품의 음악 버전으로 여긴다. **transient** 현대 음악 경향이 지닌 일시적인 성질은 음악가들이 계속해서 청중들에게 자신들의 새로운 모습을 보여 줘야 한다는 것을 의미한다. **vibrate** 내 옆집 이웃이 그의 음악 기기를 크게 틀 때마다, 내 아파트에 있는 모든 물건이 떨리기 시작한다.
virtuoso 사람들은 그 명 바이올린 연주자를 보길 기대하며 몇 시간 동안이나 공연장 밖에서 줄을 섰다.

EXERCISES

A Match each definition with the correct word.

1 an organized group of singers   ⓐ ardent

2 to become or make smaller in degree or amount   ⓑ precise

3 zealous or passionate   ⓒ diminish

4 the order in which things occur   ⓓ intermission

5 an expression of approval made by clapping   ⓔ applause

6 highly exact   ⓕ scribble

7 a break between parts of a show or performance ⓖ choir

8 to write quickly and carelessly   ⓗ sequence

B Choose the word that is closest in meaning to each underlined word.

1 The artist is <u>adept</u> at expressing his ideas with simple line drawings.
   ⓐ reluctant   ⓑ clumsy   ⓒ skilled   ⓓ interested

2 The dark colors used in the painting <u>amplify</u> its mood of grief and sadness.
   ⓐ explain   ⓑ intensify   ⓒ disperse   ⓓ calm

3 The <u>transient</u> trend of experimental art has been replaced by a new style of realism.
   ⓐ thrilling   ⓑ confusing   ⓒ fleeting   ⓓ growing

4 The dancers <u>mesmerize</u> audiences with graceful movements and synchronized jumps.
   ⓐ enchant   ⓑ amuse   ⓒ deceive   ⓓ shock

5 The director's <u>brusque</u> explanation of his film disappointed his fans at the movie festival.
   ⓐ curt   ⓑ practical   ⓒ uninformed   ⓓ friendly

6 The concert hall decided to <u>entice</u> concert-goers by lowering the ticket price.
   ⓐ tempt   ⓑ exclude   ⓒ identify   ⓓ surprise

7 The opera singer is <u>renowned</u> for her ability to hold difficult notes for an extended period.
   ⓐ tested   ⓑ mocked   ⓒ exchanged   ⓓ celebrated

ART & DESIGN

SOCIAL SCIENCE

NATURAL SCIENCE

HUMANITIES

EARTH & SPACE

SOCIAL ISSUES

Lesson 03

> 시각 예술

Visual Arts

★★

abstract

[æbstrǽkt]

[형] 추상적인

n. abstraction

adj. based on concepts rather than material objects

Although the **abstract** painting was beautiful, no one could agree on what it was supposed to represent.

syn. unreal *ant.* concrete

★★

adorn

[ədɔ́ːrn]

[동] 장식하다, 꾸미다

n. adornment

v. to add decorations to something or someone

The sculptor **adorned** his latest work with colorful pieces of broken glass that shine in the sun.

syn. decorate

★★★

aesthetic

[esθétik]

[형] 심미적인

[명] 미적 특질, 미학

adj. relating to beauty or appearance

Although these sculptures have little **aesthetic** value, they carry great social and cultural importance.

n. a set of principles followed by an art genre or movement

The modern mural **aesthetic** has been greatly influenced by the commercialization of graffiti art.

★

artistry

[ɑ́ːrtistri]

[명] 예술성

n. creative skills or abilities

Bettina Werner is known for her **artistry**, but few people realize that her work is also environmentally friendly.

★★

carve

[kɑːrv]

[동] 조각하다

v. to cut words or designs into a solid material

Thousands of years ago, ancient craftspeople **carved** realistic faces into the wood of the heavy door.

★

chisel

[tʃízəl]

[동] 끌로 깎다[새기다]

[명] 끌, (금속용) 정

v. to shape hard material using a sharp tool

As the man **chiseled** the large slab of marble into a human shape, small pieces of rock flew into the air.

n. a sharp tool used for shaping hard material

Holding the handle of the **chisel**, place the blade against the rock and hit the other end with a hammer.

---

abstract 그 추상화가 아름답기는 했지만, 아무도 그것이 원래 무엇을 나타내려고 했는지에 대해 합의하지 못했다. **adorn** 그 조각가는 햇빛에 반짝이는 형형색색의 부서진 유리 조각들로 자신의 최신작을 장식했다. **aesthetic** 이 조각들이 심미적 가치는 별로 없지만, 사회·문화적으로 아주 중요하다. / 현대 벽화의 미적 특질은 낙서 예술의 상업화에 큰 영향을 받았다. **artistry** Bettina Werner는 예술성으로 유명하지만, 그녀의 작품이 친환경적이기도 하다는 것을 알아차리는 사람은 거의 없다. **carve** 수천 년 전, 고대 장인들은 그 육중한 문의 목질부에 사실적인 얼굴들을 조각했다. **chisel** 그 남자가 끌로 그 거대한 대리석판을 인간의 형상으로 깎아 낼 때, 작은 암석 파편들이 공중에 튀었다. / 끌의 손잡이를 잡은 채, 칼날 부분을 암석에 대고 망치로 맞은편 끝을 쳐라.

★★

contrast

[kántræst]
[명] 대조, 대비
[kəntrǽst]
[동] 대조하다, 대비시키다

n. **the use of different colors or textures to enhance one another**

The painter's fondness for **contrast** can be seen in his frequent use of orange and green.

v. **to highlight the differences between two things**

The critic **contrasted** the two works of art by pointing out the differences in their compositions.

★★

depict

[dipíkt]
[동] 그리다, 묘사하다
n. depiction

v. **to show something through words or pictures**

This ancient painting **depicts** the Greek hero Heracles battling a large dog with three heads.

syn. portray

★

dimension

[diménʃən]
[명] (길이·너비 등의) 치수

n. **a type of measurement, such as length or width**

The **dimensions** of the canvas are 48 inches by 48 inches, making it too large to hang on our wall.

★★★

exhibit

[igzíbit]
[동] 1. 전시하다
2. (감정·특질 등을) 보이다[드러내다]
n. exhibition

v. **1 to display a collection of items**
2 to show a trait through one's behavior *ant.* conceal

1. The new museum will **exhibit** modern artwork by both local and international artists.
2. Van Gogh began to **exhibit** signs of madness, such as when he cut off part of his own ear.

★★★

flawless

[flɔ́:lis]
[형] 흠 없는, 완벽한

adj. **having no mistakes or errors**

The brushstrokes of the watercolor artist are **flawless**, but some of his color choices are less than impressive.

syn. perfect *ant.* flawed

★★

forge

[fɔːrdʒ]
[동] 위조하다
n. forgery

v. **to commit a crime by making something fake**

The police believe that several of the museum's paintings are fake, having been **forged** in the 19th century.

syn. counterfeit

---

contrast 그 화가가 주황색과 녹색을 자주 사용하는 것에서 그가 대조를 좋아한다는 것을 알 수 있다. / 그 비평가는 두 예술 작품의 구성 차이를 언급하며 그 둘을 대조했다. **depict** 이 고대 그림은 머리가 셋 달린 거대한 개와 싸우는 그리스 영웅 Heracles(헤라클레스)를 그린 것이다. **dimension** 그 캔버스의 치수는 폭 48인치에 길이가 48인치로, 우리 벽에 걸기에는 너무 크다. **exhibit** 1. 그 새 박물관에서 현지 및 해외 예술가들의 현대 미술 작품을 전시할 것이다. 2. Van Gogh는 자신의 귀의 일부를 잘랐을 때와 같은 정신병의 징조를 보이기 시작했다. **flawless** 그 수채화가의 붓놀림은 완벽하지만, 몇몇 색 선택은 덜 인상적이다. **forge** 경찰은 그 박물관의 그림 몇 점이 19세기에 위조된 가짜라고 믿고 있다.

★★

glimpse

[glimps]

[동] 힐끗[언뜻] 보다

[명] 힐끗[언뜻] 보기

v. to see something briefly or partially *syn.* glance

Through the half-open door of the workshop, the children **glimpsed** shelves full of pottery.

n. a quick or partial view of something *syn.* glance

The bus drove past the outdoor mural too quickly, so the passengers were able to catch only a **glimpse** of it.

Useful Tips

glimpse와는 다르게 gaze와 stare는 응시하는 것을 의미한다.

★★★

illustrate

[íləstrèit]

[동] 1. 삽화를 넣다
2. 설명하다, 예증하다

n. illustration

v. 1 to draw or provide pictures for something
2 to make something clear *syn.* clarify

1. The book is **illustrated** with reproductions of old black-and-white drawings from the 18th century.
2. The art professor **illustrated** her point about African art by giving a number of examples.

★★

inscribe

[inskráib]

[동] 새기다

n. inscription

v. to etch words into something

The jeweler **inscribes** his name and the date into the inside of every gold ring he makes.

syn. engrave

★

landscape

[lǽndskèip]

[명] 풍경화(법)

n. a painting of natural scenery

There are several **landscapes** done in oil paint, all of which show the desert at night.

★★

magnificent

[mægnífəsnt]

[형] 웅장한, 훌륭한

n. magnificence

adj. grand and impressive

This **magnificent** bronze statue of a Native American chief is considered the greatest work of its kind.

syn. outstanding *ant.* awful

★

mirror

[mírər]

[동] …와 흡사하다

v. to resemble something; to copy

The composition of this recently discovered sketch **mirrors** that of one drawn by the great Leonardo.

syn. mimic

---

glimpse 그 아이들은 그 작업실의 반쯤 열린 문을 통해 도자기로 가득한 선반들을 힐끗 보았다. / 버스가 야외 벽화를 너무 빨리 스쳐 지나가서, 승객들은 그것을 언뜻만 볼 수 있었다. **illustrate** 1. 그 책에는 오래된 18세기 흑백 소묘를 복제한 삽화가 들어 있다. 2. 그 미술과 교수는 아프리카 예술에 대한 자신의 의견을 많은 예시를 들면서 설명했다. **inscribe** 그 보석 세공인은 자신이 만든 모든 금반지 안쪽에 자신의 이름과 날짜를 새긴다. **landscape** 유화로 그린 풍경화가 몇 점 있는데, 그것들은 모두 밤의 사막을 보여 준다. **magnificent** 이 웅장한 북미 원주민 추장의 청동 조각상은 동일한 유형의 작품들 중 최고로 간주된다. **mirror** 최근 발견된 이 스케치의 구성은 위대한 Leonardo가 그린 한 스케치의 구성과 흡사하다.

mold
[mould]

ⓥ 주조하다, (…로) …을 만들다

v. to shape something

The potter carefully **molded** the clay on the wheel into a towering urn with graceful curves.

novelty
[nάvəlti]

ⓝ 1. 새로움, 참신함
2. 새로운[참신한] 것

adj. novel

n. 1 the characteristic of being new and interesting   *ant.* familiarity
2 something that is new and interesting

1. The **novelty** of modern art trends wears off quickly, with painters returning to more traditional styles.

2. The museum gift shop sells many **novelties**, such as magnets with well-known works of art printed on them.

offer
[ɔ́ːfər]

ⓥ 제안하다, 제공하다
ⓝ 제안, 제의

v. to present something to be accepted or rejected   *ant.* withhold

The art teacher **offered** his student a new pencil, but she preferred to use her old, worn-down one.

n. something presented to be accepted or rejected   *syn.* proposition

The artist turned down an **offer** from a café to display his work on its walls for a month.

pigment
[pígmənt]

ⓝ 도료, 안료, 색소

n. a substance that produces color

The **pigment** in this ink will leave a stain, so be careful not to spill it on your clothing or carpet.

Useful **Tips**

스스로 자신의 모습을 그린 것은 self-portrait, 사진으로 찍은 것은 selfie이다.

portrait
[pɔ́ːrtrit]

ⓝ 초상화

n. a painting or drawing of a person

In America, **portraits** of former presidents are traditionally hung on the walls of the White House.

proportion
[prəpɔ́ːrʃən]

ⓝ 비율, 비례

n. the relationship of the size of one measurement to that of another

The bodily **proportions** of the man in the drawing are off—his torso is too short, and his arms are too long.

---

mold 그 도공은 녹로 위에 놓인 점토를 조심스럽게 주조해 우아한 곡선이 있는 매우 훌륭한 항아리를 만들었다.   **novelty** 1. 현대 미술 동향의 참신함은 빨리 사라져 화가들은 좀 더 전통적인 방식으로 회귀한다. 2. 그 박물관의 기념품점에서는 유명한 예술 작품들이 인쇄된 자석처럼 참신한 것들을 많이 판다.   **offer** 그 미술 교사는 그의 학생에게 새 연필을 제공했지만, 그 학생은 낡고 닳은 자신의 연필을 사용하는 걸 선호했다. / 그 화가는 한 달 동안 그의 작품을 벽에 전시해 주겠다는 한 카페 측의 제안을 거절했다.   **pigment** 이 잉크의 안료는 얼룩을 남길 것이니, 옷이나 카펫에 쏟지 않도록 주의하시오.   **portrait** 미국에서는 전통적으로 전직 대통령들의 초상화를 백악관 벽에 걸어 둔다.   **proportion** 그 소묘 속의 남자의 신체 비율이 맞지 않는다. 그의 상반신은 너무 짧고, 그의 팔은 너무 길다.

★
spellbound
[spélbàund]

📖 매혹된, 홀린

adj. completely fascinated by something

Each and every visitor to the gallery was **spellbound** by the flashing lights and gentle music of the installation piece.

syn. entranced   *ant.* disinterested

★
still life
[stíl làif]

📖 정물화

n. a painting or drawing of objects that have been arranged artistically

One of the most common subjects of the traditional **still life** is a simple bowl of fruit on a table.

> **Useful Tips**
> 명사 life의 복수형은 lives지만 still life의 복수형은 still lifes이다.

★
★
★
symbolize
[símbəlàiz]

📖 상징하다

adj. symbolic
n. symbolization

v. to serve as a representation of something

In medieval art, unicorns were often used to **symbolize** purity and innocence, as well as power.

syn. represent

★
★
trace
[treis]

📖 1. 베끼다, 투사하다
　 2. (선·윤곽 등을 따라) 긋다

v. 1 to copy an image by drawing it on transparent paper
　 2 to draw along the outer edge of something

1. The apprentice placed a thin sheet of paper atop the photo and **traced** the image visible beneath it.

2. In the art class, students **traced** the outlines of their own hands with markers.

★
★
★
transform
[trænsfɔ́ːrm]

📖 변형시키다, 완전히 바꿔 놓다

n. transformation

v. to change something into something new

The paintings on the walls **transformed** the old workspace into a trendy art gallery.

syn. convert

★
★
★
vivid
[vívid]

📖 선명한, 강렬한

adj. brightly colored

Although **vivid** colors are more eye-catching, soft pastels can be used to create a more tranquil mood.

syn. intense   *ant.* dull

---

spellbound 그 미술관을 방문한 사람은 누구나 그 설치 작품의 번쩍이는 불빛과 부드러운 음악에 매혹되었다.　**still life** 전통적인 정물화의 가장 흔한 소재 중 하나는 탁자에 놓인 소박한 과일 그릇이다.　**symbolize** 중세 미술에서 유니콘은 권력뿐만 아니라 순수와 천진함을 상징하는 데 흔히 사용되었다.　**trace** 1. 그 견습생은 사진 위에 얇은 종이를 대고 그 밑에 보이는 이미지를 베꼈다. 2. 미술 시간에 학생들은 매직펜으로 자기 손의 윤곽을 따라 그렸다.　**transform** 벽에 걸린 그 그림들은 낡은 작업실을 최신 유행의 미술관으로 완전히 바꿔 놓았다.　**vivid** 강렬한 색이 좀 더 눈길을 끌긴 하지만, 좀 더 평온한 분위기를 내려면 부드러운 파스텔을 사용할 수 있다.

EXERCISES

A Match each definition with the correct word.

1 a substance that produces color

2 the characteristic of being new and interesting

3 to see something briefly or partially

4 to display a collection of items

5 completely fascinated by something

6 a painting or drawing of a person

7 to draw along the outer edge of something

8 to commit a crime by making something fake

ⓐ novelty

ⓑ forge

ⓒ glimpse

ⓓ portrait

ⓔ pigment

ⓕ trace

ⓖ spellbound

ⓗ exhibit

B Choose the word that is closest in meaning to each underlined word.

1 The woman used a sharp tool to <u>inscribe</u> her initials in the metal of the music box.

    ⓐ detect   ⓑ include   ⓒ engrave   ⓓ remove

2 The set designers <u>transformed</u> the stage into what appeared to be an urban bus stop.

    ⓐ compared   ⓑ transported   ⓒ described   ⓓ converted

3 The <u>vivid</u> pinks and yellows of the dancers' costumes stood out against the gray backdrop.

    ⓐ numerous   ⓑ intense   ⓒ traditional   ⓓ unsettling

4 These quilts are <u>adorned</u> with small pieces of fabric from the quilter's own clothing.

    ⓐ acquired   ⓑ desired   ⓒ decorated   ⓓ recognized

5 There are many <u>magnificent</u> operas that were written in the Italian language, such as *Tosca*.

    ⓐ outstanding   ⓑ modern   ⓒ productive   ⓓ sturdy

6 The singer's performance was <u>flawless</u> until she missed a note at the very end of the aria.

    ⓐ familiar   ⓑ perfect   ⓒ careless   ⓓ innovative

7 The playwright <u>depicts</u> the main character as a nervous teenager who worries about everything.

    ⓐ deceives   ⓑ induces   ⓒ approves   ⓓ portrays

ART & DESIGN

SOCIAL SCIENCE

NATURAL SCIENCE

HUMANITIES

EARTH & SPACE

SOCIAL ISSUES

Lesson 04 Performing Arts

▶ 공연 예술

---

acrobatic
[æ̀krəbǽtik]
형 곡예의, 곡예 같은

adj. relating to or able to do difficult physical movements

The **acrobatic** movements of the modern dancers resembled fallen leaves blowing in the wind.

syn. agile   *ant.* clumsy

> **Useful Tips**
> 서커스에서 매우 어려운 동작들로 관중을 즐겁게 해주는 곡예사를 acrobat이라고 한다.

---

aspect
[ǽspekt]
명 (측)면, 양상

n. a particular part or quality of something

The most interesting **aspect** of the puppet show was the clever way in which the puppeteers remained hidden.

syn. facet

---

audition
[ɔːdíʃən]
명 오디션

n. a short performance used to judge if a person is good enough for a role

During the open **audition**, hundreds of talented people waited in line for a chance to show off their skills.

syn. tryout

---

choreography
[kɔ̀ːriágrəfi]
명 안무

n. the sequence of movements performed by dancers

Many of the scenes consist of **choreography** that requires dozens of synchronized dancers.

---

conjure
[kándʒər]
동 1. …을 (마술로) 불러내다
   2. …을 상기시키다

v. 1 to make something appear as if by magic
2 to cause something to come to mind   *syn.* evoke

1. Using a table with a hole in it, the magician made it seem as if he had **conjured** a rabbit from his hat.

2. The opening scene of the performance **conjures** memories of classic ballets from the past.

---

constitute
[kánstətjùːt]
동 …을 구성하다, (일부를) 이루다

v. to be a part of something bigger

These two talented individuals **constitute** two thirds of a trio that is popular across the nation.

syn. make up

---

acrobatic 그 현대 무용가들의 곡예 동작은 바람에 흩날리는 낙엽 같았다.   **aspect** 그 인형극의 가장 흥미로운 면은 인형술사들이 숨어있는 영리한 방법이었다.   **audition** 공개 오디션 동안, 재능 있는 수많은 사람들이 자신의 기량을 뽐낼 기회를 위해 줄 서서 기다렸다.   **choreography** 많은 장면들이 동시에 같은 동작을 수행하는 수십 명의 무용수가 필요한 안무를 담고 있다.   **conjure** 1. 그 마술사는 탁자 위에 난 구멍을 이용해 토끼 한 마리를 마술로 그의 모자에서 불러낸 것처럼 보이게 했다. 2. 그 공연의 첫 장면은 과거의 전통 발레에 대한 추억을 상기시킨다.   **constitute** 이 재능 있는 두 사람은 전국적으로 인기 있는 3인조의 2/3를 구성한다.

ART & DESIGN

SOCIAL SCIENCE

NATURAL SCIENCE

HUMANITIES

EARTH & SPACE

SOCIAL ISSUES

★★ convey

[kənvéi]

ⓥ 1. (생각·감정 등을) 전달하다
2. …을 나르다, 운반하다

n. conveyance

v. 1 to communicate an idea   *syn.* express
2 to move something to another place   *syn.* carry

1. Folk dancing often **conveys** a feeling of organized joy, enticing viewers to jump on stage and join in.

2. The dance academy hired several large trucks to **convey** all of their gear to the new building.

★ dazzle

[dǽzl]

ⓥ 눈부시게 하다

adj. dazzling

v. to briefly blind with bright lights

Dazzled by the bright lights at the foot of the stage, the performer froze in an awkward silence.

★★ diminutive

[dimínjutiv]

ⓐ 아주 작은

adj. especially small

Despite her **diminutive** stature, the woman continues to impress audiences with her powerful stage presence.

syn. minuscule   *ant.* enormous

★★ dynamic

[dainǽmik]

ⓐ 1. 역동적인, 활력 있는, 힘찬
2. 동적인

adj. 1 energetic and powerful   *syn.* lively   *ant.* listless
2 continually changing

1. It is always a good idea to end a dance performance with the most **dynamic** and unforgettable piece.

2. Due to the country's **dynamic** economic situation, the national dance company is hesitant to expand its budget.

★★★ engage

[ingéidʒ]

ⓥ 1. (주의·관심을) 사로잡다
2. 관여하다, 참여하다

n. engagement

v. 1 to attract and hold someone's attention
syn. captivate   *ant.* repel

2 to take part in

1. The samba dancer **engaged** audiences with his fluid movements, earning himself several awards.

2. The young ballerinas **engaged** in a series of traditional training exercises before the performance.

★ ensemble

[ɑːnsɑ́ːmbl]

ⓝ 무용단, 합주단, 극단

n. a group of people who perform together

The **ensemble** of young ballet dancers got together to discuss the details of their upcoming show.

---

convey 1. 민속 무용은 관객들이 무대로 뛰어올라와 함께 하도록 유도하여, 종종 조직적인 즐거움을 전달한다. 2. 그 무용 학교는 새로운 건물로 모든 학교 장비들을 운반할 큰 트럭 여러 대를 빌렸다.   **dazzle** 무대 밑의 밝은 빛에 눈이 부셨던 그 공연자는 어색한 침묵 속에 얼어붙었다.   **diminutive** 그 여자는 아주 작은 키에도 강력한 무대 장악력으로 계속해서 관객들을 감동시킨다.   **dynamic** 1. 가장 역동적이고 기억에 남을 만한 작품으로 춤 공연을 마무리하는 것은 언제나 좋은 생각이다. 2. 변동성이 많은 그 나라의 경제 상황 때문에, 그 국립 무용단은 예산을 늘리는 것을 주저한다.   **engage** 1. 그 삼바 무용수는 유려한 동작으로 관객들을 사로잡아 여러 개의 상을 받았다. 2. 그 어린 발레리나들은 공연 전에 연이은 전통적 훈련 연습에 참여했다.   **ensemble** 어린 발레 무용수들로 구성된 그 무용단은 다가오는 공연의 세부 사항을 의논하기 위해 모였다.

★★★ **enthusiastic**
[inθù:ziǽstik]
[형] 열광적인, 열렬한
n. enthusiasm

adj. very excited about something

The nervous belly dancer was both thrilled and shocked by the audience's **enthusiastic** response to her performance.

syn. exuberant *ant.* lackluster

★★ **exhort**
[igzɔ́:rt]
[동] 강력히 권고하다, 권하다
n. exhortation

v. to strongly tell someone to do something

The director **exhorted** the set designers to get the stage ready as quickly as possible.

syn. urge

★★ **extent**
[ikstént]
[명] (크기·중요성·심각성 등의) 정도, 범위

n. the degree or range of something

The **extent** of the dance group's influence became clear when they went on a global tour.

syn. scope

★ **extol**
[ikstóul]
[동] 극찬하다

v. to strongly praise someone or something

Critics **extolled** the Paris Opera Ballet's latest show, with many of them calling it the best performance of the year.

syn. acclaim *ant.* denounce

★★ **illusion**
[ilú:ʒən]
[명] 환상, 환영, 오해[착각]

n. an image or idea that appears to be something it is not

The success of the local circus was merely an **illusion** created by a small group of ardent fans.

syn. misconception

★★ **incredible**
[inkrédəbl]
[형] 1. (믿기 어려울 만큼) 훌륭한
2. 믿을 수 없는

adj. 1 excellent *syn.* wonderful *ant.* awful
2 difficult to believe *syn.* unbelievable *ant.* credible

1. It was an **incredible** display of breakdancing, and the audience left the theater in a state of excitement.
2. The elderly woman's **incredible** claims of having been a world-famous ballroom dancer were quickly dismissed.

---

enthusiastic 그 긴장한 벨리 댄서는 그녀의 춤에 대한 관객들의 열광적인 반응에 전율을 느낌과 동시에 깜짝 놀랐다. **exhort** 그 감독은 무대 디자이너들에게 가능한 한 빨리 무대를 완성하라고 강력히 권고했다. **extent** 그 무용단이 끼치는 영향력의 크기가 전 세계 순회공연을 했을 때 확연히 드러났다. **extol** 비평가들은 파리 오페라 발레단의 최근 공연을 극찬했는데, 그들 중 많은 이가 그 공연을 그 해에 가장 훌륭한 공연이라고 칭했다. **illusion** 그 지역 서커스단의 성공은 소수의 열렬한 팬들이 만들어낸 착각에 지나지 않았다. **incredible** 1. 그것은 훌륭한 브레이크 댄스 공연이었고, 관객들이 흥분한 상태로 공연장을 빠져나갔다. 2. 자신이 세계적으로 유명한 사교 댄서였다는 그 노부인의 믿을 수 없는 주장은 바로 묵살되었다.

intense
[inténs]

ⓐ 극도의, 극심한, 강렬한

n. intensity

adj. extreme in degree or strength

The ballerinas were under **intense** pressure to perform well, as the queen was in attendance that evening.

in unison
[in júːnəsn]

ⓟ 1. 합심하여, 조화를 이뤄
2. 일제히

adv. 1 in harmony **2** at the same time *syn.* as one

1. During the opening scene of the ballet, a large choir sings together **in unison**.

2. The audience members rose **in unison** and applauded the cast for more than five minutes.

leap
[liːp]

ⓥ (높이 길게) 뛰다, 뛰어오르다
ⓝ 뛰어오름, 도약

v. to jump high into the air *syn.* bound

An overexcited fan **leapt** onto the stage and tried to hand the jazz dancer a bouquet of roses.

n. the act of jumping high into the air

Mikhail Baryshnikov was known for outstanding **leaps** that made it seem as though he could fly.

Useful Tips

leap의 과거형은 leapt와 leaped 둘 다 가능한데, leapt는 정통적인 과거형이고, leaped는 미국에서 많이 쓰이는 과거형이다.

portray
[pɔːrtréi]

ⓥ 1. (영화·연극에서 특정한 역할을) 연기하다
2. 묘사하다

n. portrayal

v. 1 to play the role of someone on stage, film, or TV **2** to depict in a certain way *syn.* describe

1. In this production, the veteran dancer **portrays** a beautiful swan who falls in love with a prince.

2. Although the tango dancer has been **portrayed** as an unruly troublemaker, he is actually quite quiet and shy.

renovate
[rénəvèit]

ⓥ …을 보수하다, 양호한 상태로 되돌리다

n. renovation

v. to bring something back to its original condition

There are plans to **renovate** the old theater by replacing the worn-out seats and repainting the walls and ceiling.

syn. refurbish

review
[rivjúː]

ⓝ (신간 서적·연극 따위의) 비평, 평가, 평론

n. an article in which someone gives their opinion on a book, TV show, or film

The newspaper's **review** of the production was mostly negative, which surprised many of the cast members.

syn. critique

---

intense 여왕이 그날 저녁 발레 공연을 보러 와서, 그 발레리나들은 공연을 잘해야 한다는 극심한 압박감에 사로잡혀 있었다. **in unison** 1. 그 발레의 첫 장면에서 대규모의 합창단이 다 같이 조화를 이뤄 노래를 부른다. 2. 관객들이 일제히 일어나 5분 이상 출연진들에게 박수갈채를 보냈다. **leap** 지나치게 흥분한 팬이 무대로 뛰어올라와서 그 재즈 무용수에게 장미 꽃다발을 건네려 했다. / Mikhail Baryshnikov는 마치 그가 날 수 있는 것처럼 보이게 한 뛰어난 도약으로 알려져 있었다. **portray** 1. 이 공연 작품에서 그 베테랑 무용수는 왕자와 사랑에 빠지는 아름다운 백조를 연기한다. 2. 그 탱고 무용수는 제멋대로 구는 말썽쟁이로 묘사되었지만, 사실 매우 조용하고 수줍음이 많다. **renovate** 낡은 좌석을 교체하고 벽과 천장을 다시 페인트칠하는 방식으로 그 오래된 극장을 보수하려는 계획이 있다. **review** 그 공연 작품에 대한 신문의 평가는 대부분 부정적이었는데, 이는 많은 출연진들을 놀라게 했다.

revival

[riváivəl]

똉 1. (예전 연극·영화 따위의) 재공연, 재상연
2. 부흥, 재유행

v. revive

n. 1 a new performance of an old work
2 the process of becoming popular again   *syn.* resurgence

1. The local dance company's **revival** of a classic production drew many local senior citizens.
2. The 1980s trend of breakdancing has experienced an unexpected **revival** in recent years.

---

routine

[ru:tí:n]

똉 (정해진) 순서, 과정

n. a regular, preplanned sequence of events

The magician always starts his **routine** by amusing the audience with some clever jokes.

---

sensational

[senséiʃənl]

똉 굉장한, 세상을 깜짝 놀라게 하는

n. sensation

adj. excellent and unexpected

The **sensational** dancing of the students drew praise from people throughout the community.

syn. stunning   *ant.* dull, mundane

---

sponsor

[spánsər]

똉 후원하다
똉 후원자, 후원 업체

n. sponsorship

v. to give money to support an event   *syn.* fund

A local supermarket has generously **sponsored** the town's international dance festival this year.

n. a person or company that has given money to support an event
  syn. benefactor, patron

The names of all the ballet company's **sponsors** are listed on the back page of this evening's program.

---

tremble

[trémbl]

똉 떨다, 떨리다

v. to shake slightly

The final dance included the entire cast and was so energetic that it caused the stage to **tremble**.

---

venue

[vénju:]

똉 (공연·경기·회담 등의) 장소

n. a place where events take place

This old concert hall isn't pretty, but it is the largest **venue** for live performances in the region.

---

revival 1. 그 지역 무용단의 고전 작품 재공연은 그 지역의 많은 어르신들을 끌어들였다. 2. 1980년대의 브레이크 댄스 트렌드는 최근 몇 해 동안 기대치 않게 재유행했다.   **routine** 그 마술사는 항상 기발한 농담으로 관중들을 즐겁게 하면서 그의 무대 순서를 시작한다.   **sensational** 그 학생들의 굉장한 춤이 그 지역 사회 사람들의 호평을 이끌어냈다.   **sponsor** 올해 한 지역 슈퍼마켓이 그 마을의 국제 춤 축제를 아낌없이 후원했다. / 그 발레단의 모든 후원 업체명이 오늘 저녁 프로그램의 뒤 페이지에 열거되어 있다.   **tremble** 마지막 춤은 전 출연진이 함께 했고 매우 힘이 넘쳐서 무대가 떨렸다.   **venue** 이 오래된 공연장은 아름답지는 않지만, 이 지역에서 라이브 공연을 할 수 있는 가장 큰 장소이다.

EXERCISES

A Match each definition with the correct word.

1 a regular, preplanned sequence of events   ⓐ aspect

2 especially small   ⓑ venue

3 a place where events take place   ⓒ diminutive

4 extreme in degree or strength   ⓓ renovate

5 to briefly blind with bright lights   ⓔ intense

6 to communicate an idea   ⓕ routine

7 to bring something back to its original condition   ⓖ dazzle

8 a particular part or quality of something   ⓗ convey

B Choose the word that is closest in meaning to each underlined word.

1 The veteran actor was pleased by the generally good <u>reviews</u> that his new sitcom received.
   ⓐ critiques   ⓑ requests   ⓒ awards   ⓓ expectations

2 If a photographer's hands <u>tremble</u>, the photographs will likely be blurred.
   ⓐ shake   ⓑ sweat   ⓒ wave   ⓓ freeze

3 Eco-friendly buildings and houses <u>constitute</u> the majority of the architect's portfolio.
   ⓐ break down   ⓑ look like   ⓒ make up   ⓓ detract from

4 The 16th-century painter's outstanding use of color and light is <u>extolled</u> by critics.
   ⓐ disliked   ⓑ preferred   ⓒ acclaimed   ⓓ underrated

5 The orchestra's conductor <u>exhorted</u> the musicians to play with more energy.
   ⓐ urged   ⓑ scolded   ⓒ warned   ⓓ praised

6 The <u>extent</u> of Michelangelo's influence on Renaissance art cannot be overstated.
   ⓐ motivation   ⓑ increase   ⓒ scope   ⓓ loss

7 The new musical features a lot of <u>dynamic</u> singing and dancing.
   ⓐ unique   ⓑ lively   ⓒ familiar   ⓓ popular

ART & DESIGN

SOCIAL SCIENCE

NATURAL SCIENCE

HUMANITIES

EARTH & SPACE

SOCIAL ISSUES

---

acclaimed
[əkléimd]

ⓐ 칭찬[호평]을 받는

adj. publicly praised by many people

The **acclaimed** director has won countless international awards and is considered a living legend by many film critics.

syn. lauded   *ant.* reviled

---

assemble
[əsémbl]

ⓥ 1. 모이다
   2. 조립하다

n. assembly

v. 1 to gather together in a group   *ant.* disperse
   2 to put something together

1. The members of the drama club **assembled** in the school theater to welcome their new drama teachers.
2. The tripod for the camera arrived in several pieces, so it had to be **assembled** before filming could begin.

---

bestow
[bistóu]

ⓥ 수여하다, 주다

v. to formally present an honor or gift

This was the first year that the film festival **bestowed** the title of "Best Foreign Film" on an Iranian movie.

syn. award

---

celebrity
[səlébrəti]

ⓝ 유명 인사

n. a famous person

Although she is a **celebrity**, the actress still stops to talk with her fans when she meets them on the street.

syn. star

---

collaborate
[kəlǽbərèit]

ⓥ 협력하다, 공동으로 하다

n. collaboration

v. to work with someone to create something

The two well-known screenplay writers **collaborated** to write a script based on a popular novel.

syn. cooperate

---

crucial
[krú:ʃəl]

ⓐ 매우 중요한, 결정적인

adj. extremely important

Despite not being a starring role, the part of the hero's mother-in-law is **crucial** to the success of the play.

syn. vital   *ant.* insignificant

---

acclaimed 호평 받는 그 감독은 국제적인 상을 수없이 받았고, 많은 영화 평론가들에 의해 살아있는 전설로 여겨진다.   **assemble** 1. 그 연극 동아리 회원들은 새 연극 교사들을 환영하기 위해 교내 극장에 모였다. 2. 사진기 삼각대가 몇 부분으로 분리된 상태로 도착해서, 촬영이 시작될 수 있기 전에 조립해야 했다.
bestow 올해는 그 영화제가 '최우수 외국어 영화상' 칭호를 이란 영화에 수여한 최초의 해였다.   **celebrity** 그 여배우는 유명 인사임에도, 거리에서 팬들을 만나면 여전히 발걸음을 멈추고 그들과 대화를 나눈다.   **collaborate** 유명한 두 시나리오 작가가 대중소설을 토대로 한 영화 대본을 공동 집필했다.   **crucial** 그 남자 주인공의 장모 역은 주역이 아님에도 불구하고, 그 연극의 성공에 결정적이다.

ART & DESIGN

SOCIAL SCIENCE

NATURAL SCIENCE

HUMANITIES

EARTH & SPACE

SOCIAL ISSUES

domain
[douméin]

몡 1. 분야
　2. 영토

n. 1 a specific field of knowledge
2 the area of land one owns or controls　*syn.* realm

1. In the **domain** of special effects, computer-generated images, also known as CGI, are the current hot trend.

2. At the start of the play, a king looks out across his **domain** and complains about its small size.

entertain
[èntərtéin]

통 즐겁게 해 주다

n. entertainment

v. to keep other people amused or interested

During a delay in the start of the musical, one of the actors came out on stage and **entertained** the audience with funny stories.

syn. amuse　*ant.* bore

fade
[feid]

통 흐려지다, 약해지다, 줄다

v. to diminish in strength or visibility

The popular actor waited for the applause to **fade** before he delivered the opening line of the play.

syn. lessen　*ant.* strengthen

fame
[feim]

몡 명성, 명망

n. the state of being known by many people

Some actors dream of mastering their art, while others are interested only in acquiring **fame**.

syn. renown　*ant.* obscurity

filmography
[filmágrəfi]

몡 필모그래피(특정 배우가 출연하거나 특정 감독이 만든 영화 목록)

n. a list of all the films a professional has worked on

The cinematographer's **filmography** includes several classics, along with a number of lesser-known works.

Useful **Tips**

한 작가가 쓴 책들의 목록은 bibliography, 한 음악가가 녹음한 음반들의 목록은 discography이다.

flicker
[flíkər]

통 깜박이다

v. to shine erratically

The film crew had to stop shooting the indoor scene when one of the lights began to **flicker**.

syn. blink

---

domain 1. 특수 효과 분야에서 CGI라고도 알려진 컴퓨터 생성 이미지가 현재 대세이다.　2. 그 연극의 도입부에서, 한 왕이 그의 영토를 건너다보고는 그 크기가 작다고 한탄한다.　**entertain** 그 뮤지컬의 시작이 지연되는 동안, 배우들 중 한 명이 무대로 나와 우스운 이야기로 관객을 즐겁게 했다.　**fade** 그 인기 배우는 그 연극의 첫 대사를 하기 전에, 박수가 잦아들기를 기다렸다.　**fame** 어떤 배우들은 자신의 예술을 숙달하길 꿈꾸는 반면, 명성을 얻는 것에만 관심을 갖는 배우들도 있다.　**filmography** 그 촬영감독의 필모그래피에는 다수의 덜 알려진 작품들과 몇 편의 고전 명작이 포함되어 있다.　**flicker** 조명 중 한 개가 깜박이기 시작하자 그 영화 제작진은 실내 장면 촬영을 중단해야 했다.

★
footage
[fútidʒ]

몡 (특정한 사건을 담은) 장면[화면]

n. film or video of an event

There is very little **footage** of the legendary stage actor, and what does exist is of extremely poor quality.

syn. clip

★
★
genre
[ʒá:nrə]

몡 (예술 작품의) 장르

n. a category or style of one of the arts

The actor's latest film is an interesting mix of **genres**, part comedy and part murder mystery.

syn. type

★
★
imaginative
[imǽdʒənətiv]

몡 창의적인, 상상의

adj. having or having been created by a powerful imagination

The theater company's **imaginative** stage sets are partly the result of having an unusually small budget.

syn. creative

★
★
★
integral
[íntigrəl]

몡 필수의

adj. essential to make something whole and functional

Soundtracks should be considered an **integral** part of cinema; without them, films would feel empty and lifeless.

ant. superfluous

★
★
notable
[nóutəbl]

몡 주목할 만한, 뛰어난

adj. worth noticing or mentioning

The movie includes a small but **notable** performance by the director's son, who plays a shy student.

syn. noteworthy   *ant.* unremarkable

★
ovation
[ouvéiʃən]

몡 큰 박수갈채, 열렬한 환영

n. loud and enthusiastic applause

A standing **ovation** is an audience's greatest gesture of respect, signaling that the performance was excellent.

Useful Tips

ovation과 함께 자주 사용하는 형용사에는 huge, thunderous, enthusiastic, rousing 등이 있다.

---

footage 그 전설적인 연극 배우에 관한 화면은 거의 없고, 남아 있는 것도 화질이 극도로 좋지 않다.   **genre** 그 배우의 최신 영화는 장르들이 흥미롭게 섞여 있는데, 일부는 코미디물이고 일부는 살인 미스터리물이다.   **imaginative** 그 극단의 창의적인 무대 장치는 부분적으로 매우 적은 예산에서 기인한 것이다. **integral** 영화 음악은 영화에서 필수적인 것으로 간주되어야 한다. 영화 음악이 없으면, 영화가 공허하고 활기 없게 느껴질 것이다.   **notable** 그 영화에서 감독의 아들이 적은 분량이지만 주목할 만한 연기를 하는데, 수줍음 많은 학생 역할이다.   **ovation** 기립 박수는 관객이 경의를 표하는 가장 큰 제스처로, 그 공연이 훌륭했다는 것을 뜻한다.

★ **premiere**
[primíər, -mjέər]
[명] 개봉, 초연, 첫날

n. the first public showing or performance of a movie, play, or TV show

The **premiere** of the documentary was a major event, with many actors and local celebrities in attendance.

syn. debut *ant.* finale

★★ **prior**
[práiər]
[형] 전의, 기존의, 앞서

adj. having occurred or existed previously

The director's **prior** plays were all musicals, but this one is a serious drama based on the life of a human rights activist.

syn. previous *ant.* upcoming

★ **prompt**
[prɑmpt]
[동] 1. 대사를 일러 주다
2. 촉발하다, 촉구하다
[형] 신속한, 기민한

v. 1 to remind an actor of the next line in the script
2 to cause something to happen *syn.* induce

1. Whenever the young actors forgot their lines, their drama teacher cheerfully **prompted** them from offstage.
2. The terrible reviews of the play **prompted** the director to replace all of the lead actors.

adj. on time; without delay *syn.* punctual *ant.* tardy

When asked questions by his fans online, the actor always gives a **prompt** and friendly reply.

★ **prop**
[prɑp]
[명] 소도구

n. an object used in a play, movie, or TV show

This looks like a real sword, but it is actually a plastic **prop** that has been used in several Shakespeare plays.

★ **rehearsal**
[rihə́:rsəl]
[명] 리허설, 예행 연습
v. rehearse

n. the act of practicing an event or performance before it actually occurs

The cast of the play gathered together for one final **rehearsal** on the day before opening night.

syn. practice

★★ **repertoire**
[répərtwɑ̀:r]
[명] 레퍼토리, 상연 목록

n. the complete list of songs, plays, or dances a person or company is able to perform

The Phantom of the Opera is part of the **repertoire** of the company.

---

premiere 그 다큐멘터리의 개봉은 주요 행사여서, 많은 배우들과 지역 유명 인사들이 참석했다. **prior** 그 감독의 전작들은 모두 뮤지컬이었지만, 이번 작품은 한 인권 운동가의 일생을 바탕으로 한 진지한 드라마이다. **prompt** 1. 그 어린 배우들이 대사를 잊을 때마다, 그들의 연극 교사가 무대 뒤에서 기꺼이 대사를 일러 주었다. 2. 그 연극에 대한 악평은 감독으로 하여금 주연 배우들을 모두 교체하게 했다. / 그 배우는 온라인 상에서 팬들의 질문을 받으면, 늘 신속하고 상냥하게 답한다. **prop** 이것은 진짜 검처럼 보이지만, 사실 몇몇 Shakespeare 극에서 사용되어 온 플라스틱 소도구이다. **rehearsal** 그 연극 출연자들이 개막 전날 최종 리허설을 위해 모였다. **repertoire** *오페라의 유령*은 그 극단의 상연 목록의 일부이다.

★
sequel
[síːkwəl]

ⓝ 속편, 후속

n. a play, movie, or book whose plot continues the story of a previous work

The original Harry Potter movie, *Harry Potter and the Sorcerer's Stone*, was followed by seven **sequels**.

syn. follow-up   *ant.* prequel

★
theatrical
[θiǽtrikəl]

ⓐ 1. 연극의, 극장의
2. 과장된, 연극조의

adj. 1 relating to drama or the theater
2 behaving in an extreme way to attract attention

1. The town decided to host a series of outdoor **theatrical** productions in the local park during the summer.

2. When the playwright claimed his critics were trying to destroy him, he was told to stop being so **theatrical**.

★
★
troupe
[truːp]

ⓝ 극단

n. a group of performers

The traveling **troupe** went from town to town, performing original plays for the locals.

syn. crew

★
★
unveil
[ʌnvéil]

ⓥ 공개하다, 발표하다, 밝히다

v. to reveal something formally or as part of a ceremony

The director **unveiled** the cast of his new movie, which surprisingly included several foreign actors.

ant. conceal

★
★
usher
[ʌ́ʃər]

ⓥ 안내하다

v. to politely show people where they should go

After he was announced as the winner of the Best Performance award, the overexcited actor had to be **ushered** to the stage.

syn. guide

★
★
★
versatile
[vɔ́ːrsətl]

ⓐ 다재다능한

n. versatility

adj. having a wide range of skills or abilities

Known as a **versatile** performer, Julie Andrews was able to dance and sing as well as she could act.

syn. multitalented

---

sequel 첫 번째 해리 포터 영화인 *해리 포터와 마법사의 돌* 이후, 7편의 후속 영화가 나왔다.   **theatrical** 1. 그 도시는 여름에 지역 공원에서 일련의 야외 연극 공연을 주최하기로 했다.   2. 그 극작가는 평론가들이 그를 몰락시키려 한다고 주장했을 때, 너무 과장되게 굴지 말라는 말을 들었다.   **troupe** 그 유랑 극단은 현지인들 대상으로 창작극을 공연하면서, 이 마을 저 마을을 돌아다녔다.   **unveil** 그 감독은 자신의 새 영화의 출연진을 발표했는데, 거기에는 놀랍게도 몇 명의 외국인 배우들이 포함되어 있었다.   **usher** 최우수 연기상 수상자로 호명된 후, 지나치게 흥분한 그 배우는 무대로 안내 받아야 했다.   **versatile** 다재다능한 연기자로 알려진 Julie Andrews는 연기뿐 아니라 춤과 노래도 잘했다.

EXERCISES

ART & DESIGN

SOCIAL SCIENCE

NATURAL SCIENCE

HUMANITIES

EARTH & SPACE

SOCIAL ISSUES

A Match each definition with the correct word.

1 to diminish in strength or visibility   ⓐ prop

2 an object used in a play, movie, or TV show   ⓑ fade

3 a group of performers   ⓒ celebrity

4 worth noticing or mentioning   ⓓ troupe

5 to shine erratically   ⓔ entertain

6 film or video of an event   ⓕ flicker

7 a famous person   ⓖ notable

8 to keep other people amused or interested   ⓗ footage

B Choose the word that is closest in meaning to each underlined word.

1 Because the violin is a difficult instrument to master, practicing often and regularly is crucial.
　ⓐ recommended   ⓑ challenging   ⓒ vital   ⓓ common

2 Rodin was acclaimed for the realism of his statues, which made them powerful works of art.
　ⓐ lauded   ⓑ criticized   ⓒ copied   ⓓ discussed

3 Having sprained her ankle in a prior performance, the ballerina will not dance tonight.
　ⓐ professional   ⓑ formal   ⓒ unplanned   ⓓ previous

4 The young artist's use of imaginative imagery makes his paintings both interesting and unique.
　ⓐ traditional   ⓑ amusing   ⓒ creative   ⓓ technical

5 Although the artisan never achieved fame, he did earn a great deal of money through his work.
　ⓐ satisfaction   ⓑ renown   ⓒ progress   ⓓ awards

6 The pianist and the opera singer will collaborate on a song to raise money for charity.
　ⓐ improve   ⓑ cooperate   ⓒ perform   ⓓ transform

7 A group of hip-hop dancers assembled at their studio to discuss an upcoming competition.
　ⓐ practiced   ⓑ relaxed   ⓒ argued   ⓓ gathered

A Choose the correct words.

1 The word offer has the same meaning as
   ⓐ opposition   ⓑ explanation   ⓒ condition   ⓓ proposition

2 The word leap has the same meaning as
   ⓐ fail   ⓑ bound   ⓒ mold   ⓓ reply

3 The word dedicate has the same meaning as
   ⓐ dictate   ⓑ relate   ⓒ affect   ⓓ devote

4 The word succinct has the same meaning as
   ⓐ fixed   ⓑ exquisite   ⓒ concise   ⓓ unexpected

5 The word integral has the same meaning as
   ⓐ essential   ⓑ continuous   ⓒ gigantic   ⓓ technical

6 The word ponder has the same meaning as
   ⓐ distribute   ⓑ explain   ⓒ consider   ⓓ deconstruct

7 The word abstract has the same meaning as
   ⓐ unreal   ⓑ unknown   ⓒ relaxed   ⓓ displaced

8 The word enthusiastic has the same meaning as
   ⓐ restless   ⓑ exuberant   ⓒ intelligible   ⓓ synchronized

B Fill in the blanks with the best words from the box.

1 The actor's _____ contains many songs and dance numbers from popular American musicals from the 1960s.

2 The Native American artist has the ability to _____ a simple piece of wood into a traditional work of art.

3 The actress had a hard time memorizing the _____ of the grand finale, so a dance instructor was hired to help her.

4 A former _____ of the great sculptor went on to surpass him in both artistic skill and critical acclaim.

5 The _____ of the ballet had to be postponed by a week due to an injury to one of the lead dancers.

6 Stage actors are taught to _____ if they suddenly find they have forgotten their lines in the middle of a show.

choreography	apprentice	carve	improvise	repertoire	premiere

C Read the following passages.

ART & DESIGN

SOCIAL SCIENCE

NATURAL SCIENCE

HUMANITIES

EARTH & SPACE

SOCIAL ISSUES

[1-2]   **1** Choose one word that fits both blanks.

> Beethoven needed to _____ himself after arguing with a conductor about one of his symphonies. He made himself a cup of tea and sat on his balcony. Once he had calmed down sufficiently, he walked over to his piano and began to _____ a new song.

ⓐ entice   ⓑ compose   ⓒ diminish   ⓓ amplify

2 Choose the appropriate pair of words to fill in the blanks.

> Performing magic on television is a lot easier than doing so in front of a live audience. When a TV magician seemingly _____ a large animal from out of nowhere, it could simply be an _____ created by stopping the recording, bringing the animal onstage, and then starting it again.

ⓐ conveys — audition   ⓑ renovates — ensemble
ⓒ ushers — artistry   ⓓ conjures — illusion

[3-4]

> One of the most important parts of any theater production is the moment when the curtain first rises to unveil the carefully constructed stage set. If it is particularly impressive or realistic, it can draw an ovation before the play has even begun.

3 In the context of the passage, unveil means _____.
ⓐ improve   ⓑ disregard   ⓒ reveal   ⓓ brighten

4 The word ovation in the passage could best be replaced by
ⓐ entertainment   ⓑ controversy   ⓒ criticism   ⓓ applause

[5-6]

> Goldwork is the art of weaving gold threads into fabric, usually for the purpose of making elegant clothing. The thread is merely _____, as it increases neither the strength nor durability of the fabric. However, it is highly regarded for the manner in which it can make an ordinary garment glimmer like a star.

5 Choose the word that is most suitable for the blank.
ⓐ seamless   ⓑ ornamental   ⓒ affluent   ⓓ adroit

6 The word glimmer in the passage is closest in meaning to
ⓐ flow   ⓑ transform   ⓒ intertwine   ⓓ sparkle

Lesson 06

미술사

Art History

★★★

advent
[ǽdvent]

[명] (중요 인물·시대·사건 등의) 도래, 출현

n. the arrival or beginning of something important

The **advent** of the Renaissance had a huge impact on European art, bringing about a renewed emphasis on naturalism.

syn. onset

★

aim
[eim]

[명] 목적, 목표, 의도

n. a goal or intention

The **aim** of restoration is to bring damaged artwork back to its original condition, not to improve on it.

syn. objective

★★

appall
[əpɔ́:l]

[동] 오싹하게 하다, 질겁하게 하다

adj. appalling

v. to cause feelings of shock or disapproval

Although many older critics were **appalled** by Andy Warhol's pop art, it was embraced by young people.

syn. horrify *ant.* delight

★★

appeal
[əpí:l]

[동] 관심[흥미]을 끌다

adj. appealing

v. to be found attractive or interesting

Formal portraits were meant to **appeal** to the vanity of the wealthy individuals who were willing to pay for them.

syn. captivate *ant.* repulse

★★

belief
[bilí:f]

[명] (옳다고 믿고 있는) 생각, 믿음

n. a powerful feeling that something is true or good

The **belief** that many ancient Roman statues were copies of Greek originals has been proven true.

★★

coarse
[kɔ:rs]

[형] 1. 결이 거친
2. (느낌·태도 등이) 거친, 세련되지 않은

adj. 1 having a rough texture *syn.* bumpy *ant.* smooth
2 rude or unrefined *syn.* crude *ant.* cultured

1. Marble lacks the **coarse** texture of many other kinds of rock, which made it the preferred material of many early sculptors.
2. **Coarse** brushstrokes are often used in expressionism, as they are effective at conveying strong emotions.

advent 르네상스의 도래는 자연주의에 대한 강조를 새롭게 불러일으키며, 유럽의 미술에 큰 영향을 끼쳤다. **aim** 복원의 목적은 손상된 미술품을 기존보다 향상시키는 것이 아니라, 원래의 상태로 되돌리는 것이다. **appall** 나이가 지긋한 많은 비평가들은 Andy Warhol의 팝아트에 질겁했지만, 젊은 사람들은 이를 포용했다. **appeal** 정식 초상화들은 기꺼이 값을 지불할 용의가 있는 부유한 이들의 허영심을 끌어들이도록 의도되었다. **belief** 고대 로마의 많은 조각상들이 그리스 원본들의 복제품이라는 믿음이 사실로 입증되었다. **coarse** 1. 대리석에는 많은 다른 종류의 돌에 있는 거친 질감이 없어서, 많은 초기 조각가들이 선호하는 재료가 되었다. 2. 거친 붓놀림은 강한 감정을 전달하는 데 효과적이기 때문에, 표현주의에 자주 사용된다.

***

coherent
[kouhíərənt]
[형] 논리 정연한
n. coherence

adj. clear and logical

Art historians seek to arrange centuries of changing art trends into a single **coherent** description.

syn. comprehensible *ant.* incoherent

*

composition
[kàmpəzíʃən]
[명] 구도, 배치

n. the arrangement or makeup of something

The **composition** of the objects in Dutch *vanitas* paintings was meticulously planned out by the artists.

Useful Tips

vanitas 화는 죽음을 묘사한 정물화로 주로 해골, 식물, 시계, 책 등이 많이 나온다. '공허한' 이라는 뜻의 라틴어 vanitas에서 유래했다.

**

conform
[kənfɔ́ːrm]
[동] (규칙·법 등에) 따르다
n. conformity

v. to follow a set of rules

Not wishing to **conform** to the rules of Impressionism, young artists began creating their own styles.

syn. comply

*

debunk
[diːbʌ́ŋk]
[동] (생각·믿음 등이) 틀렸음을 드러내다[밝히다]

v. to prove an idea or belief wrong

Modern art has **debunked** the idea that formal training is needed to produce artwork of great value.

syn. disprove *ant.* confirm

***

declare
[diklέər]
[동] 선언[선포·공표]하다
n. declaration

v. to announce formally

The museum **declared** its intention to look into the origins of certain pieces in its international collection.

syn. proclaim

**

defy
[difái]
[동] 반항[저항·거역]하다
n. defiance

v. to oppose or refuse to obey

Each generation of young artists **defies** the norms and expectations of those that came before them.

syn. resist *ant.* conform

---

coherent 미술 사학자들은 수 세기 동안 변화하는 미술 동향을 하나의 논리 정연한 설명으로 정리하려고 시도한다. **composition** 네덜란드의 *vanitas* 화에서 물체의 구도는 화가들에 의해 세심하게 계획되었다. **conform** 인상주의 원칙을 따르고 싶지 않아서, 젊은 예술가들은 그들만의 양식을 만들기 시작했다. **debunk** 현대 미술은 훌륭한 가치를 지닌 미술품을 만들어 내는 데에 정규 교육이 필요하다는 생각이 틀렸음을 드러냈다. **declare** 그 박물관 측은 국제 소장품들 중 특정 작품들의 출처를 조사하겠다는 의도를 공표했다. **defy** 각 세대의 젊은 예술가들은 그들 이전 세대로부터 이어져 온 기준과 기대에 저항한다.

deteriorate
★★★★

[ditíəriərèit]

(통) 악화되다, 더 나빠지다

n. deterioration

v. to worsen in condition

Due to the delicate materials used to create them, Chinese scrolls will begin to **deteriorate** if left hanging for extended periods.

syn. fall apart

emerge
★★★

[imə́ːrdʒ]

(통) 1. 드러나다, 알려지다
2. 나오다, 나타나다

n. emergence

v. 1 to become known
  2 to come out of something or become visible   *syn.* materialize

1. The first signs of Van Gogh's genius began to **emerge** during his stay in Arles in the south of France.

2. When artwork is displayed under the proper lighting, details **emerge** that would otherwise go unseen.

engrave
★★

[ingréiv]

(통) (나무·돌·쇠붙이 등에) 새기다

n. engraving

v. to cut words or images into a hard material

The poet William Blake actually began his career as an artist, **engraving** images into copper plates.

syn. inscribe

exaggerate
★★★

[igzǽdʒərèit]

(통) 과장하다

n. exaggeration

v. to make things seem bigger or more extreme than they really are

The body parts that are commonly **exaggerated** in African art are a form of symbolism rather than an indication of a lack of artistic ability.

syn. overstate

exceed
★★★

[iksíːd]

(통) 한계를 넘다, 초과하다

v. to go beyond what was planned

The demand for the work of master artists often **exceeded** their ability to produce it, so they relied on the assistance of apprentices.

ant. fall short

exceptional
★★★

[iksépʃənl]

(형) 이례적일 정도로 우수한, 특출한

adj. unusually good

The **exceptional** quality of the Korean paper known as *hanji* made it a favorite material of local artists.

syn. extraordinary   *ant.* subpar

---

deteriorate 중국의 족자들은 손상되기 쉬운 약한 재료들로 만들어졌기 때문에, 장기간 걸어 놓으면 상태가 더 나빠지기 시작한다.   **emerge** 1. Van Gogh의 천재성의 첫 번째 징후는 그가 프랑스 남부 아를에 머물 적에 드러나기 시작했다.   2. 적절한 조명 아래에 미술 작품이 전시될 때, 조명 없이는 보이지 않을 수도 있는 세부 양식들이 나타난다.   **engrave** 시인 William Blake는 사실 예술가로서 사회생활을 시작했는데, 동판에 그림을 새기는 일을 했다.   **exaggerate** 아프리카 미술에서 흔히 과장되어 있는 신체 부위는 예술 실력이 부족하다는 표시라기보다는 상징성의 한 형태이다.   **exceed** 미술계의 거장들은 그들 작품에 대한 수요가 그것을 완성해내는 능력을 종종 넘어섰기 때문에, 수제자들의 도움에 의지했다.   **exceptional** '한지'라고 알려진 한국 종이의 우수한 품질은 그것이 한국 예술가들이 가장 선호하는 재료가 되게 했다.

flaunt
[flɔːnt]
(동) 과시하다

v. to show off something you are proud of to impress others

Wealthy individuals in Florence **flaunted** their power by commissioning artwork from some of the greatest artists of the Renaissance.

geometric
[dʒìːəmétrik]
(형) 기하학의, 기하학적인

n. geometry

adj. relating to or made up of basic lines, curves, and shapes

Cubist artists were best known for changing the natural forms of objects into simple **geometric** shapes.

Useful Tips

geometry는 도형이나 공간에 대한 학문, 즉 '기하학'을 의미한다. 철자가 비슷한 geology(지질학)나 geography(지리학)와 혼동하지 않도록 주의한다.

imaginary
[imǽdʒənèri]
(형) 상상에만 존재하는, 가상적인

v. imagine

adj. not real; existing only in the mind

Imaginary creatures such as the unicorn were often used in a symbolic manner in the art of the Middle Ages.

syn. fictional, unreal

immense
[iméns]
(형) 거대한, 어마어마한

adj. very large

The people of Easter Island created **immense** rock sculptures in the shape of human heads more than 500 years ago.

syn. gigantic, enormous   *ant.* tiny

impressive
[imprésiv]
(형) 인상적인, 인상[감명] 깊은

v. impress

adj. capable of drawing the attention and admiration of others

In the late 19th century, the **impressive** artwork of Japan was introduced to Europe in the form of postcards.

syn. awe-inspiring, magnificent   *ant.* trivial

instill
[instíl]
(동) (사상·감정 등을) 서서히 불어넣다, 주입시키다

v. to cause someone to slowly feel or believe something

Apprenticeships were sometimes used to **instill** a sense of confidence in young artisans who were still learning their craft.

---

flaunt 피렌체의 부유한 사람들은 르네상스의 가장 훌륭한 몇몇 예술가들에게 미술품을 의뢰함으로써, 그들의 권력을 과시했다.   **geometric** 입체파 예술가들은 물체의 원래 형태를 단순한 기하학적 모양들로 바꾸는 것으로 가장 잘 알려졌다.   **imaginary** 유니콘과 같은 상상 속의 동물들은 중세 시대 미술에서 종종 상징적인 방식으로 사용되었다.   **immense** 이스터 섬의 사람들은 500년 보다 더 이전에 인간 머리 모양을 한 거대한 석상을 만들었다.   **impressive** 19세기 후반에, 일본의 인상적인 미술 작품이 엽서의 형태로 유럽에 소개되었다.   **instill** 수습 기간은 때로 기술을 익히고 있는 젊은 장인들에게 자신감을 심어주기 위해 사용되었다.

★

marvelous
[mά:rvələs]

[형] 아주 훌륭한, 놀라운

n. marvel

adj. wonderful; amazing

The Inca produced **marvelous** pieces of metalwork that are unlike any other ancient Mesoamerican art.

syn. astonishing *ant.* awful

★★

mimic
[mímik]

[동] …을 모방하다, 흉내를 내다

v. to copy the sound or appearance of someone or something

Many modern artists have tried to **mimic** the style of Jackson Pollock, but his creations remain unique.

★

mysterious
[mistíəriəs]

[형] 이해[설명]하기 힘든, 불가사의한

n. mystery

adj. difficult to understand or identify

A **mysterious** painting titled *Salvator Mundi* is said to be the work of Leonardo da Vinci, but some experts have expressed doubts.

syn. enigmatic

★★

obscure
[əbskjúər]

[형] 1. 분명하지 않은, 알기 어려운
2. 잘 알려져 있지 않은, 무명의

n. obscurity

adj. 1 hard to understand or see *syn.* vague *ant.* clear
2 not well known *syn.* unknown *ant.* famous

1. The origins of the piece of ancient pottery are **obscure**, but it may have been produced in Persia.
2. Frida Kahlo was an **obscure** artist for most of her life, but she has achieved great fame since her death in 1954.

★★

offensive
[əfénsiv]

[형] 1. 불쾌한, 모욕적인
2. 역겨운

adj. 1 upsetting or insulting to others *syn.* obnoxious *ant.* agreeable
2 disgusting

1. Some people consider the artwork of Damien Hirst to be **offensive**, while others find it impressive.
2. It is unfortunate that some of the substances used to preserve the ancient artwork have an **offensive** odor.

★★

outrageous
[autréidʒəs]

[형] 너무나 충격적인, 당찮은

n., v. outrage

adj. shocking and unacceptable

The **outrageous** behavior of people who have vandalized priceless works of art can never be forgiven.

syn. disgraceful

Useful Tips

outrageous는 기본적으로 부정적인 이미지를 가지고 있지만, 현대 영어에서는 종종 긍정적인 의미의 놀라움을 나타내는 데 사용되기도 한다.

---

marvelous 잉카는 다른 고대 메소아메리카 예술품들과는 다른 아주 훌륭한 금속 작품들을 만들어냈다. **mimic** 여러 현대 미술가들이 Jackson Pollock의 기법을 모방하려고 노력했지만, 그의 작품들은 여전히 독특하다. **mysterious** *Salvator Mundi*라는 제목의 불가사의한 그림은 Leonardo da Vinci의 작품이라고 하지만, 일부 전문가들은 의구심을 나타냈다. **obscure** 1. 그 고대 도기 작품의 기원은 분명하지 않지만, 페르시아에서 제작되었을 수도 있다. 2. Frida Kahlo는 그녀의 삶 대부분 동안 무명 예술가였지만, 그녀가 사망한 1954년 이래로 대단한 명성을 얻었다. **offensive** 1. 다른 이들이 Damien Hirst의 작품을 인상적이라고 느끼는 반면에, 몇몇 사람들은 그의 작품을 불쾌하다고 여긴다. 2. 고대 미술 작품을 보존하는 데 사용된 몇몇 물질에서 역겨운 냄새가 나는 것은 유감스러운 일이다. **outrageous** 대단히 귀중한 미술 작품을 훼손한 사람들의 충격적인 행동은 결코 용서받을 수 없다.

perilous
[pérələs]
⑬ 아주 위험한
n. peril

adj. full of danger

In 1891, Paul Gaugin made the **perilous** trip to Tahiti, where he found great inspiration for his later work.

syn. dangerous   *ant.* safe

perpetual
[pərpétʃuəl]
⑬ 끊임없이 계속되는

adj. happening without end; occurring repeatedly

There is a **perpetual** demand for outdoor sculptures and other large works of art that can be displayed in public.

syn. everlasting, never-ending   *ant.* finite

predecessor
[prédəsèsər]
⑬ 전임자, 전신, 앞서 있었던 것
v. precede

n. someone or something that came first

The **predecessors** of modern canvases were simple wood panels, although many works were painted directly onto walls.

syn. forerunner   *ant.* successor

rampant
[rǽmpənt]
⑬ (나쁜 것이) 걷잡을 수 없는, 만연[횡행]하는

adj. widespread and out of control

Many art movements have faced **rampant** criticism from people unwilling to accept radical change.

syn. unchecked   *ant.* constrained

rebel
[ribél]
⑤ 저항[반항]하다
[rébəl]
⑬ 반항자, 저항자
n. rebellion

v. to refuse to follow the rules   *syn.* defy, revolt

Members of the Realist movement **rebelled** against the constraints and demands of Romanticism.

n. someone who refuses to follow the rules
syn. nonconformist, insurgent

Banksy is known as an artistic **rebel** who constantly pushes the boundaries of modern art.

refer to
[rifə́ːr tu]
⑤ 1. 언급하다, 주목하게 하다
2. 문의하다
n. reference

v. 1 to mention or draw attention to   *syn.* allude
2 to consult for information

1. Many art historians have begun to **refer to** Paul Cézanne as the "father of modern art."

2. Visitors can **refer to** a list of every piece in the museum's collection, arranged by style, genre, and period.

---

perilous 1891년에 Paul Gaugin은 그의 후기 작품들에 지대한 영감을 준 장소인 타히티로의 위험천만한 여행을 떠났다.   **perpetual** 공개적으로 전시될 수 있는 실외 조각상들과 다른 거대한 미술 작품들에 대한 끊임없는 요구가 있다.   **predecessor** 많은 작품들이 곧바로 벽에 그려지기 했지만, 현대 캔버스의 전신은 단순한 나무 판자였다.   **rampant** 많은 예술 운동은 급진적 변화를 받아들이기를 꺼리는 사람들의 걷잡을 수 없는 비판에 부딪혔다.   **rebel** 사실주의 운동의 일원들은 낭만주의의 제약과 강요에 저항했다. / Banksy는 현대 미술의 지평을 끊임없이 넓혀가는 예술적 저항자로 알려져 있다.   **refer to** 1. 많은 미술 사학자들이 Paul Cézanne을 '현대 미술의 아버지'라고 언급하기 시작했다. 2. 방문자들은 양식, 부문, 시기별로 정리된 모든 박물관 소장품들의 목록을 문의할 수 있다.

★★

serene
[sərí:n]
⃝ 잔잔한, 평화로운
n. serenity

adj. calm and peaceful

The **serene** colors of Monet's paintings of lily ponds make them favorites of art lovers even today.

syn. tranquil　*ant.* chaotic

★★

strive
[straiv]
⃝ 분투하다

v. to try to do something with effort or enthusiasm

Many Westerners **strive** to understand the symbolism of early Asian art, but much of it is unfamiliar to them.

syn. endeavor

Useful Tips

본래 strive의 활용 형태는 strive-strove-striven이지만 현대영어에서 때때로 strive-strived-strived의 형태를 사용하는 경우도 있다. 하지만 이는 표준형이 아니므로 주의한다.

★

stun
[stʌn]
⃝ …을 어리벙벙하게 하다, 깜짝 놀라게 하다
adj. stunning

v. to shock someone so much that he or she cannot react

The fact that Georgia O'Keeffe's *Jimson Weed/White Flower No. 1* sold for more than $44 million **stunned** the art world.

syn. astound

★★

subtle
[sʌ́tl]
⃝ 미묘한, 감지하기 힘든
n. subtlety

adj. unclear; difficult to notice

There are some **subtle** differences between the ancient art of the Mayans and that of the Aztecs.

syn. understated, delicate　*ant.* bold

★

technique
[tekní:k]
⃝ 기법, 방법

n. a way of doing something

Some of the **techniques** used by primitive artists are still being employed today.

syn. method

★★★

transcend
[trænsénd]
⃝ (경험·이성·상상 등이) …을 넘다, 초월하다
adj. transcendental

v. to go beyond the limitations of something

Performance art is sometimes viewed as a way of **transcending** the static nature of traditional artwork.

---

serene Monet의 수련 연못 그림들의 잔잔한 색감은 오늘날까지도 많은 미술 애호가들에게 가장 사랑받고 있다.　**strive** 많은 서양인들이 초기 동양 미술의 상징적인 표현을 이해하려고 노력하지만, 대부분이 그들에게는 생소하다.　**stun** Georgia O'Keeffe의 *Jimson Weed/White Flower No. 1*이 4천4백만 달러 이상의 가격에 팔렸다는 사실은 미술계를 깜짝 놀라게 했다.　**subtle** 마야와 아즈텍의 고대 미술에는 약간의 미묘한 차이들이 있다.　**technique** 원시 시대 예술가들이 사용했던 몇몇 기법들은 요즘에도 여전히 사용되고 있다.　**transcend** 공연 예술은 때로로 전통 예술의 정적인 성격을 초월하는 하나의 방법으로 여겨진다.

EXERCISES

ART & DESIGN

SOCIAL SCIENCE

NATURAL SCIENCE

HUMANITIES

EARTH & SPACE

SOCIAL ISSUES

A Match each definition with the correct word.

1 a powerful feeling that something is true or good   ⓐ instill

2 to cause someone to slowly feel or believe something   ⓑ appall

3 the arrangement or makeup of something   ⓒ geometric

4 upsetting or insulting to others   ⓓ perpetual

5 unusually good   ⓔ offensive

6 relating to or made up of basic lines, curves, and shapes   ⓕ exceptional

7 to cause feelings of shock or disapproval   ⓖ composition

8 happening without end; occurring repeatedly   ⓗ belief

B Choose the word that is closest in meaning to each underlined word.

1 The author has the ability to transform poorly translated text into something coherent.
    ⓐ comprehensible   ⓑ unfamiliar   ⓒ illogical   ⓓ regrettable

2 The exciting scenes depicted on the movie poster were designed to appeal to teenagers.
    ⓐ frustrate   ⓑ surprise   ⓒ captivate   ⓓ disappoint

3 As the folk musicians played a serene song, audience members closed their eyes and smiled.
    ⓐ tranquil   ⓑ innovative   ⓒ sensational   ⓓ melancholy

4 The film contains a subtle message about the importance of empathizing with others.
    ⓐ unneeded   ⓑ obvious   ⓒ outdated   ⓓ understated

5 The weaver sometimes exaggerates the speed at which she can work to impress others.
    ⓐ dominates   ⓑ overstates   ⓒ improves   ⓓ communicates

6 Compared to today's models, early film cameras were immense and difficult to carry.
    ⓐ gigantic   ⓑ precious   ⓒ primitive   ⓓ efficient

7 When historical structures begin to deteriorate, architects are called in to restore them.
    ⓐ grow up   ⓑ fall apart   ⓒ come together   ⓓ show off

> 사진술
Photography

★★
affect
[əfékt]
ⓥ 영향을 미치다

v. to influence or cause a change in someone or something

The intensity and location of a light source can **affect** the overall quality and appearance of a photograph.

syn. alter

★★
augment
[ɔːgmént]
ⓥ 증강시키다, 늘리다

n. augmentation

v. to change something by making it bigger or better

There are many computer programs designed to give people the ability to **augment** their own digital photos.

syn. improve   *ant.* diminish

★
automatic
[ɔːtəmætik]
ⓐ 자동의

adj. not requiring human control

This digital camera has an **automatic** mode that chooses the proper settings for each picture.

★★
boost
[buːst]
ⓥ 늘리다, 끌어 올리다

v. to help something increase or improve

The photographer decided to **boost** the value of her photos by mounting them in attractive frames.

syn. advance

★★
candid
[kǽndid]
ⓐ 1. 자연스러운, 포즈를 취하지 않은
2. 솔직한, 진솔한

adj. 1 informal and unposed
      2 direct, open, and honest   *syn.* straightforward

1. After taking some formal pictures of the president, the photographer asked to take some **candid** shots.

2. The art students had a **candid** discussion with their professor about the quality of the photographs in the gallery.

★★
capture
[kǽptʃər]
ⓥ 포착하다, 잡다

v. to accurately record a feeling or mood

Ansel Adams' black-and-white photos **captured** the untamed beauty of the American West.

---

affect 광원의 강도와 위치가 사진의 전반적인 질과 모습에 영향을 미칠 수 있다.   **augment** 사람들이 자신의 디지털 사진을 증강시킬 수 있도록 고안된 컴퓨터 프로그램이 많이 있다.   **automatic** 이 디지털 카메라에는 각 사진에 적합한 설정을 선택하는 자동 모드가 있다.   **boost** 그 사진작가는 자신의 사진들을 멋진 액자에 끼워 그것들의 가치를 올리기로 결정했다.   **candid** 1. 그 사진작가는 공식적인 대통령 사진을 몇 장 찍은 후, 자연스러운 모습을 몇 장 찍자고 요청했다. 2. 그 미술학도들은 그 미술관에 있는 사진들의 질에 대해 교수와 진솔한 토론을 했다.   **capture** Ansel Adams의 흑백 사진들은 미국 서부의 야성 그대로의 아름다움을 포착했다.

ART & DESIGN

SOCIAL SCIENCE

NATURAL SCIENCE

HUMANITIES

EARTH & SPACE

SOCIAL ISSUES

★★★ **complex**
[kəmpléks, kámpleks]

ⓐ 복잡한

n. complexity

adj. difficult to understand due to containing many parts and details

The **complex** internal mechanism of cameras is susceptible to damage caused by extreme weather conditions.

syn. intricate   *ant.* simple

★★ **critical**
[krítikəl]

ⓐ 매우 중요한, 결정적인

adj. extremely important

Composition is **critical** when taking formal photographs of large groups of people.

syn. essential   *ant.* trivial

★★ **define**
[difáin]

ⓥ 분명히 나타내다,
규정하다

v. to describe the nature of something

The impressive photos of Annie Leibovitz **define** the creativity and excess of American celebrity culture.

★ **determine**
[ditə́ːrmin]

ⓥ 밝히다, 결정하다

v. to find out certain facts or information

The value of vintage photos is generally **determined** by their age, subject matter, and overall condition.

syn. calculate, discover

★★★ **develop**
[divéləp]

ⓥ 1. 현상하다
2. 발전하다, 발달하다

n. development

v. 1 to make photographs or negatives from film
2 to grow and progress   *syn.* flourish

1. Darkrooms have historically been used for **developing** film in an environment free from damaging light.

2. The art of photography **developed** slowly at first, partly due to the size and costliness of the necessary equipment.

★★ **distort**
[distɔ́ːrt]

ⓥ 왜곡하다, 비틀다

n. distortion

v. to change something so that it is no longer accurate

Experimental photographers will sometimes use special filters that **distort** the images in their work.

syn. twist

---

complex 카메라의 복잡한 내부 구조는 극심한 기후 조건에 의해 손상되기 쉽다.   **critical** 공식적인 대규모 인물 사진을 찍을 때, 구성이 매우 중요하다.
define Annie Leibovitz의 그 인상적인 사진들은 미국 유명인 문화의 창의성과 과잉을 분명히 나타낸다.   **determine** 빈티지 사진의 가치는 보통 그것의 연식,
소재, 그리고 전반적인 상태에 의해 결정된다.   **develop** 1. 역사적으로 암실은 손상을 입히는 빛이 없는 환경에서 필름을 현상하는 데 사용되어 왔다.   2. 처음에는
사진술이 서서히 발전했는데, 부분적으로는 필요한 장비의 크기와 비싼 가격 때문이었다.   **distort** 실험적인 사진작가들은 자기 작품 속의 이미지를 왜곡시키는 특수
필터를 때때로 사용할 것이다.

★★
exposure
[ikspóuʒər]
[명] 노출
v. expose

n. the act of allowing film to come in contact with light

A long **exposure** is ideal for landscape photography, as it brings out the details in unmoving objects.

★★★
figure
[fígjər]
[명] 1. 사람 모양[모습]
2. 명사, 거물

n. 1 a human shape *syn.* form
2 a well-known individual

1. What appeared to be a dark **figure** in the background of the photo turned out to be nothing more than a shadow.
2. Man Ray, a renowned fashion and portrait photographer, was an important **figure** in the art and fashion scene of Paris in the 1930s.

★★★
focus
[fóukəs]
[동] 1. 초점을 맞추다
2. (관심·노력 등을) 집중하다

v. 1 to sharpen a camera's image
2 to concentrate on a single thing

1. By twisting the dial located on the shaft of the lens, users can **focus** the camera quickly and easily.
2. Some photographers **focus** on a single genre throughout their careers, while others experiment with various styles.

★
hue
[*h*juː]
[명] 색조

n. a certain variation of a color; shade

The yellowish **hue** of old sepia photos was achieved through a special chemical process.

★★
ironically
[airɑ́nikəli]
[부] 반어적으로, 얄궂게도
n. irony

adv. in a way that is paradoxical or different from how it appears

Ironically, the photographer's touching pictures of families living in poverty made him a wealthy man.

★★
magnify
[mǽgnəfài]
[동] 확대하다
n. magnification

v. to make something appear larger

A telephoto lens will **magnify** images to a much greater degree than standard digital zoom lenses.

syn. enlarge *ant.* shrink

Useful Tips
magnifying glass는 '돋보기,' magnifying power는 광학에서 '배율'을 뜻한다.

---

exposure 긴 노출은 움직이지 않는 대상의 세부 요소들을 나타내 주기 때문에 풍경 사진에 이상적이다. **figure** 1. 그 사진 배경에 검은 사람 모습으로 보였던 것은 그림자에 불과했던 것으로 밝혀졌다. 2. 유명한 패션 및 인물 사진작가인 Man Ray는 1930년대 파리의 예술 및 패션계에서 중요한 거물이었다.
focus 1. 사용자들은 렌즈축 위에 있는 다이얼을 돌려, 빠르고 쉽게 그 카메라의 초점을 맞출 수 있다. 2. 어떤 사진작가들은 작업을 하는 동안 줄곧 한 가지 장르에 집중하는 반면, 다양한 스타일을 실험해 보는 작가들도 있다. **hue** 특수 화학처리 공정을 통해 오래된 적갈색 사진의 누르스름한 색조가 나왔다.
ironically 얄궂게도, 가난한 생활을 하는 가족들을 찍은 그 사진작가의 감동적인 사진들이 그를 부자로 만들었다. **magnify** 망원 렌즈는 일반적인 디지털 줌렌즈보다 이미지들을 훨씬 더 크게 확대할 것이다.

★
manual
[mǽnjuəl]
[명] 안내 책자

n. **a book that explains how to use a device or machine**

The photo editing software came with an illustrated **manual** written in several different languages.

syn. handbook

★★
memorable
[mémərəbl]
[형] 기억할 만한, 인상적인

adj. **worth remembering or easy to remember**

Neil Leifer's famous picture of the boxer Muhammad Ali is one of the most **memorable** sports photos of all time.

syn. noteworthy, catchy *ant.* insignificant, forgettable

★★
outline
[áutlàin]
[동] 약술하다, …의 개요를 설명하다

v. **to make a summary of a plan or written work**

Today the gallery will **outline** its plans for providing free exhibition space to local amateur photographers.

syn. summarize

★
patchy
[pǽtʃi]
[형] 드문드문 있는, 고르지 못한

n. patch

adj. **existing in some places but not others**

A ray of sunshine bursting through some **patchy** clouds can transform an ordinary photo into something special.

syn. spotty

★★
pertinent
[pə́ːrtənənt]
[형] 적절한, 관계가 있는

v. pertain

adj. **clearly related to the matter at hand**

All of the **pertinent** details of this photograph can be found on the plaque located just beneath it.

syn. relevant

★★★
potential
[pəténʃəl]
[형] 잠재적인, 가능성 있는
[명] 잠재력, 가능성

adj. **possibly happening in the future** *syn.* possible

The photo of the dam seems to show a **potential** disaster, as cracks are clearly visible in the concrete.

n. **the capacity to do or become something in the future**

In the late 19th century, few people believed photography had the **potential** to become a serious art form.

manual 그 사진 편집 소프트웨어에는 몇 개의 다양한 언어로 쓰여진, 삽화가 수록된 안내 책자가 딸려 있었다. **memorable** Neil Leifer가 권투 선수 Muhammad Ali를 찍은 유명한 사진은 역사상 가장 기억될 만한 스포츠 사진들 중 하나이다. **outline** 오늘 그 미술관은 현지 아마추어 사진작가들에게 무료로 전시 공간을 제공하는 계획의 개요를 설명할 것이다. **patchy** 드문드문 있는 구름 사이를 뚫고 나온 한 줄기 햇살이 평범한 사진을 특별한 것으로 변화시킬 수 있다. **pertinent** 이 사진에 관련된 모든 세부 사항은 바로 그 밑에 있는 명판에서 확인할 수 있다. **potential** 그 댐 사진에는 콘크리트에 갈라진 금들이 뚜렷이 보이기 때문에, 잠재적 재난을 보여 주는 것 같다. / 19세기 말에, 사진술이 진지한 예술 형식이 될 가능성이 있다고 믿는 사람은 거의 없었다.

privilege
★★★
[prívəlidʒ]

图 1. 특권, 특전
2. 영광, 명예

adj. privileged

n. 1 a right or benefit only certain people receive   *ant.* disadvantage
2 a desirable opportunity

1. The **privileges** of being the official photographer of the royal family included full access to private events.

2. The critic said it was a **privilege** to be one of the first people to view the museum's new photo exhibit.

resume
★★
[rizúːm]

图 다시 시작하다

n. resumption

v. to start again after a pause

The photoshoot **resumed** after the models and lighting crew were given a 30-minute break for lunch.

syn. restart

seize
★★
[siːz]

图 잡다, 포착하다

n. seizure

v. to take something suddenly and forcefully

The photographer **seized** the opportunity to take some rare photos, picking up her camera and running into the storm.

syn. grab   *ant.* release

> **Useful Tips**
> 라틴어구 carpe diem에서 유래한 seize the day는 '오늘을 즐기다, 호기를 놓치지 않다'라는 뜻이다.

spontaneous
★★★
[spɑntéiniəs]

图 자연스러운, 즉흥적인

adj. natural and unplanned

The **spontaneous** nature of Henri Cartier-Bresson's street photos has made them a favorite of many photography lovers.

syn. impromptu   *ant.* premeditated

symmetry
★
[símətri]

图 대칭, 균형

adj. symmetrical

n. the trait of being identical on either side

The photographer created **symmetry** in the photo by positioning the model between a pair of tall oak trees.

syn. balance   *ant.* imbalance

unequivocally
★
[ʌ̀nikwívəkəli]

凰 명백히, 절대적으로

adv. without any question or doubt

Dorothea Lange is **unequivocally** considered one of the most important documentary photographers of her time.

syn. unquestionably   *ant.* doubtfully

---

privilege 1. 왕실 가족의 공식 사진사가 되는 것의 특권들 중에는 사적인 행사에 전면적으로 접근할 수 있는 것이 포함되었다. 2. 그 비평가는 그 미술관의 새로운 사진전을 처음으로 관람하게 되어 영광이라고 말했다. **resume** 모델들과 조명 담당자들이 30분 간의 점심시간을 가진 후, 사진 촬영이 다시 시작됐다. **seize** 그 사진작가는 자신의 카메라를 집어 들어 폭풍우 속으로 달려 들어가 보기 드문 사진을 찍을 기회를 잡았다. **spontaneous** Henri Cartier-Bresson이 찍은 거리 사진들의 자연스러운 특성 때문에, 많은 사진 애호가들이 그 사진들을 좋아한다. **symmetry** 그 사진작가는 그 모델을 한 쌍의 큰 참나무 사이에 자리 잡게 함으로써, 그 사진에 대칭을 만들었다. **unequivocally** Dorothea Lange은 명백히 그녀 당대의 가장 중요한 다큐멘터리 사진작가들 중 하나로 간주된다.

EXERCISES

ART & DESIGN

SOCIAL SCIENCE

NATURAL SCIENCE

HUMANITIES

EARTH & SPACE

SOCIAL ISSUES

A Match each definition with the correct word.

1 to make photographs or negatives from film   ⓐ privilege

2 the act of allowing film to come in contact with light   ⓑ exposure

3 a human shape   ⓒ unequivocally

4 a right or benefit only certain people receive   ⓓ pertinent

5 clearly related to the matter at hand   ⓔ develop

6 extremely important   ⓕ focus

7 without any question or doubt   ⓖ critical

8 to sharpen a camera's image   ⓗ figure

B Choose the word that is closest in meaning to each underlined word.

1 Opera glasses were once commonly used to <u>magnify</u> the performers on the stage.
   ⓐ contact   ⓑ recreate   ⓒ identify   ⓓ enlarge

2 City planners must analyze <u>complex</u> traffic patterns before installing new traffic lights.
   ⓐ ancient   ⓑ intricate   ⓒ unexpected   ⓓ fatal

3 The director decided to use CGI to <u>augment</u> the appearance of the actor playing an alien.
   ⓐ discuss   ⓑ transport   ⓒ improve   ⓓ ridicule

4 The architects considered the <u>potential</u> drawbacks of installing large skylights in the ceiling.
   ⓐ possible   ⓑ mild   ⓒ unwanted   ⓓ repeated

5 Inspired by the beautiful scenery, the artist <u>seized</u> his easel and the nearest blank canvas.
   ⓐ blamed   ⓑ grabbed   ⓒ purchased   ⓓ copied

6 The dollmaker did some research to <u>determine</u> if there was a market for her creations.
   ⓐ deny   ⓑ proclaim   ⓒ increase   ⓓ discover

7 In the musical's most <u>memorable</u> scene, the heroine declares her love for her neighbor.
   ⓐ confusing   ⓑ noteworthy   ⓒ amusing   ⓓ questionable

Lesson 08 | Fashion & Design

---

adapt
[ədǽpt]
동 (상황에) 적응하다
n. adaptation

v. to change something to fit a new situation

Whenever global fashion trends change, designers need to quickly **adapt** to the new styles.

syn. adjust

---

anecdote
[ǽnikdòut]
명 일화
adj. anecdotal

n. a short story about an amusing or interesting incident

The fashion model told an **anecdote** about finding out all the outfits were the wrong size at a runway show.

syn. tale

---

attire
[ətáiər]
명 의복, 복장

n. the clothes someone is wearing

The **attire** of celebrities at televised events is carefully chosen by professional fashion consultants.

syn. apparel

---

avant-garde
[əvà:ntgá:rd]
형 전위적인, 선구적이고 실험적인

adj. new and experimental

The **avant-garde** interior design of the new hotel was quite a shock to guests who were used to the traditional style of most hotels.

syn. unconventional   *ant.* conventional

---

bleach
[bli:tʃ]
동 표백하다, 색을 바래게 하다

v. to cause something to lose its color and become white

The sun **bleached** all the color out of the old pair of blue jeans, giving them a casual, worn-out appearance.

syn. whiten

---

cease
[si:s]
동 중단되다, 그치다
n. cessation

v. to come to an end

Publication of *Mademoiselle*, a popular women's fashion magazine in the 1960s and 70s, **ceased** in 2001.

syn. halt   *ant.* continue

---

adapt 전 세계 패션 트렌드가 바뀔 때마다, 디자이너들은 새로운 스타일에 빨리 적응해야 한다.   **anecdote** 그 패션모델은 패션쇼에서 모든 의상이 잘못된 사이즈라는 것을 알게 되었던 일화를 들려주었다.   **attire** TV로 방송되는 행사에 참석한 유명 인사들의 의상은 전문 패션 고문들이 신중하게 선택한다. **avant-garde** 새 호텔의 전위적인 실내 디자인은 대부분의 호텔의 전통적인 양식에 익숙해 있던 손님들에게 상당한 충격을 주었다.   **bleach** 오래된 청바지의 색이 햇볕에 완전히 바래, 캐주얼하고 헤진 모습이 되었다.   **cease** 1960·70년대 인기 여성 패션 잡지였던 *Mademoiselle*의 발행은 2001년에 중단되었다.

ART & DESIGN

SOCIAL SCIENCE

NATURAL SCIENCE

HUMANITIES

EARTH & SPACE

SOCIAL ISSUES

characteristic
[kæ̀riktərístik]

ⓐ 특유의, 특징적인, 전형적인
ⓝ 특징, 특성

adj. expected of a particular person, place, or thing　*syn.* distinctive

It is **characteristic** of high-fashion brands to display shocking and unconventional clothing at their seasonal shows.

n. a distinguishing feature　*syn.* trait

One unmistakable **characteristic** of the Art Deco design style is the heavy use of chrome plating and stainless steel.

client
[kláiənt]

ⓝ (전문가의 서비스를 받는) 고객, 의뢰인

n. someone who pays for a service

The interior designer personally visits the home of each of her **clients** before making suggestions for improvements.

syn. customer

complement
[kúmpləmənt]

ⓥ 보완하다

adj. complementary

v. to complete or improve something else

Silver accessories including bracelets and a brooch were used to **complement** the deep blue of the gown.

conscious
[kánʃəs]

ⓐ 1. 신중한
　 2. 의식이 있는

adj. 1 done with careful thought
　　　 2 awake and aware　*ant.* unconscious

1. The clothing brand made the **conscious** decision to raise the prices of their products despite the economic recession.

2. After falling and hitting his head during the runway show, the model was **conscious** but in great pain.

cumbersome
[kÁmbərsəm]

ⓐ 크고 무거운, 다루기 힘든, 거추장스러운

v. encumber

adj. heavy or difficult to move or use

It was once considered fashionable for women to wear **cumbersome** hats that could barely fit through a doorway.

syn. unwieldy

customize
[kÁstəmàiz]

ⓥ 주문 제작하다, 사용자의 사정에 맞추다

v. to change something for a particular intention or person

The store's formal wear can be **customized** by having the customer's initials printed on the inside of the lapel.

syn. personalize　*ant.* standardize

---

characteristic 시즌별 패션쇼에서 파격적이고 색다른 옷을 내놓는 것이 최신 패션 브랜드들의 특징이다. / Art Deco 디자인 양식의 틀림없는 특징 중 하나는 크롬 도금과 스테인리스강을 많이 사용한다는 것이다.　**client** 그 인테리어 디자이너는 개선점을 제안하기 전에 각 고객의 집을 직접 방문한다.　**complement** 팔찌와 브로치를 포함한 은으로 만든 장신구들은 그 드레스의 짙은 푸른색을 보완하기 위해 사용되었다.　**conscious** 1. 그 의류 브랜드는 경기 침체에도 불구하고 제품 가격을 인상하기로 신중하게 결정했다. 2. 패션쇼 중에 넘어져 머리를 부딪힌 후, 그 모델은 의식이 있었지만 엄청난 고통을 느꼈다.　**cumbersome** 출입구를 간신히 통과할 수 있는 거추장스러운 모자를 쓰는 것이 한때 여성들에게 유행으로 여겨졌다.　**customize** 그 상점의 정장은 옷깃 안쪽에 고객의 이니셜을 박아 넣는 주문 제작이 가능하다.

differentiate
[dìfərénʃièit]

ⓥ …을 구별하다

n. difference

v. to show or recognize the difference between two things

It can be difficult to **differentiate** between silk and nylon from a distance, but the superior quality of silk is obvious from up close.

syn. discern, distinguish

---

elite
[ilíːt, ei-]

ⓐ 선발된, 정예의
ⓝ 최상류층 사람들

adj. among the best of its type   *syn.* first class   *ant.* inferior

An **elite** team of interior designers was brought in to the White House to prepare it for the new president and his family.

n. a small group of wealthy, powerful people
   syn. upper class   *ant.* commoner

Some fashion is still designed for the **elite**, but most brands are focused on the needs of everyday people.

---

emphasize
[émfəsàiz]

ⓥ 강조하다, 두드러지게 하다

n. emphasis

v. to make something more noticeable

Tight-fitting clothing that **emphasizes** the shape of the wearer is losing popularity to comfortable, casual styles.

syn. stress, accent   *ant.* downplay

---

enhance
[inhǽns]

ⓥ 높이다, 향상시키다

n. enhancement

v. to improve something

Patterned wallpaper was once thought to **enhance** the appearance of a room, but it has largely fallen out of style.

ant. diminish

---

exclusive
[iksklúːsiv]

ⓐ 독점적인, 한정된,
   다른 곳에서 살 수 없는

adj. available only to certain people

An **exclusive** shop in Los Angeles sells one-of-a-kind wedding gowns that only the super-wealthy can afford.

syn. restricted   *ant.* open

---

garment
[gáːrmənt]

ⓝ 의류 한 점

n. an article of clothing

Selecting an attractive **garment** from the rack, the stylist held it up in front of the model to see if its color matched her hair.

Useful Tips

attire는 한 사람이 입은 의복 전체를 가리키고, garment는 의류 한 점을 의미한다.

---

differentiate 멀리서 비단과 나일론을 구별하기 어려울 수 있지만, 가까이 보면 비단의 우수한 품질이 확연히 드러난다.　**elite** 선발된 실내 디자이너 팀이 신임 대통령과 그의 가족들을 위한 실내 공사를 하기 위해 백악관으로 투입되었다. / 일부 패션은 여전히 최상류층을 위해 디자인되지만, 대부분의 브랜드는 일반인들의 요구에 초점을 맞추고 있다.　**emphasize** 착용자의 몸매를 강조하는 딱 붙는 옷은 편안하고 캐주얼한 스타일에 인기를 잃어가고 있다.　**enhance** 한때 무늬 벽지는 방의 외관을 향상시키는 것으로 여겨졌으나, 유행에 크게 뒤떨어지게 되었다.　**exclusive** 로스앤젤레스에 있는 독점 판매점은 아주 부유한 사람들만이 살 수 있는 하나뿐인 웨딩드레스들을 판매한다.　**garment** 선반에서 매력적인 옷을 한 점 고른 스타일리스트는 그 옷의 색이 모델의 머리와 어울리는지 보려고 옷을 모델에게 대보았다.

★
★ **incorporate**
[inkɔ́ːrpərèit]
ⓥ 1. (일부로) 포함하다
　 2. …을 법인 조직으로 만들다
n. incorporation

v. 1 to use as part of something bigger　*syn.* absorb　*ant.* separate
2 to legally become a corporation

1. The exciting, new fashion line **incorporates** Asian materials and Western styles into a look that is unlike any other.
2. After deciding to **incorporate**, the design firm called its lawyers for help with the confusing paperwork.

★ **in vogue**
[in vóug]
ⓐ 유행하는

adj. currently in style

Wide neckties with bright colors and loud patterns were once **in vogue**, but today they are seen as old-fashioned and tacky.

syn. fashionable　*ant.* out of fashion

★
★ **involve**
[inválv]
ⓥ …을 포함하다
n. involvement

v. to include something as a participant or element

Modern graphic design **involves** the careful use of images and words to convey a message to viewers.

ant. exclude

★ **knack**
[næk]
ⓝ 재주, 요령

n. the ability to do something well

The design consultant has a **knack** for immediately identifying the best style for any room in a home.

syn. skill

★ **loose**
[luːs]
ⓐ 헐렁한, 헐거워진, 풀린

adj. not tight; not properly fastened

The top of the expensive dress is tight and form-fitting, but the bottom half is **loose** and flowing.

syn. baggy　*ant.* tight

★
★ **mend**
[mend]
ⓥ …을 고치다, 수선하다

v. to fix

Using a needle and thread, the tailor quickly **mended** a small tear in the blouse of the model.

syn. repair　*ant.* damage

---

incorporate 그 흥미롭고 새로운 패션 라인은 아시아적인 소재와 서양적인 스타일을 접목시켜 다른 어떤 것과도 다른 모습을 만들어 낸다. / 법인 설립을 결정한 후, 그 디자인 회사는 헷갈리는 서류 작업에 대한 도움을 요청하기 위해 회사 변호사들에게 전화했다.　**in vogue** 한때 밝은 색과 요란한 무늬의 넓은 넥타이가 유행했었지만, 요즘에는 유행에 뒤떨어지고 촌스러워 보인다.　**involve** 현대 그래픽 디자인은 보는 이들에게 메시지를 전달하기 위해 이미지와 단어를 신중하게 사용하는 것을 포함한다.　**knack** 그 디자인 상담가는 집 안의 어떤 방에든 최고의 스타일을 바로 찾아내는 재주가 있다.　**loose** 그 값비싼 드레스의 윗부분은 꽉 조이고 몸에 딱 맞는 반면, 허리 아랫부분은 헐겁게 늘어져 있다.　**mend** 그 재단사는 바늘과 실을 사용하여 모델의 블라우스에 난 작은 구멍을 재빨리 수선했다.

★★ **original**
[ərídʒənl]
[형] 1. 독창적인
2. 최초의, 본래의, 원본의

adj. 1 creative and unique *syn.* inventive *ant.* derivative
2 the first *syn.* initial

1. The designs on display at the Museum of Visual Arts are both **original** and highly appealing to most people.
2. The **original** dress cost thousands of dollars, but mass-produced copies are available at a fraction of the cost.

★ **ornate**
[ɔːrnéit]
[형] 화려하게 장식된

adj. heavily decorated

Wealthy families once insisted on **ornate** interiors for their homes, but today's millionaires generally prefer a minimalistic style.

syn. fancy *ant.* plain

★★ **participate**
[pɑːrtísəpèit]
[동] 참여하다, 참가하다

v. to take part in an event or activity

Even famous fashion designers will sometimes **participate** in the everyday tasks of the business, such as cutting and sewing.

ant. sit out

★ **probation**
[proubéiʃən]
[명] (직장에서의) 수습 기간

n. a period of time during which new employees are carefully monitored

During the new employee's **probation** period at the design firm, she had to report to her supervisor at the end of each day.

★★ **publicity**
[pʌblísəti]
[명] 언론의 관심[주목]
v. publicize

n. attention from the media

Some of the designs on display during fashion week are not actually meant to be worn; rather, they are simply a way of gaining valuable **publicity**.

★★★ **quality**
[kwáləti]
[명] 질, 품질

n. a measurement of how good or bad something is

The **quality** of the blouses is not in question, but their price is too high to appeal to most people.

original 1. 시각예술 박물관에 전시되어 있는 디자인들은 독창적임과 동시에 대부분의 사람들에게 매력적으로 다가온다. 2. 그 드레스 원품 한 벌의 가격은 수천 달러이지만, 대량 생산된 복제품은 훨씬 더 저렴한 가격으로 구매가 가능하다. **ornate** 한때 부유한 가족들은 그들의 집에 화려한 인테리어를 강조했지만, 오늘날의 백만장자들은 일반적으로 단순한 스타일을 선호한다. **participate** 유명한 패션 디자이너들조차도 때때로 재단과 바느질 같은 일상적인 작업에 참여할 것이다. **probation** 디자인 회사에서 수습 기간 동안, 그 신입사원은 매일 업무가 끝날 무렵 상사에게 보고해야 했다. **publicity** 패션 위크 기간 동안 선보여진 몇몇 디자인들은 사실 실제로 착용되기 위한 것이 아니라, 단순히 소중한 언론의 주목을 받기 위한 것이다. **quality** 그 블라우스들의 품질은 의심의 여지가 없지만, 가격이 너무 비싸서 대부분의 사람들에게 매력적이지 못했다.

ART & DESIGN

SOCIAL SCIENCE

NATURAL SCIENCE

HUMANITIES

EARTH & SPACE

SOCIAL ISSUES

simultaneously
[sàiməltéiniəsli]

⑨ 동시에, 일제히

adj. simultaneous

adv. at the same time

Walking down the catwalk side by side, the two fashion models **simultaneously** turned on their heels and continued in the opposite direction.

syn. concurrently

sleek
[sli:k]

⑨ (매끄럽고) 윤기 나는

adj. smooth and shiny

The **sleek** appearance of sharkskin suits made them a favorite of many male celebrities and politicians in the 1950s.

syn. glossy   *ant.* dull

specialize
[spéʃəlàiz]

⑤ 전공하다, 전문으로 삼다

n. specialist

v. to focus on a single field, activity, or subject

Designers that **specialize** in typography help businesses select the best fonts for their signs, websites, and packaging.

striking
[stráikiŋ]

⑨ 눈에 띄는, 두드러진

adj. noticeable due to unusual or extreme features

People couldn't stop talking about the **striking** shoe designs of the brand's recently released autumn collection.

syn. eye-catching   *ant.* ordinary

suitable
[súːtəbl]

⑨ 적합한, 적절한, 알맞은

adj. right or acceptable for the situation or a purpose

Certain color combinations that are perfectly **suitable** for one situation may not be desirable in others.

syn. appropriate, fitting   *ant.* inappropriate

tailored
[téilərd]

⑨ 1. (옷이) 잘 맞도록 만든
2. (특정한 개인·목적을 위한) 맞춤의

adj. 1 made to fit the body well
　　　2 made for a particular person or situation   *syn.* bespoke

1. The CEO's **tailored** suits make him stand out from his employees, most of whom buy their work clothes off the rack.

2. This **tailored** bathroom was designed to fit the needs of the elderly actress, who suffers from arthritis.

---

simultaneously 두 패션모델은 무대를 나란히 걸어가다가 동시에 뒤로 돌았고, 반대 방향으로 계속해서 걸어갔다.　**sleek** 상어 가죽 정장의 윤기 나는 외관은 그 정장들이 1950년대 많은 남성 유명 인사들과 정치인들에게 인기를 끄는 요인이 되었다.　**specialize** 조판 전문 디자이너들은 기업이 간판, 웹 사이트, 포장에 최상의 글꼴을 선택하도록 돕는다.　**striking** 사람들은 최근 출시된 그 브랜드의 가을 컬렉션에 있는 눈에 띄는 신발 디자인들에 대해 이야기하는 것을 멈출 수가 없었다.　**suitable** 한 가지 상황에 완벽하게 알맞은 특정 색 조합은 다른 상황들에는 바람직하지 않을 수 있다.　**tailored** 1. 그 최고 경영자의 맞춤 양복은 대부분 기성복을 구매하는 그의 직원들 사이에서 그를 두드러지게 한다.　2. 이 맞춤 욕실은 관절염을 앓고 있는 나이 든 여배우의 요구에 맞게 설계되었다.

★
trim
[trim]
[동] 다듬다, 손질하다

v. **to neaten or make smaller by cutting away parts**

Any threads hanging off the edges of the fabric must be **trimmed** before the two sections are sewn together.

syn. clip

★★
typical
[típikəl]
[형] 전형적인, 일반적인

adj. **usual; as expected**

Typical graphic design makes use of bold colors and patterns in the interest of catching the attention of purchasers.

syn. normal, standard *ant.* abnormal, unusual

★★
vice versa
[váisə vɔ́ːrsə]
[부] 반대로, 거꾸로

adv. **with the order or relationships reversed**

In order for a project to be successful, clients must be respectful of the ideas of the designers they hire, and **vice versa**.

Useful Tips

vice versa는 라틴어에서 유래한 말로, 문장의 끝에 and vice versa의 형태로 쓰여 '(앞에 언급한 내용의) 반대도 마찬가지이다'라는 의미로 쓰인다.

★
vintage
[víntidʒ]
[형] 옛 것으로 멋진[품위가 있는]

adj. **old and stylish**

This **vintage** fedora, a hat popular in the 1930s, was the inspiration for a new line of classic clothing with a modern twist.

syn. classic *ant.* brand-new

★★★
virtually
[vɔ́ːrtʃuəli]
[부] 1. 거의
2. (컴퓨터를 이용하여) 가상으로
adj. virtual

adv. **1 nearly** *syn.* almost
2 done online

1. It would be **virtually** impossible to find an evening gown more elegant than the one worn by the hostess.
2. Homeowners can now check out the latest trends in interior design **virtually**, simply by visiting a website.

★★
visualize
[víʒuəlàiz]
[동] 마음속에 떠올리다, 시각화하다
adj. visual

v. **to see something in your mind**

Fashion designers must **visualize** what they want to create before making a quick sketch of the idea on paper.

syn. imagine

---

trim 천의 가장자리에 매달려 있는 실은 두 부분을 함께 꿰매기 전에 다듬어야 한다. **typical** 일반 그래픽 디자인은 구매자들의 관심을 끌기 위해 과감한 색상과 무늬들을 사용한다. **vice versa** 하나의 프로젝트가 성공하기 위해서, 고객은 그들이 고용하는 디자이너들의 생각을 존중해야 하고, 그 반대도 마찬가지이다. **vintage** 오래되었지만 멋진 이 페도라는 1930년대에 유행했던 모자로, 현대적 요소를 가미한 새로운 클래식 의상 라인에 영감을 주었다. **virtually** 1. 그 여주인이 입은 이브닝드레스보다 더 우아한 이브닝드레스를 찾는 것은 거의 불가능할 것이다. 2. 집주인들은 간단하게 웹 사이트를 방문해서 실내 디자인의 최신 트렌드를 가상으로 확인할 수 있다. **visualize** 패션 디자이너들은 아이디어를 종이에 간단히 스케치하기 전에 그들이 만들고 싶은 것을 마음속으로 떠올려 봐야 한다.

EXERCISES

A Match each definition with the correct word.

1 to focus on a single field, activity, or subject   ⓐ specialize

2 the ability to do something well   ⓑ vice versa

3 attention from the media   ⓒ tailored

4 to complete or improve something else   ⓓ publicity

5 with the order or relationships reversed   ⓔ complement

6 to show or recognize the difference between two things   ⓕ differentiate

7 made to fit the body well   ⓖ attire

8 the clothes someone is wearing   ⓗ knack

B Choose the word that is closest in meaning to each underlined word.

1 It is difficult to find a theater suitable for performances of Cirque du Soleil.
     ⓐ fitting   ⓑ available   ⓒ inadequate   ⓓ improper

2 The violinist had his instrument customized to better fit his large hands.
     ⓐ repaired   ⓑ destroyed   ⓒ personalized   ⓓ replaced

3 The architect ordered the workers to cease construction after she found a crack in a wall.
     ⓐ accelerate   ⓑ deteriorate   ⓒ continue   ⓓ halt

4 When craftspeople move to another country, they must adapt to the materials available there.
     ⓐ pretend   ⓑ adhere   ⓒ adjust   ⓓ purchase

5 The actors perform on a bare stage, so the audience must visualize the setting.
     ⓐ virtualize   ⓑ imagine   ⓒ diminish   ⓓ improvise

6 Wooden easels are cumbersome for landscape painters, so they prefer lighter ones.
     ⓐ essential   ⓑ prodigious   ⓒ unnecessary   ⓓ unwieldy

7 The popular movie is being shown simultaneously on three different screens.
     ⓐ occasionally   ⓑ erroneously   ⓒ unexpectedly   ⓓ concurrently

ART & DESIGN

SOCIAL SCIENCE

NATURAL SCIENCE

HUMANITIES

EARTH & SPACE

SOCIAL ISSUES

Lesson 09 [건축] Architecture

★★ **adjacent**
[ədʒéisnt]
[형] 인접한, 이웃의

adj. next to or near

The new construction is **adjacent** to an apartment building whose residents have complained that their views will be blocked.

syn. bordering

★★ **blueprint**
[blú:prìnt]
[명] (건물·기계 설계용) 청사진, 계획

n. a technical plan for a building or machine

Unrolling the **blueprints** on the table, the lead architect began to point out some of the structure's planned features.

★★ **calculate**
[kǽlkjulèit]
[동] 계산하다, 산출하다
n. calculation

v. to find an amount through mathematics

The exact height of the proposed building will be **calculated** once the plan has been approved.

syn. compute

★★★ **culminate**
[kʌ́lmənèit]
[동] 정점에 달하다, 끝나다
n. culmination

v. to reach a climax

The official opening of the newly constructed bridge **culminated** with a ribbon-cutting ceremony in the middle of the structure.

syn. peak *ant.* commence

★★★ **demolish**
[dimáliʃ]
[동] 철거하다, 파괴하다
n. demolition

v. to tear down or completely destroy

Several abandoned homes are to be **demolished** to make way for the construction of a huge sports stadium.

syn. raze *ant.* erect

★★ **dense**
[dens]
[형] 1. 밀집한
2. 우둔한
n. density

adj. 1 crowded or closely compacted *ant.* sparse
2 unintelligent *syn.* stupid

1. Due to the **dense** conditions of rapidly growing cities in the late 19th century, architects began to design taller, narrower buildings.
2. People viewing the early ideas of Rem Koolhaas thought he might be **dense**, but they soon realized he was actually an unconventional genius.

adjacent 그 새 건축물은 한 아파트 건물과 인접해 있어서, 아파트 거주자들은 시야가 가려질 것이라며 항의해 왔다. **blueprint** 그 수석 설계자는 탁자 위에 청사진을 펼치며, 계획 중인 그 구조물의 특징 몇 가지를 언급하기 시작했다. **calculate** 제안된 그 건물의 정확한 높이는 그 계획이 승인된 후 산출될 것이다. **culminate** 새로 지어진 그 다리의 공식 개통식은 그 구조물의 중간에서 준공식을 하며 막을 내렸다. **demolish** 대형 종합경기장 건설을 위한 공간을 만들기 위해, 폐가 몇 채가 철거될 예정이다. **dense** 1. 19세기 말 급속도로 성장하는 도시들의 밀집 상태 때문에, 건축가들은 더 높고 폭이 더 좁은 건물들을 설계하기 시작했다. 2. Rem Koolhaas의 초기 아이디어를 본 사람들은 그가 우둔할 것이라 생각했지만, 사실은 그가 독특한 천재라는 것을 곧 깨달았다.

★★ **destitute**
[déstətjùːt]
[형] 빈곤한, 결핍한

adj. having no money or basic necessities

After his firm went bankrupt, the architect ended up **destitute**, begging for change on the street where he once worked.

syn. impoverished *ant.* affluent

★ **diagonal**
[daiǽgənl]
[형] 사선의, 대각선의

adj. connecting the opposite corners of a two-dimensional shape

The Eiffel Tower is more than 300 meters in height, with its heavy weight supported by a series of **diagonal** iron beams.

★★ **encompass**
[inkʌ́mpəs]
[동] …을 포함하다, …을 둘러싸다

v. to include within

The field of architecture **encompasses** both the design of physical structures and the actual construction of them.

syn. comprise

★★ **extremely**
[ikstríːmli]
[부] 매우, 극도로

adv. to a great degree

Frank Lloyd Wright is considered an **extremely** creative architect who helped shape the appearance of the modern world.

syn. exceedingly *ant.* barely

★ **facade**
[fəsɑ́ːd]
[명] 정면, 앞면

n. the front of a building

A new **facade** was added to the old guest house during its renovation to cover up its worn, chipped bricks.

★★★ **furnish**
[fə́ːrniʃ]
[동] 1. 가구를 비치하다
2. 제공하다
n. furnishings

v. 1 to fill with furniture
2 to provide *syn.* equip, supply

1. The couple's new home is not yet **furnished**, as the floor is still being tiled and the interior painting has not yet been completed.
2. The dormitory will be **furnished** with double-paned windows to reduce the amount of heat lost during the winter months.

destitute 그 건축가는 자신의 회사가 파산한 후, 예전에 일했던 거리에서 푼돈을 구걸하는 궁핍한 신세에 처하게 되었다. **diagonal** 에펠탑은 높이가 300미터 이상이며, 그 육중한 무게를 일련의 사선으로 된 강철 기둥들이 지탱하고 있다. **encompass** 건축 분야는 물리적 구조 디자인과 그것의 실제 공사를 모두 포함한다. **extremely** Frank Lloyd Wright은 현대 세계의 형태를 갖추도록 도운 매우 창의적인 건축가로 간주된다. **facade** 그 낡은 게스트 하우스의 닳고 깨진 벽돌을 덧입히는 수리 작업 도중에, 새로운 앞면이 추가되었다. **furnish** 1. 그 부부의 새 집에는 아직 가구가 비치되지 않았는데, 바닥에 여전히 타일을 깔고 있는 중이고 실내 페인팅도 아직 끝나지 않았기 때문이다. 2. 겨울 동안 손실되는 열의 양을 줄이기 위해, 그 기숙사에 이중 유리창이 제공될 것이다.

★★★

indicate

[índikèit]

[동] 나타내다, 보여 주다, 암시하다

n. indication

v. to point out, suggest, or imply

Polls of architectural experts **indicate** that the Parthenon in Athens, Greece, is generally considered the most beautiful building of all time.

syn. signify

★★

initial

[iníʃəl]

[형] 처음의, 초기의

adj. occurring at the beginning; first

The **initial** reaction to the proposed design of the new museum was positive, but people have begun to turn against it.

syn. preliminary *ant.* final

★★

internal

[intə́ːrnl]

[형] 내부의

adj. existing or occurring on the inside

Although the elevator on the outside of the building is less reliable than a traditional **internal** one, it is very stylish.

syn. inner *ant.* external

Useful Tips

internal과 철자가 비슷한 단어 eternal은 '영원한, 끊임없는'이란 의미이므로 혼동하지 않도록 유의한다.

★

joint

[dʒɔint]

[명] 연결 부위, 접합부

n. the place where two things are joined

The steel beams are carefully welded at each **joint** to ensure that they can withstand the effects of even a large earthquake.

syn. juncture

★★★

lavish

[lǽviʃ]

[형] 호화로운

[동] 아낌없이 주다

adj. elaborate and excessive *syn.* luxurious *ant.* austere

Antoni Gaudi was known for the **lavish** design of his buildings, especially Barcelona's impressive Sagrada Familia cathedral.

v. to give generously

The designers of the newly renovated palace were **lavished** with praise and valuable gifts from the appreciative royal family.

★★

meander

[miǽndər]

[동] 꾸불꾸불 나아가다, 굽이쳐 흐르다

v. to move or be arranged in a curving, indirect manner

The avant-garde building has few straight lines or right angles, and its hallways **meander** in large, looping curves.

---

indicate 건축 전문가들의 여론 조사는 일반적으로 그리스 아테네의 파르테논 신전이 역사상 가장 아름다운 건축물로 간주되고 있음을 보여 준다. **initial** 그 새 박물관의 제안된 디자인에 대한 초기 반응은 긍정적이었으나, 사람들은 그것에 등을 돌리기 시작했다. **internal** 그 건물 외부의 엘리베이터는 전통적인 내부 엘리베이터보다 신뢰도가 떨어지지만, 매우 멋지다. **joint** 그 철강 들보들은 큰 지진의 영향도 확실히 견딜 수 있도록 각 접합부가 세심하게 용접되어 있다. **lavish** Antoni Gaudi는 그의 건축물들, 특히 바르셀로나의 인상적인 사그라다 파밀리아 성당의 호화로운 설계로 유명했다. / 새로 개조된 그 궁전의 설계자들은 고마워하는 왕실 가족으로부터 찬사와 귀한 선물을 아낌없이 받았다. **meander** 그 전위적인 건물은 직선이나 직각이 거의 없고, 복도들은 크게 구부러진 곡선으로 굽이쳐 흐른다.

myriad

[míriəd]

명 무수함

n. a large, indefinite number

The city has a **myriad** of ugly concrete buildings that were built during an economic recession in the 1980s.

niche

[nitʃ]

명 1. 벽감(벽면을 파내어 조각품 등을
　　놓도록 만든 곳)
　　2. 아주 꼭 맞는 자리[일·분야]

n. 1 a recess in a wall where things can be kept　　*syn.* alcove
　　2 a situation that is suitable

1. The exterior of the ancient building features numerous **niches** in which statues of kings and queens once stood.

2. I.M. Pei found his architectural **niche** when he began designing museums and art galleries in the 1970s and 80s.

perforate

[pɔ́ːrfərèit]

동 …에 구멍을 뚫다

n. perforation

v. to make a hole or a line of holes in something

If you **perforate** metals, they become more durable and energy efficient, which makes them a popular architectural material.

syn. puncture　　*ant.* seal

phenomenal

[finámənl]

형 놀랄만한

adj. remarkable

The famous Blue Mosque of Istanbul, Turkey, is a **phenomenal** example of the Islamic architecture of the 17th century.

syn. extraordinary　　*ant.* awful

possess

[pəzés]

동 소유하다, 보유하다,
　 가지다

n. possession

v. to have as a feature or belonging

Traditional Korean *hanok* **possess** distinctively curved roofs that are often covered in tiles made of clay.

syn. own

prevail

[privéil]

동 우세하다, 만연하다, 이기다

adj. prevalent

v. to prove superior to or defeat opposition

When several architectural movements exist at the same time, one will usually **prevail** and become more popular than the rest.

syn. triumph　　*ant.* yield

ART & DESIGN

SOCIAL SCIENCE

NATURAL SCIENCE

HUMANITIES

EARTH & SPACE

SOCIAL ISSUES

---

myriad 그 도시에는 1980년대 경기 불황 시기에 세워진 흉한 콘크리트 건물들이 무수히 많다.　**niche** 1. 그 고대 건물의 외부에는 한때 왕과 왕비들의 동상이 그 안에 세워져 있던 수많은 벽감들이 있다. 2. I.M. Pei는 1970년대와 1980년대에 박물관과 화랑을 설계하기 시작했을 때, 자신에게 아주 꼭 맞는 건축 분야를 발견했다.　**perforate** 금속에 구멍을 뚫으면, 내구성과 에너지 효율이 좀 더 좋아져서 인기 있는 건축 자재가 된다.　**phenomenal** 터키 이스탄불의 유명한 블루모스크는 17세기 이슬람 건축의 놀랄만한 예이다.　**possess** 한국의 전통적인 한옥은 흔히 점토로 만든 기와로 덮인 독특한 곡선 지붕을 가지고 있다.　**prevail** 몇 개의 건축 동향이 동시에 존재할 때, 보통 한 가지가 우세하게 되어 나머지 것들보다 인기를 더 얻는다.

scope
[skoup]
옝 범위, 영역

n. the range that is covered by something

The architect met with the land owners to discuss shrinking the **scope** of the ambitious project that they had proposed.

syn. extent

Useful Tips

scope은 telescope(망원경), microscope(현미경), stethoscope(청진기), periscope(잠망경)처럼 의학·기술 분야의 도구를 나타내는 단어에서 사용되기도 한다.

★★
slanted
[slǽntid]
옝 경사진, 비스듬한

adj. not level; with one end higher than the other

The **slanted** roofs of the homes stopped snow from piling up during winter, which could potentially be damaging.

syn. skewed

★★
steep
[stiːp]
옝 가파른

adj. rising or falling at a sharp angle

The company's new headquarters required some innovative architecture, as it was built on a **steep** incline.

★★
structural
[strʌ́ktʃərəl]
옝 구조의, 구조적

adj. relating to the physical makeup of something

Due to their **structural** weaknesses, most wooden towers were eventually replaced by stone or metal structures.

★★
sustain
[səstéin]
용 1. 지탱하다, 지속시키다
　 2. (피해·손실 등을) 입다
adj. sustainable

v. 1 to provide ongoing support　*syn.* maintain　*ant.* hinder
2 to suffer something negative

1. The longer the museum construction project lasts, the more difficult it will be for the town to financially **sustain** it.

2. France's historic Notre-Dame de Paris cathedral **sustained** serious damage from a large fire in 2019.

★★
terrain
[təréin]
몡 지형, 지대

n. natural landscape

Green architecture seeks to cause minimal changes to the **terrain** surrounding the site of a new building.

---

scope 그 건축가는 토지 소유자들이 제안했던 야심찬 프로젝트의 범위 축소를 논의하려고 그들과 만났다.　**slanted** 그 가정들의 경사진 지붕들은 겨울 동안 피해를 줄 가능성이 있는 눈쌓임을 방지해 주었다.　**steep** 그 회사의 새 본사는 가파른 경사면에 세워져서, 혁신적인 건축 양식이 필요했다.　**structural** 대부분의 목탑들은 구조적 취약함 때문에, 결국 석재나 금속재 구조로 대체되었다.　**sustain** 1. 그 박물관 건설 프로젝트가 더 길어질수록, 그 도시가 그것을 재정적으로 지속시키는 것이 더 어려워질 것이다. 2. 역사적으로 중요한 프랑스의 노트르담 대성당은 2019년에 큰 화재로 심각한 손상을 입었다.　**terrain** 친환경 건축은 새 건물 부지 주변의 지형에 변화를 최소화하려고 노력한다.

EXERCISES

ART & DESIGN

SOCIAL SCIENCE

NATURAL SCIENCE

HUMANITIES

EARTH & SPACE

SOCIAL ISSUES

A Match each definition with the correct word.

1 natural landscape   ⓐ structural

2 the place where two things are joined   ⓑ blueprint

3 relating to the physical makeup of something   ⓒ joint

4 a recess in a wall where things can be kept   ⓓ calculate

5 to find an amount through mathematics   ⓔ initial

6 to provide ongoing support   ⓕ niche

7 a technical plan for a building or machine   ⓖ sustain

8 occurring at the beginning; first   ⓗ terrain

B Choose the word that is closest in meaning to each underlined word.

1 The oil painting shows a <u>lavish</u> feast, with tables covered in plates of delicious food.
   ⓐ religious   ⓑ luxurious   ⓒ bizarre   ⓓ distasteful

2 As the character in the play is supposed to be <u>destitute</u>, the actor is dressed in rags.
   ⓐ extroverted   ⓑ unintelligent   ⓒ impoverished   ⓓ infamous

3 A new four-lane highway connecting the city to an <u>adjacent</u> town is currently being planned.
   ⓐ emerging   ⓑ thriving   ⓒ bordering   ⓓ struggling

4 Opera is popular because it <u>encompasses</u> elements of both classical music and drama.
   ⓐ overshadows   ⓑ reimagines   ⓒ dismisses   ⓓ comprises

5 The painting whose canvas was accidently <u>perforated</u> by a nail is being repaired.
   ⓐ punctured   ⓑ suspended   ⓒ tightened   ⓓ flooded

6 When a city's suburbs begin to grow too <u>dense</u>, they tend to spread into rural areas.
   ⓐ upscale   ⓑ reviled   ⓒ remote   ⓓ crowded

7 The dancers complained about the choreography, but the director <u>prevailed</u> in the end.
   ⓐ triumphed   ⓑ withdrew   ⓒ apologized   ⓓ reconsidered

City Planning

★
★
★
accelerate

[æksélərèit, ək-]

ⓥ 가속하다, …의 속도를 늘리다

n. acceleration

v. to go faster or make something go faster

The planned expansion of the city's greenspaces has been **accelerated** by an unexpected increase in the project's budget.

syn. hasten   *ant.* delay

★
★
approval

[əprúːvəl]

ⓝ 승인, 허가

v. approve

n. the act of officially accepting something

Once the project receives **approval** from the mayor's office, large solar panels will be set up atop City Hall.

syn. authorization   *ant.* denial, disapproval

★
★
arduous

[áːrdʒuəs]

ⓐ 몹시 힘든, 고된

adj. difficult, requiring a lot of effort

Updating an aging highway system is an **arduous** task, but leaving it unmaintained can lead to serious traffic issues.

syn. strenuous   *ant.* effortless

★
★
colossal

[kəlásəl]

ⓐ 거대한, 엄청난

n. colossus

adj. extraordinarily large

Building a rotary around the **colossal** monument in the center of the city will help avoid traffic jams in that area.

syn. gigantic   *ant.* minuscule, tiny

★
★
commute

[kəmjúːt]

ⓥ 통근하다

v. to travel to and from work

The larger the percentage of people who **commute** to work is, the more important an emphasis on improving public transportation becomes.

★
★
concentrate

[kánsəntrèit]

ⓥ …에 집중하다

n. concentration

v. to focus one's attention on a single thing

The city planners were asked to **concentrate** on finding cost-efficient ways to make the city more pedestrian-friendly.

---

accelerate 계획된 도시 녹지 확장은 그 프로젝트 예산의 예상치 못한 증가로 가속화되었다.　**approval** 일단 그 사업이 시장실의 승인을 받고 나면, 커다란 태양 전지판이 시청 꼭대기에 설치될 것이다.　**arduous** 노후된 고속도로 시스템을 새롭게 고치는 것은 매우 고된 일이지만, 이를 그대로 방치하면 심각한 교통 문제를 초래할 수 있다.　**colossal** 도심에 있는 거대한 기념비 주위에 로터리를 만드는 것은 그 지역의 교통 체증을 방지하는 데 도움이 될 것이다.　**commute** 통근하는 사람들의 비율이 더 커질수록, 대중교통의 개선을 강조하는 것이 더 중요해진다.　**concentrate** 도시 계획가들은 도시를 보다 보행자 친화적으로 만들기 위해 비용 효율적인 방법을 찾는 데 집중하도록 요청받았다.

coordinate
[kouɔ́ːrdənèit]
ⓥ 조정하다, 조직화하다, 조화롭게 하다

n. coordination

v. to organize multiple things and make them work together

A meeting was held in the interest of **coordinating** the city's numerous ongoing neighborhood improvement projects.

demand
[dimǽnd]
ⓥ 요구하다
ⓝ 요구, 수요

adj. demanding

v. to forcefully request something

Modern people **demand** fast and efficient public transportation systems that have a minimal impact on the environment.

n. the overall need for a product or service

The **demand** for public spaces where residents can gather can be satisfied by the establishment of a central plaza.

Useful **Tips**

demand(수요)는 경제학에서 supply(공급)와 함께 자주 쓰인다. demand와 supply는 제품과 서비스의 가격을 결정짓는 데 중요한 역할을 한다.

devote
[divóut]
ⓥ (시간·노력·돈 등을) 바치다, 쏟다

n. devotion

v. to give all of one's time, effort, or energy to something or someone

Australia's first highway lanes that were **devoted** to vehicles carrying multiple passengers were opened in the early 1990s.

syn. dedicate

dismantle
[dismǽntl]
ⓥ 분해하다, 해체하다

v. to take apart

The barriers surrounding the vacant lot were **dismantled** by city officials, allowing residents to change the land into a community garden.

syn. disassemble   *ant.* assemble

drainage
[dréinidʒ]
ⓝ 배수 (장치)

n. a system or process of removing unwanted water

The **drainage** of surface and sub-surface water from vacant land is required before development can begin.

encourage
[inkɔ́ːridʒ]
ⓥ 용기를 북돋우다, 고무하다

n. encouragement

v. to give courage or support

The city planners were **encouraged** by the unexpected popularity of the city's recently revitalized waterfront.

syn. inspire   *ant.* discourage

---

coordinate 그 도시의 진행 중인 수많은 인근 지역 개선 사업들을 조정하기 위한 회의가 열렸다.   **demand** 1. 현대인들은 환경에 가장 적은 영향을 주는, 빠르고 효율적인 대중교통 체계를 요구한다. 2. 거주민들이 모일 수 있는 공용 공간에 대한 요구는 중앙 광장의 설립으로 충족될 수 있다.   **devote** 호주에서는 다수의 승객들을 실어 나르는 교통수단 전용인 고속도로가 1990년대 초에 처음 개통되었다.   **dismantle** 공터를 둘러싸고 있던 장벽들이 시 공무원들에 의해 해체되어, 거주민들이 그 땅을 공동 정원으로 바꿀 수 있게 되었다.   **drainage** 개발이 시작되기 전에 공한지의 지표수와 지하수의 배수가 필요하다.   **encourage** 그 도시 계획가들은 최근 활기를 되찾은 해안가의 기대치 못한 인기에 고무되었다.

★★★

endeavor

[indévər]

[동] 노력하다, 애쓰다

v. to make a serious attempt to do something

The planners of Chandigarh, India, **endeavored** to create a new state capital that would be the pride of the entire nation.

syn. strive

★★★

exert

[igzə́ːrt]

[동] (힘·능력·권력 등을) 쓰다, 행사하다

n. exertion

v. to use some kind of force or power

The planning ideas of the ancient Greeks, who placed their city streets at right angles, still **exert** an influence on modern cities.

syn. expend

★

fairly

[fέərli]

[부] 1. 상당히, 꽤
2. 공평하게

adv. 1 to a somewhat large degree
2. in a just manner *syn.* equitably

1. The construction of canal systems in cities was **fairly** common in the past, but they have now fallen out of fashion.
2. If the undeveloped land within a city's limits is not divided **fairly**, it can lead to public dissatisfaction.

★

hallmark

[hɔ́ːlmɑ̀ːrk]

[명] 특징, 특성

n. a typical quality or feature

A central main street lined with shops has become a recognizable **hallmark** of American towns and small cities.

★★

impetus

[ímpətəs]

[명] 원동력, (일의 추진에 필요한) 자극(제)

n. a force that causes something to happen quickly

The rise of car culture in the 1940s and 50s was the **impetus** behind several major shifts in city-planning trends.

syn. motivation

★★

infrastructure

[ínfrəstrʌ̀ktʃər]

[명] 사회 기반 시설

n. the basic system that allows a city or country to work properly

Every city manager knows that the maintenance and modernization of **infrastructure** is absolutely essential to a well-run city.

Useful Tips

국가의 사회 기반 시설(infrastructure)이라는 것은 도로망, 다리, 철도, 공공 시설, 전기 시설 등을 의미한다.

---

endeavor 인도 찬디가르 주의 도시 계획가들은 온 국민의 자부심이 될 새로운 주도를 만들려고 애썼다. **exert** 도시의 거리들을 직각으로 배치했던 고대 그리스인들의 도시 계획 아이디어는 현대 도시에도 여전히 영향을 미친다. **fairly** 1. 도시에 운하 시스템을 건설하는 것이 과거에는 상당히 흔했지만, 지금은 유행이 지났다. 2. 도시 내 미개발 토지가 공평하게 분할되지 않으면, 대중의 불만으로 이어질 수 있다. **hallmark** 상점들이 늘어서 있는 중심 도로는 미국의 도시와 소도시들의 눈에 띄는 특징이 되었다. **impetus** 1940년대와 50년대의 자동화 문화의 부상은 도시 계획 동향의 여러 주요한 변화를 일으킨 원동력이었다. **infrastructure** 모든 도시 관리자들은 사회 기반 시설의 유지와 현대화가 운영이 잘 되는 도시에 절대적으로 필요하다는 것을 알고 있다.

ART & DESIGN

SOCIAL SCIENCE

NATURAL SCIENCE

HUMANITIES

EARTH & SPACE

SOCIAL ISSUES

integrate
[íntəgrèit]

동 통합하다

n. integration

v. to combine two or more things into a whole

The layout of a downtown area should **integrate** the needs of businesses with the leisure and entertainment desires of residents.

syn. assimilate, incorporate   *ant.* separate

inundate
[ínəndèit]

동 1. 범람시키다, 침수시키다
2. 밀려들다, 쇄도하다

v. 1 to flood with water
2 to give or provide in overly large quantities

1. To prevent parts of the town from being **inundated** by floodwaters, updates are being made to the drainage system.

2. To stop the city from being **inundated** by trucks, a bypass has been constructed.

irreversible
[ìrivə́:rsəbl]

형 변경할 수 없는, 취소할 수 없는

adj. impossible to change or erase

No city-planning decision is **irreversible**, but it can take a great deal of time and money to correct serious missteps.

ant. reversible

mechanism
[mékənìzm]

명 1. 기계 (장치), 기계 부품
2. 방법, 메커니즘

adj. mechanical

n. 1 a machine or part of one
2 something that achieves a task within a system

1. A drawbridge is a bridge that has been fitted with a **mechanism** that can raise the two ends of the span to allow tall ships to pass.

2. The city has a **mechanism** for dealing with situations where a property owner fails to perform a basic level of maintenance.

metropolitan
[mètrəpúlitən]

형 대도시의, 수도권의

adj. in or relating to a big city

The **metropolitan** area of New York City is home to about 20 million people and includes parts of the states of New Jersey and Connecticut.

overwhelm
[òuvərhwélm]

동 …을 압도하다, 제압하다

adj. overwhelming

v. to defeat through superior force or numbers

Efforts to reduce air pollution in major cities have been **overwhelmed** by the ever-growing number of cars on the road.

syn. overpower

---

integrate 도심지의 배치는 사업체들의 요구와 거주민들의 여가 및 오락적 욕구를 통합해야 한다.   **inundate** 1. 그 도시의 일부가 홍수로 인해 침수되는 것을 막기 위해서 배수 시설을 새롭게 고치고 있다. 2. 그 도시에 트럭들이 밀려드는 것을 멈추기 위해 우회로가 건설되었다.   **irreversible** 도시 계획 결정이 변경될 수 없는 것은 아니지만, 심각한 실수를 바로잡는 데는 상당한 시간과 비용이 들 수 있다.   **mechanism** 1. 도개교는 높은 배가 지나갈 수 있도록 다리 경간의 양쪽 끝을 올릴 수 있는 기계 장치가 장착된 다리이다. 2. 그 도시는 부동산 소유자가 기본적인 유지 보수를 수행하지 않는 상황에 대처하기 위한 방법을 가지고 있다.   **metropolitan** 뉴욕 대도시 지역은 약 2천만 명의 사람들이 살고 있으며, 뉴저지와 코네티컷 주의 일부를 포함한다.   **overwhelm** 주요 도시들에서 대기오염을 줄이려는 노력은 점점 증가하는 도로 위의 자동차 수에 압도당했다.

★★ **permit**
[pərmít]
[동] 허락하다, 허가하다

v. to allow something to happen

Revitalizing neighborhoods in economic decline **permits** a city to grow without expanding beyond its existing boundaries.

ant. prohibit, forbid

★ **residential**
[rèzədénʃəl]
[형] 주거의, 거주의
n. resident

adj. designed to be lived in

Highway noise barriers are large walls designed to reduce the amount of noise experienced in **residential** areas near a major road.

ant. commercial

★★★ **restrict**
[ristríkt]
[동] 제한하다
n. restriction

v. to limit what can be done

The development of certain towns and cities can be **restricted** by local geographic features, such as cliffs, valleys, or swamps.

★★ **threat**
[θret]
[명] 위협, (나쁜 일의) 징조, 조짐

n. a possibility of danger

Climate change poses a serious **threat** to the Italian city of Venice, as rising water levels have been causing its canals to flood.

★★ **undergo**
[ʌ̀ndərgóu]
[동] (변화·안 좋은 일 등을) 겪다

v. to experience something unpleasant

Small towns that **undergo** a rapid decline in population due to young people moving away often fall into disrepair as homes are left abandoned.

★★ **urban**
[ə́ːrbən]
[형] 도시의

adj. in or relating to a town or city

Urban areas need greater attention to the efficient use of space, as uncontrolled growth can lead to overcrowding.

ant. rural

permit 경기 쇠퇴기의 지역 활성화는 도시가 기존의 한계를 넘어 확장되지 않고 성장할 수 있도록 허용한다. **residential** 고속도로 방음벽은 주요 도로 인근 주택가에서 겪는 소음의 양을 줄이기 위해 설계된 대형 벽이다. **restrict** 특정 마을과 도시의 개발은 절벽, 계곡, 습지와 같은 그 지역의 지형적 특징에 따라 제한될 수 있다. **threat** 기후 변화는 이탈리아 도시 베네치아에 심각한 위협이 되고 있는데, 상승하는 수위가 운하의 범람을 야기하기 때문이다. **undergo** 젊은이들의 이주로 급속한 인구 감소를 겪고 있는 소도시들은 주택이 버려지기 때문에 황폐화되기 일쑤이다. **urban** 도시 지역은 효율적인 공간 사용에 더 많은 주의가 필요한데, 무절제한 성장이 인구 과밀로 이어질 수 있기 때문이다.

EXERCISES

ART & DESIGN

SOCIAL SCIENCE

NATURAL SCIENCE

HUMANITIES

EARTH & SPACE

SOCIAL ISSUES

A Match each definition with the correct word.

1 a possibility of danger		ⓐ hallmark
2 designed to be lived in		ⓑ residential
3 to forcefully request something		ⓒ commute
4 to a somewhat large degree		ⓓ threat
5 difficult, requiring a lot of effort		ⓔ fairly
6 a machine or part of one		ⓕ demand
7 a typical quality or feature		ⓖ arduous
8 to travel to and from work		ⓗ mechanism

B Choose the word that is closest in meaning to each underlined word.

1 Photographers <u>endeavor</u> to capture special moments in images that will last a lifetime.
  ⓐ strive   ⓑ resolve   ⓒ gather   ⓓ spurt

2 After the band's outdoor performance ended, the stage was <u>dismantled</u> by the park staff.
  ⓐ enhanced   ⓑ renovated   ⓒ disassembled   ⓓ relocated

3 It is a challenging task to <u>coordinate</u> the schedules of multiple theaters during a film festival.
  ⓐ share   ⓑ adjust   ⓒ receive   ⓓ organize

4 Due to a sore knee, the ballerina has been <u>restricted</u> to less demanding roles.
  ⓐ overwhelmed   ⓑ limited   ⓒ requested   ⓓ criticized

5 If the town receives the artist's <u>approval</u>, the new statue will be unveiled tomorrow.
  ⓐ authorization   ⓑ recommendation   ⓒ instigation   ⓓ explanation

6 No one but the architect and construction manager is <u>permitted</u> inside the unfinished building.
  ⓐ allowed   ⓑ engaged   ⓒ escorted   ⓓ encouraged

7 The craftsperson's unique work, which <u>integrates</u> weaving with sculpture, is on display.
  ⓐ displaces   ⓑ accelerates   ⓒ assimilates   ⓓ instructs

A **Choose the correct words.**

1 The word advent has the same meaning as

ⓐ action   ⓑ pitfall   ⓒ onset   ⓓ consequence

2 The word undergo has the same meaning as

ⓐ decrease   ⓑ repeat   ⓒ update   ⓓ experience

3 The word conform has the same meaning as

ⓐ surpass   ⓑ comply   ⓒ proclaim   ⓓ oppose

4 The word furnish has the same meaning as

ⓐ equip   ⓑ detract   ⓒ stack   ⓓ inscribe

5 The word resume has the same meaning as

ⓐ restart   ⓑ rethink   ⓒ undo   ⓓ uncover

6 The word culminate has the same meaning as

ⓐ inquire   ⓑ transform   ⓒ peak   ⓓ submerge

7 The word spontaneous has the same meaning as

ⓐ obnoxious   ⓑ imminent   ⓒ impromptu   ⓓ engaging

8 The word incorporate has the same meaning as

ⓐ surround   ⓑ absorb   ⓒ detach   ⓓ inundate

B **Fill in the blanks with the best words from the box.**

1 The perfect _____ of the ancient building was ruined when one of the three columns to the left of the entrance fell over in the 1960s.

2 Few artists approach a blank canvas without knowing what they're going to paint, as it takes _____ planning to create a great work of art.

3 The streets of a planned city rarely _____; they tend to be straight lines that cross one another at right angles.

4 The emperor decided to _____ his great wealth and power by having a gold-plated statue of himself erected in the city center.

5 Frida Kahlo's desire to express herself while hospitalized after an accident gave her the _____ to return to her childhood hobby of painting.

6 Although the photo is said to be a(n) _____ shot, the fact that most of the people are looking directly into the camera makes it look posed.

impetus	symmetry	meander	candid	conscious	flaunt

C Read the following passages.

ART & DESIGN

SOCIAL SCIENCE

NATURAL SCIENCE

HUMANITIES

EARTH & SPACE

SOCIAL ISSUES

[1-2] **1** Choose one word that fits both blanks.

> During the war, a bomb was dropped near a village's church, causing it to _____ minor damage to its woodwork. A local woman offered to repair it for free. Having done an excellent job, she received enough work to _____ her career as a woodworker.

ⓐ sustain   ⓑ integrate   ⓒ boost   ⓓ perforate

2 Choose the appropriate pair of words to fill in the blanks.

> Most directors agree that editing is a _____ part of filmmaking, and some would even argue that it is the most important step of the process. The length of the shots and the order that they appear on the screen can directly _____ how audiences perceive the action.

ⓐ cumbersome — involve   ⓑ geometric — appall

ⓒ dense — indicate   ⓓ critical — affect

[3-4]

> The field of fashion is more tolerant of rebels than most others, mainly because it relies on continuous innovation to drive it forward. The CEOs of top brands might complain about coarse stitching or other sloppy work, but they will overlook it if the designs break the rules in an exciting way.

3 In the context of the passage, rebels means _____.

ⓐ swindlers   ⓑ experts   ⓒ nonconformists   ⓓ amateurs

4 The word coarse in the passage could best be replaced by

ⓐ unexpected   ⓑ crude   ⓒ smooth   ⓓ sleek

[5-6]

> Conceiving, designing, and constructing new buildings is not easy for architects, but renovating historic structures is even more challenging. The tiniest details must be carefully noted, such as the _____ of the bricks. If they have been bleached by the sun over the years, the new bricks must match them exactly to avoid making the restorations stick out.

5 Choose the word that is most suitable for the blank.

ⓐ niche   ⓑ threat   ⓒ hue   ⓓ aim

6 The word bleached in the passage is closest in meaning to

ⓐ whitened   ⓑ chipped   ⓒ engraved   ⓓ enlarged

83

Anglo-Saxon **Prefixes**
앵글로색슨어 접두사

접두사는 주로 고대 영어인 앵글로색슨어나 라틴어, 또는 고대 그리스어에서 유래하는데, Chapter 1에서 배운 engage, outline, overwhelm, unveil은 앵글로색슨어에서 유래한 접두사인 en-, out-, over-, un-이 사용된 단어들이다. 주요 앵글로색슨어 접두사들의 고유 의미를 살펴보고, 그 접두사가 사용된 단어들도 함께 숙지해 보자.

PREFIXES	EXAMPLES
be- *to make, completely*	befall 닥치다 befriend 친구가 되어 주다 beguile 구슬리다 behold 보다 bejeweled 보석을 두른 besiege 포위하다 beware 조심하다
en- *to make*	enable …할 수 있게 하다 enforce 시행하다 engage (주의·관심을) 사로잡다 enlarge 확장하다 enrich 풍부하게 하다 ensure 보장하다
fore- *before, earlier, front*	forecast 예측 forefront 선두 foregoing 앞서 가는 foremost 가장 앞선 foresight 선견지명 foreword 서문
mis- *bad, badly, wrongly*	misbelief 잘못된 생각 misdeed 나쁜 짓 misfire 불발하다 misgiving 불길한 예감 mishap 불행 mislead 오도하다
out- *beyond, out, more than*	outcome 결과 outgrow …보다 커지다 outline 약술하다 outlook 전망 output 출력 outrun 넘어서다 outstanding 뛰어난
over- *too, excessively, beyond*	overcome 극복하다 overconfident 지나치게 자신만만한 overdose 과다복용 overtake 추월하다 overwhelm …을 압도하다
un- *not, lack of, remove from*	unbiased 편견 없는 unconcerned 무관심한 unfortunate 불운한 unlock 열다 unusual 유별난 unveil 밝히다
under- *beneath, lower, insufficient*	underdeveloped 저개발의 undergo 겪다 underpayment 저임금 underscore 강조하다 understatement 절제된 표현 undertake 떠맡다
up- *up, upward*	upcoming 다가오는 update 최신의 것으로 하다 upgrade 향상시키다 upheaval 소란 uphold 지지하다 upkeep 유지 upset 기분 상한
with- *back, away, against*	withdraw 철회하다 withhold 억제하다 withstand 견뎌내다

CHAPTER

SOCIAL SCIENCE

Lesson 11

스포츠

Sports

★★★

advantage

[ædvǽntidʒ]

[명] 장점, 이점

adj. advantageous

n. a condition that makes success more likely

Being very tall is an **advantage** in sports such as basketball and volleyball, but it can be a disadvantage in others.

syn. edge *ant.* disadvantage, hindrance

★★★

athlete

[ǽθliːt]

[명] 운동선수

adj. athletic

n. someone who excels at sports

Not every child will grow up to be an **athlete**, but everyone can benefit from taking part in team sports at an early age.

★

attain

[ətéin]

[동] 획득하다, 이루다

v. to get something after making an effort

The tennis player's dream of **attaining** the top ranking in the world was crushed when she lost in the first round of the tournament.

syn. achieve *ant.* fail

★★

breathe

[briːð]

[동] 숨쉬다, 호흡하다

n. breath

v. to take air into the lungs and then release it

Some people believe it is best to **breathe** in through your nose and out through your mouth when running long distances.

syn. respire

Useful Tips

들숨을 쉬는 것(breathe in)은 inhale, 날숨을 쉬는 것(breathe out)은 exhale이라 한다.

★★★

competitive

[kəmpétətiv]

[형] 경쟁적인, 경쟁의

v. compete

adj. strongly desiring to beat others in games and contests

Many great Olympians were very **competitive** as children, but this quality can also lead to bad sportsmanship.

★★

considerable

[kənsídərəbl]

[형] 상당한, 꽤

adj. large in size or degree

Even though baseball has a **considerable** following in certain parts of the world, it cannot match the global popularity of soccer.

syn. sizeable *ant.* negligible

---

advantage 키가 아주 큰 것은 농구와 배구 같은 운동에서 장점이지만, 다른 운동들에서는 단점이 될 수 있다. **athlete** 모든 아이가 자라서 운동선수가 되는 건 아니지만, 어린 나이에 팀 스포츠에 참여하는 것은 모두에게 득이 될 수 있다. **attain** 세계 랭킹 1위를 이루겠다는 그 테니스 선수의 꿈은 그 시합 1차전에서 졌을 때 산산조각 났다. **breathe** 어떤 사람들은 장거리를 달릴 때, 코로 숨을 들이마시고 입으로 숨을 내쉬는 것이 가장 좋다고 믿는다. **competitive** 많은 훌륭한 올림픽 경기 출전 선수들은 어릴 때 매우 경쟁적이었는데, 이런 자질은 불량한 스포츠맨 정신을 초래할 수도 있다. **considerable** 야구가 세계의 특정 지역들에서 상당한 팬들을 거느리고 있음에도 불구하고, 축구의 세계적 인기에는 필적하지는 못한다.

★

contestant

[kəntéstənt]

[명] 참가자, 경쟁자

n. a person taking part in a contest

All of the **contestants** in the annual marathon must have a piece of paper with their registration number printed on it pinned to their shirt.

syn. participant

★★

defeat

[difíːt]

[동] 이기다, 패배시키다
[명] 패배

v. to achieve victory over someone or something *syn.* beat

In 1986, Mike Tyson **defeated** Trevor Berbick at the age of 20 to become the youngest heavyweight boxing champion of all time.

n. a failure to achieve victory *syn.* loss

After the team's humiliating **defeat**, none of the coaches or players wanted to talk to the journalists waiting outside the locker room.

★★★

endure

[indjúər]

[동] 견디다, 겪다

adj. endurable

v. to experience something unpleasant for a long period

The goalkeeper had to **endure** the jeers and insults of a group of fans behind the goal throughout the entire game.

syn. suffer

★

fortitude

[fɔ́ːrtətjùːd]

[명] 불굴의 용기, 꿋꿋함

n. strength and bravery during a difficult situation

Few people have the **fortitude** to compete in the Iditarod, a 1,500-kilomter sled dog race across the snow-covered state of Alaska.

syn. courage *ant.* cowardice

★

gear

[giər]

[명] 장비, 기어

n. the physical accessories needed for a certain activity

While soccer requires a minimum of **gear**, there are many things needed to take part in an official game of American football.

syn. equipment

★★

infallible

[infǽləbl]

[형] 결코 틀리지[실수하지] 않는

adj. never failing or making a mistake

There are some ice hockey coaches who always seem to know the right decision to make during a game, but no one is **infallible**.

syn. unerring *ant.* imperfect

---

contestant 그 연례 마라톤의 모든 참가자들은 등록 번호가 인쇄된 종이를 셔츠에 부착해야 한다. **defeat** 1986년에 Mike Tyson이 20세의 나이에 Trevor Berbick을 이기고 역대 최연소 헤비급 권투 챔피언이 되었다. / 그 팀의 굴욕적인 패배 이후, 코치나 선수들 중 그 누구도 라커룸 밖에서 기다리고 있는 기자들에게 이야기하고 싶어하지 않았다. **endure** 그 골키퍼는 그 경기 내내 골문 뒤에 있던 팬 무리의 야유와 모욕을 견뎌야 했다. **fortitude** 눈 덮인 알래스카 주를 가로지르는 1,500 킬로미터의 개썰매 경주인 아이디타로드에서 경쟁할 불굴의 용기를 가진 사람은 거의 없다. **gear** 축구에는 최소의 장비가 필요한 반면, 정식 미식축구 경기에 참가하는 데는 많은 것들이 필요하다. **infallible** 몇몇 아이스하키 코치는 경기 중 항상 옳은 결정을 내릴 줄 아는 것처럼 보이지만, 실수하지 않는 사람은 아무도 없다.

injury
★★★
[índʒəri]

ⓝ 부상, 상처

adj. injured

n. physical damage to the body

The great skier Lindsey Vonn made the difficult decision to sit out the 2014 Winter Olympics due to a knee **injury**.

syn. damage

Useful Tips

누군가 평소에 자주 부상을 입는 경우, injury prone이라는 표현을 쓴다.

linger
★★
[líŋgər]

ⓥ 남아 있다, 서성대다

v. to stay in a place after an event or activity has ended

Dozens of fans **lingered** outside the stadium after the game had ended, hoping for a glimpse of their favorite players.

syn. loiter

mediocre
★
[mì:dióukər]

ⓐ 평범한, 보통밖에 안 되는

adj. average in a negative sense

After years of **mediocre** performances, the Korean men's national soccer team surprised the world with a fourth-place finish in the 2002 World Cup.

syn. adequate

morale
★
[mərǽl]

ⓝ 사기, 의욕

n. a person or group's overall feeling of enthusiasm

Sensing a drop in **morale**, the volleyball player gathered her teammates together on the court for some words of encouragement.

syn. mood

Useful Tips

morale과 철자가 비슷한 moral은 '도덕적인, 도의상의'라는 의미이므로 혼동하지 않도록 유의한다.

myopic
★
[maiápik]

ⓐ 근시의

adj. unable to clearly see things that are far away

Prescription sports goggles are now available for **myopic** individuals who find contact lenses too uncomfortable to wear.

syn. nearsighted

opponent
★★★
[əpóunənt]

ⓝ 상대, 경쟁자

v. oppose

n. someone who fights or competes against another

Despite being fierce **opponents** on the basketball court, NBA stars Magic Johnson and Larry Bird were close friends off the court.

syn. foe

---

injury 훌륭한 스키 선수인 Lindsey Vonn은 무릎 부상으로 2014 동계 올림픽에 불참하겠다는 어려운 결정을 내렸다.   **linger** 그 경기가 끝난 후, 많은 팬들이 좋아하는 선수들을 잠깐 볼 수 있길 바라며 경기장 밖에 남아 있었다.   **mediocre** 수년 동안 평범한 성적을 내던 한국 남자 축구 대표팀이 2002 월드컵에서 4위로 마무리하며 세계를 깜짝 놀라게 했다.   **morale** 사기가 떨어진 것을 알아챈 그 배구 선수는 격려의 말을 하려고 팀 동료들을 경기장에 불러 모았다.
myopic 콘택트렌즈 착용을 너무 불편해하는 근시인 사람들은 이제 처방된 스포츠용 고글을 사용할 수 있다.   **opponent** NBA 스타인 Magic Johnson과 Larry Bird는 농구 경기장에서는 치열한 경쟁자였음에도 불구하고, 경기장 밖에서는 친한 친구였다.

★

oversight
[óuvərsàit]

[명] 1. 감독, 관리
2. 실수, 간과

n. **1 the act of monitoring a process or system** *syn.* supervision
2 an accidental failure to see or do something *syn.* omission

1. The committee charged with **oversight** of the sporting event will hold its first meeting tomorrow evening.
2. The team was shocked when their best player's name was left off the all-star list, but it turned out to be a simple **oversight**.

★★

plunge
[plʌndʒ]

[동] 뛰어들다, 떨어지다

v. **to drop a great distance suddenly**

The high diver performed a series of spins in midair before **plunging** into the swimming pool 27 meters below.

syn. plummet *ant.* soar

★★★

positive
[pázətiv]

[형] 긍정적인

n. positivity

adj. **helpful, optimistic, or agreeable** *ant.* negative

Limiting the number of games played per week is a **positive** step toward protecting the health of players, but more needs to be done.

★★

procedure
[prəsíːdʒər]

[명] 절차, 과정, 처리

n. **the accepted or official way of completing a task**

If the proper registration **procedures** are not followed, teams will not be allowed to play in the regional rugby tournament.

syn. process

★★

qualify
[kwáləfài]

[동] 자격을 얻다

adj. qualified

v. **to be allowed to advance to the next round of a competition**

Unless the home team wins tonight, they will not **qualify** for the semifinal round of the national field hockey tournament.

★★

relentless
[riléntlis]

[형] 끈질긴, 가차없는

v. relent

adj. **aggressive and refusing to give up**

The Brazilian soccer team's **relentless** attack resulted in several shots on goal, but the other team's keeper stopped every single one.

syn. persistent

oversight 1. 그 스포츠 행사의 관리를 맡은 위원회는 내일 저녁 첫 회의를 열 것이다. 2. 그 팀은 팀의 최우수 선수 이름이 올스타 목록에서 빠졌을 때 충격을 받았지만, 그것은 단순한 실수였음이 밝혀졌다. **plunge** 그 하이 다이빙 선수는 27 미터 아래 수영장에 뛰어들기 전에 공중에서 연이은 회전을 했다. **positive** 한 주에 뛰는 경기의 수를 제한하는 것은 선수들의 건강을 보호하기 위한 긍정적인 조치지만, 더 많은 일들이 이루어져야 한다. **procedure** 적절한 등록 절차를 따르지 않으면, 팀들이 그 지역 럭비 시합에서 경기하는 것이 허용되지 않을 것이다. **qualify** 오늘밤에 홈팀이 승리하지 않으면, 그들은 전국 필드하키 시합 준결승전에 출전할 자격을 얻지 못할 것이다. **relentless** 그 브라질 축구팀의 끈질긴 공격으로 몇 개의 슛이 골대로 날아갔지만, 상대팀의 골키퍼가 모든 슛을 막아냈다.

★ **rigorous**
[rígərəs]
[형] 면밀한, 엄격한

adj. thorough and accurate

After a **rigorous** investigation into accusations of cheating, the cyclist was cleared to continue competing.

syn. exhaustive

★★ **spectator**
[spékteitər]
[명] 관객, 구경꾼

n. someone who watches an event

Additional netting has been erected in many professional baseball stadiums to prevent **spectators** from being struck by foul balls.

syn. viewer

★★ **steady**
[stédi]
[형] 1. 안정된, 확고한
2. 끊임없는

adj. 1 solidly in place or unshaking *syn.* stable
2 occurring or progressing at an even pace *syn.* uninterrupted

1. An archer needs a **steady** hand, as well as significant arm strength, to hit the bull's-eye of a target from 70 meters away.
2. Three minutes of **steady** cheering from the fans caused the legendary player to step out of the dugout and tip his hat to the crowd.

★★★ **strategy**
[strǽtədʒi]
[명] 전략, 전술
v. strategize

n. a plan for achieving something

Down by a score of eight points to none, the table-tennis player decided to change her **strategy**.

syn. approach

★★ **strenuous**
[strénjuəs]
[형] 힘이 많이 드는, 격렬한

adj. requiring large amounts of effort and energy

Without the use of motorized carts to get around and caddies to carry one's clubs, golf is actually a fairly **strenuous** sport that can provide a good workout.

syn. laborious

★★★ **surmount**
[sərmáunt]
[동] 극복하다
adj. surmountable

v. to successfully deal with a problem

Female players have had to **surmount** many barriers over the years, but women's sports are finally getting the recognition they deserve.

syn. conquer

---

rigorous 부정행위 혐의에 대한 면밀한 조사 후, 그 사이클 선수는 계속 시합해도 좋다는 허가를 받았다. **spectator** 관중이 파울볼을 맞는 것을 방지하기 위해, 많은 프로 야구 경기장에 추가 그물망이 세워졌다. **steady** 1. 70 미터 떨어진 과녁 정중앙을 명중시키기 위해, 양궁 선수는 상당한 팔의 힘뿐만 아니라 흔들리지 않는 손도 필요하다. 2. 3분 동안 끊임없는 팬들의 환호가 이어지자, 그 전설적인 선수는 선수 대기석에서 나와 모자를 조금 올려 관중에게 인사했다. **strategy** 0대 8의 점수로 뒤지고 있던 그 탁구 선수는 전략을 바꾸기로 결정했다. **strenuous** 돌아다니는데 사용되는 동력이 달린 카트들과 골프채를 운반해 주는 캐디들이 없으면, 골프는 사실 상당한 운동량을 제공해 줄 수 있는 힘이 꽤 많이 드는 스포츠이다. **surmount** 여자 선수들은 수년 간 많은 장벽을 극복해와야 했지만, 여성 스포츠는 마침내 받아 마땅한 인정을 받고 있다.

EXERCISES

ART & DESIGN

SOCIAL SCIENCE

NATURAL SCIENCE

HUMANITIES

EARTH & SPACE

SOCIAL ISSUES

A Match each definition with the correct word.

1 someone who watches an event

2 strongly desiring to beat others in games and contests

3 unable to clearly see things that are far away

4 to stay in a place after an event or activity has ended

5 someone who excels at sports

6 strength and bravery during a difficult situation

7 never failing or making a mistake

8 someone who fights or competes against another

ⓐ competitive

ⓑ spectator

ⓒ athlete

ⓓ opponent

ⓔ fortitude

ⓕ myopic

ⓖ linger

ⓗ infallible

B Choose the word that is closest in meaning to each underlined word.

1 Running for public office requires a <u>considerable</u> amount of money in many countries.
   ⓐ unexpected   ⓑ unspecified   ⓒ variable   ⓓ sizeable

2 Finding nothing valuable at the site, the anthropologists packed up their <u>gear</u> and left.
   ⓐ artifacts   ⓑ paperwork   ⓒ vehicles   ⓓ equipment

3 It took the man three years of law school to <u>attain</u> his goal of becoming an attorney.
   ⓐ bury   ⓑ renew   ⓒ achieve   ⓓ mold

4 In a psychology lab report, each of the experiment's <u>procedures</u> must be described.
   ⓐ participants   ⓑ objects   ⓒ processes   ⓓ results

5 An ethical business <u>strategy</u> respects the rights of both employees and customers.
   ⓐ partner   ⓑ approach   ⓒ executive   ⓓ contact

6 The food company's <u>relentless</u> advertising campaign helped improve their reputation.
   ⓐ persistent   ⓑ hasty   ⓒ careless   ⓓ organized

7 When a nation's GDP begins to <u>plunge</u>, decisive steps must be taken to quickly stabilize it.
   ⓐ wander   ⓑ plummet   ⓒ decelerate   ⓓ escalate

Lesson 12

인류학과 고고학

Anthropology & Archaeology

★★

accidental

[æksədéntl]

[형] 우연한, 우발적인

adj. happening by chance or by mistake

An **accidental** discovery of an archaeological site occurred when some Chinese farmers stumbled across the Terra Cotta Army in 1974.

syn. unintended *ant.* deliberate

★★★

ancestor

[ǽnsestər]

[명] 조상, 선조

adj. ancestral

n. a relative who lived a long time ago

Cultures all around the world celebrate holidays during which families gather to remember and honor their **ancestors**.

syn. forefather *ant.* descendant

★★

artifact

[ɑ́ːrtəfæ̀kt]

[명] 인공 유물

n. an object made by humans in the past

Some of the most important Mesoamerican **artifacts** ever found are on display at the National Museum of Anthropology in Mexico City.

syn. relic

★★

associate

[əsóuʃièit, -si-]

[동] 연상하다, 결부 짓다

n. association

v. to mentally connect one thing with another

Many people **associate** anthropologists with the study of ancient cultures, but they also study the behavior of modern humans.

syn. correlate

★

burial

[bériəl]

[명] 매장

v. bury

n. the act of putting a dead body into the ground

The mask of Tutankhamun, which was worn by the ancient Egyptian pharaoh during his **burial**, was discovered by Howard Carter in 1925.

syn. interment

★

caste

[kæst]

[명] (힌두 문화의) 카스트 제도, 신분 제도

n. a social class that people are born into, especially in Hindu societies

Although the Indian **caste** system dates back to ancient times, the modern version we know today was shaped by British colonialism.

---

accidental 고고학 유적지의 우연한 발견은 1974년 몇몇 중국 농민들이 Terra Cotta Army(병마용갱)를 우연히 발견했을 때 일어났다. **ancestor** 전 세계의 문화들은 가족들이 모여 조상들을 기억하고 기리는 휴일을 기념한다. **artifact** 지금까지 발견된 가장 중요한 메소아메리카 유물 중 몇 가지가 멕시코시티에 있는 국립 인류학 박물관에 전시되어 있다. **associate** 많은 사람들이 인류학자들을 고대 문화 연구와 연관 짓지만, 그들은 현대 인류의 행동도 연구한다. **burial** 투탕카멘의 가면은 고대 이집트 파라오가 매장될 때 썼던 것으로, 1925년 Howard Carter에 의해 발견되었다. **caste** 인도의 카스트 제도는 고대까지 거슬러 올라가지만, 오늘날 우리가 알고 있는 현대판은 영국의 식민주의에 의해 형성되었다.

★★ **ceremonial**
[sèrəmóuniəl]
[형] 의식의, 예식의

adj. involving formal rites and other traditions

In many Western countries, **ceremonial** robes are still worn by judges as a symbol of their power and importance.

syn. ritual

★★ **civilization**
[sìvəlizéiʃən]
[명] 문명 (사회)
adj. civilized

n. an advanced society

It is believed that some of the earliest **civilizations** formed between the Tigris and Euphrates rivers.

syn. culture

★ **crypt**
[kript]
[명] (특히 과거 묘지로 쓰이던 교회의) 지하실

n. an underground room beneath a church where dead bodies are placed

The bones of ancient monks can still be found arranged along the walls of a **crypt** beneath one Roman church.

syn. catacomb

Useful Tips
'무덤'을 의미하는 단어로 grave와 tomb이 있는데, grave는 시신을 땅 아래 매장한 것이고, 지상에 매장한 것은 tomb이라고 한다.

★★ **descendant**
[diséndənt]
[명] 자손, 후손, 후예
v. descend

n. a person related to someone from the past

Some scientists believe that about one of every 200 modern men is a direct **descendant** of Genghis Khan.

syn. relative *ant.* ancestor

★★ **deserted**
[dizə́ːrtid]
[형] 사람이 없는, 인적이 끊긴
v. desert

adj. having no people

Although it has been **deserted** since the 16th century, Machu Picchu was once home to about 750 people.

syn. abandoned

★★ **domesticated**
[dəméstikèitid]
[형] 길든, 길들여진

adj. trained to live with or be used by humans

Sheep have long been thought to be the first **domesticated** animals, but some evidence suggests it may actually have been dogs.

syn. tame *ant.* wild

---

ceremonial 많은 서양 국가들에서, 판사들은 그들의 권력과 중요성의 상징으로 여전히 예복을 착용한다. **civilization** 가장 초기 문명들의 일부가 티그리스강과 유프라테스강 사이에 형성되었다고 여겨진다. **crypt** 고대 수도사들의 유골이 한 로마 교회 아래에 있는 지하 묘소 벽면을 따라 여전히 나열되어 있다. **descendant** 일부 과학자들은 대략 현대인의 200명 중 한 명이 Genghis Khan의 직계 후손이라고 생각한다. **deserted** 마추픽추는 16세기 이래로 인적이 끊겼지만, 한때 약 750명의 사람이 살았다. **domesticated** 양은 오랫동안 최초로 길들여진 동물이라고 여겨져 왔지만, 몇몇 증거가 사실은 그것이 개였을 것이라고 시사한다.

dwell
[dwel]

ⓥ (…에) 살다, 거주하다

n. dwelling

v. to live in a particular place

People that **dwell** deep in the Amazon rainforest have had little exposure to the modern world.

syn. inhabit

elapse
[ilǽps]

ⓥ (시간이) 경과하다

v. to go by, in terms of time

More than 20,000 years have **elapsed** since the first humans arrived in North America via a land bridge connecting it to Asia.

syn. pass

ethnic
[éθnik]

ⓐ 민족의, 종족의

adj. relating to a group of people with a shared culture

The Merina are the predominant **ethnic** group of Madagascar, having founded a kingdom there in the 15th century.

excavate
[ékskəvèit]

ⓥ (구멍을) 파다, 발굴하다

n. excavation

v. to dig a hole; to dig up objects from the past

While construction workers tend to use heavy machinery to **excavate**, archaeologists often rely on hand tools such as shovels.

ant. bury

expedition
[èkspədíʃən]

ⓝ 탐험, 원정

n. an organized journey with a specific purpose

An underwater **expedition** beneath the waves of the Black Sea led to the discovery of 60 ancient ships.

syn. excursion

flourish
[flə́:riʃ]

ⓥ 번성하다, 번영하다

v. to grow or develop well

Unlike most animal species, human beings have the ability to **flourish** in nearly any environmental conditions.

syn. prosper, thrive   *ant.* wither

---

dwell 아마존 열대 우림 깊은 곳에 사는 사람들은 현대 세계에 거의 노출되지 않았다.   **elapse** 최초의 인류가 아시아로 연결된 육교를 통해 북미에 도착한 지 2만 년이 넘는 세월이 흘렀다.   **ethnic** 메리나 족은 마다가스카르의 지배적인 민족인데, 15세기에 그곳에 왕국을 세웠다.   **excavate** 건설 노동자들이 땅에 구멍을 뚫기 위해 중장비를 이용하는 경향이 있는 반면, 고고학자들은 종종 삽과 같은 수공구를 이용한다.   **expedition** 흑해 해저 탐험은 60척의 고대 선박의 발견으로 이어졌다.   **flourish** 대부분의 동물 종들과는 다르게, 인간은 거의 모든 환경적 조건에서도 번성할 수 있는 능력을 가지고 있다.

ART & DESIGN

SOCIAL SCIENCE

NATURAL SCIENCE

HUMANITIES

EARTH & SPACE

SOCIAL ISSUES

forage
[fɔ́ːridʒ]
ⓥ (먹이 등을) 찾다

v. to search for food or other needed items

Before agriculture, people used to wander from place to place, **foraging** for whatever food they needed.

genetic
[dʒənétik]
ⓐ 유전(학)의, 유전적인

n. gene

adj. relating to the act of passing on genes to offspring

Genetic study suggests that modern humans originated in Africa and later spread out across the planet.

syn. hereditary

genuine
[dʒénjuin]
ⓐ 진짜의, 진품의

adj. not fake or deceptive

Using cutting-edge technology, the museum determined that the ancient jade statue was not **genuine**.

syn. authentic   *ant.* counterfeit

hieroglyph
[háiərəglìf]
ⓝ 상형 문자

n. a picture used as part of a writing system

It was the discovery of the Rosetta Stone that eventually allowed researchers to understand ancient Egyptian **hieroglyphs**.

syn. pictograph

homogeneous
[hòumədʒíːniəs]
ⓐ 동종의, 동질의

adj. all similar or of the same kind

In anthropology, a **homogeneous** culture is one with a predominant way of thinking that offers little room for deviation.

ant. heterogeneous

indigenous
[indídʒənəs]
ⓐ 토착의, 어느 지역 원산의

adj. occurring naturally in a certain area

The Sámi people, formerly known as Lapps, are an **indigenous** group inhabiting the northern regions of the Scandinavian peninsula.

syn. native   *ant.* foreign

Useful **Tips**

동식물을 이야기할 때, indigenous species라고 하면 토착종을 일컫고, invasive species는 침입종을 의미한다.

---

forage 사람들은 농경 사회 이전에 그들이 필요로 하는 음식을 찾아 이곳 저곳을 떠돌아다니곤 했다.   **genetic** 유전자 연구는 현대 인류가 아프리카에서 시작되어 추후에 전 세계로 퍼져나갔다는 것을 시사한다.   **genuine** 그 박물관은 최첨단 기술을 사용하여 그 고대 비취 석상이 진품이 아니라는 것을 밝혀냈다.
hieroglyph 로제타석의 발견은 마침내 연구자들이 고대 이집트 상형 문자를 이해할 수 있게 해 주었다.   **homogeneous** 인류학에서 동질 문화는 편차의 여지를 거의 두지 않는, 지배적인 사고방식을 가진 문화이다.   **indigenous** 이전에 라프 족으로 알려졌던 사미 족은 스칸디나비아 반도의 북쪽 지역에 사는 토착민들이다.

★

lineage
[líniidʒ]
[명] 혈통, 일족

n. the line of individuals and families one is descended from

DNA testing technology has made it easier than ever for everyday people to trace their **lineage** back for several generations.

syn. ancestry

★

matriarchal
[mèitriá:rkəl]
[형] 모계 중심의
n. matriarch

adj. led or ruled by females

The Mosuo people of China have what is sometimes described as a **matriarchal** society, although Mosuo men also hold positions of power.

ant. patriarchal

★★★

method
[méθəd]
[명] 방법
adj. methodical

n. a way of doing something

One of the most common **methods** of modern anthropologists is to spend time in the culture they are studying.

syn. means

★★

monumental
[mànjuméntl]
[형] 기념비적인, 대단한
n. monument

adj. of great importance

The **monumental** discoveries made by Louis and Mary Leakey in the Olduvai Gorge changed the way we look at human evolution.

syn. significant *ant.* insignificant

★

Paleolithic
[pèiliəlíθik]
[형] 구석기 시대의

adj. relating to the earliest era of the Stone Age

Paleolithic humans were hunter-gatherers who used tools made of stone and created art on the walls of caves.

Useful Tips

Mesolithic은 '중석기 시대의'란 의미이고, Neolithic은 '신석기 시대의'란 의미이다. 이들 단어에 공통적으로 쓰인 접미사 -lithic은 '돌의'라는 뜻이다.

★★

penetrate
[pénətrèit]
[동] 관통하다, 꿰뚫다

v. to pass through the surface of something

An auger is a tool that can **penetrate** solid rock and bring up soil samples from deep beneath the Earth's surface.

syn. pierce

---

lineage DNA 검사 기술은 일반인들이 수 세대에 걸친 그들의 혈통을 추적하는 것을 그 어느 때보다도 쉽게 해 주었다. **matriarchal** 중국의 모수오 족은 모수오 남성들 또한 권력을 쥐고 있음에도 불구하고, 가끔 모계 사회로 묘사된다. **method** 현대 인류학자들이 사용하는 가장 일반적인 방법 중 하나는 그들이 연구하고 있는 문화권에서 시간을 보내는 것이다. **monumental** 올두바이 협곡에서 Louis와 Mary Leakey가 이룬 기념비적인 발견으로 우리가 인류의 진화를 바라보는 방식이 바뀌었다. **Paleolithic** 구석기인들은 돌로 만든 도구를 사용하고, 동굴 벽에 예술을 창조한 수렵·채집가들이었다. **penetrate** 나사송곳은 단단한 돌을 뚫고 들어가 지표면 아래 깊은 곳에서 토양 샘플을 채취할 수 있는 도구이다.

ART & DESIGN

SOCIAL SCIENCE

NATURAL SCIENCE

HUMANITIES

EARTH & SPACE

SOCIAL ISSUES

★
★
★ **permanent**
[pə́ːrmənənt]
ⓐ 영구적인, 영속적인

n. permanence

adj. lasting forever or for a long time

The first **permanent** human settlements are thought to have been built in modern-day Turkey nearly 10,000 years ago.

syn. everlasting, perpetual   *ant.* temporary

★
★
★ **prehistoric**
[prìːhistɔ́ːrik]
ⓐ 선사 시대의

n. prehistory

adj. relating to the time before written history

There are no agreed upon dates defining the **prehistoric** era, as each culture views this period in a different light.

★ **prestige**
[prestíːʒ]
ⓝ 위신, 위세, 명망

adj. prestigious

n. the level of respect and admiration someone or something receives

Cattle are historically a symbol of **prestige** in many cultures, as great wealth and power are needed in order to tend a large herd.

syn. status

★
★ **probable**
[prábəbl]
ⓐ 있을 법한, …할 듯한

adj. expected to occur or be true

It is **probable** that globalization and technological advancements will continue to reduce cultural distinctions in the future.

syn. likely   *ant.* improbable

★ **relatively**
[rélətivli]
ⓐ 비교적으로, 상대적으로

adv. in comparison to something similar

It is **relatively** easy to study the traditions and beliefs of a culture that continues to exist in the modern world.

syn. comparatively

★
★ **remains**
[riméinz]
ⓝ 유물, 유적, 유해

n. the still existing parts of something dead or ruined

Whenever the **remains** of ancient humans are uncovered, forensic anthropologists are called in to determine when and how they died.

syn. remnant

Useful**Tips**

remain이 '유물, 유적'의 의미일 때 항상 복수형인 remains로 사용되는데, 비슷한 의미를 가진 단어 leftover와 ruin도 항상 복수형으로 쓰인다.

---

permanent 인류 최초의 영구 정착은 대략 1만년 전 오늘날의 터키에서 이뤄졌다고 여겨진다.   **prehistoric** 각각의 문화권에서 선사 시대를 서로 다른 관점으로 보기 때문에, 이 시대를 규정하는 날짜는 합의된 것이 없다.   **prestige** 거대한 무리의 소떼를 돌보기 위해서는 엄청난 부와 권력이 필요하기 때문에, 역사적으로 소는 많은 문화권에서 위세의 상징이다.   **probable** 미래에 세계화와 기술의 발전은 문화적 차이를 지속적으로 줄여나갈 것으로 보인다.   **relatively** 현대 세계에 계속 존재하는 어떤 문화의 전통과 신념을 연구하는 것은 비교적 쉽다.   **remains** 고대 인류의 유해가 발견될 때마다, 언제, 어떻게 그들이 사망했는지를 밝혀내기 위해 법의학 인류학자들이 소환된다.

★ **scrutiny**
[skrú:təni]
[명] 정밀 조사
v. scrutinize

n. close observation or inspection

Hours of **scrutiny** with a powerful microscope revealed that the ancient scrolls were not nearly as old as had been believed.

★★ **sediment**
[sédəmənt]
[명] 퇴적물, 침전물
adj. sedimentary

n. solid matter carried by wind and water or located at the bottom of a liquid

Scientists have developed a way to find and remove human DNA from **sediment** collected from caves used by ancient people.

syn. silt

★ **shaman**
[ʃá:mən]
[명] 주술사, 무속인

n. a person who claims to communicate with spirits to help or heal others

Shamans played many important roles in early Mongolian society, serving as leaders, healers, and fortunetellers.

★ **shard**
[ʃa:rd]
[명] (유리·금속 등의) 조각, 파편

n. a sharp piece of a broken object

The archaeologist noticed a **shard** of light blue pottery sticking out from the side of a recently dug hole.

syn. fragment

★★ **site**
[sait]
[명] (건물·도시 등이 들어설 혹은 있던) 위치, 장소

n. the place where something is occurring or has occurred

Stonehenge is believed to have been an important **site** during the Bronze Age, but what it was used for is still a mystery.

syn. locale

★ **vestige**
[véstidʒ]
[명] 자취, 흔적
adj. vestigial

n. a very small sign of something that no longer exists

Aerial photography can be used to allow researchers to find **vestiges** of ancient settlements hidden in the dense jungle.

syn. trace

---

scrutiny 성능 좋은 현미경을 사용해 몇 시간 동안 정밀 조사한 결과, 그 고대 족자들은 믿었던 것만큼 오래되지 않았다는 사실이 드러났다.
sediment 과학자들은 고대인들이 사용했던 동굴에서 수집된 퇴적물에서 인간의 DNA를 찾아 옮기는 방법을 개발했다. **shaman** 주술사들은 초기 몽골 사회에서 지도자, 치료사, 그리고 점쟁이로서 많은 중요한 역할을 했다. **shard** 그 고고학자는 최근에 파낸 구멍의 측면에 옅은 파란색 도기 조각 하나가 튀어나와 있는 것을 알아챘다. **site** 스톤헨지는 청동기 시대의 중요한 유적지였다고 여겨지지만, 무엇을 위한 장소였는지는 아직도 수수께끼로 남아있다. **vestige** 항공 사진은 연구자들이 울창한 밀림 속에 숨겨진 고대 정착지의 흔적을 발견하는 데 사용될 수 있다.

EXERCISES

A Match each definition with the correct word.

1 the line of individuals and families one is descended from   ⓐ prehistoric

2 close observation or inspection   ⓑ site

3 all similar or of the same kind   ⓒ lineage

4 relating to the time before written history   ⓓ flourish

5 the act of putting a dead body into the ground   ⓔ homogeneous

6 having no people   ⓕ burial

7 to grow or develop well   ⓖ deserted

8 the place where something is occurring or has occurred   ⓗ scrutiny

B Choose the word that is closest in meaning to each underlined word.

1 The <u>probable</u> cause of the economic depression was a sudden rise in bankruptcies.
   ⓐ likely   ⓑ original   ⓒ primary   ⓓ damaging

2 The oil company sponsored an <u>expedition</u> into the unexplored area to search for oil.
   ⓐ excursion   ⓑ endorsement   ⓒ framework   ⓓ proposition

3 The arrow failed to <u>penetrate</u> the target, bouncing off and landing on the ground.
   ⓐ overtake   ⓑ subdue   ⓒ shatter   ⓓ pierce

4 The teacher asked the students to guess what the ancient <u>artifact</u> was used for.
   ⓐ laborer   ⓑ relic   ⓒ tome   ⓓ settlement

5 The lawyer argued that her client's regret was <u>genuine</u>, but few people believed her.
   ⓐ unforeseen   ⓑ beneficial   ⓒ authentic   ⓓ imminent

6 The advertisement is aimed at people who <u>dwell</u> in rural areas and own farm animals.
   ⓐ inhabit   ⓑ toil   ⓒ invade   ⓓ desire

7 The business closed down and moved out, leaving behind only <u>vestiges</u> of its existence.
   ⓐ accounts   ⓑ traces   ⓒ stockpiles   ⓓ consequences

ART & DESIGN

SOCIAL SCIENCE

NATURAL SCIENCE

HUMANITIES

EARTH & SPACE

SOCIAL ISSUES

Lesson 13

[>] 교육

Education

★★★ **academic**
[ӕkədémik]
[형] 학업의, 학문적인
n. academy

adj. relating to education

Despite his impressive **academic** record, the young man had difficulty finding a suitable position for his particular set of skills.

syn. scholastic

★★ **admission**
[ædmíʃən]
[명] 1. 입학, 입장
2. (잘못 등에 대한) 시인
v. admit

n. 1 the process of allowing someone to enter or join
syn. admittance
2 the act of acknowledging that something is true

1. After applying for **admission** to a university, high school students must wait nervously to find out if they have been accepted.
2. The student's **admission** that she had cheated on the final exam shocked her classmates, who had believed her to be honest.

★★ **aptitude**
[ǽptətjùːd]
[명] 재능, 소질, 적성

n. a natural ability

Having an **aptitude** for writing clearly and concisely provides a student with a considerable advantage in many types of classes.

syn. talent

★ **aspire**
[əspáiər]
[동] 열망하다, 바라다
n. aspiration

v. to desire to achieve something

Some teachers **aspire** to become principals or administrators, but others are content to remain in the classroom.

★★ **assignment**
[əsáinmənt]
[명] 과제, 임무
v. assign

n. work or a task that must be done

The students' **assignment** was to interview an elderly relative about what life was like for young people in the past.

★★ **comprehensive**
[kɑ̀mprihénsiv]
[형] 종합적인, 포괄적인

adj. covering all parts of something

This history class provides a **comprehensive** overview of not only the Great Depression but also the numerous events that led up to it.

syn. inclusive

---

academic 인상적인 학업 성적에도 불구하고, 그 청년은 그의 특정 기술에 적합한 자리를 구하는 데 어려움을 겪었다. **admission** 1. 대학 입학 지원 후, 고등학생들은 합격 여부를 알 때까지 초조하게 기다려야 한다. 2. 기말시험에서 부정행위를 했다는 그 학생의 시인은 그녀가 정직하다고 믿고 있었던 급우들에게 충격을 줬다. **aptitude** 분명하고 간결하게 글을 쓰는 재능을 가진 것은 여러 종류의 수업에서 학생에게 상당한 이점을 준다. **aspire** 어떤 교사들은 교장이나 행정가가 되길 열망하지만, 다른 교사들은 교직에 남는 것에 만족해한다. **assignment** 그 학생들의 과제는 과거 청년들의 삶이 어땠는지에 대해 나이 든 친척 어른을 인터뷰하는 것이었다. **comprehensive** 이 역사 수업은 대공황뿐 아니라 그것을 촉발한 수많은 사건들에 대해서도 종합적 개요를 제공한다.

compulsory
[kəmpʌ́lsəri]
⑩ 의무적인, 필수의

adj. required by law; not optional

In some countries around the world, learning a second language in middle school is encouraged but not **compulsory**.

syn. mandatory   *ant.* voluntary

degree
[digríː]
⑩ 학위

n. a qualification received after completing a course of higher education

Without a college **degree**, it can sometimes be challenging to find a rewarding and well-paying job.

diploma
[diplóumə]
⑩ 졸업장, 수료증

n. a certificate received after completing a course of study

All of the high school principal's **diplomas** have been framed and are hanging on the walls of his office.

discipline
[dísəplin]
⑩ 단련, 수양, 통제
⑤ 징계하다

n. the ability to control one's behavior

It requires **discipline** to sit through an hour-long lesson, and this is something many young children do not have.

v. to punish someone

Several students were **disciplined** for using their smartphones in class after having been told to turn them off.

dissertation
[dìsərtéiʃən]
⑩ 논문

n. an extended essay on an academic topic

Although the length of a doctoral **dissertation** depends on a number of factors, it is generally expected to be between 150 and 300 pages.

syn. treatise

enroll
[inróul]
⑤ 입학시키다, 등록하다

n. enrollment

v. to officially become or make someone become a member of a class or school

When moving to a new town, parents should be sure to **enroll** their kids in the local school as soon as possible.

syn. register

ART & DESIGN | SOCIAL SCIENCE | NATURAL SCIENCE | HUMANITIES | EARTH & SPACE | SOCIAL ISSUES

---

compulsory 전 세계의 몇몇 나라에서는 중학교에서 제2외국어를 배우는 것이 권장되지만 의무적이지는 않다.   **degree** 학사 학위가 없으면, 보람 있고 보수가 좋은 직업을 찾기가 때때로 힘들 수 있다.   **diploma** 그 고등학교 교장의 모든 수료증들이 액자에 담겨 그의 집무실 벽에 걸려 있다.   **discipline** 한 시간짜리 수업을 끝까지 들으려면 단련이 필요한데, 이것은 많은 어린아이들이 갖고 있지 않은 점이다. / 학생 몇 명이 스마트폰을 끄라는 말을 듣고도 수업 중에 사용해서 징계를 받았다.   **dissertation** 박사 논문의 길이는 많은 요인에 따라 달라지지만, 일반적으로 150-300쪽 사이로 예상된다.   **enroll** 새로운 도시로 이사할 때, 부모는 가능한 한 빨리 자녀들을 그 지역 학교에 입학시켜야 한다.

★★

extracurricular

[èkstrəkəríkjulər]

[형] 과외의, 정규 교과 외의

adj. after or outside of class

Participation in **extracurricular** activities such as school clubs and sports teams can help students get into a good college.

Useful Tips

faculty는 집합명사로 단수 동사와 함께 사용되며, 개인을 나타낼 때는 faculty member라고 한다.

★★

faculty

[fǽkəlti]

[명] 교수진

n. the teaching staff at a school

Several different members of the school's **faculty** have won state and national teaching awards in recent years.

★★★

graduate

[grǽdʒuèit]

[동] 졸업하다

n. graduation

v. to complete a course of study at a school

Due to her intense schedule, the woman was able to **graduate** from a four-year school in only three years.

★

grant

[grænt]

[명] 보조금, 기부금

[동] 주다, 승인하다

n. money given for a specific purpose *syn.* donation

Thanks to a generous **grant** from the government, the university was able to start a new online program for part-time students.

v. to give or allow something *syn.* permit *ant.* refuse

The professor was **granted** permission to take a six-month leave of absence while she recovered from a serious illness.

★★★

imperative

[impérətiv]

[형] 필수적인, 중요한

adj. extremely important or urgent

Most educators agree that it is **imperative** to keep young learners interested and engaged in the material they are studying.

ant. trivial

★★★

institution

[ìnstətjúːʃən]

[명] 기관, 협회

n. a large, important organization

Considered the oldest continuously operating educational **institution** in the world, the University of Bologna was founded in 1088.

syn. establishment

---

extracurricular 학교 동호회와 스포츠팀 같은 과외 활동 참여는 학생들이 좋은 대학에 입학하는 데 도움이 될 수 있다. **faculty** 그 학교의 서로 다른 교수진 몇 명이 최근 몇 년 동안 주 단위 및 전국 교직상을 받았다. **graduate** 그 여자는 강도 높게 일정을 잡은 덕분에, 4년제 학교를 3년 만에 졸업할 수 있었다. **grant** 후한 정부 보조금 덕에, 그 대학은 시간제 학생들을 위한 신설 온라인 프로그램을 시작할 수 있었다. / 그 교수는 심각한 병에서 회복하면서 6개월 간 휴직할 수 있는 허가를 받았다. **imperative** 대부분의 교육자들은 어린 학습자들이 자신들이 공부하고 있는 자료에 계속 흥미와 관심을 갖도록 하는 것이 필수적이라는 점에 동의한다. **institution** 지속적으로 운영 중인 교육 기관 중 세계에서 가장 오래된 곳으로 여겨지는 볼로냐 대학은 1088년에 설립되었다.

★★ **lecture**
[léktʃər]
[명] 강의, 강연

n. an educational talk

Some students took notes during the professor's **lecture**, but others simply recorded it with their phones or laptops.

syn. lesson

★★ **major**
[méidʒər]
[명] 전공

n. a chosen course of study

According to the latest data, business is the most popular **major** among American college students.

★ **prodigy**
[prádədʒi]
[명] 신동, 천재

n. someone who can do something well at a young age

Blaise Pascal, the famous French mathematician, was a math **prodigy** who wrote a treatise on geometry at the age of 16.

ant. late bloomer

★★★ **require**
[rikwáiər]
[동] 1. 필요하다
2. (법·규칙에 따라) 요구하다
n. requirement

v. 1 to need or depend on 2 to call for or demand

1. Some young readers **require** extra time to sound out words, but this is not necessarily indicative of a problem.
2. The university library used to **require** a student ID for entry, but it now welcomes local residents and other non-students.

★★ **scholarship**
[skálərʃip]
[명] 장학금

n. money given to help pay for someone's education

Oprah Winfrey grew up poor, but her hard work in the classroom earned her a full **scholarship** to Tennessee State University.

★★ **submit**
[səbmít]
[동] 제출하다
n. submission

v. to hand in

Modern technology allows some students to **submit** homework to their teachers online rather than in person.

lecture 어떤 학생들은 그 교수의 강의 도중 필기를 했지만, 다른 학생들은 단순히 자신의 전화기나 노트북으로 녹음을 했다. **major** 최신 자료에 따르면, 경영학이 미국 대학생들 사이에서 가장 인기 있는 전공이다. **prodigy** 유명한 프랑스 수학자 Blaise Pascal은 열여섯 살 때 기하학에 대한 논문을 쓴 수학 신동이었다. **require** 1. 어떤 어린 독자들은 단어를 소리 내어 읽느라 시간을 더 필요로 하지만, 이것이 꼭 문제가 있다는 것은 아니다. 2. 그 대학 도서관은 입장할 때 학생증을 요구했었지만, 지금은 지역 거주자들과 학생이 아닌 사람들도 받아들인다. **scholarship** Oprah Winfrey는 가난하게 자랐지만, 열심히 공부해 테네시 주립 대학의 전액 장학금을 받았다. **submit** 현대 과학 기술 덕분에, 일부 학생들은 교사에게 숙제를 직접 제출하기보다 온라인 상으로 제출할 수 있다.

★★

tedious

[tíːdiəs]

[형] 지루한, 장황한

adj. lengthy and uninteresting

Students who find their history textbooks **tedious** could benefit from watching lively and engaging historical documentaries.

syn. tiresome *ant.* thrilling

★

transcript

[trǽnskript]

[명] 1. 성적증명서
2. 글로 옮긴 기록

v. transcribe

n. 1 an official record of a student's grades
2 a written copy of spoken material

1. Along with a résumé and cover letter, some human resources departments will ask for the college **transcripts** of applicants.
2. A **transcript** of two intelligent scholars debating an arguable issue can make good reading material for students.

★★★

transfer

[trænsfə́ːr]

[동] 전학하다, 옮기다

v. to switch from one school to another

Students attending community colleges often **transfer** to four-year schools after a few semesters.

★

truancy

[trúːənsi]

[명] 무단결석

n., adj. truant

n. the act of being absent from school without authorization

In order to combat **truancy**, school officials will sometimes visit students' homes to speak to their parents directly.

Useful Tips

playing hooky, skipping school, cutting class는 truancy와 같은 의미를 가지고 있다.

★★

tuition

[tjuːíʃən]

[명] 등록금, 수업료

n. the money paid to take classes

Rising college **tuition** costs have caused many young people to take out student loans that they may never be able to pay back.

★★

vocational

[voukéiʃənl]

[형] 직업의

n. vocation

adj. relating to a specific occupation

A **vocational** school can be an excellent alternative for students who do not perform well in a traditional classroom environment.

syn. occupational

---

tedious 역사 교과서가 지루한 학생들은 생생하고 흥미로운 역사 다큐멘터리를 시청하며 도움을 받을 수 있다. **transcript** 1. 어떤 인사부서에서는 이력서 및 자기소개서와 함께 지원자들의 대학 성적증명서를 요구할 것이다. 2. 논란의 여지가 있는 문제에 관한 총명한 두 학자의 논쟁을 글로 옮긴 기록은 학생들에게 좋은 읽을거리가 될 수 있다. **transfer** 지역 전문 대학에 다니는 학생들은 종종 몇 학기 후 4년제 학교로 편입한다. **truancy** 무단결석을 방지하기 위해, 학교 관계자들은 학부모와 직접 면담하려고 가끔 학생들의 집을 방문할 것이다. **tuition** 인상되고 있는 대학 등록금 비용 때문에 많은 청년들은 절대 갚지 못할 수도 있는 학자금 대출을 받아왔다. **vocational** 직업학교는 전통적인 수업 환경에서 기량을 잘 발휘하지 못하는 학생들에게 훌륭한 대안이 될 수 있다.

EXERCISES

A Match each definition with the correct word.

1 to switch from one school to another   ⓐ lecture

2 an educational talk   ⓑ scholarship

3 a certificate received after completing a course of study   ⓒ require

4 to need or depend on   ⓓ diploma

5 a natural ability   ⓔ aptitude

6 money given to help pay for someone's education   ⓕ graduate

7 to complete a course of study at a school   ⓖ extracurricular

8 after or outside of class   ⓗ transfer

B Choose the word that is closest in meaning to each underlined word.

1 There is an <u>imperative</u> need for qualified lawyers willing to represent low-income clients.
    ⓐ expanding   ⓑ historical   ⓒ urgent   ⓓ unexpected

2 Journalists were denied <u>admission</u> to the archaeological site because of security issues.
    ⓐ information   ⓑ contribution   ⓒ venue   ⓓ admittance

3 Although ethics debates may seem <u>tedious</u>, they are essential to understanding human nature.
    ⓐ tiresome   ⓑ unfamiliar   ⓒ aggressive   ⓓ intellectual

4 <u>Vocational</u> counselors provide advice to individuals who are uncertain about their future.
    ⓐ educational   ⓑ recreational   ⓒ additional   ⓓ occupational

5 Due to widespread cheating, drug tests are now <u>compulsory</u> at many sporting events.
    ⓐ mandatory   ⓑ despised   ⓒ amplified   ⓓ introductory

6 The business encouraged its employees to <u>enroll</u> in classes that would develop their skills.
    ⓐ discuss   ⓑ register   ⓒ conduct   ⓓ participate

7 The politician bragged about his <u>academic</u> achievements, but voters wanted to hear about his policies.
    ⓐ interpersonal   ⓑ monetary   ⓒ scholastic   ⓓ rampant

ART & DESIGN

SOCIAL SCIENCE

NATURAL SCIENCE

HUMANITIES

EARTH & SPACE

SOCIAL ISSUES

> 비즈니스
Business

---

accurate
[ǽkjurət]
혱 정확한, 정밀한

n. accuracy

adj. correct in every detail

Modern businesses use accounting software in order to keep an **accurate** record of their earnings, expenses, and losses.

syn. precise   *ant.* inaccurate

---

adamant
[ǽdəmənt]
혱 요지부동의, 단호한

adj. refusing to change one's mind or position

The board of directors did not like the CEO's new business plan, but she was **adamant** that it would be successful.

syn. determined, insistent

---

affiliate
[əfílièit]
뗑 계열사, 자회사

adj. affiliated

n. a smaller organization closely related to a larger one

The television network is based in New York City, but it has local **affiliates** located in nearly every major city.

---

assent
[əsént]
됭 찬성하다

v. to agree to or officially permit something

The small business's loyal employees **assented** to a minor decrease in their salaries in order to help the owners avoid bankruptcy.

ant. refuse

Useful Tips
assent를 동음이의어인 ascent(상승)와 혼동하지 않도록 유의한다.

---

barter
[báːrtər]
됭 물물교환하다

v. to exchange goods or services without using money

Before modern money systems, individuals and businesses simply **bartered** what they had for what they needed.

syn. swap

---

capital
[kǽpətl]
뗑 자본

n. the wealth available to a business

In order to raise **capital** to expand into the international market, the owners began to sell shares in their company.

---

accurate 현대 기업체들은 그들의 수입, 지출 및 손해를 정확하게 기록하기 위해 회계 소프트웨어를 사용한다.   **adamant** 이사회는 최고경영자의 새로운 사업 계획이 마음에 들지 않았지만, 그 최고경영자는 그 사업 계획이 성공할 것이라는 단호한 태도를 보였다.   **affiliate** 그 텔레비전 방송국은 뉴욕시에 기반을 두고 있지만, 거의 모든 주요 도시에 지역 계열사가 있다.   **assent** 그 소기업의 충성도 높은 직원들은 사업주들의 파산을 막기 위해 자신들의 급여를 소폭 삭감하는 데 찬성했다.   **barter** 현대 화폐 제도 이전에, 개인과 기업들은 단순하게 자신들이 가지고 있던 물건을 필요한 물건과 교환했다.   **capital** 국제 시장 진출에 필요한 자본 확충을 위해, 사업주들은 자사주를 팔기 시작했다.

ART & DESIGN

SOCIAL SCIENCE

NATURAL SCIENCE

HUMANITIES

EARTH & SPACE

SOCIAL ISSUES

★★★ **commercial**
[kəmɔ́:rʃəl]
ⓐ 상업의, 상업적인
ⓝ (TV·라디오의) 광고 (방송)

n. commerce

adj. relating to business

The French term *laissez faire* is used to refer to an informal governmental policy of not interfering in **commercial** activities.

n. an advertisement on television or the radio

It cost more than $5 million to run a 30-second **commercial** during the Super Bowl, the championship game of American football, in 2020.

★★★ **consolidate**
[kənsálədèit]
ⓥ 통합하다

n. consolidation

v. to combine several things into one

As the company begins to downscale, many smaller factories will be closed down and **consolidated** into a single facility.

syn. combine   *ant.* separate

★★★ **contract**
[kántrækt]
ⓝ 계약(서)

n. a written legal agreement

Once a **contract** has been properly signed and dated, it becomes a binding agreement in the eyes of the law.

★★ **corporate**
[kɔ́:rpərət]
ⓐ 기업의

n. corporation

adj. relating to large companies

The idea behind **corporate** social responsibility is that large businesses have an obligation to have a positive influence on the community.

★★ **debt**
[det]
ⓝ 빚, 부채, 채무

n. money that is owed

Unable to pay off its **debts**, the small business closed its doors for good.

> Useful**Tips**
> 빚을 진 상태를 말할 때 in debt라는 표현을 사용한다.

★★ **dispense**
[dispéns]
ⓥ 나누어 주다, 분배하다

v. to give out something to many different people

Some restaurant chains have a central warehouse from which they can **dispense** supplies to individual branches.

syn. distribute

---

commercial *laissez faire*(자유방임주의)라는 프랑스 용어는 상업 활동에 간섭하지 않는 비공식적인 정부 정책을 가리키는 데 사용된다. / 2020년 미식축구 챔피언 결정전인 슈퍼볼에서 30초짜리 광고 한 편을 내보내는 데 5백만 달러 이상의 비용이 들었다.　**consolidate** 그 회사가 규모를 줄이기 시작하면, 많은 소규모 공장들이 문을 닫고 하나의 시설로 통합될 것이다.　**contract** 일단 계약서에 제대로 사인하고 날짜를 기입하면, 법률상으로 구속력이 있는 계약이 된다. **corporate** 기업의 사회적 책임 이면에 깔린 개념은 대기업들이 지역 사회에 긍정적인 영향을 줄 의무가 있다는 것이다.　**debt** 빚을 갚을 수 없어서, 그 소기업은 영구적으로 문을 닫았다.　**dispense** 일부 레스토랑 체인들은 물품을 개별 지점에 분배할 수 있는 중앙 창고가 있다.

★★
entrepreneur
[à:ntrəprənə́:r]
[명] 기업가, 기업인
adj. entrepreneurial

n. someone who starts a business

Bill Gates started out as a teenage **entrepreneur** running a computer business out of a garage with Paul Allen.

Useful Tips

real estate(부동산)는 일반적인 땅과 건물을 가리키며, 사람들이 부동산을 사거나 임대하게 도와주는 부동산 중개 업체를 real estate agency라고 한다.

★★
estate
[istéit]
[명] 사유지, 토지

n. a piece of land with a large home on it

The Rockefellers, who made their fortune in oil, own a large **estate** in upstate New York that is now a museum.

★
freight
[freit]
[명] 운송 화물

n. goods that are being shipped

Businesses that regularly ship **freight** long distances incur high costs.

syn. shipment

★
frivolous
[frívələs]
[형] 시시한, 하찮은

adj. lacking seriousness

Dreaming up new and unusual toys may seem like a **frivolous** hobby, but it has the potential to lead to billion-dollar businesses.

syn. trivial *ant.* solemn

★★★
guarantee
[gæ̀rəntí:]
[동] 보장[약속]하다, 보증하다
[명] 굳은 약속, 보장, 보증

v. to assure that something will happen

Some companies **guarantee** that they will return all of your money if you are not completely satisfied with their products.

n. an assurance that something will happen *syn.* pledge

A warranty is a **guarantee** that a business will repair or replace a product at no charge for a certain period of time.

★
incentive
[inséntiv]
[명] 장려책, 우대책

n. something that serves as encouragement

Local governments often offer tax **incentives** to businesses as a way of encouraging them to create new jobs in the area.

syn. inducement *ant.* deterrent

---

entrepreneur Bill Gates는 Paul Allen과 함께 차고에서 컴퓨터 사업체를 운영하며 십 대 기업가로 출발했다. **estate** 석유로 재산을 모은 Rockefeller 가문은 뉴욕주 북부에 현재는 박물관으로 쓰이는 거대한 토지를 소유하고 있다. **freight** 정기적으로 화물을 장거리 운송하는 기업체들은 높은 비용을 낸다. **frivolous** 새롭고 특이한 장난감을 생각해 내는 것은 하찮은 취미처럼 보일지도 모르지만, 그것은 10억 달러 규모의 사업들로 이어질 잠재력을 가지고 있다. **guarantee** 몇몇 회사들은 당신이 그들의 제품에 완전히 만족하지 않으면, 당신의 돈을 모두 돌려줄 것이라고 보증한다. / 품질보증서는 회사가 특정 기간 동안 제품을 무상으로 수리하거나 교환해 주겠다는 약속이다. **incentive** 지방 정부는 그 지역에 새로운 일자리 창출을 독려하는 방법으로 기업들에게 종종 세금 우대책을 제공한다.

★★★

invest
[invést]
[동] 투자하다
n. investment

v. **to spend money, time, or energy in the hope of earning a profit**

If you had **invested** $1,000 in Amazon in 1997, the shares would have been worth more than $1.3 million twenty years later.

ant. divest

★★

lay off
[léi ɔ́:f]
[동] 정리 해고하다
n. layoff

v. **to end a worker's employment due to financial problems**

Due to the severe economic depression, many companies had to **lay off** workers, which made the situation even worse.

syn. dismiss *ant.* hire

★

lease
[li:s]
[명] 임대차 계약

n. **an agreement to pay to use something for a particular period of time**

The company has just signed a five-year **lease** on a large warehouse in which it will store its equipment.

syn. rent

★

lenient
[lí:niənt]
[형] 관대한

adj. **not harsh or strict**

Lenient laws regarding environmental protection do little to stop large businesses from polluting the air and water.

★

liability
[làiəbíləti]
[명] 법적 책임
adj. liable

n. **a legal responsibility for something**

Unwilling to accept **liability** for the accident caused by their product, the company hired a legal team.

syn. culpability

★★

loan
[loun]
[동] 빌려주다
[명] 대출금

v. **to allow someone to borrow money with interest** *syn.* lend

Banks are willing to **loan** large amounts of money to businesses due to the interest they will be able to collect.

n. **an amount of money borrowed with interest**

After getting a startup **loan**, the couple started a small business out of the basement of their own home.

Useful Tips
돈을 대출해 주는 사람이나 기관을 lender라고 부르며, 대출을 받는 사람이나 기업을 borrower라 부른다.

invest 만약 당신이 1997년에 아마존에 천 달러를 투자했다면, 20년 후 그 주식의 가치는 130만 달러 이상이 되었을 것이다. **lay off** 심각한 경기 침체 때문에, 많은 기업들이 근로자를 정리 해고해야 했고, 이는 상황을 더욱 악화시켰다. **lease** 그 회사는 장비를 보관할 대형 창고의 5년짜리 임대차 계약을 막 체결했다. **lenient** 환경보호에 대해 관대한 법률은 대기업들이 공기와 물을 오염시키는 것을 막는 데 거의 도움이 되지 않는다. **liability** 그 회사는 자신들의 제품 때문에 일어난 사고에 대한 법적 책임을 지고 싶지 않아 법무팀을 고용했다. **loan** 은행들은 그들이 받을 수 있는 이자 때문에 기업들에게 큰 돈을 기꺼이 빌려준다. / 그 부부는 창업 대출금을 받은 후, 그들의 집 지하실에서 작은 사업을 시작했다.

★★

maneuver

[mənúːvər]

[동] 잘 처리하다
[명] 책략, 술책

v. to move or accomplish something in a skillful way *syn.* navigate

When new businesses find it difficult to **maneuver** through the licensing process, they often hire lawyers to guide them.

n. a planned movement or action used to gain a benefit *syn.* tactic

It took some clever financial **maneuvers**, but the businesswoman finally found a way to fund her project.

★★★

manufacture

[mæ̀njufǽktʃər]

[동] (대량으로) 제조하다

v. to make large amounts of something through an industrial process

Although most of the individual parts of the automobiles are **manufactured** abroad, the vehicles are assembled locally.

syn. mass produce

★★

mortgage

[mɔ́ːrgidʒ]

[명] 담보 대출

n. a legal agreement to borrow money to purchase real estate

Shop owners who want to avoid paying monthly rental fees can apply for a business **mortgage** in order to purchase their own space.

★

novice

[nɑ́vis]

[명] 초보자

n. a person who is new to or inexperienced with something

Many nations have a government agency that provides free guidance and advice to business owners who are **novices**.

syn. beginner *ant.* veteran

★

pompous

[pɑ́mpəs]

[형] 젠체하는, 거만한

adj. full of self-importance

The company's founder is brilliant, but his **pompous** attitude has made him unpopular with most of his employees.

syn. pretentious *ant.* humble

★★★

profitable

[prɑ́fitəbl]

[형] 수익성이 있는

n., v. profit

adj. successful in a way that creates financial gain

The business consultant claims that she can make any business **profitable** in under six months.

syn. lucrative *ant.* unprofitable

---

maneuver 신규 사업체들은 인허가 절차를 잘 처리하는 것이 어려울 때, 조언해 줄 변호사들을 종종 고용한다. / 약간의 교묘한 재정적 술책이 필요했지만, 그 여성 기업가는 마침내 그녀의 프로젝트에 자금을 댈 방법을 찾았다. **manufacture** 자동차 개별 부품들의 대부분은 해외에서 제조되지만, 차량은 현지에서 조립된다. **mortgage** 월세 내는 것을 피하고자 하는 점주들은 자신들의 공간을 매입하기 위해 사업 담보 대출을 신청할 수 있다. **novice** 많은 국가들이 초보 사업주들에게 무료 지도와 상담을 제공하는 정부 기관을 두고 있다. **pompous** 그 회사의 설립자는 뛰어나지만, 그의 거만한 태도로 인해 대부분의 직원들에게 인기가 없다. **profitable** 그 사업 상담가는 6개월 이내에 어떠한 사업체라도 수익을 내게 할 수 있다고 주장한다.

provoke
[prəvóuk]

ⓥ 유발하다, (반응을) 불러일으키다

n. provocation

v. to cause a negative reaction in others

Publicly announcing an increase in prices is often avoided, as it is likely to **provoke** a negative reaction in customers.

syn. inflame *ant.* appease

recruit
[rikrúːt]

ⓥ 모집하다

v. to seek out people to join something

When top companies want to **recruit** new employees, they head to the campuses of the nation's best universities.

redundant
[ridΛndənt]

ⓐ 불필요한, 여분의

n. redundancy

adj. not needed

Employees made **redundant** by the new automated system will either be released or retrained for new positions.

syn. superfluous

register
[rédʒistər]

ⓥ 등록하다, 신고하다
ⓝ 기록부, 명부

v. to add one's name to an official list *syn.* sign up

All new small businesses should immediately **register** with the government for tax and licensing purposes.

n. a list of names *syn.* registry

A **register** of customers containing up-to-date contact information can be a powerful marketing tool for businesses.

reimburse
[rìːimbə́ːrs]

ⓥ 배상하다, (비용을) 갚다

n. reimbursement

v. to repay someone who has spent money because of you

Employee expenses incurred during business trips will only be **reimbursed** if the proper documentation is submitted.

syn. compensate

speculate
[spékjulèit]

ⓥ 1. 투기하다
2. 추측하다, 짐작하다

n. speculation

v. 1 to buy and sell for profit in a risky way
2 to guess without being certain

1. People who **speculate** in the stock market purchase risky stocks in the hope that their value will rise dramatically.

2. Some people **speculate** that the Great Depression could easily have been avoided, but there is no way of knowing whether this is true.

ART & DESIGN

SOCIAL SCIENCE

NATURAL SCIENCE

HUMANITIES

EARTH & SPACE

SOCIAL ISSUES

---

provoke 가격 인상을 공개적으로 알리는 것은 종종 꺼려지는데, 고객들에게 부정적인 반응을 유발할 수 있기 때문이다. **recruit** 일류 기업들이 신입 사원들을 모집하기 원할 때, 국내 최고 대학들의 캠퍼스로 향한다. **redundant** 새로운 자동화 시스템으로 인해 불필요해진 직원들은 방출되거나 새로운 직책을 위해 재교육을 받을 것이다. **register** 모든 신규 소규모 사업체는 즉시 정부에 세금과 인허가 목적을 등록해야 한다. / 최신 연락 정보를 포함한 고객 명부는 기업의 강력한 마케팅 도구가 될 수 있다. **reimburse** 직원의 출장 기간 동안 발생한 비용은 올바른 서류가 제출되었을 때에만 환급될 것이다. **speculate** 1. 주식 시장에서 투기하는 사람들은 그 가치가 급격하게 상승할 것을 바라면서 위험한 주식을 구매한다. 2. 일부 사람들은 대공황을 쉽게 피할 수 있었을 것이라고 추측하지만, 이것이 사실인지 알 길이 없다.

★

staple

[stéipl]

[명] 주된 요소, 주요 산물

n. a common and important element of something

Online shopping has become a **staple** of modern businesses, but at one time it was considered a passing trend.

syn. mainstay

★

stipulate

[stípjulèit]

[동] 규정하다, 명기하다

n. stipulation

v. to demand or state something as part of a larger agreement

Trade agreements between countries sometimes **stipulate** that protective customs duties be removed from certain products.

★

subsidy

[sʌ́bsədi]

[명] (국가·기관이 제공하는) 보조금

v. subsidize

n. money given to an essential business by the government

The United States government regularly gives **subsidies** to farmers who grow corn, soybeans, wheat, cotton, or rice.

syn. aid

★

transaction

[trænsǽkʃən]

[명] 거래

n. a single act of buying and selling

It has been estimated that more than one billion credit card **transactions** take place across the globe every single day.

★★

unscrupulous

[ʌ̀nskrú:pjuləs]

[형] 부도덕한, 비양심적인

n. scruple

adj. lacking moral principles

The government plans to crack down on **unscrupulous** companies that aim their advertisements at young children.

syn. unethical *ant.* principled

★★

wholesale

[hóulsèil]

[형] 도매의, 대량의

adj. relating to the sale of goods to businesses rather than consumers

Wholesale prices will always be lower than retail prices, but they are generally unavailable to most people.

ant. retail

---

staple 온라인 쇼핑은 현대 비즈니스의 주된 요소가 되었지만, 한때는 그저 지나가는 유행이라고 여겨졌다. **stipulate** 국가 간 무역 협정은 때때로 특정 물품에서 보호관세를 없애도록 규정하고 있다. **subsidy** 미국 정부는 옥수수, 콩, 밀, 목화, 혹은 쌀을 재배하는 농민들에게 정기적으로 보조금을 지급한다. **transaction** 전 세계적으로 매일 10억 건 이상의 신용카드 거래가 이루어지고 있는 것으로 추정된다. **unscrupulous** 정부는 어린아이들을 대상으로 광고를 하는 부도덕한 기업들을 엄중히 단속할 예정이다. **wholesale** 도매가격은 항상 소매가격보다 낮을 테지만, 일반적으로 대부분의 사람들에게는 제공되지 않는다.

EXERCISES

A Match each definition with the correct word.

1 a smaller organization closely related to a larger one   ⓐ entrepreneur

2 the wealth available to a business   ⓑ affiliate

3 lacking seriousness   ⓒ mortgage

4 to end a worker's employment due to financial problems   ⓓ stipulate

5 a legal agreement to borrow money to purchase real estate   ⓔ provoke

6 to cause a negative reaction in others   ⓕ capital

7 to demand or state something as part of a larger agreement   ⓖ lay off

8 someone who starts a business   ⓗ frivolous

B Choose the word that is closest in meaning to each underlined word.

1 Novices who struggle with problems can get advice from their more experienced coworkers.
     ⓐ pupils   ⓑ beginners   ⓒ assistants   ⓓ researchers

2 Tired of the lies of unscrupulous politicians, voters are eager for someone they can trust.
     ⓐ unethical   ⓑ inexperienced   ⓒ unexpected   ⓓ incompatible

3 Installing machines that dispense cash in shopping malls encourages shoppers to spend more.
     ⓐ accumulate   ⓑ distribute   ⓒ organize   ⓓ accrue

4 Deciding which industries to give subsidies to can be difficult for any government.
     ⓐ advice   ⓑ punishment   ⓒ aid   ⓓ regulations

5 The coach decided to consolidate all of her knowledge and experiences into a book.
     ⓐ reveal   ⓑ conceal   ⓒ promote   ⓓ combine

6 The archaeologists were adamant that they were in the right place, but they found nothing.
     ⓐ deceived   ⓑ uncertain   ⓒ insistent   ⓓ reassured

7 A good advertisement will provide an accurate description of the product and its features.
     ⓐ brief   ⓑ detailed   ⓒ precise   ⓓ exclusive

ART & DESIGN

SOCIAL SCIENCE

NATURAL SCIENCE

HUMANITIES

EARTH & SPACE

SOCIAL ISSUES

경제학

Lesson 15 Economics

★

anomaly
[ənɑ́məli]
[명] 이례, 변칙

n. something that is different from what usually occurs

Experts are trying to determine whether the sudden economic slowdown was an **anomaly** or part of a larger pattern.

syn. deviation

★★

asset
[ǽset]
[명] 자산, 재산

n. money or something valuable that is owned by a person or company

For many young families struggling to get by, the house that they live in is their only significant **asset**.

ant. liability

★

censure
[sénʃər]
[동] 견책하다, 불신임하다

v. to strongly blame or criticize

The CEOs of several large banks were **censured** by Congress for providing investors with misleading information.

syn. condemn *ant.* commend

Useful Tips
censure는 '검열하다, 삭제하다'라는 의미의 censor와 철자가 비슷하므로 혼동하지 않도록 유의한다.

★★

collapse
[kəlǽps]
[동] 붕괴하다, 무너지다

v. to completely fall apart

To stop their economies from **collapsing**, some countries are forced to turn to international organizations for help.

syn. crumble

★★★

competent
[kɑ́mpətənt]
[형] 유능한
n. competence

adj. able to do something well

Any **competent** economist can analyze past depressions, but it takes an expert to predict one before it occurs.

syn. capable *ant.* incompetent

★★

contradict
[kɑ̀ntrədíkt]
[동] 부정하다, 모순되다
n. contradiction

v. to state or suggest the opposite of something

The politician's cheerful assurances that the economy was fine **contradicted** the harsh reality faced by many people.

---

anomaly 전문가들은 그 갑작스러운 경기 침체가 이례적인 것이었는지 또는 더 큰 패턴의 일부였는지 알아내려고 애쓰고 있다. **asset** 자녀가 아직 어린, 그럭저럭 살아가는 많은 가정들에게 그들이 살고 있는 집은 유일한 중요 자산이다. **censure** 몇몇 거대 은행들의 최고경영자들은 투자자들에게 오해의 소지가 있는 정보를 제공해 의회의 견책을 받았다. **collapse** 경제가 붕괴되는 것을 막기 위해, 몇몇 나라들은 국제 기구에 원조를 요청해야만 한다. **competent** 유능한 경제학자라면 누구나 과거의 불황을 분석할 수 있지만, 불황이 발생하기 전에 그것을 예견하려면 전문가가 필요하다. **contradict** 경기가 좋다는 그 정치인의 쾌활한 장담은 많은 사람들이 직면한 가혹한 현실과 모순되었다.

★★★ **currency**
[kə́:rənsi]
[명] 통화, 화폐

n. **the system of money used in a particular place**

Having an extremely strong **currency** usually means a country's citizen can buy foreign goods at lower prices.

syn. cash

★★ **curtail**
[kə:rtèil]
[동] 줄이다, 삭감하다

v. **to decrease or reduce something**

In order to **curtail** uncontrolled spending, members of the government sought to make amendments to the budget.

syn. diminish *ant.* strengthen

★ **debit**
[débit]
[명] 차변

n. **an amount of money that has been removed**

The accountants went through all of the **debits** and credits for the year and tried to figure out what had been miscalculated.

ant. credit

★★ **deficit**
[défəsit]
[명] 적자, 결손

n. **the amount by which spending exceeds earnings**

In 2019, the United States had a **deficit** of $984 million, an increase of more than $200 million from the previous year.

syn. shortfall

★★ **deposit**
[dipázit]
[명] 예금
[동] 예금하다

n. **an amount of money added to an account** *ant.* withdrawal

The **deposits** of account holders are what banks use to make loans to both consumers and large organizations.

v. **to add an amount of money to an account** *ant.* withdraw

When consumers **deposit** their paychecks rather than spending them, it can cause a slowdown in the economy.

★★★ **discrepancy**
[diskrépənsi]
[명] 차이, 불일치

n. **a difference between two things that are supposed to be the same**

A large **discrepancy** in the monthly unemployment rates reported by the federal government caused a great deal of confusion.

syn. disparity

---

currency 아주 강력한 통화를 가지고 있다는 것은 보통 한 나라의 국민이 더 낮은 가격에 외국 제품을 살 수 있다는 뜻이다. **curtail** 걷잡을 수 없는 지출을 줄이기 위해, 정부 관리들은 예산을 수정하려고 했다. **debit** 그 회계사들은 그 해의 모든 대변차변을 검토하고, 어떤 것이 잘못 계산되었는지 찾아내려고 애썼다. **deficit** 2019년에 미국은 9억 8천 4백만 달러의 적자를 냈는데, 그것은 이전 해보다 2억 달러 이상 증가한 액수이다. **deposit** 예금주들의 예금은 은행들이 소비자들과 거대 조직체 모두에게 대출을 해 주는 데 사용된다. / 소비자들이 그들의 급료를 쓰지 않고 예금을 하면, 경기를 둔화시킬 수 있다.
discrepancy 연방 정부가 보고한 월간 실업률 간의 큰 차이는 엄청난 혼란을 야기시켰다.

★★
endorse
[indɔ́ːrs]
[동] 승인하다, 지지하다
n. endorsement

v. to publicly state one's support

Several notable politicians have **endorsed** the plan to lower interest rates in order to boost economic growth.

★★★
finance
[finǽns, fáinæns]
[명] 재정, 재원
n. financial

n. the management of how money is spent or invested

The decision to appoint a new minister of **finance** was not surprising considering the weak state of the economy.

★★
fiscal
[fískəl]
[형] 재정의, 회계의

adj. relating to money matters

Practicing **fiscal** responsibility is the only guaranteed way for the government to lead the country out of its current economic situation.

★★
forfeit
[fɔ́ːrfit]
[동] 몰수[박탈] 당하다

v. to give something up as a penalty

There are fears that the inability to keep up with rising tax rates may force many families to **forfeit** their homes.

syn. relinquish *ant.* retain

★★
frugal
[frúːgəl]
[형] 알뜰한, 검소한

adj. unwilling to spend money or use something

Frugal government spending helped balance the budget, but it caused dissatisfaction among many taxpayers.

syn. thrifty

Useful Tips
지나치게 frugal한 사람을 miser, 그 반대 성향의 사람을 spendthrift라 한다.

★★★
import
[impɔ́ːrt]
[동] 수입하다

v. to bring goods into a country

Several countries **imported** more than $1 billion of rice in 2019, making it an extremely important global commodity.

ant. export

---

endorse 몇몇 유명한 정치인들이 경제 성장을 부양하기 위해 이율을 낮추는 계획을 승인했다. **finance** 취약한 경제 상태를 감안할 때, 새 재무 장관을 임명하겠다는 결정은 놀랍지 않았다. **fiscal** 재정적인 책임을 다하는 것은 정부가 나라를 현재 경제 상황에서 벗어나게 하는 유일하게 보장된 방법이다. **forfeit** 인상되는 세율을 감당하지 못해서 많은 가정들이 집을 몰수 당할 수 있다는 우려가 있다. **frugal** 정부의 알뜰한 지출 덕분에 예산이 균형 있게 유지되었지만, 많은 납세자들 사이에서는 불만을 야기했다. **import** 2019년에 몇몇 국가들이 10억 달러어치 이상의 쌀을 수입해, 쌀이 극히 중요한 국제적 상품이 되었다.

impose
[impóuz]

ⓥ (의무·세금 등을) 지우다, 부과하다

n. imposition

v. to force people to accept something

Countries sometimes **impose** strict restrictions on trade in order to protect domestic industries.

---

initiative
[iníʃiətiv]

ⓝ 조치, 새로운 계획

v. initiate

n. a new plan or strategy to accomplish something

Economic **initiatives** aimed at helping small businesses survive during difficult times tend to be widely popular.

syn. scheme

---

innovation
[ìnəvéiʃən]

ⓝ 1. 획기적인 것
2. 혁신, 쇄신

v. innovate
adj. innovative

n. 1 a new method or item
2 the introduction of new methods or items

1. The use of energy-saving **innovations** such as LED light bulbs could ultimately save the nation billions of dollars.

2. **Innovation** is sometimes blocked by established companies that feel threatened by the new technology.

---

inventory
[ínvəntɔ̀:ri]

ⓝ 재고(품)

n. all of the goods currently on hand

The government's **inventory** of meat, cheese, and milk is used to help feed poor families during hard times.

syn. supply

---

irresolute
[irézəlù:t]

ⓐ 우유부단한

adj. uncertain or hesitant

An **irresolute** approach to economic reform is likely to be challenged by political rivals who sense a weakness.

syn. indecisive

---

manageable
[mǽnidʒəbl]

ⓐ 관리할 수 있는

v. manage

adj. capable of being handled

The current national debt may seem impossibly large, but some economists insist that it is still at a **manageable** level.

syn. feasible

ART & DESIGN

SOCIAL SCIENCE

NATURAL SCIENCE

HUMANITIES

EARTH & SPACE

SOCIAL ISSUES

---

impose 국가들은 국내 산업을 보호하기 위해 때때로 무역에 엄격한 제약을 가한다. **initiative** 힘든 시기에 소기업이 존속하도록 돕기 위한 경제 조치들은 널리 인기 있는 경향이 있다. **innovation** 1. LED 전구 같이 에너지를 절약하는 획기적인 것들을 사용하면, 궁극적으로 그 나라는 수십억 달러를 절약할 수 있을 것이다. 2. 혁신은 새 기술에 위협을 느끼는 기존 회사들에 의해 때때로 저지된다. **inventory** 정부의 고기, 치즈, 우유 재고는 불경기에 가난한 가정들에 식량 조달을 돕는 데 사용된다. **irresolute** 경제 개혁에 대한 우유부단한 접근은 약점을 감지한 정치적 경쟁자들의 이의 제기를 받을 수 있다. **manageable** 현재 국가 부채는 어처구니없이 큰 것 같지만, 몇몇 경제학자들은 그것이 아직 관리 가능한 수준이라고 주장한다.

★★ **monopoly**
[mənápəli]
ⓝ 독점, 전매
v. monopolize

n. complete control of a commodity or service

The government has the right to break up any **monopoly** that is formed, in the interest of protecting consumers.

★ **plummet**
[plʌ́mit]
ⓥ 폭락하다, 급감하다

v. to drop a long distance in a short time

In the early 1930s, both money supply and real output unexpectedly **plummeted**, leading to the Great Depression.

syn. plunge

★ **predicament**
[pridíkəmənt]
ⓝ 곤경, 어려움

n. a bad situation that is difficult to escape

The government faced a **predicament**—making large budget cuts would help the economy, but it would also anger many people.

syn. dilemma

★★★ **property**
[prápərti]
ⓝ 재산, 소유

n. things that are owned

People in debt are sometimes forced to sell their personal **property** in order to raise money to pay back their loans.

syn. possession

★★★ **prosper**
[práspər]
ⓥ 번영하다, 발전하다
adj. prosperous

v. to experience financial success

When a country's middle class expands and **prospers**, it is a positive sign for the overall health of the economy.

syn. flourish   *ant.* languish

★★ **provision**
[prəvíʒən]
ⓝ 1. 규정, 조항
   2. 지원

n. 1 a requirement in an agreement
   2 the act of supplying something needed

1. Due to a **provision** in their contract with the government, the company had to freeze the cost of their services.

2. The government is responsible for the **provision** of a safe and modern infrastructure paid for with taxpayer money.

---

monopoly 정부에게는 소비자 보호를 위해 기존의 어떤 독점도 해체시킬 권리가 있다.   **plummet** 1930년대 초에, 자금 공급과 실제 생산량이 뜻밖에 급감하여 대공황을 초래했다.   **predicament** 정부는 곤경에 직면했는데, 그것은 대규모 예산 삭감이 경제에 도움이 되겠지만 또한 많은 사람들을 분노하게 만들 것이라는 사실이었다.   **property** 빚을 진 사람들은 때때로 융자금을 갚을 돈을 마련하기 위해 개인 재산을 팔아야만 한다.   **prosper** 한 나라의 중산층이 확장되고 번영하는 것은 전반적인 경제 번영의 긍정적 징후이다.   **provision** 1. 그 회사는 정부와의 계약상 규정 때문에, 서비스 비용을 동결해야 했다.   2. 정부는 납세자들의 세금으로 지불한 안전하고 현대적인 기반 시설을 지원할 책임이 있다.

★

quota

[kwóutə]

[명] 할당(량), 쿼터

n. a limit on the amount of something

Because trade **quotas** were not being uniformly enforced, several countries threatened to pull out of the trade agreement.

★★

recession

[riːséʃən]

[명] 불황, 불경기

n. a period during which a national economy is doing poorly

One of the biggest global **recessions** took place between 2007 and 2009, although some large countries were unaffected.

Useful Tips

recession은 일상적인 경기 순환의 일부지만, depression은 그보다 심각한 경기 불황 상태를 나타낸다.

★★★

revenue

[révənjùː]

[명] 세입, 매출, 수입

n. money that is taken in

Annual tax **revenues** are what allow a government to undertake many of the projects it has planned.

syn. earnings

★★

shrink

[ʃriŋk]

[동] 줄다, 감소하다

v. to make or become smaller

An economy is said to **shrink** when consumer demand significantly lowers while manufacturing continues at the same rate.

syn. contract *ant.* expand

★★

soar

[sɔːr]

[동] 급등하다, 상승하다

v. to rise or increase rapidly

Soaring joblessness rates can have a lasting effect on the economy if enough new jobs aren't created in response.

syn. skyrocket

★★★

stagnant

[stǽgnənt]

[형] 정체된, 불경기의

n. stagnation

adj. showing little movement, improvement, or activity

When an economy grows at a rate of less than 2% annually, experts will consider it to be **stagnant**.

syn. sluggish *ant.* active

quota 무역 할당이 균등하게 시행되지 않고 있었기 때문에, 몇몇 나라들이 그 무역 협정에서 탈퇴하겠다고 위협했다. **recession** 가장 큰 국제적 불황들 중 하나가 2007년에서 2009년 사이에 발생했는데, 그럼에도 몇몇 큰 나라들은 영향을 받지 않았다. **revenue** 정부가 계획한 많은 프로젝트를 착수할 수 있게 해 주는 것은 연간 세금 수입이다. **shrink** 제조가 동일한 비율로 지속되는 반면 소비자 수요가 상당히 감소할 때, 경제가 위축된다고 한다. **soar** 급등하는 실업률은 충분한 새 일자리가 그에 대응해 창출되지 않으면, 경제에 지속적인 영향을 미칠 수 있다. **stagnant** 경제 성장률이 연간 2% 미만이면, 전문가들은 불경기로 간주할 것이다.

★★★ **stock**
[stɑk]
[명] 주식, 증권

n. a share of ownership in a company

Rather than saving their money in bank accounts with low interest rates, many individuals choose to invest it in **stocks**.

★ **stringent**
[stríndʒənt]
[형] 엄격한, 까다로운

adj. strict and demanding

Global organizations like the IMF and the World Bank often have **stringent** conditions attached to the loans they provide.

syn. severe *ant.* lenient

★ **surplus**
[sə́ːrplʌs]
[명] 과잉, 잉여

n. an extra amount of something

It has been established that a **surplus** of goods will eventually lead to a decrease in prices.

syn. excess

★★ **tariff**
[tǽrif]
[명] 관세

n. a tax on goods being brought into a country

Removing high **tariffs** on goods coming into the country would have both positive and negative effects.

syn. tax

★★ **treasury**
[tréʒəri]
[명] 재무부, 재정

n. the government agency in charge of financial matters

The government's department of the **treasury** is responsible for both the production of money and the borrowing of funds.

★★★ **validate**
[vǽlədèit]
[동] (…의 정당성을) 확인하다, 입증하다
n. validation

v. to prove that something is true or accurate

The economic measures taken by the prime minister were **validated** by the recovery that began shortly after.

syn. verify

---

stock 많은 개인들이 이율이 낮은 은행 계좌에 돈을 저축하기보다 주식 투자를 선택한다. **stringent** IMF와 세계은행 같은 국제 기구들은 종종 그들이 제공하는 융자에 까다로운 조건들을 붙인다. **surplus** 제품 과잉이 결국 가격 인하로 이어질 것이라는 것이 확립되어 있다. **tariff** 그 나라에 유입되는 제품에 대한 높은 관세를 철회하는 것은 긍정적 효과와 부정적 효과를 모두 낳을 것이다. **treasury** 정부의 재무부는 화폐 발행과 기금 차용을 모두 책임지고 있다. **validate** 그 수상이 취한 경제 조치는 그 직후에 시작된 (경기) 회복으로 그 정당성이 확인되었다.

EXERCISES

A Match each definition with the correct word.

1 to bring goods into a country   ⓐ endorse

2 a limit on the amount of something   ⓑ import

3 a period during which a national economy is doing poorly   ⓒ contradict

4 the amount by which spending exceeds earnings   ⓓ anomaly

5 to state or suggest the opposite of something   ⓔ quota

6 complete control of a commodity or service   ⓕ recession

7 something that is different from what usually occurs   ⓖ monopoly

8 to publicly state one's support   ⓗ deficit

B Choose the word that is closest in meaning to each underlined word.

1 After its advertising campaign, the tech company's popularity with teens began to <u>soar</u>.
    ⓐ skyrocket   ⓑ spread   ⓒ loom   ⓓ reverse

2 Students who attend the academy tend to <u>prosper</u> in the business world after graduation.
    ⓐ strive   ⓑ panic   ⓒ invest   ⓓ flourish

3 Some otherwise <u>competent</u> people freeze up in fear at the prospect of speaking in public.
    ⓐ uninformed   ⓑ arrogant   ⓒ capable   ⓓ imaginative

4 <u>Irresolute</u> individuals give the impression that they are questioning their own judgment.
    ⓐ hasty   ⓑ impolite   ⓒ indecisive   ⓓ exceptional

5 Singapore has some of the most <u>stringent</u> laws in the world, which keeps crime rates low.
    ⓐ candid   ⓑ severe   ⓒ renowned   ⓓ modern

6 Faced with a <u>surplus</u> of shirts, the company decided to donate the goods to needy countries.
    ⓐ demand   ⓑ range   ⓒ shipment   ⓓ excess

7 The basketball game was stopped when a referee noticed a <u>discrepancy</u> between the two scoreboards.
    ⓐ refrain   ⓑ potential   ⓒ disparity   ⓓ contingency

ART & DESIGN

SOCIAL SCIENCE

NATURAL SCIENCE

HUMANITIES

EARTH & SPACE

SOCIAL ISSUES

A Choose the correct words.

1 The word strenuous has the same meaning as

  ⓐ durable   ⓑ repetitive   ⓒ protective   ⓓ laborious

2 The word accidental has the same meaning as

  ⓐ average   ⓑ inaccessible   ⓒ dubious   ⓓ unintended

3 The word institution has the same meaning as

  ⓐ concept   ⓑ establishment   ⓒ request   ⓓ framework

4 The word forfeit has the same meaning as

  ⓐ obtain   ⓑ scatter   ⓒ relinquish   ⓓ permit

5 The word guarantee has the same meaning as

  ⓐ pledge   ⓑ apology   ⓒ destination   ⓓ foundation

6 The word censure has the same meaning as

  ⓐ slumber   ⓑ pierce   ⓒ reinforce   ⓓ condemn

7 The word comprehensive has the same meaning as

  ⓐ defective   ⓑ inclusive   ⓒ hesitant   ⓓ restricted

8 The word surmount has the same meaning as

  ⓐ observe   ⓑ mimic   ⓒ conquer   ⓓ deny

B Fill in the blanks with the best words from the box.

1 Despite the fact that only a single _____ of pottery has been uncovered so far, the archaeologists hope they will be able to find an entire ancient vase eventually.

2 Because they _____ to play professional basketball someday, the three teenagers spend hours together at the local gym, working out and perfecting their skills.

3 The rites performed by the modern-day _____ are based on the natural healing traditions of her people, which are believed to date back thousands of years.

4 Informed that he had been made _____ by an improvement to the company's manufacturing process, the factory worker immediately began searching for a new job.

5 There were many citizens who were willing to _____ years of economic hardship if it would allow their country to keep its independence and national identity.

6 _____ teachers are adept at finding ways to make professional-looking educational materials on their own, rather than purchasing them from a store or website.

| shard | endure | frugal | aspire | redundant | shaman |

C Read the following passages.

ART & DESIGN

SOCIAL SCIENCE

NATURAL SCIENCE

HUMANITIES

EARTH & SPACE

SOCIAL ISSUES

[1-2]

1 Choose one word that fits both blanks.

Some young students don't have the _____ to sit down and silently read a long story on their own. Teachers should not _____ them for this inability. Instead, they should find other ways to deal with the material, such as having students take turns reading sentences aloud.

ⓐ grant   ⓑ loan   ⓒ discipline   ⓓ maneuver

2 Choose the appropriate pair of words to fill in the blanks.

After purchasing some expensive supplies for a presentation, the employees were surprised when the company failed to _____ them. Knowing that complaining loudly might _____ a bad reaction from their boss, they instead wrote a formal letter explaining the situation.

ⓐ reimburse — provoke   ⓑ contradict — affiliate

ⓒ defeat — consolidate   ⓓ submit — linger

[3-4]

Early humans were nomadic. When they finally began to form settlements, they probably expected their descendants to live there for a generation or two and then move on. Little did they know that they would remain there and flourish for thousands of years.

3 In the context of the passage, descendants means _____.

ⓐ relatives   ⓑ enemies   ⓒ ancestors   ⓓ neighbors

4 The word flourish in the passage could best be replaced by

ⓐ escalate   ⓑ diversify   ⓒ thrive   ⓓ dwindle

[5-6]

When the team found out that they had failed to _____ for the national tournament, they were shocked and upset. At the next practice, the coach noticed that their morale was extremely low, so he decided to do something about it. He gathered the players together and gave them an inspirational speech about the importance of never giving up.

5 Choose the word that is most suitable for the blank.

ⓐ qualify   ⓑ associate   ⓒ penetrate   ⓓ endorse

6 The word morale in the passage is closest in meaning to

ⓐ strength   ⓑ mood   ⓒ popularity   ⓓ concentration

Lesson 16

마케팅과 홍보

Marketing & Public Relations

★★

activate

[ǽktəvèit]

[동] 활성화시키다, (반응을) 촉진하다

n. activation

v. to make something begin to move or start working

A well-crafted commercial **activates** the interest of consumers, driving them to seek out more information.

syn. trigger *ant.* deactivate

★★★

advertise

[ǽdvərtàiz]

[동] 광고하다

v. to make something publicly known, usually in order to sell it

In the past, companies primarily **advertised** their products in newspapers and on large billboards in public places.

syn. publicize

★★

agency

[éidʒənsi]

[명] 대리점, 서비스 제공 회사

n. a business that represents clients

A large company whose CEO was involved in a scandal contacted a powerful public relations **agency** for assistance.

Useful Tips

흔히 사용되는 agency의 종류에는 travel agency(여행사), real estate agency(부동산 중개소), 그리고 temp agency(임시직 취업 알선소) 등이 있다.

★★

astound

[əstáund]

[동] 경악시키다, 큰 충격을 주다

adj. astounding

v. to shock or surprise

People were **astounded** by the number of famous celebrities who appeared in the tech company's television commercials.

syn. astonish

★★

complaint

[kəmpléint]

[명] 불만, 불평

v. complain

n. a statement of dissatisfaction

By personally addressing the **complaints** of consumers, the business hopes to improve its poor public image.

syn. grievance

★★

consult

[kənsʌ́lt]

[동] 상담하다, 상의하다

n. consultation

v. to seek advice or an opinion from an expert

After **consulting** with their lawyers, the corporation agreed to remove some of the claims they had made in their latest ad.

syn. confer

---

activate 잘 만들어진 광고는 소비자들의 관심을 촉진시켜 더 많은 정보를 찾게 만든다. **advertise** 과거에 회사들은 주로 신문과 공공장소의 커다란 옥외 광고판에 그들의 제품을 광고했다. **agency** 스캔들에 연루된 최고경영자가 있는 대기업이 도움을 받기 위해 영향력이 강한 홍보회사와 접촉했다. **astound** 사람들은 그 기술 회사의 TV 광고에 출연한 유명 인사들의 수에 깜짝 놀랐다. **complaint** 그 회사는 소비자들의 불만을 직접 해결함으로써, 좋지 못한 기업 이미지가 개선되기를 희망한다. **consult** 그 회사는 변호사들과 상의한 후, 그들의 최근 광고에서 제작한 선전 문구 중 일부를 삭제하는 데 동의했다.

★★ **crisis**
[kráisis]
[명] 위기

n. **a time of great difficulty**

During a national **crisis**, businesses will often alter their marketing messages to make them more uplifting and inspirational.

syn. emergency

★ **depreciate**
[diprí:ʃièit]
[동] 가치가 떨어지다

v. **to decrease in value**

It takes a special marketing approach to make new cars and other expensive products that **depreciate** rapidly appealing to consumers.

syn. devalue

★★ **distribute**
[distríbju:t]
[동] 나누어 주다, 분배하다
n. distribution

v. **to give something to numerous people**

Whenever it opens a factory in a new region, the company **distributes** press materials highlighting its contributions to communities.

syn. dispense

★ **fiasco**
[fiǽskou]
[명] 대실패, 낭패

n. **an embarrassing failure**

After the **fiasco** of the release of its new smartphone, the company shifted its emphasis back to personal computers.

syn. debacle *ant.* success

★★★ **lucrative**
[lú:krətiv]
[형] 수익성이 좋은

adj. **leading to a large profit**

Signing the global soccer star to a **lucrative** ten-year contract was one of the best PR moves the sneaker company ever made.

syn. fruitful, profitable *ant.* unprofitable

★★ **maintenance**
[méintənəns]
[명] 유지, 관리
v. maintain

n. **the act of keeping something in good condition**

Once a positive corporate image has been created, it requires continued **maintenance** year after year.

syn. upkeep *ant.* neglect

crisis 국가적 위기 동안, 기업들은 자신들이 좀 더 희망적이고 고무적으로 보일 수 있게 종종 마케팅 메시지를 고칠 것이다. **depreciate** 급격하게 가치가 하락하는 신차들과 다른 고가 제품들을 소비자들에게 어필하기 위해서는 특별한 마케팅 접근법이 필요하다. **distribute** 그 회사는 새로운 지역에 공장을 열 때마다 지역 사회에 대한 기여도를 강조하는 보도자료를 배포한다. **fiasco** 새로운 스마트폰 출시의 대실패 이후, 그 회사는 주안점을 다시 개인용 컴퓨터로 옮겼다. **lucrative** 그 세계적인 축구 스타와 수익성 좋은 10년짜리 계약을 체결한 것은 그 운동화 회사가 한 최고의 홍보 조치 중 하나였다. **maintenance** 일단 긍정적인 기업 이미지가 만들어지면, 매년 지속적인 관리가 필요하다.

★

market share

[má:rkit ʃɛər]

[명] 시장 점유율

n. the percentage of an industry's sales controlled by a particular company

With its **market share** decreasing, the electronics company decided to completely rebrand its line of televisions.

★★

merchandise

[mə́:rtʃəndàis]

[명] 상품, 물품

n. things that are bought and sold

The first 100 visitors to the new sports apparel store were given gift bags stuffed with free **merchandise**.

syn. goods

★

objectivity

[àbdʒektívəti]

[명] 객관성, 객관적인 것

n., adj. objective

n. the state of being unbiased

The CEO's lack of **objectivity** kept her from fully understanding why her products were inferior to those of her rival.

syn. impartiality

★★

offset

[ɔ́:fsèt]

[동] 상쇄하다

v. to balance out the effect of something else

The expected spike in sales is forecasted to **offset** the extremely high cost of the new television commercials.

syn. counterbalance

★★★

opportunity

[àpərtjú:nəti]

[명] 기회

adj. opportune

n. a chance to do something desirable or valuable

Given the **opportunity** to switch to a new brand at a lower cost, loyal customers will often stick with their favorite products.

★

optimize

[áptəmàiz]

[동] 최적화하다, 최대한 활용하다

n., adj. optimum

v. to make something as good as it can possibly be

In order to **optimize** the results of its email marketing, the business put together a list of its most active customers.

---

market share 시장 점유율이 감소함에 따라, 그 전자 회사는 텔레비전 라인의 브랜드 이미지를 전면 쇄신하기로 결정했다. **merchandise** 새로운 스포츠 의류 매장을 방문한 고객 중 첫 100명이 무료 상품으로 가득 찬 선물 가방을 받았다. **objectivity** 그 최고경영자는 객관성이 부족하여 자신의 제품들이 경쟁사 제품보다 떨어지는 이유를 완전히 이해하지 못했다. **offset** 예상되는 매출의 급증은 새로운 TV 광고의 극도로 높은 비용을 상쇄할 것이라 예견된다. **opportunity** 보다 저렴한 가격에 새 브랜드로 전환할 수 있는 기회가 주어져도, 충성도 높은 고객들은 흔히 그들이 선호하는 상품을 고수할 것이다. **optimize** 이메일 마케팅의 결과를 최적화하기 위해, 그 기업은 가장 활동적인 고객 명단을 만들었다.

★★

preference

[préfərəns]

[명] 선호(도)

v. prefer

n. a feeling that one would rather do or have something

A growing **preference** for one-stop shopping has led to the rise of superstores that sell nearly everything imaginable.

syn. predilection

★★★

promote

[prəmóut]

[동] 1. 홍보하다
2. 촉진하다, 증진하다, 장려하다

n. promotion

v. 1 to give publicity to something *syn.* advertise
2 to help something improve or develop *syn.* bolster

1. To **promote** its new breakfast menu, the fast-food restaurant began giving away small toys with every purchase.
2. Some hotel chains claim to **promote** eco-friendly behavior, but their actions rarely match their words.

★★★

recognize

[rékəgnàiz]

[동] 1. …을 알다, 알아보다
2. 인정하다

n. recognition

v. 1 to know an identity from past experience
2 to show approval of an achievement or ability

1. If people don't instantly **recognize** the name of a brand, they are less likely to purchase one of its products.
2. For more than 60 years, the annual Clio Awards ceremony has **recognized** excellence in the field of advertising.

★★

refund

[rí:fʌnd]

[명] 환불금

n. an amount of money that is returned

Along with a **refund** for their purchase of the defective game system, the company is offering customers a discount on future purchases.

★★

reputation

[rèpjutéiʃən]

[명] 평판, 명성

n. the overall opinion that people have of someone or something

If a company's **reputation** has been damaged beyond repair, it may decide to change its name for a fresh start.

★

spokesperson

[spóukspə̀:rsn]

[명] 대변인

n. a person who officially represents an organization

As the new **spokesperson** for the milk industry, the actress will appear in a number of ads both in print and on TV.

Useful Tips
과거에는 '대변인'이란 단어로 spokesman이 주로 사용되었지만, 성차별 문제를 피하기 위해 점차 spokesperson을 사용하게 되었다.

---

preference 원스톱 쇼핑의 선호도 증가가 상상 가능한 거의 모든 것을 판매하는 슈퍼스토어의 등장으로 이어졌다. **promote** 1. 그 패스트푸드점은 새 아침 메뉴를 홍보하기 위해 모든 구매 고객에게 작은 장난감들을 나눠 주기 시작했다. 2. 몇몇 호텔 체인들은 친환경적인 태도를 장려한다고 주장하지만, 그들의 행동은 그들의 말과 거의 일치하지 않는다. **recognize** 1. 만약 사람들이 어떤 브랜드의 이름을 즉시 알아보지 못한다면, 그 회사의 제품들 중 하나를 구매할 가능성은 더 적다. 2. 매년 열리는 Clio Awards 시상식은 60년 넘게 광고 분야에서 (광고들과 광고를 만든이들의) 우수성을 인정해 왔다. **refund** 그 회사는 고객들에게 불량 게임 시스템 구매에 대한 환불과 함께 추후 구매 제품에 대한 할인도 제공하고 있다. **reputation** 만약 회사의 평판이 회복할 수 없을 정도로 손상되었다면, 새로운 출발을 위해 회사 이름을 바꾸기로 결정할 수도 있다. **spokesperson** 우유 산업의 새로운 대변인으로서, 그 여배우는 지면과 TV의 많은 광고에 출연할 것이다.

★★

stabilize

[stéibəlàiz]

[동] 안정되다

adj. stable

v. to become steady and predictable

Sales of the company's new products have been up and down, but they are expected to **stabilize** once customers grow familiar with them.

★★★

survey

[sərvéi]

[명] 설문 조사

n. a set of questions about people's opinions

A **survey** of shoppers revealed that white packaging gives an impression of purity, while black packaging makes a product look luxurious.

syn. poll

★★

tactic

[tǽktik]

[명] 전략, 전술

adj. tactical

n. an approach used to get something done

Guerilla marketing **tactics**, such as disguising ads as graffiti, are designed to draw attention with their creativity.

syn. strategy

Useful Tips

보통 트레이드마크 표시는 상표의 심볼이나 단어 옆에 약자 TM이 작은 글씨로 붙는다. 법적으로 정부에 등록된 트레이드마크의 경우, ®이 사용된다.

★

trademark

[tréidmà:rk]

[명] 상표, 트레이드마크

n. a symbol, word, or phrase that represents a product or company

The **trademarks** of large companies like Nike and Apple are instantly identifiable to people around the world.

★

tycoon

[taikú:n]

[명] (실업계의) 거물

n. a wealthy person involved in a certain industry

There are fears that media **tycoons** have too much power over the public's impression of their businesses.

syn. magnate

Useful Tips

'go viral'이란 표현은 주로 인터넷 상에서 사용되는데, 입소문 등이 매우 빠른 속도로 퍼지고 있다는 것을 의미한다.

★★

viral

[váiərəl]

[형] 바이러스(성)의

adj. spreading rapidly from one person to another like virus

Viral advertisements cost little money to make, but there is no guarantee that the public will spread them.

---

stabilize 그 회사의 신제품 매출은 오르내렸지만, 고객들이 그 신제품들에 익숙해지면 안정될 것이라 예상된다. **survey** 구매자를 대상으로 하는 설문 조사에서 흰색 포장은 순수한 느낌을 주는 반면, 검은색 포장은 제품을 고급스러워 보이게 한다는 것이 드러났다. **tactic** 광고를 그래피티로 위장하는 것과 같은 게릴라 마케팅 전략들은 그것들의 창의성으로 이목을 끌도록 고안되었다. **trademark** 나이키와 애플 같은 대기업의 상표들은 전 세계 사람들이 즉시 식별할 수 있다. **tycoon** 언론계 거물들이 그들 기업들에 대한 대중의 인상을 지나치게 좌지우지한다는 우려가 있다. **viral** 바이럴(입소문) 광고는 만드는 데 돈이 거의 들지 않지만, 대중들이 그 광고를 퍼트릴 것이라는 보장이 없다.

EXERCISES

A Match each definition with the correct word.

1 to make something as good as it can possibly be   ⓐ recognize

2 leading to a large profit   ⓑ agency

3 to know an identity from past experience   ⓒ optimize

4 spreading rapidly from one person to another like virus   ⓓ viral

5 to make something begin to move or start working   ⓔ reputation

6 a business that represents clients   ⓕ activate

7 the overall opinion that people have of someone or something   ⓖ promote

8 to give publicity to something   ⓗ lucrative

B Choose the word that is closest in meaning to each underlined word.

1 Lawyers interview potential jurors to make sure they will listen with total <u>objectivity</u>.
ⓐ attentiveness   ⓑ impartiality   ⓒ ingenuity   ⓓ collaboration

2 Decision-making during a <u>crisis</u> can be tricky, as unexpected ethical questions may arise.
ⓐ reunion   ⓑ examination   ⓒ emergency   ⓓ tournament

3 Professional sports teams rely on a variety of <u>merchandise</u> to help pay their high costs.
ⓐ rivals   ⓑ goods   ⓒ auctions   ⓓ sectors

4 Parents planning to teach their children at home should <u>consult</u> with professionals first.
ⓐ publicize   ⓑ distribute   ⓒ envision   ⓓ confer

5 When the soccer coach wants the team to use a new <u>tactic</u>, she waves her arms.
ⓐ strategy   ⓑ assembly   ⓒ opportunity   ⓓ accomplishment

6 The young politician's first speech was a <u>fiasco</u>, full of mistakes and awkward silences.
ⓐ revelation   ⓑ debacle   ⓒ oddity   ⓓ modification

7 Museum visitors were <u>astounded</u> by the beauty of the ancient Greek sculptures.
ⓐ satisfied   ⓑ astonished   ⓒ stabilized   ⓓ unconvinced

ART & DESIGN

SOCIAL SCIENCE

NATURAL SCIENCE

HUMANITIES

EARTH & SPACE

SOCIAL ISSUES

abuse
[əbjúːz]
ⓥ 학대하다
adj. abusive

v. to treat someone cruelly

People who have been **abused** in the past sometimes need professional help to move forward with their lives.

syn. harm

acknowledge
[æknálidʒ]
ⓥ 인정하다, 승인하다
n. acknowledgement

v. to indicate that something exists or is true

It is often said that the first step toward improving bad behavior is **acknowledging** that you have a problem.

syn. admit   *ant.* deny

averse
[əvə́ːrs]
ⓥ 싫어하는, 반대하는
n. aversion

adj. disliking or opposing something

People who are **averse** to small spaces will go out of their way to avoid elevators, even if it means walking up several flights of stairs.

ant. agreeable

confidential
[kànfədénʃəl]
ⓥ 비밀의, 내밀한
v. confide

adj. not meant to be shared with others

The psychologist starts all of her sessions by reminding her patients that everything they say is completely **confidential**.

syn. secret

cordial
[kɔ́ːrdʒəl]
ⓥ 다정한, 따뜻한
n. cordiality

adj. friendly and welcoming

Although he was **cordial** to all of his coworkers, the man's body language made it clear that he was uncomfortably shy.

syn. congenial   *ant.* hostile

delusional
[dilúːʒənəl]
ⓥ 망상의
n. delusion

adj. unable to tell fantasy from reality

Delusional individuals sometimes believe that characters on television shows are sending them secret messages.

ant. lucid

---

abuse 과거에 학대 받은 적이 있는 사람들은 인생에서 전진하기 위해 때때로 전문적 도움을 필요로 한다.   **acknowledge** 나쁜 행동을 개선하는 첫 단계는 자신에게 문제가 있다는 것을 인정하는 것이라고 흔히들 말한다.   **averse** 좁은 공간을 싫어하는 사람들은 몇몇 층계참을 걸어 올라가야 하더라도, 일부러 엘리베이터를 피하려고 할 것이다.   **confidential** 그 심리학자는 환자들에게 그들이 말하는 모든 것이 완전히 비밀이라는 것을 상기시키면서 모든 상담을 시작한다. **cordial** 그 남자는 모든 동료들에게 다정하게 대했지만, 그의 몸짓 언어는 그가 참을 수 없을 만큼 수줍어했다는 것을 확실히 나타냈다.   **delusional** 망상에 사로잡힌 사람들은 때때로 텔레비전 쇼의 등장인물들이 그들에게 비밀 메시지를 보내고 있다고 믿는다.

★★ **denial**
[dináiəl]
[명] 부정, 부인
v. deny

n. the state of refusing to believe something

Denial is a natural and expected reaction to hearing tragic news, but this stage can be unhealthy if it lasts too long.

ant. acceptance

★★★ **depressed**
[diprést]
[형] 우울한, 의기소침한
n. depression

adj. feeling unhappy and hopeless

Being **depressed** is a mental condition, but it can lead to a lack of physical energy that is difficult to overcome.

syn. dejected *ant.* cheerful

★ **dilemma**
[dilémə]
[명] 딜레마, 어려운 문제

n. a situation that involves a difficult choice

Few **dilemmas** turn out to have a simple solution; the best course of action is often to make a decision and live with it.

syn. predicament

★★★ **disorder**
[disɔ́ːrdər]
[명] 1. 질환, 장애
2. 혼란, 어수선함

n. 1 a physical or mental problem *syn.* affliction
2 a state of confusion and poor organization *syn.* chaos

1. It is believed that many creative people in the past secretly suffered from mental **disorders**.
2. Unable to deal with **disorder**, the woman was constantly rearranging the papers and pencils on her desk.

★ **disposition**
[dìspəzíʃən]
[명] 성격, 기질

n. a person's general mood and character

A sunny **disposition** can sometimes be used to hide personal problems from the rest of the world.

syn. temperament

★★ **distraught**
[distrɔ́ːt]
[형] 마음이 산란해진

adj. extremely worried and upset

Distraught over the loss of his grandmother, the man made an appointment with a local grief counselor.

syn. distressed *ant.* calm

denial 부정은 비극적인 소식을 듣는 것에 대한 자연스럽고 예상되는 반응이지만, 이 단계가 너무 길게 지속되면 유해할 수 있다. **depressed** 우울한 것은 정신적 상태지만, 극복하기 힘든 체력 고갈을 초래할 수 있다. **dilemma** 간단한 해결책이 있는 것으로 밝혀지는 딜레마는 거의 없어서, 종종 최선의 행동 방침은 결정을 내리고 그것을 감수하는 것이다. **disorder** 1. 과거의 많은 창의적인 사람들이 남모르게 정신 질환을 앓았다고 여겨진다. 2. 그 여자는 어수선한 것을 참을 수 없어서, 책상 위의 종이와 연필들을 계속 재배치하고 있었다. **disposition** 명랑한 성격은 때때로 개인적 문제들을 세상으로부터 숨기는 데 사용될 수 있다. **distraught** 할머니를 여의고 마음이 산란해진 그 남자는 현지의 슬픔 극복 상담가와 약속을 잡았다.

★★ **dubious**
[djú:biəs]
[형] 1. 의심스럽게 생각하는
2. 의심쩍은, 수상한

adj. 1 hesitant or doubtful *ant.* certain
2 untrustworthy or suspicious *syn.* shady *ant.* trustworthy

1. Many people are **dubious** when they first meet with a psychologist, expecting mind games or some sort of trick.
2. **Dubious** individuals claiming to be doctors will sometimes offer expensive treatments for common mental issues.

★★★ **empathy**
[émpəθi]
[명] 공감, 감정 이입
v. empathize
adj. empathetic

n. the ability to understand how other people feel

It is **empathy** that allows human beings to form close social bonds with individuals to whom they are not related.

Useful Tips
empathy는 타인의 감정을 이해하는 것인 반면 sympathy는 타인의 감성을 공유하는 것이다.

★★ **esteem**
[istí:m]
[명] 존중, 존경

n. feelings of respect and admiration

Although Sigmund Freud was held in high **esteem** by many of his peers, much of his work was later rejected.

★ **exhilarate**
[igzílərèit]
[동] 고무하다, 활기를 불어넣다
n. exhilaration

v. to make someone very happy and excited

Exhilarated by the idea of being freed from mental torment, the patients volunteered to receive the experimental psychological treatments.

syn. elate *ant.* depress

★★★ **frustration**
[frʌstréiʃən]
[명] 좌절감, 불만
v. frustrate

n. a feeling of anger or annoyance due to being unable to do something

Frustration can motivate us to seek out innovative solutions, but it can also cause us to quit or become discouraged.

ant. satisfaction

★ **gratify**
[grǽtəfài]
[동] 기쁘게 하다, 만족시키다
n. gratification

v. to create a feeling of pleasure or satisfaction

Human beings are social animals, so it **gratifies** us to be praised and admired by others of our kind.

syn. please

---

dubious 1. 많은 사람들이 처음으로 심리학자와 만나면, 심리전이나 모종의 속임수를 예상하면서 의심스러워 한다. 2. 의사라고 주장하는 의심쩍은 사람들은 때때로 흔한 정신적 문제들에 대해 비싼 치료들을 제안할 것이다. **empathy** 인간이 자신과 관련이 없는 사람들과 친밀한 사회적 유대를 형성하도록 해 주는 것은 바로 공감이다. **esteem** Sigmund Freud는 많은 동료들에게 매우 존경을 받았지만, 후에 그의 연구의 많은 부분이 인정되지 않았다. **exhilarate** 정신적 고통에서 벗어난다는 생각에 고무된 그 환자들은 그 실험적 심리 치료를 받겠다고 자원했다. **frustration** 좌절감은 우리가 혁신적인 해결책들을 찾도록 동기를 부여할 수 있지만, 그만두거나 낙심하게 만들 수도 있다. **gratify** 인간은 사회적 동물이기 때문에, 다른 사람들의 찬사와 존경을 받는 것이 우리를 기쁘게 한다.

haunt
[hɔːnt]
ⓥ 계속 괴롭히다[떠오르다]

adj. haunted

v. to continue to bother someone for a long time

Soldiers who have fought in battle are often **haunted** by what they saw long after the war has ended.

syn. torment

hypnosis
[hipnóusis]
ⓝ 최면

v. hypnotize

n. the act of putting someone into a highly suggestible state

Treatments involving **hypnosis** have showed some success in helping individuals break harmful habits such as smoking.

hysteria
[histériə]
ⓝ 히스테리, 광적 흥분

adj. hysterical

n. extreme uncontrolled emotion

During emergency situations, certain people will experience **hysteria** that prevents them from making logical decisions.

Useful **Tips**

대규모의 사람들이 동일한 히스테리 증상을 보이는 것을 mass hysteria라 한다.

impulsive
[impʌ́lsiv]
ⓐ 충동적인

n. impulse

adj. acting on a sudden urge rather than a logical plan

Avoiding **impulsive** decisions can allow people to take greater control of their own lives.

syn. impetuous   *ant.* deliberate

instinct
[ínstiŋkt]
ⓝ 본능, 직감

adj. instinctual

n. a natural response that does not involve thought

Human babies are born with certain **instincts**, such as gripping things and putting them in their mouths, that help them survive.

introvert
[íntrəvə̀ːrt]
ⓝ 내성적인 사람

adj. introverted

n. a person who avoids social situations

Introverts may naturally seek out isolation from time to time, but they also enjoy normal social interaction.

ant. extrovert

ART & DESIGN

SOCIAL SCIENCE

NATURAL SCIENCE

HUMANITIES

EARTH & SPACE

SOCIAL ISSUES

---

haunt 전투에 참전했던 군인들은 종종 전쟁이 끝난 지 오랜 후에, 그들이 목격했던 것 때문에 종종 괴로워한다.   **hypnosis** 최면을 수반하는 치료법들은 사람들이 흡연 같은 해로운 습관들을 고치도록 돕는 데 어느 정도 성공적이었다.   **hysteria** 응급 상황에서, 어떤 사람들은 논리적인 결정을 내리지 못하게 하는 히스테리를 경험할 것이다.   **impulsive** 충동적인 결정을 피하는 것은 사람들이 자신의 삶을 더 잘 통제하게 해 줄 수 있다.   **instinct** 인간 아기들은 물건들을 움켜쥐고 그것들을 입에 넣는 것과 같이 그들이 생존할 수 있도록 돕는 특정 본능들을 가지고 태어난다.   **introvert** 내성적인 사람들은 물론 때때로 고립을 추구하지만, 평범한 사회적 교류도 즐긴다.

★★

menace

[ménis]

[동] 위협하다

[명] 위협

adj. menacing

v. to threaten or be likely to cause harm *syn.* imperil

After he stopped taking his medication, the man began to believe he was being **menaced** by invisible enemies.

n. a threat or something likely to cause harm *syn.* hazard

The **menace** of hungry predators played a large role in the development of the brains of early humans.

★★★

obsession

[əbséʃən]

[명] 집착, 강박

adj. obsessed

n. an unhealthy inability to stop thinking about something

An **obsession** with acquiring and keeping objects of little value can make a person's home more or less uninhabitable.

syn. fixation

★★

phobia

[fóubiə]

[명] 공포증

n. an extreme and irrational fear of something specific

It is believed that up to 5% of the population suffers from a fear of heights, making it one of the most common **phobias**.

★★

psychiatrist

[saikáiətrist]

[명] 정신과 의사

n. a doctor who treats mental illnesses

Carl Jung was a 20th-century Swiss **psychiatrist** whose work has had a great influence on numerous fields of science.

Useful Tips

psychologist는 psychiatrist와 비슷한 일을 하지만, medical doctor는 아니다.

★

psychosomatic

[sàikousəmǽtik]

[형] 심리적 문제로 인한

adj. caused by mental issues rather than physical ones

Psychosomatic illnesses often have their roots in stress, and they can have very real effects on a person's physical health.

★★

recoil

[rikɔ́il]

[동] 움츠러들다

v. to pull away in fear, pain, or disgust

People will involuntarily **recoil** from sights and sounds that have caused them harm or fear in the past.

syn. flinch

---

menace 약 복용을 멈춘 후, 그 남자는 자신이 보이지 않는 적들에 의해 위협받고 있다고 믿기 시작했다. / 굶주린 포식자들의 위협이 초기 인간의 두뇌 발달에 지대한 역할을 했다. **obsession** 가치가 거의 없는 물건을 획득해 간직하려는 집착은 한 사람의 집을 거의 살 수 없을 지경으로 만들 수 있다. **phobia** 인구의 5%에 이르는 사람들이 고소공포증에 시달린다고 여겨지는데, 그 수치는 고소공포증을 가장 흔한 공포증들 중 하나로 만든다. **psychiatrist** Carl Jung은 자신의 연구로 수많은 과학 분야들에 큰 영향을 미친 20세기 스위스 정신과 의사였다. **psychosomatic** 심리적 문제로 인한 병들은 흔히 스트레스가 원인이며, 개인의 육체적 건강에 매우 실질적인 영향을 미칠 수 있다. **recoil** 사람들은 과거에 그들에게 피해나 공포를 야기시켰던 광경이나 소리에 자신도 모르게 움츠러들 것이다.

responsive
[rispánsiv]
® 즉각 반응하는
v. respond

adj. quick to react to the needs of others

Parents tend to be more **responsive** to their children than they are to their partners, which can sometimes cause tension.

ant. indifferent

stigma
[stígmə]
® 오명, 불명예

n. an association of disgrace with a certain action or condition

Times have changed, and visiting a psychologist no longer carries the **stigma** that it once did.

stimulate
[stímjulèit]
® 자극하다, 촉진시키다
n. stimulation

v. to cause to become more active or energetic

A visit from family members, especially young children, can **stimulate** the minds of patients struggling with mental issues.

syn. arouse   *ant.* deaden

Useful **Tips**

stimulate와 철자가 비슷한 simulate는 '모의실험하다, 가장하다'라는 의미이므로 혼동하지 않도록 유의한다.

strain
[strein]
® 중압(감)

n. mental or physical pressure caused by a difficult situation

The **strain** of their jobs can cause police officers, firefighters, and EMTs to suffer emotional breakdowns.

syn. stress

succumb
[səkám]
® 굴복하다

v. to give in to a strong force

The patient initially refused to take the medication her doctor had given her, but she eventually **succumbed** to the pressure of her family.

syn. capitulate   *ant.* resist

suppress
[səprés]
® 참다, 억누르다
n. suppression

v. to prevent something from forming

Anger management classes teach people how to **suppress** sudden anger and later release it in a more appropriate way.

syn. quell

ART & DESIGN

SOCIAL SCIENCE

NATURAL SCIENCE

HUMANITIES

EARTH & SPACE

SOCIAL ISSUES

---

responsive 부모들은 자신의 배우자들에게보다 자녀에게 좀 더 즉각적으로 반응하는 경향이 있는데, 이것은 때때로 갈등을 야기할 수 있다.   **stigma** 시대가 변해, 심리학자를 방문하는 것은 이제 과거에 그랬던 것처럼 오명이 따르지는 않는다.   **stimulate** 가족 구성원, 특히 어린아이들의 방문은 정신적 문제로 힘들어하는 환자들의 정신을 자극할 수 있다.   **strain** 경찰, 소방관, 전문 응급 구조원들은 그들의 직업이 주는 중압감 때문에 정신 쇠약을 겪을 수 있다.   **succumb** 그 환자는 의사가 준 약을 복용하는 것을 처음에는 거부했지만, 결국 가족의 압력에 굴복했다.   **suppress** 분노 조절 수업은 사람들에게 갑작스러운 분노를 참고 나중에 더 적절한 방식으로 분출하는 법을 가르쳐 준다.

★★ **therapeutic**
[θèrəpjú:tik]
[형] 긴장을 푸는 데 도움이 되는, 치료의
n. therapy

adj. relating to healing
Creating artwork can be **therapeutic**, allowing patients to express things that are difficult to say with words.
syn. curative

★★ **trance**
[træns]
[명] 무아지경, 최면 상태

n. a state of semi-consciousness
The patient sat quietly in his bed, staring at the blank wall in front of him as if he were in a **trance**.
syn. stupor

★★ **trauma**
[tráumə, trɔ:-]
[명] 1. 충격
2. 외상
adj. traumatic

n. 1 shock caused by an upsetting experience
2 a severely upsetting experience
1. The emotional **trauma** of witnessing a serious accident should not be underestimated.
2. Teachers need to be aware of the signs of childhood **trauma** and to look for them in their young students.

★★★ **unconscious**
[ʌnkánʃəs]
[형] 의식을 잃은
n. unconsciousness

adj. in a state in which the senses cannot be perceived
After being knocked **unconscious** in a fall, the woman began to show subtle changes in her personality.
ant. conscious

★★ **vacillate**
[vǽsəlèit]
[동] 망설이다, 흔들리다
n. vacillation

v. to switch back and forth between two things
Constantly **vacillating** between choices without making a decision can eventually undermine a person's self-confidence.

★ **vilify**
[víləfài]
[동] 비난하다, 비방하다
n. vilification

v. to damage someone's reputation with harsh statements
The serial killer's psychologist was **vilified** by members of the media who felt he could have done something to stop him.
syn. slander *ant.* glorify

---

therapeutic 예술 작품을 만드는 것은 환자들이 말하기 힘든 것들을 표현하게 해서 치료법이 될 수 있다. **trance** 그 환자는 자기 침대에 조용히 앉아, 마치 무아지경에 빠진 듯 앞쪽의 빈 벽을 응시하고 있었다. **trauma** 1. 심각한 사고를 목격한 정서적 충격은 과소평가되어서는 안 된다. 2. 교사들은 유아기 외상의 징후들을 숙지하고 어린 학생들에게서 찾아봐야 한다. **unconscious** 추락하며 의식을 잃은 이후, 그 여자는 미묘한 성격 변화를 보이기 시작했다. **vacillate** 결정을 내리지 않고 선택권들 사이에서 계속 망설이는 것은 결국 한 사람의 자신감을 약화시킬 수 있다. **vilify** 그 연쇄 살인범의 심리학자는 그를 막기 위해 뭔가를 할 수도 있었을 거라 생각하는 언론인들의 비난을 받았다.

EXERCISES

ART & DESIGN

SOCIAL SCIENCE

NATURAL SCIENCE

HUMANITIES

EARTH & SPACE

SOCIAL ISSUES

A Match each definition with the correct word.

1 the state of refusing to believe something   ⓐ unconscious

2 to make someone very happy and excited   ⓑ denial

3 in a state in which the senses cannot be perceived   ⓒ psychosomatic

4 a person who avoids social situations   ⓓ exhilarate

5 to switch back and forth between two things   ⓔ vacillate

6 the act of putting someone into a highly suggestible state   ⓕ therapeutic

7 relating to healing   ⓖ introvert

8 caused by mental issues rather than physical ones   ⓗ hypnosis

B Choose the word that is closest in meaning to each underlined word.

1 Despite being criticized for <u>vilifying</u> his opponent in ads, the politician easily won the election.
   ⓐ deceiving   ⓑ enlarging   ⓒ slandering   ⓓ stimulating

2 The students say studying philosophy makes it easier to deal with life's moral <u>dilemmas</u>.
   ⓐ triumphs   ⓑ predicaments   ⓒ introductions   ⓓ shortcomings

3 It was the judge's amiable <u>disposition</u> that created a relaxed mood in the courtroom.
   ⓐ salutation   ⓑ visage   ⓒ temperament   ⓓ facility

4 The star hockey player was kicked off his team after he was arrested for <u>abusing</u> his children.
   ⓐ embarrassing   ⓑ supporting   ⓒ abandoning   ⓓ harming

5 The chairperson slammed her hand onto the table in anger, causing everyone to <u>recoil</u>.
   ⓐ grovel   ⓑ clamor   ⓒ flinch   ⓓ menace

6 The company's new products appeal to the public's sudden <u>obsession</u> with cleanliness.
   ⓐ attribution   ⓑ fixation   ⓒ disappointment   ⓓ contentment

7 The anthropologists were <u>dubious</u> of the claims about the tribe's traditions, but they agreed to look into them.
   ⓐ doubtful   ⓑ conscious   ⓒ ashamed   ⓓ envious

Lesson 18 Ethics

> 윤리

altruism
[ǽltruːìzm]
명 이타주의, 이타심
adj. altruistic

n. concern for the happiness and well-being of others

Modern consumers know better than to trust businesses that claim they are acting purely out of **altruism**.

syn. benevolence

arbitrary
[áːrbətrèri]
명 임의의

adj. having no particular reason

What had appeared to be an **arbitrary** decision turned out to be part of complex plan to influence public opinion.

syn. random

assumption
[əsʌ́mpʃən]
명 가정, 추측, 추정
v. assume

n. the act of believing something to be true without proof

We often act under the **assumption** that others have the same motivations and desires as we do.

syn. supposition

avarice
[ǽvəris]
명 탐욕

n. a strong desire for wealth

History teaches us that unchecked **avarice** is the most likely cause when the powerful suffer a downfall.

syn. greed   *ant.* generosity

awaken
[əwéikən]
동 1. 깨닫게 하다, …에 눈뜨게 하다
2. 깨우다
adj. awake

v. 1 to become aware of something   *syn.* arouse
2 to make someone stop sleeping   *syn.* arouse

1. Even the smallest positive social interactions can **awaken** feelings of goodwill in otherwise coldhearted people.

2. When we are **awakened** from a deep sleep, we sometimes see difficult situations more clearly than before.

benevolent
[bənévələnt]
명 자애로운, 자비로운
n. benevolence

adj. having good intentions toward others

Offering the nervous strangers a **benevolent** smile, the kindly man asked them if they needed assistance.

syn. benign   *ant.* malevolent

---

altruism 현대 소비자들은 기업들이 순전히 이타심에서 행동한다는 주장을 신뢰할 정도로 어리석지 않다.   **arbitrary** 임의적 결정으로 보였던 것이 여론에 영향을 미치기 위한 복잡한 계획의 일부라는 것으로 밝혀졌다.   **assumption** 우리는 종종 다른 이들도 우리와 같은 동기와 욕구를 가지고 있다는 가정하에 행동한다.   **avarice** 역사는 권력자들이 몰락할 때 억제되지 않은 탐욕이 유력한 원인이라는 것을 우리에게 가르쳐 준다.   **awaken** 1. 가장 사소한 긍정적인 사회적 상호작용조차도 냉정한 사람들에게 호의적 감정을 일깨울 수 있다. 2. 우리가 깊은 잠에서 깨어나면, 때때로 어려운 상황을 전보다 더 명확하게 볼 수 있다.
benevolent 그 친절한 남성은 긴장한 낯선 이들에게 자애로운 미소를 보이면서, 도움이 필요한지 물었다.

★★ **blurry**
[bló:ri]
[형] 흐릿한, 모호한
n., v. blur

adj. difficult to see

There is a **blurry** line that exists between a healthy level of self-interest and harmful selfishness.

syn. unclear *ant.* sharp

★★ **compassionate**
[kəmpǽʃənət]
[형] 연민 어린, 동정하는
n. compassion

adj. feeling or showing sympathy toward others

Compassionate individuals will give up their own comfort and safety to help people who are less fortunate.

syn. sympathetic *ant.* uncaring

★★★ **compromise**
[kámprəmàiz]
[동] 타협하다, 절충하다
[명] 타협, 절충

v. to reach an agreement through concessions on both sides

Children must be taught how to **compromise**; otherwise, they will find themselves trapped in bitter disagreements without end.

n. an agreement reached through concessions on both sides

Once two sides reach an initial **compromise**, feelings of distrust tend to fade into the background.

★★ **conscientious**
[kànʃiénʃəs]
[형] 1. 양심적인
2. 성실한, 꼼꼼한

adj. 1 guided by a sense of right and wrong
2 hard-working and thorough *syn.* meticulous *ant.* careless

1. Soldiers who express the **conscientious** belief that all killing is wrong are usually excused from combat duties.
2. **Conscientious** employees who finish their own work usually check with their coworkers to see if they need help.

★★ **conviction**
[kənvíkʃən]
[명] (강한) 신념, 확신

n. a strong belief or opinion

Even when faced with evidence that they are wrong, people are reluctant to abandon their personal **convictions**.

★★★ **deceit**
[disí:t]
[명] 속임수, 기만
adj. deceitful

n. dishonest behavior used to fool others

Apologizing for her **deceit**, the woman tried to explain why she had misled her friends and neighbors for so long.

syn. deception *ant.* honesty

---

blurry 건전한 수준의 사리 추구와 해로운 이기주의 사이의 경계는 모호하다. **compassionate** 동정심이 많은 사람들은 불우한 사람들을 돕기 위해 그들 자신의 안위와 안전을 포기할 것이다. **compromise** 아이들은 타협하는 방법을 배워야 하는데, 그렇지 않으면 그들은 끝없는 격렬한 의견 충돌에 빠질 것이다. / 일단 양측이 초기 합의에 도달하면, 불신의 감정은 뒤로 사라지는 경향이 있다. **conscientious** 1. 모든 살생이 잘못된 것이라는 양심적 신념을 표현하는 병사들은 보통 전투 의무에서 면제된다. 2. 자신의 일을 마친 성실한 직원들은 보통 동료 직원들이 도움이 필요한지를 확인한다. **conviction** 사람들은 자신들이 틀렸다는 증거에 직면할 때조차도, 개인적 신념을 버리는 것을 꺼려 한다. **deceit** 그 여자는 자신의 기만을 사과하면서, 자신이 왜 친구들과 이웃들을 오랫동안 오도했는지 설명하려 애썼다.

★★

decent

[dí:snt]

[형] 1. (사회 기준에) 맞는, 점잖은
2. 상당한, 충분한, 꽤 좋은

n. decency

adj. 1 socially acceptable; respectable *syn.* proper *ant.* improper
2 fairly good *syn.* satisfactory

1. Even **decent** men and women can be made to do bad things by extreme social pressure.
2. There is a **decent** chance that you would lie to friends in order to keep an unpleasant truth from them.

Useful Tips

일상적으로 decent는 'Don't come in yet. I'm not decent.'에서와 같이 '옷을 완전히 입은'의 의미로 사용되기도 한다.

★★

deprive

[dipráiv]

[동] 빼앗다, 박탈하다

v. to take or withhold something essential

Children who are **deprived** of affection by their parents may have trouble telling the difference between right and wrong.

★★★

dignity

[dígnəti]

[명] 품위, 위엄

adj. dignified

n. the state of being worthy of respect

Political leaders should act with **dignity** at all times to set an example for the rest of the country.

syn. respectability

★★

discreet

[diskrí:t]

[형] (언행이) 신중한, 조심스러운

adj. careful to avoid revealing secrets or offending others

To avoid conflict, it is best to be **discreet** about your political beliefs when you are in the workplace.

syn. tactful *ant.* inconsiderate

★

heed

[hi:d]

[동] 주의를 기울이다

v. to follow someone's advice or pay attention to a warning

Those who fail to **heed** the advice of their more experienced elders have no one to blame but themselves.

ant. disregard

★★

honorable

[ánərəbl]

[형] 존경할 만한, 명예로운

n. honor

adj. worthy of respect

Because she was an **honorable** person, the woman refused to accept payment for work that was not up to standard.

syn. respectable *ant.* dishonorable

---

decent 1. 점잖은 성인들조차도 극심한 사회적 압력에 의해 나쁜 짓을 하게 될 수 있다. 2. 친구들에게 불쾌한 진실을 감추기 위해 거짓말을 하게 될 가능성이 충분히 있다. **deprive** 부모로부터 사랑을 받지 못한 아이들은 옳고 그름의 차이를 구별하는 데 어려움을 겪을지도 모른다. **dignity** 정치 지도자들은 국민들에게 모범이 되기 위해 늘 품위 있게 행동해야 한다. **discreet** 갈등을 피하기 위해, 직장 내에서 자신의 정치적 신념에 대해 신중한 것이 (언행을 삼가는 것이) 최선이다. **heed** 경험이 더 많은 어르신들의 충고에 주의를 기울이지 않는 사람들은 그들 자신 외에는 탓할 사람이 없다. **honorable** 그 여자는 명예로운 사람이었기 때문에, 기준에 미치지 못하는 일에 대한 보수를 받는 것을 거부했다.

ART & DESIGN

SOCIAL SCIENCE

NATURAL SCIENCE

HUMANITIES

EARTH & SPACE

SOCIAL ISSUES

immoral
[imɔ́:rəl]

ⓐ 비도덕적인, 부도덕한

n. immorality

adj. not following society's standards of right and wrong

Some of what was considered **immoral** behavior in the past may be socially acceptable today.

syn. wicked, corrupt   *ant.* moral

imperil
[impérəl]

ⓥ 위험에 빠뜨리다, 위태롭게 하다

n. peril

v. to put someone or something in danger

We should always avoid actions that could **imperil** others, even if they will bring us great rewards.

syn. endanger   *ant.* protect

justice
[dʒʌ́stis]

ⓝ 정의, 공평성, 합법성

adj. just

n. lawfulness and fair play

People within a culture tend to share a common sense of **justice**, although it may change slightly over time.

ant. injustice

lofty
[lɔ́:fti]

ⓐ 1. 고귀한, 고결한
   2. 아주 높은, 우뚝 선

adj. 1 admirable and important   *syn.* exalted   *ant.* modest
    2 very high   *syn.* elevated   *ant.* low

1. It feels good to sometimes set **lofty** goals for ourselves, but it is unfair to do so for others.

2. Looking down on the city from a **lofty** height, the woman realized how crowded the poorer sections had become.

noble
[nóubl]

ⓐ 고결한, 숭고한

adj. good in the way that is brave and generous

Volunteering for a year in a poor country is a **noble** aspiration, but not everyone is able to handle such a stressful situation.

syn. virtuous

oblige
[əbláidʒ]

ⓥ 의무적으로 …하게 하다

v. to force someone to do something by law or principle

Although doctors are **obliged** to treat the sick and injured, some hospitals turn away patients who can't afford to pay their bills.

syn. obligate

Useful **Tips**

oblige는 주로
'be obliged to + 부정사'의
형태로 많이 쓰인다.

---

immoral 과거에 비도덕적인 행동으로 여겨졌던 것들의 일부는 오늘날 사회적으로 용인될 수 있다.   **imperil** 엄청난 보상을 가져다 줄지라도, 다른 이들을 위험에 빠뜨릴 수 있는 행동들을 항상 피해야 한다.   **justice** 비록 시간이 지남에 따라 조금씩 바뀔 수 있지만, 한 문화권 안의 사람들은 동일한 정의감을 갖고 있는 경향이 있다.   **lofty** 1. 때때로 자신을 위해 고귀한 목표를 세우는 것은 기분이 좋지만, 남들에게 그렇게 하는 것은 불공평하다. 2. 아주 높은 곳에서 도시를 내려다보면서, 그 여성은 빈민촌이 얼마나 혼잡해졌는지 깨달았다.   **noble** 가난한 나라에서 1년 동안 자원봉사하는 것은 고결한 포부이지만, 모두가 그렇게 스트레스를 많이 받는 상황을 감당할 수 있는 것은 아니다.   **oblige** 의사들이 병들고 다친 환자들을 의무적으로 치료해야 하지만, 일부 병원들은 치료비를 지불할 수 없는 환자들을 받지 않는다.

pertain

[pǝrtéin]

통 …에 관계하다, 상관하다

adj. pertinent

v. to be related to

There are many things that **pertain** to the moral decisions we make, and they will all be discussed in this ethics course.

prerequisite

[pri:rékwǝzit]

명 전제 조건, 필수 조건
형 미리 필요한, …에 필수적인

n. something that must be done before something else can happen
   syn. requirement

It is unethical for hiring departments to overlook missing **prerequisites** for some applicants but not others.

adj. necessary before something else can happen
   syn. mandatory   *ant.* optional

Without the **prerequisite** background knowledge, students will have trouble following the lecture on ethics.

restrain

[ristréin]

통 저지하다, 억제하다, 억누르다

v. to hold back or control

The woman **restrained** her desire to shout at the unruly teens and tried to explain why their behavior was unacceptable instead.

syn. curb

situate

[sítʃuèit]

통 …을 어느 장소에 놓다, 위치시키다

v. to be in a specific location

Situated just behind the forehead, the frontal lobe is believed to be the part of the brain that controls moral behavior.

syn. locate

stealthy

[stélθi]

형 몰래 하는, 은밀한

n. stealth

adj. difficult to see or hear

With **stealthy** movements, the man slid some bread into his jacket, allowing his hunger to defeat his moral principles.

vice

[vais]

명 악, 악덕 행위

n. a bad habit that shows weakness

Smoking hasn't always been considered a **vice**; in the past it was considered a sign of sophistication or rebellion.

Useful Tips

vice squad(풍기 사범 단속반)는 불법 도박이나 마약 사범과 같은 문제들을 전담하는 경찰들이다.

---

pertain 우리가 내리는 도덕적 결정과 관련된 많은 것들이 있는데, 그것들은 모두 이 윤리 강좌에서 논의될 것이다.   **prerequisite** 채용 부서가 몇몇 지원자들의 누락된 필수조건을 눈감아 주면서 다른 지원자들에게는 그렇게 하지 않는 것은 비윤리적이다. / 필수 배경지식이 없으면, 학생들은 그 윤리 강의를 따라가는 데 어려움을 겪을 것이다.   **restrain** 그 여자는 제멋대로인 십 대들에게 소리치고 싶은 욕구를 자제했고, 대신 그들의 행동이 용납될 수 없는 이유를 설명하려 애썼다.   **situate** 이마 바로 뒤에 위치한 전두엽은 도덕적 행동을 관장하는 뇌의 한 부분이라고 여겨진다.   **stealthy** 그 남자는 배고픔이 그의 도덕적 원칙을 무너뜨리는 것을 용인하며, 은밀하게 약간의 빵을 상의 안에 슬쩍 넣었다.   **vice** 흡연이 항상 나쁜 것으로 여겨진 것은 아니다. 과거에는 교양이나 반항의 표시로 여겨졌다.

EXERCISES

ART & DESIGN

SOCIAL SCIENCE

NATURAL SCIENCE

HUMANITIES

EARTH & SPACE

SOCIAL ISSUES

A Match each definition with the correct word.

1 to be related to   ⓐ vice

2 having no particular reason   ⓑ deprive

3 a bad habit that shows a weakness   ⓒ compromise

4 to reach an agreement through concessions on both sides   ⓓ justice

5 lawfulness and fair play   ⓔ pertain

6 good in the way that is brave and generous   ⓕ heed

7 to follow someone's advice or pay attention to a warning ⓖ noble

8 to take or withhold something essential   ⓗ arbitrary

B Choose the word that is closest in meaning to each underlined word.

1 Economists warned that the collapse of a single major bank would <u>imperil</u> the entire economy.
   ⓐ endanger   ⓑ enclose   ⓒ enlarge   ⓓ enforce

2 Denounced for <u>deceit</u> by its rivals, the company attempted to improve its image.
   ⓐ inspection   ⓑ rejection   ⓒ defection   ⓓ deception

3 Before the game was standardized, the rules of football were <u>blurry</u> and inconsistent.
   ⓐ conscientious   ⓑ unclear   ⓒ sophisticated   ⓓ decent

4 The teenager's interest in archaeology was <u>awakened</u> by a visit to a museum.
   ⓐ satisfied   ⓑ concluded   ⓒ redirected   ⓓ aroused

5 Praised for her <u>altruism</u>, the billionaire is now considering running for president.
   ⓐ leadership   ⓑ fame   ⓒ benevolence   ⓓ enforcement

6 It is up to schools to ensure that children understand that <u>avarice</u> is not socially acceptable.
   ⓐ greed   ⓑ bribery   ⓒ prejudice   ⓓ aggression

7 Despite the <u>assumption</u> that he is a criminal, the man maintains his innocence.
   ⓐ connection   ⓑ termination   ⓒ position   ⓓ supposition

Lesson 19 ▶법 Law

★
adjourn
[ədʒə́ːrn]
ⓥ 휴정하다, 휴회하다
n. adjournment

v. to end a meeting or other event until a later time

At the end of the day, the judge announced that court would be **adjourned** until next Monday.

★★★
advocate
[ǽdvəkèit]
ⓥ 지지하다, 옹호하다
adj. advocative

v. to publicly support or recommend something

A group **advocating** for the passage of the new law created an ad that will be run on a major network.

syn. back *ant.* oppose

★★
authority
[əθɔ́ːrəti]
ⓝ 1. 권한, 직권
　　2. 권력자
v. authorize

n. 1 the power to make others follow laws or rules
　　2 someone with the power to make others follow laws or rules

1. The attorney argued that the police did not have the **authority** to enter his client's apartment.

2. Local **authorities** asked the federal government for help due to a sudden rise in gun crimes.

★★
bill
[bil]
ⓝ 법안

n. a proposal for a new law

In order for the **bill** to pass, it must receive a majority of votes from the state representatives.

★★
constitution
[kùnstət/úːʃən]
ⓝ 헌법
adj. constitutional

n. a nation's set of basic laws and principles

After the country became a democracy, the newly elected government went to work on writing a **constitution**.

★★
contempt
[kəntémpt]
ⓝ (법규·위험 등을) 개의치 않음, 무시
adj. contemptuous

n. a strong feeling that someone or something does not deserve respect

Some of the town's residents showed their **contempt** for the new parking laws by refusing to follow them.

syn. disdain *ant.* admiration

> **Useful Tips**
> 법원의 규칙과 명령에 불복하거나 법정의 질서를 어지럽히는 것을 contempt of court라 한다.

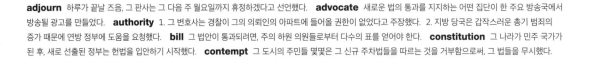

adjourn 하루가 끝날 즈음, 그 판사는 그 다음 주 월요일까지 휴정하겠다고 선언했다.　**advocate** 새로운 법의 통과를 지지하는 어떤 집단이 한 주요 방송국에서 방송될 광고를 만들었다.　**authority** 1. 그 변호사는 경찰이 그의 의뢰인의 아파트에 들어올 권한이 없었다고 주장했다.　2. 지방 당국은 갑작스러운 총기 범죄의 증가 때문에 연방 정부에 도움을 요청했다.　**bill** 그 법안이 통과되려면, 주의 하원 의원들로부터 다수의 표를 얻어야 한다.　**constitution** 그 나라가 민주 국가가 된 후, 새로 선출된 정부는 헌법을 입안하기 시작했다.　**contempt** 그 도시의 주민들 몇몇은 그 신규 주차법들을 따르는 것을 거부함으로써, 그 법들을 무시했다.

ART & DESIGN

SOCIAL SCIENCE

NATURAL SCIENCE

HUMANITIES

EARTH & SPACE

SOCIAL ISSUES

★
contravene
[kὰntrəvíːn]

ⓥ 위반하다, 위배하다

n. contravention

v. to act in a way that goes against a law or an order

The nation warned its neighbor that sending troops across the border would **contravene** international law.

syn. defy   *ant.* obey

★
★
decree
[dikríː]

ⓝ 법령, 칙령

n. an official order

The king, who was a bird lover, issued a **decree** making it illegal to kill swans on his land.

syn. mandate

★
★
★
defend
[difénd]

ⓥ 변호하다

n. defense

v. to argue in support of an accused person in court

The Internet influencer accused of not paying his taxes hired a famous attorney to **defend** him in court.

★
★
dissent
[disént]

ⓝ 반대, 이의
ⓥ 반대하다

n. an expression of disagreement or disapproval   *syn.* opposition

After the case was decided, one of the Supreme Court justices wrote a long opinion expressing her **dissent**.

v. to disagree or disapprove   *syn.* oppose

The bill was passed by the Senate almost unanimously, with only a single senator **dissenting**.

★
★
enact
[inǽkt]

ⓥ 제정하다, 입법하다

n. enactment

v. to officially turn a proposal into a law

The Stamp Act, which was **enacted** by the British government in 1765, imposed a tax on the American colonies.

syn. ratify

★
★
★
enforce
[infɔ́ːrs]

ⓥ 시행하다

n. enforcement

v. to ensure that a rule or law is being followed

It is the job of the police department to **enforce** the laws that are made by the government.

---

contravene 그 나라는 이웃 나라에게 군대를 국경 너머로 보내면 국제법을 위반하는 것이라고 경고했다.   **decree** 새를 좋아했던 그 왕은 그의 영토에서 백조를 죽이는 것을 불법화하는 법령을 포고했다.   **defend** 세금 미납으로 기소된 그 인터넷 인플루언서는 법정에서 그를 변호할 유명한 변호사를 고용했다.   **dissent** 그 소송에 판결이 내려진 후, 대법관들 중 한 명이 이의를 표명하는 긴 의견을 썼다. / 그 법안은 거의 만장일치로 상원에 의해 통과되었는데, 오직 한 명의 상원 의원만 반대했다.   **enact** 1765년 영국 정부에 의해 제정된 인지조례는 미국 식민지들에 세금을 부과했다.   **enforce** 정부가 만든 법들을 시행하는 것이 바로 경찰서의 일이다.

★
entail
[intéil]
동 수반하다

v. to involve as a requirement or result

Filing a lawsuit against someone **entails** filling out the necessary paperwork and submitting it to the court.

★
★
exempt
[igzémpt]
형 면제된

n. exemption

adj. free from a requirement or rule

The lawyer explained to his client that not being aware of a law does not make you **exempt** from it.

★
★
★
guilty
[gílti]
형 유죄의

n. guilt

adj. responsible for a crime or other negative act

Having been found **guilty** in a court of law, the murderer was sent away to prison for the rest of his life.

ant. innocent

★
illicit
[ilísit]
형 불법의

adj. illegal or socially unacceptable

The newspaper is full of articles about powerful people who have been caught engaging in **illicit** activity.

syn. forbidden   *ant.* acceptable

★
★
jurisdiction
[dʒùərisdíkʃən]
명 1. 사법권, 관할권
    2. 관할 구역

n. 1 the right to make legal decisions
       2 the area in which one can make legal decisions

1. Local court systems do not have the **jurisdiction** to try people who are accused of federal crimes.

2. The police officer was unable to arrest the woman after she crossed the state line, as she was no longer in his **jurisdiction**.

★
★
★
jury
[dʒúəri]
명 배심원단

n. a group of people who decide the outcome of a legal case

A **jury** of twelve men and women will listen to the case and decide on the outcome.

---

entail 어떤 사람을 상대로 소송을 제기하는 것은 필요한 서류를 작성해 그것을 법원에 제출하는 일을 수반한다.   **exempt** 그 변호사는 그의 의뢰인에게 어떤 법을 모른다고 해서 그 법에서 면제되는 것은 아니라고 설명했다.   **guilty** 법정에서 유죄가 인정된 그 살인자는 무기징역에 처해졌다.   **illicit** 그 신문은 불법 행위에 연루된 것이 포착된 권력자들에 대한 기사로 가득하다.   **jurisdiction** 1. 지방 법원 제도들은 연방 범죄들로 기소된 사람들을 재판할 사법권을 갖고 있지 않다. 2. 그 경찰관은 그 여자가 주 경계선을 넘은 후 그녀를 체포할 수 없었는데, 그녀가 더 이상 그의 관할 구역 내에 있지 않았기 때문이다.   **jury** 12명의 남녀로 이루어진 배심원단이 그 사건을 듣고 평결을 내릴 것이다.

ART & DESIGN

SOCIAL SCIENCE

NATURAL SCIENCE

HUMANITIES

EARTH & SPACE

SOCIAL ISSUES

★
★
legislation
[lèdʒisléiʃən]
ⓝ 법률, 법규

v. legislate
adj. legislative

n. a law or set of laws

For many years, people have been demanding an overall simplification of the national tax **legislation**.

★
★
★
legitimate
[lidʒítəmət]
ⓐ 합법적인

n. legitimacy

adj. legally acceptable

If you have a **legitimate** excuse for parking in a disabled space, you can present it to the judge in traffic court.

syn. legal　*ant.* illegitimate

★
lucid
[lúːsid]
ⓐ 1. 명료한, 명쾌한
　 2. 의식이 또렷한

n. lucidity

adj. 1 clear and easy to understand　*ant.* murky
　　　2 aware and thinking clearly　*syn.* clearheaded　*ant.* irrational

1. The judge writes his legal opinions in an extremely **lucid** style, which makes them easy for anyone to understand.

2. The police decided to place the drunken man in a cell and question him when he was **lucid**.

★
★
parliament
[páːrləmənt]
ⓝ 국회, 의회

adj. parliamentary

n. the group responsible for making a nation's laws and policies

The **parliament** of the United Kingdom is divided into two parts: the House of Commons and the House of Lords.

syn. legislature

★
★
★
plead
[pliːd]
ⓥ 탄원하다, 간청하다

n. plea

v. to ask for something urgently or emotionally

The young man who had been arrested at a protest **pleaded** with the judge not to send him to prison.

syn. appeal

Useful Tips

피고가 유죄를 인정하는 것은 plead guilty, 무죄를 주장하는 것은 plead innocent라고 한다.

★
★
refute
[rifjúːt]
ⓥ 반박하다

adj. refutable

v. to prove something wrong

There was evidence that **refuted** the man's claim of having spent the evening at home watching TV.

syn. disprove　*ant.* confirm

---

legislation 오랫동안 사람들은 전반적인 국세 법규 간소화를 요구해 왔다.　**legitimate** 장애인 주차 공간에 주차할 합법적인 이유가 있다면, 교통 위반 즉결 재판소의 판사에게 그것을 제시할 수 있다.　**lucid** 1. 그 판사는 매우 명료한 방식으로 그의 법적 견해들을 작성해, 누구나 그것을 이해하기 쉽게 만든다. 2. 경찰은 그 주취자를 감방에 넣었다가 그가 의식이 또렷할 때 취조하기로 결정했다.　**parliament** 영국의 의회는 두 부분, 즉 하원과 상원으로 나뉜다.　**plead** 시위하다 구속된 그 청년은 자신을 감옥에 보내지 말아달라고 판사에게 탄원했다.　**refute** 집에서 TV를 보며 그날 저녁을 보냈다는 그 남자의 주장을 반박할 증거가 있었다.

★

reparation

[rèpəréiʃən]

[명] 배상금

adj. reparative

n. money paid for damage or harm

The man asked the judge to award him **reparation** of $20,000 for the injuries he suffered in the attack.

syn. compensation

Useful Tips

reparation의 복수형 reparations는 전쟁 배상금 같은 국가 차원의 배상금을 뜻한다.

★★

sentence

[séntəns]

[명] 형벌, 형

[동] (형을) 선고하다

n. the punishment assigned to someone who broke the law

The prosecuting attorney asked for a life **sentence** without parole, but the judge gave the man 15 years in prison instead.

v. to assign a punishment to someone who broke the law

People who are **sentenced** to community service must volunteer with local organizations for a certain number of hours.

★★★

sue

[suː]

[동] 고소하다

v. to open a legal case against someone

The woman wanted to **sue** the corporation for damaging her home, but she could not afford the legal fees.

★★★

trial

[tráiəl]

[명] 재판, 공판

v. try

n. the legal process of deciding if someone has committed a crime

During a **trial**, spectators are instructed to sit quietly and refrain from reacting in any noticeable way.

★★

verdict

[vəːrdikt]

[명] 판결, 심판

n. an official decision on a legal case

After a three-hour wait, the judge returned to the courtroom in order to issue his **verdict** on the case.

syn. ruling

★★

vindicate

[víndəkèit]

[동] 무죄를[…의 정당성을] 입증하다

n. vindication

v. to prove that an accused person is innocent or correct

The woman accused of theft hoped that the testimony of the witnesses would **vindicate** her.

syn. exonerate

---

reparation 그 남자는 그 공격으로 입은 부상에 대해 2만 달러의 배상금 지급 판정을 내려 달라고 판사에게 요청했다. **sentence** 그 검사는 가석방 없는 종신형을 요청했으나, 판사는 대신 그 남자에게 징역 15년을 구형했다. / 사회 봉사를 선고 받은 사람들은 특정 시간 동안 지역 단체들에서 자원봉사를 해야 한다. **sue** 그 여자는 그녀의 가정에 해를 끼친 혐의로 그 회사를 고소하고 싶었지만, 수임료를 감당할 수 없었다. **trial** 재판 도중, 방청객들은 조용히 앉아서 눈에 띄게 반응하지 말라는 지시를 받는다. **verdict** 3시간의 기다림 후, 그 사건에 대한 판결을 내리기 위해 판사가 법정으로 돌아왔다. **vindicate** 절도죄로 기소된 그 여자는 그 증인의 증언이 자신의 무죄를 입증하기를 바랐다.

EXERCISES

A Match each definition with the correct word.

1 to open a legal case against someone   ⓐ sentence

2 free from a requirement or rule   ⓑ sue

3 a law or set of laws   ⓒ legislation

4 a group of people who decide the outcome of a legal case   ⓓ contravene

5 to act in a way that goes against a law or an order   ⓔ decree

6 an official order   ⓕ jurisdiction

7 the right to make legal decisions   ⓖ exempt

8 to assign a punishment to someone who broke the law   ⓗ jury

B Choose the word that is closest in meaning to each underlined word.

1 It is the economist's <u>lucid</u> writing style that makes his complex theories so easy to understand.
   ⓐ dynamic   ⓑ familiar   ⓒ clear   ⓓ untraditional

2 The politician threatened to shut the business down, but he doesn't have the <u>authority</u> to do so.
   ⓐ ambition   ⓑ power   ⓒ sponsorship   ⓓ verdict

3 The instant replay <u>vindicated</u> the referee for her decision to call a penalty on the play.
   ⓐ replicated   ⓑ renovated   ⓒ deviated   ⓓ exonerated

4 The psychologist tried to figure out why the troubled boy showed <u>contempt</u> for his family.
   ⓐ sympathy   ⓑ conflict   ⓒ despair   ⓓ disdain

5 New research <u>refutes</u> the explorer's claims that he discovered the lost city of Atlantis.
   ⓐ disproves   ⓑ analyzes   ⓒ reinforces   ⓓ recreates

6 The group <u>advocates</u> stricter regulations on commercials shown during children's shows.
   ⓐ innovates   ⓑ backs   ⓒ relocates   ⓓ understands

7 Since the bill was <u>enacted</u> in 1987, it has helped increase the recycling rates of plastic bottles in California.
   ⓐ supported   ⓑ omitted   ⓒ ratified   ⓓ transported

ART & DESIGN

SOCIAL SCIENCE

NATURAL SCIENCE

HUMANITIES

EARTH & SPACE

SOCIAL ISSUES

Lesson 20 Politics

정치

★
abate
[əbéit]
[동] (강도가) 약해지다, 줄다

v. to become less severe

The flood of political ads on TV won't begin to **abate** until after the election in November.

syn. diminish

★★
amnesty
[ǽmnəsti]
[명] 사면, 특사

n. forgiveness granted to political prisoners

The president granted **amnesty** to dozens of jailed opposition leaders as a gesture of goodwill.

★★
ballot
[bǽlət]
[명] 1. 무기명 투표
2. 투표용지

n. 1 the process of voting secretly
2 the paper on which a vote is recorded

1. City council members were selected by the mayor in the past, but now they are elected by **ballot**.
2. After filling out and signing your mail-in **ballot**, you must place it inside the accompanying envelope.

Useful Tips

과거에 투표용지는 위에 구멍이 있는 밀봉된 상자에 들어 있는 경우가 많았는데, 이러한 이유로 the ballot box(투표함)라는 단어가 일반적인 '선거'를 가리키는 데 사용되기도 한다.

★★
cabinet
[kǽbənit]
[명] (정부의) 내각, 각료

n. a group of people who advise a leader and make policies

The president will meet with his **cabinet** tomorrow evening to discuss the issue of closing the borders.

★★★
campaign
[kæmpéin]
[명] (사회·정치적) 운동

n. an organized effort to achieve a goal or get elected

After receiving little support from the public, the former governor ended his presidential **campaign**.

★★★
candidate
[kǽndidèit, -dət]
[명] (선거의) 입후보자

n. a person running for political office or applying for a job

The two leading **candidates** have agreed to have a televised debate two weeks from tomorrow.

---

abate TV의 정치 광고 홍수는 11월 선거가 끝날 때까지 줄어들기 시작하지 않을 것이다. **amnesty** 대통령은 호의의 표시로 수십 명의 수감된 야당 지도자들을 사면시켰다. **ballot** 1. 과거에는 시장이 시 위원들을 선출했지만, 현재는 무기명 투표로 선출된다. 2. 우편 투표용지를 기입하고 서명한 후에, 반드시 그 투표용지를 동봉된 봉투에 넣어야 한다. **cabinet** 대통령은 국경을 폐쇄하는 문제를 논의하기 위해 내일 저녁 각료들을 만날 것이다. **campaign** 대중들의 지지를 거의 받지 못하자, 전 주지사는 본인의 대선 운동을 접었다. **candidate** 두 유력 후보는 내일로부터 2주 후에 TV 토론회를 하기로 합의했다.

ART & DESIGN

SOCIAL SCIENCE

NATURAL SCIENCE

HUMANITIES

EARTH & SPACE

SOCIAL ISSUES

coalition
[kòuəlíʃən]
ⓝ 연합, 연대, 통합

n. a short-term union of groups with a shared goal

The leaders of several political parties met to discuss forming a **coalition**, but they could not reach a formal agreement.

syn. alliance

confront
[kənfrʌ́nt]
ⓥ (문제나 힘든 상황에) 맞서다

n. confrontation

v. to deal with a difficult person or problem directly

The politician was surprised to be **confronted** by an angry citizen who demanded that he release his tax returns.

syn. challenge   *ant.* avoid

corruption
[kərʌ́pʃən]
ⓝ 부패, 부정

v., adj. corrupt

n. dishonest or illegal behavior by people in power

Some journalists pride themselves on their ability to find and expose political **corruption**.

delegate
[déligət]
ⓝ 대표

n. delegation

n. a person chosen to represent a group at a meeting

At the start of the conference, all of the **delegates** gathered together for an introductory meeting.

syn. representative

dictator
[díkteitər]
ⓝ 독재자

v. dictate

n. a leader with unlimited power who rules through force

Joseph Stalin was a **dictator** who ruled the Soviet Union from 1927 until his death in 1953.

syn. autocrat

diplomacy
[diplóuməsi]
ⓝ 외교(술)

adj. diplomatic

n. the skillful management of relationships

Due to the prime minister's international **diplomacy**, the country enjoyed a long period of peace with its neighbors.

syn. tact

---

coalition 여러 정당의 대표들이 연합 구성을 논의하기 위해 만났지만, 정식 합의에 도달할 수 없었다.   **confront** 그 정치인은 분개한 한 시민이 그의 소득 신고서를 공개하라고 요구하며 맞서자, 놀랐다.   **corruption** 일부 언론인들은 정치적 부패를 찾아 폭로하는 능력에 자부심을 느낀다.   **delegate** 회담이 시작되자, 모든 대표자들이 첫 회의를 위해 한자리에 모였다.   **dictator** Joseph Stalin은 1927년부터 그가 사망한 1953년까지 소련을 통치한 독재자였다.   **diplomacy** 그 나라는 총리의 국제 외교 덕분에 이웃 나라들과의 평화 기간을 오랫동안 누렸다.

★
electorate
[iléktərət]
몡 유권자

n. all the people who are eligible to vote

Some of the president's policies were well thought out, but many of them were simply designed to appeal to the **electorate**.

★
★
★
exile
[égzail]
동 망명시키다, 추방하다
몡 망명, 추방

v. to ban someone from their own country

In the past, defeated leaders were sometimes **exiled** by their rivals, who wanted to ensure they would not return to power.

n. the state of being forced to live outside one's own country

After the people rose up against him, the leader escaped to a neighboring country and lived out the rest of his life in **exile**.

★
faction
[fǽkʃən]
몡 당파, 파벌

n. a small opposition group within a larger group

A **faction** within the political party opposes the plan to raise the taxes of wealthy individuals.

★
fanatical
[fənǽtikəl]
몡 광(신)적인

n. fanatic

adj. excessively and unreasonably enthusiastic about something

Refusing to accept that he had lost the election, the president's **fanatical** followers took to the streets in protest.

syn. rabid   *ant.* indifferent

Useful Tips

특정 사람이나 단체를 매우 좋아하는 사람을 fan이라고 지칭하는데, 이는 fanatic(광신도)이란 단어의 줄임말이다.

★
fugitive
[fjúːdʒətiv]
몡 도망자, 탈주자

n. a person who is trying to avoid the police by running away or hiding

Once a respected politician, the ex-mayor became a **fugitive** after he was accused of misusing political donations.

★
hegemony
[hidʒémoni]
몡 패권, 헤게모니

n. the state of being greater in strength and having control over others

During the Cold War between the US and the USSR, the two superpowers imposed their **hegemony** on the rest of the world.

syn. dominion

---

electorate 그 대통령의 몇몇 정책들은 세심히 계획되었지만, 다수는 그저 유권자들의 관심을 끌기 위해 만들어졌다.   **exile** 과거에 패배한 지도자들은 때때로 그들이 권좌로 돌아오지 않는 것을 확실히 하길 원했던 정적들에 의해 추방당했다. / 그 지도자는 국민들이 궐기하자 이웃 나라로 탈출했고, 망명한 상태로 여생을 살았다.   **faction** 그 정당 안의 한 계파는 부유층에 대한 그 세금 인상 계획에 반대한다.   **fanatical** 그 대통령의 광적인 추종자들은 그가 선거에서 졌다는 사실을 받아들이기를 거부하며 거리로 나와 시위했다.   **fugitive** 한때 존경받는 정치인이었던 전 시장은 정치 후원금 남용으로 기소 당한 후, 도망자가 되었다.
hegemony 미국과 소련의 냉전 기간 동안에 이 두 초강대국은 전 세계의 나머지 국가들에게 그들의 패권을 강요했다.

impeach

[impíːtʃ]

ⓥ 탄핵하다, 고발하다

n. impeachment

v. to formally accuse an elected official of a serious crime

Due to the political scandal, several members of the president's own party voted to **impeach** him.

---

inaugurate

[inɔ́ːgjurèit]

ⓥ 1. 취임시키다
   2. …을 개시하다, 발족시키다

n. inauguration

v. 1 to formally begin the term of an elected official
2 to officially start something

1. The president and vice president were **inaugurated** in a lavish ceremony that was broadcast live.

2. The prime minister hopes to **inaugurate** her new immigration policies at the start of the new year.

---

incumbent

[inkʌ́mbənt]

ⓝ 재임자

n. the person holding a position at present

Although the challenger received 47% of the votes in the mayoral election, the **incumbent** received 49%.

---

liberal

[líbərəl]

ⓐ 진보적인, 진보주의적인
ⓝ 진보주의자

adj. socially progressive and open to new ideas   *ant.* conservative

Due to the president's unpopular policies, some people with **liberal** views cast their votes for his conservative rival.

n. a person with socially progressive political beliefs
   ant. conservative

The politician was a **liberal** when she was young, but she changed her views several years ago.

---

multiple

[mʌ́ltəpl]

ⓐ 다수의, 많은

adj. more than one or two

The politician claimed that some people had voted **multiple** times in the election.

syn. numerous   *ant.* single

---

negotiate

[nigóuʃièit, -si-]

ⓥ 협상하다, 교섭하다

n. negotiation

v. to reach an agreement through formal discussions

The vice president met with members of both parties to help them **negotiate** a solution to their disagreement.

SOCIAL SCIENCE

NATURAL SCIENCE

HUMANITIES

EARTH & SPACE

SOCIAL ISSUES

---

impeach 정치 스캔들로 인해 대통령 소속 정당의 여러 당원들이 그를 탄핵하는 데 투표했다.   **inaugurate** 1. 생방송으로 진행된 호화로운 기념식에서 대통령과 부통령이 취임했다. 2. 그 총리는 자신의 새로운 이민 정책을 새해 시작과 함께 시행하기를 희망한다.   **incumbent** 시장 선거에서 도전자가 47%의 득표율을 얻었지만, 재임자는 49%를 얻었다.   **liberal** 1. 대통령의 인기 없는 정책들 때문에 진보적인 견해를 가진 일부 사람들이 그의 보수 경쟁자에게 표를 던졌다. 2. 그 정치인은 젊었을 때 진보주의자였지만, 몇 년 전에 자신의 견해를 바꾸었다.   **multiple** 그 정치인은 선거에서 일부 사람들이 여러 번 투표했다고 주장했다.
negotiate 부통령은 양당 의원들의 의견 차이 해결을 위한 협상을 돕기 위해 그들과 만났다.

★★ **nominee**
[nɑ̀məníː]
[명] (직책·수상 등에) 지명된 사람, 후보
v. nominate

n. **someone who has been officially suggested for a position or award**
Each political party holds a primary election to decide who their presidential **nominee** will be.

★★ **oath**
[ouθ]
[명] 맹세, 서약, 선서

n. **a formal promise**
During the ceremony, each new member of parliament will take an **oath** pledging to be loyal to the country.
syn. vow

★★ **oppress**
[əprés]
[동] 억압하다, 탄압하다
n. oppression

v. **to treat a group of people in an unfair way**
Complaining that they had been politically **oppressed** for decades, members of the ethnic group demanded equality.
syn. subjugate

★ **ostracize**
[ástrəsàiz]
[동] …을 배척하다, 추방하다

v. **to drive an individual out of a group**
The young politician was **ostracized** by his own party after voting against a popular bill.
syn. exclude *ant.* accept

★★ **overpower**
[òuvərpáuər]
[동] 압도하다, 이기다

v. **to defeat through greater force**
The crowd protesting the election results **overpowered** the security guards and rushed forward.
syn. subdue

★ **partisan**
[pɑ́ːrtizən]
[형] 편파적인, 당파적인
n. partisanship

adj. **showing preference for one side without considering the other**
People often complain about **partisan** politics, wishing their leaders would put the country before their political parties.
syn. one-sided *ant.* unbiased

nominee 각 정당은 그들 정당의 대통령 후보가 누가 될지를 결정하기 위해 경선을 한다. **oath** 기념식 중에 각 신임 국회의원이 나라에 충성을 맹세하는 서약을 할 것이다. **oppress** 그 민족 구성원들은 수십 년 동안 정치적으로 탄압을 받아왔다고 호소하며 평등을 요구했다. **ostracize** 그 젊은 정치인은 인기 있는 법안에 반대 투표한 후, 그의 정당에서 배척당했다. **overpower** 선거 결과에 항의하는 군중들이 보안 요원들을 제압하고 앞으로 돌진했다. **partisan** 사람들은 종종 지도자들이 국가를 자신의 정당보다 더 우선시하기를 바라며, 파벌 정치에 대해 불만을 토로한다.

★★★

patriot

[péitriət]

[명] 애국자

n. patriotism

n. someone who is strongly loyal to their country

Calling themselves **patriots**, the group tried to persuade shoppers to buy only products that were made in the country.

syn. nationalist

★★

poll

[poul]

[명] 1. 여론 조사
2. 투표소

n. 1 a survey of public opinion
2 a place where people vote

1. According to the latest **polls**, the prime minister's approval ratings are at an all-time high.
2. In just three days, millions of citizens will be heading to the **polls** to cast their votes for a new president.

Useful Tips
poll이 '투표소'라는 의미일 때는 복수형인 polls로 사용한다는 점을 유의한다.

★★★

proclaim

[proukléim]

[동] 선언하다, 공표하다

n. proclamation

v. to publicly announce

The president **proclaimed** that she would raise the national minimum wage in order to lower poverty rates.

syn. declare

★

prone

[proun]

[형] …하기 쉬운

adj. likely to do something

People who don't keep up with the news are **prone** to vote for whoever's name is most familiar.

Useful Tips
prone은 항상 'be prone to + 부정사'의 형태로 사용된다.

★

propaganda

[prὰpəgǽndə]

[명] (주의·주장 등의) 선전,
(비방·선전 목적의) 유포된 정보

n. false information that supports a political cause

The political group's claim that the government was hiding secrets from the public was dismissed as **propaganda**.

syn. disinformation

★

referendum

[rèfəréndəm]

[명] 국민 투표, 총선거

n. a general vote on a single issue

The question of whether or not the country should leave the European Union will be decided by national **referendum**.

---

patriot 그 단체는 자신들을 애국자라 지칭하며, 쇼핑객들이 국산품들만 사도록 설득하려고 애썼다. **poll** 1. 최근 여론 조사에 의하면, 총리의 지지율이 역대 최고치를 기록하고 있다. 2. 불과 3일 후에, 수백만의 시민들이 새 대통령을 선출하기 위해 투표소로 향할 것이다. **proclaim** 그 대통령은 빈곤율을 낮추기 위해 국가 최저임금을 인상하겠다고 선언했다. **prone** 뉴스를 계속해서 보지 않는 사람들은 누구든 가장 익숙한 이름의 후보에게 투표하기 쉽다. **propaganda** 정부가 대중으로부터 비밀을 숨기고 있다는 그 정치 단체의 주장은 정치 선전이라며 묵살당했다. **referendum** 그 나라의 유럽연합 탈퇴 여부에 대한 문제는 국민 투표에 의해 결정될 것이다.

★★ **regime**
[reiʒíːm]
[명] 정권

n. **the government running a country**
Since the **regime** took power five years ago, the country's economy has nearly collapsed.
syn. administration

Useful Tips
regime은 부정적인 의미가 있는 반면, 동의어인 administration은 중립적인 의미를 내포한다.

★ **secession**
[siséʃən]
[명] (주·국가 등의) 분리 독립
v. secede

n. **the act of leaving a county or union**
Many people in the United Kingdom are worried about the possibility of Scottish **secession** in the near future.

★ **suffrage**
[sʌ́fridʒ]
[명] 선거권, 참정권

n. **the right to vote**
Susan B. Anthony is remembered as one of the leaders of the woman's **suffrage** movement in the United States.
ant. disenfranchisement

★★ **treason**
[tríːzn]
[명] 반역죄
adj. treasonous

n. **the crime of betraying one's country**
The government worker who sold state secrets to the enemy was charged with **treason**.
syn. sedition

★★ **veto**
[víːtou]
[명] 거부권
[동] (거부권을 행사하여) 거부하다

n. **the authority to reject an official decision**
It rarely happens, but a presidential **veto** can be defeated by a two-thirds vote in Congress.

v. **to reject an official decision**
Although the spending bill was passed last night, the president has said that he will **veto** it.

★★ **wield**
[wiːld]
[동] (권력·권위 등을) 행사하다

v. **to have or use a particular power**
Generals control the military, but only politicians **wield** the power to declare war against another nation.

regime 이 정권이 5년 전에 집권한 이후로, 국가 경제가 거의 무너졌다. **secession** 많은 영국 국민들은 가까운 장래에 스코틀랜드가 분리 독립할 가능성에 대해 우려한다. **suffrage** Susan B. Anthony는 미국 여성 참정권 운동의 지도자 중 한 명으로 기억된다. **treason** 국가 기밀을 적에게 팔아 넘긴 정부 직원은 반역죄로 기소되었다. **veto** 그런 일은 거의 일어나지 않지만, 대통령의 거부권은 국회에서 2/3의 표결로 부결될 수 있다. / 지난밤에 지출 법안이 통과되었지만, 대통령은 그 법안에 거부권을 행사하겠다고 말했다. **wield** 장군들이 군대를 통제하지만, 오직 정치인들만이 다른 나라와의 전쟁을 선포하는 권한을 행사한다.

EXERCISES

ART & DESIGN

SOCIAL SCIENCE

NATURAL SCIENCE

HUMANITIES

EARTH & SPACE

SOCIAL ISSUES

A Match each definition with the correct word.

1 a general vote on a single issue

2 to have or use a particular power

3 dishonest or illegal behavior by people in power

4 forgiveness granted to political prisoners

5 a person who is trying to avoid the police by running away or hiding

6 a person running for political office or applying for a job

7 to reach an agreement through formal discussions

8 to formally accuse an elected official of a serious crime

ⓐ referendum

ⓑ corruption

ⓒ impeach

ⓓ wield

ⓔ negotiate

ⓕ fugitive

ⓖ candidate

ⓗ amnesty

B Choose the word that is closest in meaning to each underlined word.

1 The product's bold packaging proclaims that it is new and improved.
  ⓐ confronts   ⓑ declares   ⓒ propels   ⓓ regains

2 The report's grim economic numbers conflict with the government's cheery propaganda.
  ⓐ secession   ⓑ policy   ⓒ culmination   ⓓ disinformation

3 As the course grew more difficult, the students' early enthusiasm began to abate.
  ⓐ diminish   ⓑ advance   ⓒ intensify   ⓓ merge

4 A coalition of chemical companies funded the study concerning the safety of the weed killer.
  ⓐ formation   ⓑ reservoir   ⓒ alliance   ⓓ auditor

5 When dealing with someone stubborn, diplomacy is more useful than force.
  ⓐ logic   ⓑ tact   ⓒ trickery   ⓓ lawfulness

6 Fanatical support of a belief can drive an individual to behave in an unethical manner.
  ⓐ rabid   ⓑ hesitant   ⓒ coordinated   ⓓ conventional

7 In some countries around the world, execution is considered a suitable punishment for treason.
  ⓐ homicide   ⓑ bribery   ⓒ vandalism   ⓓ sedition

A Choose the correct words.

1 The word oath has the same meaning as

   ⓐ vow   ⓑ claim   ⓒ stupor   ⓓ ease

2 The word reparation has the same meaning as

   ⓐ separation   ⓑ inclination   ⓒ compensation   ⓓ revelation

3 The word prerequisite has the same meaning as

   ⓐ prearranged   ⓑ fragile   ⓒ enigmatic   ⓓ mandatory

4 The word complaint has the same meaning as

   ⓐ grievance   ⓑ proclamation   ⓒ triumph   ⓓ analysis

5 The word impulsive has the same meaning as

   ⓐ benevolent   ⓑ impetuous   ⓒ obstinate   ⓓ exhausted

6 The word restrain has the same meaning as

   ⓐ crush   ⓑ curb   ⓒ expel   ⓓ surround

7 The word dissent has the same meaning as

   ⓐ acceptance   ⓑ curiosity   ⓒ opposition   ⓓ intention

8 The word oppress has the same meaning as

   ⓐ relegate   ⓑ interpret   ⓒ subjugate   ⓓ penalize

B Fill in the blanks with the best words from the box.

1 It is human nature to try to _____ the feelings of guilt created by our bad behavior with the positive emotions created by socially acceptable activities.

2 There is a(n) _____ of senators within Congress that has chosen to obstruct daily activities as a form of protest against certain rules.

3 It is a basic principle of leadership that you should never make any rules that you aren't ready and willing to _____ with some kind of punishment.

4 The nervous man was ensured that he would be _____ from arrest if he agreed to testify against the defendant at the trial.

5 Once she learned that everything would be kept _____, the patient began to tell the psychologists secrets she had kept hidden for years.

6 The company has had an excellent _____ with consumers, primarily due to the fact that its products are made with an emphasis on durability.

enforce	reputation	offset	exempt	faction	confidential

C Read the following passages.

[1-2] **1** Choose one word that fits both blanks.

> In our modern society, _____ people refuse to speak or behave in ways that will offend others or make them feel uncomfortable. As long as someone makes a(n) _____ effort to avoid social conflicts, it is easy to get along with others.

    ⓐ dubious   ⓑ viral   ⓒ decent   ⓓ arbitrary

2 Choose the appropriate pair of words to fill in the blanks.

> Lawyers often find themselves engaged in heated arguments in the courtroom. Once the trial has ended, however, they are expected to be _____ to each other whenever they meet, no matter how they really feel. Nevertheless, this can cause a(n) _____ on their relationship.

    ⓐ liberal — coalition   ⓑ lucrative — objectivity
    ⓒ cordial — strain   ⓓ immoral — conviction

[3-4]

> It is never easy for people to confront a superior, even when they know they are right. This is especially true in politics. If, for example, a dictator supported a policy that was harmful to the country, few people in the government would be willing to say something.

3 In the context of the passage, confront means _____.
    ⓐ consult   ⓑ challenge   ⓒ insult   ⓓ imitate

4 The word dictator in the passage could best be replaced by
    ⓐ executive   ⓑ barbarian   ⓒ announcer   ⓓ autocrat

[5-6]

> As the economy had been rising and falling in an erratic manner, the president asked his top economists to find a way to _____ it. After discussing a number of possible approaches, they advised finding a way to distribute government funds to middle-class families who would immediately spend the money, putting it back into the economy.

5 Choose the word that is most suitable for the blank.
    ⓐ stabilize   ⓑ advertise   ⓒ promote   ⓓ depreciate

6 The word distribute in the passage is closest in meaning to
    ⓐ activate   ⓑ optimize   ⓒ dispense   ⓓ recognize

ART & DESIGN

SOCIAL SCIENCE

NATURAL SCIENCE

HUMANITIES

EARTH & SPACE

SOCIAL ISSUES

라틴어 접두사
Latin **Prefixes**

영어에는 라틴어 접두사가 사용된 단어들이 상당히 많기 때문에, 라틴어 접두사의 의미를 알면 처음 보는 단어들의 의미를 추측해 볼 수 있어 매우 유용하다. Chapter 2에서 배운 averse, benevolent, multiple, permanent, submit, transfer는 라틴어에서 유래한 접두사인 a-/ab-, bene-, multi-, per-, sub-, trans-가 사용된 단어들이다. 주요 라틴어 접두사들의 고유 의미를 살펴보고, 그 접두사가 사용된 단어들도 함께 숙지해 보자.

PREFIXES	EXAMPLES
a-/ab- *away, from*	abrupt 갑작스러운　absent 결석한　abstain 자제하다　abstract 추상적인 averse 싫어하는　avert 피하다
bene- *good, well*	benediction 축복　benefactor 후원자　beneficial 이로운 beneficiary 수혜자　benefit 혜택　benevolent 자애로운
co-/col-/com-/con-/cor- *with, together*	coherent 논리 정연한　collaborate 협력하다　collide 충돌하다 combine 결합하다　concord 화합　correspond 일치하다
dis- *not*	disagree 동의하지 않다　disclose 드러내다　discourage 좌절시키다 dishonor 불명예　disorder 질환, 장애　distract 주의를 돌리게 하다
e-/ex- *out of*	emigrate 이민을 가다　evict 쫓아내다　evoke 떠올려 주다 excavate 발굴하다　exclusive 독점적인　exhale 내쉬다　extract 추출하다
multi- *many*	multicolored 다색의　multimedia 멀티미디어　multiple 다수의 multiply 곱하다　multipurpose 다목적　multitude 다수
per- *through*	perennial 다년생의　permanent 영구적인　persist 계속되다 pertinent 적절한　pervade 만연하다
pre- *before, in front of*	precede …에 앞서다　precocious 조숙한　prediction 예측 prelude 서곡　prepare 준비하다　preview 시사회
re- *again, back*	reaction 반응　repeat 반복하다　response 응답, 반응 return 돌아오다　review 비평　rewind 되감다
sub- *under*	subconscious 잠재의식　submerge 잠수하다　submit 제출하다 subordinate 종속된　subscribe 구독하다　subsidy 보조금
trans- *across, beyond, through*	transfer 전학하다　transform 변형시키다　translate 번역하다 transparent 투명한　transplant 이식하다　transport …을 수송하다

CHAPTER

NATURAL SCIENCE

● 생물학
Biology

★★
adequate
[ǽdikwət]
③ 충분한, 적당한

adj. enough or acceptable for a particular purpose

People who do not drink an **adequate** amount of water each day will likely suffer from a number of physical issues.

syn. sufficient   *ant.* lacking

★★
adverse
[ædvə́ːrs]
③ 부정적인, 유해한

n. adversity

adj. having a harmful or unfavorable effect

The cancer treatments can have some **adverse** medical effects, including nausea and physical exhaustion.

ant. beneficial

★★
aerobic
[ɛəróubik]
③ 유산소의

adj. relating to oxygen

During **aerobic** exercise, your heart rate goes up, maximizing the amount of oxygen in the blood.

ant. anaerobic

★
arboreal
[ɑːrbɔ́ːriəl]
③ 나무 위에 사는, 수목의

adj. living in or relating to trees

Studying the anatomy of several **arboreal** species gave the students a better understanding of how animals move between trees.

★★★
cell
[sel]
③ 세포

adj. cellular

n. the smallest structural unit of a living thing

Although individual **cells** are microscopic, they are an essential component of all bodily functions.

★
chromosome
[króuməzòum]
③ 염색체

n. a thread-like structure that contains genetic information

Human beings have 23 pairs of **chromosomes**, while our close relative the chimpanzee has 24.

---

adequate 매일 충분한 물을 마시지 않는 사람들은 여러 신체적 문제들을 겪을 수 있을 것이다.   **adverse** 그 암 치료들에는 메스꺼움과 체력 소모를 포함한 몇몇 약리적 부작용들이 있을 수 있다.   **aerobic** 유산소 운동 중에는 심박수가 증가해 혈중 산소량이 극대화된다.   **arboreal** 나무 위에 사는 몇몇 종(種)들의 신체 구조에 대한 연구는 동물들이 나무 사이를 이동하는 방법을 그 학생들이 더 잘 이해할 수 있게 했다.   **cell** 개체 세포들은 미세하지만, 모든 신체 기능의 필수 구성 요소이다.   **chromosome** 인간은 23쌍의 염색체를 가지고 있는 반면, 인간과 가까운 동류인 침팬지는 24쌍을 가지고 있다.

★★

dissect

[disékt]

[동] 해부하다

n. dissection

v. to cut open an animal or plant to study it

The teacher swiftly **dissected** the frog to allow the class to examine its internal organs.

syn. take apart

★★★

dominant

[dámənənt]

[형] 지배적인, 우세한

v. dominate

adj. more powerful or successful than others

Dominant individuals within a species are more likely to have the opportunity to breed, passing their superior genes on to the next generation.

syn. supreme

★★

embryo

[émbriòu]

[명] 배아, 수정란

adj. embryonic

n. an unborn human or animal in the early stages of development

The parents had to wait for the **embryo** to develop more before they could know its sex.

Useful Tips

수정된 human embryo는 첫 8주 이후 fetus(태아)가 된다.

★

entity

[éntəti]

[명] 존재, 실재

n. something or someone that exists independently

The doctors believed that the rash on the patient's skin was being caused by some kind of biological **entity**.

★★★

evolve

[iválv]

[동] 진화하다, 발달하다

n. evolution

v. to develop gradually

If a single group of animals is separated geographically, it will eventually **evolve** into two different species.

ant. regress

★★

filter

[fíltər]

[동] 정화하다

v. to remove unwanted items

It was Marcello Malpighi who discovered how the air sacs in our lungs **filter** the air to obtain fresh oxygen.

syn. purify

---

dissect 그 교사는 그 학급이 개구리의 내장들을 살펴 볼 수 있도록 그것을 신속히 해부했다. **dominant** 어떤 종에서 우세한 개체들은 번식할 기회를 잡아 그들의 우수한 유전자들을 다음 세대에 물려줄 가능성이 더 많다. **embryo** 그 부모는 배아의 성별을 알 수 있기 전에, 그것이 더 성장하기를 기다려야 했다. **entity** 그 의사들은 그 환자의 피부 발진이 어떤 생물학적 존재 때문에 야기되고 있다고 믿었다. **evolve** 어떤 단일한 동물 집단이 지리적으로 분리되면, 그것은 결국 두 개의 서로 다른 종으로 진화할 것이다. **filter** 우리 폐에 있는 폐포들이 신선한 산소를 얻기 위해 어떻게 공기를 정화시키는지를 알아낸 이는 바로 Marcello Malpighi였다.

★★ **fission**
[fíʃən]
[명] (세포의) 분열

n. the division of a cell for reproduction

When a single cell divides through binary **fission**, its internal structures must be reproduced as well.

ant. fusion

★★ **fragment**
[frǽgmənt]
[명] 조각, 일부분

n. a piece, shard, or particle

Platelets are small cell **fragments** in the blood that form clots in order to prevent excessive bleeding.

ant. whole

★★ **impermeable**
[impə́ːrmiəbl]
[형] 불침투성의
n. impermeability

adj. not allowing gas or liquid to pass through

Our skin is an **impermeable** layer of tissue that keeps unwanted substances out of our internal system.

syn. impenetrable

★ **incubate**
[ínkjubèit]
[동] 품다, 배양하다
n. incubation

v. to help something develop, such as an egg

Birds **incubate** their eggs by sitting on top of them, which keeps them at the proper temperature.

★★★ **inherit**
[inhérit]
[동] 물려받다
n. inheritance

v. to receive physical or mental characteristics from one's parents or ancestors

The members of a family tend to look similar to one another, since the children **inherit** their parent's physical characteristics.

★★ **luminescent**
[lùːmənésnt]
[형] 발광성의, 빛나는

adj. emitting light not resulting from heat

It was discovered that some living creatures produce **luminescent** materials for self-defense.

syn. glowing

---

fission 한 개의 세포가 이분열을 통해 나눠질 때, 그 내부 구조들도 복제되어야 한다. **fragment** 혈소판은 과다 출혈을 막기 위해 혈전을 형성하는 혈액 내의 작은 세포 조각들이다. **impermeable** 우리 피부는 원치 않는 물질들의 체내 유입을 막는 불침투성 조직막이다. **incubate** 새들은 알들 위에 앉아 알을 품는데, 이것은 그 알들을 적정 온도로 유지시켜 준다. **inherit** 자녀가 부모의 신체적 특성들을 물려받기 때문에, 한 가족의 구성원들은 서로 닮아 보이는 경향이 있다. **luminescent** 몇몇 생물들이 자기방어를 위해 발광성 물질들을 만들어낸다는 것이 밝혀졌다.

★
malignant
[məlígnənt]
[형] 악성의

adj. dangerous or cruel

The doctors discovered that the woman had a **malignant** form of cancer that was difficult to treat.

syn. harmful, malevolent *ant.* harmless, benign

★★
metabolism
[mətǽbəlìzm]
[명] 신진대사
adj. metabolic

n. the chemical process of converting food into energy

Cardiovascular exercise increases the **metabolism**, helping people lose weight by burning more calories.

★★★
organism
[ɔ́:rgənìzm]
[명] 생물, 유기체

n. a living thing

There are some tiny **organisms** that are made up of a single cell, including bacteria.

★
osmosis
[ɑzmóusis]
[명] 삼투

n. the process by which a liquid gradually moves through a barrier

Nutrients and essential vitamins enter the body's system through the process of **osmosis** in the digestive system.

★★
parasite
[pǽrəsàit]
[명] 기생충

n. a plant or animal that lives off another type of plant or animal

Some **parasites** do not seriously affect their hosts, while others can cause significant problems.

★★
reflex
[rí:fleks]
[명] 반사

n. an automatic physical reaction

Physicians use a rubber hammer to check the natural **reflexes** of patients by tapping them on the knee.

malignant 그 의사들은 그 여자에게 치료하기 힘든 악성 종양이 있다는 것을 발견했다. **metabolism** 유산소 운동은 신진대사를 증대시켜, 사람들이 더 많은 칼로리를 소모함으로써 체중을 줄이도록 도와준다. **organism** 단세포로 된 아주 작은 생물들이 박테리아를 포함해 몇몇 있다. **osmosis** 영양소와 필수 비타민들은 소화 기관 내의 삼투 작용을 통해 신체 체계로 들어간다. **parasite** 어떤 기생충들은 숙주들에게 심각하게 영향을 미치지 않는 반면, 다른 것들은 중대한 문제를 일으킬 수 있다. **reflex** 내과 의사들은 고무 망치를 사용해 환자들의 무릎을 두드려 자연 반사를 확인한다.

★★

replicate

[réplikèit]

[동] 복제하다

n. replica

v. to duplicate or reproduce something

The mitochondria within the animal cell **replicated** its DNA and divided itself in two.

syn. copy

★★★

respiration

[rèspəréiʃən]

[명] 1. 호흡
2. 호흡 작용

v. respire
adj. respiratory

n. 1 the action of breathing
2 the process of producing energy through the intake of oxygen

1. Human beings have a pair of lungs, important organs that play a primary role in **respiration**.
2. Cells obtain energy through **respiration**, consuming oxygen and then releasing carbon dioxide.

★★

rudimentary

[rù:dəméntəri]

[형] 미발달의, 흔적의

adj. not very well developed

The spleen was once considered a **rudimentary** organ of little value, but it is now believed to be an essential part of the immune system.

syn. primitive *ant.* advanced

★★

shed

[ʃed]

[동] (껍질·가죽 등을) 갈다, 벗다

v. to cast off or get rid of

As a snake develops, it will **shed** its skin multiple times to accommodate its growth.

syn. discard *ant.* retain

★★

symbiotic

[sìmbiátik, -bai-]

[형] 공생의

n. symbiosis

adj. involving a mutually beneficial interaction between different organisms

Clownfish and anemone have a **symbiotic** relationship, providing each other with nutrients and shelter.

★★★

trait

[treit]

[명] 형질

n. a characteristic that is passed from parent to child

Characteristics such as straight hair, dark eyes, and attached earlobes are **traits** that can be inherited.

---

replicate 그 동물 세포 안의 미토콘드리아는 DNA를 복제해 두 개로 분열했다. **respiration** 1. 인간은 호흡에 주된 역할을 하는 중요한 장기인 폐 한 쌍을 가지고 있다. 2. 세포들은 산소를 소비한 후 이산화탄소를 배출하는 호흡 작용을 통해 에너지를 얻는다. **rudimentary** 비장은 한때 별 가치가 없는 흔적 기관으로 여겨졌지만, 지금은 면역 체계의 필수 부분으로 여겨진다. **shed** 뱀은 성장하면서, 성장에 맞추기 위해 수차례 탈피한다. **symbiotic** 흰동가리와 말미잘은 공생 관계를 맺고 있어서, 서로에게 영양분과 피신처를 제공해 준다. **trait** 직모, 검은 눈동자, 부착된 귓불 같은 특성들은 유전될 수 있는 형질들이다.

EXERCISES

ART & DESIGN

SOCIAL SCIENCE

NATURAL SCIENCE

HUMANITIES

EARTH & SPACE

SOCIAL ISSUES

A Match each definition with the correct word.

1 emitting light not resulting from heat   ⓐ rudimentary

2 an automatic physical reaction   ⓑ trait

3 living in or relating to trees   ⓒ evolve

4 relating to oxygen   ⓓ luminescent

5 to develop gradually   ⓔ reflex

6 not very well developed   ⓕ arboreal

7 the division of a cell for reproduction   ⓖ aerobic

8 a characteristic that is passed from parent to child   ⓗ fission

B Choose the word that is closest in meaning to each underlined word.

1 If a plant's roots were <u>impermeable</u>, they would not be able to extract water from the soil.
   ⓐ impenetrable   ⓑ important   ⓒ instantaneous   ⓓ immobile

2 Each ant carried a <u>fragment</u> of the dead grasshopper's body back to the nest.
   ⓐ pollutant   ⓑ subject   ⓒ estate   ⓓ piece

3 The <u>dominant</u> animal in a hunting group will usually be the first to eat from the prey.
   ⓐ outcast   ⓑ supreme   ⓒ aspiring   ⓓ distinct

4 Without an <u>adequate</u> level of water, none of the fish will be able to survive in the pond.
   ⓐ qualified   ⓑ beneficial   ⓒ certified   ⓓ sufficient

5 Crabs and other crustaceans periodically <u>shed</u> their hard outer layer and grow a new one.
   ⓐ spread   ⓑ reveal   ⓒ discard   ⓓ shrink

6 The primary role of the kidneys is to <u>filter</u> blood by removing toxins and waste material.
   ⓐ distribute   ⓑ purify   ⓒ spread   ⓓ extract

7 The cells in a <u>malignant</u> tumor will multiply uncontrollably, destroying other tissues in the process.
   ⓐ pungent   ⓑ invasive   ⓒ harmful   ⓓ lethargic

> 식물학
Botany

★★★
absorb
[æbsɔ́ːrb, əb-]
동 흡수하다, 빨아들이다

v. to take something in

The roots of a plant **absorb** not only water from the soil but also some of the minerals found in it.

syn. soak up   *ant.* reflect

★★
aquatic
[əkwǽtik, əkwátik]
형 물의, 수생의

adj. relating to or living in water

There are some rootless **aquatic** plants, such as the bladderwort, that float freely on the water's surface.

ant. terrestrial

★★
bark
[baːrk]
명 나무 껍질

n. the rough covering on the surface of a tree

When a tree's trunk is stripped of its **bark**, the tree becomes dangerously vulnerable to external threats.

★★
barren
[bǽrən]
형 척박한, 황량한

adj. unable to grow or produce anything

Although this land is currently **barren**, it was once covered in fields of grass and wildflowers.

★★★
blossom
[blásəm]
명 꽃
동 꽃이 피다, 꽃을 피우다

n. a flower on a tree or bush

The **blossoms** of the cherry tree vary in color from pure white to a vibrant shade of pink.

v. to produce flowers

When the fruit trees begin to **blossom** in spring, the orchard is filled with the sound of buzzing bees.

★
bore
[bɔːr]
동 구멍을 뚫다

v. to make a deep hole in a hard material

Woodpeckers use their beaks to **bore** holes in trees, searching for insects that live inside the wood.

syn. drill

---

absorb 식물의 뿌리는 흙에서 나오는 수분뿐만 아니라, 그 안에서 발견되는 일부 무기질도 흡수한다.   **aquatic** 통발처럼, 수면을 자유롭게 떠다니는 몇몇 뿌리 없는 수생 식물들이 존재한다.   **bark** 나무 기둥의 껍질이 벗겨지면, 나무는 외부 위협에 위험할 정도로 취약해진다.   **barren** 이 땅은 현재 황량하지만, 한때 풀과 야생화로 뒤덮여 있었다.   **blossom** 벚나무의 꽃들은 순백색부터 선명한 핑크빛에 이르기까지 색이 다양하다. / 봄에 과일나무의 꽃이 피기 시작하면, 과수원은 윙윙거리는 벌 소리로 가득 찬다.   **bore** 딱따구리들은 부리를 사용해 나무에 구멍을 뚫고, 그 안에 서식하는 곤충들을 찾는다.

★★ **bud**
[bʌd]
[명] 싹, 꽃봉오리

n. an undeveloped leaf or flower

The green growths that have begun to appear on the bare branches of the forest's trees are the **buds** of young leaves.

★ **canopy**
[kǽnəpi]
[명] 캐노피(숲의 나뭇가지들이 지붕 모양으로 우거진 것)

n. the covering of branches and leaves high above the forest floor

The rainforest **canopy** is alive with the cries of the creatures that live there, including small monkeys and colorful birds.

★★ **cellulose**
[séljulòus]
[명] 섬유소

n. a substance that makes up the walls of plant cells

The cotton that is used to make our clothing is made from the **cellulose** found in the fiber of the cotton plant.

★★ **cluster**
[klʌ́stər]
[명] 무리, (작은 열매의) 송이
[동] 모이다

n. a group of things positioned close together *syn.* clump

The Hawaiian leis used to welcome visitors are made of plumeria flowers, which grow in large, brightly colored **clusters**.

v. to gather close together *ant.* spread out

When it began to rain, the botanists **clustered** together at the base of the tree to keep dry.

★★ **coniferous**
[kouníf ərəs, kə-]
[형] 침엽수의

adj. producing cones and needle-like leaves that do not fall off in winter

Coniferous forests are mostly found in the northernmost regions of North America, Europe, and Asia.

Useful Tips
coniferous tree(침엽수)와 반대로 매년 낙엽이 지는 나무를 deciduous tree(낙엽수)라고 부른다.

★ **distill**
[distíl]
[동] 1. 추출하다
2. 증류하다, 정제하다
n. distillation

v. 1 to remove the liquid from something *syn.* extract
2 to purify liquid by heating and then cooling it

1. People have long been **distilling** the essential oils from plants, as they have a wide variety of practical uses.
2. Due to the plant life and algae living in the pond, its water must be **distilled** before you drink it.

bud 숲 속 나무들의 빈 가지에 돋아나기 시작한 녹색 식물들은 어린 잎의 싹이다. **canopy** 열대 우림의 캐노피는 작은 원숭이들과 형형색색의 새들을 포함해 그곳에 살고 있는 동물들의 울음소리로 활기가 넘친다. **cellulose** 우리 의복을 만드는 데 사용되는 면화는 목화의 섬유에서 발견되는 섬유소로 만들어진다. **cluster** 방문객들을 환영하는 데 쓰이는 하와이 레이는 푸루메리아로 만드는데, 이 꽃은 커다랗고 밝은 색의 꽃송이들이 무리를 지어 자란다. / 비가 내리기 시작하자, 식물학자들은 비에 젖지 않기 위해 나무 아래로 모였다. **coniferous** 침엽수림은 대부분 북미, 유럽, 그리고 아시아의 최북단에서 발견된다. **distill** 1. 사람들은 오래도록 식물에서 에센셜 오일을 추출해 왔는데, 그것들이 다양한 실용적 용도를 가지고 있기 때문이다. 2. 연못에 사는 식물과 조류 때문에, 연못 물은 마시기 전에 반드시 정제해야 한다.

dormant
[dɔ́ːrmənt]
휑 휴면기의, 휴지 상태의

adj. alive but inactive

Some plants and trees may seem to die in winter, but they have simply entered a **dormant** state.

syn. inert   *ant.* active

dwindle
[dwíndl]
통 점점 줄어들다[작아지다]

v. to become smaller in amount or size

As the region's native grasses **dwindle**, they are being aggressively replaced by invasive varieties.

syn. lessen   *ant.* expand

efficacy
[éfikəsi]
휑 효능, 효과, 효험

n. the ability to achieve a desired result

The botanists experimented with new methods of growing plants indoors in order to test their **efficacy**.

syn. efficiency   *ant.* inefficiency

elastic
[ilǽstik]
휑 1. 탄성 있는, 탄력 있는
2. 융통성 있는, 적응성 있는

adj. 1 able to stretch but retain its original shape
    syn. malleable   *ant.* stiff

    2 able to change easily   *syn.* adaptable   *ant.* inflexible

1. The stems of most plants are **elastic**, allowing them to bend in strong winds without sustaining any damage.

2. The exact sunlight and water requirements of some houseplants are **elastic**, depending on a number of factors.

evergreen
[évərgriːn]
휑 상록수

n. a tree that does not lose its leaves or change color in winter

The color of the **evergreens** contrasts sharply with the white snow blanketing the mountain landscape.

exotic
[igzátik]
휑 외국의, 이국적인

adj. native to a distant region

Alongside the native plants, you'll find some **exotic** flowers in the gardens, including orchids from Madagascar.

syn. alien   *ant.* commonplace

---

dormant 일부 식물과 나무들은 겨울에 죽은 것처럼 보일지 모르지만, 그것들은 단순히 휴면 상태에 돌입한 것일 뿐이다.   **dwindle** 그 지역의 토종 풀들이 점점 줄어들면서, 침입종들이 그것들을 공격적으로 대체하고 있다.   **efficacy** 식물학자들은 실내에서 식물을 키우는 새로운 방법들이 효과가 있는지 시험하기 위해 실험을 했다.   **elastic** 1. 대부분 식물들의 줄기는 탄성이 있어서, 강한 바람에도 아무런 손상을 입지 않고 구부러질 수 있다. 2. 몇몇 가정용 화초들의 정확한 일조량과 용수량은 여러 요인들에 따라 변할 수 있다.   **evergreen** 상록수의 색은 산 풍경을 뒤덮은 하얀 눈과 뚜렷이 대비된다.   **exotic** 당신은 그 정원에서 토종 식물들과 더불어 마다가스카르 산 난초를 포함한 몇몇 이국적인 꽃들을 발견할 것이다.

flora
[flɔ́:rə]
ⓝ 식물군

n. the plants and trees of a certain area

The region's **flora** is typical of desert areas, consisting mostly of sparse grasses, low shrubs, and tall cacti.

syn. vegetation

Useful**Tips**

flora(식물군)는 주로 fauna(동물군)와 함께 사용된다.

---

fragrant
[fréigrənt]
ⓐ 향기로운, 향긋한

n. fragrance

adj. having a pleasant smell

The more **fragrant** a flower is, the more successful it will be at attracting bees and hummingbirds.

syn. aromatic   *ant.* foul-smelling

---

germinate
[dʒə́:rmənèit]
ⓥ 싹트다, 싹트게 하다

v. to begin to grow (from a seed) or to cause a seed to begin to grow

The seeds will **germinate** after a few weeks if you keep them wrapped in a wet paper towel.

syn. sprout

---

graft
[græft]
ⓥ 접목하다, 이식하다

v. to join a piece of skin, bone, or plant matter to a larger whole

The branches taken from nearby fruit trees were **grafted** onto the trunks of young trees growing in the yard.

syn. transplant

---

horticulture
[hɔ́:rtəkʌ̀ltʃər]
ⓝ 원예(학·술)

adj. horticultural

n. the study or practice of growing plants in a garden

The woman has a degree in **horticulture**, which explains why her backyard garden is so impressive.

syn. gardening

---

lush
[lʌʃ]
ⓐ 무성한, 우거진

adj. growing healthily and in abundance

The **lush** jungle that begins just beyond the beach is so full of vines, trees, and plants that it is impossible to pass through.

syn. verdant   *ant.* barren

ART & DESIGN

SOCIAL SCIENCE

NATURAL SCIENCE

HUMANITIES

EARTH & SPACE

SOCIAL ISSUES

---

flora 그 지역의 식물군은 사막 지역의 전형으로, 대부분 드문드문 난 풀과 키 작은 관목들, 그리고 큰 선인장들로 이루어져 있다.   **fragrant** 꽃이 더 향기로울수록, 벌들과 벌새들을 더 잘 끌어들일 것이다.   **germinate** 그 씨앗들을 젖은 종이 수건으로 감싸 두면, 몇 주 후에 싹이 틀 것이다.   **graft** 근처 과일나무에서 떼온 가지들은 정원에서 자라고 있는 어린 나무들의 기둥에 접목되었다.   **horticulture** 그 여자는 원예학 학위가 있는데, 그것이 왜 그녀의 뒷마당 정원이 그토록 인상적인지를 말해 준다.   **lush** 해변 바로 너머로 시작되는 무성한 밀림은 덩굴, 나무, 그리고 식물들로 가득 차 있어 통행이 불가능하다.

★★
membrane
[mémbrein]
[명] (동·식물 조직의) 막

n. a thin layer of tissue acting as a boundary

Plant cells have both a cell wall and a **membrane**, while animal cells have only a **membrane**.

★★★
moisture
[mɔ́istʃər]
[명] 수분, 습기
adj. moist

n. small amounts of water in the air or on a surface

Cacti can live in extremely dry climates, but they do need at least a little **moisture** in order to survive.

syn. dampness *ant.* dryness

★★
nectar
[néktər]
[명] 꽃의 꿀, 화밀

n. a sweet liquid produced by flowers

Honeybees gather **nectar** from flowers and bring it back to their hive, where it is turned into honey.

★★★
perennial
[pəréniəl]
[형] 1. 다년생의
2. (아주 오랫동안) 지속되는, 계속 반복되는

adj. 1 living for a period of several years
2 lasting a long time or happening again and again

1. Because sage and thyme are **perennial** herbs, they are a favorite of amateur gardeners who are also chefs.
2. Flower trends come and go, but roses are a **perennial** favorite, mainly due to their associations with romantic love.

Useful Tips
한해살이 식물은 annual plants, 두해살이 식물은 biennial plants, 다년생 식물은 perennial plants라고 표현한다.

★★
pesticide
[péstəsàid]
[명] 살충제, 농약
n. pest

n. a chemical used to kill insects

Commercial **pesticides** may be effective in protecting plants in the short term, but they cause long-term damage to the soil and water.

★★
petal
[pétl]
[명] 꽃잎

n. one of the colored segments of a flower

The shape, color, and size of a flower's **petals** depends on the type of insect or bird it is trying to attract.

---

membrane 식물 세포에는 세포벽과 세포막이 있는 반면에, 동물 세포에는 세모막만 있다. **moisture** 선인장은 극도로 건조한 기후에서 살 수 있지만, 살아남기 위해서는 적어도 아주 약간의 수분이 필요하다. **nectar** 꿀벌들은 꽃에서 화밀을 모아 그것이 꿀로 바뀌는 장소인 벌집으로 가져온다. **perennial** 1. 세이지와 백리향은 다년생 허브이기 때문에, 요리사인 아마추어 정원사들이 가장 좋아한다. 2. 꽃의 유행이 돌고 돌지만, 장미는 주로 낭만적인 사랑이 연상되기 때문에 지속적으로 사랑 받고 있다. **pesticide** 상업적인 살충제는 단기적으로는 식물 보호에 효과적일 수 있지만, 토양과 물에 장기적인 피해를 입힌다. **petal** 꽃잎의 모양, 색, 그리고 크기는 그 꽃이 끌어들이려 하는 곤충이나 새의 종류에 따라 다르다.

★★★

photosynthesis

[fòutəsínθəsis]

[명] 광합성

n. the process of converting sunlight into food

Because most plants survive through **photosynthesis**, they must be planted in a location that receives some sunlight.

★★

pollen

[pálən]

[명] 꽃가루, 화분

n. a powder produced by flowers in order to reproduce

As bees fly from flower to flower, they gather and disperse **pollen**—this is what allows flowers to reproduce.

★★

pollinate

[pálənèit]

[동] …을 수분하다

v. to help flowers reproduce by distributing pollen

In the absence of insects and birds, gardeners will sometimes **pollinate** their flowers by hand.

★

prune

[pru:n]

[동] 가지치기하다, 전지하다

v. to remove parts of a plant to help it grow

If trees are not properly **pruned**, they may end up growing in a manner that weakens their overall structure.

syn. trim

★★

pungent

[pʌ́ndʒənt]

[형] (맛·냄새가) 톡 쏘는 듯한, 자극성의

adj. having a taste or smell that is strong and sharp

There are some flowers with a very **pungent** odor that reproduce by attracting flies rather than bees.

syn. acrid

★★

resin

[rézin]

[명] 나무의 진, 송진

n. a sticky substance produced by certain trees and plants

If a pine tree is cut or otherwise seriously damaged, it is likely that **resin** will ooze out of the wound.

photosynthesis 대부분의 식물들은 광합성을 통해 생존하기 때문에, 어느 정도 햇빛이 드는 장소에 심어야 한다. **pollen** 벌들은 꽃들 사이를 날아다니면서 꽃가루를 모으고 퍼트리는데, 이로 인해 꽃들이 번식할 수 있다. **pollinate** 곤충들과 새들이 없을 때, 정원사들은 이따금씩 수작업으로 꽃들을 수분시킬 것이다. **prune** 나무가 제대로 가지치기되지 않으면, 결국 전체적인 구조를 약화시키는 쪽으로 자라게 될 수도 있다. **pungent** 벌보다는 파리들을 유인해 번식하는, 톡 쏘는 듯한 냄새가 나는 몇몇 꽃들이 있다. **resin** 만약 소나무가 잘리거나 심하게 손상되면, 그 상처에서 송진이 흘러나올 가능성이 높다.

★★★ **ripe**
[raip]
[형] 익은, 숙성한
v. ripen

adj. fully grown or matured

Once the fruit on a tree is **ripe**, its weight will cause it to detach from the branch, unless it is picked first.

ant. unripe

★★ **sap**
[sæp]
[명] 수액

n. a watery, sugary substance found inside plants and trees

When insects attack a plant, it is often to feed on the **sap** found inside its stems and leaves.

★★★ **thorn**
[θɔːrn]
[명] 가시
adj. thorny

n. a sharp point on a stem or branch

Animals are discouraged from eating the tree's leaves by the sharp **thorns** growing on its branches.

★★★ **thrive**
[θraiv]
[동] 번성하다, 잘 자라다
adj. thriving

v. to survive and do well

Mangroves, small trees with partially exposed roots, **thrive** in marshy areas and along shorelines.

syn. flourish

★ **transpiration**
[trӕnspəréiʃən]
[명] 증발, 증산 (작용)

n. the process through which plants release water

Most of the water a plant takes in through its roots is later released via the process of **transpiration**.

★★ **wither**
[wíðər]
[동] 시들다, 쭈그러들다

v. to become dry and wrinkled

Once a flower has been cut from the rest of the plant, it will begin to **wither** in a day or two.

syn. shrivel *ant.* flourish

---

ripe 일단 나무의 열매가 익은 후 그것을 먼저 따지 않는다면, 그 무게 때문에 열매가 가지에서 떨어질 것이다. **sap** 곤충들이 식물에 달려들면, 그것은 종종 식물의 줄기와 잎에 있는 수액을 먹기 위해서이다. **thorn** 동물들은 나뭇가지에서 자라는 날카로운 가시로 인해 나뭇잎을 먹는 것을 단념한다. **thrive** 부분적으로 뿌리가 드러나 있는 작은 나무인 맹그로브는 늪지대와 물가를 따라 번성한다. **transpiration** 식물이 뿌리를 통해 빨아들인 대부분의 수분은 추후 증산 과정을 통해 발산된다. **wither** 일단 꽃 한 송이가 나머지 식물에서 잘려 나가면, 하루나 이틀 안에 시들기 시작할 것이다.

EXERCISES

ART & DESIGN

SOCIAL SCIENCE

NATURAL SCIENCE

HUMANITIES

EARTH & SPACE

SOCIAL ISSUES

A Match each definition with the correct word.

1 the process through which plants release water   ⓐ ripe

2 fully grown or matured   ⓑ membrane

3 a thin layer of tissue acting as a boundary   ⓒ petal

4 a sweet liquid produced by flowers   ⓓ transpiration

5 a chemical used to kill insects   ⓔ photosynthesis

6 the process of converting sunlight into food   ⓕ coniferous

7 one of the colored segments of a flower   ⓖ nectar

8 producing cones and needle-like leaves that   ⓗ pesticide
   do not fall off in winter

B Choose the word that is closest in meaning to each underlined word.

1 As predator populations begin to <u>dwindle</u>, the populations of their prey are growing.
   ⓐ migrate   ⓑ recover   ⓒ lessen   ⓓ concentrate

2 Light that isn't reflected by the surface of an object is <u>absorbed</u> and converted into heat.
   ⓐ spread out   ⓑ soaked up   ⓒ slowed down   ⓓ turned over

3 If the muscles of the body go unused or underused for long periods, they can begin to <u>wither</u>.
   ⓐ swell   ⓑ shrivel   ⓒ ache   ⓓ elongate

4 <u>Fragrant</u> chemical compounds are blended together and mixed with alcohol to make perfume.
   ⓐ toxic   ⓑ priceless   ⓒ pragmatic   ⓓ aromatic

5 During severe flooding, certain species of ants will <u>cluster</u> together to form living rafts.
   ⓐ gather   ⓑ withdraw   ⓒ construct   ⓓ reproduce

6 Scientists have created laser beams that can <u>bore</u> a hole straight through solid material.
   ⓐ seal   ⓑ distill   ⓒ broaden   ⓓ drill

7 When the human eye produces too much <u>moisture</u>, it is expelled in the form of tears.
   ⓐ dampness   ⓑ intensity   ⓒ vision   ⓓ energy

[동물학]

Lesson 23 Zoology

★★
amphibian
[æmfíbiən]
[명] 양서 동물
adj. amphibious

n. a cold-blooded animal that lives both on land and in water

Most **amphibians** spend the early parts of their life cycle living in the water and later live on the land.

★★
armor
[áːrmər]
[명] (껍질·가시 등) 방호 기관

n. a hard outer layer that provides protection

The **armor** of rhinoceroses is so thick that it protects them from each other's horns when they battle over mates.

★
biped
[báiped]
[명] 두 발 동물
adj. bipedal

n. an animal that walks on two legs

Few mammals other than humans are true **bipeds**, although many, such as bears and apes, sometimes move around on two legs.

★★
breed
[briːd]
[동] 새끼를 낳다, 번식하다

v. to mate and give birth

Some species **breed** so quickly that a single pair released into the wild can turn into a large population in just a few years.

syn. reproduce

★★★
camouflage
[kǽməflàːʒ]
[명] 위장

n. something that makes an animal or object blend in with its surroundings

A tiger's stripes act as **camouflage**, allowing it to blend in with the shapes and shadows of tall grasses.

★★
carnivorous
[kaːrnívərəs]
[형] 육식성의
n. carnivore

adj. feeding on meat

Carnivorous creatures are usually equipped with sharp claws and teeth that help them hunt and kill efficiently.

syn. meat-eating *ant.* vegetarian

Useful Tips
인간처럼 육식과 채식을 같이 하는 잡식성을 나타내는 단어는 omnivorous이다.

---

amphibian 대부분의 양서 동물들은 초기 생활 주기를 물 속에서 보내고 그 후에는 땅 위에서 산다. **armor** 코뿔소의 방호 기관은 아주 두꺼워서 짝을 두고 싸울 때 서로의 뿔로부터 보호해 준다. **biped** 곰과 유인원 같은 많은 포유동물이 때때로 두 다리로 돌아다니긴 해도, 순수 두 발 동물인 포유동물은 인간 외에는 거의 없다. **breed** 몇몇 종들은 너무 빨리 번식해서, 야생에 방사된 한 쌍이 몇 년 만에 큰 개체군이 될 수 있다. **camouflage** 호랑이의 줄무늬는 위장하는 역할을 해, 큰 풀들의 모양 및 그늘에 섞여 들게 해 준다. **carnivorous** 육식성 동물들은 보통 효과적으로 사냥하고 죽이는 것을 돕는 날카로운 발톱과 이빨을 갖고 있다.

★★★ **distinguish**
[distíŋgwiʃ]
[동] 구별하다, 구분하다

v. to tell something apart from other things
One way to **distinguish** leopards from cheetahs is by the shape of the spots on their fur.
syn. differentiate

★★ **divergent**
[divə́ːrdʒənt, dai-]
[형] 다른, 분기하는
v. diverge

adj. moving or developing in a different direction
The species found on the Galapagos Islands are **divergent** from those living on the mainland.
syn. differing *ant.* convergent

★★ **fearsome**
[fíərsəm]
[형] 무서운
n. fear

adj. causing a lot of fright
Although they are portrayed as being cute and friendly in cartoons, hippos are actually **fearsome** creatures that kill many people.
syn. terrifying

★ **haven**
[héivən]
[명] 피난처, 안식처

n. a safe place
The wildlife sanctuary serves as a **haven** for many local species that would otherwise be hunted for their fur.
syn. refuge

★★ **herbivore**
[hə́ːrbəvɔ̀ːr]
[명] 초식 동물
adj. herbivorous

n. an animal that eats only plants
Some of Africa's largest animals, including elephants and rhinoceroses, are actually **herbivores**.
syn. vegetarian *ant.* carnivore

★★★ **hibernate**
[háibərnèit]
[동] 동면하다
n. hibernation

v. to remain inactive in winter
Before an animal **hibernates**, it will eat as much food as possible in order to store up fat in its body.

distinguish 표범과 치타를 구별하는 한 가지 방법은 털 위 반점들의 모양을 이용하는 것이다. **divergent** 갈라파고스 제도에서 발견된 종들은 본토에 살고 있는 종들과 다르다. **fearsome** 하마가 만화에서는 귀엽고 상냥하게 묘사되지만, 실제로는 많은 사람을 죽이는 무서운 동물이다. **haven** 그 야생 동물 보호 구역은 그 구역이 없었으면 털 때문에 사냥되었을 많은 현지 종들을 위한 피난처 역할을 한다. **herbivore** 코끼리와 코뿔소들을 포함한 아프리카의 가장 큰 동물들 중 일부는 사실 초식 동물이다. **hibernate** 동물은 동면하기 전에, 체내에 지방을 축적하기 위해 가능한 한 많은 먹이를 먹을 것이다.

hoard

[hɔ:rd]

ⓥ 저장하다

ⓝ 저장물, 축적

v. to collect and store large amounts of something   *syn.* amass

Some squirrels **hoard** acorns in the hollow parts of trees to ensure that they have food all winter.

n. a collection of things that have been stored   *syn.* stockpile

The children's pet hamster keeps a **hoard** of food hidden in one of the corners of its cage.

imitate

[ímətèit]

ⓥ 모방하다

n. imitation

v. to copy the appearance or behavior of something

Certain birds **imitate** the songs of other species, and some will even attempt to recreate human speech.

syn. mimic

imprint on

[imprínt ɔn]

ⓥ …에 각인하다

v. to become fixated on something

It is said that ducklings will **imprint** themselves **on** the first thing they see after hatching from their eggs.

marsupial

[mɑːrsúːpiəl]

ⓝ 유대목 동물

n. a mammal that carries its young in a pouch

In terms of wildlife, Australia is best known for the many species of **marsupials** that are found nowhere else.

Useful Tips

유대목 동물의 대표적인 예는 캥거루와 주머니두더지이다.

migrate

[máigreit]

ⓥ 이동하다

n. migration

v. to move to a new area because of the season

Every winter, humpback whales **migrate** from northern parts of the oceans to the warm waters of the tropics.

nocturnal

[nɑktɔ́ːrnl]

ⓝ 야간에 활동하는, 야행성의

adj. active at night

It is believed that bats are **nocturnal** so that they won't have to compete with birds for food.

ant. diurnal

---

hoard 어떤 다람쥐들은 겨우내 먹을 먹이를 확보하려고 나무의 빈 부분들에 도토리들을 저장한다. / 그 아이들의 애완용 햄스터는 우리 한 구석에 먹이 비축물을 보관한다.   **imitate** 특정 새들은 다른 종들의 노래들을 모방하는데, 어떤 새들은 인간의 말까지 따라하려 할 것이다.   **imprint on** 새끼 오리들은 알에서 부화한 후 처음 보는 것에 각인할 것이라고 한다.   **marsupial** 야생 동물에 관해서는, 호주가 다른 곳에서 발견되지 않는 많은 종의 유대목 동물들로 가장 유명하다.   **migrate** 매년 겨울, 혹등고래들은 북부 대양 해역들에서 따뜻한 열대해로 이동한다.   **nocturnal** 박쥐들은 먹이를 놓고 새들과 경쟁하지 않아도 되도록 야간에 활동한다고 여겨진다.

★

poach

[poutʃ]

[동] 밀렵하다

v. to illegally kill or catch an animal

Park rangers in some African countries are armed with machine guns to scare off people trying to **poach** animals.

★★★

prey

[prei]

[명] (육식 동물의) 사냥감[먹이]

[동] 잡아먹다

n. animals that are hunted and eaten by other animals

Crocodiles grab their **prey** in their powerful jaws and drag it underwater, holding it there until it drowns.

v. to hunt and kill another animal for food

Because cats **prey** on mice and other pests, ancient people began keeping them in their homes.

Useful Tips

fall prey to는 '…의 희생양이 되다'라는 의미로 사용된다.

★★

primate

[práimeit]

[명] 영장류

n. a member of the group of animals that includes humans and apes

Not many people realize that the lemurs of Madagascar, an island nation off the coast of Africa, are also **primates**.

★★

prolific

[prəlífik]

[형] 많이 산출하는, 다산하는

adj. producing a lot of something

Cows are **prolific** producers of methane, one of the greenhouse gases currently causing climate change.

syn. fruitful *ant.* barren

★★

rodent

[róudnt]

[명] 설치류 동물

n. a member of the group of small mammals that includes rats and mice

Rodents constantly gnaw on wood and other hard materials to keep their teeth from growing too long.

★

ruminant

[rú:mənənt]

[명] 반추 동물

n. a member of the group of animals that includes cattle and deer

The stomachs of **ruminants** are divided into four separate sections, which helps them digest grass.

poach 몇몇 아프리카 나라들의 공원 경비원들은 동물들을 밀렵하려는 사람들을 겁주기 위해 기관총으로 무장하고 있다. **prey** 악어는 강한 주둥이 안에 사냥감을 물고 물밑으로 끌고 들어가, 그것이 익사할 때까지 그곳에 붙잡고 있는다. / 고양이가 쥐와 다른 유해 동물들을 잡아먹기 때문에, 고대인들은 고양이를 가정에서 기르기 시작했다. **primate** 아프리카 연안의 섬나라 마다가스카르의 여우원숭이들도 영장류라는 것을 알고 있는 이들은 그리 많지 않다. **prolific** 암소는 현재 기후 변화를 야기하는 온실가스들 중 하나인 메탄을 많이 배출한다. **rodent** 설치류 동물은 이빨이 너무 길게 자라지 않도록 목재와 다른 딱딱한 물질들을 계속 물어뜯는다. **ruminant** 반추 동물의 위장은 네 개의 분리된 부분으로 나뉘어 있는데, 이것이 풀을 소화하는 것을 돕는다.

scavenger
[skǽvindʒər]
⑩ 청소 동물

v. scavenge

n. an animal that feeds on decaying things

Vultures are **scavengers** that fly in circles looking for the corpses of animals that have been recently killed.

---

specimen
[spésəmən]
⑩ 표본, 견본

n. an example of something that is used for scientific purposes

The museum displays stuffed **specimens** from nearly every species found in the country.

syn. sample

---

tendency
[téndənsi]
⑩ 성향, 기질

v. tend

n. a likelihood to behave in a certain way

Wild animals have a **tendency** to avoid human beings, but some grow to view them as a source of food.

syn. inclination

---

territorial
[tèrətɔ́:riəl]
⑩ 세력권을 주장하는

n. territory

adj. living in and being aggressively protective of a certain area

Chimpanzees live in extremely **territorial** groups that will attack and even kill the members of other groups.

---

vertebrate
[vɔ́:rtəbrət]
⑩ 척추동물

n. an animal with a backbone

All mammals, including human beings, are **vertebrates**, while insects and shellfish are invertebrates.

ant. invertebrate

---

vigorous
[vígərəs]
⑩ 활기찬, 활발한

n. vigor

adj. with or full of energy and enthusiasm

Along with singing, some birds will use **vigorous** dancing in order to attract and impress potential mates.

syn. energetic   *ant.* sluggish

---

scavenger 독수리들은 최근 죽임을 당한 동물들의 사체를 찾아 원을 그리며 나는 청소 동물이다.   **specimen** 그 박물관에는 그 나라에서 발견된 거의 모든 종의 박제 표본들이 전시되어 있다.   **tendency** 야생 동물들은 인간을 피하는 성향이 있지만, 일부는 인간을 식량원으로 여기게 된다.   **territorial** 침팬지들은 다른 무리들의 구성원들을 공격하거나 죽이기까지 할, 극단적으로 세력권을 주장하는 무리 안에서 생활한다.   **vertebrate** 인간을 포함한 모든 포유동물은 척추동물인 반면, 곤충과 갑각류는 무척추동물이다.   **vigorous** 어떤 새들은 짝이 될 가능성이 있는 새들의 주의를 끌고 깊은 인상을 주기 위해 노래와 함께 활기찬 춤을 사용할 것이다.

EXERCISES

ART & DESIGN

SOCIAL SCIENCE

NATURAL SCIENCE

HUMANITIES

EARTH & SPACE

SOCIAL ISSUES

A Match each definition with the correct word.

1 a hard outer layer that provides protection   ⓐ biped

2 active at night   ⓑ marsupial

3 an animal that walks on two legs   ⓒ scavenger

4 an animal that feeds on decaying things   ⓓ divergent

5 animals that are hunted and eaten by other animals   ⓔ armor

6 to collect and store large amounts of something   ⓕ nocturnal

7 moving or developing in a different direction   ⓖ hoard

8 a mammal that carries its young in a pouch   ⓗ prey

B Choose the word that is closest in meaning to each underlined word.

1 Some insects <u>imitate</u> the leaves of the plants they live on in order to avoid being seen.
   ⓐ consume   ⓑ transform   ⓒ mimic   ⓓ collaborate

2 People have a <u>tendency</u> to mistrust medications whose effects they can't directly feel.
   ⓐ memory   ⓑ inclination   ⓒ resistance   ⓓ similarity

3 <u>Vigorous</u> shaking speeds up chemical reactions by causing the compounds to mix together.
   ⓐ occasional   ⓑ mechanical   ⓒ energetic   ⓓ prolonged

4 The trees of the Amazon rainforest provide a <u>haven</u> for more than 1,200 species of birds.
   ⓐ refuge   ⓑ nutrient   ⓒ diversity   ⓓ experiment

5 Mosquitos <u>breed</u> so quickly that subsequent generations soon develop a resistance to pesticides.
   ⓐ feed   ⓑ maneuver   ⓒ subside   ⓓ reproduce

6 Upon seeing a <u>fearsome</u> animal, most people will experience a burst of adrenaline.
   ⓐ cowardly   ⓑ terrifying   ⓒ familiar   ⓓ sluggish

7 Physicists are trying to develop a more powerful microscope that will make it easier to <u>distinguish</u> various particles.
   ⓐ illustrate   ⓑ destroy   ⓒ merge   ⓓ differentiate

Lesson 24

[>] 곤충학

Entomology

★

abdomen
[ǽbdəmən, æbdóu-]

[명] 1. (곤충의) 복부
2. 배, 복부

n. 1 the rear part of an insect's body
2 the part of the body containing the internal organs

1. Both the digestive and reproductive systems of most insects can be found inside their **abdomens**.
2. After spending the night in the jungle, the man had insect bites all across his **abdomen**.

★★

abundant
[əbʌ́ndənt]

[형] 많은, 풍부한

n. abundance

adj. existing in large amounts

It is believed that ants are the most **abundant** insects on Earth, with a total population of about one quadrillion.

syn. plentiful *ant.* meager

★★★

adopt
[ədɑ́pt]

[동] 채택하다, 차용하다

n. adoption

v. to begin using or doing something new

When humans drastically change environmental conditions, insects are forced to **adopt** new feeding habits.

★★

appendage
[əpéndidʒ]

[명] (다리·꼬리·지느러미 등의) 부속지

v. append

n. a part of the body that extends from the main part

Scorpions have claws located on the end of two of their **appendages**, which they use for grabbing prey.

syn. limb

★★★

attack
[ətǽk]

[동] 공격하다, 덤벼들다

v. to aggressively attempt to cause harm

If their hive is disturbed or threatened, bees will **attack** the intruder by inflicting painful stings.

★★★

attract
[ətrǽkt]

[동] 끌어들이다

n. attraction

v. to cause to come closer

It is the heat of the human body that **attracts** hungry mosquitoes looking to feed on warm blood.

syn. entice *ant.* repel

---

abdomen 1. 대부분 곤충들의 소화 기관들과 생식 기관들 모두 복부 내에서 발견될 수 있다. 2. 밀림에서 밤을 보낸 후, 그 남자의 배 전체에 벌레 물린 자국이 생겼다. **abundant** 개미는 지구상에서 가장 수가 많은 곤충이라고 알려져 있는데, 총 개체수는 약 1,000조 마리이다. **adopt** 인간들이 환경 조건을 급격히 변화시킬 때, 곤충들은 새로운 먹이 섭취 습성을 채택할 수밖에 없다. **appendage** 전갈은 두 부속지(다리) 끝에 집게발을 지니고 있는데, 먹이를 잡을 때 사용한다. **attack** 벌집이 방해받거나 위협받으면, 벌들은 고통스러운 침을 쏘아 침입자를 공격할 것이다. **attract** 따뜻한 피를 먹으려 하는 굶주린 모기들을 끌어들이는 것은 인체의 열이다.

ART & DESIGN

SOCIAL SCIENCE

NATURAL SCIENCE

HUMANITIES

EARTH & SPACE

SOCIAL ISSUES

biodiversity
[bàioudivə́ːrsəti, -dai-]
ⓝ 생물의 다양성

n. a wide variety of species living in an environment

Insects account for more than half of the planet's total **biodiversity**, representing more than one million species.

bristle
[brísl]
ⓝ 짧고 억센 털, 강모

n. a short, stiff hair

Common house flies usually have a row of **bristles** located along the top of their thoraxes.

classify
[klǽsəfài]
ⓥ 분류하다, 구분하다

n. classification

v. to put something in a certain category

Spiders are not true insects, as they are **classified** as arachnids, along with scorpions and ticks.

syn. categorize

cocoon
[kəkúːn]
ⓝ 고치

n. a case that protects developing insects

Once a caterpillar has enclosed itself in a **cocoon**, it will stay there for about two weeks before emerging as a moth.

colony
[káləni]
ⓝ 군집, 군체, 집단

v. colonize

n. a group of people or animals living together in a certain place

Within a **colony** of ants, there is often a single queen that lays all of the eggs; the rest of the females are workers.

syn. community

conceal
[kənsíːl]
ⓥ 감추다, 숨기다

v. to keep something from view

Like many small creatures, insects tend to **conceal** themselves by blending in with their surroundings.

syn. hide   *ant.* expose

---

biodiversity 곤충들은 지구 전체 생물 다양성의 절반 이상을 차지하는데, 100만 종 이상이 이에 해당한다.   **bristle** 일반적인 집파리들에게는 보통 흉부의 윗부분을 따라 강모 한 줄이 나 있다.   **classify** 거미는 전갈, 진드기와 함께 거미류로 분류되기 때문에 순수 곤충이 아니다.   **cocoon** 애벌레가 고치 안에 에워싸이면, 나방이 되어 나오기 전까지 약 2주 정도 그 안에 있을 것이다.   **colony** 개미 군체 안에는 보통 모든 알들을 낳는 한 마리의 여왕개미가 있다. 나머지 암컷들은 일꾼들이다.   **conceal** 많은 작은 생명체들처럼, 곤충은 주변 환경에 섞여 자신을 숨기는 경향이 있다.

devour
[diváuər]

Ⓥ 게걸스럽게 먹다

v. to eat hungrily and quickly

Gypsy moth caterpillars can **devour** the leaves of trees at an alarming rate, causing serious damage to forests.

ant. nibble

disseminate
[disémənèit]

Ⓥ 퍼트리다, 전파하다

v. to spread something widely

A number of deadly diseases are **disseminated** by insects, including malaria and yellow fever.

syn. disperse   *ant.* concentrate

distract
[distrǽkt]

Ⓥ 주의를 돌리게 하다, 산란하게 하다

n. distraction

v. to draw someone's attention away from what they are doing

The brown marmorated stink bug **distracts** hungry predators by releasing an extremely unpleasant odor.

syn. divert

elongated
[iló:ŋgeitid]

Ⓐ 아주 가늘고 긴, 길쭉한

v. elongate

adj. unusually long and thin

The sawyer beetle is a small, black insect with a pair of **elongated** antennae that are longer than its body.

equip
[ikwíp]

Ⓥ (장비·준비를) 갖추다

n. equipment

v. to provide with tools or abilities

Some insects are **equipped** with two pairs of wings that allow them to fly quickly through the air.

exoskeleton
[èksouskélətn]

Ⓝ 외골격

n. a hard, protective outer covering

The **exoskeletons** of insects are made of a material called chitin, which does not grow with the rest of the body.

ant. endoskeleton

---

devour 매미나방 애벌레는 급속도로 나뭇잎들을 먹어 치울 수 있어, 숲에 심각한 피해를 입힌다.   **disseminate** 말라리아와 황열병을 포함한 다수의 치명적인 질병들이 곤충들에 의해 전파된다.   **distract** 갈색 방귀벌레는 매우 불쾌한 악취를 뿜어 굶주린 포식자들을 산란시킨다.   **elongated** 수염하늘소는 자신의 몸보다 긴 한 쌍의 아주 길쭉한 더듬이를 가진 작고 검은 곤충이다.   **equip** 몇몇 곤충들은 공중을 빠르게 날 수 있게 해 주는 두 쌍의 날개를 갖추고 있다.
exoskeleton 곤충들의 외골격은 키틴이라는 물질로 이루어져 있는데, 이것은 몸의 나머지 부분과 함께 자라지 않는다.

★★★ **flexible**
[fléksəbl]
[형] 1. 유연한, 잘 구부러지는
2. 융통성 있는, 적응성 있는
v. flex

adj. **1 able to bend without breaking** *syn.* pliable *ant.* rigid
2 able to deal with different conditions *syn.* adaptable

1. Aerodynamics experts are studying the **flexible** wings of insects to better understand how they aid flight.
2. While some insects need specific environmental conditions to survive, others are more **flexible**.

★★★ **fragile**
[frǽdʒəl]
[형] 부서지기 쉬운, 취약한

adj. **easily broken**

The flying wings of beetles are thin and **fragile**, so they remain covered by a pair of hard outer wings when not in use.

syn. delicate *ant.* durable

★ **gait**
[geit]
[명] 걸음걸이, 걷는 모양

n. **the manner in which a person or animal walks**

When fleeing danger, some insects will change their **gait** by running with three legs touching the ground at all times.

syn. stride

★★★ **hatch**
[hætʃ]
[동] 1. (알이) 부화되다
2. (새·곤충 등이) 부화하다

v. **1 to open up and release young** **2 to come out of an egg**

1. Mosquito eggs, which can be found in stagnant water, usually **hatch** within 72 hours of being laid.
2. Once cicada young **hatch** from eggs laid in trees, they fall to the ground and immediately begin burrowing into the dirt.

★ **infested**
[inféstid]
[형] 들끓는
v. infest

adj. **having large numbers of something harmful or negative**

A pet dog or cat that has fleas can quickly cause the entire house to become **infested**.

syn. overrun

★★ **invasive**
[invéisiv]
[형] 침입하는, 침해의
v. invade

adj. **not native to the area**

Invasive fruit flies are a huge problem in the state of California, where they cause millions of dollars of damage to fruit.

ant. indigenous

flexible 1. 기체 역학 전문가들은 곤충들의 유연한 날개가 어떻게 비행을 돕는지 더 잘 이해하기 위해 연구하고 있다. 2. 어떤 곤충들은 살아남기 위해 특정한 환경 조건을 필요로 하지만, 다른 곤충들은 더 쉽게 적응한다. **fragile** 딱정벌레의 비행을 위한 날개는 얇고 약해서, 사용하지 않을 때는 한 쌍의 단단한 바깥 날개로 덮여 있다. **gait** 위험에서 달아날 때, 몇몇 곤충들은 항상 세 다리가 땅에 닿은 채 뛰는 방식으로 걸음걸이를 바꿀 것이다. **hatch** 1. 고인 물에서 발견될 수 있는 모기 알들은 보통 알을 낳은 지 72시간 안에 부화된다. 2. 나무에 낳아 놓은 알에서 새끼 매미들이 부화하면, 그것들은 땅으로 떨어져 바로 흙으로 파고들기 시작한다. **infested** 벼룩이 있는 애완견이나 애완 고양이는 빠르게 온 집안을 벼룩으로 들끓게 할 수 있다. **invasive** 침습성 초파리는 캘리포니아 주에서 큰 골칫거리인데, 과일에 수백만 달러의 손해를 끼친다.

★★

larva

[lά:rvə]

[명] 유충, 애벌레

n. **the immature form of an insect**

The **larva** of an insect often has an appearance that is totally different from that of a fully mature adult.

Useful Tips

larva의 복수형은 larvae이다.

★

mesh

[meʃ]

[동] 딱 들어맞다, 맞물리다

[명] 그물망

v. **to fit together**

A tiny species of planthopper has gears in its legs that **mesh** when it hops, keeping the insect steady.

n. **a structure of interlaced material** *syn.* netting

In countries where malaria is a problem, people sleep beneath mosquito nets or some other kind of **mesh** material.

★★

metamorphosis

[mètəmɔ́:rfəsis]

[명] 탈바꿈, 변태

n. **the act of changing or developing into something new**

After undergoing **metamorphosis**, a butterfly must wait for its new wings to dry before it can fly away.

syn. transformation

★★

olfactory

[ɑlfǽktəri]

[형] 후각의

adj. **relating to odors or the sense of smell**

An ant that finds a source of food can create an **olfactory** trail for other ants to follow by releasing pheromones.

syn. odorous

★★

paralyze

[pǽrəlàiz]

[동] 마비시키다

n. paralysis

v. **to cause someone to be unable to move**

Some species of wasps **paralyze** spiders with their sting before feeding them to their young.

syn. immobilize

★★

pierce

[piərs]

[동] 뚫다

v. **to pass through a hard surface**

Insects such as aphids **pierce** the surface of plants in order to feed on the liquids within.

syn. penetrate

---

larva 곤충의 유충은 종종 다 자란 성충과는 완전히 다른 모습을 지니고 있다. **mesh** 플랜트호퍼 소형 종의 다리에는 깡충 뛸 때 맞물리는 톱니바퀴가 있어서, 그 곤충을 안정적으로 유지시켜 준다. / 말라리아 문제가 있는 나라들에서는 사람들이 모기장이나 다른 종류의 그물망 안에서 잔다. **metamorphosis** 나비는 변태 과정을 겪은 후 날 수 있게 되기 전까지 새 날개가 마르기를 기다려야 한다. **olfactory** 식량원을 찾는 개미는 페로몬을 내뿜음으로써 다른 개미들이 쫓아올 수 있는 후각적인 자취를 만들 수 있다. **paralyze** 몇몇 말벌 종들은 새끼들에게 거미를 먹이로 주기 전에 침을 쏘아 마비시킨다. **pierce** 진딧물 같은 곤충들은 식물에 있는 수분을 섭취하기 위해 식물의 표면을 뚫는다.

★
raptorial
[ræptɔ́ːriəl]
⒜ 생물을 잡아 먹는, 육식의

n. raptor

adj. relating to the seizing of prey

Praying mantises are **raptorial** insects that use their curved forelegs to reach out and grab their prey.

syn. predatory

Useful **Tips**

보통 raptor는 매나 독수리와 같은 '맹금류'를 나타낼 때 쓰이며, 때로는 공룡의 한 종류를 말할 때 쓰이기도 한다.

★
★
★
repel
[ripél]
ⓝ 쫓아 버리다

n., adj. repellant

v. to drive someone or something away

Many companies sell sprays and lotions that are designed to **repel** insects, but not all of them are effective.

syn. repulse   *ant.* attract

★
scuttle
[skʌ́tl]
ⓥ (빠르게) 종종걸음 치다

v. to move with short, quick steps

Once the lights were turned on, all of the cockroaches in the room **scuttled** into dark corners.

syn. scamper

★
★
secrete
[sikríːt]
ⓥ 분비하다

v. to produce and release a substance

Aphids **secrete** a sweet liquid called honeydew, which is a favorite food of some ant species.

★
★
segment
[ségmənt]
ⓝ 부분, 조각
ⓥ 나누다, 분할하다

n. one distinct part of a whole   *syn.* section

One pair of legs is attached to each of the three **segments** of the insect's thorax.

v. to divide a whole into distinct parts

All true insects have six legs, and their bodies are **segmented** into three main parts.

★
★
signal
[sígnəl]
ⓥ 신호를 보내다

v. to communicate through a gesture or sound

Certain termites **signal** that there is danger by violently shaking their heads, which sends shockwaves through the nest.

syn. indicate

---

raptorial 사마귀는 구부러진 앞다리들을 뻗어 먹이를 잡는 데 사용하는 육식 곤충이다.   **repel** 많은 회사들이 벌레를 쫓아 버리도록 만들어진 스프레이와 로션들을 판매하지만, 그것들 모두가 효과 있는 것은 아니다.   **scuttle** 불이 켜지자, 방에 있는 모든 바퀴벌레들이 어두운 구석으로 빠르게 움직였다.
secrete 진딧물은 감로라는 단물을 분비하는데, 이는 몇몇 개미 종들이 좋아하는 먹이이다.   **segment** 곤충 흉부의 세 부분에는 각각 한 쌍의 다리가 달려 있다. / 모든 순수 곤충은 다리가 여섯 개 있고, 몸은 세 개의 주요 부분들로 나눠진다.   **signal** 어떤 흰개미들은 머리를 세게 흔들어 개미굴 전체에 충격파를 보내 위험이 있다는 신호를 보낸다.

ART & DESIGN

SOCIAL SCIENCE

NATURAL SCIENCE

HUMANITIES

EARTH & SPACE

SOCIAL ISSUES

suck
★★★★
[sʌk]

동 빨다, 빨아들이다

v. to remove a gas or liquid using the mouth or suction

Bed bugs are tiny creatures that survive by **sucking** blood from the bodies of sleeping people.

syn. extract

---

suspend
★★
[səspénd]

동 1. 매달다, 걸다
2. (일시적으로) 중단하다, 유예하다

n. suspension

v. 1 to hang from above   *syn.* dangle
2 to temporarily stop something   *syn.* delay

1. While weaving its web in the upper corner of the doorway, the spider **suspended** itself from a single thread.
2. The baseball game was **suspended** after a large number of bees flew onto the field.

---

swarm
★★
[swɔːrm]

동 떼를 지어 다니다
명 (곤충의) 떼, 무리

v. to gather together in a large group and go somewhere

Flying ants **swarm** once a year, usually in mid-summer, taking to the air in order to find a mate.

n. a large gathering that moves together

A single **swarm** of locusts can contain more than ten billion individual insects.

---

terminate
★★
[tɔ́ːrmənèit]

동 끝내다, 종료하다

n. termination

v. to end something

As each successive stage in an insect's life cycle is **terminated**, a new one immediately begins.

syn. discontinue   *ant.* establish

---

transparent
★★
[trænspɛ́ərənt]

형 투명한, 속이 보이는

n. transparency

adj. capable of being seen through

The glasswing butterfly of South and Central America is the only butterfly species that has **transparent** wings.

syn. clear   *ant.* opaque

---

venomous
★
[vénəməs]

형 독이 있는

n. venom

adj. capable of producing and injecting poison

Centipedes are multi-legged creatures that are feared for their **venomous** bites, which can be very painful.

---

suck 빈대는 잠자는 사람들의 몸에서 피를 빨아먹으며 사는 아주 작은 생물이다.   **suspend** 1. 그 거미는 출입구의 위쪽 모퉁이에 거미줄을 짜는 동안, 한 가닥의 줄에 매달려 있었다.   2. 그 야구 경기는 많은 벌들이 경기장에 날아 들어온 후 중단되었다.   **swarm** 날개미는 일 년에 한 번, 보통 한여름에 짝을 찾기 위해 떼를 지어 날아 다닌다. / 하나의 메뚜기 무리에는 100억 마리 이상의 메뚜기들이 있을 수 있다.   **terminate** 곤충 생활 주기에서 연이은 각각의 단계가 끝나면, 새로운 단계가 바로 시작된다.   **transparent** 남아메리카와 중앙아메리카에 사는 유리 날개 나비는 투명한 날개를 지닌 유일한 나비 종이다.   **venomous** 지네는 물리면 아주 고통스러울 수 있는 독성으로 두려움의 대상이 된, 다족류 생물이다.

EXERCISES

ART & DESIGN

SOCIAL SCIENCE

NATURAL SCIENCE

HUMANITIES

EARTH & SPACE

SOCIAL ISSUES

A Match each definition with the correct word.

1 the immature form of an insect   ⓐ invasive

2 to eat hungrily and quickly   ⓑ exoskeleton

3 not native to the area   ⓒ bristle

4 a hard, protective outer covering   ⓓ secrete

5 unusually long and thin   ⓔ devour

6 to produce and release a substance   ⓕ larva

7 a short, stiff hair   ⓖ equip

8 to provide with tools or abilities   ⓗ elongated

B Choose the word that is closest in meaning to each underlined word.

1 Red blood cells have <u>flexible</u> membranes, allowing them to squeeze through capillaries.
   ⓐ massive   ⓑ crooked   ⓒ uneven   ⓓ pliable

2 The bright colors and fragrant smells of flowers <u>attract</u> not only insects but also humans.
   ⓐ entice   ⓑ gratify   ⓒ nourish   ⓓ perplex

3 Some drugs can temporarily <u>paralyze</u> parts of the body by blocking nerve impulses.
   ⓐ terminate   ⓑ immobilize   ⓒ soothe   ⓓ diagnose

4 Animals constantly seek out places where predators are scarce and food is <u>abundant</u>.
   ⓐ distinctive   ⓑ plentiful   ⓒ diverse   ⓓ meager

5 Some plastics are durable and <u>transparent</u>, making them potential substitutes for glass.
   ⓐ lightweight   ⓑ common   ⓒ clear   ⓓ inexpensive

6 When criminals seek to <u>conceal</u> their identities, the police now turn to genetic testing.
   ⓐ transform   ⓑ expose   ⓒ explain   ⓓ hide

7 The rib cage is designed to encase and protect the body's <u>fragile</u> internal organs.
   ⓐ vital   ⓑ varied   ⓒ delicate   ⓓ interconnected

189

atom
[ǽtəm]
ⓝ 원자
adj. atomic

n. the smallest unit of a chemical element

It is an established scientific fact that, with the exception of energy, everything in the universe is made up of **atoms**.

collide
[kəláid]
ⓥ 충돌하다
n. collision

v. to make contact with great force

When two moving bodies **collide**, they each exert force on the other, causing changes to their motion.

syn. crash

compact
[kəmpǽkt]
ⓐ 조밀한, 빽빽한

adj. small or tightly packed

White dwarfs are **compact** stars that are about the size of the Earth but have a mass similar to that of the Sun.

syn. condensed

conduct
[kándʌkt]
ⓥ 1. (열이나 전기를) 전도하다
2. (특정한 활동을) 하다
n. conductor

v. 1 to allow heat or electricity to pass through
2 to organize and carry out a complex activity

1. Metal **conducts** electricity more efficiently than wood for a number of reasons, including the fact that it is denser.

2. The Large Hadron Collider is used to **conduct** experiments involving the movement and behavior of particles.

deviate
[díːvièit]
ⓥ 벗어나다
n. deviation

v. to behave in an unexpected way

When the behavior of a substance **deviates** from the norm during a physics experiment, further investigation is warranted.

syn. differ

disturb
[distə́ːrb]
ⓥ 교란하다, 방해하다
n. disturbance

v. to affect something's position or interfere with its functioning

When a balanced system is **disturbed** by an external force, it will likely adjust to the change in conditions.

syn. upset

---

atom 에너지를 제외한 우주의 모든 것은 원자로 만들어졌다는 것이 과학적으로 확립된 사실이다.　**collide** 움직이는 두 물체가 충돌하면, 각 물체는 상대편에 힘을 행사해 움직임에 변화를 준다.　**compact** 백색 왜성들은 크기가 지구와 비슷하지만 질량은 태양과 비슷한 고밀도 항성들이다.　**conduct** 1. 금속은 밀도가 더 높다는 점을 포함한 여러 가지 이유로 목재보다 더 효율적으로 전기를 전도한다.　2. 대형 강입자 충돌기는 미립자들의 운동과 작용에 관한 실험을 하는 데 사용된다. **deviate** 물리 실험 중 어떤 물질의 작용이 표준에서 벗어나면, 심층 조사를 하게 된다.　**disturb** 어떤 균형 잡힌 체계가 외부의 힘에 의해 교란될 때, 그 체계는 조건 변화에 적응할 가능성이 높다.

ART & DESIGN

SOCIAL SCIENCE

NATURAL SCIENCE

HUMANITIES

EARTH & SPACE

SOCIAL ISSUES

★
electrolyte
[iléktrəlàit]
ⓝ 전해액[질]

n. a liquid that electricity can pass through
Electrolytes are present throughout the human body, as they are found in blood, tissue, and bodily fluids.

★
★
equilibrium
[ìːkwəlíbriəm]
ⓝ 평형, 균형
adj. equal

n. a state of balance
When all of the forces acting on an object are in balance, the object is said to be in a state of **equilibrium**.
syn. stability   *ant.* instability

★
★
facilitate
[fəsílətèit]
ⓥ 용이하게 하다
n. facilitation

v. to help something occur more easily
Today's physicists possess the distinct advantage of having access to supercomputers that can **facilitate** their complex calculations.
syn. expedite   *ant.* impede

★
★
factor
[fǽktər]
ⓝ 요인, 인자

n. something that influences an outcome
The temperature of a material is an important **factor** to consider when determining its density.
syn. aspect

★
★
frequency
[fríːkwənsi]
ⓝ 1. (전자파·소리 등의) 진동수, 주파수
　 2. 빈도
adj. frequent

n. 1 the rate of vibration of a wave
　 2 how often something occurs over a period of time
1. As the **frequency** of the wave begins to decrease, its wavelength will be observed to increase.
2. As the rate of technological development sped up, breakthroughs in the field of physics occurred with greater **frequency**.

★
★
friction
[fríkʃən]
ⓝ 마찰(력)

n. the resistance that occurs when an object moves across a surface
Friction occurs due to electromagnetic attraction between charged particles in the two objects that have come in contact.

---

electrolyte 전해액은 인체 전체에 퍼져 있어, 혈액, 조직, 체액에서 발견된다.　**equilibrium** 한 물체에 작용하는 모든 힘들이 균형을 이룰 때, 그 물체는 평형 상태에 있다고 한다.　**facilitate** 오늘날의 물리학자들은 복잡한 계산을 용이하게 할 수 있는 슈퍼 컴퓨터들에 접속하는 분명한 이점을 갖고 있다.　**factor** 어떤 물질의 온도는 그것의 밀도를 측정할 때 고려해야 할 중요한 요인이다.　**frequency** 1. 그 파의 진동수가 줄어들기 시작하면, 파장이 증가하는 것을 보게 될 것이다. 2. 기술 발전 속도가 빨라지면서, 물리학 분야의 획기적 발전들이 더 많은 빈도로 나왔다.　**friction** 서로 접촉하게 된 두 물체 내 하전 입자들 사이의 전자기적 인력 때문에 마찰이 발생한다.

★

inertia
[inə́ːrʃə]
[명] 관성

n. the tendency of objects to stay still or in uniform motion unless acted on by an external force

In terms of motion, the principle of **inertia** applies only to objects moving in a straight line.

★★★

infinite
[ínfənət]
[형] 무한한
n. infinity

adj. having no limit

The amount of stars in the universe may seem **infinite**, but an estimate of their number can be calculated.

syn. limitless *ant.* finite

★★

inquiry
[inkwáiəri, ínkwəri]
[명] 연구, 조사
v. inquire

n. an investigation or request for information

Students of physics are encouraged to make **inquiries** about the concepts they are learning.

syn. question *ant.* response

★★

inverse
[invə́ːrs]
[형] 반대의, 역의
n. inversion

adj. occurring in a wholly opposite way

When it comes to the forces that are known to science, acceleration can be said to be **inverse** to mass.

syn. contrary

★

irradiate
[iréidièit]
[동] 방사능 처리를 하다

v. to treat with or expose to radiation

Food is sometimes **irradiated** to protect it from pests and slow down the rate at which it decays.

★

jettison
[dʒétəsn]
[동] (필요 없는 것을) 버리다, 폐기하다

v. to abandon or get rid of something unwanted

After a launched rocket has used up its fuel, the tank will be **jettisoned** to decrease the rocket's weight.

syn. discard *ant.* retain

Useful Tips

배에서 고의적으로 버려져 해안으로 떠밀려 오는 표류 화물을 jetsam이라 하는 반면, 고의적으로 버려진 것이 아닌 표착 화물은 flotsam이라 한다.

---

inertia 운동 면에서, 관성의 법칙은 직선으로 움직이는 물체에만 적용된다. **infinite** 우주 항성들의 총계는 무한한 것처럼 보일 수 있지만, 대략적인 수치는 계산될 수 있다. **inquiry** 물리학을 배우는 학생들에게 그들이 배우고 있는 개념들에 대해 조사할 것이 권장된다. **inverse** 힘에 관해 과학에 알려진 바로는, 가속도는 질량에 반한다. **irradiate** 식품을 해충으로부터 보호하고 부패 속도를 늦추기 위해 때때로 방사능 처리한다. **jettison** 발사된 로켓이 연료를 다 소진한 후, 로켓 무게를 줄이기 위해 연료 탱크는 버려질 것이다.

ART & DESIGN

SOCIAL SCIENCE

NATURAL SCIENCE

HUMANITIES

EARTH & SPACE

SOCIAL ISSUES

magnitude

[mǽgnətʃùːd]

몡 규모, 정도

n. the size, degree, or importance of something

The **magnitude** of an earthquake is determined by measuring the amount of energy that is released in the form of waves.

syn. degree

---

melt

[melt]

통 1. 녹다
2. 녹이다

v. 1 to change from a solid to a liquid   *syn.* liquefy   *ant.* solidify
2 to turn a solid into a liquid   *syn.* liquefy   *ant.* solidify

1. Upon reaching a certain temperature, many solid materials will begin to **melt** into a liquid form.

2. It requires a temperature of approximately 1510 ℃ to **melt** stainless steel.

---

modulate

[mádʒulèit]

통 조절하다, 바꾸다

n. modulation

v. to change or vary something to achieve an effect

It is by **modulating** radio waves that information can be transmitted to devices such as radios, televisions, and cell phones.

---

molecule

[máləkjùːl]

몡 분자

adj. molecular

n. the smallest unit of a chemical compound

The experiment showed the students how to produce hydrogen by splitting water **molecules** using electricity.

---

nucleus

[njúːkliəs]

몡 핵

adj. nuclear

n. the central core of something

In 1911, Ernest Rutherford discovered the atomic **nucleus**, the dense region made up of both protons and neutrons at the center of an atom.

---

oscillate

[ásəlèit]

통 진동하다

n. oscillation

v. to vary regularly in size, position, or degree around a central point

As a wave moves in a given direction, the particles within it will **oscillate** back and forth.

---

magnitude 지진의 규모는 진동파 형태로 방출되는 에너지의 양을 측정해 결정된다.   **melt** 1. 많은 고체 물질들이 특정 온도에 도달하면, 액체 형태로 녹기 시작할 것이다. 2. 스테인리스 스틸을 녹이려면 섭씨 1510도 정도의 온도가 필요하다.   **modulate** 정보가 라디오, 텔레비전, 휴대전화 같은 기기로 전송될 수 있는 것은 바로 전파 조절에 의해서이다.   **molecule** 그 실험은 전기를 사용해 물 분자들을 쪼갬으로써 수소를 발생시키는 법을 학생들에게 보여 주었다.
nucleus 1911년에 Ernest Rutherford가 원자핵을 발견했는데, 그것은 원자 중심에 있는 양성자와 중성자로 이루어진 밀도가 높은 부분이다.   **oscillate** 어떤 파가 특정 방향으로 움직일 때, 그 안의 입자들은 앞뒤로 진동할 것이다.

★★★

random

[rǽndəm]

[형] 무작위의

adj. without method or pattern

The idea that quantum mechanics is truly **random** is not consistent with the laws of physics.

syn. haphazard *ant.* methodical

★★

refract

[rifrǽkt]

[동] 굴절시키다

n. refraction

v. to change the direction of light

When beams of sunlight pass through a glass of water on a table, they will be **refracted**.

★★★

rotate

[róuteit]

[동] 회전하다, 회전시키다

n. rotation

v. to move or be moved in a circle around an axis

An object moving through space will **rotate** around an axis passing through the center of its mass.

syn. spin

★★

stationary

[stéiʃənèri]

[형] 정지된

adj. unmoving

A **stationary** wave is formed by two similar waves that are moving in opposite directions.

syn. immobile *ant.* mobile

Useful Tips

stationary와 철자가 비슷한 stationery는 '문구류'라는 의미이므로 혼동하지 않도록 유의한다.

★★

variation

[vὲəriéiʃən]

[명] 변화, 차이

v. vary

n. changes or differences in amount, type, or level

Variations in the Earth's orbit around the Sun can significantly affect the distance between the two bodies.

syn. fluctuation *ant.* uniformity

★★

velocity

[vəlɑ́səti]

[명] 속도

n. the speed at which something moves in a certain direction

The constant speed that is reached by a falling object is known as its terminal **velocity**.

---

random 양자역학이 순전히 무작위라는 개념은 물리 법칙들에 위배된다. **refract** 햇살이 식탁에 놓인 물잔을 통과할 때, 굴절될 것이다. **rotate** 우주에서 이동하는 물체는 그 질량의 중심을 지나는 축을 중심으로 회전할 것이다. **stationary** 정상파는 서로 반대 방향으로 움직이는 두 개의 유사한 파들에 의해 형성된다. **variation** 태양 주위를 도는 지구 궤도상의 변화는 그 두 천체(태양과 지구) 간의 거리에 상당한 영향을 줄 수 있다. **velocity** 낙하하는 물체가 도달하는 일정한 속도를 종단 속도라고 한다.

EXERCISES

ART & DESIGN

SOCIAL SCIENCE

NATURAL SCIENCE

HUMANITIES

EARTH & SPACE

SOCIAL ISSUES

A Match each definition with the correct word.

1 to treat with or expose to radiation   ⓐ frequency

2 the smallest unit of a chemical element   ⓑ electrolyte

3 a liquid that electricity can pass through   ⓒ atom

4 the rate of vibration of a wave   ⓓ refract

5 to change or vary something to achieve an effect   ⓔ friction

6 the size, degree, or importance of something   ⓕ irradiate

7 to change the direction of light   ⓖ magnitude

8 the resistance that occurs when an object moves across a surface   ⓗ modulate

B Choose the word that is closest in meaning to each underlined word.

1 Scientists suspect that there are complex patterns behind so-called random mutations.
   ⓐ singular   ⓑ haphazard   ⓒ compact   ⓓ destructive

2 Certain kinds of geckos will sometimes jettison their tails to confuse an attacking predator.
   ⓐ discard   ⓑ wiggle   ⓒ lengthen   ⓓ contort

3 When humans upset the ecosystem, it is their responsibility to restore its equilibrium.
   ⓐ scope   ⓑ strength   ⓒ stability   ⓓ scale

4 The human genome was mapped in order to facilitate our understanding of genetics.
   ⓐ expedite   ⓑ administer   ⓒ scrutinize   ⓓ reconstruct

5 When particles collide during chemical reactions, they require energy to break their bonds.
   ⓐ merge   ⓑ disturb   ⓒ crash   ⓓ expand

6 As the snow begins to melt and the frozen soil softens, early blooming flowers emerge.
   ⓐ reposition   ⓑ thicken   ⓒ increase   ⓓ liquefy

7 If human beings are forced to remain stationary for extended periods, their muscles will begin to atrophy.
   ⓐ solitary   ⓑ finite   ⓒ contrary   ⓓ immobile

A Choose the correct words.

1 The word deviate has the same meaning as

    ⓐ adjust   ⓑ differ   ⓒ analyze   ⓓ pursue

2 The word suspend has the same meaning as

    ⓐ continue   ⓑ suggest   ⓒ divide   ⓓ dangle

3 The word carnivorous has the same meaning as

    ⓐ cold-blooded   ⓑ meat-eating   ⓒ well-behaved   ⓓ fast-moving

4 The word replicate has the same meaning as

    ⓐ block   ⓑ break   ⓒ copy   ⓓ delete

5 The word variation has the same meaning as

    ⓐ generation   ⓑ reformation   ⓒ acclimation   ⓓ fluctuation

6 The word disseminate has the same meaning as

    ⓐ extend   ⓑ meld   ⓒ peel   ⓓ disperse

7 The word prolific has the same meaning as

    ⓐ fruitful   ⓑ respected   ⓒ adept   ⓓ remote

8 The word efficacy has the same meaning as

    ⓐ efficiency   ⓑ indecision   ⓒ nostalgia   ⓓ controversy

B Fill in the blanks with the best words from the box.

1 Giraffes use their long, maneuverable tongues to avoid the _____ of acacia trees when feeding.

2 Plants can be _____, as they need to protect resources such as water from nearby competitors.

3 _____ insects, such as dragonflies, spend the early portion of their lives living in the water.

4 Centrifuge machines _____ at great speed to separate the components of substances.

5 Fish _____ to protect themselves from predators, which are confused by the movements of the group.

6 There are many different kinds of tiny _____, including fungi and mites, that live on human skin.

| aquatic | territorial | swarm | rotate | thorns | organisms |

C Read the following passages.

ART & DESIGN

SOCIAL SCIENCE

NATURAL SCIENCE

HUMANITIES

EARTH & SPACE

SOCIAL ISSUES

[1-2] **1** Choose one word that fits both blanks.

> Ornamental pear trees, which are popular with gardeners and landscapers, usually _____ in early spring. Although they are quite beautiful, each white _____ has only a mild scent. In fact, some species are said to possess a rather unpleasant smell.

    ⓐ bark   ⓑ blossom   ⓒ segment   ⓓ cluster

2 Choose the appropriate pair of words to fill in the blanks.

> Scientists cannot _____ insect-like creatures as true insects unless they meet certain criteria, such as having six legs. Another criterion is that their bodies must contain three distinct sections. The first is the head, the second is the thorax, and the last part is the _____.

    ⓐ nurture — hoard   ⓑ classify — abdomen

    ⓒ facilitate — armor   ⓓ perceive — exoskeleton

[3-4]

> White mice are often used for experiments. There are two main reasons for this. The first is that they share many characteristics, both genetic and behavioral, with humans. The second is that they breed quickly. This gives scientists specimens from multiple generations to work with.

3 In the context of the passage, breed means _____.

    ⓐ devour   ⓑ infest   ⓒ conceal   ⓓ reproduce

4 The word specimens in the passage could best be replaced by

    ⓐ vertebrates   ⓑ rates   ⓒ inquiries   ⓓ samples

[5-6]

> The atom is said to be the building block of the universe. And at the very center of every atom, you will find the _____. Despite the fact that it represents only a tiny portion of the atom's size, it contains almost all of its mass. This is because it is very compact, packed full of protons and neutrons.

5 Choose the word that is most suitable for the blank.

    ⓐ nucleus   ⓑ molecule   ⓒ electrolyte   ⓓ magnitude

6 The word compact in the passage is closest in meaning to

    ⓐ stationary   ⓑ condensed   ⓒ intense   ⓓ drastic

Lesson 26 Chemistry

[>] 화학

★

affinity
[əfínəti]
[명] 친화력

n. a measure of the tendency of chemical substances to combine

The element fluorine has a high **affinity** for hydrogen, with which it combines to form HF, or hydrogen fluorine.

★★

bind
[baind]
[동] 결합하다
n. bond

v. to join or unite

There are a number of different kinds of proteins that can cause two or more molecules to **bind** together.

syn. fasten *ant.* separate

★

cohesion
[kouhíːʒən]
[명] 응집력
adj. cohesive

n. the act of fitting together to form a whole

Water has a higher **cohesion** than many other substances, which is the reason it tends to form droplets.

★★

compound
[kámpaund]
[명] 화합물, 혼합물

n. a whole made of two or more combined parts

Table salt is an example of a chemical **compound**, as it is made up of one sodium atom and one chloride atom.

syn. composite

★★★

dissolve
[dizálv]
[동] 녹다, 용해되다

v. to incorporate a solid into a liquid

Most of the material **dissolved** in the water, but some solid particles remained visible at the bottom of the glass.

★★★

emit
[imít]
[동] 내뿜다, 방출하다
n. emission

v. to produce and release something

Atoms **emit** energy in the form of light after they have been excited to an unusually high level.

syn. discharge *ant.* absorb

---

affinity 불소 원소는 수소에 대한 높은 친화력을 가지는데, 수소와 결합하여 플루오르화[불화] 수소(HF)가 된다. **bind** 두 개 이상의 분자를 서로 결합하게 할 수 있는 여러 다른 종류의 단백질들이 있다. **cohesion** 물은 다른 많은 물질들보다 높은 응집력을 가지고 있는데, 그것이 작은 물방울들을 형성하기 쉬운 이유이다. **compound** 식용 소금은 화학 화합물의 한 예인데, 한 개의 나트륨 원자와 한 개의 염소[염화물] 원자로 구성되어 있기 때문이다. **dissolve** 대부분의 물질은 물에 용해되었지만, 일부 고체 입자들은 눈에 보일 정도로 유리 바닥에 남아 있었다. **emit** 원자들은 매우 높은 수준으로 자극받은 후, 빛의 형태로 에너지를 방출한다.

ART & DESIGN

SOCIAL SCIENCE

NATURAL SCIENCE

HUMANITIES

EARTH & SPACE

SOCIAL ISSUES

exothermic
[èksəθɔ́ːrmik]
📰 발열성의

adj. involving the release of heat

A burst of brightly colored fireworks exploding in the sky is a prime example of an **exothermic** process.

ant. endothermic

extinguish
[ikstíŋgwiʃ]
📰 불을 끄다

v. to put out a fire

Instead of water, dry chemicals such as sodium bicarbonate are sometimes used to **extinguish** fires.

Useful Tips
우리가 불을 끌 때 사용하는 소화기는 영어로 fire extinguisher라고 한다.

flammable
[flǽməbl]
📰 가연성의, 인화성의
n., v. flame

adj. capable of easily catching fire

Chlorine fluoride, which is used to make rocket fuel, is believed to be the most **flammable** of all the chemical gases.

syn. combustible   *ant.* fireproof

formula
[fɔ́ːrmjulə]
📰 화학식, 공식

n. a set of chemical symbols showing the components of a substance

One of the first chemical **formulas** learned by schoolchildren is CO_2, which is more commonly known as carbon dioxide.

hydrolysis
[haidráləsis]
📰 가수 분해

n. a chemical reaction caused by water

Hydrolysis is used to break chemical bonds, which means it can be considered the opposite of a condensation reaction.

hydrophobic
[hàidrəfóubik]
📰 소수성(물과의 친화력이 적은 성질)의

adj. unable to mix with water

It is the **hydrophobic** molecules that are found in oil that famously prevent it from mixing with water.

ant. hydrophilic

Useful Tips
hydrophobic은 hydrophobia(광견병)의 형용사형으로도 쓰인다.

---

exothermic 하늘에서 터지는 화려한 색의 불꽃놀이 폭발은 발열 과정의 전형적인 예이다.   **extinguish** 물 대신, 때때로 중탄산나트륨과 같은 건조한 화학 물질이 불을 끄는 데 사용된다.   **flammable** 로켓 연료를 만드는 데 사용되는 플루오르화 염소는 모든 화학 가스들을 통틀어 가장 가연성이 높다고 여겨진다.   **formula** 학생들이 배우는 첫 화학식 중 하나는 흔히 이산화탄소로 알려진 CO_2이다.   **hydrolysis** 가수 분해는 화학적 결합을 깨는 데 사용되는데, 이는 축합 반응의 반대라고 간주될 수 있다는 것을 의미한다.   **hydrophobic** 기름이 물과 잘 섞이지 않도록 하는 것은 기름에서 발견되는 소수성 분자들이다.

★

inorganic

[ìnɔːrgǽnik]

[형] 무기물의

adj. not made of living matter

The primary characteristic of **inorganic** compounds, which include metals and minerals, is that they are not carbon-based.

ant. organic

★

insulation

[ìnsəléiʃən]

[명] 절연[단열·방음] 처리재

adj. insulated

n. material used to block electricity, heat, or sound

Thermal **insulation** is designed to reduce heat transfer, while electrical **insulation** blocks the flow of electricity.

★★★

linear

[líniər]

[형] 1. 직선의
2. 연속적인

n. line

adj. 1 arranged or moving in a straight line
2 occurring in a series of steps

1. **Linear** molecules comprise a pair of atoms arranged at a 180-degree angle around a central atom.
2. Most chemistry experiments require researchers to follow a **linear** process if they want to receive consistent results.

★★★

mixture

[míkstʃər]

[명] 혼합(물)

v. mix

n. a combination of things

A **mixture** occurs when two or more substances are physically combined, but not at a chemical level.

syn. blend

★★

neutral

[njúːtrəl]

[형] (산성도 염기성도 아닌) 중성의

n. neutrality

adj. existing between two extremes

If there is a substance that shows neither acid nor base properties, it is said to be **neutral**.

★★

oxidize

[ɑ́ksədàiz]

[동] 산화하다, 녹슬다

n. oxidization

v. to combine with oxygen and become another substance

Exposure to oxygen and atmospheric moisture causes metals to **oxidize**, a condition commonly known as rust.

---

inorganic 금속과 광물을 포함하는 무기 화합물의 주요 특징은 그것들이 탄소 기반이 아니라는 것이다. **insulation** 단열재는 열전달을 줄이도록 설계된 반면, 전기 절연재는 전기의 흐름을 막는다. **linear** 1. 직선형 분자는 중심 원자 주위에 180도의 각도로 배열된 한 쌍의 원자로 이루어져 있다. 2. 연구원들이 일관된 결과를 얻기 원한다면, 그들은 대부분의 화학 실험에서 연속적인 과정을 따르도록 요구된다. **mixture** 혼합물은 두 개 이상의 물질이 물리적으로 결합될 때 발생하지만, 화학적 수준에서는 아니다. **neutral** 산성으로도 염기성으로도 보이지 않는 물질이 있다면, 그것은 중성이라고 한다. **oxidize** 금속이 산소와 대기 중 수분에 노출되면 흔히 녹슨다는 것으로 알려진 상태인 산화를 초래한다.

★

plasma
[plǽzmə]
[명] 1. 플라즈마(고도로 이온화된 기체)
2. 혈장

n. 1 a gas with little or no electrical charge
2 a clear liquid found in blood

1. Along with solids, liquids, and gases, **plasma** is the fourth state of natural matter present in the universe.
2. In terms of its chemical composition, blood **plasma** is mostly water, along with some electrolytes and carbon dioxide.

★★

portion
[pɔ́ːrʃən]
[명] (더 큰 것의) 일부, 부분

n. one part of a whole

Each **portion** of the modern periodic table consists of families of elements that share certain properties.

syn. section

★★

radiant
[réidiənt]
[형] (열·에너지 등의) 복사의
n. radiation

adj. transmitted through radiation

Without the **radiant** energy constantly being emitted by the sun, there could be no life on Earth.

★★★

reaction
[riǽkʃən]
[명] (화학적인) 반응

n. an interaction in which two chemical substances are changed

In a chemical **reaction**, no new atoms are created and none of the existing atoms are destroyed.

★★★

retain
[ritéin]
[동] 함유하다, 유지하다
n. retention

v. to keep something

An atom is the smallest particle of an element that still **retains** the element's basic properties.

syn. hold on to *ant.* release

★★

saturated
[sǽtʃərèitid]
[형] 포화된
v. saturate

adj. containing the maximum amount of something

When no more material can be dissolved into a liquid, the liquid is said to be **saturated**.

plasma 1. 고체, 액체, 기체와 함께 플라즈마는 우주상에 존재하는 네 번째 자연 물질 상태이다. 2. 화학적 성분 면에서 볼 때, 혈장은 약간의 전해질, 이산화탄소와 더불어 거의 대부분 물로 이루어져 있다. **portion** 현대 주기율표의 각 부분은 특정한 성질을 공유하는 원소 족(族)으로 구성된다. **radiant** 태양으로부터 지속적으로 방출되는 복사 에너지가 없다면, 지구상에는 생명체가 존재할 수 없을 것이다. **reaction** 화학 반응에서는 새로운 원자가 생성되지도, 기존의 원자 중 어떤 것이 파괴되지도 않는다. **retain** 원자는 그 원소의 기본 성질을 가지고 있는 가장 작은 원소 입자이다. **saturated** 더 이상의 물질이 액체에 용해될 수 없을 때, 그 액체는 포화 상태라고 한다.

★★

soluble

[sáljubl]

[형] (액체에) 녹는, 수용성의

adj. capable of being dissolved

Sugar and salt are common examples of **soluble** substances, as they can easily be dissolved in water.

★★

solution

[səlú:ʃən]

[명] 용액

n. a mixture of a liquid and a dissolved solid

The concentration of a **solution** will be reduced if it is diluted by the addition of more liquid.

★★

solvent

[sálvənt]

[명] 용제, 용매

n. a liquid that can dissolve certain solids

The most common **solvent** in our everyday lives is water, as it is used in the process of making tea and coffee.

★★★

tension

[ténʃən]

[명] 팽팽함, 장력

adj. tense

n. a state of tightness from being stretched

The surface **tension** of a liquid is an elastic force that is caused by a strong attraction between molecules.

Useful Tips

긴장성 두통을 영어로 tension headache라고 부르는데, 머리 둘레를 꽉 조이는 밴드로 묶은 듯이 아픈 것이 특징이다.

★★★

vapor

[véipər]

[명] 증기

v. vaporize

n. diffused matter suspended in the air

Vapor, which is a visible gas-like substance, can be created by boiling a liquid or solid at high temperatures.

★★

volatile

[válətl]

[형] 휘발성의

adj. capable of easily being turned into a gaseous form

Volatile liquids such as ethanol have an extremely low boiling point, meaning they will quickly evaporate.

---

soluble 설탕과 소금은 쉽게 물에 용해될 수 있기 때문에, 수용성 물질의 일반적인 예이다. **solution** 만약 더 많은 액체를 추가해 용액이 희석된다면, 그 용액의 농도는 줄어들 것이다. **solvent** 우리 일상생활에서 가장 흔한 용매는 물인데, 차와 커피를 만드는 과정에서 사용되기 때문이다. **tension** 액체의 표면 장력은 분자들 사이의 강력한 인력에 의해 생기는 탄성력이다. **vapor** 눈에 보이는 기체와 같은 물질인 증기는 높은 온도에서 액체나 고체를 끓여서 만들어 낼 수 있다. **volatile** 에탄올과 같은 휘발성 액체들은 끓는점이 극도로 낮은데, 이는 그 액체들이 빠르게 증발할 것이라는 것을 의미한다.

EXERCISES

A Match each definition with the correct word.

1   a state of tightness from being stretched   ⓐ saturated

2   a gas with little or no electrical charge   ⓑ linear

3   containing the maximum amount of something   ⓒ dissolve

4   material used to block electricity, heat, or sound   ⓓ inorganic

5   to put out a fire   ⓔ extinguish

6   to incorporate a solid into a liquid   ⓕ insulation

7   arranged or moving in a straight line   ⓖ tension

8   not made of living matter   ⓗ plasma

B Choose the word that is closest in meaning to each underlined word.

1   The cerebellum is the portion of the human brain that is responsible for motor skills.
    ⓐ section   ⓑ function   ⓒ resource   ⓓ damage

2   Trees will sometimes retain their leaves after they have dried up and turned brown.
    ⓐ run out of   ⓑ let go of   ⓒ cut down on   ⓓ hold on to

3   Plastics that are highly flammable are considered to be unsuitable for construction.
    ⓐ bendable   ⓑ combustible   ⓒ usable   ⓓ recyclable

4   Oranges contain citric acid, which is a compound of carbon, oxygen, and hydrogen atoms.
    ⓐ imitation   ⓑ byproduct   ⓒ nutrition   ⓓ composite

5   When a skunk feels threatened, it will emit a foul-smelling substance in self-defense.
    ⓐ absorb   ⓑ peruse   ⓒ discharge   ⓓ elude

6   The drugs bind with proteins in blood plasma, which helps enable their distribution.
    ⓐ liquidate   ⓑ compete   ⓒ replace   ⓓ fasten

7   Bees produce something called "bee bread," which is a mixture of pollen and nectar.
    ⓐ forgery   ⓑ blend   ⓒ cavity   ⓓ tribute

ART & DESIGN

SOCIAL SCIENCE

NATURAL SCIENCE

HUMANITIES

EARTH & SPACE

SOCIAL ISSUES

Lesson 27

[>] 생화학

Biochemistry

★★★

acid

[ǽsid]

[명] 산(酸), 산성물

adj. acidic

n. a chemical substance that reacts with bases to form salts

A substance called acetic **acid** is what gives common household vinegar its sharp taste and distinctive odor.

★

align

[əláin]

[동] 정렬시키다, 일직선으로 세우다

n. alignment

v. to form a straight line or move into the proper position

In a magnet, the atoms are **aligned** in such a way that they are all facing the same direction, which is what creates the magnetic force.

syn. line up

★★

assert

[əsə́:rt]

[동] 주장하다

n. assertion

v. to state a fact firmly and confidently

It was the 17th-century chemist Robert Boyle who **asserted** that all matter consists of atoms in motion.

syn. declare

★★

attach

[ətǽtʃ]

[동] 붙이다, 달라붙게 하다

n. attachment

v. to join together

Once a virus enters the human body, it will attempt to **attach** itself to one of the host's cells.

syn. adhere *ant.* detach

★★

capacity

[kəpǽsəti]

[명] 1. 용량, 수용력
2. 능력

adj. capacious

n. 1 the maximum amount that can be contained or produced
2 the ability to do something

1. Once air has reached its **capacity** to hold water, some of the moisture will be released through condensation.
2. Hydrogen is the simplest atom, so it has the **capacity** to form only a single bond with another atom.

★★

carbohydrate

[kɑ̀:rbouháidreit]

[명] 탄수화물

n. an organic compound that provides energy

Carbohydrates are burned by the cells of the body, creating the energy that an organism needs to survive.

Useful Tips

일상적인 대화를 할 때, 흔히 carbohydrates를 carbs로 줄여 말한다.

---

acid 초산이라 불리는 물질은 흔한 가정용 식초에 강렬한 맛과 독특한 냄새를 부여해 준다. **align** 자석 안에서 원자들은 모두 동일한 곳을 향하도록 정렬되어 있는데, 이것이 자력을 생성시킨다. **assert** 모든 물체는 움직이는 원자들로 이루어져 있다고 주장한 사람은 바로 17세기 화학자 Robert Boyle이었다. **attach** 바이러스가 체내에 들어가면, 숙주 세포들 중 하나에 붙으려고 할 것이다. **capacity** 1. 공기가 함수 용량에 다다르면, 그 수분의 일부는 응결을 통해 분출될 것이다. 2. 수소는 가장 단순한 원자이기 때문에, 또 다른 원자와 단일 결합만 할 수 있다. **carbohydrate** 탄수화물은 체세포들에 의해 연소되어, 한 생명체가 생존하는 데 필요한 에너지를 만든다.

★★ **catalyst**
[kǽtəlist]
[명] 촉매

n. a substance that speeds up a chemical reaction without being affected itself

All living organisms contain special proteins that act as **catalysts** for the various chemical reactions taking place in the body.

syn. stimulant

★ **congeal**
[kəndʒíːl]
[동] 응고하다

v. to thicken into a semi-solid state

Blood begins to **congeal** and form clots that can stop bleeding when platelets and proteins come together.

syn. coagulate

★★ **constituent**
[kənstítʃuənt]
[명] 구성 요소, 성분

n. one element of a complex whole

Nitrogen and oxygen are the two main **constituents** of the air that human beings must breathe in order to survive.

syn. component

★★★ **decomposition**
[diːkɑ̀mpəzíʃən]
[명] 1. 분해
2. 부패
v. decompose

n. **1** the process of breaking down into smaller parts
2 the process of rotting or decaying

1. It is the **decomposition** of potassium chlorate in the presence of heat that produces oxygen gas.
2. During **decomposition**, cells begin a process of self-digestion due to oxygen deprivation.

★ **denature**
[diːnéitʃər]
[동] 변성시키다
n. denaturation

v. to change or destroy the characteristics of (a protein)

The application of extreme heat will **denature** proteins, breaking their bonds and deforming their structure.

★★ **derive**
[diráiv]
[동] 얻다, 나오다

v. to obtain something from something else

The fact that biofuels can now be **derived** from simple algae could change the face of the energy industry in the future.

syn. extract

catalyst 모든 생명체들은 체내에서 일어나는 다양한 화학 반응들의 촉매로 작용하는 특수 단백질들을 갖고 있다. **congeal** 혈소판과 단백질이 결합하면, 혈액이 응고하기 시작해 출혈을 멈출 수 있는 응혈을 형성한다. **constituent** 질소와 산소는 인간이 생존하기 위해 호흡해야 하는 공기의 두 가지 주요 구성 요소이다. **decomposition** 1. 산소 가스를 발생시키는 것은 바로 열이 있는 곳에서의 염소산칼륨의 분해이다. 2. 부패하는 동안, 산소 부족 때문에 세포들이 자기 소화 과정을 시작한다. **denature** 극도로 강한 열을 가하면 단백질의 결합을 깨서 그 구조를 변형시켜, 단백질을 변성시킬 것이다. **derive** 현재 바이오 연료를 단순한 조류에서 얻을 수 있다는 사실은 앞으로 에너지 산업의 모습을 바꿀 수 있을 것이다.

★★ **enclose**
[inklóuz]
[동] 둘러싸다
n. enclosure

v. to surround on all sides

The nucleus of a cell is **enclosed** by a double membrane, which serves to keep the chromosomes separate from the rest of the cell.

syn. encase *ant.* release

★★★ **enzyme**
[énzaim]
[명] 효소
adj. enzymatic

n. a substance produced by living creatures that causes chemical reactions without being affected itself

Pepsin is an **enzyme** that is produced in the human stomach in order to assist in the digestion of proteins.

★★ **feasible**
[fí:zəbl]
[형] 실행할 수 있는
n. feasibility

adj. capable of being done

A chemical reaction is not considered **feasible** at a given temperature unless it can occur without the addition of extra energy.

syn. possible *ant.* impossible

★★ **fermentation**
[fə̀:rmentéiʃən]
[명] 발효
v. ferment

n. a chemical breakdown caused by yeast or bacteria

During one kind of **fermentation**, sugars are converted into cellular energy and lactic acid.

★★ **fundamental**
[fʌ̀ndəméntl]
[형] 핵심적인, 근본적인

adj. of central importance

Carbon is found in macromolecules, which are the **fundamental** building blocks of all living things.

syn. basic

★★★ **generate**
[dʒénərèit]
[동] 만들어 내다, 생성하다
n. generation

v. to create or cause to occur

Mitochondria **generate** adenosine triphosphate, commonly known as ATP, which is used as energy by cells.

syn. produce *ant.* consume

enclose 세포핵은 이중 세포막으로 둘러싸여 있는데, 이것이 염색체를 세포의 나머지 부분과 분리해 준다. **enzyme** 펩신은 단백질의 소화를 돕기 위해 인간의 위에서 만들어지는 효소이다. **feasible** 화학 반응은 여분의 에너지 추가 없이 일어날 수 있는 경우가 아니면, 특정 온도에서 실행할 수 있다고 간주되지 않는다. **fermentation** 한 가지 발효가 일어나는 동안, 당분은 세포 에너지와 젖산으로 전환된다. **fundamental** 탄소는 모든 생명체의 핵심 구성 요소인 고분자에서 발견된다. **generate** 미토콘드리아는 흔히 ATP라고 알려진 아데노신3인산을 만들어 내는데, 그것은 세포들에 의해 에너지로 사용된다.

★★ **glucose**
[glúːkous]
[명] 포도당

n. **a type of sugar that provides energy**

Glucose is a simple carbohydrate, often referred to as "blood sugar," that is regulated by a hormone called insulin.

★ **homeostasis**
[hòumioustéisis]
[명] 생체 항상성

n. **the process by which biological systems remain stable despite changes in external conditions**

One of the most basic examples of **homeostasis** is the raising and lowering of body temperature to counteract outside temperatures.

★★ **induce**
[indjúːs]
[동] 유발하다, 유도하다

v. **to cause something to occur**

When nicotine, an extremely addictive chemical, enters the bloodstream, it **induces** the release of adrenaline.

ant. prevent

★★★ **initiate**
[iníʃièit]
[동] 시작하다
n. initiation

v. **to begin something**

The process of cell death, known as apoptosis, is **initiated** when certain signals are received from other cells.

syn. trigger *ant.* conclude

★★ **ion**
[áiən]
[명] 이온
adj. ionic

n. **an atom or molecule that has an electrical charge**

Substances such as sodium, potassium, and calcium exist within the human body in the form of **ions**.

★ **lipid**
[lípid]
[명] 지질

n. **a compound that is insoluble in water but dissolves in alcohol**

During the process of human digestion, the fat found in the food we eat is broken down into fatty acids, a type of **lipid**.

glucose 포도당은 흔히 '혈당'으로 일컬어지는 단순 탄수화물로, 인슐린이라는 호르몬에 의해 조절된다. **homeostasis** 생체 항상성의 가장 기본적인 예들 중 하나는 외부 기온에 대응하기 위해 체온을 높이고 낮추는 것이다. **induce** 중독성이 강한 화학 물질인 니코틴이 혈류에 들어가면, 아드레날린 분비를 유발한다. **initiate** 세포 자멸사로 알려진 세포사의 과정은 다른 세포들에게서 특정 신호들을 받으면 시작된다. **ion** 나트륨, 칼륨, 칼슘 같은 물질들은 이온 형태로 인간의 체내에 존재한다. **lipid** 인간의 소화 과정 동안, 우리가 먹는 음식에 있는 지방이 지질의 한 유형인 지방산으로 분해된다.

★★★

merge

[məːrdʒ]

[동] 융합하다, 합치다

n. merger

v. to combine with something else to form a new entity

In a synthesis reaction, energy is released as multiple reactants **merge** together to form a single substance.

syn. consolidate *ant.* divide

★★★

resist

[rizíst]

[동] 저항하다

n. resistance

v. to fight against or refuse to accept something

Covalent bonds are much stronger than noncovalent bonds, so they **resist** being pulled apart by thermal motion.

syn. oppose *ant.* accept

★★

split

[split]

[동] 나누다, 나뉘다

v. to break or be broken into two or more parts

Carbohydrates, fats, and proteins can be **split** by adding water molecules, a process that is known as hydrolysis.

syn. separate *ant.* combine

★

starch

[stɑːrtʃ]

[명] 전분, 녹말

n. a complex carbohydrate found in plants

The **starch** from plants that is consumed by humans is broken down into sugars that are then used for energy.

★★

superfluous

[supə́ːrfluəs]

[형] 여분의, 불필요한

adj. unneeded and serving no purpose

Enzymatic activity in a cell produces no byproducts, so there are not any **superfluous** molecules present.

syn. useless *ant.* vital

★★

transmit

[trænsmít]

[동] 전달하다

n. transmission

v. to send something from one place to another

There are special chemicals in the brain that **transmit** signals from one nerve cell to another.

syn. transfer

---

merge 합성 반응에서, 여러 반응 물질들이 융합되어 단일 물질을 만들면서 에너지가 방출된다. **resist** 공유 결합은 비공유 결합보다 훨씬 더 강력해서, 열운동에 의해 분리되는 것에 저항한다. **split** 탄수화물, 지방, 단백질은 물 분자를 추가함으로써 나뉠 수 있는데, 이 과정은 가수분해라고 알려져 있다. **starch** 인간이 먹는 식물에서 나오는 전분은 후에 에너지를 내는 데 사용되는 당분으로 분해된다. **superfluous** 세포 내 효소 활동은 부산물을 배출하지 않아서, 여분의 분자가 전혀 없다. **transmit** 뇌 안에는 하나의 신경 세포에서 또 다른 신경 세포로 신호들을 전달하는 특수 화학 물질들이 있다.

EXERCISES

A Match each definition with the correct word.

1 a chemical substance that reacts with bases to form salts   ⓐ denature

2 to change or destroy the characteristics of (a protein)   ⓑ carbohydrate

3 an organic compound that provides energy   ⓒ acid

4 to join together   ⓓ lipid

5 a type of sugar that provides energy   ⓔ attach

6 a chemical breakdown caused by yeast or bacteria   ⓕ glucose

7 a compound that is insoluble in water but dissolves in alcohol   ⓖ induce

8 to cause something to occur   ⓗ fermentation

B Choose the word that is closest in meaning to each underlined word.

1 Cell fusion is a process by which two or more cells <u>merge</u> to form a single multinuclear cell.
ⓐ consolidate   ⓑ vanish   ⓒ mutate   ⓓ separate

2 Vaccines <u>initiate</u> an immune response without causing any symptoms of the disease.
ⓐ suspend   ⓑ halt   ⓒ mimic   ⓓ trigger

3 There are some medicines that people can take to help their blood <u>congeal</u> more effectively.
ⓐ circulate   ⓑ coagulate   ⓒ regenerate   ⓓ extract

4 Albert Einstein <u>asserted</u> that the speed of light is constant and cannot be exceeded.
ⓐ declared   ⓑ suspected   ⓒ misstated   ⓓ disproved

5 All living creatures reproduce in order to <u>transmit</u> their genes to the next generation.
ⓐ enhance   ⓑ expand   ⓒ transfer   ⓓ design

6 As wisdom teeth are considered to be <u>superfluous</u>, they are often removed by dentists.
ⓐ fatal   ⓑ unique   ⓒ useless   ⓓ crucial

7 One of the <u>fundamental</u> characteristics of plants is the ability to convert sunlight into food through photosynthesis.
ⓐ archaic   ⓑ uncommon   ⓒ fragile   ⓓ basic

ART & DESIGN

SOCIAL SCIENCE

NATURAL SCIENCE

HUMANITIES

EARTH & SPACE

SOCIAL ISSUES

[>] 의학

Medicine

★

administer

[ædmínistər]

[동] (약을) 투여하다

v. to give a drug or treatment to a patient

After carefully applying alcohol, the nurse **administered** the vaccine to each child via a shot in the arm.

syn. provide

★★

alleviate

[əlí:vièit]

[동] 완화하다

v. to reduce the degree of something negative

Although the medication **alleviated** some of the patient's discomfort, it did not lower her fever.

syn. relieve *ant.* worsen

★★

antibiotic

[æ̀ntibaiátik, -tai-]

[명] 항생제

n. medicine that kills disease-causing bacteria

Strep throat is a bacterial infection of the throat and tonsils that is commonly treated with **antibiotics**.

★★

antibody

[ǽntibàdi]

[명] 항체

n. a substance produced by the body to fight a specific illness

After the body has experienced a virus, it will be able to produce **antibodies** quickly in the future.

ant. antigen

★

antiseptic

[æ̀ntəséptik]

[명] 소독제, 소독약

n. a substance that prevents bacteria from causing infections

Before bandaging a wound, it should be thoroughly cleaned with an **antiseptic**, such as a spray or a lotion.

★★★

benefit

[bénəfit]

[명] 혜택, 이득

[동] …에게 도움이 되다, …에게 이롭다

adj. beneficial

n. an advantage that something provides
syn. asset *ant.* disadvantage

One of the **benefits** of capsules over tablets is that they are cheaper and easier for pharmaceutical companies to manufacture.

v. to help someone or improve something *syn.* aid *ant.* harm

This medication **benefits** patients by reducing both the inflammation in their joints and the pain they experience.

---

administer 그 간호사는 알코올을 조심스럽게 바른 후, 각 아이의 팔에 주사로 백신을 투여했다. **alleviate** 약물이 그 환자의 통증을 일부 완화시키긴 했지만, 열은 내리지 못했다. **antibiotic** 패혈성 인두염은 보통 항생제로 치료되는 목과 편도선의 세균성 감염증이다. **antibody** 몸이 바이러스를 겪고 나면, 향후 빠르게 항체를 형성할 수 있을 것이다. **antiseptic** 상처에 붕대를 감기 전에, 그 상처를 스프레이나 액상 타입과 같은 소독제로 철저히 닦아야 한다. **benefit** 캡슐이 정제보다 더 나은 이유 중 하나는, 제약회사들이 제조하기에 비용이 더 저렴하고 더 쉽다는 점이다. / 이 약은 관절의 염증과 환자들이 겪는 통증을 완화시켜 그들에게 도움이 된다.

cure
[kjuər]

ⓝ 치료(제·법)

ⓥ 낫게 하다, 치료하다

n. something that eliminates the symptoms of a disease

syn. remedy

The ultimate goal of many modern researchers is to eventually find a **cure** for all types of cancer.

v. to eliminate the symptoms of a disease

The doctor was able to **cure** the sick children simply by putting them on a nutrient-rich diet.

detect
[ditékt]

ⓥ 발견하다, 찾아내다

n. detection

v. to discover something that is hard to notice

Once a doctor **detects** abnormalities in a patient's blood, the proper medication must be determined.

syn. spot   *ant.* overlook

diagnose
[dáiəgnòus, -nòuz]

ⓥ 진단하다

n. diagnosis

v. to identify the illness or condition someone is suffering from

Rare illnesses are extremely difficult to **diagnose** because only a handful of doctors are aware of their characteristics.

dose
[dous]

ⓝ (약의) 복용량, 투여량

n. a specific amount of a drug or medicine to be taken

The nurse recommended that each **dose** of the powerful medicine be taken only after eating a meal.

Useful Tips

dose와 dosage는 비슷해 보이지만, 차이점이 있다. dose는 약을 얼마만큼 투여해야 하는지만 알려주고, dosage는 약을 얼마만큼, 얼마나 자주 투여해야 하는지 둘 다 알려 준다.

effective
[iféktiv]

ⓐ 효과적인

n. effectiveness

adj. able to successfully perform an intended purpose

There is a long and rigorous process that every new medication must undergo to determine whether it is safe and **effective**.

syn. efficient   *ant.* ineffective

extract
[ikstrǽkt]

ⓥ 추출하다

n. extraction

v. to remove something from something else

Quinine, which is a medication used to treat malaria, is **extracted** from the bark of a Peruvian tree.

ant. insert

ART & DESIGN

SOCIAL SCIENCE

NATURAL SCIENCE

HUMANITIES

EARTH & SPACE

SOCIAL ISSUES

---

cure 많은 현대 연구원들의 궁극적 목표는 결국 모든 종류의 암에 대한 치료법을 찾아내는 것이다. / 그 의사는 단순히 영양가가 풍부한 음식을 아픈 아이들에게 제공함으로써, 그들을 낫게 할 수 있었다.　**detect** 의사가 환자의 혈액에서 이상한 점을 발견하면, 적절한 약물을 결정해야 한다.　**diagnose** 희귀 질환들은 소수의 의사들만이 그 병의 특징들을 알고 있기 때문에 진단하기가 매우 어렵다.　**dose** 그 간호사는 식후에만 그 강력한 약의 1회 분을 복용할 것을 권고했다.　**effective** 모든 새로운 약물이 안전하고 효과적인지 판단하기 위해 반드시 거쳐야 하는 길고 엄격한 과정이 있다.　**extract** 말라리아를 치료하는 데 사용되는 약물인 퀴닌은 페루 나무의 껍질에서 추출된다.

★★
fatigue
[fətí:g]
[명] 피로

n. a feeling of extreme tiredness

Patients may experience some **fatigue** after taking the drug, but this will usually wear off over time.

syn. exhaustion

★
geriatric
[dʒèriǽtrik]
[형] 노인병(학)의

adj. relating to the health of elderly people

The field of **geriatric** medicine is focused on preventing, diagnosing, and treating diseases that primarily affect the elderly.

★★
hinder
[híndər]
[동] 방해하다, 막다
n. hindrance

v. to make something difficult to do

The goal of most of the cancer drugs currently in development is to **hinder** the growth of tumors.

syn. impede *ant.* facilitate

★★
inject
[indʒékt]
[동] 주사하다, 주입하다
n. injection

v. to force a substance into something

When medicine is **injected** directly into the muscle, it is quickly absorbed into the bloodstream.

syn. insert *ant.* withdraw

★★
intravenously
[ìntrəví:nəsli]
[부] 정맥으로, 정맥 안으로, 정맥 주사로
adj. intravenous

Useful Tips
흔히 우리가 말하는 링거는 intravenous(ly)의 약자인 IV로 표기한다.

adv. through a vein

Some drugs are best delivered **intravenously**, while others are considered most effective when taken orally.

★★
mitigate
[mítəgèit]
[동] 경감시키다, 완화시키다

v. to make something less severe, harmful, or unpleasant

Vaccination is one of several methods that can be used to **mitigate** the spread of a virus during a pandemic.

syn. lessen *ant.* intensify

Useful Tips
mitigate는 재앙이나 위기 같은 좋지 않은 상황이 나아지는 것을 표현할 때 사용하고, 우리말로 비슷한 뜻의 alleviate는 고통과 같이 사람이 느끼는 안 좋은 것을 경감시키는 데 사용한다.

---

fatigue 환자들은 그 약을 복용한 후에 약간의 피로감을 느낄 수 있지만, 보통 시간이 지나면 그 피로감은 점점 줄어든다. **geriatric** 노인 의학 분야는 주로 노인들에게 영향을 미치는 질병의 예방과 진단, 치료에 초점이 맞춰져 있다. **hinder** 현재 개발 중인 대부분의 암 치료제의 목표는 종양의 성장을 막는 것이다. **inject** 약을 근육에 직접 주사하면, 빠르게 혈류에 흡수된다. **intravenously** 일부 약물들은 정맥 주사로 가장 잘 전달되는 반면에, 다른 약물들은 경구 복용했을 때 가장 효과적이라고 여겨진다. **mitigate** 백신 접종은 팬데믹(전 세계적 유행병) 상황 중에 바이러스의 확산을 경감시키는 데 사용할 수 있는 여러 방법들 중 하나이다.

ART & DESIGN

SOCIAL SCIENCE

NATURAL SCIENCE

HUMANITIES

EARTH & SPACE

SOCIAL ISSUES

★★ noxious
[nάkʃəs]
ⓐ 유해한, 유독한

adj. harmful or poisonous

People will sometimes have adverse reactions to drugs, meaning that they are **noxious** and unintended.

syn. toxic

★ panacea
[pὰnəsíːə]
ⓝ 만병통치약

n. something said to solve all problems or cure all illnesses

If someone says that they have found a miracle substance that acts as a **panacea**, you can be sure that their claims are false.

syn. cure-all

★ pioneer
[pὰiəníər]
ⓝ 선구자, 개척자

n. someone who does something or goes somewhere first

Edward Jenner, an English physician, was a medical **pioneer** who created a smallpox vaccine in 1796.

★ placebo
[pləsíːbou]
ⓝ 위약, 가짜 약

n. fake medicine designed to have a psychological benefit

Sugar pills are sometimes given as a **placebo** to patients who suffer from chronic pain of an unknown origin.

★★★ prescribe
[priskráib]
ⓥ 처방하다

n. prescription

v. to suggest and authorize a patient's use of a certain medicine

When doctors **prescribe** medicine for a patient, it is essential that no one else takes it.

★★★ prevent
[privént]
ⓥ 막다, 방지하다, 예방하다

n., adj. preventative

v. to stop something from happening

There are many different medications that travelers can take to **prevent** the common problem of motion sickness.

syn. thwart   *ant.* allow

---

noxious 사람들은 가끔 약물들에 대해 부작용을 일으키는데, 이것은 그 약물들이 유해하며 의도되지 않은 효과를 낸다는 것을 의미한다.   **panacea** 만약 어떤 사람이 만병통치약으로 작용하는 기적적인 물질을 발견했다고 말한다면, 당신은 그들의 주장이 거짓임을 확신할 수 있다.   **pioneer** 영국의 내과 의사인 Edward Jenner는 1796년에 천연두 백신을 발명한 의학계의 선구자였다.   **placebo** 설탕 알약은 원인을 알 수 없는 만성적 통증을 겪는 환자들에게 가끔 위약(가짜 약)으로 제공된다.   **prescribe** 의사들이 환자에게 약을 처방할 때, 다른 사람이 그 약을 복용하지 않는 것이 필수적이다.   **prevent** 흔한 멀미 문제를 예방하기 위해 여행자들이 복용할 수 있는 많은 다양한 약들이 있다.

recipient
[risípiənt]

명 (어떤 것을) 받는 사람,
수령[수취]인

n. someone who receives something

The **recipient** of a blood transfusion must first take certain medications that reduce the chance of an allergic reaction.

syn. beneficiary   *ant.* donor

recuperate
[rikjú:pərèit, -kú:-]

동 (건강·원기를) 회복하다

v. to recover from an illness or injury

While **recuperating** from a complex surgical procedure, the patient was given a daily dose of painkillers.

syn. heal

remission
[rimíʃən]

명 (병의) 차도

n. a period during which the symptoms of an illness become less severe

Cancer treatments will sometimes result in partial or even total **remission**, but this cannot be guaranteed.

sedate
[sidéit]

동 진정제를 주다

n. sedation

v. to make someone calm down or fall asleep by giving them a drug

Although the procedure is relatively painless, some patients opt to be lightly **sedated** beforehand.

syn. tranquilize

side effect
[sáid ifèkt]

명 부작용

n. an unintended consequence

All prescription drugs have potential **side effects**, some of which can be severe or even fatal.

symptom
[símptəm]

명 증상

n. an outward sign of a disease or illness

Perhaps the most obvious **symptom** of chicken pox is an itchy rash of blisters all across the patient's skin.

---

recipient 수혈을 받는 사람은 알레르기 반응의 가능성을 줄이는 특정 약물을 먼저 투약 받아야 한다.　**recuperate** 그 환자는 복잡한 외과 수술에서 회복하는 동안, 매일 진통제를 투여받았다.　**remission** 암 치료는 때때로 병에 부분적 혹은 전체적인 차도를 보이게 할 수 있지만, 이를 장담할 수는 없다.　**sedate** 그 시술은 비교적 통증이 없지만, 몇몇 환자들은 사전에 진정제를 가볍게 투여받는 것을 택한다.　**side effect** 모든 처방약들은 일부 심각하거나 치명적일 수도 있는 잠재적 부작용이 있다.　**symptom** 수두의 가장 명백한 증상은 환자의 피부 전반에 생기는 가려운 물집성 발진일 것이다.

EXERCISES

ART & DESIGN

SOCIAL SCIENCE

NATURAL SCIENCE

HUMANITIES

EARTH & SPACE

SOCIAL ISSUES

A Match each definition with the correct word.

1 a specific amount of a drug or medicine to be taken   ⓐ geriatric

2 to discover something that is hard to notice   ⓑ dose

3 to suggest and authorize a patient's use of a certain medicine   ⓒ antiseptic

4 a substance produced by the body to fight a specific illness   ⓓ intravenously

5 relating to the health of elderly people   ⓔ prescribe

6 someone who does something or goes somewhere first   ⓕ detect

7 a substance that prevents bacteria from causing infections   ⓖ pioneer

8 through a vein   ⓗ antibody

B Choose the word that is closest in meaning to each underlined word.

1 Attempts to gather genetic information globally have been <u>hindered</u> by mistrust.
   ⓐ reinforced   ⓑ commenced   ⓒ impeded   ⓓ replicated

2 The risk of contamination in labs can be <u>mitigated</u> by following safety procedures.
   ⓐ questioned   ⓑ disinfected   ⓒ discerned   ⓓ lessened

3 The ancient Greeks believed that oregano was a <u>cure</u> for a variety of stomach ailments.
   ⓐ source   ⓑ device   ⓒ remedy   ⓓ misconception

4 Muscle <u>fatigue</u> generally occurs due to exercise, although it could have other causes.
   ⓐ injury   ⓑ expansion   ⓒ exhaustion   ⓓ length

5 Many insects have stingers that can be used to <u>inject</u> venom in self-defense.
   ⓐ spray   ⓑ insert   ⓒ inhale   ⓓ spread

6 Zoo animals must be <u>sedated</u> before they can be given a medical examination.
   ⓐ analyzed   ⓑ apprehended   ⓒ tranquilized   ⓓ rinsed

7 An unintended chemical reaction released a cloud of <u>noxious</u> fumes in the factory.
   ⓐ toxic   ⓑ transparent   ⓒ aromatic   ⓓ massive

215

> 해부학
Anatomy

anesthesia
[ǽnəsθíːʒə]
명 마취

n. the loss of feeling in the body or part of the body

Although many operations require **anesthesia**, some procedures can be performed while the patient is awake.

syn. numbness

appendix
[əpéndiks]
명 맹장

n. a small tube attached to the intestines

Because the **appendix** is believed to have little or no purpose, it is usually removed if it becomes infected.

Useful Tips

appendix에 생기는 염증성 질환인 맹장염은 appendicitis이다.

artery
[áːrtəri]
명 동맥
adj. arterial

n. a tube in the body that carries blood away from the heart

The aorta, which is connected directly to the left ventricle of the heart, is the largest **artery** in the body.

ant. vein

balm
[baːm]
명 연고

n. an oil or lotion used to soothe the skin

By applying a **balm** to the affected area twice a day, the woman was able to reduce the irritation caused by her rash.

syn. salve

bronchial
[bráŋkiəl]
명 기관지의
n. bronchus

adj. relating to the tubes that carry air to the lungs

Bronchitis is a common **bronchial** infection that tends to result in a cough, a sore throat, and wheezing.

cardiac
[káːrdiæk]
명 심장의

adj. relating to the heart

While a heart attack is caused by a blocked artery, **cardiac** arrest occurs when the heart fails to pump properly.

---

anesthesia 많은 수술에 마취가 필요하지만, 어떤 수술들은 환자가 깨어 있는 상태에서 집도된다.　**appendix** 맹장은 용도가 거의 없거나 전혀 없다고 여겨지기 때문에, 염증이 생기면 보통 제거된다.　**artery** 심장 좌심실에 바로 연결되어 있는 대동맥은 인체에서 가장 큰 동맥이다.　**balm** 그 여자는 하루에 두 번 환부에 연고를 발라, 발진으로 인한 염증을 줄일 수 있었다.　**bronchial** 기관지염은 기침, 인후염, 천명을 유발하는 경향이 있는 흔한 기관지 감염이다.　**cardiac** 심근 경색이 막힌 동맥에 의해 일어나는 반면, 심장 마비는 심장이 제대로 뛰지 않을 때 일어난다.

ART & DESIGN

SOCIAL SCIENCE

NATURAL SCIENCE

HUMANITIES

EARTH & SPACE

SOCIAL ISSUES

concussion
[kənkʌ́ʃən]
ⓝ 뇌진탕

adj. concussed

n. a head injury that causes temporary damage to the brain

Doctors believe that people who suffer multiple **concussions** may experience serious long-term effects.

excessive
[iksésiv]
ⓐ 과도한, 지나친

n. excess

adj. more than is needed

An **excessive** amount of cholesterol in the body can have an adverse effect on the flow of blood through the arteries.

fluid
[flúːid]
ⓝ 수액, 유체

n. a substance that has no fixed shape, such as a liquid or gas

Two of the roles of bodily **fluids** are transporting essential nutrients and getting rid of unwanted waste.

ant. solid

function
[fʌ́ŋkʃən]
ⓝ 기능, 역할
ⓥ 기능하다, 작용하다

n. the activity or task something is intended to do   *syn.* purpose

The primary **function** of the pancreas is to produce enzymes that aid in the digestion of sugars, fats, and starches.

v. to work properly   *syn.* operate   *ant.* malfunction

If one of the kidneys fails to **function** properly, the body is usually able to adapt with only moderate health consequences.

gland
[glænd]
ⓝ 선(腺), 샘

adj. glandular

n. a bodily organ that produces chemical substances

The pituitary **gland**, located at the base of the brain, produces hormones that regulate the growth of the body.

implant
[implǽnt]
ⓥ 주입하다, 심다

n. implantation

v. to put an object into the body

If the heart fails to beat regularly on its own, doctors may decide to **implant** a pacemaker to assist it.

syn. insert   *ant.* remove

---

concussion 의사들은 뇌진탕을 여러 번 겪은 사람들이 심각한 장기적 영향을 받을 수 있다고 믿는다.   **excessive** 과도한 양의 체내 콜레스테롤은 동맥을 지나는 혈류에 부정적인 영향을 미칠 수 있다.   **fluid** 체액의 역할들 중 두 가지는 필수 영양소를 운반하고 불필요한 노폐물을 제거하는 것이다.   **function** 췌장의 주된 기능은 당분, 지방, 탄수화물의 소화를 돕는 효소를 만드는 것이다. / 신장들 중 한 개가 제대로 기능하지 않아도, 대개는 건강에 큰 영향 없이 몸이 적응할 수 있다.   **gland** 뇌 기저부에 있는 뇌하수체는 신체 성장을 조절하는 호르몬을 만든다.   **implant** 심장이 스스로 규칙적으로 뛰지 못하면, 의사들은 그것을 도와줄 심박 조율기를 주입하기로 결정하기도 한다.

★★
incision
[insíʒən]
[명] 절개

n. a precise cut made with a scalpel during an operation

The surgeon made a 10-centimeter-long **incision** in the skin of the patient's abdomen.

★★★
inflammation
[ìnfləméiʃən]
[명] 염증
v. inflame

n. a swollen, red, and painful area on or in the body

Crohn's disease, which is caused by **inflammation** of the digestive tract, can lead to serious stomach pain.

syn. irritation

★★
limb
[lim]
[명] 사지, 팔다리

n. something that sticks out from the main body

Human **limbs** are very different from those of our closest animal relatives—our legs are quite long and our arms unusually short.

★
lobe
[loub]
[명] (폐·뇌의) 엽

n. a rounded part of a larger whole

The human brain is split into two hemispheres, each of which can be further divided into four **lobes**.

★★★
nerve
[nəːrv]
[명] 신경
adj. nervous

n. a fiber that carries messages throughout the body

The body's **nerves** connect the central nervous system to the rest of the body, carrying impulses back and forth.

Useful Tips
뻔뻔하거나 배짱 좋은 태도를 보이는 것을 have a lot of nerve라고 표현한다.

★★
ooze
[uːz]
[동] 흘러나오다, 스며 나오다

v. to flow very slowly due to being thick

Pus, a yellowish substance that sometimes **oozes** from infected wounds, is part of the immune system's response.

---

incision 그 외과의는 그 환자의 복부 피부를 10 센티미터 절개했다. **inflammation** 소화관의 염증에 의해 발생하는 크론병은 심각한 복통을 야기할 수 있다. **limb** 인간의 사지는 가장 가까운 동물 동족의 사지와 매우 달라서, 다리는 아주 길고 팔은 매우 짧다. **lobe** 인간의 뇌는 두 개의 반구로 나누어져 있고, 각 반구는 네 개의 뇌엽으로 더 세분될 수 있다. **nerve** 몸의 신경들은 자극을 이리저리 전달하면서, 중추 신경계와 몸의 나머지 부분을 연결한다. **ooze** 감염된 상처에서 때때로 흘러나오는 노르스름한 물질인 고름은 면역체계 반응의 일부이다.

★★★

organ

[ɔ́ːrgən]

[명] 장기, 기관

n. a body part that performs a specific function

The human body's largest **organ** is the skin, but the largest internal **organ** is the liver.

★★

perspire

[pərspáiər]

[동] 땀을 흘리다

n. perspiration

v. to release liquid through the skin

When human beings **perspire**, the process of evaporation on the surface of the skin lowers the body's temperature.

syn. sweat

★

pulmonary

[pʌ́lmənèri]

[형] 폐의

adj. relating to the lungs

Pulmonary circulation makes use of blood cells to carry the oxygen brought into the body from the lungs to the heart.

★

robust

[roubʌ́st]

[형] 튼튼한, 강건한

adj. strong and healthy

People with a **robust** immune system are less likely to get sick and tend to recover from illnesses more quickly.

syn. vigorous *ant.* sickly

★

sever

[sévər]

[동] 절단하다, 잘라내다

v. to cut something off from the main part

Thanks to modern medical techniques, fingers that have been **severed** can often be reattached to the hand.

syn. disconnect *ant.* attach

★★

spine

[spain]

[명] 척추

adj. spinal

n. the row of bones along an animal's back

Because we have a **spine**, human beings are classified as vertebrates, along with all other mammals.

syn. backbone

organ 인체의 가장 큰 장기는 피부지만, 가장 큰 내장은 간이다. **perspire** 사람들이 땀을 흘릴 때, 피부 표면에서의 증발 과정이 체온을 낮춰 준다. **pulmonary** 폐순환은 혈구들을 이용해 체내에 들어온 산소를 폐에서 심장까지 운반한다. **robust** 면역체계가 튼튼한 사람들은 병에 걸릴 가능성이 더 적고, 병에서 더 빨리 회복되는 경향이 있다. **sever** 현대 의학 기술 덕분에, 절단된 손가락들은 흔히 손에 다시 접합될 수 있다. **spine** 인간은 척추가 있기 때문에, 다른 모든 포유동물들과 더불어 척추동물로 분류된다.

★★ **surgical**
[sə́:rdʒikəl]
[형] 수술의, 외과의
n. surgery

adj. relating to a medical operation

The patient underwent a minor **surgical** procedure to remove a non-cancerous tumor from her neck.

★★★ **tissue**
[tíʃu:]
[명] 조직

n. a substance in animals and plants made up of cells that share a purpose

Connective **tissue**, which is found throughout the body, is made up of both organic and inorganic matter.

★★ **transplant**
[trænsplǽnt]
[동] 옮겨 심다, 이식하다

v. to remove something from one place and move it to another

There are many organs that can be **transplanted**, including livers, kidneys, hearts, and lungs.

syn. relocate

★★★ **vein**
[vein]
[명] 정맥

n. a tube in the body that carries blood to the heart

Veins are generally located relatively close to the surface of the skin, which makes them highly visible.

ant. artery

★ **viable**
[váiəbl]
[형] 독자 생존 가능한

adj. capable of living or functioning

Once an organ has been removed from a body, it can remain **viable** for only a limited period of time.

★★ **wrinkle**
[ríŋkl]
[명] 주름

n. a line or fold in a surface

The **wrinkles** in the cortex of the brain make it possible for more cells to fit in the relatively small space of the human skull.

---

surgical 그 환자는 목에서 양성 종양을 제거하는 가벼운 외과 시술을 받았다. **tissue** 몸 전체에서 발견되는 결합 조직은 유기물과 무기물로 이루어져 있다. **transplant** 간, 신장, 심장, 폐를 포함해 이식 가능한 장기들이 많다. **vein** 일반적으로 정맥은 피부 표면에 비교적 가까이 있어서, 아주 잘 보인다. **viable** 일단 장기가 몸에서 제거되면, 제한된 시간 동안만 독자 생존이 가능하다. **wrinkle** 뇌 피질의 주름 덕분에 인간 두개골의 비교적 작은 공간 안에 더 많은 세포들이 들어갈 수 있다.

EXERCISES

A Match each definition with the correct word.

1 relating to a medical operation

2 a small tube attached to the intestines

3 to flow very slowly due to being thick

4 relating to the heart

5 more than is needed

6 a bodily organ that produces chemical substances

7 a tube in the body that carries blood to the heart

8 a head injury that causes temporary damage to the brain

ⓐ gland

ⓑ excessive

ⓒ appendix

ⓓ vein

ⓔ surgical

ⓕ concussion

ⓖ cardiac

ⓗ ooze

B Choose the word that is closest in meaning to each underlined word.

1 The gardener will <u>transplant</u> the sunflowers growing in pots on her porch to her garden.
 ⓐ harvest ⓑ derive ⓒ relocate ⓓ coordinate

2 The main <u>function</u> of the burners is to heat chemicals to the proper temperature.
 ⓐ flaw ⓑ purpose ⓒ expense ⓓ resource

3 In an experiment, scientists <u>implanted</u> special computer chips in the brains of monkeys.
 ⓐ inserted ⓑ measured ⓒ charged ⓓ detected

4 Chemists have found ways to <u>sever</u> even the strongest chemical bonds.
 ⓐ reproduce ⓑ disconnect ⓒ lengthen ⓓ reinforce

5 Applying a <u>balm</u> made with garlic to mosquito bites will decrease the itching.
 ⓐ liquid ⓑ powder ⓒ salve ⓓ cube

6 Jellyfish venom can cause some mild <u>inflammation</u> of the skin, but the pain may be intense.
 ⓐ restoration ⓑ layer ⓒ cut ⓓ irritation

7 The medicine causes a loss of energy, so even the most <u>robust</u> patients will find themselves feeling lethargic.
 ⓐ vigorous ⓑ careful ⓒ infirm ⓓ cooperative

ART & DESIGN

SOCIAL SCIENCE

NATURAL SCIENCE

HUMANITIES

EARTH & SPACE

SOCIAL ISSUES

Lesson 30

유전학

Genetics

★★
albino
[ælbáinou]
[명] 알비노, 선천성 색소 결핍증에 걸린 사람[동물]
n. albinism

n. a person or animal with a condition that causes an absence of color in the skin, hair, and eyes

If an animal is an **albino**, the lack of coloration from its genetic disorder may act as a severe survival disadvantage.

★★★
alter
[ɔ́:ltər]
[동] 바꾸다, 변경하다
n. alteration

v. to make small changes to something

It is believed that prolonged exposure to certain environmental toxins can **alter** a person's DNA over time.

syn. modify

★
analogous
[ənǽləgəs]
[형] 유사한, 비슷한, 닮은
n. analogy

adj. comparable to something else

In a simplified explanation of genetics, a DNA sequence is **analogous** to a recipe that must be copied.

syn. corresponding *ant.* dissimilar

Useful Tips

analogous는 주로 전치사 to와 함께 쓰인다.

★★
antigen
[ǽntidʒən]
[명] 항원(체내로 들어가 항체 형성을 촉진하는 독소·세균)

n. a harmful substance that enters the body

Genetic makeup has a strong influence on the ability of the body to effectively respond to the presence of **antigens**.

syn. allergen *ant.* antibody

★★
commence
[kəméns]
[동] 시작되다, 시작하다
n. commencement

v. to start something

DNA replication will **commence** at certain locations where genetic material exists, known as "origins of replication."

syn. begin *ant.* conclude

★★★
conspicuous
[kənspíkjuəs]
[형] 눈에 잘 띄는, 뚜렷한

adj. easy to notice

A genetic trait that makes an individual more **conspicuous** to predators is unlikely to be passed down to the next generation.

syn. obvious *ant.* inconspicuous

---

albino 만약 어떤 동물이 알비노라면, 유전적 장애로 생긴 색의 결핍은 생존에 심각한 불이익으로 작용할 수 있다. **alter** 특정 환경적 독소에 장기간 노출되는 것은 오랜 시간에 걸쳐 사람의 DNA를 변하게 할 수 있다고 여겨진다. **analogous** 유전학을 단순하게 설명하자면, DNA 염기 서열은 똑같이 베껴야 하는 조리법과 유사하다. **antigen** 유전적 구성은 항원의 존재에 효과적으로 반응할 수 있는 신체 능력에 강한 영향을 미친다. **commence** DNA 복제는 '복제 기점'이라 알려진 유전 물질이 존재하는 특정 위치에서 시작될 것이다. **conspicuous** 한 개체를 포식자의 눈에 더 잘 띄게 하는 유전적 특성은 다음 세대에 전해질 가능성이 낮다.

ART & DESIGN

SOCIAL SCIENCE

NATURAL SCIENCE

HUMANITIES

EARTH & SPACE

SOCIAL ISSUES

correspond
[kɔ̀ːrəspánd]

ⓥ 일치하다, 부합하다

n. correspondence

v. to be very similar to something else

Although many of the genes found in animal species **correspond** to human genes, not all do.

syn. correlate

discrete
[diskríːt]

ⓐ 별개의, 불연속의

adj. separate and distinct from other things

Discrete traits are usually determined by a single gene and are either present or absent in an individual.

syn. individual

Useful **Tips**

discrete을 동음이의어인 discreet(신중한, 조심스러운)과 혼동하지 않도록 주의한다.

dissimilar
[dissímələr]

ⓐ 같지 않은, 다른

adj. very different from something else

It has been shown that partners who are genetically **dissimilar** in significant ways produce the most "successful" offspring.

syn. disparate   *ant.* analogous

encode
[inkóud]

ⓥ 암호화하다, 부호화하다

v. to create the genetic code of something

DNA stores vital information and **encodes** the sequences of amino acids in proteins using the genetic code.

fertile
[fɔ́ːrtl]

ⓐ 생식력 있는, 가임의

n. fertility

adj. capable of producing things

Whether or not an individual is **fertile** depends on many factors, but genetics does play a role.

syn. fruitful   *ant.* barren

genome
[dʒíːnoum]

ⓝ 게놈(최소한의 유전자군을 가진 염색체의 한 세트)

n. a complete set of genetic material

The human **genome** is believed to contain 23 pairs of chromosomes and anywhere from 20,000 to 50,000 genes.

---

correspond 비록 동물 종에서 발견되는 많은 유전자들이 인간의 유전자와 일치할지라도, 모든 유전자가 그런 것은 아니다.   **discrete** 불연속 형질은 보통 단일 유전자에 의해 결정되고, 한 개체에 존재할 수도, 존재하지 않을 수도 있다.   **dissimilar** 유전적으로 서로 상당히 다른 배우자들이 가장 '성공적인' 자손을 낳는 것으로 나타났다.   **encode** DNA는 중요한 정보를 저장하고, 유전적 암호를 이용해 단백질에 있는 아미노산의 염기 서열을 암호화한다.   **fertile** 한 개체가 생식력이 있는지 여부는 많은 요인에 달려있지만, 유전도 한 몫을 한다.   **genome** 인간 게놈은 23쌍의 염색체와 2만에서 5만 개 가량의 유전자를 포함하는 것으로 알려져 있다.

govern
[gʌ́vərn]

ⓥ 지배하다, 통제하다

n. government

v. to control how something works

A living organism's genetic makeup **governs** not only its appearance but also its health and behavior.

syn. regulate

hereditary
[hərédətèri]

ⓐ 유전적인

adj. passed down from one's parents before birth

Doctors often ask for a detailed family medical history in order to determine a patient's risk level for **hereditary** diseases.

syn. inherited

hybrid
[háibrid]

ⓝ 잡종

n. a mix of two different things

Hybrids, offspring of parents from two genetically different species, rarely have the ability to reproduce.

syn. composite

identical
[aidéntikəl]

ⓐ 동일한, 똑같은

adj. exactly the same

Although **identical** twins start with the same genetic material, changes to their individual DNA occur in the womb.

syn. indistinguishable   *ant.* different

impervious
[impə́ːrviəs]

ⓐ …에 영향받지 않는

adj. unaffected by something

It is believed that genetic modification will one day make human beings **impervious** to many serious diseases.

syn. immune   *ant.* susceptible

infant
[ínfənt]

ⓝ 유아, 아기

adj. infantile

n. a very young child

The DNA of nearly every **infant** that is born in the United States is collected and tested soon after birth.

ant. adult

Useful Tips

영어에도 아기를 지칭하는 여러 단어들이 있는데, 보통 생후 2개월이 안된 아기는 newborn(신생아), 생후 2개월에서 1년 사이의 아기는 infant(유아), 걷기 시작할 때부터 3세 전까지의 아기는 toddler라고 부른다.

---

govern 생명체의 유전적 구성은 그 생명체의 외향뿐만 아니라 건강과 행동까지도 지배한다.   **hereditary** 의사들은 환자의 유전 질환에 대한 위험 수준을 알아내기 위해서 보통 상세한 가족 병력을 요구한다.   **hybrid** 유전적으로 다른 두 종의 부모로부터 나온 자손인 잡종은 번식 능력이 거의 없다.   **identical** 일란성 쌍둥이들은 동일한 유전 물질로부터 시작되지만, 자궁 내에서 각각의 DNA에 변화가 발생한다.   **impervious** 유전자 조작은 언젠가 인간이 많은 심각한 질병들에 영향받지 않도록 할 것이라고 여겨진다.   **infant** 미국에서 태어나는 거의 모든 아기의 DNA는 출생 후 얼마 되지 않아 수집되고 검사된다.

★★ **innate**
[inéit]
[형] 타고난, 선천적인

adj. natural; unlearned

Innate immunity is present at birth and does not require previous exposure to the specific antigens involved.

syn. inborn *ant.* acquired

★★ **invoke**
[invóuk]
[동] (이론이나 예를) 들다, 언급하다

v. to refer to something to support an argument

Scientists often **invoke** Darwin's *Origin of the Species* when trying to explain the impact of natural selection.

★★ **latent**
[léitnt]
[형] 잠재하는, 잠복해 있는
n. latency

adj. present but undeveloped or hidden

Without DNA testing, **latent** genetic conditions are likely to go undetected until it is too late.

syn. dormant *ant.* active

★★ **lethal**
[lí:θəl]
[형] 치명적인

adj. capable of causing death

Cystic fibrosis is a **lethal** genetic disorder that affects the lungs and digestive system of sufferers.

syn. deadly

Useful Tips

lethal은 lethal weapon(흉기)과 같이 위협적인 것을 나타낼 때 사용되지만, 비슷한 단어인 fatal은 fatal accident(사망 사고)에서처럼 이미 인명 피해를 일으킨 사건을 설명할 때 흔히 사용한다.

★★ **manifest**
[mǽnəfèst]
[동] 나타나다, 분명해지다
n. manifestation

v. to become apparent

There are some inherited traits in human beings that **manifest** due to the expression of multiple genes.

syn. reveal *ant.* conceal

★★ **meager**
[mí:gər]
[형] 결핍한, 불충분한

adj. insufficient in quality or quantity

Inbreeding within a population creates a **meager** gene pool that can adversely affect the health of subsequent generations.

syn. inadequate *ant.* ample

---

innate 선천적 면역은 태어날 때에 존재하며, 관련된 특정한 항원에 대한 사전 노출을 필요로 하지 않는다. **invoke** 과학자들은 자연 선택의 영향을 설명하려고 할 때 Darwin의 *종의 기원*을 종종 근거로 든다. **latent** DNA 검사를 하지 않으면, 잠재된 유전적 조건들이 아주 늦게까지 발견되지 않을 가능성이 크다. **lethal** 낭포성 섬유증은 환자의 폐와 소화기관에 영향을 미치는 치명적인 유전 질환이다. **manifest** 인간에게는 여러 유전자의 발현 때문에 나타나는 몇몇 유전적 특성들이 있다. **meager** 집단 내의 근친 교배는 후세대의 건강에 부정적 영향을 미칠 수 있는 불충분한 유전자 풀을 만든다.

meiosis
[maióusis]

(명) (세포핵의) 감수 분열

n. a type of cell division that results in four cells with half as many chromosomes as the original

Unlike mitosis, which is a multipurpose means of cell division, **meiosis** occurs only in reproductive functions.

mutation
[mju:téiʃən]

(명) 돌연변이, 변화

v. mutate

n. a genetic change in an organism

The ability of some adults to digest milk is due to a genetic **mutation** believed to have occurred in Europe a few thousand years ago.

obliterate
[əblítərèit]

(동) (흔적을) 없애다, 지우다

v. completely destroy

Even the smallest change to the genome's sequence has the potential to **obliterate** vital bodily functions.

syn. eradicate

phenotype
[fí:nətàip]

(명) 표현형, 형태

n. the characteristics resulting from interactions between genes and the environment

By observing **phenotypes**, scientists can make reasonable inferences about the genetic makeup of organisms.

postulate
[pástʃulèit]

(동) …을 가정하다

n. postulation

v. to suggest that something is true or exists

Gregor Mendel, a 19th-century scientist who experimented with pea plants, **postulated** three laws of inheritance.

syn. hypothesize

prevalent
[prévələnt]

(명) 일반적인, 널리 퍼져 있는

n. prevalence

adj. common or widespread

Highly **prevalent** gene variants in minority populations can cause disproportional suffering of certain conditions.

syn. ubiquitous   *ant.* rare

---

meiosis 다목적 세포 분열 수단인 체세포 분열과는 다르게, 감수 분열은 생식 기능으로서만 발생한다.   **mutation** 일부 성인들의 우유를 소화시키는 능력은 몇 천년 전에 유럽에서 발생한 것으로 여겨지는 유전적 돌연변이 때문이다.   **obliterate** 게놈 서열에 생기는 가장 작은 변화조차도 중요한 신체 기능을 없앨 수 있는 잠재력을 가지고 있다.   **phenotype** 과학자들은 표현형을 관찰함으로써 생물의 유전적 구성에 대한 합리적인 추론을 할 수 있다.   **postulate** 완두를 가지고 실험했던 19세기의 과학자 Gregor Mendel은 세 가지 유전 법칙을 가정했다.   **prevalent** 소수 개체군에 매우 널리 퍼져있는 유전자 변이는 특정 질환들로 인한 불균형적인 피해를 야기할 수 있다.

★★ **progeny**
[prádʒəni]
[명] 자손

n. young or offspring

Early scientists knew that parents pass down traits to their **progeny**, but they didn't understand how this occurs.

syn. descendants

★★ **recessive**
[risésiv]
[형] 열성의

adj. inheritable only if present in both parents

A **recessive** trait cannot be observed in offspring unless the gene that causes it is carried by both parents.

ant. dominant

★ **relapse**
[rilǽps]
[명] 재발, 되돌아감

n. an instance of becoming sick again after showing improvement

Genetic mutations, along with other factors, can be the cause of a patient's unexpected **relapse**.

syn. regression

★★★ **remarkable**
[rimáːrkəbl]
[형] 주목할 만한, 놀랄 만한, 비범한
n., v. remark

adj. extremely unusual or special

Although Darwin's theories were not without flaws, they represent a **remarkable** step forward in human knowledge.

syn. extraordinary *ant.* commonplace

★★ **remnant**
[rémnənt]
[명] 나머지, 남은 부분

n. a small remaining part of something

Many modern humans carry a **remnant** of Neanderthal DNA, due to interbreeding that occurred in the distant past.

syn. remains

★★★ **reproduce**
[rìːprədjúːs]
[동] 1. 번식하다
2. 복제하다
n. reproduction

v. **1** to produce offspring *syn.* breed
2 to make a copy of something *syn.* duplicate

1. Only the strongest wild animals are able to **reproduce**, ensuring that the next generation will inherit favorable traits.
2. Some cells **reproduce** by making an exact copy of their DNA before splitting into two parts.

---

progeny 초기 과학자들은 부모가 그들의 자손에게 형질을 물려준다는 것은 알았지만, 이것이 어떻게 일어나는지는 이해하지 못했다. **recessive** 열성 형질은 그것을 일으키는 유전자를 양쪽 부모에서 물려받지 않는 한, 자손에게서 관찰될 수 없다. **relapse** 유전적 돌연변이는 다른 요인들과 더불어 환자의 예상치 못한 재발 원인이 될 수 있다. **remarkable** Darwin의 이론들이 결점이 없는 것은 아니지만, 그 이론들은 인간 지식의 주목할 만한 진보를 보여 준다. **remnant** 많은 현대인들은 먼 과거에 발생한 이종 교배로 인해 네안데르탈인 DNA의 일부분을 지니고 있다. **reproduce** 1. 오직 제일 강한 야생 동물만이 번식할 수 있고, 다음 세대가 유리한 특성을 물려받을 것을 보장한다. 2. 일부 세포들은 두 부분으로 나누어지기 전에 그들과 똑같은 DNA를 만들어 냄으로써 복제한다.

★★★

responsible

[rispάnsəbl]

[형] …의 원인이 되는, 책임지고 있는

n. responsibility

adj. being the cause of something

A cell's mitochondria, which is **responsible** for the production of energy, contains a small amount of DNA.

★

reversal

[rivə́ːrsəl]

[명] 뒤바꿈, 역전, 반전

v., adj. reverse

n. the act of changing to the opposite

Devolution is the concept of evolutionary **reversal**, in which a species would reacquire traits it had lost in the past.

★★

scarce

[skɛərs]

[형] 드문, 부족한

n. scarcity

adj. existing in small quantities; not enough

It is important to note that much of human evolution took place in a time when food was **scarce**.

syn. insufficient *ant.* ample

★★

synthesis

[sínθəsis]

[명] 합성

v. synthesize

n. the act of producing something through chemical reactions

Gene **synthesis** is an application of genetic engineering that involves the creation and assembly of artificial genes.

★★

tremendous

[triméndəs]

[형] 거대한, 엄청난

adj. extremely large

Genetic engineering has taken a **tremendous** leap forward in recent years, raising many ethical concerns.

syn. huge *ant.* tiny

★★

worthwhile

[wə́ːrθhwáil]

[형] 가치 있는

adj. good enough to do or buy

Home genetic tests are now available to consumers, but many experts question whether they are **worthwhile**.

syn. valuable *ant.* worthless

---

responsible 에너지 생성의 역할을 하는 세포의 미토콘드리아는 소량의 DNA를 지니고 있다. **reversal** 퇴행적 진화란 어떤 하나의 종이 과거에 잃어버렸던 특성을 다시 획득하는 진화 역전의 개념이다. **scarce** 인류 진화의 많은 부분이 식량이 부족한 시기에 발생했다는 점에 주목하는 것이 중요하다. **synthesis** 유전자 합성은 인공 유전자의 생성과 조합을 수반하는 유전 공학의 응용이다. **tremendous** 유전 공학은 최근 몇 년 동안 윤리적 우려들을 일으키며 엄청나게 도약했다. **worthwhile** 이제 소비자들이 가정용 유전자 검사를 이용할 수 있지만, 많은 전문가들은 그것이 가치 있는 것인지에 대해 의문을 제기한다.

EXERCISES

A Match each definition with the correct word.

1 a complete set of genetic material   ⓐ reversal

2 to become apparent   ⓑ recessive

3 comparable to something else   ⓒ genome

4 a genetic change in an organism   ⓓ progeny

5 the act of changing to the opposite   ⓔ mutation

6 young or offspring   ⓕ analogous

7 inheritable only if present in both parents   ⓖ manifest

8 a mix of two different things   ⓗ hybrid

B Choose the word that is closest in meaning to each underlined word.

1 Prolonged exposure to sunlight will <u>alter</u> the skin's appearance by making it darker.
   ⓐ enhance   ⓑ damage   ⓒ modify   ⓓ intensify

2 It would be dangerous if pills with different purposes were <u>identical</u> in appearance.
   ⓐ replaceable   ⓑ indistinguishable   ⓒ controversial   ⓓ advantageous

3 When water becomes <u>scarce</u> during dry season, animals gather around watering holes.
   ⓐ unhygienic   ⓑ tepid   ⓒ submerged   ⓓ insufficient

4 The experiment was canceled due to suggestions that it wasn't a <u>worthwhile</u> use of time.
   ⓐ comprehensible   ⓑ valuable   ⓒ standard   ⓓ unexpected

5 The substances present before the chemical reaction <u>commences</u> will undergo changes.
   ⓐ begins   ⓑ concludes   ⓒ falters   ⓓ repeats

6 Antibodies protect the body, but they don't make it <u>impervious</u> to disease.
   ⓐ fragile   ⓑ connected   ⓒ immune   ⓓ parallel

7 Rock doves, which are better known as pigeons, are <u>prevalent</u> in urbanized areas.
   ⓐ detested   ⓑ precarious   ⓒ invasive   ⓓ ubiquitous

ART & DESIGN

SOCIAL SCIENCE

NATURAL SCIENCE

HUMANITIES

EARTH & SPACE

SOCIAL ISSUES

A Choose the correct words.

1 The word align has the same meaning as
   ⓐ move around   ⓑ line up   ⓒ turn over   ⓓ slow down

2 The word perspire has the same meaning as
   ⓐ reproduce   ⓑ escape   ⓒ sweat   ⓓ construct

3 The word emit has the same meaning as
   ⓐ melt   ⓑ release   ⓒ revolve   ⓓ disappear

4 The word alleviate has the same meaning as
   ⓐ elevate   ⓑ redirect   ⓒ summarize   ⓓ relieve

5 The word postulate has the same meaning as
   ⓐ disagree   ⓑ recalculate   ⓒ hypothesize   ⓓ liquidate

6 The word prevent has the same meaning as
   ⓐ thwart   ⓑ warp   ⓒ secure   ⓓ cease

7 The word incision has the same meaning as
   ⓐ decision   ⓑ procedure   ⓒ tool   ⓓ cut

8 The word feasible has the same meaning as
   ⓐ possible   ⓑ weak   ⓒ upcoming   ⓓ unknown

B Fill in the blanks with the best words from the box.

1 The central nervous system _____ messages from the brain throughout the body.

2 Scientists believe the fish may have died from eating _____ material such as microplastics.

3 Even though she wasn't showing any _____, the patient tested positive for the disease.

4 The _____ of koalas are curved, which makes it easier for them to live in the branches of trees.

5 There are some red dyes that are made with carminic acid _____ from the bodies of small insects.

6 A _____ number of termites can live in a single nest, with estimates as high as several million.

| spines | symptoms | tremendous | transmits | inorganic | derived |

C Read the following passages.

ART & DESIGN

SOCIAL SCIENCE

NATURAL SCIENCE

HUMANITIES

EARTH & SPACE

SOCIAL ISSUES

[1-2] **1** Choose one word that fits both blanks.

The _____ of the lungs is to take air into the body in order to extract vital oxygen from it. Without a sufficient supply of oxygen, the body would not be able to _____ properly, and death would soon follow. Therefore, healthy lungs are essential to survival.

ⓐ function   ⓑ implant   ⓒ relapse   ⓓ cure

2 Choose the appropriate pair of words to fill in the blanks.

Quick action is crucial during a medical emergency. Once a patient has been admitted into a hospital, doctors must _____ his or her condition as soon as possible. This allows them to determine the proper treatment or medication, which they will then quickly _____.

ⓐ attach — generate   ⓑ diagnose — administer

ⓒ sever — transplant   ⓓ oxidize — retain

[3-4]

In parts of the world, insects are expected to replace cows as a primary food source in the future. An important benefit of raising insects is that they don't require land for grazing. By reducing the number of cows, people would give damaged ecosystems a chance to recuperate.

3 In the context of the passage, benefit means _____.

ⓐ requirement   ⓑ objective   ⓒ consequence   ⓓ asset

4 The word recuperate in the passage could best be replaced by

ⓐ broaden   ⓑ shift   ⓒ heal   ⓓ regress

[5-6]

Radiation has useful applications in a variety of fields, from medicine to energy production. However, it also has a serious downside—the unwanted _____ of radioactive material left behind by these activities. This waste can remain lethal for many years, so it must be disposed of in special storage facilities designed to minimize the possibility of leakage.

5 Choose the word that is most suitable for the blank.

ⓐ starches   ⓑ panaceas   ⓒ lipids   ⓓ remnants

6 The word lethal in the passage is closest in meaning to

ⓐ deadly   ⓑ effective   ⓒ hidden   ⓓ unpredictable

그리스어 접두사
Greek **Prefixes**

영어에서 그리스어 접두사도 상당히 중요한 부분을 차지하는데, 의학, 수학, 과학, 그리고 정치와 관련된 많은 전문 용어들이 그리스어 접두사를 사용하기 때문이다. Chapter 3에서 배운 antibody, biodiversity, hydrophobic, panacea는 그리스어에서 유래한 접두사인 anti-, bio-, hydr-/hydro-, pan-이 사용된 단어들이다. 주요 그리스어 접두사들의 고유 의미를 살펴보고, 그 접두사가 사용된 단어들도 함께 숙지해 보자.

PREFIXES	EXAMPLES
anti- *against, opposite of*	antibacterial 항균성의　antibody 항체　antipathy 혐오, 반감 antiseptic 소독제　antisocial 반사회적인　antivirus 바이러스 퇴치용의
auto- *self*	autobiography 자서전　autocrat 전제 군주　autograph 서명 autoimmune 자가 면역의　automatic 자동의　autonomy 자치(권)
bio- *life, living matter*	biodiversity 생물의 다양성　biochemical 생화학의　biography 전기, 일대기 biology 생물학　biomass 바이오매스　biotoxin 생물 독소
dia- *across, between, through*	diabetes 당뇨병　diagnosis 진단　diagram 도표　dialect 방언 dialogue 대화　diameter 지름
geo- *earth, soil, global*	geocentric 지구 중심적인　geography 지리학　geology 지질학 geometric 기하학의　geomorphic 지구 모양의　geoscience 지구 과학
hydr-/hydro- *water, liquid*	hydrate 수화시키다　hydraulic 수압의　hydrogen 수소 hydrolysis 가수 분해　hydrophobic 소수성의　hydropower 수력
pan- *all, any, everyone*	panacea 만병통치약　pandemic 전 세계적인 유행병　pandemonium 대소란 panorama 전경　pantheism 다신교　pantomime 무언극
poly- *many, more than one*	polychrome 여러 가지 색채의　polyester 폴리에스테르　polygamy 일부다처제 polyglot 여러 언어를 사용하는　polygon 다각형　polygraph 거짓말 탐지기
syl-/sym-/syn-/sys- *together, with, same*	syllable 음절　symmetry 대칭　sympathy 동정, 연민 synergy 동반 상승효과　synonym 동의어　system 제도
tele- *far, distant*	telecommuting 재택 근무　telegram 전보　telepathy 텔레파시 telephone 전화　telescope 망원경　television 텔레비전

CHAPTER

HUMANITIES

[>] 미디어와 저널리즘

Lesson 31 Media & Journalism

★★
biased
[báiəst]
[형] 편향된, 선입견 있는
n. bias

adj. **unfairly prejudiced for or against someone or something**

Many people complained that the cable news show presented a **biased** view of the presidential elections.

syn. partisan *ant.* unbiased

★★
censor
[sénsər]
[동] 삭제하다, 검열하다
n. censorship

v. **to stop images, text, or video from being seen by the public**

If the newspaper articles seemed incomplete, it was probably because some sensitive information had been **censored**.

syn. forbid

★
circulation
[sə̀ːrkjuléiʃən]
[명] 발행 부수, 판매 실적
v. circulate

n. **the number of copies of a newspaper or magazine that are sold**

Nearly every newspaper in the world has experienced a decline in **circulation** with the rise of the Internet.

syn. readership

Useful Tips
circulation은 인쇄된 출판물에 대해서만 사용되며, 온라인 뉴스 매체는 subscriber나 page view의 숫자가 circulation을 대신한다.

★★
commentary
[kámənteri]
[명] 논평, 시사 평론
n., v. comment

n. **an opinion about an issue or event**

The news anchor's passionate **commentary** on the political situation was widely praised by viewers.

★★★
coverage
[kʌ́vəridʒ]
[명] 보도, 취재 범위
v. cover

n. **the attention that the media gives to an issue or event**

There was a lot of local **coverage** of the forest fire, but it received little attention from the national news.

syn. reporting

★★
credibility
[krèdəbíləti]
[명] 신뢰성, 진실성
adj. credible

n. **the quality of being seen as believable and trustworthy**

After admitting to adding false details to one of her stories, the journalist lost **credibility** with the public.

syn. believability

---

biased 그 케이블 뉴스 방송이 대통령 선거에 대해 편향된 시각을 보였다고 많은 사람들이 불평했다. **censor** 신문 기사들이 미비해 보인다면, 일부 민감한 정보가 삭제되었기 때문일 것이다. **circulation** 인터넷의 부상으로 세계 거의 모든 신문의 발행 부수가 감소했다. **commentary** 그 정치 상황에 대한 뉴스 앵커의 열정적 논평은 시청자들로부터 널리 호평을 받았다. **coverage** 그 산불에 대한 지역 보도는 많았지만, 전국 뉴스에서는 거의 주목을 받지 못했다. **credibility** 그 기자는 자신의 기사들 중 하나에 허위 세부 내용들을 추가했다고 인정한 후, 대중의 신뢰를 잃었다.

ART & DESIGN

SOCIAL SCIENCE

NATURAL SCIENCE

HUMANITIES

EARTH & SPACE

SOCIAL ISSUES

divulge
[diváldʒ]
ⓥ (비밀 등을) 누설하다, 알려 주다

v. to share a secret or private information

Celebrities sometimes **divulge** unintended information when they become too comfortable with an interviewer.

syn. disclose   *ant.* withhold

edit
[édit]
ⓥ 편집하다, 교정하다

n. editor

v. to alter a piece of writing, film, or video to make it better or shorter

The stunning footage of the protests had to be **edited** for length before it was shown on the evening news.

syn. refine

feature
[fíːtʃər]
ⓝ 특집 기사[방송]

n. an in-depth analysis of a specific issue in print or on TV

This month's issue of the news magazine includes a **feature** about the housing problems faced by poor families.

syn. piece

freelance
[fríːlæns]
ⓐ 프리랜서로 일하는

n. freelancer

adj. relating to independently produced work from an outside source

The television network contacted a local **freelance** journalist about conducting interviews with earthquake survivors.

impartial
[impáːrʃəl]
ⓐ 공정한

n. impartiality

adj. fair and unprejudiced

Most television newsreaders strive to appear **impartial** without giving the impression of a lack of interest.

syn. unbiased   *ant.* partial

influential
[influénʃəl]
ⓐ 영향력 있는, 유력한

n., v. influence

adj. having the power to affect the beliefs and opinions of others

The New York Times is considered one of the most respected and **influential** newspapers in the United States.

syn. significant   *ant.* obscure

---

divulge 유명 인사들이 인터뷰 진행자와 지나치게 편안해지면, 때때로 의도하지 않은 정보를 누설한다.   **edit** 그 시위들을 찍은 충격적인 장면은 길이 때문에, 저녁 뉴스에 나가기 전에 편집되어야 했다.   **feature** 그 시사 잡지의 이번 달 호에는 빈곤 가정들이 직면한 주택 문제에 대한 특집 기사가 포함되어 있다.
freelance 그 텔레비전 방송국은 지진 생존자들과의 인터뷰 진행과 관련해 현지 프리랜서 기자에게 연락했다.   **impartial** 대부분의 텔레비전 아나운서들은 무관심하다는 인상을 주지 않으면서 공정하게 보이려고 노력한다.   **influential** 뉴욕 *타임즈*는 미국에서 가장 높이 평가되고 영향력 있는 신문들 중 하나로 간주된다.

★
★ ★
integrity
[intégrəti]

ⓝ 진실성, 고결

n. the quality of having strong moral principles

The **integrity** of journalists can be challenged when they report on matters that affect them personally.

syn. honor *ant.* corruption

★
libel
[láibəl]

ⓝ 명예 훼손

adj. libelous

n. the illegal act of publicly making false accusations

The magazine was sued for **libel** after publishing a false report about the personal life of a famous actor.

syn. defamation

★ ★
literacy
[lítərəsi]

ⓝ 읽고 쓰는 능력

adj. literate

n. the ability to read and write

With the rise of **literacy** in Europe, more and more weekly newspapers began to be published.

ant. illiteracy

★ ★
mainstream
[méinstrìːm]

ⓝ 주류, 대세

n. behavior, activities, and ideas that are typical and widely accepted

Although people were hesitant to abandon print newspapers at first, online news soon became part of the **mainstream**.

★ ★
★ ★
manipulate
[mənípjulèit]

ⓥ 조종하다

n. manipulation

v. to skillfully control a person or situation in a dishonest way

The politician attempted to **manipulate** reporters by offering favors to those who wrote positive articles about him.

★ ★
misleading
[mislíːdiŋ]

ⓝ 오해의 소지가 있는, 오도하는

adj. causing people to draw false conclusions

There was nothing controversial about the article itself, but readers complained about its **misleading** headline.

syn. deceitful

---

integrity 본인들에게 개인적으로 영향을 미치는 문제들에 대해 보도할 때, 기자들의 진실성이 시험 받을 수 있다.　**libel** 그 잡지는 한 유명 배우의 사생활에 대한 허위 기사를 게재한 후, 명예 훼손으로 피소되었다.　**literacy** 유럽에서 읽고 쓰는 능력이 높아지면서, 점점 더 많은 주간지들이 발간되기 시작했다.
mainstream 사람들이 처음에는 인쇄된 신문을 포기하는 것을 주저했지만, 곧 온라인 뉴스가 주류에 편입했다.　**manipulate** 그 정치인은 자신에 대해 긍정적인 기사를 쓴 사람들에게 호의를 베풀어 기자들을 조종하려 했다.　**misleading** 그 기사 자체에는 논란거리가 없었지만, 독자들은 오해의 소지가 있는 헤드라인에 대해 항의했다.

★
★
plagiarism

[pléidʒərìzm]

몡 표절, 도용

v. plagiarize

n. the act of copying the work of others and pretending it is your own

Failure to properly cite his sources led to charges of **plagiarism** being leveled against the reporter.

★
★
★
privacy

[práivəsi]

몡 사생활

adj. private

n. the state of being unseen and undisturbed by others

Despite the public's demand for details about the lives of popular celebrities, journalists must respect their right to **privacy**.

syn. confidentiality

★
publicist

[pʌ́bləsist]

몡 홍보 담당자

n. a person whose job is to get media attention for a person or organization

The company hired a **publicist** to ensure that they received adequate coverage of their charitable initiatives.

syn. press agent

★
★
quote

[kwout]

됭 인용하다

n. quotation

v. to write or refer to the words of someone else

The television news reporter began her piece by **quoting** a past president who is still widely respected.

syn. cite

★
★
ratings

[réitiŋz]

몡 시청률

n. a measure of the size of the estimated audience of a television show

The morning news show's **ratings** skyrocketed when it switched to a more upbeat and youthful format.

★
★
★
reliable

[riláiəbl]

몡 신뢰할 수 있는

v. rely

adj. consistent and trustworthy

The public craves a **reliable** source of news that does not attempt to sway the opinions of its readers.

syn. dependable   *ant.* unreliable

---

plagiarism 그 기자는 출처들을 제대로 인용하지 않아, 표절 혐의를 받았다.   **privacy** 대중은 인기 있는 유명 인사들의 삶에 대한 자세한 내용들을 요구하지만, 기자들은 그들의 사생활권을 존중해야 한다.   **publicist** 그 회사는 자선 계획들에 대한 적절한 보도가 확실히 이루어지도록 홍보 담당자를 채용했다.   **quote** 그 텔레비전 뉴스 기자는 여전히 널리 존경 받고 있는 전직 대통령의 말을 인용하면서 보도를 시작했다.   **ratings** 그 아침 뉴스 방송이 좀 더 발랄하고 젊은 감각의 형식으로 전환하자, 시청률이 급등했다.   **reliable** 대중은 독자들의 의견을 조종하려 하지 않는 신뢰할 수 있는 소식통을 원한다.

★
retraction
[ritrǽkʃən]

ⓝ 철회, 취소

v. retract

n. the act of withdrawing a statement because it was false

The news site issued a **retraction** and a formal apology after posting a story based on untruthful information.

★
★
★
scandalous
[skǽndləs]

ⓐ 불명예스러운, 수치스러운

n. scandal

adj. causing public outrage due to shocking behavior

The **scandalous** behavior of the wealthy CEO made front-page headlines all across the globe.

syn. disreputable

★
★
sensationalism
[senséiʃənəlìzm]

ⓝ 선정주의

adj. sensational

n. the use of shocking information to get the attention of readers or viewers

Unfortunately, many online news sources resort to **sensationalism** in order to entice readers to click on their articles.

★
sound bite
[sáund bàit]

ⓝ 방송용으로 발췌한
짧은 영상이나 어구

n. a short excerpt from a longer statement

The evening news program reduced the two-hour presidential debate into a handful of entertaining **sound bites**.

★
★
tabloid
[tǽblɔid]

ⓝ 타블로이드 신문

n. a newspaper that publishes shocking and sometimes inaccurate stories

Many readers of weekly **tabloids** are fully aware that some of the stories they are reading are untrue.

Useful Tips

tabloid는 원래 보통 신문의 절반 크기인 신문을 뜻했으나, 지금은 흥미 위주의 짧은 기사와 유명인의 사진을 크게 싣는 신문이라는 뜻으로 더 많이 쓰인다.

★
★
★
verify
[vérəfài]

ⓥ 확인하다, 검증하다

n. verification

v. to check something to ensure it is true

It is the responsibility of journalists to **verify** all of the information that they receive from outside sources.

syn. confirm

---

retraction 그 뉴스 사이트는 허위 정보에 근거한 기사를 게시한 후, 철회와 공식적인 사과를 발표했다. **scandalous** 그 부유한 최고 경영자의 불명예스러운 행동은 전 세계 신문 1면 기사로 떴다. **sensationalism** 유감스럽게도, 많은 온라인 뉴스 매체들은 독자들이 기사들을 클릭하게 하려고 선정주의를 이용한다. **sound bite** 그 저녁 뉴스 프로그램은 2시간짜리 대통령 후보 토론을 방송용으로 발췌한 몇 개의 재미난 짧은 영상들로 줄였다. **tabloid** 주간 타블로이드 신문들을 읽는 많은 독자들은 자신이 읽고 있는 기사들의 일부가 사실이 아니라는 것을 충분히 인식하고 있다. **verify** 외부 정보원들로부터 받는 모든 정보를 검증하는 것이 기자들의 의무이다.

EXERCISES

A Match each definition with the correct word.

1 a short excerpt from a longer statement

2 causing people to draw false conclusions

3 an opinion about an issue or event

4 the ability to read and write

5 to share a secret or private information

6 the act of withdrawing a statement because it was false

7 fair and unprejudiced

8 to skillfully control a person or situation in a dishonest way

ⓐ retraction

ⓑ manipulate

ⓒ literacy

ⓓ commentary

ⓔ sound bite

ⓕ divulge

ⓖ misleading

ⓗ impartial

B Choose the word that is closest in meaning to each underlined word.

1 The novel *Don Quixote* is considered one of the most <u>influential</u> books of all time.
   ⓐ controversial   ⓑ significant   ⓒ complicated   ⓓ overrated

2 The classic myths in this collection have been <u>edited</u> to make them suitable for children.
   ⓐ refined   ⓑ removed   ⓒ researched   ⓓ entered

3 Due to inaccuracies, this book is no longer considered a <u>reliable</u> source of information.
   ⓐ collective   ⓑ traditional   ⓒ widespread   ⓓ dependable

4 Philosophers such as Aristotle and Socrates are still commonly <u>quoted</u> in modern times.
   ⓐ cited   ⓑ honored   ⓒ defended   ⓓ skewed

5 During media <u>coverage</u> of important events, words are used to evoke an emotional response.
   ⓐ monitor   ⓑ censor   ⓒ reporting   ⓓ interpretation

6 It is difficult to <u>verify</u> the authenticity of folk art whose creators are unknown.
   ⓐ share   ⓑ declare   ⓒ inspect   ⓓ confirm

7 Critics called the mayor's autobiography <u>biased</u> for its depiction of his political rivals.
   ⓐ legendary   ⓑ partisan   ⓒ beneficial   ⓓ appreciative

> 현대 문학

Modern Literature

★★
appreciate
[əprí:ʃièit]
ⓥ 진가를 알아보다, 높이 평가하다

n. appreciation

v. to recognize the worth of someone or something

People tend to **appreciate** books that reflect the current mood of society in new and interesting ways.

★
avid
[ǽvid]
ⓐ 열심인, 열렬한

adj. very enthusiastic about an activity

Avid readers are constantly searching for interesting authors whose books they have not yet read.

syn. keen   *ant.* disinterested

★★
cliché
[kli:ʃéi]
ⓝ 상투적인 문구, 진부한 표현

n. something overused and unoriginal

Critics complained about the book's main character, calling her an outdated **cliché** with little connection to reality.

★★★
consistent
[kənsístənt]
ⓐ 한결 같은, 일관된

adj. showing little change

The celebrated mystery writer has been releasing books at a **consistent** rate for more than 30 years now.

syn. steady   *ant.* erratic

★★★
contemporary
[kəntémpərèri]
ⓐ 현대의, 동시대의

adj. relating to the present day

Many of the most common **contemporary** themes in literature would have been considered shocking in the past.

syn. modern   *ant.* archaic

★★
copyright
[kápiràit]
ⓝ 저작권, 판권

n. the legal right to use an artistic, literary, or musical work

Because the book's **copyright** expired a couple of years ago, it is now available online for free.

---

appreciate 사람들은 사회의 현재 분위기를 새롭고 흥미로운 방법으로 반영하는 책들을 높이 평가하는 경향이 있다.   **avid** 열렬한 독자들은 그들이 아직 읽지 않은 책들을 쓴 흥미로운 작가들을 끊임없이 찾고 있다.   **cliché** 비평가들은 그 책의 주인공에 대해 불만을 나타내며, 그녀를 현실과 관련성이 거의 없는 시대에 뒤떨어진 진부한 인물이라고 칭했다.   **consistent** 그 유명한 추리 소설 작가는 지금까지 30년 이상 한결 같이 책을 출간해 오고 있다.   **contemporary** 가장 흔한 현대 문학 주제 중 다수가 과거에는 충격적으로 여겨졌을 것이다.   **copyright** 그 책의 저작권이 몇 년 전에 만료되었기 때문에, 현재 온라인에서 무료로 이용할 수 있다.

cynical
[sínikəl]
ⓐ 냉소적인, 자기 이익만 생각하는

n. cynic

adj. believing or based on the belief that all people are selfish

As the novel offers a **cynical** view of the modern movie industry, even the protagonists are unlikable.

syn. misanthropic

Useful Tips

cynical은 부정적인 마음의 상태를 의미하고, sarcastic은 단순히 생각을 부정적인 방법으로 표현하는 것을 의미한다.

dystopian
[distóupiən]
ⓐ 반(反)이상향의

n. dystopia

adj. relating to an imaginary future in which everything is bad

Novels with **dystopian** settings have been unusually popular with young adults and teens in recent years.

ant. utopian

excerpt
[éksəːrpt]
ⓝ 발췌[인용] (부분)

n. a short section taken from a larger work

The author granted a magazine permission to publish an **excerpt** from his upcoming book about the American Civil War.

fictional
[fíkʃənl]
ⓐ 허구적인

n. fiction

adj. imagined; not real

There are many **fictional** characters from novels that have become influential figures in modern society.

syn. imaginary   *ant.* real

figurative
[fígjurətiv]
ⓐ 비유적인

adj. representing something outside its normal meaning

The author's creative use of **figurative** language transforms dry historical facts into an entertaining story.

syn. symbolic   *ant.* literal

Useful Tips

homage라는 단어가 불어에서 유래했기 때문에 두 가지의 발음을 들을 수 있다. 전통적으로 영어에서는 'h'를 발음하지만, 요즘에는 묵음으로 발음하는 경우도 흔하다.

homage
[hámidʒ, ám-]
ⓝ 경의, 존경의 표시

n. something said or done to show respect

Some biographies treat their subjects unkindly, but this one comes across more as an **homage** to the legendary actor.

syn. tribute

---

cynical 그 소설이 현대 영화 산업을 냉소적으로 바라보기 때문에, 주인공들조차도 호감이 가지 않는다. **dystopian** 반(反)이상향적 배경의 소설들은 최근 몇 년 동안 젊은이들과 십 대들에게 이례적으로 인기가 있었다. **excerpt** 그 작가는 출간을 앞둔 미국 남북 전쟁에 대한 그의 책에서 발췌한 부분을 잡지사가 게재하도록 허락했다. **fictional** 현대 사회에서 영향력 있는 인물이 된 소설 속 허구적인 등장인물들이 많다. **figurative** 그 작가의 창의적인 비유적 언어 사용은 무미건조한 역사적 사실을 재미있는 이야기로 바꿔 준다. **homage** 몇몇 전기들은 그 대상을 불친절하게 다루지만, 이 전기는 그 전설적인 배우에 대한 존경의 표시라는 인상을 더 준다.

★★★
inspire
[inspáiər]
[동] 영감을 주다, 고무[격려]하다
n. inspiration

v. to motivate someone to do or create something

Inspired by his writing instructor, the young man published his first short story at the age of 22.

syn. encourage *ant.* dissuade

★★
literary
[lítərèri]
[형] 문학의, 문필의, 문예의
n. literature

adj. relating to reading, writing, or studying books

The Booker Prize, based in the United Kingdom, is one of the most prestigious awards in the **literary** world.

★★
masterpiece
[mǽstərpìːs]
[명] 걸작, 명작

n. an exceptional work of art

The Color Purple, written by Alice Walker and published in 1982, is considered a modern **masterpiece**.

★★
memoir
[mémwaːr]
[명] 회고록, 전기

n. a written account based on personal experiences

A Moveable Feast, Ernest Hemingway's 1964 **memoir**, recounts his life as an American expat in Paris in the 1920s.

Useful Tips

memoir(회고록)는 특정 시간과 사건을 둘러싼 감정과 경험에 중점을 두는 데 반해, autobiography(자서전)는 작가의 삶에 걸쳐 있었던 일들을 시간 순서대로 나타낸다.

★★
monologue
[mánəlɔ̀ːg]
[명] 독백

n. an extended speech given by a single person

Much of the novel takes the form of an interior **monologue** given by the main character during a long train ride.

syn. soliloquy *ant.* dialogue

★★
motif
[moutíːf]
[명] 주제

n. a repeated idea in a written work

The book's **motif** of a loss of identity is symbolized by the characters' quest for meaning online.

syn. theme

---

inspire 그 젊은이는 그의 작문 강사에게 고무되어 22세의 나이에 그의 첫 단편 소설을 출간했다. **literary** 영국에 기반을 둔 부커 상은 문학계에서 가장 권위 있는 상들 중 하나이다. **masterpiece** Alice Walker가 집필하고 1982년에 출판된 *컬러 퍼플*은 현대 걸작으로 여겨진다. **memoir** Ernest Hemingway의 1964년 회고록인 *파리는 날마다 축제*는 1920년대 파리에 거주했던 미국인으로서의 그의 삶에 대해 이야기한다. **monologue** 그 소설의 많은 부분이 긴 기차 여행을 하는 동안 주인공이 하는 내적 독백의 형식을 띠고 있다. **motif** 정체성의 상실이라는 그 책의 주제는 온라인에서 등장인물들이 (삶의) 의미를 탐구하는 것으로 상징된다.

narrative
★★★
[nǽrətiv]
몡 묘사, 서술, 이야기

v. narrate

n. a spoken or written description of a series of events

The writer offers a straightforward **narrative** from the point of view of a Native American teenager.

syn. account

overview
★★★
[óuvərvjùː]
몡 개관, 개요

n. a general description of something as a whole

The opening chapter of the book presents an **overview** of the historical events that led up to dropping of the atomic bomb.

syn. summary

parody
★★
[pǽrədi]
몡 패러디(다른 것을 풍자적으로 모방한 연극, 글, 예술 작품)

n. a film, book, or work of art that imitates something to make fun of it

The book is a **parody** of every Victorian novel in which a hardheaded young woman finds true love.

syn. spoof

plot
★★★
[plɑt]
몡 (소설·극·영화 등의) 구성, 줄거리

n. the story of a book or film

The **plot** of the novel involves a group of friends who witness a crime but decide to keep it a secret.

syn. storyline

proofread
★★
[prúːfrìːd]
통 교정을 보다

v. to check a written work for errors

The writer explained that her husband **proofread** the entire 600-page manuscript of her latest book.

pseudonym
★
[súːdənìm]
몡 필명, 가명

n. a false name

Horror writer Stephen King published several novels under the **pseudonym** Richard Bachman in the 1970s and 80s.

syn. alias

ART & DESIGN | SOCIAL SCIENCE | NATURAL SCIENCE | HUMANITIES | EARTH & SPACE | SOCIAL ISSUES

---

narrative 그 작가는 십 대 미국 원주민의 관점에서 직설적으로 서술한다.　**overview** 그 책의 첫 장은 원자 폭탄 투하로 이어진 역사적 사건들을 개괄적으로 보여 준다.　**parody** 그 책은 냉철한 젊은 여성이 진정한 사랑을 찾는 모든 빅토리아 시대 소설의 패러디이다.　**plot** 그 소설의 줄거리는 범죄를 목격했지만 비밀에 부치기로 한 무리의 친구들과 관련이 있다.　**proofread** 그 작가는 그녀의 남편이 자신의 600 페이지짜리 최근 저서 원고를 전부 교정했다고 설명했다.
pseudonym 공포물 작가인 Stephen King은 1970년대와 80년대에 Richard Bachman이란 필명으로 몇 편의 소설을 출간했다.

publication
[pÀbləkéiʃən]
ⓝ 출판, 발행

v. publish

n. the process of making a written work available for purchase

Publication of the former prime minister's autobiography has been delayed by legal issues.

relevant
[réləvənt]
ⓝ 관련 있는, 적절한

n. relevancy

adj. connected to a topic or situation

Despite being nearly 50 years old, the young adult novel is still **relevant** to the lives of teenagers today.

syn. pertinent   *ant.* irrelevant

revision
[rivíʒən]
ⓝ 개정, 수정

v. revise

n. a change made to improve a written work

The author's publisher returned his latest manuscript along with a long list of **revisions** they deemed necessary.

syn. modification

simile
[síməli]
ⓝ 직유

n. a comparison made using either "as" or "like"

"As busy as a bee" may seem like a modern **simile**, but it was used by Chaucer in the 14th century.

subtext
[sÁbtèkst]
ⓝ 언외의 의미, 작품 속에 숨은 의미

n. something that is unwritten or unspoken but understood

The **subtext** of the author's latest book is that human beings need to start working together in order to survive.

terse
[tə:rs]
ⓝ (예의에 어긋날 정도로) 간결한

adj. brief and unfriendly

The writer's **terse** sentences may be cold and uninviting to readers, but they do convey the facts effectively.

---

publication 전 총리의 자서전 출판이 법적인 문제로 연기되었다.   **relevant** 그 청소년 소설은 거의 50년이 되었음에도 불구하고, 여전히 오늘날 십 대들의 삶과 관련이 있다.   **revision** 그 작가의 출판사는 그들이 필요하다고 생각하는 긴 수정 목록과 함께 그의 최근 원고를 돌려주었다.   **simile** '벌처럼 바쁜'은 현대적 직유처럼 보일지 모르나, 14세기에 Chaucer에 의해 사용되었다.   **subtext** 그 저자의 최신작 속에 숨겨진 의미는 인간이 생존하기 위해 함께 힘을 모으기 시작해야 한다는 것이다.   **terse** 그 작가의 간결한 문장들이 독자들에게는 차갑고 매력 없을지 모르지만, 사실들을 매우 효과적으로 전달한다.

EXERCISES

ART & DESIGN

SOCIAL SCIENCE

NATURAL SCIENCE

HUMANITIES

EARTH & SPACE

SOCIAL ISSUES

A Match each definition with the correct word.

1 to recognize the worth of someone or something   ⓐ pseudonym

2 a false name   ⓑ memoir

3 a repeated idea in a written work   ⓒ excerpt

4 something overused and unoriginal   ⓓ proofread

5 a change made to improve a written work   ⓔ appreciate

6 a short section taken from a larger work   ⓕ motif

7 to check a written work for errors   ⓖ cliché

8 a written account based on personal experiences   ⓗ revision

B Choose the word that is closest in meaning to each underlined word.

1 Contemporary philosophers struggle to make their ideas accessible to everyday people.
     ⓐ acclaimed   ⓑ amateur   ⓒ modern   ⓓ cooperative

2 Some religious teachings are designed to inspire people to be better neighbors.
     ⓐ endorse   ⓑ encourage   ⓒ prevent   ⓓ dissuade

3 Avid travelers avoid touristy areas, instead seeking out the authentic culture of places.
     ⓐ intrusive   ⓑ keen   ⓒ cautious   ⓓ domestic

4 Due to the regional nature of folk art, its national characteristics are rarely consistent.
     ⓐ recognized   ⓑ appealing   ⓒ ornate   ⓓ steady

5 Critics accused the novelist of copying Hemingway, but he said his book was an homage.
     ⓐ blunder   ⓑ request   ⓒ sequel   ⓓ tribute

6 Some of the fictional heroes of mythology may have been based on historical figures.
     ⓐ imaginary   ⓑ courageous   ⓒ ancient   ⓓ mundane

7 The most important lessons taught to us by history have remained relevant over the centuries.
     ⓐ ambiguous   ⓑ troublesome   ⓒ pertinent   ⓓ archaic

[>] 고전

Classics

★★ **accessible**
[æksésəbl]
[형] 접근[이용] 가능한
n. accessibility

adj. **easy to reach, interact with, or use**

Some classics have been shortened and rewritten in simple language in order to make them more **accessible**.

syn. approachable *ant.* inaccessible

★ **allegory**
[ǽligɔ̀:ri]
[명] 우화, 풍자
adj. allegorical

n. **writing or art in which characters or events have symbolic meanings**

George Orwell's *Animal Farm* is commonly understood as an **allegory** criticizing authoritarian governments.

★★ **anonymously**
[ənɑ́nəməsli]
[부] 작자 미상으로, 익명으로

adv. **done in a way that keeps a person's identity hidden**

The acclaimed novel *Frankenstein* was written by Mary Shelley, although it was originally published **anonymously**.

syn. namelessly

★★★ **antique**
[æntí:k]
[형] 1. 골동의
2. 고대 그리스·로마의

adj. **1 old and valuable 2 relating to ancient Greece or Rome**

1. **Antique** books are often treated as collectible objects by their owners, rather than as works of literature.
2. The *Iliad* and the *Odyssey,* renowned examples of **antique** literature, were written in the 8th century BC.

★★ **banish**
[bǽniʃ]
[동] 추방하다
n. banishment

v. **to expel someone from their country and forbid them from returning**

Numerous works of art and literature have been created by people who were **banished** from their homelands.

syn. exile

★★★ **concept**
[kɑ́nsept]
[명] 개념
adj. conceptual

n. **a general thought or idea**

In Franz Kafka's *Metamorphosis*, the author writes about the **concept** of transformation both literally and figuratively.

syn. notion

accessible 어떤 고전 작품들은 좀 더 접근 가능하도록 길이가 줄고 이해하기 쉬운 말로 다시 쓰여졌다. **allegory** George Orwell의 *동물 농장*은 보통 독재 정부들을 비판하는 우화로 이해된다. **anonymously** 호평을 받은 소설 *프랑켄슈타인*은 Mary Shelley가 썼으나, 원래는 작자 미상으로 출간됐다.
antique 1. 고서 소장인들은 흔히 그것들을 문학 작품이라기보다 수집품으로 취급한다. 2. 고대 그리스·로마 문학의 유명한 예인 *일리아드*와 *오디세이*는 기원전 8세기에 쓰여졌다. **banish** 많은 예술 작품과 문학 작품들이 고향에서 추방당한 사람들에 의해 창작되었다. **concept** Franz Kafka의 *변신*에서, 작가는 변신의 개념에 대해 문자 그대로, 또 비유적으로도 서술한다.

★★ **descriptive**
[diskríptiv]
[형] 서술하는, 설명적인
n. description

adj. showing exactly how something appears or what it is like
The works of Charles Dickens are known for their **descriptive** passages depicting life in the Victorian era.
syn. vivid

★★ **epic**
[épik]
[명] 서사시

n. a long poem about heroic events
The well-known **epic** *Beowulf* was written in Old English towards the end of the 10th century.
syn. saga

★★★ **evoke**
[ivóuk]
[동] (감정·기억 등을) 떠올려 주다, 환기시키다
adj. evocative

v. to produce or summon a certain feeling or impression
Many of William Wordsworth's most famous poems **evoke** feelings of nostalgia for childhood.
syn. elicit

★★★ **explore**
[iksplɔ́ːr]
[동] 1. 탐사하다, 탐험하다 2. 탐구하다
n. exploration

v. 1 to travel to an unfamiliar location to learn about it
2 to examine and learn about something *syn.* investigate

1. In Jules Verne's *Twenty Thousand Leagues Under the Sea*, the main characters **explore** the ocean in Captain Nemo's ship.
2. The Romantic era of literature was characterized by its celebration of nature and attempts to **explore** individual experiences.

★★ **fantasy**
[fǽntəsi]
[명] 상상, 공상

n. something imagined that has no basis in reality
The writer's stories are pure **fantasy**, which is one reason younger readers have such a strong affinity for them.
ant. reality

★★ **foundation**
[faundéiʃən]
[명] 토대, 기초

n. the basis upon which something is built
Some might argue that William Shakespeare established the **foundation** of modern English literature.
syn. base

descriptive Charles Dickens의 작품들은 빅토리아 시대의 삶을 묘사하는 서술적 구절들로 유명하다. **epic** 유명한 서사시 *베어울프*는 10세기말 무렵에 고대 영어로 쓰여졌다. **evoke** William Wordsworth의 가장 유명한 시들 중 많은 것들이 유년 시절에 대한 향수의 감정을 떠올리게 한다. **explore** 1. Jules Verne의 *해저 2만리*에서, 주인공들은 Nemo 선장의 배를 타고 대양을 탐사한다. 2. 문학에서 낭만주의 시대는 자연에 대한 찬양과 개인의 경험을 탐구하려는 시도들이 특징이다. **fantasy** 그 작가의 이야기들은 완전히 상상이며, 그것이 어린 독자들이 그 이야기들에 강하게 공감하는 이유이다. **foundation** 어떤 이들은 William Shakespeare가 현대 영문학의 토대를 세웠다고 주장할 수도 있다.

★★ **gothic** [gά θik]
[형] 고딕풍의(괴기스럽고 퇴폐적인 분위기의)

adj. relating to horror, death, and mystery
Edgar Allen Poe's **gothic** short stories brought about new interest in gloomy and disturbing tales.

Useful Tips
대문자로 시작하는 Gothic은 12-16세기에 유행했던 고딕 건축 양식이나 고대 게르만 부족인 고트족을 가리키는 형용사로 사용된다.

★ **imagery** [ímidʒəri]
[명] 비유적 묘사, 수사적 표현

n. words or pictures used to describe something
The vivid use of **imagery** in Oscar Wilde's *The Picture of Dorian Gray* draws the reader into this chilling tale.

★ **in-depth** [índépθ]
[형] 심층의, 면밀한

adj. thorough and in great detail
The article offers an **in-depth** investigation of the idea of modernity in Bram Stoker's *Dracula*.
syn. comprehensive *ant.* shallow

★★ **manuscript** [mǽnjuskrìpt]
[명] 원고

n. the original text of a writer's work before it is printed
The **manuscripts** of some famous literary works have been sold for a high price or are displayed in museums.

★★ **metaphor** [métəfɔ̀ːr]
[명] 은유
adj. metaphorical

n. a figure of speech in which one thing is likened to another
In the romantic poem, the moon serves as a **metaphor** for feelings of love that have begun to fade.

★ **minstrel** [mínstrəl]
[명] 음유 시인

n. a traveling musician who sang songs or recited poetry in the Middle Ages
Some **minstrels** created their own tales about distant places or historical events, while others embellished existing works.

---

gothic Edgar Allen Poe의 고딕풍 단편 소설들은 음울하고 불안감을 주는 소설들에 대한 새로운 관심을 유발했다. **imagery** Oscar Wilde는 *도리안 그레이의 초상*에서 생생한 비유적 묘사를 이용해 독자를 이 으스스한 이야기 속으로 끌어들인다. **in-depth** 그 기사는 Bram Stoker의 *드라큘라*에 내재된 현대성 개념에 대한 심층 연구를 제공한다. **manuscript** 몇몇 유명한 문학 작품들의 원고는 높은 가격에 팔렸거나 박물관에 전시되어 있다. **metaphor** 그 낭만주의 시에서 달은 점점 희미해지기 시작한 사랑의 감정들에 대한 은유 역할을 한다. **minstrel** 어떤 음유 시인들은 멀리 떨어진 장소나 역사적 사건들에 대해 자신만의 이야기들을 만들어 낸 반면, 다른 음유 시인들은 기존 작품들을 윤색했다.

★

pretense
[priténs]
[명] 가식, 겉치레

n. behavior meant to deceive others

Jane Austen's characters are marked by their sincerity in a society where **pretense** was considered the norm.

syn. charade

★★★

rare
[rɛər]
[형] 드문, 희귀한
n. rarity

adj. uncommon or occurring infrequently

It is quite **rare** to see young writers with no previous publishing experience suddenly succeed.

syn. unusual *ant.* common

★★

readability
[rìːdəbíləti]
[명] 가독성
adj. readable

n. the quality of being easily comprehensible to readers

This new edition includes footnotes that are intended to improve the **readability** of John Milton's poems.

syn. clarity

★★

reflective
[rifléktiv]
[형] 사색적인, 묵상적인
n. reflection

adj. showing or engaging in careful thinking

One could easily make the argument that the author's later works are centered around **reflective** thoughts about her life.

syn. contemplative

★★

rhyme
[raim]
[동] 운이 맞다, 각운을 이루다

v. to have an ending sound that is similar to that of another word

While some poets do tend to use words that **rhyme**, doing so is not an integral part of writing poetry.

★★

satire
[sǽtaiər]
[명] 풍자
adj. satirical

n. the use of humor and irony to criticize something or someone

The writer's use of social **satire** delights her readers but sometimes angers the targets of her sharp humor.

ART & DESIGN | SOCIAL SCIENCE | NATURAL SCIENCE | HUMANITIES | EARTH & SPACE | SOCIAL ISSUES

pretense Jane Austen 작품의 등장인물들은 가식이 일반적인 것으로 간주되던 사회에서 정직함을 특징으로 한다. **rare** 이전 출판 경험이 없는 젊은 작가들이 갑자기 성공하는 것을 보는 일은 매우 드물다. **readability** 이 신판에는 John Milton이 쓴 시들의 가독성을 향상시키기 위한 주석들이 포함되어 있다. **reflective** 그 작가의 후기 작품들이 자신의 인생에 대한 사색적인 생각들에 중점을 두고 있다는 주장을 쉽게 할 수 있을 것이다. **rhyme** 어떤 시인들은 운이 맞는 단어들을 사용하는 경향이 있지만, 그렇게 하는 것이 시 쓰기의 필수 요소는 아니다. **satire** 그 작가가 사회 풍자를 사용하는 것은 독자들을 즐겁게 하지만, 때로는 그 날카로운 유머의 대상들을 화나게 한다.

★

scripture

[skríptʃər]

[명] 경전

n. religious writing

It is important to respect the **scriptures** of other religions even if you do not agree with them.

★★

shallow

[ʃǽlou]

[형] 피상적인, 얄팍한

adj. superficial and devoid of careful thought

The author's **shallow** description of the novel's historical setting left some readers struggling to follow the plot.

ant. in-depth

★★

timeless

[táimlis]

[형] 세월이 흘러도 변치 않는, 영원한

adj. remaining consistent throughout the passage of time

While the novel's characters may seem dated to today's readers, the message it delivers is **timeless**.

syn. eternal

★★★

tragedy

[trǽdʒədi]

[명] 1. 비극 (작품)
2. 비극(적 사건)

adj. tragic

n. 1 a literary genre that deals with sorrow and suffering
2 a sad or horrific event *syn.* catastrophe

1. *Death of a Salesman* by Arthur Miller is a **tragedy** that offers us a glimpse into the sad realities of everyday life.
2. The novel ends in **tragedy**, with one of the main characters succumbing to a deadly illness.

★★

universal

[jùːnəvə́ːrsəl]

[형] 보편적인

n. universe

adj. applicable everywhere and involving everyone

While literature deals with culturally specific characters and events, the messages it conveys tend to be **universal**.

★★★

virtue

[və́ːrtʃuː]

[명] 미덕, 덕목

adj. virtuous

n. righteousness or the moral quality of a person

Although it may be viewed as a cliché, a hero full of **virtue** defeating the forces of evil still resonates with today's readers.

syn. goodness *ant.* vice

---

scripture 다른 종교들의 경전들을 따르지 않는다 해도, 그 경전들을 존중하는 것은 중요하다. **shallow** 그 소설의 역사적 배경에 대한 작가의 피상적인 묘사 때문에 몇몇 독자들은 그 줄거리를 따라가기 힘들어했다. **timeless** 그 소설의 등장인물들이 오늘날의 독자들에게 구식으로 보일 수 있지만, 그 소설이 전하는 메시지는 세월이 흘러도 변치 않는다. **tragedy** 1. Arthur Miller의 *세일즈맨의 죽음*은 일상생활의 슬픈 현실을 일별할 수 있게 해 주는 비극 작품이다. 2. 그 소설은 주인공들 중 한 명이 치명적인 병에 굴복하는 비극으로 끝난다. **universal** 문학은 문화적으로 특정한 인물들과 사건들을 다루지만, 그것이 전달하는 메시지들은 보편적인 경향이 있다. **virtue** 상투적으로 보일 수 있지만, 악의 세력을 물리치는 미덕을 겸비한 주인공은 여전히 오늘날의 독자들에게 반향을 불러일으킨다.

EXERCISES

ART & DESIGN

SOCIAL SCIENCE

NATURAL SCIENCE

HUMANITIES

EARTH & SPACE

SOCIAL ISSUES

A Match each definition with the correct word.

1 a long poem about heroic events   ⓐ satire

2 a figure of speech in which one thing is likened to another   ⓑ antique

3 something imagined that has no basis in reality   ⓒ epic

4 relating to horror, death, and mystery   ⓓ metaphor

5 religious writing   ⓔ gothic

6 the use of humor and irony to criticize something or someone   ⓕ fantasy

7 applicable everywhere and involving everyone   ⓖ universal

8 old and valuable   ⓗ scripture

B Choose the word that is closest in meaning to each underlined word.

1 The Bible has been translated into modern English to make it more <u>accessible</u> to young people.
ⓐ popular   ⓑ affordable   ⓒ educational   ⓓ approachable

2 Many of the great mythological heroes were defined by both their courage and their <u>virtue</u>.
ⓐ goodness   ⓑ strength   ⓒ intelligence   ⓓ weakness

3 For centuries, philosophers have been eager to <u>explore</u> the question of what makes us human.
ⓐ celebrate   ⓑ promote   ⓒ dismiss   ⓓ investigate

4 These traditional costumes are seldom worn, but they <u>evoke</u> a feeling of cultural pride.
ⓐ curtail   ⓑ elicit   ⓒ negate   ⓓ challenge

5 Ovid was a Roman poet who was <u>banished</u> to a distant province by the emperor himself.
ⓐ assigned   ⓑ originated   ⓒ exiled   ⓓ appraised

6 A reporter wrote an <u>in-depth</u> article about the causes of the chemical plant explosion.
ⓐ reflective   ⓑ lengthy   ⓒ unusual   ⓓ comprehensive

7 Some people think that much of the formal language we use is simply a <u>pretense</u>.
ⓐ notion   ⓑ taunt   ⓒ charade   ⓓ pretext

Mythology

---

abduct
[æbdʎkt]
ⓥ 유괴하다, 납치하다

n. abduction

v. to take someone away by force

Zeus turned into a white bull and **abducted** Europa, carrying her away to the Greek island of Crete.

syn. kidnap

---

abyss
[əbís]
ⓝ 깊은 구렁, 심연

n. a deep hole

After the Titans were defeated by the Greek gods, they were imprisoned in a deep **abyss** known as Tartarus.

syn. chasm

---

archaic
[ɑːrkéiik]
ⓐ 구식의, 낡은, 폐물이 된

adj. old-fashioned and no longer commonly used

The word "wight" refers to an undead creature in mythology, but it also has an **archaic** usage meaning "a human being."

syn. obsolete   *ant.* contemporary

---

archetype
[ɑːrkitàip]
ⓝ 전형, 모범

n. a typical example of something

Ares, the Greek god of war, is also considered a classic warrior **archetype** of ancient mythology.

---

assault
[əsɔ́ːlt]
ⓥ 폭행하다, 공격하다
ⓝ 폭행, 공격

v. to physically attack someone or something

For the crime of stealing fire, Prometheus was chained to a rock and **assaulted** by a giant eagle every day.

n. a physical attack

During the Trojan War, King Agamemnon led a huge Greek army in an **assault** of the city of Troy.

---

calamity
[kəlǽməti]
ⓝ 재앙, 재난

n. a terrible disaster

Many ancient cultures have similar myths about a **calamity** that left the entire Earth flooded.

syn. tragedy

---

abduct Zeus(제우스)는 하얀 황소로 변해서 Europa(에우로페)를 납치했고, 그녀를 그리스의 크레타 섬으로 데리고 갔다.　**abyss** 티탄 족은 그리스 신들에게 패배한 후, 타르타로스라고 알려진 깊은 구렁에 유폐되었다.　**archaic** 'wight'라는 단어는 신화에서 완전히 죽지 않은 생명체를 의미하지만, 그것은 또한 '인간'이라는 오래된 뜻을 가지고 있다.　**archetype** 그리스 전쟁의 신인 Ares(아레스)는 고대 신화에서 고전적 전사의 전형으로 여겨지기도 한다.　**assault** 불을 훔친 죄로, Prometheus(프로메테우스)는 바위에 묶여 매일같이 거대 독수리에게 공격당했다. / 트로이 전쟁 동안, Agamemnon(아가멤논) 왕은 트로이 시를 공격하기 위해 거대한 그리스 군대를 이끌었다.　**calamity** 많은 고대 문화들에는 지구 전체가 물에 잠기는 재앙에 관한 비슷한 신화들이 있다.

conquer
[kánkər]
ⓥ 정복하다

v. to defeat and take control of
It is said that the Amazons, a race of female warriors, **conquered** many kingdoms across Europe and Asia Minor.

conspire
[kənspáiər]
ⓥ 음모를 꾸미다, 공모하다

n. conspiracy

v. to make plans to do something bad or illegal
Loki **conspired** to murder Baldur, who was one of the sons of the great Norse god Odin.

syn. scheme

curse
[kəːrs]
ⓥ 저주를 내리다, 악담을 퍼붓다
ⓝ 저주, 악담

v. to cast an evil spell on
The goddess Hera **cursed** Echo by preventing her from saying anything but the last words that were spoken to her.

n. an evil spell
Medusa was once a beautiful young woman, but a **curse** turned her hair into a nest of terrible snakes.

Useful**Tips**

curse는 현대 영어에서 종종 '욕을 하다'라는 의미로 사용되며, 동의어로는 swear가 있다.

deity
[díːəti]
ⓝ 신, 하느님

n. a god or goddess
One of the **deities** of ancient Aztec mythology was said to take the form of a giant feathered snake.

syn. divinity

descent
[disént]
ⓝ 내려오기, 하강

v. descend

n. the act of moving downward
Orpheus made the dangerous **descent** into Hades in order to bring his beloved wife back to life.

ant. ascent

disguise
[disgáiz]
ⓥ 변장하다, 위장하다

v. to change an appearance to fool others
The gods were said to sometimes **disguise** themselves as mortals in order to walk among human beings.

ART & DESIGN

SOCIAL SCIENCE

NATURAL SCIENCE

HUMANITIES

EARTH & SPACE

SOCIAL ISSUES

---

conquer 여전사 종족인 아마존은 유럽과 소아시아 전역에 걸쳐 많은 왕국을 정복했다고 한다. **conspire** Loki(로키)는 Baldur(발데르)를 죽이려는 음모를 꾸몄는데, 그는 위대한 북유럽 신인 Odin(오딘)의 아들 중 하나였다. **curse** 여신 Hera(헤라)는 Echo(에코)가 자신에게 한 마지막 말 이외에 아무 말도 못 하게 막는 저주를 내렸다. / Medusa(메두사)는 한때 아름다운 젊은 여인이었지만, 저주로 인해 그녀의 머리카락이 끔찍한 뱀의 둥지로 바뀌었다. **deity** 고대 아즈텍 신화의 신들 중 하나는 깃털이 있는 거대한 뱀의 형상을 취했다고 한다. **descent** Orpheus(오르페우스)는 자신의 사랑하는 아내를 되살리기 위해서 Hades(죽은자들의 나라)로의 위험한 강하를 감행했다. **disguise** 신들은 인간들 사이를 다니기 위해 때때로 사람으로 변장했다고 한다.

★★★ **fate**
[feit]
[명] 운명

n. things that are predestined to happen

Characters in myths often learn of their unpleasant **fates** but are unable to avoid them in the end.

★★★ **immortal**
[imɔ́ːrtl]
[형] 불멸의, 불사의
n. immortality

adj. able to live forever

The gods made Tithonus **immortal**, but they didn't give him eternal youth, so he grew weaker and weaker.

syn. eternal *ant.* mortal

★★ **invincible**
[invínsəbl]
[형] 천하무적의, 불패의

adj. incapable of being defeated

The warrior Achilles seemed to be **invincible**, but he had a vulnerable spot on the heel of one foot.

syn. indomitable *ant.* vulnerable

★ **labyrinth**
[lǽbərìnθ]
[명] 미로

n. a network of paths that is difficult to navigate

The Minotaur, who was a man with a bull's head, lived in a **labyrinth** beneath the palace of the King of Crete.

syn. maze

★★ **nemesis**
[néməsis]
[명] (이길 수 없는) 강적

n. a powerful opponent or enemy

The biggest **nemesis** of the Norse god Thor was a giant sea monster that he battled several times.

ant. ally

★★ **ominous**
[ɑ́mənəs]
[형] 불길한

adj. creating the feeling that something bad is going to happen

Pandora was given the **ominous** warning that she must never open the box she had been given.

syn. foreboding *ant.* hopeful

---

fate 신화 속의 등장인물들은 종종 불쾌한 운명을 알게 되지만, 결국에는 그 운명을 피할 수 없다. **immortal** 신들이 Tithonus(티토노스)를 불멸로 만들었지만, 그에게 영원한 젊음은 주지 않았기에 그는 점점 약해져 갔다. **invincible** 전사 Achilles(아킬레스)는 천하무적처럼 보였지만, 한쪽 발뒤꿈치에 약점이 있었다. **labyrinth** 황소 머리를 가진 인간인 Minotaur(미노타우로스)는 크레타 왕궁 아래에 있는 미로에서 살았다. **nemesis** 북유럽 신 Thor(토르)의 가장 강력한 적은 그가 여러 번 싸웠던 거대 바다 괴물이었다. **ominous** Pandora(판도라)는 그녀에게 주어진 그 상자를 절대 열면 안 된다는 불길한 경고를 받았다.

★★ **ordeal**
[ɔːrdíːəl]
[명] 시련, 고난, 고생

n. a prolonged and extremely difficult situation

Mythical heroes must undergo many **ordeals** before they can achieve their goals or complete their journeys.

syn. trial

★★★ **passion**
[pǽʃən]
[명] 열정
adj. passionate

n. strong emotions or extreme enthusiasm

Arachne weaved with great skill and **passion**, and it was said that her work was more beautiful than that of the gods.

syn. fervor *ant.* indifference

★★★ **prominent**
[prámənənt]
[형] 1. 중요한, 유명한
2. 눈에 잘 띄는, 두드러진

adj. 1 important and well known *syn.* eminent *ant.* unknown
2 easily noticeable *syn.* obtrusive *ant.* inconspicuous

1. Huang Di, sometimes called the Yellow Emperor in English, is a **prominent** figure in Chinese mythology.
2. The most **prominent** feature of the Cyclops was the single eye located in the middle of his forehead.

★★ **prophecy**
[práfəsi]
[명] 예언
v. prophesize

n. a statement about what will happen in the future

The oracle's **prophecies** always came true, but sometimes their exact meaning was difficult to decipher.

syn. prediction

★★ **protagonist**
[proutǽgənist]
[명] (연극·영화·책 등의) 주인공

n. the main character of a tale

The **protagonist** of the *Odyssey* is Ulysses, a Greek king who must undertake a great journey before returning home.

syn. hero *ant.* antagonist

★★★ **punish**
[pʌ́niʃ]
[동] 처벌하다, 벌주다
n. punishment

v. to make someone suffer for having done something wrong

Zeus **punished** evil King Sisyphus by forcing him to push a large boulder up a hill for eternity.

syn. discipline *ant.* reward

ordeal 신화 속 영웅들은 그들의 목표를 달성하거나 여정을 완수하기 전까지 많은 시련을 겪어야 한다. **passion** Arachne(아라크네)는 훌륭한 기술과 열정으로 천을 짰는데, 그녀의 작품이 신들의 작품보다 더 아름다웠다고 한다. **prominent** 1. 영어로 종종 Yellow Emperor라고 불리는 황제(중국 신화에 나오는 신 중 하나)는 중국 신화에서 중요한 인물이다. 2. Cyclops(키클롭스)의 가장 두드러진 특징은 그의 이마 한 가운데에 위치한 외눈이었다. **prophecy** 신탁의 예언들은 항상 실현되었지만, 때때로 그 예언들의 정확한 의미는 해독하기가 어려웠다. **protagonist** *오디세이*의 주인공은 고향으로 돌아오기 전에 위대한 여정을 해야 하는 그리스의 왕인 Ulysses(율리시스)이다. **punish** Zeus(제우스)는 사악한 왕 Sisyphus(시시포스)에게 영원히 거대한 바위를 언덕으로 밀어 올리게 하는 벌을 내렸다.

★★
quest
[kwest]
[명] 탐색, 탐구, 모험 여행

n. a long, difficult search for something

King Arthur's **quest** for the Holy Grail is one of the most important stories in British mythology.

★★★
revenge
[rivéndʒ]
[명] 복수, 보복

n. the act of hurting someone because they have hurt you

Hephaestus was rejected by his mother, Hera, but he got his **revenge** by making a throne that trapped her.

syn. vengeance

★★
riddle
[rídl]
[명] 수수께끼

n. a question asked in an intentionally puzzling way

The Sphinx was a creature that guarded the city of Thebes, allowing travelers to pass only if they could solve a **riddle**.

★
saga
[sá:gə]
[명] 영웅 이야기, 무용담

n. a long story about heroic events of the past

It is believed that the great Icelandic **sagas** of the 13th century are a mix of historical facts and mythology.

syn. epic

★★
sanction
[sǽŋkʃən]
[동] 허가하다, 승인하다

v. to give official approval

Although the gods did not **sanction** relationships with mortals, they occur in numerous tales.

Useful Tips

신문이나 뉴스에 sanction이 복수로 사용되어 다른 국가에 가하는 '제재'를 의미하기도 하는데, 주로 'impose sanctions on + 제재의 대상'의 형태로 쓰인다.

★★★
scar
[ska:*r*]
[동] 흉터를 남기다, 상처를 남기다
[명] 흉터, 상처

adj. scarred

v. to wound someone and leave a permanent mark

There are multiple myths about individuals who were **scarred** by bolts of lightning from the heavens.

n. a permanent mark from a wound

Daedalus, the father of Icarus, was a great inventor who had a **scar** shaped like a bird on his shoulder.

---

quest Arthur(아서)왕의 성배의 탐색은 영국 신화에서 가장 중요한 이야기 중 하나이다. **revenge** Hephaestus(헤파이스토스)는 자신의 어머니인 Hera(헤라)에게 버림받았지만, 그녀를 옭아맨 왕좌를 만들어 복수했다. **riddle** Sphinx(스핑크스)는 테베 시를 지켰던 동물이었는데, 여행자들이 수수께끼를 풀어야만 지나가도록 허락했다. **saga** 13세기의 위대한 아이슬란드 영웅 이야기는 역사적 사실과 신화가 혼합된 것이라고 여겨진다. **sanction** 신들은 인간들과의 관계를 허락하지 않았지만, 이러한 관계가 수많은 이야기에서 일어난다. **scar** 하늘에서 떨어진 번개에 맞아 흉터를 지니게 된 사람들에 대한 다수의 신화가 있다. / Icarus(이카로스)의 아버지인 Daedalus(다이달로스)는 어깨에 새 모양의 흉터를 가진 위대한 발명가였다.

serpent
[sə́ːrpənt]

명 뱀

adj. serpentine

n. a long, legless reptile

Asclepius, the Greek god of medicine, carried a staff with a long **serpent** coiled around it.

syn. snake

slay
[slei]

동 …을 죽이다

v. to kill someone or something violently

Apollo sent Hercules to Nemea to **slay** a giant lion that was terrorizing the people of the region.

syn. murder

Useful Tips

slay는 불규칙 동사로 slay-slew-slain의 형태로 활용하는데, 일상적인 미국 영어에서는 규칙동사처럼 slayed의 형태로 쓰일 때도 있다.

slumber
[slʌ́mbər]

명 잠, 수면

n. the act of resting in a natural unconscious state

If someone caught Proteus during his afternoon **slumber**, they could force him to foretell the future.

syn. sleep

snare
[snɛər]

명 덫, 올가미
동 덫으로 잡다

n. a trap used to catch small animals

Apollo freed a raven that had been caught in a **snare** because it promised to make an offering to him.

v. to catch something

In Polynesian mythology, Maui **snared** the Sun in order to slow it down as it traveled across the sky.

tantalize
[tǽntəlàiz]

동 애태우게 하여 괴롭히다, 감질나게 하다

v. to cruelly taunt someone with a promise of something they can't have

The word "**tantalize**" comes from Tantalus, a hero who was punished with a great thirst but the inability to reach water.

tenacity
[tənǽsəti]

명 고집, 끈기, 불굴

adj. tenacious

n. the quality of not giving up easily

Ares, the god of war, was greatly admired by the warlike Greeks for his **tenacity** in battle.

syn. determination

---

serpent 그리스 의술의 신인 Asclepius(아스클레피오스)는 긴 뱀이 휘감고 있는 지팡이를 들고 다녔다.　**slay** Apollo(아폴론)는 네메아 지역의 사람들을 공포에 떨게 만들고 있었던 거대 사자를 죽이기 위해 Hercules(헤라클레스)를 그곳으로 보냈다.　**slumber** 만약 Proteus(프로테우스)가 낮잠을 자고 있는 동안 누군가 그를 붙잡는다면, 그들은 Proteus(프로테우스)에게 미래를 예언하도록 강요할 수 있었다.　**snare** Apollo(아폴론)는 덫에 걸린 큰 까마귀를 풀어 주었는데, 그 까마귀가 그에게 제물을 바치겠다고 약속했기 때문이다. / 폴리네시아 신화에서 Maui(마우이)는 태양이 하늘을 가로질러 갈 때, 이를 늦추기 위해 덫으로 태양을 잡았다.
tantalize 'tantalize'라는 단어는 엄청난 갈증을 느끼면서도 물에 가까이 갈 수 없는 형벌을 받은 영웅인 Tantalus(탄탈로스)에서 유래되었다.　**tenacity** 전쟁의 신 Ares(아레스)는 전투에서의 끈기로 호전적인 그리스인들에게 매우 존경 받았다.

toil
[tɔil]
ⓥ 힘들게 일하다

v. to work hard

Vulcan, the Roman god of fire, carried a blacksmith's hammer and **toiled** in a fiery underground forge.

treachery
[trétʃəri]
ⓝ 배반, 배신

adj. treacherous

n. a betrayal of someone's trust

Clever mortals who attempt to fool or outwit the gods end up being punished for their **treachery**.

syn. disloyalty   *ant.* fidelity

underworld
[ʌ́ndərwə̀ːrld]
ⓝ 지옥, 저승

n. an imaginary place where people go after they die

The mythologies of most cultures include some kind of **underworld**, such as China's Youdu and Egypt's Duat.

syn. hell   *ant.* heaven

valiant
[vǽljənt]
ⓐ 용맹한, 단호한

adj. brave and determined

Agamemnon, who was both a respected king and a **valiant** hero, is one of the main characters in the *Iliad*.

syn. courageous   *ant.* cowardly

vigilant
[vídʒələnt]
ⓐ 빈틈없는, 방심하지 않는

n. vigilance

adj. alert and on guard

Argos was a **vigilant** watchman due to the fact that he was a giant with 100 eyes scattered across his body.

syn. watchful   *ant.* unobservant

winged
[wiŋd]
ⓐ 날개가 달린

adj. having wings

Pegasus was a white, **winged** horse that was ridden by the hero Bellerophon during his epic adventures.

---

toil 로마의 불의 신인 Vulcan(불카누스)은 대장장이 망치를 들고, 불타는 듯한 지하 대장간에서 힘들게 일했다.　**treachery** 신들을 속이거나 이기려고 시도한 약삭빠른 인간들은 결국 그들의 배반에 대한 형벌을 받게 된다.　**underworld** 대부분 문화들의 신화에는 중국의 Youdu나 이집트의 Duat과 같은 일종의 지옥이 포함되어 있다.　**valiant** 존경받는 왕이자 용맹한 영웅이었던 Agamemnon(아가멤논)은 *일리아드*의 주인공들 중 하나이다.　**vigilant** Argos(아르고스)는 온몸에 100개의 눈이 산재해 있던 거인이었기 때문에, 빈틈없는 감시자였다.　**winged** Pegasus(페가수스)는 영웅 Bellerophon(벨레로폰)이 그의 장대한 모험 중에 탄 날개가 달린 백마였다.

EXERCISES

ART & DESIGN

SOCIAL SCIENCE

NATURAL SCIENCE

HUMANITIES

EARTH & SPACE

SOCIAL ISSUES

A Match each definition with the correct word.

1 a question asked in an intentionally puzzling way   ⓐ toil

2 the act of moving downward   ⓑ ordeal

3 a trap used to catch small animals   ⓒ scar

4 a typical example of something   ⓓ riddle

5 to work hard   ⓔ descent

6 to wound someone and leave a permanent mark   ⓕ archetype

7 a prolonged and extremely difficult situation   ⓖ snare

8 to make plans to do something bad or illegal   ⓗ conspire

B Choose the word that is closest in meaning to each underlined word.

1 The folk artist is known for disdaining technology and using <u>archaic</u> techniques instead.
   ⓐ artistic   ⓑ unreliable   ⓒ authentic   ⓓ obsolete

2 *The Count of Monte Cristo* is a novel about a man who waited years to get his <u>revenge</u>.
   ⓐ vengeance   ⓑ collision   ⓒ compensation   ⓓ malady

3 The Roman Empire once seemed <u>invincible</u>, but it eventually collapsed.
   ⓐ unavoidable   ⓑ indomitable   ⓒ indeterminate   ⓓ unsophisticated

4 The <u>tenacity</u> of the reporter allowed her to uncover important information.
   ⓐ perception   ⓑ determination   ⓒ fortitude   ⓓ momentum

5 The 1931 China floods were a terrible <u>calamity</u>, resulting in the deaths of many people.
   ⓐ aberration   ⓑ acquisition   ⓒ reminder   ⓓ tragedy

6 Many philosophers share the <u>ominous</u> view that we're headed toward self-destruction.
   ⓐ foreboding   ⓑ communal   ⓒ incisive   ⓓ optimistic

7 The people tried to retain their traditions after they were <u>conquered</u> by a powerful nation.
   ⓐ contacted   ⓑ emulated   ⓒ assisted   ⓓ defeated

★
★ **abbreviate**
[əbríːvìèit]
ⓥ (단어·구 등을) 줄여 쓰다
n. abbreviation

v. to make shorter

In very informal spoken English, the title of "doctor" may sometimes be **abbreviated** as "doc."

syn. shorten   *ant.* lengthen

★
★ **acquire**
[əkwáiər]
ⓥ 습득하다, 얻다
n. acquisition

v. to get something

It is a well-known fact that young children **acquire** new languages faster and more easily than adults.

syn. obtain   *ant.* lose

★
★ **ambiguous**
[æmbígjuəs]
ⓐ 모호한, 애매한
n. ambiguity

adj. not clearly defined

If the meaning of a sentence is **ambiguous**, it is a good idea to rephrase it in a clearer way.

syn. vague   *ant.* definite

★ **articulate**
[ɑːrtíkjulèit]
ⓥ 분명히 표현하다

v. to put into words clearly

People who struggle to **articulate** their feelings may turn to art as a form of personal expression.

syn. enunciate

★
★ **barrier**
[bǽriər]
ⓝ 장애물, 장벽
v. bar

n. something that blocks movement, communication, or progress

Language can sometimes be a **barrier** for international travelers, but there are many ways to get around it.

syn. impediment

★
★ **colloquial**
[kəlóukwiəl]
ⓐ 구어체의

adj. used in everyday speech

Many formal words, including "thus" and "whom," have fallen out of use in **colloquial** English.

syn. conversational   *ant.* formal

---

abbreviate 아주 일상적인 구어체 영어에서는 'doctor'라는 직함을 때로 'doc'으로 줄여 쓸 수도 있다.   **acquire** 어린아이들이 성인들보다 더 빠르고 쉽게 새 언어들을 습득한다는 것은 잘 알려진 사실이다.   **ambiguous** 어떤 문장의 의미가 모호하다면, 더 명확한 방식으로 바꾸어 말하는 것이 좋은 방안이다.
articulate 자신의 감정을 분명히 표현하는 것을 힘들어하는 사람들은 개인적 표현 방식으로 예술에 의지할 수도 있다.   **barrier** 해외 여행자들에게 때로 언어가 장애물이 될 수도 있지만, 그것을 해결할 방법들은 많다.   **colloquial** 'thus'와 'whom'을 포함한 많은 문어체 단어들이 구어체 영어에서 쓰이지 않게 되었다.

ART & DESIGN

SOCIAL SCIENCE

NATURAL SCIENCE

HUMANITIES

EARTH & SPACE

SOCIAL ISSUES

diction
[díkʃən]
ⓝ 발음, 말투

n. the way in which someone's words are pronounced

The school's speech therapist works with certain students once a week to improve their **diction**.

syn. pronunciation

discourse
[dískɔːrs]
ⓝ 담화, 담론

n. the discussion around an issue

When the topic of conversation turns to politics or religion, the **discourse** may grow heated.

syn. dialogue

eloquent
[éləkwənt]
ⓐ 감정을 드러내는, 감명적인
n. eloquence

adj. expressing or able to express ideas in an attractive way

People used to write **eloquent** letters by hand in the past, but now they are satisfied with sending a quick text message.

extinct
[ikstíŋkt]
ⓐ 사라진, 멸종한
n. extinction

adj. no longer existing

Many indigenous cultures are making renewed efforts to prevent their traditional languages from becoming **extinct**.

syn. dead   *ant.* extant

illegible
[ilédʒəbl]
ⓐ 읽기 어려운, 알아볼 수 없는

adj. difficult or impossible to read

Because they spend so much time using keyboards, the handwriting of many young people has become **illegible**.

syn. unreadable   *ant.* readable

inflected
[infléktid]
ⓐ (어형이) 굴절된
n. inflection

adj. changed from its normal form or tone

Words are **inflected** for a number of reasons, such as to express a change in tense, number, or voice.

syn. altered

---

diction 그 학교의 언어치료사는 특정 학생들의 발음을 향상시키려고 일주일에 한 번 그들과 작업한다.   **discourse** 대화의 주제가 정치나 종교가 되면, 그 담화는 격렬해질 수 있다.   **eloquent** 과거에는 사람들이 감정이 담긴 자필 편지를 쓰곤 했지만, 지금은 빠른 문자 메시지를 보내는 것에 만족한다.   **extinct** 많은 토착 문화들이 자신들의 전통 언어가 사라지는 것을 막기 위해 새로운 노력을 기울이고 있다.   **illegible** 많은 젊은이들이 너무 많은 시간을 키보드를 사용하며 보내기 때문에, 그들의 필적이 읽기 어렵게 되었다.   **inflected** 단어들은 시제나 수, 또는 태(態)의 변화를 나타내기 위함과 같은 많은 이유들로 굴절된다.

★★★ **inherent**
[inhíərənt, -hér-]

형 내재된, 선천적인

adj. naturally existing and essential

Several renowned linguists, including Noam Chomsky, have argued that language is **inherent** in humans.

syn. fundamental

★★ **interpret**
[intə́ːrprit]

동 1. 해석하다, 이해하다
2. 통역하다

n. interpretation

v. 1 to explain what something means   *syn.* decipher
2 to translate from one language to another

1. Poetry differs from prose in that it is written in a style of language that requires the reader to **interpret** it.

2. The UN ambassador listened to a version of her colleague's speech that was being **interpreted** in real time.

★ **jargon**
[dʒáːrgən]

명 (특정 분야의 전문) 용어

n. language used in a specific field or industry

It is a common complaint that legal **jargon** is used by lawyers in order to make their services necessary to the average person.

Useful Tips
전문가 집단이 사용하는 jargon과 달리 slang은 표준어가 아닌 비속어이다.

★ **lexicon**
[léksəkàn]

명 어휘

n. all of the words used in something

Recent research has shown that the modern English **lexicon** is actually expanding and has now surpassed one million words.

syn. vocabulary

★ **linguistic**
[liŋgwístik]

형 언어의, 언어적인

adj. relating to language

It can be said that speaking grammatically is the **linguistic** equivalent of knowing how and when to dress properly.

★ **literal**
[lítərəl]

형 문자 그대로의

adj. used in its standard sense

There are some cases in which a word's **literal** meaning has become less commonly used than its metaphorical one.

ant. figurative

---

inherent Noam Chomsky를 포함한 몇몇 유명 언어학자들은 인간이 언어(능력)를 선천적으로 타고났다고 주장해 왔다.   **interpret** 1. 시는 독자가 그것을 해석해야 하는 형식의 언어로 쓰여져 있다는 점에서 산문과 다르다. 2. 그 UN 대사는 실시간으로 통역되고 있는 동료의 연설본을 들었다.   **jargon** 일반인에게 그들의 서비스가 필요하도록 만들기 위해 변호사들이 법률 용어를 이용한다는 것이 공통적으로 제기되는 불만 사항이다.   **lexicon** 최근 연구는 현대 영어 어휘가 실제로 확장되고 있으며 현재 백만 단어가 넘는다는 것을 보여 주었다.   **linguistic** 문법에 맞게 말하는 것은 언어적으로 보았을 때 어떻게, 언제 제대로 옷을 갖춰 입어야 하는지를 아는 것과 같다고 할 수 있다.   **literal** 어떤 단어의 문자 그대로의 의미가 그 단어의 은유적 의미보다 덜 보편적으로 쓰이게 된 경우가 몇 있다.

★★

multilingual

[mʌltilíŋgwəl]

[형] 다중 언어의

adj. speaking or using more than two languages

Although the device comes with a detailed, **multilingual** manual, users still complain that it is difficult to use.

Useful Tips

bilingual은 '이중 언어를 하는'의 뜻으로, monolingual은 '단일어를 하는'의 뜻으로 사용된다.

★★★

originate

[ərídʒənèit]

[동] 유래하다

n. origin

v. to begin to exist

English may have **originated** in England, but it was shaped by the languages brought by foreign invaders.

syn. emerge *ant.* cease

★★

outspoken

[áutspóukən]

[형] 노골적인, 거리낌 없는

adj. unafraid to speak one's mind

As an **outspoken** critic of social media, the college professor urges people to spend less time staring at a screen.

syn. forthright *ant.* timid

★★

perception

[pərsépʃən]

[명] 인식, 지각

v. perceive

n. a specific way of viewing or understanding something

Our **perception** of others is strongly influenced by the way they use language in different situations.

syn. viewpoint

★★

phonetic

[fənétik]

[형] 표음식의, 음성의

adj. relating to spoken sounds

Dictionaries often present the **phonetic** spelling of a word to help learners struggling with pronunciation.

★

pidgin

[pídʒən]

[명] 혼성어, 피진어

n. a common language used by people who speak different languages

You will commonly hear **pidgin** spoken in marketplaces where buyers and sellers from different cultures converge.

syn. patois

---

multilingual 그 장치에는 상세한 다중 언어 설명서가 딸려 있지만, 그래도 이용자들은 사용하기 불편하다고 불만을 나타낸다. **originate** 영어는 영국에서 유래했을 수 있지만, 외국 침입자들이 유입해 온 언어들에 의해 형태를 갖추게 되었다. **outspoken** 그 대학 교수는 소셜 미디어에 대한 노골적인 비판가로서, 사람들에게 스크린을 응시하는 시간을 줄이라고 충고한다. **perception** 타인들에 대한 우리의 인식은 다양한 상황에서 그들이 언어를 사용하는 방식에 의해 강하게 영향을 받는다. **phonetic** 발음을 어려워하는 학습자들을 돕기 위해, 사전들은 흔히 단어의 표음식 철자를 제공한다. **pidgin** 서로 다른 문화 출신의 구매자와 판매자가 모이는 시장에서는 혼성어를 말하는 것을 일상적으로 들을 것이다.

proficiency
[prəfíʃənsi]
ⓝ 기량, 숙달

adj. proficient

n. the ability to do something well

Due to her grammatical **proficiency**, the student is often asked to proofread the essays of her classmates.

syn. aptitude

rectify
[réktəfài]
ⓥ …을 바로 잡다, 교정하다

v. to fix a mistake or a bad situation

A written or spoken apology can be an effective way of **rectifying** a social misstep, but only if it is sincere.

syn. amend   *ant.* worsen

rhetoric
[rétərik]
ⓝ 미사여구

n. language intended to influence or persuade others

Tired of political **rhetoric**, the nation's people want to hear a substantial debate about today's issues.

semantic
[simǽntik]
ⓐ 의미론의, 어의의

adj. relating to the meaning of words

Semantic arguments over the intended meaning of regional slang phrases seldom end in agreement.

stammer
[stǽmər]
ⓝ 말더듬증
ⓥ 말을 더듬다

n. a speech problem that causes people to hesitate and repeat sounds   *syn.* stutter

King George VI famously dreaded public speech due to his lifelong struggles with a **stammer**.

v. to hesitate and repeat sounds when speaking   *syn.* stutter

It is not unusual for individuals to **stammer** when they are nervous, deprived of sleep, or under great stress.

vernacular
[vərnǽkjulər]
ⓝ 토착어, 방언

n. a dialect widely used by common people

Modern scientists have found that writing in the **vernacular** allows their ideas to reach a wider audience.

---

proficiency 그 학생은 문법적 기량 때문에, 반 친구들의 에세이를 교정해 달라는 부탁을 자주 받는다.   **rectify** 서면이나 말로 하는 사과는 사회적 실수를 바로 잡는 효과적인 방법이 될 수 있지만, 그것이 진심일 때만 그렇다.   **rhetoric** 정치적 미사여구에 진절머리가 난 그 나라 국민들은 현재의 문제점들에 대한 현실적인 토론을 듣고 싶어한다.   **semantic** 지방 속어 어구들이 어떤 의미를 나타내는지에 대한 의미론적 논쟁이 합의적으로 끝나는 경우는 거의 없다.
stammer George 6세는 일생 동안 씨름했던 말더듬증 때문에, 공개 연설을 두려워한 것으로 유명하다. / 사람들이 긴장하거나, 수면 부족이거나, 심한 스트레스를 받고 있을 때 말을 더듬는 것은 드문 일이 아니다.   **vernacular** 현대 과학자들은 토착어로 글을 쓰는 것이 그들의 생각을 더 광범위한 청중에게 닿을 수 있게 해 준다는 것을 발견했다.

EXERCISES

A Match each definition with the correct word.

1 relating to spoken sounds   ⓐ interpret

2 a dialect widely used by common people   ⓑ multilingual

3 to explain what something means   ⓒ vernacular

4 all of the words used in something   ⓓ jargon

5 language used in a specific field or industry   ⓔ phonetic

6 used in its standard sense   ⓕ literal

7 speaking or using more than two languages   ⓖ discourse

8 the discussion around an issue   ⓗ lexicon

B Choose the word that is closest in meaning to each underlined word.

1 Characters in myths who <u>acquire</u> supernatural powers often use them in foolish ways.
   ⓐ observe   ⓑ impede   ⓒ obtain   ⓓ allow

2 Journalists sometimes have to <u>abbreviate</u> words to make headlines fit the page.
   ⓐ delete   ⓑ rearrange   ⓒ explain   ⓓ shorten

3 Neat handwriting used to be essential, as an <u>illegible</u> manuscript had no value.
   ⓐ unreadable   ⓑ illegal   ⓒ undesirable   ⓓ deformed

4 It is easier for people with a <u>proficiency</u> in foreign languages to travel internationally.
   ⓐ timidity   ⓑ obligation   ⓒ refusal   ⓓ aptitude

5 Religious texts with <u>ambiguous</u> meanings have been understood differently in different eras.
   ⓐ harsh   ⓑ vague   ⓒ natural   ⓓ alluring

6 The characters speak <u>colloquial</u> English that is different from the author's formal style.
   ⓐ flawless   ⓑ altered   ⓒ conversational ⓓ educated

7 Throughout history, people have had unrealistic <u>perceptions</u> about distant lands.
   ⓐ intentions   ⓑ viewpoints   ⓒ origins   ⓓ expectations

A Choose the correct words.

1 The word libel has the same meaning as
  ⓐ incarceration   ⓑ reclamation   ⓒ concentration   ⓓ defamation

2 The word extinct has the same meaning as
  ⓐ current   ⓑ dead   ⓒ threatened   ⓓ widespread

3 The word figurative has the same meaning as
  ⓐ significant   ⓑ symbolic   ⓒ unclear   ⓓ disconnected

4 The word abduct has the same meaning as
  ⓐ assist   ⓑ reset   ⓒ kidnap   ⓓ dismantle

5 The word protagonist has the same meaning as
  ⓐ professional   ⓑ author   ⓒ investigator   ⓓ hero

6 The word narrative has the same meaning as
  ⓐ account   ⓑ service   ⓒ obstacle   ⓓ conclusion

7 The word inflected has the same meaning as
  ⓐ reversed   ⓑ rejected   ⓒ altered   ⓓ improved

8 The word anonymously has the same meaning as
  ⓐ carefully   ⓑ namelessly   ⓒ fluently   ⓓ gradually

B Fill in the blanks with the best words from the box.

1 In the classic novel *1984*, a man lives in a _____ society where people are constantly watched.

2 Most folk art is considered to be outside of the _____, so it does not get a lot of attention.

3 Philosophy guides us away from _____ ideas and shows us how to become deep thinkers.

4 News shows deliver important information to viewers, but they also focus on getting high _____.

5 Modern governments sometimes seek to _____ serious mistakes the nation made in the past.

6 In the novel, a group of kids must find their way out of a _____ in order to win a prize.

labyrinth	mainstream	ratings	dystopian	rectify	shallow

C Read the following passages.

[1-2] **1** Choose one word that fits both blanks.

> Bob Woodward is a(n) _____ American journalist who currently works for the *Washington Post*. In the early 1970s, he, along with his colleague Carl Bernstein, played a(n) _____ role in the Watergate scandal, which prematurely ended the presidency of Richard Nixon.

ⓐ contemporary   ⓑ antique   ⓒ ominous   ⓓ prominent

2 Choose the appropriate pair of words to fill in the blanks.

> Literary _____ has been used to make fun of foolish attitudes and unfair social practices for centuries. Some of this writing deals with issues that no longer exist, so modern readers struggle to understand it. However, when it addresses human nature, it has a _____ quality.

ⓐ subtext — misleading   ⓑ jargon — fictional

ⓒ satire — timeless   ⓓ plagiarism — reflective

[3-4]

> Spoken language is the primary mode of communication for human beings. Unfortunately, some people, especially young children, suffer from speech problems, such as a stammer. Not only does this make it harder to communicate, it can also be a barrier to establishing social relationships.

3 In the context of the passage, stammer means _____.

ⓐ stutter   ⓑ phobia   ⓒ injury   ⓓ meekness

4 The word barrier in the passage could best be replaced by

ⓐ rationale   ⓑ alternative   ⓒ consideration   ⓓ impediment

[5-6]

> *The Great Gatsby* was written by F. Scott Fitzgerald in 1925. It received mixed reviews when it was first published, but it is now considered one of the great literary _____ of the 20th century. The novel's main motif is money. It tells the story of a man who has recently become wealthy but cannot gain social acceptance from people who were born into rich families.

5 Choose the word that is most suitable for the blank.

ⓐ tabloids   ⓑ masterpieces   ⓒ scriptures   ⓓ sagas

6 The word motif in the passage is closest in meaning to

ⓐ conflict   ⓑ pretext   ⓒ theme   ⓓ rhetoric

Lesson 36 [>] 민속 예술 Folk Art

★★★

accomplish
[əkɑ́mpliʃ, əkʌ́m-]

[동] 이루다, 성취하다

n. accomplishment

v. to successfully complete a task or reach a goal

The folk artist **accomplished** her goal of having her wood carvings displayed in a nearby gallery.

syn. achieve *ant.* fail

★★

allure
[əlúər]

[명] 매력

n. a quality that attracts people

For collectors, the **allure** of the dolls is that they are handmade using only natural materials.

syn. appeal

★★

attempt
[ətémpt]

[동] 시도하다

v. to try to do something

Many people have **attempted** to locate the creator of the mural painted on the side of the old building, but all have failed.

syn. endeavor

★

auspicious
[ɔːspíʃəs]

[형] 길조의, 전조가 좋은, 순조로운

adj. suggesting that something is likely to be successful

The regional art festival got off to an **auspicious** beginning, with visitors lining up to enter the fairgrounds.

syn. promising *ant.* inauspicious

★★

authentic
[ɔːθéntik]

[형] 진짜의, 진품의

n. authenticity

adj. being exactly what it claims to be

The leatherwork isn't considered **authentic** unless it bears the artist's monogram on the back.

syn. genuine *ant.* false

★★

basis
[béisis]

[명] 기초, 기본, 기반

n. the underlying foundation of something

Maintaining traditional methods of producing crafts is the **basis** of the folk art classes at the community center.

---

accomplish 그 민속 작가는 그녀의 나무 조각품들을 인근 갤러리에 전시하고자 하는 자신의 목표를 이뤘다. **allure** 수집가들에게 그 인형들의 매력은 오로지 천연 재료만 사용해서 수제로 만들어진다는 것이다. **attempt** 많은 사람들이 그 오래된 건물 벽에 그려진 벽화의 원작자를 찾으려고 시도했지만, 모두 실패했다. **auspicious** 그 지역의 예술 축제는 축제 장소로 입장하기 위해 줄을 선 방문자들로 순조롭게 시작했다. **authentic** 가죽 작품은 예술가의 모노그램(두 개 이상의 글자를 합쳐 한 글자 모양으로 도안한 글자)이 그 뒷면에 없으면 진품으로 여겨지지 않는다. **basis** 공예품 제작의 전통적 방법을 유지하는 것이 주민 센터 민속 예술 수업의 기본이다.

★★ **calligraphy**
[kəlígrəfi]
[명] 서예

n. the art of producing beautiful writing with ink and a pen or brush
The special brushes that the artist uses for his **calligraphy** are made of bamboo and white goat hair.

★★★ **cherish**
[tʃériʃ]
[동] 소중히 여기다, 아끼다

v. to love and protect someone or something
The family **cherishes** the antique weathervanes, as they were made by a relative more than 100 years ago.

★★★ **comprise**
[kəmpráiz]
[동] …으로 구성되다, …으로 이루어지다

v. to be made up of
The primitive art painting **comprises** four separate panels, each of which shows a different village scene.
syn. consist

Useful Tips
comprise는 타동사로 뒤에 바로 목적어가 오지만, consist는 'The series consists of five books.'에서와 같이 자동사로 전치사 of와 함께 쓰인다.

★★ **conventional**
[kənvénʃənl]
[형] 평범한, 인습적인, 관습적인

adj. done or appearing in the standard way
Conventional handmade baskets are made of natural materials, but plastic or metal can also be used.
syn. normal *ant.* unconventional

★★★ **deserve**
[dizə́ːrv]
[동] …을 받을 만하다, …을 누릴 자격이 있다

v. to have earned or be worthy of something
Everyone agreed that the silversmith's turquoise jewelry **deserved** to win first prize at the craft fair.

★★ **distinct**
[distíŋkt]
[형] 뚜렷한, 분명한
n. distinction

adj. easily recognizable as being different from others
There are several **distinct** styles of blankets that are made by the indigenous people of this region.
syn. unmistakable *ant.* indistinct

calligraphy 그 작가가 그의 서예 작품에 사용하는 특별한 붓들은 대나무와 흰 염소 털로 만들어졌다. **cherish** 그 가족은 고풍스러운 풍향계들을 소중히 여기는데, 그들의 친척이 100여 년 전에 그것들을 만들었기 때문이다. **comprise** 그 원시 미술화는 4개의 분리된 판으로 구성되어 있으며, 각각의 판은 서로 다른 마을 풍경을 보여 준다. **conventional** 평범한 수제 바구니는 천연 재료로 만들어지지만, 플라스틱이나 금속 또한 사용될 수 있다. **deserve** 그 은세공인의 터키석 장신구가 공예 박람회에서 대상을 받을 만하다고 모두가 동의했다. **distinct** 이 지역의 원주민들이 만든 몇 가지 뚜렷한 스타일의 담요들이 있다.

diverse
[divə́:rs, dáivərs]

ⓐ 다양한

n. diversity

adj. having a great deal of variety

Creative activities as **diverse** as tile making and ironwork can fall under the umbrella of folk art.

duplicate
[djú:plikèit]

ⓥ 복제하다, 복사하다

[djú:plikət]

ⓝ 복제(품)

n. duplication

v. to recreate an object or situation   *syn.* replicate

The young bellmaker tried to **duplicate** an ancient brass bell he had seen during his travels.

n. an exact recreation of something   *syn.* reproduction

A **duplicate** of this beautiful woodprint is hanging in the Folk Art Museum in New York City.

embroidery
[imbrɔ́idəri]

ⓝ 자수

v. embroider

n. the act of stitching designs into cloth with thread

Although women were discouraged from making art in the past, they were able to express themselves through **embroidery**.

etch
[etʃ]

ⓥ 식각하다(약물 등을 사용해 유리나 금속에 조각하다)

v. to cut a design or pattern into a hard surface

The local artist meticulously **etched** a detailed image of a barn owl into the copper plate.

extensive
[iksténsiv]

ⓐ 광범위한, 폭넓은, 대규모의

adj. covering a large area or a wide range of something

The museum houses an **extensive** collection of folk art created by local farmers during the 19th century.

syn. wide-ranging   *ant.* limited

flamboyant
[flæmbɔ́iənt]

ⓐ 화려한

n. flamboyance

adj. behaving or appearing in a way that attracts attention

These **flamboyant** traditional costumes are handstitched in the village and colored with natural dyes.

syn. extravagant   *ant.* plain

---

diverse 타일 만들기, 철 세공과 같은 다양한 창작 활동은 민속 예술 산하에 속할 수 있다.   **duplicate** 그 젊은 종 제작자는 그가 여행 중에 본 고대 황동 종을 복제하려고 했다. / 이 아름다운 목판화의 복제품이 뉴욕 시에 있는 민속 예술 박물관에 걸려 있다.   **embroidery** 과거에는 여성들이 예술품을 만드는 것이 환영받지 못하였음에도 불구하고, 그들은 자수를 통해 자신을 표현할 수 있었다.   **etch** 그 지역 예술가는 원숭이 올빼미의 상세한 이미지를 동판에 꼼꼼하게 식각했다.
extensive 그 박물관은 19세기에 지역 농부들이 만든 광범위한 민속 예술 수집품들을 소장하고 있다.   **flamboyant** 이 화려한 전통 의상들은 그 마을에서 손으로 꿰매고, 천연염료로 염색한다.

★★

folklore

[fóuklɔ̀ːr]

[명] 민속, 민간 전승

n. the traditional stories and beliefs of a culture or region

The collector of local **folklore** travels from small village to small village recording tales told by the older generations.

★★

intricate

[íntrikət]

[형] 복잡한

n. intricacy

adj. detailed and complicated

The **intricate** patterns in the lace of this handmade dress make it both extremely beautiful and dangerously fragile.

syn. elaborate *ant.* simple

★★

lively

[láivli]

[형] 활기 넘치는, 활발한

adj. cheerful and energetic

The elderly storyteller was joined by a musical trio that played **lively** music to accompany his tales.

syn. bustling *ant.* somber

★

luxuriant

[lʌgʒúəriənt]

[형] (식물·머리카락이) 풍성한, 무성한

adj. growing or arranged in a full or thick way

These **luxuriant** wreaths of local grasses and colorful wildflowers were created by a group of folk artists.

syn. lush *ant.* sparse

★★★

native

[néitiv]

[형] 원주민의, 토착의

adj. coming from or naturally existing in a certain area

The **native** crafts of the island are made mostly with seashells, coral, and small pieces of driftwood.

syn. indigenous *ant.* imported

Useful Tips

가끔 native가 '다른 나라에서 온 백인이 아닌 사람'이란 뜻으로 사용되는 경우가 있는데, 이는 시대에 뒤떨어지고 인종 차별적인 느낌을 주므로 주의한다.

★★

neglect

[niglékt]

[동] (돌보지 않고) 방치하다, 등한시하다

[명] 방치, 소홀

v. to fail to give enough care or attention

Because they **neglected** their local artisans for so long, the people of the city have lost touch with their past.

n. the state of failing to give enough care or attention

Despite years of **neglect** and abuse, the ornate ironwork of the old house is still quite attractive.

folklore 그 지역 민간 전승 수집가는 기성세대들이 들려주는 이야기들을 녹음하며 작은 마을들을 옮겨 다닌다. **intricate** 레이스에 있는 복잡한 무늬 때문에 이 핸드메이드 드레스는 매우 아름다우면서도 위태로울 정도로 약하다. **lively** 그 나이 든 이야기꾼은 자신의 이야기에 활기 넘치는 음악 반주를 넣어 주는 삼인조 악단과 함께 했다. **luxuriant** 지역에서 나는 풀과 형형색색의 야생화로 이루어진 이 풍성한 화환들은 한 무리의 민속 예술가들이 만들었다. **native** 그 섬의 토착 공예품은 대부분 조개껍질, 산호, 그리고 작은 유목 조각들로 만들어졌다. **neglect** 그 도시의 사람들은 그들의 지역 장인들을 오랫동안 등한시했기 때문에, 그들의 과거와 단절되었다. / 수년간의 방치와 오용에도 불구하고, 그 오래된 집의 화려하게 꾸며진 철제 장식은 여전히 꽤 매력적이다.

practicality
[præktikǽləti]
ⓝ 실용성
adj. practical

n. the quality of being useful in certain situations

It is the **practicality** of many pieces of folk art that sets them apart from the "high art" found in galleries.

prestigious
[prestídʒəs]
ⓐ 명성 있는, 일류의
n. prestige

adj. being admired or having high status

Some artists graduate from **prestigious** art schools, while others learn their craft from hands-on work experience.

syn. distinguished

puppetry
[pʌ́pitri]
ⓝ 인형극, 인형을 만들고 조종하는 기술

n. the art of making puppets or putting on puppet shows

Perhaps the most striking example of regional **puppetry** is Vietnam's unique water-puppet tradition.

tapestry
[tǽpəstri]
ⓝ 태피스트리(여러 가지 색실로 그림을 짜 넣은 직물)

n. a large piece of cloth with images sewn or woven into it

A large **tapestry** depicting the westward journey of the town's original settlers hangs in a local museum.

tribe
[traib]
ⓝ 부족, 종족
adj. tribal

n. a large group that is related by blood and shares a culture

Members of the **tribe** still carve colorful and engaging totem poles that have deep symbolic meaning.

syn. clan

weave
[wi:v]
ⓥ 1. (옷감 등을) 짜다, 엮다
2. 엮어 만들다

v. 1 to make cloth by crossing threads over one another
2 to make an object by crossing strips of material over one another

1. It can take several people working together more than a year to **weave** a single Persian rug.

2. By **weaving** palm fronds together, local children make traditional baskets that are sold to tourists.

---

practicality 많은 민속 예술 작품들을 갤러리에서 볼 수 있는 '순수 예술'과 구분 짓는 것은 민속 예술 작품들의 실용성이다. **prestigious** 어떤 예술가들은 명문 예술 학교를 졸업하지만, 다른 예술가들은 실제 작업 경험을 통해 그들의 기술을 익힌다. **puppetry** 아마도 지역 인형극의 가장 두드러진 예는 베트남의 독특한 수상 인형 전통일지도 모른다. **tapestry** 그 마을 최초 정착자들의 서부로의 여정을 묘사한 거대한 태피스트리가 한 지역 박물관에 걸려 있다. **tribe** 그 부족원들은 깊은 상징적 의미를 지닌 화려하고 매력 있는 토템 기둥을 여전히 조각한다. **weave** 1. 페르시아 양탄자 하나를 짜는 데 여러 사람이 함께 일해서 1년 이상이 걸릴 수 있다. 2. 지역 아이들은 야자 나뭇잎을 엮어서 관광객들에게 판매할 전통 바구니들을 만든다.

EXERCISES

A Match each definition with the correct word.

1 the underlying foundation of something   ⓐ tribe

2 to have earned or be worthy of something   ⓑ diverse

3 having a great deal of variety   ⓒ basis

4 a large group that is related by blood and shares a culture   ⓓ tapestry

5 to fail to give enough care or attention   ⓔ folklore

6 to love and protect someone or something   ⓕ cherish

7 a large piece of cloth with images sewn or woven into it   ⓖ deserve

8 the traditional stories and beliefs of a culture or region   ⓗ neglect

B Choose the word that is closest in meaning to each underlined word.

1 The colorful domes of Russian Orthodox cathedrals give them a <u>distinct</u> appearance.
     ⓐ gorgeous   ⓑ everchanging   ⓒ deceptive   ⓓ unmistakable

2 Part of the <u>allure</u> of Greek mythology is that few characters are purely good or evil.
     ⓐ foundation   ⓑ appeal   ⓒ intention   ⓓ control

3 The university has one of the most <u>prestigious</u> philosophy departments in the world.
     ⓐ ancient   ⓑ respective   ⓒ distinguished   ⓓ resurgent

4 The traditional medicine of most cultures is based on the use of <u>native</u> herbs and roots.
     ⓐ medicinal   ⓑ common   ⓒ stable   ⓓ indigenous

5 The author's debut novel was a bestseller, but she was unable to <u>duplicate</u> her success.
     ⓐ replicate   ⓑ appreciate   ⓒ disseminate   ⓓ evade

6 The collector thought he had purchased an <u>authentic</u> whalebone carving, but it was fake.
     ⓐ genuine   ⓑ exclusive   ⓒ concave   ⓓ affordable

7 The Khoisan languages of Africa use an <u>intricate</u> system of clicking sounds.
     ⓐ silent   ⓑ vacillating   ⓒ artificial   ⓓ elaborate

Lesson 37

[>] 문화와 전통

Cultures & Traditions

★★ **acceptable**
[ækséptəbl]
[형] 용인되는
v. accept

adj. approved of or allowed

What is considered **acceptable** in one culture may be viewed as strange or rude in another.

★★ **ascribe**
[əskráib]
[동] (결과 등을) …의 탓으로 돌리다

v. to indicate a cause or source

The tensions between the two ethnic groups can be **ascribed** to significant differences in their cultural traditions.

syn. attribute

★ **binding**
[báindiŋ]
[형] 의무적인, 구속력이 있는
v. bind

adj. being necessary to follow or obey

Although it is not a **binding** rule, visitors to the ancient temple are encouraged to dress modestly.

syn. mandatory *ant.* optional

★★★ **conflict**
[kάnflikt]
[명] 갈등, 충돌
[kənflíkt]
[동] 상충하다

n. a heated disagreement between two parties *syn.* clash

In the past, the traditional dance was used as a means of resolving **conflicts** without resorting to violence.

v. to be unable to coexist *syn.* clash

Even if your personal beliefs **conflict** with those of the local population, you need to respect the traditions of your hosts.

★★ **contribute**
[kəntríbju:t]
[동] 기여하다, 주다
n. contribution

v. to give something to a cause or effort

Many different ethnic groups from across the region have **contributed** to the modern culture of the nation.

syn. provide

★★ **copious**
[kóupiəs]
[형] 많은, 풍부한

adj. present in large amounts

There are **copious** reasons to visit the national museum, including the cultural workshops it offers.

syn. abundant *ant.* lacking

---

acceptable 한 문화권에서 용인된다고 여겨지는 것이 다른 문화권에서는 이상하거나 무례한 것으로 여겨질 수 있다. **ascribe** 그 두 종족들 간의 갈등은 문화적 전통의 큰 차이 탓일 수 있다. **binding** 의무적인 규칙은 아니지만, 그 고대 신전의 방문객들은 옷을 단정하게 입도록 권장된다. **conflict** 그 전통 무용은 과거에 폭력에 의존하지 않고 갈등을 해소하는 방편으로 사용되었다. / 개인적 신념이 현지인들의 신념과 상충한다 해도, 초대한 사람들의 전통을 존중해야 한다. **contribute** 그 지역 전체의 많은 다양한 종족들은 그 나라의 현대 문화에 기여해 왔다. **copious** 그 국립 박물관이 제공하는 문화 워크숍들을 포함해 그곳을 방문할 많은 이유들이 있다.

★

cosmopolitan

[kὰzməpάlətn]

[형] 국제적인, 세련된

adj. containing or influenced by people from a variety of countries

The nation's capital has a **cosmopolitan** atmosphere, but the people of rural regions still have traditional lifestyles.

syn. sophisticated *ant.* unsophisticated

★★

courtesy

[kɔ́ːrtəsi]

[명] 예의, 정중한 행동

adj. courteous

n. polite behavior that shows respect for others

In some nations, holding a door open for strangers is a common **courtesy**, but in others it is not.

syn. deference

Useful Tips

(by) courtesy of는 '…의 호의로, … 덕분에, …이 제공한'의 뜻으로 사용된다.

★★★

deliberate

[dilíbərət]

[형] 고의의

[dilíbərèit]

[동] 숙고하다

n. deliberation

adj. done on purpose *syn.* intentional *ant.* accidental

The region's government made a **deliberate** attempt to downplay the influence of the ethnic minority.

v. to think carefully before making a decision *syn.* contemplate

After **deliberating** for several days, the committee proposed that the traditional holiday be given a new name.

★

embody

[imbάdi]

[동] 상징하다, 포함하다

n. embodiment

v. to represent a quality or characteristic

The hero of the revolution was said to **embody** all of the national characteristics that people held dear.

syn. exemplify

★★

feast

[fiːst]

[명] 잔치, 만찬

n. a large meal eaten on a special occasion

In both Canada and the United States, families get together to enjoy a turkey **feast** on Thanksgiving.

syn. banquet

★★

halt

[hɔːlt]

[동] 중단하다, 멈추다

v. to stop or put a stop to something

The tradition of holding large street parties was **halted** after drunken revelers smashed windows and fought the police.

syn. cease *ant.* continue

---

cosmopolitan 그 나라 수도의 분위기는 국제적이지만, 시골 지역 사람들은 여전히 전통적인 생활방식을 고수하고 있다. **courtesy** 몇몇 나라들에서는 타인들에게 문을 잡아 주는 것이 일반적인 예의이지만, 다른 나라들에서는 그렇지 않다. **deliberate** 그 지방 정부는 소수 민족의 영향력을 고의적으로 경시하려 했다. / 그 위원회는 며칠 동안의 숙고 끝에, 그 고유 명절에 새로운 이름을 붙이자고 제안했다. **embody** 그 혁명의 영웅은 국민이 소중하게 여기는 모든 국민성을 지니고 있다고 일컬어졌다. **feast** 캐나다와 미국에서는, 추수감사절에 가족들이 모여 칠면조 만찬을 즐긴다. **halt** 대규모 길거리 파티를 여는 전통은 술에 취해 흥청거리는 사람들이 창문을 박살내고 경찰과 다툰 이후 중단되었다.

★★★ heritage
[hératidʒ]

명 (국가·사회의) 유산

n. everything that is valued and passed on from one generation to the next

In an effort to protect its **heritage**, the nation introduced a new cultural curriculum for schools.

★★ immerse
[imə́ːrs]

동 …에 몰두시키다

v. to become deeply involved in something

On the night before the festival, local artists were **immersed** in the task of painting giant papier-mâché puppets.

syn. engross

★★★ immigrant
[ímigrənt]

명 이민자

n. someone who has moved to a place from another country

Since the late 19th century, Asian **immigrants** have had a strong influence on the cuisine of Hawaii.

ant. emigrant

★★ intact
[intǽkt]

형 손상되지 않은

adj. unbroken and without any missing parts

Despite the persecution of the occupiers, the local people managed to keep their traditions **intact**.

syn. undamaged   *ant.* damaged

★★ isolation
[àisəléiʃən]

명 고립, 소외

v. isolate

n. the state of being alone and cut off from others

Having developed in **isolation**, the religious ceremonies of the islanders are unlike those found on the mainland.

syn. seclusion

★ luster
[lʌ́stər]

명 광택, 광채

n. a shiny or glowing appearance

It is the natural **luster** of silk that makes it a favorite material in many cultures around the world.

syn. shimmer

---

heritage 유산을 보호하기 위한 노력으로, 그 나라는 학교에 새로운 문화 교육 과정을 도입했다.   **immerse** 그 축제 전날 밤에, 현지 예술가들은 혼응지로 만든 거대한 꼭두각시들을 칠하는 작업에 몰두했다.   **immigrant** 19세기 말 이래로, 아시아인 이민자들은 하와이 요리에 강한 영향을 미쳐 왔다.   **intact** 점령군들의 박해에도 불구하고, 그 지역 사람들은 그들이 전통이 손상되지 않도록 지켜냈다.   **isolation** 그 섬사람들의 종교 의식들은 고립된 상태로 발전해서, 본토에서 발견되는 종교 의식들과는 다르다.   **luster** 비단을 전 세계 많은 문화권에서 사랑 받는 직물로 만드는 요인은 바로 그것의 천연 광택이다.

★ **milieu**
[miljú]
[명] 환경

n. **the people, things, and activities around someone**

The wide range of social **milieus** that make up a single culture shapes the lifestyles of individuals.

syn. surroundings

Useful Tips
milieu의 복수형은 milieus와 milieux인데, milieus는 미국에서, milieux는 영국에서 흔히 사용된다.

★ **multitude**
[mʌ́ltətjùːd]
[명] 다수

n. **a large number of something**

The Philippines is made up of a **multitude** of islands, both large and small, each with its own traditions.

syn. myriad *ant.* handful

★★ **polish**
[pɑ́liʃ]
[동] 1. 닦다, 윤내다
2. 다듬다
adj. polished

v. **1 to rub something until it becomes shiny and reflective** *syn.* buff
2 to make something more refined *syn.* enhance

1. As Hanukkah approaches, Jewish families **polish** their menorahs, which are traditional candleholders.
2. The drummers got together to **polish** their routine a few days before the festival began.

★★★ **preserve**
[prizə́ːrv]
[동] 보존하다
n. preservation

v. **to keep something safe from harm or extinction**

The villagers believe that the best way to honor their ancestors is by **preserving** the ways of the past.

syn. conserve *ant.* neglect

★★ **prodigious**
[prədídʒəs]
[형] 막대한
n. prodigy

adj. **very large or impressive**

During Oktoberfest, Germans sing and dance to traditional music while drinking **prodigious** amounts of beer.

syn. tremendous *ant.* underwhelming

★★★ **ritual**
[rítʃuəl]
[명] 의식, 제사

n. **a series of actions or activities done in a certain way**

The **ritual** of burning effigies on Guy Fawkes Night dates back to an attempted bombing in 1605.

syn. ceremony

---

milieu 단일 문화권을 구성하는 다양한 사회 환경들이 개개인의 생활 방식을 형성한다. **multitude** 필리핀은 크고 작은 다수의 섬들로 이루어져 있는데, 각 섬에는 고유의 전통들이 있다. **polish** 1. 하누카가 다가오면, 유대인 가정들은 전통 촛대인 메노라(여러 갈래로 나뉜 큰 촛대)를 닦는다. 2. 축제가 시작되기 며칠 전에, 그 드럼 연주자들은 같이 모여 공연 루틴을 다듬었다. **preserve** 그 마을 주민들은 조상을 기리는 최고의 방안이 과거의 방식을 보존하는 것이라고 믿는다. **prodigious** 10월제 동안, 독일인들은 막대한 양의 맥주를 마시면서 전통 음악에 맞춰 노래하고 춤을 춘다. **ritual** 가이 포크스의 밤에 모형들을 불태우는 의식은 1605년에 미수에 그친 폭파 사건으로 거슬러 올라간다.

★★★ **separate**
[sépərèit]
[동] 분리하다
[sépərət]
[형] 별개의, 서로 다른
n. separation

v. to break into two or more or move away from each other

Although Ireland has been **separated** into two countries, they share a culture, a language, and many traditions.

adj. not connected *syn.* detached

Halloween and the Day of the Dead are celebrated at the same time, but they are two **separate** holidays.

★★★ **succeed**
[səksíːd]
[동] 성공하다
n. success

v. to achieve a goal

People are sometimes given good-luck charms, such as four-leaf clovers, to help them **succeed**.

syn. prevail *ant.* fail

★★ **taboo**
[təbúː, tæ-]
[명] 금기

n. something prohibited or frowned upon within a society

There are many theories surrounding the precise origins of the religious **taboo** against eating pork.

★★ **tangible**
[tǽndʒəbl]
[형] 유형의

adj. existing in a form that can be perceived by the senses

Examples of a nation's **tangible** cultural heritage include works of art, ancient manuscripts, and religious artefacts.

syn. material *ant.* intangible

★ **upbringing**
[ʌ́pbrìŋiŋ]
[명] 양육, 훈육

n. the way in which a person was raised as a child

A child's **upbringing** helps determine how much of a cultural connection he or she feels as an adult.

★★ **vanish**
[vǽniʃ]
[동] 사라지다

v. to no longer exist or be able to be seen

The American tradition of giving an apple to the teacher has completely **vanished** from today's society.

syn. disappear *ant.* appear

separate 아일랜드가 두 나라로 분리되긴 했지만, 그 두 나라는 문화와 언어, 그리고 많은 전통들을 공유한다. / 핼로윈과 망자의 날은 같은 때에 기념되지만, 두 개의 서로 다른 휴일이다. **succeed** 사람들은 때로 네잎클로버 같이 성공을 돕기 위한 행운의 부적들을 받는다. **taboo** 돼지고기를 먹는 것을 금하는 종교적 금기의 정확한 기원을 둘러싼 이론들이 많이 있다. **tangible** 한 나라의 유형 문화 유산의 예로는 예술 작품, 고문서, 종교적 공예품들이 있다. **upbringing** 아이의 양육은 성인이 돼서, 얼마나 많은 문화적 유대감을 느끼는지 결정하는 데 도움을 준다. **vanish** 선생님에게 사과를 주는 미국의 전통은 현재 사회에서 완전히 사라졌다.

EXERCISES

ART & DESIGN

SOCIAL SCIENCE

NATURAL SCIENCE

HUMANITIES

EARTH & SPACE

SOCIAL ISSUES

A Match each definition with the correct word.

1 someone who has moved to a place from another country   ⓐ milieu

2 a large number of something   ⓑ courtesy

3 a shiny or glowing appearance   ⓒ acceptable

4 polite behavior that shows respect for others   ⓓ luster

5 the way in which a person was raised as a child   ⓔ upbringing

6 something prohibited or frowned upon within a society   ⓕ multitude

7 approved of or allowed   ⓖ immigrant

8 the people, things, and activities around someone   ⓗ taboo

B Choose the word that is closest in meaning to each underlined word.

1 A number of different major religions incorporate the burning of incense into their <u>rituals</u>.
   ⓐ structures   ⓑ narratives   ⓒ ceremonies   ⓓ lectures

2 Many Native American languages have <u>vanished</u>, but others have been kept alive.
   ⓐ disappeared   ⓑ emerged   ⓒ reshaped   ⓓ contracted

3 Some freelance journalists <u>contribute</u> articles to both magazines and newspapers.
   ⓐ analyze   ⓑ criticize   ⓒ edit   ⓓ provide

4 Folk art doesn't get attention in <u>cosmopolitan</u> social circles, but it still has considerable value.
   ⓐ tedious   ⓑ sophisticated   ⓒ inclusive   ⓓ reanimated

5 Medusa had to live in <u>isolation</u>, as the sight of her face turned people to stone.
   ⓐ terror   ⓑ contentment   ⓒ seclusion   ⓓ anticipation

6 The author Ernest Hemingway <u>embodied</u> traditional masculinity for many people.
   ⓐ neglected   ⓑ exemplified   ⓒ disputed   ⓓ rehabilitated

7 It is not true that the library burned down with none of its manuscripts surviving <u>intact</u>.
   ⓐ unopened   ⓑ undamaged   ⓒ unexamined   ⓓ unknown

Lesson 38 Philosophy

[>] 철학

★

cogent
[kóudʒənt]
[형] 설득력 있는

adj. logical and convincing

It is easy to be swayed by **cogent** philosophical arguments, but that doesn't necessarily mean they are correct.

syn. compelling *ant.* ineffective

★★★

confine
[kənfáin]
[동] 국한시키다
n. confinement

v. to keep someone or something within certain limits

People sometimes **confine** their thoughts to material matters, as they find deeper issues overly intimidating.

syn. restrict

★

contemplate
[kántəmplèit]
[동] 생각하다, 고려하다
adj. contemplative

v. to think deeply about something

No matter how much we **contemplate** the reasons for our existence, we will never have all the answers.

syn. ponder

★

credence
[krí:dəns]
[명] 신빙성, 믿음, 신임

n. the belief that something is true

In spite of advances in human knowledge, Aristotle's philosophical ideas have gained **credence** over the centuries.

★★

deductive
[didʌ́ktiv]
[형] 추론적인, 연역적인
v. deduce

adj. relating to the act of drawing a conclusion based on logic

When faced with a great unknown, wise individuals use **deductive** reasoning to come to a logical conclusion.

syn. analytical

Useful Tips
deductive는 주로 deductive reasoning (연역적 추론)이라는 용어로 많이 쓰인다.

★★

despite
[dispáit]
[전] …임에도 불구하고

prep. without being affected by

Despite being called a "dumb ox" by his classmates, Thomas Aquinas went on to become a respected philosopher and theologian.

syn. in spite of *ant.* because of

---

cogent 설득력 있는 철학적 주장들에 휘둘리기 쉽지만, 그렇다고 해서 그 주장들이 반드시 옳다는 것은 아니다. **confine** 사람들은 그들의 생각을 때때로 물질적인 문제에 국한시키는데, 더 깊은 문제들에서 대해서는 지나치게 위협적이라 생각하기 때문이다. **contemplate** 우리가 아무리 우리 존재의 이유를 생각하더라도, 결코 모든 답을 얻지는 못할 것이다. **credence** 인간 지식의 진보에도 불구하고, Aristotle(아리스토텔레스)의 철학 사상은 수 세기에 걸쳐 신임을 얻어 왔다. **deductive** 엄청난 미지의 것을 마주할 때, 현명한 사람들은 논리적인 결론에 도달하기 위해 연역적 추론을 사용한다. **despite** 동급생들에게 '바보'라고 불렸음에도 불구하고, Thomas Aquinas는 존경받는 철학자이자 신학자가 되었다.

★

didactic

[daidǽktik]

[형] 교훈적인, 가르치려 드는

adj. done in a way intended to teach a lesson

Philosophical lectures are **didactic** by nature, but they can also be engaging and enjoyable.

★★

doctrine

[dáktrin]

[명] 교리, 정책, 주의

n. a set of beliefs held by a religion or other organized group

Many philosophers who believed in God still found themselves challenging the religious **doctrines** of their time.

syn. principle

★★

dogmatic

[dɔːgmǽtik]

[형] 독단적인

n. dogma

adj. expressing opinions as absolute truths

Making **dogmatic** assertions can be seen as a heavy-handed attempt to stifle the ideas of others.

★

empirical

[impírikəl]

[형] 경험에 의거한, 실증적인

adj. based on practical experience

Once a theoretical idea has been put forward, efforts should be made to support it with **empirical** evidence.

ant. theoretical

★★

enlighten

[inláitn]

[동] …을 계몽하다

n. enlightenment

v. to impart important information or knowledge

The philosophical writings of Simone de Beauvoir **enlightened** many people in the first half of the 20th century.

syn. educate

★★★

equality

[ikwáləti]

[명] 평등, 균등, 동등

adj. equal

n. the state of being treated the same way as others

Although the great Greek philosophers spoke of **equality**, few of them considered women or slaves worthy of it.

syn. fairness *ant.* inequality

didactic 철학 강의는 본래 교훈적이지만, 매력적이고 즐거울 수도 있다. **doctrine** 하느님을 믿었던 많은 철학자들은 그럼에도 당대의 종교적 교리에 이의를 제기했다. **dogmatic** 독단적인 주장을 하는 것은 다른 사람들의 생각을 억누르려는 고압적인 시도로 보일 수 있다. **empirical** 일단 이론적인 개념이 제시되면, 실증적 증거로 그것을 뒷받침하려는 노력을 해야 한다. **enlighten** Simone de Beauvoir의 철학적 저술은 20세기 전반기에 많은 사람들을 계몽시켰다. **equality** 위대한 그리스 철학자들이 평등에 대해 말했음에도 불구하고, 그들 중 여성이나 노예가 평등을 누릴 가치가 있다고 생각하는 사람은 거의 없었다.

generalize

[dʒénərəlàiz]

동 일반화하다

adj. general

v. to make a broad statement about a group

It is sometimes necessary to **generalize** in philosophy, but this puts us at risk of formulating fallacies.

glean

[gliːn]

동 (지식·정보 등을) 모으다, 얻다

v. to gather information slowly and carefully

By poring over books on philosophy in the library, the student was able to **glean** a great deal of knowledge.

hypothesis

[haipάθəsis]

명 가설

v. hypothesize

n. a possible explanation that is suggested without hard evidence

Due to the limited amount of information available, we can only create a **hypothesis** of what may have occurred.

ideal

[aidíːəl]

형 이상적인, 가장 알맞은

adj. perfect or perfectly suited for something

Plato believed that **ideal** forms can exist only in ideas, and that physical objects are merely representations of them.

syn. optimal

idle

[áidl]

형 1. 게으른, 나태한
2. 쉬고 있는

adj. 1 unwilling to work   *syn.* lazy   *ant.* hardworking
2 not currently active   *syn.* inactive   *ant.* active

1. **Idle** individuals have a lot of time on their hands, but they rarely use it to ponder the mysteries of life.

2. It has been argued that an **idle** mind is actually more open and receptive to new ideas than a working one.

Useful Tips

idol(우상, 우상 숭배)과 idyll(목가시, 전원시)은 idle과 발음은 같으나 의미가 다른 동음이의어이다.

ignorant

[íɡnərənt]

형 무지한, 무식한

n. ignorance

adj. lacking knowledge

Once people become aware that they are **ignorant**, they have the capacity to go forth and gather knowledge.

syn. uneducated   *ant.* educated

---

generalize 철학에서는 일반화하는 것이 때때로 필요하지만, 이는 우리를 오류 형성의 위험에 빠뜨린다.   **glean** 그 학생은 도서관에서 철학에 관한 책들을 세세히 읽음으로써 많은 지식을 얻을 수 있었다.   **hypothesis** 이용할 수 있는 정보의 양이 제한되어 있기 때문에, 우리는 일어났을지도 모르는 것에 대한 가설을 세울 수 있을 뿐이다.   **ideal** Plato(플라톤)는 이상적인 형태들은 오직 이데아로만 존재할 수 있고, 현실의 사물은 단지 그것들의 표현일 뿐이라고 믿었다.
idle 1. 게으른 사람들은 많은 시간이 있음에도, 그 시간을 삶의 신비에 대해 곰곰이 생각해 보는 데 좀처럼 사용하지 않는다. 2. 사실 쉬고 있는 뇌가 활동하고 있는 뇌보다 새로운 의견들에 더 개방적이고 수용적이라는 주장이 제기되어 왔다.   **ignorant** 일단 사람들은 자신이 무지하다는 것을 알게 되면, 앞으로 나아가 지식을 얻을 수 있는 능력을 갖게 된다.

interfere

★★★

[ìntərfíər]

ⓥ 1. 간섭하다, 개입하다
   2. 방해하다

n. interference

v. 1 to get involved in a situation without being welcome
   syn. meddle
   2 to prevent a process from taking place properly   *syn.* obstruct

1. The students asked their professor not to **interfere** with their argument over the meaning of justice.

2. Our worries about everyday needs often **interfere** with our attempts to better understand the nature of existence.

---

in vain

★★

[in vein]

ⓐ 헛되이, 허사가 되어

adv. without achieving the intended result

Even if your search for an answer ends **in vain**, you will likely have learned other things along the way.

syn. fruitlessly   *ant.* successfully

---

merit

★★★

[mérit]

ⓝ 장점, 가치 있는 요소

n. an advantage or worthy quality

The **merits** of generosity may be obvious, but there are also advantages to being somewhat selfish.

syn. strong point

---

perplexing

★★

[pərpléksiŋ]

ⓐ 당황하게 하는, 난처하게 하는

v. perplex

adj. causing extreme confusion

Many **perplexing** questions inevitably arise when we attempt to create precise definitions of good and evil.

syn. baffling

---

perspective

★★

[pərspéktiv]

ⓝ 관점, 시각

n. a specific way of viewing something

From the **perspective** of the ancient Chinese philosopher Sun Tzu, war has the ability to teach us about life.

syn. point of view

---

pragmatic

★★

[prægmǽtik]

ⓐ 실용적인, 실제적인

adj. employing basic common sense to deal with things in a realistic way

There are some **pragmatic** approaches to problem-solving that tend to have a high success rate.

syn. practical   *ant.* impractical

---

interfere 1. 그 학생들은 정의의 의미에 대한 자신들의 논쟁에 개입하지 말아 달라고 교수님께 부탁드렸다. 2. 일상적 욕구에 대한 우리의 걱정은 종종 존재의 본질을 더 잘 이해하려는 우리의 시도를 방해한다. **in vain** 비록 해답을 찾는 것이 헛되이 끝나더라도, 그 과정에서 다른 것들을 배웠을 것이다. **merit** 관대함의 장점들은 명백할 수 있지만, 다소 이기적인 것 역시 장점들이 있다. **perplexing** 우리가 선과 악의 정확한 정의를 내리려고 시도할 때, 당혹스러운 많은 질문들이 불가피하게 발생한다. **perspective** 고대 중국의 철학자인 손자(손무)의 관점에서, 전쟁은 우리에게 삶에 대해 가르쳐 줄 수 있다. **pragmatic** 문제 해결에 성공률이 높은 몇 가지 실용적인 접근법들이 있다.

pronounce

[prənáuns]

ⓥ 선언하다, 표명하다

n. pronouncement

v. to make a formal announcement

The German philosopher Friedrich Nietzsche **pronounced** that God was dead, shocking many of his contemporaries.

syn. declare

---

pursue

[pərsú:]

ⓥ 추구하다

n. pursuit

v. to attempt to catch or achieve something

Epicurus was an ancient Greek philosopher who believed that people should **pursue** happiness in their lives.

syn. chase after

---

rational

[rǽʃənl]

ⓐ 합리적인, 이성적인

adj. based on sound logic

In the past, it was believed that humankind's capacity for **rational** thought is what separates us from animals.

syn. logical   *ant.* irrational

---

reason

[rí:zn]

ⓥ (논리적인 근거에 따라) 판단하다, 추론하다

ⓝ 이성

adj. reasonable

v. to make a decision based on logic   *syn.* figure out

Around 400 BC, Democritus **reasoned** that everything in the universe must be made of individual atoms.

n. the ability to make decisions based on logic   *syn.* sense

By using our **reason** to honestly assess our own behavior, we can begin to make ourselves better people.

---

skeptical

[sképtikəl]

ⓐ 의심 많은, 회의적인

n. skeptic

adj. having strong doubts about something

Many modern people are **skeptical** about the value of philosophy, preferring to put their faith in science.

syn. doubtful   *ant.* convinced

---

stoic

[stóuik]

ⓐ 금욕의, 극기의

adv. stoically

adj. having firm control over one's emotions

There are some who believe that remaining **stoic** is the best way to prevent emotions from overwhelming logic.

syn. unemotional

Useful Tips

stoic(금욕주의자)의 형용사형은 원래 stoical이지만, 최근에는 stoic이 형용사형으로 더 많이 사용된다.

---

pronounce 독일의 철학자 Friedrich Nietzsche(니체)는 신은 죽었다고 선언하여 당시 많은 사람들에게 충격을 주었다.   **pursue** Epicurus(에피쿠로스)는 사람들은 살면서 행복을 추구해야 한다고 믿었던 고대 그리스의 철학자였다.   **rational** 과거에는 이성적인 생각을 할 수 있는 인류의 능력이 우리를 동물과 구분 짓는 것이라고 간주되었다.   **reason** 기원전 400년 즈음에 Democritus(데모크리토스)는 우주[세계]의 모든 것은 개별적인 원자로 만들어졌다고 추론했다. / 우리의 행동을 정직하게 평가하는 데 이성을 사용함으로써, 우리 자신을 더 나은 사람으로 만들기 시작할 수 있다.   **skeptical** 많은 현대인들은 철학의 가치에 대해 회의적이며, 과학을 믿는 것을 선호한다.   **stoic** 금욕적인 상태를 유지하는 것은 감정이 논리를 압도하지 못하게 하는 최상의 방법이라고 믿는 일부 사람들이 있다.

EXERCISES

ART & DESIGN

SOCIAL SCIENCE

NATURAL SCIENCE

HUMANITIES

EARTH & SPACE

SOCIAL ISSUES

A Match each definition with the correct word.

1 to make a decision based on logic   ⓐ reason

2 without achieving the intended result   ⓑ hypothesis

3 logical and convincing   ⓒ cogent

4 to gather information slowly and carefully   ⓓ empirical

5 the belief that something is true   ⓔ enlighten

6 to impart important information or knowledge   ⓕ credence

7 based on practical experience   ⓖ in vain

8 a possible explanation that is suggested without hard evidence   ⓗ glean

B Choose the word that is closest in meaning to each underlined word.

1 In spite of the horrors he had seen, the Greek hero remained calm and stoic.
   ⓐ disenchanted   ⓑ deflated   ⓒ reenergized   ⓓ unemotional

2 Attila contemplated invading Persia but attacked the Eastern Roman Empire instead.
   ⓐ pondered   ⓑ regretted   ⓒ endorsed   ⓓ impeded

3 Small villages are ideal places to track down eccentric folk art found nowhere else.
   ⓐ outlandish   ⓑ precarious   ⓒ optimal   ⓓ antiquated

4 Some religions encourage believers to pursue spiritual goals rather than material ones.
   ⓐ turn down   ⓑ chase after   ⓒ think over   ⓓ change into

5 The cultural traditions that we take for granted might seem perplexing to visitors.
   ⓐ dazzling   ⓑ inviting   ⓒ disparaging   ⓓ baffling

6 It is troubling that people are becoming skeptical about what they read in the news.
   ⓐ unimpressed   ⓑ enthusiastic   ⓒ doubtful   ⓓ cooperative

7 Edith Wharton did not confine herself to writing novels—she also wrote short stories.
   ⓐ restrict   ⓑ arrange   ⓒ praise   ⓓ deter

Lesson 39

종교

Religion

★★

abstain

[æbstéin]

[동] 자제하다, 피하다

v. to stop doing something enjoyable

Catholics **abstain** from eating meat on Ash Wednesday and every Friday during the six weeks of Lent.

syn. refrain

★★

altar

[ɔ́:ltər]

[명] 제단

n. a table used for religious ceremonies

The priests placed the bread and wine for communion on the **altar** before the mass began.

★

atheist

[éiθiist]

[명] 무신론자

n. someone who does not believe in God

Although he was raised in a religious household, the famous writer now considers himself an **atheist**.

syn. nonbeliever

Useful Tips

agnostic은 인간이 신의 존재 여부를 알 수 없다는 '불가지론자'를 뜻한다.

★★

baptize

[bæptáiz]

[동] 세례를 주다

v. to bring someone into the Christian Church by pouring water on their head

There are some Christian churches that **baptize** their new members outdoors in a nearby river or lake.

★★

blasphemy

[blǽsfəmi]

[명] 신성 모독

n. words or actions that are offensive to members of a religion

Galileo's proclamation that the Earth revolves around the Sun was considered a form of **blasphemy** by the Church.

★

canonize

[kǽnənàiz]

[동] (…을) 성인으로 공표하다

v. to officially make someone a saint

In 2016, Mother Teresa was **canonized** as Saint Teresa of Calcutta by the Catholic Church.

---

abstain 가톨릭 교인들은 사순절 6주 동안 재의 수요일과 모든 금요일에 육식을 자제한다. **altar** 그 신부들은 미사가 시작되기 전에 성찬식용 빵과 포도주를 제단 위에 올려 놓았다. **atheist** 그 유명 작가는 독실한 가정에서 자랐지만, 지금은 자신을 무신론자로 여긴다. **baptize** 가까운 강이나 호수에서 새 교인들에게 야외 세례를 주는 몇몇 기독교 교회들이 있다. **blasphemy** 지구가 태양 주위를 돈다는 Galileo의 선언은 교회에 의해 일종의 신성 모독으로 간주되었다. **canonize** 2016년에, Teresa 수녀가 가톨릭 교회에 의해 캘커타의 성 Teresa라는 성인으로 공표되었다.

confess

[kənfés]

ⓥ 고해하다, 고백하다

n. confession

v. to admit to bad things you have done

Catholics are expected to formally **confess** all of their sins to a priest at least once a month.

---

cult

[kʌlt]

ⓝ 사이비 종교 집단

n. a small religious group with practices that are considered strange

While the group calls itself a church, critics say it is a kind of **cult** that is run like a business.

---

disciple

[disáipl]

ⓝ 제자

n. a follower of someone's teachings

According to the Bible, Jesus Christ was betrayed by Judas Iscariot, who was one of his early **disciples**.

syn. adherent

---

dispel

[dispél]

ⓥ 없애다, 털어 버리다

v. to drive away a belief or feeling

The young pastor **dispelled** all doubt about his speaking ability by giving the congregation a moving sermon.

---

divine

[diváin]

ⓐ 신의, 인간을 초월한

n. divinity

adj. relating to a god or like a god

Miracles are **divine** acts that cannot be explained by the laws of nature, such as the parting of the Red Sea.

syn. supernatural

---

elevate

[éləvèit]

ⓥ 높이다, 올리다

n. elevation

v. to lift up, either physically or in terms of status

The status of the church has been **elevated** in the eyes of the community due to its numerous charitable activities.

syn. raise   *ant.* lower

ART & DESIGN

SOCIAL SCIENCE

NATURAL SCIENCE

HUMANITIES

EARTH & SPACE

SOCIAL ISSUES

confess 가톨릭 교인들은 적어도 한 달에 한 번 신부에게 모든 죄를 정식으로 고해하도록 되어 있다.   **cult** 그 집단은 스스로 교회라 칭하지만, 비판자들은 그것이 사업처럼 운영되는 일종의 사이비 종교 집단이라고 말한다.   **disciple** 성서에 의하면, 예수는 그의 초기 제자들 중 하나인 Judas Iscariot에 의해 배신 당했다.   **dispel** 그 젊은 목사는 신자들에게 감동적인 설교를 해서 그의 연설 능력에 대한 모든 의구심을 없앴다.   **divine** 기적은 홍해를 가르는 것 같이 자연 법칙으로 설명될 수 없는 신의 행위이다.   **elevate** 수많은 자선 활동 덕에 지역 사회의 시각으로 보는 그 교회의 지위가 높아졌다.

★★ **eternal**
[itə́ːrnl]
[형] 영원한, 불변의

adj. lasting forever

Some religions teach that people go to some kind of paradise after they die, where they enjoy **eternal** happiness.

syn. everlasting *ant.* finite

★★★ **faith**
[feiθ]
[명] 신앙, 믿음
adj. faithful

n. a strong belief based on feelings rather than proof

While scientific beliefs are based on experimentation and evidence, religious beliefs are based on **faith**.

★ **fervent**
[fə́ːrvənt]
[형] 열렬한

adj. very enthusiastic about something

When the church's choir breaks into song, the people in the pews rise up and join in with **fervent** intensity.

syn. passionate *ant.* apathetic

★★ **gospel**
[gáspəl]
[명] 복음

n. the teachings of Jesus Christ

Traveling preachers used to roam through the American West, sharing the **gospel** with settlers.

★★ **heretic**
[hérətik]
[명] 이단자
n. heresy

n. someone who goes against religious or social beliefs

During its three centuries of existence, the Spanish Inquisition imprisoned about 150,000 people as **heretics**.

ant. believer

★ **hermit**
[hə́ːrmit]
[명] 은둔자

n. someone who chooses to live in isolation

Some **hermits** simply dislike the company of their fellow human beings, while others have religious motives.

syn. recluse

eternal 어떤 종교들은 사람들이 사후에 영원한 행복을 누리는 일종의 천국에 간다고 가르친다. **faith** 과학적 믿음들이 실험과 증거에 기반을 두고 있는 반면, 종교적 믿음들은 신앙에 기반을 둔다. **fervent** 그 교회 성가대가 노래를 시작하면, 신도석의 사람들이 일어나 열렬하게 노래에 참여한다. **gospel** 순회 전도사들은 정착민들에게 복음을 나누며 미국 서부 전역을 돌아다니곤 했다. **heretic** 스페인 종교 재판이 3세기에 걸쳐 지속되는 동안, 약 15만 명의 사람들이 이단자로 투옥되었다. **hermit** 어떤 은둔자들은 단지 다른 사람들과 함께 있는 것을 싫어하는 반면, 다른 은둔자들은 종교적 동기들을 가지고 있다.

★★ **karma**
[kɑ́ːrmə]
[명] 업보, 카르마

n. the idea that past actions or past lives affect what happens to a person

Numerous religions believe that **karma** has an effect on the quality of our life after we are reborn.

★★ **martyr**
[mɑ́ːrtər]
[명] 순교자

n. someone who suffers or is killed for a belief

A statue atop the hill memorializes the deaths of several Christian **martyrs** who were executed 200 years ago.

★★★ **mercy**
[mə́ːrsi]
[명] 자비, 은총
adj. merciful

n. the act of showing compassion or forgiveness toward wrongdoers

People who have lived bad lives sometimes beg their god for **mercy** when they are facing death.

syn. benevolence *ant.* malevolence

★★ **missionary**
[míʃənèri]
[명] 선교사

n. a person who visits a foreign country to promote Christianity

David Livingston was a doctor and **missionary** who explored Africa in search of the source of the Nile.

★ **omnipresent**
[àmniprézənt]
[형] 편재하는, 어디에나 있는

adj. everywhere at all times

The idea that there is a single **omnipresent** god can be found in most mainstream Western religions.

★★ **orthodox**
[ɔ́ːrθədàks]
[형] 정통의, 전통적인

adj. relating to older, more traditional methods and beliefs

Due to their **orthodox** beliefs, members of the religious group are forbidden to wear modern clothing.

karma 많은 종교에서 우리가 다시 태어난 후에 업보가 우리 삶의 질에 영향을 미친다고 믿는다. **martyr** 그 언덕 위의 동상은 200년 전에 처형된 몇몇 기독교 순교자들의 죽음을 추모한다. **mercy** 악하게 산 사람들은 죽음에 직면하면, 때로 그들의 신에게 자비를 구한다. **missionary** David Livingston은 나일 강의 근원을 찾아 아프리카를 탐사했던 의사이자 선교사였다. **omnipresent** 편재하는 유일신이 있다는 개념은 대부분의 주류 서양 종교들에서 찾아볼 수 있다. **orthodox** 그 종교 집단의 교인들은 그들의 정통 신앙 때문에, 현대 복장 착용이 금지되어 있다.

pagan
[péigən]
ⓐ 이교도의

adj. relating to non-mainstream religions that worship nature and multiple gods

Many modern Christian holidays are on the same day as **pagan** festivals that were celebrated long ago.

Useful Tips

The Pantheon은 고대 로마 신들에게 바치는 신전으로 사용된 건축물로, 7세기 이후에는 로마 가톨릭 교회의 성당으로 사용되었다.

pantheon
[pǽnθiàn]
ⓝ (한 민족·국가의 모든) 신들

n. all of the gods of a religion

It is generally agreed that the Hindu **pantheon** consists of 33 gods, including Vishnu and Indra.

persecution
[pə̀ːrsikjúːʃən]
ⓝ 박해, 핍박

v. persecute

n. the act of maltreating a group of people because of their beliefs

Some of the earliest settlers of the United States are said to have been fleeing religious **persecution** in England.

syn. oppression

pilgrimage
[pílgrəmidʒ]
ⓝ 순례, 성지 참배

n. a journey to a holy site

Every year, millions of Muslims make a **pilgrimage** to Mecca, Saudi Arabia, the holiest city of Islam.

pious
[páiəs]
ⓐ 독실한

n. piety

adj. having strict religious beliefs

Although all of her grandparents were quite **pious**, the woman was raised without a religion.

syn. devout

prophet
[práfit]
ⓝ 예언자

n. a person who claims to know what God wants people to do

Moses, the most important **prophet** in Judaism, also plays an important role in Islam and Christianity.

---

pagan 많은 현대 기독교의 축일들은 오래 전에 기념되었던 이교도의 축제들과 날짜가 동일하다.   **pantheon** 힌두교 신들이 Vishnu와 Indra를 포함해 33의 신들로 이루어져 있다는 것이 일반적으로 합의된 사실이다.   **persecution** 가장 초기의 미국 정착민들 중 일부는 영국에서 있었던 종교적 박해를 피해서 왔다고들 한다.   **pilgrimage** 매년, 수백만 명의 이슬람교도들이 이슬람교의 가장 성스러운 도시인 사우디 아라비아의 메카를 순례한다.   **pious** 조부모가 모두 매우 독실함에도 불구하고, 그 여자는 종교 없이 자랐다.   **prophet** 유대교에서 가장 중요한 예언자인 Moses는 이슬람교와 기독교에서도 중요한 역할을 한다.

★★ **redeem**
[ridíːm]
[동] 속죄하다, 구원하다
n. redemption

v. to compensate for bad behavior in the past
The greedy businessman donated money to the church, in an effort to **redeem** himself in the eyes of God.
syn. atone

★ **reincarnation**
[rìːinkɑːrnéiʃən]
[명] 환생

n. the act of being reborn in a new body after death
The belief in **reincarnation** is predicated on the idea that we possess a soul that can inhabit a new body.

★★ **repent**
[ripént]
[동] 회개하다, 뉘우치다

v. to seek forgiveness for bad behavior in the past
The priest urged the prisoner, who was on her deathbed, to **repent** her sins before she died.

★★ **rite**
[rait]
[명] 의식

n. a traditional ceremony
Bar mitzvahs and bat mitzvahs are religious **rites** for Jewish children who are approaching adulthood.
syn. ritual

★★ **sacred**
[séikrid]
[형] 신성한

adj. considered to be connected to God
Aboriginal Australians have been seeking to legally protect certain sites that they consider **sacred**.
syn. holy *ant.* profane

★★★ **sacrifice**
[sǽkrəfàis]
[동] 제물로 바치다
[명] 제물
adj. sacrificial

v. to kill an animal for or offer an object to a god
It was believed that **sacrificing** a domesticated animal such a goat would appease the angry gods.

n. an animal or object killed for or offered to a god
The villagers left their valuable items on the altar as a **sacrifice** to God.

redeem 그 탐욕스러운 사업가는 하나님의 관점에서 속죄하려는 노력의 일환으로 교회에 돈을 기부했다. **reincarnation** 환생에 대한 믿음은 우리가 새로운 몸에 들어가 살 수 있는 영혼을 가지고 있다는 개념에 근거한다. **repent** 그 신부는 임종을 맞은 그 죄수에게 죽기 전에 죄를 회개하라고 강권했다. **rite** 바르 미츠바와 바트 미츠바는 곧 성인이 될 유대교 아이들을 위한 종교 의식이다. **sacred** 오스트레일리아 원주민들은 그들이 신성하게 여기는 특정 장소들을 법적으로 보호해 달라고 요청해 왔다. **sacrifice** 염소 같이 길들여진 동물을 제물로 바치는 것이 분노한 신들을 달래 줄 것이라고 믿어졌다. / 그 마을 사람들은 하나님에게 바치는 제물로 그들의 귀중품들을 제단 위에 두었다.

★★ salvation
[sælvéiʃən]
몡 구원

n. the act of being saved from a bad situation

Some people who have had difficult lives claim that they found their **salvation** in religion.

syn. deliverance

★★ sanctuary
[sǽŋktʃuèri]
몡 피난처, 성역

n. a place that offers protection

During the street fighting between the government and the rebels, many citizens sought **sanctuary** in churches.

syn. asylum

★ schism
[sízm, skízm]
몡 분립, 분열, 불화

n. the division of one group into two, based on differing beliefs

In the year 1054, a **schism** took place in Catholicism, leading to the formation of the Eastern Orthodox Church.

syn. rift   *ant.* unity

★★ secular
[sékjulər]
휑 세속적인

adj. not connected to religion

Christmas is traditionally a religious holiday, but many modern Christmas celebrations are **secular** in nature.

ant. religious

★★ shrine
[ʃrain]
몡 성당, 사당, 신전

n. a religious place where a person is remembered

A **shrine** to the Virgin Mary was erected in the spot where several schoolchildren claimed she appeared to them.

★★ worship
[wɔ́ːrʃip]
통 숭배하다

v. to show respect to a god

In many early religions, some of which still exist today, people **worshiped** rocks and trees.

---

salvation 삶이 힘들었던 몇몇 사람들은 종교에서 구원을 찾았다고 주장한다.   **sanctuary** 정부와 저항 세력 간의 시가전 동안, 많은 시민들이 교회 안의 피난처를 찾았다.   **schism** 1054년에 가톨릭교에서 분립이 일어나, 동방 정교회의 설립으로 이어졌다.   **secular** 크리스마스는 전통적으로 종교적 축일이지만, 많은 현대의 크리스마스 기념 행사는 사실상 세속적이다.   **shrine** 학생 몇 명이 성모 마리아가 그들에게 나타났다고 주장했던 곳에 성모 마리아 성당이 세워졌다.   **worship** 오늘날까지 그 일부가 존재하는 많은 초기 종교들에서, 사람들은 바위와 나무들을 숭배했다.

EXERCISES

ART & DESIGN

SOCIAL SCIENCE

NATURAL SCIENCE

HUMANITIES

EARTH & SPACE

SOCIAL ISSUES

A Match each definition with the correct word.

1 not connected to religion   ⓐ confess

2 a strong belief based on feelings rather than proof   ⓑ blasphemy

3 someone who suffers or is killed for a belief   ⓒ pantheon

4 to kill an animal for or offer an object to a god   ⓓ secular

5 everywhere at all times   ⓔ faith

6 all of the gods of a religion   ⓕ omnipresent

7 to admit to bad things you have done   ⓖ martyr

8 words or actions that are offensive to members of a religion   ⓗ sacrifice

B Choose the word that is closest in meaning to each underlined word.

1 In Greek myths, heroes facing certain death are often saved by <u>divine</u> intervention.
  ⓐ auspicious   ⓑ supernatural   ⓒ undesirable   ⓓ uncertain

2 <u>Fervent</u> enthusiasts of military history sometimes gather together to recreate famous battles.
  ⓐ youthful   ⓑ passionate   ⓒ disinterested   ⓓ argumentative

3 A controversial article by a professor created a <u>schism</u> in the field of philosophy.
  ⓐ marvel   ⓑ annex   ⓒ rift   ⓓ debit

4 *Walden* is Thoreau's account of his life as a <u>hermit</u> while living in seclusion in the woods.
  ⓐ laborer   ⓑ scribe   ⓒ hostage   ⓓ recluse

5 The reporter interviewed the leaders of an ethnic group that is facing <u>persecution</u>.
  ⓐ deportation   ⓑ commendation   ⓒ oppression   ⓓ assimilation

6 The theme of the classic novel is the <u>eternal</u> question: "What is the meaning of life?"
  ⓐ exclusive   ⓑ vulgar   ⓒ everlasting   ⓓ rhetorical

7 If you visit a Muslim country during Ramadan, you must <u>abstain</u> from eating in public.
  ⓐ refrain   ⓑ regret   ⓒ sustain   ⓓ commend

Lesson **40**

> 역사
History

★★★ **advanced**
[ædvǽnst]
ⓐ 앞선, 발달한, 선진의
n. advancement

adj. highly developed

Math and science were more **advanced** in India and China than they were in other ancient civilizations.

ant. primitive

★ **annihilate**
[ənáiəlèit]
ⓥ 전멸시키다, 멸망시키다
n. annihilation

v. to completely destroy or eliminate

General Custer's army was **annihilated** by Native American warriors in the Battle of Little Bighorn in 1876.

syn. obliterate

★★ **appoint**
[əpɔ́int]
ⓥ 임명하다, 지명하다
n. appointment

v. to place someone in an official position or role

Sandra Day O'Connor, America's first female Supreme Court justice, was **appointed** by Ronald Reagan in 1981.

★★ **archive**
[ɑ́ːrkaiv]
ⓝ 옛 기록, 공문서

n. a collection of historical records or documents

The official national historical **archives** of some countries are now accessible on the Internet.

★ **aristocratic**
[ərìstəkrǽtik]
ⓝ 귀족(적)인
n. aristocracy

adj. belonging or relating to a privileged class

During the French Revolution, many **aristocratic** individuals were executed, while others fled the country.

syn. noble   *ant.* common

★★ **autonomy**
[ɔːtánəmi]
ⓝ 자치(권)
adj. autonomous

n. a state of self-rule

Greenland, the world's largest island, was granted **autonomy** by the Kingdom of Denmark in 1979.

syn. independence   *ant.* dependence

---

advanced 수학과 과학은 다른 고대 문명들에서보다 인도와 중국에서 더 많이 앞서 있었다.　**annihilate** Custer 장군의 군대는 1876년 리틀 빅혼 전투에서 아메리카 원주민 전사들에게 전멸되었다.　**appoint** 미국 최초의 여성 대법관인 Sandra Day O'Connor는 1981년에 Ronald Reagan 대통령에 의해 임명되었다. **archive** 이제 일부 국가의 공식적인 국가 역사 기록물들을 인터넷에서 볼 수 있다.　**aristocratic** 프랑스 혁명이 진행되는 동안에 많은 귀족들이 처형되었고, 다른 귀족들은 나라를 떠났다.　**autonomy** 세계에서 가장 큰 섬인 그린란드는 1979년 덴마크 왕국에 의해 자치권을 부여받았다.

avert

[əvə́ːrt]

ⓥ 피하다, 방지하다

v. to avoid something undesirable

During the Cuban Missile Crisis of 1962, a nuclear war between the USSR and the USA was narrowly **averted**.

syn. prevent   *ant.* allow

chronological

[krànəládʒikəl]

ⓐ 시간 순서로 된, 연대순의

adj. occurring in or relating to a specific time order

This **chronological** timeline is designed to help students better understand the history of Argentina.

conquest

[kánkwest, káŋ-]

ⓝ (다른 나라·민족에 대한) 정복

v. conquer

n. a victory in which control is assumed over a land and its people

The Roman Empire's **conquest** of Britain began in 43 AD, when the Roman army crossed the English Channel.

syn. subjugation

crusade

[kruːséid]

ⓝ (개혁·숙청·박멸) 운동

n. a prolonged attempt to reach a strongly desired outcome

After the Holy Land fell under Muslim rule, Europeans began discussing a **crusade** to reclaim it.

Useful **Tips**

십자군 전쟁은 대문자를 사용하여 the Crusades라고 표기한다.

demonstrate

[démənstrèit]

ⓥ (행동으로) 보여 주다, 입증하다

v. to show something through actions or make something clear

Time after time, all across the globe, it has been **demonstrated** that history does indeed repeat itself.

dispute

[dispjúːt]

ⓝ 분쟁, 논쟁
ⓥ 반박하다, 이의를 제기하다

n. a heated disagreement over facts   *syn.* conflict

A **dispute** between the UK and Norway over an Antarctic island ended when the UK renounced its claim in 1929.

v. to disagree with what someone else states is true

Some people claim that Columbus set out to prove that the world isn't flat, but historians **dispute** this.

ART & DESIGN

SOCIAL SCIENCE

NATURAL SCIENCE

HUMANITIES

EARTH & SPACE

SOCIAL ISSUES

---

avert 1962년 쿠바 미사일 위기 동안, 소련과 미국 간의 핵전쟁을 가까스로 방지했다.　**chronological** 이 시간순으로 된 연대표는 학생들이 아르헨티나의 역사를 더 잘 이해하도록 돕기 위해 고안되었다.　**conquest** 로마 제국의 영국 정복은 로마 군대가 영국 해협을 건넜던 서기 43년에 시작되었다.　**crusade** 성지가 이슬람의 지배에 들어간 후, 유럽인들은 성지를 되찾기 위한 (십자군) 운동을 논의하기 시작했다.　**demonstrate** 시간이 흐르면서 전 세계에 걸쳐, 정말로 역사는 반복된다는 것이 입증되었다.　**dispute** 남극섬에 대한 영국과 노르웨이 사이의 분쟁은 영국이 1929년 영유권 주장을 포기하면서 종결되었다. / 일부 사람들은 Columbus가 지구가 평평하지 않다는 것을 증명하기 위해 탐험에 나섰다고 주장하지만, 역사가들은 이에 이의를 제기한다.

★★★

dynasty

[dáinəsti, dín-]

[명] 왕조

n. a period of time during which a single family rules a country

Shah Mir, who was the sultan of Kashmir, founded the **dynasty** that would take his name in 1339.

★★

emancipate

[imǽnsəpèit]

[동] 해방시키다

n. emancipation

v. to grant freedom to someone

Slaves in ancient Rome who were **emancipated** became "freedmen" and were given many rights.

syn. liberate *ant.* enslave

Useful Tips

1863년 링컨 대통령이 발표한 '노예 해방 선언'을 영어로는 The Emancipation Proclamation이라고 한다.

★

epoch

[épək]

[명] (중요한 사건·변화들이 일어난) 시대

n. a long period of time during which important events occurred

For better or for worse, the Industrial Revolution marked a new **epoch** in the history of humankind.

★

espouse

[ispáuz, -páus]

[동] 지지하다, 옹호하다

v. to support a cause, method, or belief

Many youths who **espoused** revolution and the counterculture in the 1960s later joined the mainstream.

syn. advocate *ant.* oppose

★★★

establish

[istǽbliʃ]

[동] 세우다, 설립하다

n. establishment

v. to set up or create

It is believed that Norsemen **established** settlements in North America in the late 10th century.

syn. found

★★

evict

[ivíkt]

[동] (주택이나 땅에서) 쫓아내다, 퇴거시키다

n. eviction

v. to forcefully remove someone from their home

After the Nazis took power, Jewish families were **evicted** from their homes and sent to concentration camps.

syn. throw out

---

dynasty 카슈미르의 술탄이었던 Shah Mir는 1339년에 자신의 이름을 딴 왕조를 세웠다. **emancipate** 해방된 고대 로마의 노예들은 '자유인'이 되었고, 많은 권리를 부여받았다. **epoch** 좋든 나쁘든 간에, 산업혁명은 인류 역사의 새로운 시대를 열었다. **espouse** 1960년대에 혁명과 반체제 문화를 지지했던 많은 젊은이들이 후에 주류로 합류했다. **establish** 노르인(고대 노르웨이인)들이 10세기 후반에 북미에 정착했다고 여겨진다. **evict** 나치가 권력을 잡은 후, 유대인 가족들은 집에서 쫓겨나 강제 수용소로 보내졌다.

★★
feudalism
[fjúːdəlìzm]
[명] 봉건 제도
adj. feudal

n. a social system in which common people lived on land owned by nobles

Feudalism lasted for several centuries in Europe before it was officially ended by Napoleon in 1789.

★
futile
[fjúːtl]
[형] 헛된, 소용없는
n. futility

adj. without success

After several **futile** attempts, the first major undersea communications cable was laid in 1851.

syn. fruitless *ant.* fruitful

★
hierarchy
[háiərɑ̀ːrki]
[명] 계급
adj. hierarchical

n. a status system in which people are ranked above or below one another

In the social **hierarchy** of ancient Egypt, soldiers enjoyed higher status than educated scribes.

★★★
hostile
[hɑ́stl]
[형] 적대적인
n. hostility

adj. showing anger or aggression

The people of some Pacific islands welcomed the first European explorers, while those of others were **hostile**.

syn. belligerent *ant.* friendly

★★
ignite
[ignáit]
[동] 1. …에 불이 붙다, 점화하다
2. (감정을) 타오르게 하다, 촉발하다
n. ignition

v. 1 to cause something to start burning
2 to cause a volatile situation to worsen

1. According to legend, a lantern knocked over by a cow **ignited** the Great Chicago Fire of 1871.
2. France's decision to test a nuclear weapon in the South Pacific in 1995 **ignited** a firestorm of international criticism.

Useful Tips
ignition은 자동차에 시동을 거는 '점화 장치'를 의미하기도 한다.

★★
imperialism
[impíəriəlìzm]
[명] 제국주의
adj. imperial

n. the practice of occupying and controlling weaker countries

In the 18th and 19th centuries, European **imperialism** divided Africa up into colonies to be exploited.

---

feudalism 봉건 제도는 1789년 Napoleon에 의해 공식적으로 끝나기 전까지 유럽에서 수 세기 동안 지속되었다. **futile** 몇 번의 헛된 시도 끝에, 최초의 주요 해저 통신 케이블이 1851년에 놓였다. **hierarchy** 고대 이집트의 사회 계급에서 군인들은 교육받은 사본 필경사들보다 더 높은 지위를 누렸다. **hostile** 몇몇 태평양 섬의 사람들은 최초의 유럽 탐험가들을 환영했지만, 다른 섬사람들은 적대적이었다. **ignite** 1. 전해오는 이야기에 따르면, 젖소 한 마리가 넘어뜨린 등불이 1871년 시카고 대화재에 처음 불을 붙였다고 한다. 2. 1995년에 남태평양 바다에서 핵실험을 하기로 한 프랑스의 결정은 거센 국제적 비판을 촉발했다. **imperialism** 18세기와 19세기에 유럽의 제국주의는 착취를 위해 아프리카를 식민지들로 갈라놓았다.

★★★ **justify**
[dʒʌ́stəfài]
[동] 정당화하다
n. justification

v. to prove that something was done for a good reason

It is widely considered to be unethical to attempt to **justify** a nation's past aggressions in a history book.

syn. rationalize

★★ **keen**
[ki:n]
[형] 1. 열정적인
2. 예민한, 예리한

adj. 1 motivated and enthusiastic *syn.* eager *ant.* apathetic
2 highly developed *syn.* sharp *ant.* dull

1. **Keen** followers of history tend to enjoy the historical documentaries of American filmmaker Ken Burns.
2. It takes a **keen** mind to spot some of the minor historical inaccuracies in our nation's textbooks.

★★ **medieval**
[mì:dií:vəl, méd-]
[형] 중세의

adj. relating to the Middle Ages

Medieval villagers led hard lives centered around farming land that belonged to a knight or nobleman.

★★ **monarchy**
[mánərki]
[명] 군주제, 군주국, 왕정

n. a government led by a king or queen

Oliver Cromwell helped overthrow the English **monarchy** in 1649, but it was later restored.

★★ **paradox**
[pǽrədàks]
[명] 역설, 모순

n. something with aspects that seem to contradict each other

Some people consider it a **paradox** that the ancient Greeks invented democracy while practicing slavery.

syn. contradiction

★★★ **predict**
[pridíkt]
[동] 예언하다, 예측하다
n. prediction

v. to say what you think will happen in the future

While historians record and analyze events of the past, futurists **predict** what will happen in the future.

syn. prognosticate

---

justify 역사책에서 한 국가의 과거 침략을 정당화하려는 시도는 비윤리적이라고 널리 알려져 있다. **keen** 1. 역사의 열렬한 추종자들은 미국 영화 제작자인 Ken Burns의 역사 다큐멘터리를 즐겨 보는 경향이 있다. 2. 우리나라의 교과서에서 사소한 역사적 오류를 발견하기 위해서는 예리한 지력이 필요하다. **medieval** 중세 마을 주민들은 기사나 귀족이 소유한 농경지에 집중된 고된 삶을 살았다. **monarchy** Oliver Cromwell이 1649년에 영국 왕정을 전복하는 것을 도왔지만, 이후에 왕정은 다시 복구되었다. **paradox** 몇몇 사람들은 고대 그리스인들이 노예제를 실행하면서 민주주의를 고안한 것을 역설이라 생각한다. **predict** 역사가들은 과거의 사건들을 기록하고 분석하지만, 미래학자들은 미래에 어떤 일이 일어날지 예측한다.

ART & DESIGN

SOCIAL SCIENCE

NATURAL SCIENCE

HUMANITIES

EARTH & SPACE

SOCIAL ISSUES

reform
[rifɔ́ːrm]
ⓥ 개혁하다, 개선하다

v. to improve a system or institution through change

The goal of the Young Turks was to **reform** the crumbling political systems of the Ottoman Empire.

syn. rehabilitate

reign
[rein]
ⓝ 통치 기간, 치세
ⓥ 군림하다, 통치하다

n. the period during which a king or queen rules a country

The **reign** of Sejong the Great began in 1418 and ended with his death in 1450.

v. to be the king or queen of a country   *syn.* rule

Louis XIV **reigned** as king of France for more than 70 years, longer than any monarch in modern history.

relinquish
[rilíŋkwiʃ]
ⓥ (마지못해 소유권을) 포기하다, 내주다

v. to give something up

Queen Liliuokalani of Hawaii was imprisoned and forced to **relinquish** her claim to the throne in 1895.

ant. hold on to

retrospect
[rétrəspèkt]
ⓝ 회상, 회고
n., adj. retrospective

n. a look back at the past

When viewed in **retrospect**, the events leading up to the First World War seem to have been avoidable.

Useful **Tips**

retrospect는 in retrospect(돌이켜 생각해 보면)의 형태로 자주 사용된다.

revolution
[rèvəlúːʃən]
ⓝ 1. 혁명
2. 대변혁, 개혁
v. revolt

n. 1 an uprising against a government   *syn.* rebellion
2 a period of great change

1. In the early 20th century, Vladimir Lenin led a **revolution** against the Imperial Russian government.

2. It was the invention of the printing press that led to a **revolution** in the way information was shared.

solidarity
[sɑ̀lədǽrəti]
ⓝ 연대, 결속

n. a deep feeling of affinity and togetherness

Feelings of **solidarity** between the citizens of the UK and the USA were strengthened by World War II.

syn. unity   *ant.* discord

---

reform 청년 투르크당의 목표는 오스만 제국의 흔들리는 정치 시스템을 개혁하는 것이었다.   **reign** 세종대왕의 치세는 1418년에 시작하여 1450년 그의 서거와 함께 끝났다. / Louis 14세는 근대사의 그 어떤 군주보다도 긴 70년 이상을 프랑스의 왕으로 군림했다.   **relinquish** 하와이의 여왕 Liliuokalani는 1895년에 감금되었고, 그녀의 왕좌에 대한 주장을 포기해야만 했다.   **retrospect** 돌이켜 보면, 제1차 세계 대전으로 이어지는 사건들은 피할 수 있었던 것처럼 보인다.
revolution 1. 20세기 초에 Vladimir Lenin은 제정 러시아 정부에 대항하는 혁명을 이끌었다. 2. 정보의 공유 방식에 대변혁을 가져온 것은 인쇄기의 발명이었다.
solidarity 영국과 미국 국민들 사이의 연대감은 제2차 세계 대전에 의해 강화되었다.

★★ tolerance
[tálərəns]

ⓝ 용인, 관용, 아량

v. tolerate

n. the trait of accepting things you don't agree with or approve of

The Dutch Republic was known for its religious **tolerance**, allowing people of all faiths to live side by side.

★ treacherous
[trétʃərəs]

ⓐ 1. 위험한
2. 기만적인, 신뢰할 수 없는

n. treachery

adj. 1 dangerous and unpredictable　*syn.* hazardous　*ant.* safe
　　　　2 untrustworthy and prone to betrayal　*syn.* disloyal

1. Explorers feared the Drake Passage, the body of water between South America and Antarctica, for its **treacherous** currents.

2. Benedict Arnold, who betrayed the American Revolution, is considered one of the most **treacherous** figures in American history.

★★ triumph
[tráiəmf]

ⓝ 승리
ⓥ 승리를 거두다, 극복하다

adj. triumphant

n. an important victory　*syn.* success　*ant.* failure

The **triumph** of the Greek navy at the Battle of Salamis helped forestall the Persian invasion.

v. to win an important victory　*syn.* prevail　*ant.* fail

Roald Amundsen **triumphed** over the elements to become the first explorer to reach the North Pole in 1926.

★★ turmoil
[tɔ́ːrmɔil]

ⓝ 소란, 혼란

n. uncontrolled activity and disturbances

The **turmoil** created by the Partition of India of 1947 led to the tragic loss of hundreds of thousands of lives.

syn. unrest　*ant.* tranquility

★ tyranny
[tírəni]

ⓝ 폭정, 압제, 폭압

n. harsh and cruel rule

The United States claimed that it invaded Iraq in 2003 in order to free its people from **tyranny**.

★★ usurp
[juːsɔ́ːrp]

ⓥ (왕권·권좌 등을) 빼앗다, 찬탈하다

v. to unlawfully take a position of power from someone

King Henry IV of England **usurped** the throne from Richard II, who was his cousin and childhood friend.

---

tolerance 네덜란드 공화국은 종교적 관용으로 알려져 있었는데, 모든 종교의 사람들이 함께 살 수 있도록 허락했기 때문이다.　**treacherous** 1. 탐험가들은 위험한 조류 때문에 남아메리카와 남극 사이의 수역인 드레이크 해협을 두려워했다. 2. 미국 독립 혁명을 배신한 Benedict Arnold는 미국 역사상 가장 기만적인 인물 중 하나로 여겨진다.　**triumph** 살라미스 해전에서 그리스 해군의 승리는 페르시아의 침공을 막는 데 기여했다. / Roald Amundsen은 악천후를 이겨내고 1926년에 북극에 도달한 최초의 탐험가가 되었다.　**turmoil** 1947년 인도의 분할에 의해 야기된 혼란은 수십만 명의 목숨을 비극적으로 앗아갔다.　**tyranny** 미국은 폭정으로부터 이라크인들을 해방시키기 위해 2003년에 이라크를 침공했다고 주장했다.　**usurp** 영국의 Henry 4세는 자신의 사촌이자 어릴 적 친구였던 Richard 2세에게서 왕권을 찬탈했다.

EXERCISES

ART & DESIGN

SOCIAL SCIENCE

NATURAL SCIENCE

HUMANITIES

EARTH & SPACE

SOCIAL ISSUES

A Match each definition with the correct word.

1 to cause something to start burning   ⓐ reign

2 relating to the Middle Ages   ⓑ monarchy

3 the practice of occupying and controlling weaker countries   ⓒ ignite

4 the period during which a king or queen rules a country   ⓓ usurp

5 a long period of time during which important events occurred   ⓔ imperialism

6 a collection of historical records or documents   ⓕ epoch

7 to unlawfully take a position of power from someone   ⓖ archive

8 a government led by a king or queen   ⓗ medieval

B Choose the word that is closest in meaning to each underlined word.

1 The novel takes place during the turmoil of the 1968 Prague Spring.
   ⓐ onset   ⓑ conclusion   ⓒ unrest   ⓓ gratification

2 A dispute over the construction of a new mosque has caused religious tensions.
   ⓐ delay   ⓑ proposal   ⓒ conflict   ⓓ condition

3 Mark Twain's keen wit is what has made his satirical novels popular for more than 100 years.
   ⓐ sharp   ⓑ unusual   ⓒ old-fashioned   ⓓ unclear

4 According to one Native American myth, the moon is captured by a hostile tribe each night.
   ⓐ adjacent   ⓑ legendary   ⓒ enigmatic   ⓓ belligerent

5 Addressing others as family members creates feelings of solidarity in some languages.
   ⓐ uncertainty   ⓑ unity   ⓒ levity   ⓓ superiority

6 In order to avert a lawsuit, the newspaper printed an apology for publishing false information.
   ⓐ publicize   ⓑ analyze   ⓒ initiate   ⓓ prevent

7 Even when young people turn their backs on traditions, older people refuse to relinquish them.
   ⓐ seek out   ⓑ put off   ⓒ work on   ⓓ give up

REVIEW TEST

A Choose the correct words.

1 The word autonomy has the same meaning as

ⓐ mechanism　　　ⓑ independence　　　ⓒ efficiency　　　ⓓ aggression

2 The word auspicious has the same meaning as

ⓐ suspicious　　　ⓑ ambiguous　　　ⓒ promising　　　ⓓ refined

3 The word equality has the same meaning as

ⓐ achievement　　　ⓑ calculation　　　ⓒ timeliness　　　ⓓ fairness

4 The word ascribe has the same meaning as

ⓐ compile　　　ⓑ disinfect　　　ⓒ attribute　　　ⓓ sojourn

5 The word pious has the same meaning as

ⓐ illustrious　　　ⓑ serene　　　ⓒ devout　　　ⓓ fatal

6 The word doctrine has the same meaning as

ⓐ operation　　　ⓑ principle　　　ⓒ commander　　　ⓓ ambition

7 The word halt has the same meaning as

ⓐ cease　　　ⓑ spill　　　ⓒ stretch　　　ⓓ petition

8 The word sanctuary has the same meaning as

ⓐ fracture　　　ⓑ truancy　　　ⓒ creator　　　ⓓ asylum

B Fill in the blanks with the best words from the box.

1 The remote region's unique traditions have been _____ for future generations to enjoy.

2 The visiting students examined a beautiful quilt that _____ the skill of local artists.

3 People from other cultures may seem _____, but they simply possess different knowledge.

4 The _____ read Bible stories to the local people and invited them to visit his church.

5 The _____ of the cruel king was finally ended when the people rose up in rebellion.

6 Having a(n) _____ vocabulary allows you to express your ideas and opinions more vividly.

| missionary | extensive | demonstrated | preserved | ignorant | tyranny |

C Read the following passages.

ART & DESIGN

SOCIAL SCIENCE

NATURAL SCIENCE

HUMANITIES

EARTH & SPACE

SOCIAL ISSUES

[1-2] **1** Choose one word that fits both blanks.

> Alsace-Lorraine was a territory that caused a(n) _____ between France and the German Empire. After France was defeated in the Franco-Prussian War, the German Empire claimed the territory. France later seized it back, but some people _____ the region's borders even today.

ⓐ attempt ⓑ dispute ⓒ neglect ⓓ reign

2 Choose the appropriate pair of words to fill in the blanks.

> It is the duty of philosophers to _____ the meaning of life and to try to draw lines between what is right and what is wrong. When they _____ something to be a fundamental truth, they are actually inviting us to think about what they have said and to draw our own conclusions.

ⓐ relinquish — ignite ⓑ contemplate — pronounce
ⓒ generalize — pursue ⓓ immerse — contribute

[3-4]

> There are many different traditions surrounding the agreement to marry. In most cosmopolitan societies, getting engaged is simply a formality. It is not considered a legally binding agreement. In other places, however, it can involve the signing of an enforceable contract.

3 In the context of the passage, cosmopolitan means _____.
ⓐ secluded ⓑ powerful ⓒ gregarious ⓓ sophisticated

4 The word binding in the passage could best be replaced by
ⓐ agreeable ⓑ coordinated ⓒ mandatory ⓓ cohesive

[5-6]

> _____ folk art is commonly viewed as being practical and predictable, as it tends to follow closely to standards and methods that have existed for centuries. However, a new generation of folk artists are changing this perception. Their artwork is flamboyant and unusual, incorporating bright colors and modern imagery that is both unexpected and appealing.

5 Choose the word that is most suitable for the blank.
ⓐ Conventional ⓑ Hostile ⓒ Intact ⓓ Didactic

6 The word flamboyant in the passage is closest in meaning to
ⓐ economical ⓑ minuscule ⓒ extravagant ⓓ obedient

303

라틴어 어근
Latin Roots

어근이란 단어의 실질적인 의미를 나타내는 중심 부분을 일컫는데, 어근에 여러 접사가 붙어 다른 의미의 단어를 형성한다. Chapter 4에서 배운 abduct, confine, reform, emancipate, ascribe는 라틴어 어근인 duc/duct, fin, form, man/manu, scrib/script를 포함한 단어들이다. 주요 라틴어 어근들의 고유 의미를 살펴보고, 그 어근이 사용된 단어들도 함께 숙지해 보자.

ROOTS	EXAMPLES
act *to do*	activate 활성화시키다　actual 실제의　counteract 대응하다 enact 제정하다　interaction 상호 작용　radioactive 방사성의
dict *to speak*	contradict 부정하다　dictation 받아쓰기　dictator 독재자　diction 발음 dictionary 사전　unpredictable 예측할 수 없는　verdict 판결
duc/duct *to lead*	abduct 유괴하다　conduct 전도하다　deductive 연역적인　induce 유도하다 introduce 소개하다　produce 생산하다　reduce 줄이다
fin *end, boundary, limit*	affinity 친화력　confine 국한시키다　definitive 확정적인　final 마지막의 finish 끝나다　infinite 무한한
form *shape*	conform 따르다　format 구성 방식　formula 공식　inform 알리다 reform 개혁하다　transform 변형시키다　uniform 제복, 교복
ject *to throw*	abject 극도로 비참한　eject 쫓아내다　inject 주입하다　objectivity 객관성 project 계획, 과제　rejection 거절　subject 주제
man/manu *hand*	emancipate 해방시키다　maneuver 책략　manipulate 조종하다 manual 안내 책자　manufacture 제조하다　manuscript 원고
rupt *to break*	bankrupt 파산한　corruption 부패　disruption 붕괴 eruption 분출　interrupt 방해하다　rupture 파열
scrib/script *to write*	ascribe …의 탓으로 돌리다　describe 묘사하다　inscribe 새기다 prescribe 처방하다　scribble …을 휘갈겨 쓰다　scripture 경전
sect *to cut*	bisect 2등분 하다　dissect 해부하다　insect 곤충　intersect 교차하다 section 부분, 구획　transect 횡단하다
vid/vis *to see*	envision 마음속에 그리다　evidence 증거　invisible 보이지 않는 revise 수정하다　televise TV로 방송하다　video 비디오

CHAPTER

EARTH & SPACE

Lesson 41

> 지질학

Geology

★

aquifer
[ǽkwəfər]

[명] 대수층

n. a layer of rock that holds water or allows water to pass through it

When an **aquifer** becomes contaminated from exposure to pollutants, it can negatively impact a region's groundwater.

★

boulder
[bóuldər]

[명] 큰 바위, 거석

n. a large rock

The earthquake dislodged a **boulder**, which rolled down the hill and into the middle of the highway.

★★

caldera
[kældέərə]

[명] 칼데라(화산 폭발로 생긴 대규모 함몰지)

n. the crater left behind by a volcano that erupts and collapses

Crater Lake, a well-known **caldera** in the United States, was formed when Mount Mazama collapsed about 7,000 years ago.

★★

crevice
[krévis]

[명] (바위·벽 등의) 갈라진 틈

n. a narrow crack in a rock or a wall

There are many small creatures that make their homes deep within **crevices**, where predators cannot reach them.

★★

crumble
[krʌ́mbl]

[동] 부스러지다, 부스러뜨리다

n. crumb

v. to fall apart into small pieces or to break something into small pieces

Erosion is causing the cliffs to slowly **crumble**, which is why the area is now closed off to tourists.

syn. break up

★★★

debris
[dəbríː]

[명] 잔해, 쓰레기

n. the waste left behind after something explodes or is destroyed

The ancient Roman city of Pompeii was completely buried in volcanic **debris** about 2,000 years ago.

syn. rubble

---

aquifer 대수층이 오염 물질에 노출돼 오염되면, 한 지역의 지하수에 부정적으로 영향을 미칠 수 있다. **boulder** 지진으로 큰 바위가 제자리에서 벗어나, 언덕 아래로 굴러내려 고속도로 중앙에 놓이게 되었다. **caldera** 미국에 있는 유명한 칼데라인 크레이터 호수는 약 7천년 전 마자마산이 붕괴됐을 때 형성되었다. **crevice** 포식자들이 들어갈 수 없는 갈라진 틈들 안의 깊은 곳에 집을 짓는 작은 동물들이 많이 있다. **crumble** 침식으로 그 절벽들이 서서히 부스러지고 있는데, 그 때문에 현재 그 지역이 관광객들에게 폐쇄되었다. **debris** 약 2천년 전에 고대 로마 도시 폼페이가 화산 잔해에 완전히 묻혔다.

★
devoid
[divɔ́id]
[형] 전혀 없는

adj. completely lacking something

Although Death Valley is the hottest place on Earth, it is not **devoid** of life—many animal species live there.

★★
emanate
[émənèit]
[동] 나오다, 비롯되다

v. to come from somewhere

Most rivers **emanate** from mountainous areas, flowing downward across the land and into the sea.

syn. originate

★
epicenter
[épəsèntər]
[명] 진원지, 진앙

n. the exact spot where an earthquake occurs

The **epicenter** of the earthquake that caused the Boxing Day Tsunami of 2004 was located off the coast of Sumatra.

Useful Tips
epicenter는 'Seoul is the epicenter of the K-pop revolution.'에서처럼 은유적으로 '…의 중심지'를 나타내기도 한다.

★★★
eruption
[irʌ́pʃən]
[명] 분출, 분화
v. erupt

n. an event in which materials are expelled from a volcano

The ash cloud from the **eruption** of a volcano in Iceland seriously disrupted European air traffic in 2010.

★★★
fault
[fɔːlt]
[명] 단층

n. an extended crack in the surface of a planet

There are many cities around the world that have been built on geological **faults**, including Los Angeles and Tokyo.

★★
gem
[dʒem]
[명] 보석

n. a precious or semi-precious stone

One of the most valuable types of **gem** is the emerald, which is prized for its deep green color.

syn. jewel

---

devoid 데스 밸리는 지구상에서 가장 온도가 높은 곳이지만, 생명체가 전혀 없지는 않아서 많은 동물 종들이 그곳에 산다. **emanate** 대부분의 강들은 산악 지역에서 나와, 육지를 가로질러 바다를 향해 아래로 흘러내린다. **epicenter** 2004년 복싱 데이 쓰나미를 일으켰던 그 지진의 진원지는 수마트라 앞바다였다. **eruption** 2010년에 아이슬란드의 한 화산 분출에서 나온 화산재 구름은 유럽의 항공 교통에 심각한 지장을 주었다. **fault** 로스앤젤레스와 도쿄를 포함해 지질 단층들 위에 세워진 도시들이 전 세계에 많이 있다. **gem** 가장 값비싼 보석 종류 중 하나는 에메랄드인데, 그것은 진한 녹색 때문에 귀하게 여겨진다.

★★★

glacier
[gléiʃər]
[명] 빙하

n. a large, slow-moving mass of ice

Many of the most noticeable geological features of the Earth were created by the movement of **glaciers**.

Useful Tips
glacier의 형용사형인 glacial은 '매우 느린'이라는 뜻으로도 자주 사용된다.

★

granite
[grǽnit]
[명] 화강암

n. a hard rock often used in construction

Granite is a common igneous rock that is unusually durable and has an attractive appearance when polished.

★★

gravel
[grǽvəl]
[명] 자갈

n. small, smooth pieces of rock

Much of the rock dug up at the quarry will be crushed into **gravel** and used to pave roads and paths.

★★

innumerable
[injúːmərəbl]
[형] 셀 수 없이 많은

adj. too many to be counted

Rock was a favored material of early humans, who used it to create **innumerable** tools and structures.

syn. countless

★★★

lava
[láːvə]
[명] 용암

n. melted rock that has been forced to the surface of the planet

When flowing **lava** is exposed to air, it gradually forms a solid crust and loses its liquid qualities.

★★

magnetic
[mægnétik]
[형] 자기의
n. magnet

adj. having the quality of attracting or repelling iron and steel

Some rocks are naturally **magnetic**, but most magnets are artificially created using a special process.

---

glacier 지구의 가장 중요한 지질들 중 많은 것들이 빙하들의 이동에 의해 생성되었다. **granite** 화강암은 내구성이 매우 강하고 광택을 내면 외관이 멋진 흔한 화성암이다. **gravel** 채석장에서 캐낸 많은 암석이 자갈로 파쇄되어 도로와 길을 포장하는 데 사용될 것이다. **innumerable** 암석은 초기 인류에게 선호되었던 물질로, 그들은 암석을 사용해 셀 수 없이 많은 도구들과 구조물들을 만들었다. **lava** 유동 용암이 공기에 노출되면, 서서히 고체 표면을 형성하면서 액체의 특성을 잃는다. **magnetic** 어떤 암석들은 자연 발생적으로 자기를 띠지만, 대부분의 자석들은 특수 공정을 이용해 인공적으로 만들어진다.

★★ **mantle**

[mǽntl]

[명] 맨틀(지각과 중심핵의 중간부)

n. the layer of a planet that surrounds the core

The Earth's **mantle** has a temperature of over 1000 °C and is primarily made up of oxygen, silicon, and magnesium.

★★ **mineral**

[mínərəl]

[명] 광물, 무기질

n. a substance that is natural, solid, and inorganic

Few people have heard of bridgmanite, but it is believed to be the most common **mineral** on Earth.

★★ **molten**

[móultən]

[형] 용해된, 열로 녹은

adj. liquefied by the application of heat

Magma, which is **molten** rock beneath the Earth's surface, is called lava once it has been expelled.

syn. melted *ant.* frozen

★ **protrude**

[proutrúːd]

[동] 튀어나오다, 돌출되다

n. protrusion

v. to extend beyond a surface

In geology, an outcrop is the section of an underground rock formation that **protrudes** above the surface.

syn. stick out

★★ **purify**

[pjúərəfài]

[동] 정화하다

n. purifier

v. to remove harmful or unwanted substances from something

Fine-grained rock can **purify** water that passes through it by acting as a sort of natural filter.

syn. cleanse *ant.* pollute

★ **relocate**

[rìːloukéit]

[동] 이전하다, 이동하다

v. to move to a new place

People who have built their homes on the river's floodplain are being urged to **relocate** by the authorities.

mantle 지구의 맨틀은 온도가 섭씨 1000도 이상이며 주로 산소, 규소, 마그네슘으로 이루어져 있다. **mineral** 브리지마나이트에 대해 들어 본 사람은 거의 없지만, 그것은 지구상에서 가장 흔한 광물로 여겨진다. **molten** 지구 표면 아래에 있는 용해된 암석인 마그마는 일단 분출되면 용암으로 불린다. **protrude** 지질학에서 노두(광맥·암석 등의 노출부)는 지하 암반층이 지면 위로 튀어나온 부분이다. **purify** 결이 고운 암석은 일종의 천연 필터 역할을 함으로써 그것을 통과하는 물을 정화할 수 있다. **relocate** 그 강의 범람원 위에 집을 지은 사람들은 당국에 의해 이주할 것을 종용 받고 있다.

★

rim

[rim]

[명] 가장자리

n. the outside edge of a circular object

Some tourists make the questionable decision to photograph one another on the **rim** of the volcano.

★★

rupture

[rʌ́ptʃər]

[동] 파열하다
[명] 파열

v. to suddenly break or burst open

When the San Andreas fault line **ruptured** in 1906, the resulting earthquake nearly destroyed San Francisco.

n. an instance of something suddenly breaking or bursting open
syn. fracture

Strong earthquakes sometimes cause surface **ruptures**, which leave visible scars on the ground.

★★★

seismic

[sáizmik]

[형] 지진의

adj. relating to earthquakes

Earthquakes produce several different kinds of **seismic** waves, each of which moves in a different manner.

★

stratum

[stréitəm]

[명] (암석 등의) 층

n. a layer of rock

By examining each **stratum** in the exposed rock wall, the geologist can learn about the region's ancient past.

★★

strip

[strip]

[동] 벗기다, 제거하다

v. to remove something from a surface

Erosion caused by wind, rain, and waves is constantly **stripping** away the outermost layer of the Earth.

syn. peel

★★

subterranean

[sʌ̀btəréiniən]

[형] 지하의

adj. beneath the surface of the planet

The explorers discovered a huge **subterranean** cavern filled with stalagmites and stalactites.

syn. underground   *ant.* aboveground

---

rim 몇몇 관광객들은 그 화산 가장자리에서 서로 사진을 찍어 주겠다는 문제가 되는 결정을 한다. **rupture** 샌앤드레어스 단층이 1906년에 파열했을 때, 그로 인해 발생한 지진이 샌프란시스코를 거의 다 파괴했다. / 강한 지진들은 때때로 지면 파열을 일으키는데, 이는 땅에 뚜렷한 흔적을 남긴다. **seismic** 지진들은 몇몇 서로 다른 종류의 지진파들을 생성하는데, 각 지진파는 서로 다른 양식으로 움직인다. **stratum** 그 지질학자는 노출된 암석 벽의 각 층을 조사함으로써, 그 지역의 아주 오래된 과거에 대해 알아낼 수 있다. **strip** 바람, 비, 파도에 의해 야기된 침식은 지구의 가장 바깥쪽 층을 끊임없이 제거하고 있다. **subterranean** 그 탐험가들은 석순과 종유석으로 가득 찬 거대한 지하 동굴을 발견했다.

EXERCISES

A Match each definition with the correct word.

1 the layer of a planet that surrounds the core   ⓐ boulder

2 a large rock   ⓑ glacier

3 relating to earthquakes   ⓒ aquifer

4 a substance that is natural, solid, and inorganic   ⓓ mineral

5 a narrow crack in a rock or a wall   ⓔ mantle

6 completely lacking something   ⓕ devoid

7 a large, slow-moving mass of ice   ⓖ seismic

8 a layer of rock that holds water or allows water to pass through it   ⓗ crevice

B Choose the word that is closest in meaning to each underlined word.

1 After a hurricane tore through the seaside town, the streets were littered with <u>debris</u>.
ⓐ media   ⓑ flora   ⓒ rubble   ⓓ liquid

2 The paleontologist was shocked to see a fossilized dinosaur bone <u>protruding</u> from the ground.
ⓐ falling off   ⓑ breaking up   ⓒ sticking out   ⓓ turning over

3 Hungry bears emerging from hibernation sometimes <u>strip</u> the bark off trees.
ⓐ peel   ⓑ elevate   ⓒ squeeze   ⓓ defend

4 A freak snowstorm caused pipes to freeze and <u>rupture</u> in many people's homes.
ⓐ leak   ⓑ burst   ⓒ retreat   ⓓ slide

5 There are estimated 200 billion galaxies in the universe, which contain <u>innumerable</u> stars.
ⓐ brilliant   ⓑ diverse   ⓒ countless   ⓓ occasional

6 Enormous drills are traditionally used to access <u>subterranean</u> reserves of oil.
ⓐ ancient   ⓑ minuscule   ⓒ profitable   ⓓ underground

7 Small mines created by people searching for <u>gems</u> constitute a serious threat to the local environment.
ⓐ resources   ⓑ coins   ⓒ fossils   ⓓ jewels

311

> 지리학
Geography

★★★ agricultural
[ǽgrikʌ́ltʃərəl]
ⓐ 농업의, 농사의
n. agriculture

adj. relating to farming

This **agricultural** land is vital for sustaining the large populations of the nation's coastal cities.

★★ avalanche
[ǽvəlæ̀ntʃ]
ⓝ (산·눈) 사태

n. a large amount of rocks or snow that slides down a mountain

Several cross-country skiers who had strayed off the trail inadvertently caused a major **avalanche** to occur.

★ cascade
[kæskéid]
ⓝ 작은 폭포

n. a small waterfall

This mountain is popular with local hikers due to the numerous **cascades** located along its streams.

★★ channel
[tʃǽnl]
ⓝ 물길, 수로

n. a narrow strip of water between two large bodies of water

The government wants to deepen the **channel** so that large boats carrying freight can pass through it.

Useful Tips

channel은 자연적으로 생긴 물길을 의미하고, canal은 인간이 만든 물길을 의미한다.

★ chasm
[kǽzm]
ⓝ (땅·바위·얼음 등에 난) 아주 깊은 틈, 협곡

n. a deep, narrow hole in the ground

The shepherd lost several of her sheep when they wandered away from the flock and stumbled down a **chasm**.

syn. ravine

★★ cleave
[kliːv]
ⓥ (둘로) 쪼개지다, 갈라지다

v. to break in two

Any significant pressure applied to a slab of slate will cause it to **cleave** along a line between two of its layers.

syn. split

---

agricultural 이 농경지는 그 나라 해안 도시들의 많은 인구가 살아가는 데 필수적이다. **avalanche** 길을 벗어난 몇몇 크로스컨트리 스키어들이 부주의로 큰 눈사태를 일으켰다. **cascade** 이 산은 냇물을 따라 위치한 수많은 작은 폭포들 때문에 지역 등산객들에게 인기가 있다. **channel** 그 정부는 화물을 실은 거대한 선박들이 지나갈 수 있도록 수로를 더 깊게 만들기를 원한다. **chasm** 그 양치기는 그녀의 양 몇 마리가 무리에서 처진 뒤, 협곡 아래로 떨어져 그 양들을 잃었다. **cleave** 어떤 상당한 압력이 점판암 한 장에 가해지면, 그 판이 두 층 사이의 선을 따라 쪼개질 것이다.

ART & DESIGN

SOCIAL SCIENCE

NATURAL SCIENCE

HUMANITIES

EARTH & SPACE

SOCIAL ISSUES

delta
[déltə]
몡 삼각주

n. the area where a river splits up before emptying into the ocean

The Nile River has one of the world's largest **deltas**, spreading out across 240 kilometers of coastline.

desolate
[désələt, déz-]
톙 황량한, 적막한
n. desolation

adj. empty and bleak

Although these areas are **desolate** today, they were once home to several lakes and small forests.

syn. barren

dissipate
[dísəpèit]
똉 소멸되다

v. to weaken and gradually disappear

Due to a spit of sand located just offshore, ocean waves tend to **dissipate** before reaching the beach.

syn. disperse

edge
[edʒ]
몡 가장자리, 모서리

n. the outer border of something

Small villages that were once located just beyond the **edge** of the Sahara have since been swallowed up.

syn. fringe   *ant.* center

embedded
[imbédid, em-]
톙 박힌
v. embed

adj. firmly stuck in something solid

Many rocks and boulders are so deeply **embedded** in the ground here that they cannot be moved.

syn. fixed

equator
[ikwéitər]
몡 (지구의) 적도
adj. equatorial

n. the imaginary line of latitude running around the middle of the Earth

The **equator** stretches for more than 40,000 kilometers and passes through 13 different countries.

---

delta 나일강에는 240 킬로미터의 해안선을 가로질러 뻗어 있는 세계에서 가장 큰 삼각주 중 하나가 있다.   **desolate** 비록 오늘날 이 지역들은 황량하지만, 한때는 여러 호수와 작은 숲들이 있었다.   **dissipate** 사취(砂嘴)가 바로 앞바다에 위치하기 때문에, 파도는 바닷가에 닿기 전에 소멸되기 쉽다.   **edge** 한때 사하라 사막 가장자리 바로 너머에 위치했던 작은 마을들은 그 후 모래에 묻혔다.   **embedded** 많은 돌과 바위들이 이 땅 속에 매우 깊이 박혀 있어 옮길 수가 없다.
equator 적도는 4만 킬로미터 이상을 뻗어 있고, 13개국을 통과한다.

★★★ **erode**
[iróud]
[동] 침식시키다
n. erosion

v. to gradually wear something away
Over centuries, the softer rock was **eroded** by the elements, leaving only the harder rock behind.
syn. deteriorate

★ **estuary**
[éstʃuèri]
[명] (강이 바다로 들어 가는) 어귀, 강 하구
adj. estuarine

n. the place where a river's water meets the ocean's tide
Only certain fish can live in **estuaries**, as they contain a mix of fresh water and salt water.

★ **geyser**
[gáizər]
[명] 간헐 온천

n. a hot spring that periodically sprays water into the air
The **geyser** known as Old Faithful got its name from the fact that it erupts on a predictable schedule.

★★ **gorge**
[gɔːrdʒ]
[명] 협곡

n. a narrow valley with steep walls
This **gorge** was considered impassible until a footbridge was built across it about 50 years ago.
syn. canyon

★★★ **horizon**
[həráizn]
[명] 지평선, 수평선
adj. horizontal

n. the line in the distance where the sky meets the land or sea
The state of Montana is known as Big Sky Country because you can see the **horizon** in all directions.

★★ **jut**
[dʒʌt]
[동] 돌출하다, 튀어나오다

v. to stick out
Some small plants are growing on a rock that **juts** out from the midsection of the towering cliffs.
syn. protrude

---

erode 수 세기 동안, 무른 바위는 비바람에 침식되었고, 오직 단단한 바위만이 남았다. **estuary** 오직 특정 물고기들만이 강 하구에서 살 수 있는데, 그곳은 민물과 바닷물이 섞여 있기 때문이다. **geyser** Old Faithful이라 알려진 간헐천은 예측 가능한 일정으로 분출한다는 사실에서 그 이름이 생겼다. **gorge** 이 협곡은 약 50년 전에 이곳을 가로지르는 육교가 세워질 때까지 지나갈 수 없다고 여겨졌다. **horizon** 몬타나 주는 사방에서 지평선을 볼 수 있기 때문에 Big Sky Country라고 알려져 있다. **jut** 몇몇 작은 식물들이 우뚝 솟은 절벽 중간에 돌출된 바위에서 자라고 있다.

★★
lagoon
[ləgúːn]
[명] 석호(만의 입구가 막혀 바다와 분리되어 생긴 호수)

n. part of the ocean separated by rocks, sand, or a coral reef

While the ocean is rough, the protected waters of the **lagoon** are calm and perfect for swimming in.

★★★
landmark
[lǽndmɑ̀ːrk]
[명] 주요 지형지물

n. a noticeable object, structure, or geological feature

Due to the rock formation's height and whitish coloration, it serves as a **landmark** for hikers.

★★
marsh
[mɑːrʃ]
[명] 습지

n. an area of wet land

The soil of the **marsh** is too soft to build on, so it has become a haven for local birds and animals.

syn. swamp

Useful Tips
marsh에는 풀과 초본 식물이 많이 있지만, 나무는 매우 적거나 없다. 반면, 비슷한 단어인 swamp에는 앞서 언급한 식물들이 모두 많이 있다.

★
moraine
[məréin]
[명] 빙퇴석

n. a mass of rock or soil deposited by a glacier

This thin stretch of land sticking out into the ocean is actually the **moraine** left behind by an ancient glacier.

★★
plateau
[plætóu]
[명] 고원

n. an area of flat land elevated above the surrounding land

The ancient people built a fortress atop this **plateau**, which allowed them to spot distant invaders.

★
proximity
[prɑksíməti]
[명] 근접, 가까움

n. the quality of being nearby

Hot springs are often found in the **proximity** of volcanic activity that is occurring underground.

syn. closeness *ant.* distance

lagoon 바다는 파도가 심한 반면에, 석호가 감싼 물은 잔잔해서 수영하기에 완벽하다. **landmark** 그 바위 층은 높이와 희끄무레한 색 때문에 등산객들에게 주요 지형지물이 된다. **marsh** 그 습지의 토양은 너무 물러 건물을 지을 수가 없기 때문에, 그 지역 새들과 동물들의 안식처가 되었다. **moraine** 바다로 돌출되어 가늘게 뻗은 이 땅은 사실 아주 오래된 빙하가 남긴 빙퇴석이다. **plateau** 고대인들은 이 고원 꼭대기에 요새를 지었는데, 그것은 멀리 있는 침략자들을 발견할 수 있게 해 주었다. **proximity** 온천은 지하에서 일어나고 있는 화산 활동의 근접 지역에서 종종 발견된다.

★★ **recede**
[riːsíːd]
[동] 감소하다, 물러나다
n. recession

v. to lessen or move away

The Dead Sea is **receding** at a rapid rate, having lost about 400 square kilometers of surface area since 1930.

syn. diminish, withdraw *ant.* expand, approach

★★ **scrape**
[skreip]
[동] (떼어내기 위해) 긁다, 긁어내다

v. to remove a layer from a surface by moving along it

As a glacier moves across the land, the rocks beneath it **scrape** deep striations into the ground.

★ **silt**
[silt]
[명] 침니(모래보다 잘고, 진흙보다 거친 침적토)

n. solid materials carried and deposited by running water

Deposits of **silt** can accumulate in bodies of water over time, causing major changes to the ecosystem.

★★ **slope**
[sloup]
[명] 경사지

n. a surface that rises on one end

The southern **slope** of the mountain is far steeper and more dangerous than other routes to the peak.

syn. incline

★★ **sunken**
[sʌ́ŋkən]
[형] 침몰한, 움푹 들어간
v. sink

adj. lower than the surrounding area

There is a **sunken** area in the landscape that may have been formed by an asteroid strike in the distant past.

syn. depressed *ant.* raised

★★★ **vast**
[væst]
[형] 거대한, 광대한, 광활한

adj. extremely large

The **vast** taiga forests of Siberia have been expanding northward due to warming caused by climate change.

syn. enormous *ant.* tiny

---

recede 사해는 급속도로 감소하고 있는데, 1930년 이래로 표면적의 약 400 평방 킬로미터가 소실되었다. **scrape** 빙하가 육지를 가로질러 움직일 때, 그 아래 있던 돌들이 땅을 긁어 깊은 줄무늬가 생긴다. **silt** 침니의 퇴적물은 시간이 지남에 따라 수역에 축적되어, 생태계에 큰 변화를 일으킨다. **slope** 그 산의 남쪽 경사지는 산 정상에 이르는 다른 길들보다 훨씬 더 가파르고 위험하다. **sunken** 그 지역에는 먼 옛날 소행성 충돌 때문에 생겼을지도 모르는 움푹 들어간 구역이 있다. **vast** 시베리아의 광활한 타이가(북반구 냉대 기후 지역의 침엽수림) 숲은 기후 변화에 의해 발생한 온난화 때문에 북쪽으로 확장되어 왔다.

EXERCISES

ART & DESIGN

SOCIAL SCIENCE

NATURAL SCIENCE

HUMANITIES

EARTH & SPACE

SOCIAL ISSUES

A Match each definition with the correct word.

1 relating to farming   ⓐ equator

2 solid materials carried and deposited by running water   ⓑ landmark

3 the line in the distance where the sky meets the land or sea   ⓒ agricultural

4 the place where a river's water meets the ocean's tide   ⓓ estuary

5 a noticeable object, structure, or geological feature   ⓔ scrape

6 a hot spring that periodically sprays water into the air   ⓕ horizon

7 to remove a layer from a surface by moving along it   ⓖ silt

8 the imaginary line of latitude running around the middle of the Earth   ⓗ geyser

B Choose the word that is closest in meaning to each underlined word.

1 Sand is created when waves <u>erode</u> rocks and shells over an extended period of time.
  ⓐ envelope   ⓑ deteriorate   ⓒ transport   ⓓ reinforce

2 The universe is constantly expanding, causing other galaxies to <u>recede</u> from ours.
  ⓐ illuminate   ⓑ swivel   ⓒ withdraw   ⓓ enlarge

3 The aurora borealis lit up the night sky before <u>dissipating</u> a short time later.
  ⓐ intensifying   ⓑ transforming   ⓒ dispersing   ⓓ reproducing

4 The continental shelf extends outward from the shore and ends in a sudden <u>slope</u>.
  ⓐ incline   ⓑ delta   ⓒ fissure   ⓓ plateau

5 An enormous iceberg <u>cleaved</u> off a glacier and floated away on the ocean's currents.
  ⓐ split   ⓑ ascended   ⓒ bounced   ⓓ evolved

6 A peninsula <u>juts</u> out from a landmass and is surrounded by water on three sides.
  ⓐ accelerates   ⓑ plummets   ⓒ circumvents   ⓓ protrudes

7 It is a <u>desolate</u> place, but the discovery of underground water reserves may change that.
  ⓐ glamorous   ⓑ barren   ⓒ relevant   ⓓ unspoiled

Lesson 43

[>] 기상학

Meteorology

★★

abrupt

[əbrʌ́pt]

[형] 갑작스러운

adj. sudden and unexpected

Any significant shift in the jet stream could cause **abrupt** changes in local weather patterns.

syn. unforeseen

★★

altitude

[ǽltət/jùːd]

[명] 고도

n. height above sea level

Even in extremely warm climates, it is not uncommon to experience annual snow at high **altitudes**.

syn. elevation

★★★

anticipate

[æntísəpèit]

[동] 예상하다

n. anticipation

v. to expect something to happen

Weather experts are **anticipating** an unusually active hurricane season this year, so everyone should be prepared.

★

arid

[ǽrid]

[형] 불모의, 메마른

adj. lacking rain

Farming is a challenge in **arid** lands, as irrigation systems must be used to make up for a lack of rainfall.

syn. dry *ant.* moist

★★

assess

[əsés]

[동] 평가하다, 산정하다

n. assessment

v. to look over and make a judgment

The government will **assess** the damage caused by the blizzard and provide the appropriate relief aid.

syn. evaluate

★★★

atmosphere

[ǽtməsfìər]

[명] 대기

adj. atmospheric

n. the area of gas surrounding a planet

The troposphere, which is the lowest layer of the **atmosphere**, is where most weather occurs.

abrupt 제트 기류의 큰 변화는 현지 기상 패턴에 갑작스러운 변화를 가져올 수 있다. **altitude** 극히 온난한 기후에서도, 높은 고도에서 매년 눈이 내리는 것을 경험하는 일이 드물지는 않다. **anticipate** 기상 전문가들이 올해 유난히 격심한 허리케인 시즌을 예상하고 있으므로, 모두 대비해야 한다. **arid** 부족한 강우를 보충하기 위해 관개 시스템을 사용해야 하므로, 불모의 땅에 농사를 짓는 것은 어려운 일이다. **assess** 정부는 눈보라로 인한 피해를 산정하여 적절한 구호 지원을 할 것이다. **atmosphere** 대기의 가장 낮은 층인 대류권은 대부분의 기상이 발생하는 곳이다.

breeze
[briːz]

ⓝ 산들바람

adj. breezy

n. a light wind

This morning's gentle **breeze** is expected to turn into damaging winds by late this evening.

---

drizzle
[drízl]

ⓝ 보슬비, 이슬비

n. a light rain

There has been no rain for over a month, with the exception of a brief **drizzle** last week.

---

drought
[draut]

ⓝ 가뭄

n. an extended period without rain

Cloud seeding, a method of artificially inducing rain, has been used to help end serious **droughts**.

syn. dry spell

---

evident
[évədənt]

ⓐ 명백한, 분명한

adj. easily seen or understood

It is **evident** that our climate is changing, but efforts to slow the change have met with some resistance.

syn. obvious   *ant.* obscure

---

exacerbate
[igzǽsərbèit]

ⓥ 악화시키다

v. to make a bad situation worse

A hurricane is expected to slam into the island tomorrow, with an unusually high tide **exacerbating** the situation.

syn. worsen   *ant.* alleviate

---

forecast
[fɔ́ːrkæ̀st]

ⓝ 예보, 예측
ⓥ 예보하다, 예측하다

n. a statement about what is probably going to happen
    syn. prediction

Boaters should always check the latest weather **forecast** for the region before heading out to sea.

v. to make a statement about what is probably going to happen
    syn. predict

The National Weather Center is **forecasting** a heatwave for the southern coast starting next week.

ART & DESIGN | SOCIAL SCIENCE | NATURAL SCIENCE | HUMANITIES | EARTH & SPACE | SOCIAL ISSUES

---

breeze 오늘 아침의 부드러운 산들바람이 오늘 저녁 늦게 피해를 끼치는 바람으로 변할 것으로 예상된다. **drizzle** 지난주에 잠깐 보슬비가 내린 것을 제외하고, 한 달 넘게 비가 오지 않았다. **drought** 인공적으로 비를 일으키는 방법인 구름 씨 뿌리기는 심각한 가뭄 종식을 돕는 데 사용되어 왔다. **evident** 우리 기후가 변하고 있는 것은 명백하지만, 그런 변화를 늦추려는 노력들이 약간의 저항에 부딪혀 왔다. **exacerbate** 허리케인이 내일 그 섬을 강타할 것으로 예상되는데, 매우 높은 조수가 상황을 악화시킬 것으로 보인다. **forecast** 보트 타는 사람들은 바다로 나가기 전에 현지의 최신 일기 예보를 항상 확인해야 한다. / 국립 기상국은 다음 주부터 남부 해안에 폭염이 올 것을 예보하고 있다.

319

★★
harsh
[hɑːrʃ]
[형] 혹독한

adj. rough and unpleasant

Harsh weather conditions for eight months a year discourage people from living in the area.

syn. severe *ant.* mild

★★
humidity
[hjuːmídəti]
[명] 습도

n. the amount of moisture in the air

High **humidity** can make hot weather even more uncomfortable because the body is unable to cool off.

★★★
imply
[implái]
[동] 암시하다, 시사하다
n. implication

v. to suggest something without stating it directly

Issuing a severe weather warning **implies** that the approaching thunderstorms have intensified.

syn. indicate

★
inclement
[inklémənt]
[형] 궂은, 험악한

adj. cold, wet, or windy

Due to **inclement** conditions across the state, significant delays are expected on all train lines today.

syn. nasty

★★
latitude
[lǽtətjùːd]
[명] 위도

n. the distance of a point from the equator

Although New York and Madrid are located at about the same **latitude**, their climates are quite different.

Useful Tips
latitude와 함께 longitude(경도)를 사용해 지구상의 위치를 나타낸다.

★
marginally
[mɑ́ːrdʒinəli]
[부] 아주 조금, 미미하게

adv. by a small amount

Although today's temperature is only **marginally** lower than yesterday's, the wind makes it feel much colder.

syn. barely

---

harsh 연간 8개월 간의 혹독한 기상 조건 때문에 사람들이 그 지역에 살지 못한다. **humidity** 높은 습도는 더운 날씨를 훨씬 더 불쾌하게 만드는데, 신체가 체온을 낮출 수 없기 때문이다. **imply** 심각한 기상 경보 발효는 접근 중인 뇌우들이 강력해졌음을 암시한다. **inclement** 그 주 전역에 걸친 궂은 날씨 때문에, 오늘 모든 철도 노선들이 상당히 지연될 것으로 예상된다. **latitude** 뉴욕과 마드리드는 거의 동일한 위도상에 있지만, 그 두 곳의 기후는 매우 다르다. **marginally** 오늘 기온이 어제 기온보다 아주 조금 낮지만, 바람 때문에 훨씬 더 춥게 느껴진다.

ART & DESIGN

SOCIAL SCIENCE

NATURAL SCIENCE

HUMANITIES

EARTH & SPACE

SOCIAL ISSUES

★★★ **measure**
[méʒər]
ⓥ 측정하다

n. measurement

v. to determine the precise size or degree of something

A barometer is a scientific instrument that is used by meteorologists to **measure** the air pressure.

syn. calculate

★ **mist**
[mist]
ⓝ 엷은 안개

adj. misty

n. a mass of tiny water droplets suspended in the air near the ground

Nearly every morning at this time of year, the tops of the distant mountains are shrouded in **mist**.

Useful **Tips**

fog는 mist와 비슷하지만 더 짙으며 지속 시간이 더 길다.

★★★ **observe**
[əbzɔ́ːrv]
ⓥ 관찰하다, 관측하다

n. observation

v. to watch something closely

These windsocks allow people to easily **observe** changes in wind direction and speed.

syn. monitor

★★ **phase**
[feiz]
ⓝ 단계, 형세, 위상

n. a distinct period during a process of change or development

Scientists now believe that the **phases** of the moon have an effect on the amount of rain that falls on Earth.

syn. stage

★★ **precipitation**
[prisìpətéiʃən]
ⓝ 강수, 강수량

n. water that falls from the sky

Antarctica is technically considered a desert due to the fact that it receives so little **precipitation**.

★ **presumably**
[prizúːməbli]
ⓐ 아마, 추측하건대

v. presume

adv. likely to be true but not certain

The start of the soccer game has been delayed by one hour, **presumably** due to a passing storm.

syn. probably

---

measure 기압계는 기상학자들이 기압을 측정하는 데 사용하는 과학 기기이다.　**mist** 연중 이맘때면 거의 매일 아침에 먼 산들의 꼭대기가 엷은 안개로 뒤덮인다.
observe 이 풍향계들은 사람들이 풍향과 풍속의 변화를 쉽게 관측할 수 있게 해 준다.　**phase** 현재 과학자들은 달의 위상이 지구에 내리는 강우량에 영향을
준다고 믿는다.　**precipitation** 강수량이 거의 없다는 사실 때문에, 남극은 엄밀히 따지면 사막으로 간주된다.　**presumably** 추측하건대 지나가는 폭풍우
때문에, 그 축구 경기의 시작이 한 시간 늦춰졌다.

prospect

prospect
[práspekt]
® 가능성, 예상
adj. prospective

n. the possibility that something will happen

The **prospect** of an early-season snowstorm was enough to make most drivers switch to their snow tires.

realm

realm
[relm]
® 영역

n. an area of interest or activity

In the **realm** of meteorology, some storm chasers have a bad reputation for their risky behavior.

syn. field

render

render
[réndər]
® (어떤 상태가 되게) 만들다

v. to transform something into a new state

An unexpected hailstorm can **render** a beautiful summer day at the park into an icy mess.

simulate

simulate
[símjulèit]
® 시뮬레이션하다, 모의실험하다
n. simulation

v. to create an artificial version of something

There are computer programs that can **simulate** wind patterns to help predict unforeseen weather.

syn. replicate

soak

soak
[souk]
® 흠뻑 적시다

v. to make something extremely wet

A band of rainstorms passed over the forest, **soaking** the ground and turning trails into mud.

syn. drench   *ant.* dry out

statistics

statistics
[stətístiks]
® 통계
adj. statistical

n. the science of collecting and analyzing numbers

Statistics show that the 10 hottest Augusts in the Northern Hemisphere have all occurred after 1998.

---

prospect 조기 눈보라가 칠 가능성은 대부분의 운전자들이 스노타이어로 바꾸게 하기에 충분했다.   **realm** 기상학의 영역에서, 폭풍을 쫓는 몇몇 사람들은 그들의 위험한 행동으로 평판이 나쁘다.   **render** 예기치 않은 우박을 동반한 폭풍은 공원에서의 아름다운 여름날을 얼음에 뒤덮여 엉망이 된 상황으로 만들 수 있다.   **simulate** 뜻밖의 날씨를 예측하는 것을 돕기 위해 바람의 패턴들을 시뮬레이션할 수 있는 컴퓨터 프로그램들이 있다.   **soak** 일단의 폭풍우가 그 숲 위로 지나가면서, 지면을 흠뻑 적시고 오솔길들을 진흙탕으로 만들었다.   **statistics** 통계에 따르면 북반구에서 가장 더운 열 번의 8월이 모두 1998년 이후에 일어났다.

★★ **steer**
[stiər]
[동] 몰고 가다, 이끌다

v. to control the direction of something

At the last minute, a high pressure system **steered** the storm away from the coast and out to sea.

syn. guide

★ **strictly**
[stríktli]
[부] 엄격히, 엄밀히

adv. in a way that adheres closely to the rules

Strictly speaking, the terms "climate" and "weather," although similar, have very different meanings.

★★ **superficial**
[sù:pərfíʃəl]
[형] 피상[표면]적인, 가벼운

adj. existing only on the surface

A powerful storm passed through the town, but it caused only **superficial** damage to a few buildings.

syn. trivial *ant.* deep

★★ **tornado**
[tɔ:rnéidou]
[명] 회오리바람, 토네이도

n. a spinning funnel of wind that can cause great damage

Tornados are measured on the Fujita scale, with the most damaging receiving a rating of F5.

syn. twister

★★ **torrential**
[tɔ:rénʃəl]
[형] 억수 같은, 급류의
n. torrent

adj. flowing or pouring down in great quantities

Three days of **torrential** rain caused severe flooding around the river, as well as several landslides.

★★★ **tropical**
[trápikəl]
[형] 열대의
n. tropics

adj. relating to areas near the equator

A mass of **tropical** air moving northward is expected to drive local temperatures to unseasonable highs.

steer 마지막 순간에, 고기압이 그 폭풍우를 해안에서 방향을 돌려 바다로 몰고 갔다. **strictly** 엄밀히 말해서, '기후'와 '기상'이라는 용어는 비슷하지만 아주 다른 의미를 가지고 있다. **superficial** 강한 폭풍우가 그 도시를 관통했지만, 건물 몇 채에 가벼운 피해만 입혔다. **tornado** 회오리바람은 푸지타 스케일(강도계)로 측정되는데, 가장 심한 피해를 입히는 것이 F5 등급을 받는다. **torrential** 3일 간의 억수 같은 비가 몇 차례의 산사태뿐만 아니라 그 강 주위에 심각한 홍수를 일으켰다. **tropical** 북쪽으로 이동 중인 열대 기단 덩어리가 현지 온도를 철에 맞지 않는 고온으로 만들 것으로 예상된다.

★★★ **typhoon**
[taifúːn]
[명] 태풍

n. a powerful tropical storm in the Indian Ocean or Western Pacific Ocean

Once a **typhoon** passes over land or cold water, it gradually begins to lose its structure and windspeed.

syn. cyclone

★★ **unprecedented**
[ʌ̀nprésədèntid]
[형] 전례 없는
n. precedent

adj. having never happened before

After an **unprecedented** series of powerful snowstorms, the town was buried under five feet of snow.

★ **utmost**
[ʌ́tmòust]
[형] 최고의, 극도의

adj. to the highest degree

It is of **utmost** importance that we carefully track and record changes in weather patterns.

syn. ultimate

★★ **vague**
[veig]
[형] 막연한, 모호한

adj. hard to understand or possessing few details

Most people have a **vague** understanding of what causes lightning, but few truly understand the phenomenon.

syn. unclear *ant.* precise

★★ **variable**
[vέəriəbl]
[형] 변동이 심한, 가변적인

adj. prone to change

Expect **variable** winds this morning, with the most powerful gusts coming from the southwest.

syn. volatile *ant.* stable

★ **void**
[vɔid]
[명] 허공, 빈 공간

n. an empty space

Weather does not occur in a **void**—it is the product of a large number of factors and conditions.

syn. vacuum

---

typhoon 태풍이 육지나 차가운 바다 위를 지나면, 그 구조와 풍속을 서서히 잃기 시작한다. **unprecedented** 전례 없는 일련의 강한 눈보라 후에, 그 도시는 5피트의 눈에 파묻혔다. **utmost** 기상 패턴의 변화를 세심하게 추적해 기록하는 것이 최고로 중요하다. **vague** 대부분의 사람들이 무엇이 번개를 일으키는지에 대해 막연한 이해를 하고 있지만, 그 현상을 정확히 아는 사람은 거의 없다. **variable** 오늘 아침에는 남서쪽에서 불어오는 가장 강한 돌풍을 동반한, 변동이 심한 바람을 예상하시오. **void** 기상은 허공에서 일어나는 것이 아니라, 다수의 요인들과 조건들의 산물이다.

EXERCISES

A Match each definition with the correct word.

1 relating to areas near the equator   ⓐ statistics

2 a light wind   ⓑ latitude

3 the distance of a point from the equator   ⓒ breeze

4 the amount of moisture in the air   ⓓ drizzle

5 the science of collecting and analyzing numbers   ⓔ tropical

6 the possibility that something will happen   ⓕ mist

7 a light rain   ⓖ humidity

8 a mass of tiny water droplets suspended in the air near the ground   ⓗ prospect

B Choose the word that is closest in meaning to each underlined word.

1 Local authorities have yet to <u>assess</u> the extent of damage from yesterday's tsunami.
  ⓐ deliver   ⓑ assume   ⓒ evaluate   ⓓ predict

2 As undersea vehicles improve, oceanographers <u>anticipate</u> discovering new species.
  ⓐ expect   ⓑ regret   ⓒ recall   ⓓ announce

3 Corn ethanol is only <u>marginally</u> more environmentally friendly than fossil fuels.
  ⓐ massively   ⓑ barely   ⓒ gradually   ⓓ fortunately

4 Despite <u>superficial</u> improvements, modern automobiles are still major polluters.
  ⓐ momentous   ⓑ obvious   ⓒ technical   ⓓ trivial

5 The paleontologist <u>soaked</u> the fossils from the beach in fresh water to remove the salt.
  ⓐ drenched   ⓑ twisted   ⓒ bleached   ⓓ stretched

6 This beach was already polluted, but the recent oil spill <u>exacerbated</u> the situation.
  ⓐ indicated   ⓑ deviated   ⓒ worsened   ⓓ resolved

7 The artificial lights of cities make the stars appear as little more than <u>vague</u> glimmers of light.
  ⓐ flashing   ⓑ numerous   ⓒ attractive   ⓓ unclear

ART & DESIGN

SOCIAL SCIENCE

NATURAL SCIENCE

HUMANITIES

EARTH & SPACE

SOCIAL ISSUES

> 해양학

Lesson 44 Oceanography

★★★

Arctic

[ɑ́ːrktik]

[형] 북극의

adj. relating to the area around the North Pole

The Beaufort Gyre is a massive **Arctic** current that moves in a circular, clockwise pattern.

Useful Tips

arctic은 '극도로 추운'이란 의미로 쓰이기도 하는데, 이런 경우 대문자 A를 소문자로 쓴다.

★★

buoyant

[bɔ́iənt]

[형] (물에) 떠 있는, 부력이 있는

adj. capable of floating

Because phytoplankton are **buoyant**, they float near the ocean's surface where sunlight can reach them.

★★

consecutive

[kənsékjutiv]

[형] 연이은

adj. occurring one after the other

Warm ocean water caused coral reef bleaching for three **consecutive** years, between 2015 and 2018.

syn. successive

★★

crack

[kræk]

[명] (무엇이 갈라져 생긴) 금, 틈
[동] 깨지다, 금이 가다

n. a narrow break in a hard surface *syn.* fracture

The Mariana Trench is a deep **crack** in the ocean floor that stretches for more than 2,500 kilometers.

v. to cause a narrow break in a hard surface *syn.* fracture

The mantis shrimp can **crack** a clam's thick shell simply by striking it with its powerful claws.

★★

diameter

[daiǽmətər]

[명] 지름

n. the distance of a horizontal line drawn across the center of something

Weathervanes, the largest scallops in the world, have an average shell **diameter** of about 25 centimeters.

syn. width

★★

dim

[dim]

[형] (빛이) 어두한, 흐릿한

adj. poorly lit

In the **dim** light of the deep sea, many fish create their own light through bioluminescence.

syn. faint *ant.* bright

Arctic 보퍼트 환류는 둥글게 시계 방향 패턴으로 움직이는 거대한 북극 해류이다. **buoyant** 식물성 플랑크톤은 부력이 있기 때문에, 햇빛이 닿을 수 있는 해수면 근처를 떠다닌다. **consecutive** 따뜻한 바닷물이 2015년에서 2018년까지 3년 연속으로 산호초 표백을 유발했다. **crack** 마리아나 해구는 해저에 2,500 킬로미터 이상 뻗어 있는 깊은 균열이다. / 갯가재는 강력한 집게발로 조개의 두꺼운 껍질을 때려서 간단히 깰 수 있다. **diameter** 세계에서 가장 큰 가리비인 weathervane은 껍데기 평균 지름이 약 25 센티미터이다. **dim** 심해의 흐릿한 빛 속에서 많은 물고기들이 생물 발광을 통해 스스로 빛을 만든다.

drift
[drift]
ⓥ (물·공기에) 떠가다, 표류하다

v. to move by floating on the air or water

Jellyfish don't simply **drift** in the water—they move around by navigating the ocean's currents.

---

exorbitant
[igzɔ́ːrbətənt]
ⓐ 과도한, 지나친

adj. unreasonably high

There's an **exorbitant** amount of plastic waste floating in the ocean, and it's causing severe damage.

syn. excessive   *ant.* reasonable

---

favorable
[féivərəbl]
ⓐ 유리한, 좋은

n., v. favor

adj. having a beneficial effect

Female sea turtles crawl onto remote beaches looking for a **favorable** place to lay their eggs.

syn. advantageous   *ant.* unhelpful

---

fluctuate
[flʌ́ktʃuèit]
ⓥ 변동을 거듭하다

n. fluctuation

v. to change frequently and irregularly

The populations of sea creatures **fluctuate** widely, although the reasons for this aren't always clear.

syn. vary

---

inert
[inə́ːrt]
ⓐ 비활성의, 부동의

n. inertia

adj. inactive or unmoving

Some species of lungfish burrow into the mud during dry season, where they remain **inert** until the rains return.

syn. immobile   *ant.* active

---

instantaneous
[instəntéiniəs]
ⓐ 즉각적인, 즉시의

adj. occurring right away

Mass extinctions of ocean species are not **instantaneous** events; they sometimes take place over millions of years.

syn. immediate   *ant.* gradual

---

drift 해파리는 단순히 물에서 떠다니지 않고, 해류의 방향을 읽으면서 이동한다.   **exorbitant** 바다에 지나치게 많은 양의 플라스틱 쓰레기가 떠다니는데, 그것은 심각한 피해를 유발하고 있다.   **favorable** 암컷 바다거북이들은 알을 낳기에 좋은 장소를 찾아 외딴 해변으로 기어간다.   **fluctuate** 바다 생물들의 개체수는 큰 변동을 거듭하는데, 그 이유가 항상 명확하지만은 않다.   **inert** 몇몇 폐어 종들은 건기에 진흙을 파고들어 가는데, 비가 다시 내릴 때까지 그곳에서 비활성 상태로 지낸다.   **instantaneous** 해양 종들의 대량 멸종은 즉각적인 사건이 아니며, 때때로 수백만 년 이상에 걸쳐 일어난다.

★★★ **marine**
[mərí:n]
[형] 바다의, 해양의

adj. relating to the ocean

Marine environments are generally divided into four zones, which can be differentiated by their depth.

★ **negligible**
[néglidʒəbl]
[형] (중요성·규모가 작아) 무시해도 될 정도의

adj. so small as to have no effect

Oceanographers have found that there is gold in seawater, but it exists only in **negligible** amounts.

syn. insignificant *ant.* significant

★★★ **occur**
[əkə́:r]
[동] 일어나다, 발생하다
n. occurrence

v. to take place

Ocean acidification **occurs** when excessive amounts of carbon dioxide are absorbed by seawater.

syn. happen

★ **placid**
[plǽsid]
[형] 차분한, 잔잔한

adj. calm and peaceful

The **placid** waters of the Gulf of Mexico are home to more than 15,000 species, including 29 types of marine mammals.

syn. serene *ant.* turbulent

★ **posit**
[pázit]
[동] …을 사실로 가정하다

v. to put forth an idea as a basic fact

Alfred Wegener **posited** that the modern oceans began to form when a single land mass called Pangaea split apart.

syn. postulate

★★ **probe**
[proub]
[명] 무인 탐사선
[동] 조사하다, 탐사하다

n. an unmanned vehicle used for exploration

In 2009, a deep-sea **probe** called Nereus dove to a depth of more than 10,000 meters beneath the ocean's surface.

v. to explore thoroughly *syn.* investigate

Oceanographers have now begun to **probe** the ocean floor, one of last unexplored regions of the planet.

---

marine 해양 환경은 일반적으로 4개의 구역으로 나뉘는데, 그 깊이에 따라 구분될 수 있다. **negligible** 해양학자들은 바닷물에 금이 있다는 것을 알아냈지만, 무시해도 좋을 정도로 적은 양만이 존재한다. **occur** 해양 산성화는 과도한 양의 이산화탄소가 바닷물에 흡수될 때 발생한다. **placid** 멕시코 만의 그 잔잔한 바다는 29가지 종류의 해양 포유류를 포함한 15,000 종 이상의 서식지이다. **posit** Alfred Wegener는 판게아라고 불리는 하나의 육지 덩어리가 갈라지면서 현대 바다가 형성되기 시작했다는 것을 사실로 가정했다. **probe** 2009년에 네레우스라고 불리는 심해 무인 탐사선이 해저 10,000 미터 이상의 깊이까지 잠수했다. / 해양학자들은 이제 지구의 마지막 미탐험 지역 중 하나인 해저 면을 탐사하기 시작했다.

reduce
★★★
[ridʒúːs]
ⓥ 줄이다, 감소시키다

n. reduction

v. to make something smaller in size, degree, or number

Melting icebergs and glaciers release fresh water, which can **reduce** the salinity of seawater.

syn. decrease   *ant.* increase

reservoir
★★
[rézərvwàːr]
ⓝ (많은 양의) 비축, 저장(소)

n. a large supply of something

The ocean is considered a vast **reservoir** of carbon dioxide, which it absorbs and stores.

syn. stockpile

Useful **Tips**

reservoir는 '저수지'라는 의미로 사용되기도 한다.

rugged
★★
[rʌ́gid]
ⓐ 울퉁불퉁한

adj. having an uneven surface

Efforts to accurately map the ocean floor have been unsuccessful because the seabed is so **rugged**.

syn. jagged   *ant.* smooth

semblance
★
[sémbləns]
ⓝ (진실을 위장한) 외관, 겉모습

n. an outward appearance that is misleading

While some declining fish populations have shown a **semblance** of recovery, the situation as a whole remains dire.

syn. pretense

source
★★★
[sɔːrs]
ⓝ 원천, 근원

n. the place where something comes from

One of the primary **sources** of the ocean's salt is eroded rock that has been washed into the sea.

syn. origin

submarine
★★
[sʌ̀bməríːn]
ⓝ 잠수함

n. a boat that can travel beneath the surface of the ocean

Oceanographers often use **submarines** designed for a single person, but the largest ones can carry 160 people.

ART & DESIGN

SOCIAL SCIENCE

NATURAL SCIENCE

HUMANITIES

EARTH & SPACE

SOCIAL ISSUES

---

reduce 녹아내리는 빙산과 빙하에서 담수가 나오는데, 그로 인해 바닷물의 염도가 낮아질 수 있다.   **reservoir** 바다는 이산화탄소를 흡수하고 저장하는 거대한 저장소로 여겨진다.   **rugged** 해저면이 너무 울퉁불퉁하기 때문에, 해저면 지도를 정확하게 만드는 노력은 성공적이지 못했다.   **semblance** 일부 물고기 개체 수의 감소는 겉으로 회복하는 것처럼 보였지만, 전체적인 상황은 여전히 심각하다.   **source** 해양 소금의 주된 원천 중 하나는 바다로 씻겨 들어간 침식된 암석이다.   **submarine** 해양학자들은 흔히 1인용으로 고안된 잠수함을 이용하지만, 가장 큰 것은 160명을 태울 수 있다.

superior
★★
[səpíəriər]

혱 (…보다 더) 우수한, 상위의

n. superiority

adj. of high quality or better than others of its kind

Some researchers believe that the echolocation used by dolphins may be **superior** to human sonar technology.

ant. inferior

surge
★★
[səːrdʒ]

혱 급증, 밀려듦
통 급증하다, 밀려들다

n. a sudden increase or movement forward

An unexpected **surge** in the ocean's surface temperature occurred in the North Pacific in July of 2013.

v. to suddenly increase or move forward

Billions of tons of ocean water **surge** into and out of Canada's Bay of Fundy every single day.

thaw
★★
[θɔː]

통 녹다

v. to become unfrozen

The permafrost in the Arctic is **thawing**, which may have significant effects on our planet's oceans.

syn. unfreeze, melt   *ant.* freeze

tide
★★
[taid]

혱 조수(의 간만)

adj. tidal

n. the regular change in the level of the ocean

The Earth's **tides** are caused by the gravitational effects of not only the Moon but also the Sun.

trivial
★★
[tríviəl]

혱 사소한, 하찮은

adj. having little significance or importance

Tracking the migration patterns of marine mammals such as humpback whales is not a **trivial** task.

syn. unimportant   *ant.* significant

vent
★
[vent]

혱 통풍구, 환기구

v. ventilate

n. an opening through which gas or liquid can flow

The areas around the hydrothermal **vents** found on the ocean floor are home to unusual forms of life.

syn. outlet

---

superior 일부 연구자들은 돌고래가 사용하는 반향 위치 측정이 인간의 수중 음파 탐지 기술보다 더 우수하다고 믿는다.   **surge** 예상치 못한 해수면 온도의 급등은 2013년 7월에 북태평양에서 일어났다. / 수십억 톤의 바닷물이 매일 캐나다의 펀디만을 드나든다.   **thaw** 북극의 영구 동토층이 녹고 있는데, 이는 지구 해양에 상당한 영향을 미칠지도 모른다.   **tide** 지구 조수의 간만은 달의 인력 작용뿐만 아니라 태양의 인력 작용으로도 발생한다.   **trivial** 혹등고래와 같은 해양 포유류의 이동 패턴을 추적하는 것은 사소한 임무가 아니다.   **vent** 해저 면에서 발견된 열수 분출공 주위 지역은 특이한 생물들의 서식지이다.

EXERCISES

A Match each definition with the correct word.

1 of high quality or better than others of its kind   ⓐ surge

2 an outward appearance that is misleading   ⓑ semblance

3 relating to the ocean   ⓒ marine

4 an unmanned vehicle used for exploration   ⓓ buoyant

5 a sudden increase or movement forward   ⓔ tide

6 to move by floating on the air or water   ⓕ probe

7 the regular change in the level of the ocean   ⓖ drift

8 capable of floating   ⓗ superior

B Choose the word that is closest in meaning to each underlined word.

1 Sirius B, the companion star of Sirius A, is so <u>dim</u> that it can barely be seen.
   ⓐ nimble   ⓑ erratic   ⓒ faint   ⓓ scarce

2 Heat lightning was the <u>source</u> of the strange lights in the sky that many people saw.
   ⓐ result   ⓑ origin   ⓒ continuation   ⓓ error

3 The area's annual snowfall amounts are <u>negligible</u>, but it does occasionally get flurries.
   ⓐ insignificant   ⓑ innumerable   ⓒ increasing   ⓓ unexpected

4 Despite the region's <u>placid</u> exterior, it is teeming with underground volcanic activity.
   ⓐ frosty   ⓑ bizarre   ⓒ serene   ⓓ captivating

5 Amy wants to tow icebergs to dry areas, where they would <u>thaw</u> and provide clean water.
   ⓐ sink   ⓑ enlarge   ⓒ refract   ⓓ unfreeze

6 The large <u>cracks</u> in the rock were caused by water that seeped in and then froze.
   ⓐ ridges   ⓑ hues   ⓒ formations   ⓓ fractures

7 The fossil discovery had an <u>instantaneous</u> effect, turning the town into a tourist attraction.
   ⓐ positive   ⓑ immediate   ⓒ gradual   ⓓ devastating

Lesson 45 Ecology

★★ **aggravate**
[ǽgrəvèit]
[동] 악화시키다
n. aggravation

v. to make something bad become worse
Human activity can **aggravate** the soil erosion that is naturally caused by wind and water.
syn. exacerbate *ant.* improve

★★ **biome**
[báioum]
[명] 생물 군계

n. a specific type of environment and the plants and animals that live there
The plants of the desert **biome** have evolved unique methods of surviving with a minimum of water.
syn. ecosystem

★ **bog**
[bɑg]
[명] 늪지, 습지

n. an area in which the land is wet mud
Peat moss that grows in the vast **bogs** of Canada is sold to gardeners in the United States.
syn. fen

★★ **damp**
[dæmp]
[형] 습기 찬, 축축한

adj. slightly wet in an unpleasant way
Mushrooms and other types of fungi grow best in environments that are both dark and **damp**.
syn. soggy *ant.* dry

★ **defoliate**
[diːfóulièit]
[동] …에서 잎을 없애다
n. defoliant

v. to remove the leaves from plants and trees
Grazing animals, especially large herds of domesticated herbivores, can **defoliate** large areas of land.

★★★ **desertification**
[dizə̀ːrtəfikéiʃən]
[명] 사막화

n. a process in which land becomes dry and infertile
Desertification is causing local people to abandon land that they have farmed for generations.

---

aggravate 인간의 활동은 바람과 물에 의해 자연적으로 발생하는 토양 침식을 악화시킬 수 있다. **biome** 사막 생물 군계의 식물들은 최소한의 물로 생존할 수 있는 독특한 방법들을 발달시켰다. **bog** 캐나다의 광활한 늪지들에서 자라는 초탄은 미국의 정원사들에게 판매된다. **damp** 버섯 및 다른 유형들의 균류는 어두우면서 습기 찬 환경에서 가장 잘 자란다. **defoliate** 방목 가축, 특히 대규모의 길든 초식 동물 떼들은 넓은 지역의 땅에서 잎을 없앨 수 있다. **desertification** 사막화로 인해 현지인들이 몇 대에 걸쳐 농사지어 온 땅을 버리고 떠나고 있다.

★★★ **destroy**
[distrɔ́i]
[동] 파괴하다
n. destruction

v. to completely ruin something by damaging it

Once the balance of an ecosystem has been **destroyed**, there is little that can be done to restore it.

syn. demolish *ant.* fix

★ **discard**
[diskɑ́:rd]
[동] 버리다

v. to get rid of something unwanted

Because people casually **discard** disposable plastic products, they often find their way into the ecosystem.

syn. dump

★★ **evacuate**
[ivǽkjuèit]
[동] 피난하다, 대피시키다
n. evacuation

v. to leave a structure or area due to impending danger

Humans can be **evacuated** when wildfires occur, but plants and animals are at the mercy of the flames.

syn. vacate

★★ **evaporate**
[ivǽpərèit]
[동] 증발하다
n. evaporation

v. to change from a liquid to a gas

The water cycle begins when the heat from sunlight causes water to **evaporate** and rise into the air.

ant. condensate

★★★ **habitat**
[hǽbitæ̀t]
[명] 서식지

n. the area where a species naturally lives

A species allowed to live in its natural **habitat** free from human interference will likely thrive.

★★ **havoc**
[hǽvək]
[명] 큰 피해, 대파괴

n. confusion, destruction, and disorder

Animal overpopulation can wreak **havoc** with the entire ecosystem, thereby posing a threat to biodiversity.

syn. chaos *ant.* order

Useful Tips
havoc은 보통 동사 wreak이나 play와 함께 사용되어 '…에 큰 피해를 초래하다, …을 엉망으로 만들다'의 뜻을 나타낸다.

destroy 일단 생태계의 균형이 파괴되면, 그것을 복원하기 위해 할 수 있는 일이 거의 없다. **discard** 사람들이 일회용 플라스틱 제품들을 무심코 버리기 때문에, 그것들은 자주 생태계에 유입된다. **evacuate** 들불이 발생하면 사람들은 대피시킬 수 있지만, 동식물은 불길 앞에 속수무책이다. **evaporate** 햇빛의 열기로 물이 증발해 공기 중에 상승할 때, 물순환이 시작된다. **habitat** 인간의 간섭 없이 자연 서식지에서 살도록 허용된 종은 아마 번성할 것이다. **havoc** 동물의 개체수 과잉은 전체 생태계에 큰 피해를 초래할 수 있어서, 생물의 다양성에 위협이 된다.

infiltrate

★★

[ínfiltreit]

ⓥ 스며들다, 침투하다

n. infiltration

v. to gradually enter something

Rainwater **infiltrates** the soil, working its way down to where it can be absorbed by the roots of plants.

syn. penetrate

innocuous

★

[inákjuəs]

ⓐ 무해한

adj. presenting no threat or causing no offense

Although some invasive species may seem to be **innocuous**, they represent competition to native fauna.

syn. harmless　*ant.* malicious

intermittent

★

[intərmítnt]

ⓐ 간헐적인

adj. happening at irregular intervals

Intermittent fish die-offs in the lake have been blamed on algae blooms that deplete oxygen levels.

syn. sporadic　*ant.* regular

irrigation

★★

[irəgéiʃən]

ⓝ 관개

v. irrigate

n. the act of supplying crops with water

An increase in **irrigation** in the area has had a damaging effect on the quality of the local water and soil.

microbe

★★

[máikroub]

ⓝ 미생물

n. a microscopic organism

Microbes may be unseen, but they are present in every ecosystem and play many important roles.

syn. microorganism

notion

★★★

[nóuʃən]

ⓝ 생각, 개념

n. a belief about something

The **notion** that human beings are meant to be guardians of the environment is not a new idea.

syn. concept

---

infiltrate 빗물은 땅에 스며들어, 식물의 뿌리에 흡수될 수 있는 곳으로 흘러내린다.　**innocuous** 일부 침입종이 무해하게 보일 수 있어도, 그들은 토종 동물군에 경쟁 상대가 된다.　**intermittent** 호수 어류 종의 간헐적인 자연 소멸은 산소 농도를 대폭 감소시키는 녹조 현상 탓으로 돌려져 왔다.　**irrigation** 그 지역의 관개 증가는 현지의 수질과 토질에 유해한 영향을 끼쳐 왔다.　**microbe** 미생물은 보이지 않을지라도, 모든 생태계에 존재하면서 많은 중요한 역할을 한다.
notion 인간이 환경의 수호자가 되어야 한다는 생각은 새로운 발상이 아니다.

onset
[ánsèt]
명 시작

n. the beginning of something

The **onset** of an ecological crisis may go unrecognized if humans continue to focus only on their own needs.

syn. commencement   *ant.* conclusion

optimistic
[ὰptəmístik]
형 낙관적인

n. optimist

adj. having positive feelings about the future

Environmentalists are **optimistic** that the reintroduction of locally extinct species will have positive effects.

syn. hopeful   *ant.* pessimistic

pest
[pest]
명 해충, 유해 동물

n. a small creature that causes harm

Insects that farmers consider **pests** cannot be eliminated without severely damaging the ecosystem.

Useful **Tips**

남을 성가시게 하는 사람을 pest라고 칭하기도 한다.

predicate
[prédəkèit]
동 근거를 두다, 입각시키다

v. to depend on as a precondition

The ecological health of any wilderness area is **predicated** on the careful maintenance of a delicate balance.

profound
[prəfáund]
형 1. 심오한
2. 엄청난

adj. 1 having intellectual depth   *syn.* deep   *ant.* shallow
    2 strong or extreme   *syn.* great   *ant.* trivial

1. The keynote speaker introduced her **profound** ideas about reestablishing a natural harmony between species.
2. Habitat availability can have a **profound** effect on a species' ability to thrive and expand its population.

protect
[prətékt]
동 보호하다

n. protection

v. to keep from harm

By **protecting** an umbrella species, conservationists can indirectly keep other species safe from harm as well.

syn. defend   *ant.* attack

---

onset 인간이 계속 자신의 욕구에만 집중한다면, 생태 위기의 시작이 인식되지 못할 수도 있다.   **optimistic** 환경 운동가들은 현지에서 멸종된 종들을 재도입하는 것이 긍정적인 효과를 낼 것으로 낙관한다.   **pest** 생태계를 심각하게 훼손하지 않으면서 농부들이 해충으로 간주하는 곤충들을 제거할 수는 없다.
predicate 자연 보호 구역의 생태학적 건강은 미묘한 균형을 세심하게 유지하는 것에 근거한다.   **profound** 1. 그 기조 연설자는 종들 간의 자연스러운 조화를 재건하는 것에 대한 자신의 심오한 개념들을 소개했다.   2. 서식지 이용 가능성은 한 종이 번성하고 개체수를 확장하는 능력에 엄청난 영향을 미칠 수 있다.
protect 환경 보호 활동가들은 우산종(생물 보전을 위해 선정된 종)을 보호함으로써, 다른 종들도 해를 입지 않도록 간접적으로 보호할 수 있다.

★★ **reap**
[riːp]
[동] 수확하다

v. **to gather crops from a field**
Using traditional methods to **reap** crops reduces the negative impact farmers have on the ecosystem.
syn. harvest

★ **regardless of**
[rigáːrdlis əv]
[전] …에 상관없이

prep. **without taking something into account**
Regardless of the season, species must work to find food sources that can sustain their populations.
syn. irrespective of

★ **repercussion**
[rìːpərkʌ́ʃən]
[명] (좋지 못한) 영향

n. **a negative result of an action**
The possible **repercussions** of releasing genetically modified mosquitos into the wild are not fully understood.
syn. consequence *ant.* benefit

★★ **secure**
[sikjúər]
[형] 안전한
[동] 확보하다, 획득하다

adj. **safe from danger** *syn.* sheltered *ant.* at risk
Secure in their burrows beneath the ground, many species can simply wait for dangerous conditions to pass.

v. **to get something needed** *syn.* obtain
In order to **secure** enough calories to survive, most animals spend the majority of their days searching for food.

★★ **summit**
[sʌ́mit]
[명] 정점

n. **the top of something**
At the **summit** of the region's food chain, you will find large predators such as eagles and wolves.
syn. peak *ant.* nadir

★★★ **vegetation**
[vèdʒətéiʃən]
[명] 초목, 식물

n. **plants and trees**
The forest's thick **vegetation** provides small animals with both sustenance and shelter from the elements.
syn. flora

---

reap 전통적 작물 수확 방식을 사용하면 농부들이 생태계에 미치는 부정적 영향이 감소된다. **regardless of** 계절에 상관없이, 종들은 개체수를 유지할 수 있는 식량원을 찾기 위해 노력해야 한다. **repercussion** 유전자가 조작된 모기들을 야생에 방출하는 것이 초래할 수 있는 영향은 완전히 밝혀지지 않았다. **secure** 많은 종들은 지하 굴 속의 안전한 상태에서, 위험한 상황들이 지나가기를 그저 기다리기만 하면 된다. / 대부분의 동물들은 생존하기에 충분한 열량을 확보하기 위해, 태반의 날들을 먹이 찾기에 보낸다. **summit** 그 지역 먹이 사슬의 정점에, 독수리나 늑대 같이 덩치가 큰 포식자들이 있을 것이다. **vegetation** 그 숲의 울창한 초목은 작은 동물들에게 자양물과 비바람을 피할 수 있는 피신처를 제공한다.

EXERCISES

ART & DESIGN

SOCIAL SCIENCE

NATURAL SCIENCE

HUMANITIES

EARTH & SPACE

SOCIAL ISSUES

A Match each definition with the correct word.

1 an area in which the land is wet mud   ⓐ irrigation

2 to keep from harm   ⓑ bog

3 the act of supplying crops with water   ⓒ habitat

4 plants and trees   ⓓ vegetation

5 to change from a liquid to a gas   ⓔ desertification

6 a small creature that causes harm   ⓕ pest

7 the area where a species naturally lives   ⓖ evaporate

8 a process in which land becomes dry and infertile   ⓗ protect

B Choose the word that is closest in meaning to each underlined word.

1 When city lights <u>infiltrate</u> the water, they disrupt the life processes of organisms.
   ⓐ ignite   ⓑ illuminate   ⓒ penetrate   ⓓ bypass

2 Geologists forced to work in <u>damp</u> conditions must be careful to avoid slipping and falling.
   ⓐ elevated   ⓑ soggy   ⓒ unpredictable   ⓓ frigid

3 Few environmentalists are <u>optimistic</u> about the way businesses are addressing climate change.
   ⓐ convinced   ⓑ uncertain   ⓒ hopeful   ⓓ outraged

4 Seized by the <u>notion</u> that the desert mirages were real, the travelers tried to reach them.
   ⓐ caution   ⓑ expectation   ⓒ concept   ⓓ explanation

5 The <u>repercussions</u> of extracting a fossilized skeleton too hastily could include damaging it.
   ⓐ consequences   ⓑ prerequisites   ⓒ accolades   ⓓ motivations

6 Due to the tornado warning, everyone is being advised to move to a <u>secure</u> location.
   ⓐ distant   ⓑ regular   ⓒ convenient   ⓓ sheltered

7 The factories will continue to burn fossil fuels <u>regardless of</u> the pollution they cause.
   ⓐ because of   ⓑ irrespective of   ⓒ instead of   ⓓ by means of

A Choose the correct words.

1 The word emanate has the same meaning as
ⓐ originate   ⓑ consider   ⓒ displace   ⓓ dominate

2 The word gorge has the same meaning as
ⓐ creek   ⓑ canyon   ⓒ ridge   ⓓ peninsula

3 The word realm has the same meaning as
ⓐ uniform   ⓑ profession   ⓒ field   ⓓ analysis

4 The word discard has the same meaning as
ⓐ slice   ⓑ reduce   ⓒ dump   ⓓ preserve

5 The word summit has the same meaning as
ⓐ closure   ⓑ peak   ⓒ expedition   ⓓ bulletin

6 The word exorbitant has the same meaning as
ⓐ excessive   ⓑ pragmatic   ⓒ elusive   ⓓ faulty

7 The word proximity has the same meaning as
ⓐ creativity   ⓑ ease   ⓒ defect   ⓓ closeness

8 The word crumble has the same meaning as
ⓐ turn over   ⓑ cool down   ⓒ spin around   ⓓ break up

B Fill in the blanks with the best words from the box.

1 There is a(n) _____ difference between our warm, mild climate and that of Antarctica.

2 The rangers _____ enforce the rule that the birds' nesting areas may not be approached.

3 The villagers decided to _____ when a nearby volcano began to rumble and emit smoke.

4 Measuring the _____ of the stone, the geologist found that it was larger than average.

5 It was raining so hard that water began to leak through a(n) _____ in the classroom's wall.

6 At the _____ of winter, many of the region's birds begin to migrate to the south coast.

| diameter | strictly | relocate | vast | vent | onset |

C Read the following passages.

[1-2] **1** Choose one word that fits both blanks.

> An unexpected _____ in local temperatures this week has caused an acceleration in the melting rates of mountain snow. As a result, local officials are warning that local rivers may _____ this weekend and cause flooding in low-lying areas to the south of the city.

ⓐ cascade ⓑ forecast ⓒ surge ⓓ rupture

2 Choose the appropriate pair of words to fill in the blanks.

> Fracking, which involves injecting fluids into rock to release natural gas, may _____ our region's already serious groundwater problems. It is said that the process can contaminate groundwater with chemicals. Even though we need natural gas, we must _____ our local water supply.

ⓐ aggravate — protect ⓑ purify — soak
ⓒ strip — fluctuate ⓓ render — probe

[3-4]

> Last month, an earthquake caused a large rockslide in the mountains. Some local gold-mining enthusiasts began picking through the debris, looking for gold nuggets. There was no gold to be found among the rocks, but they did find a rare gem thought to be worth thousands of dollars.

3 In the context of the passage, debris means _____.
ⓐ shaft ⓑ void ⓒ pathway ⓓ rubble

4 The word gem in the passage could best be replaced by
ⓐ gravel ⓑ fossil ⓒ jewel ⓓ organism

[5-6]

> In one of our country's _____ communities, a tense standoff between farmers and bison has developed. The bison live within a nearby national park, where they are legally protected. However, they have begun grazing in farm fields located near the park's edge. The farmers, fed up with losing a significant amount of their harvest, want permission to shoot any bison that leave the park.

5 Choose the word that is most suitable for the blank.
ⓐ agricultural ⓑ subterranean ⓒ superficial ⓓ instantaneous

6 The word edge in the passage is closest in meaning to
ⓐ apex ⓑ fringe ⓒ portal ⓓ core

ART & DESIGN

SOCIAL SCIENCE

NATURAL SCIENCE

HUMANITIES

EARTH & SPACE

SOCIAL ISSUES

★
★
alloy
[ǽlɔi, əlɔ́i]
ⓝ 합금

n. a combination of two or more metals

Bronze, which was the first **alloy** created by human beings, is a combination of copper and tin.

★
★
alternative
[ɔːltə́ːrnətiv, æl-]
ⓐ 대체의, 대안이 되는
v. alternate

adj. having the potential to serve as a substitute

More and more communities are beginning to rely on **alternative** energy sources such as wind and water.

★
★
average
[ǽvəridʒ]
ⓐ 보통의, 일반적인
ⓝ 평균

adj. typical of its kind   *syn.* standard   *ant.* exceptional

The **average** human has no idea how the electricity he or she uses every day has been generated.

n. the central point in a set of numbers   *syn.* mean

In 2020, the **average** cost of electricity in the United States was about 10.66 cents per kilowatt-hour.

★
biomass
[báioumæs]
ⓝ 바이오매스(에너지원으로 이용되는 생물 자원)

n. organic matter used to generate energy

Wood is the most widely used **biomass** globally, but more efficient materials are being developed.

★
★
blackout
[blǽkàut]
ⓝ 정전

n. a temporary loss of electricity

Energy suppliers sometimes resort to short-term, planned **blackouts** during times of unusually high demand.

syn. power cut

★
★
capable
[kéipəbl]
ⓐ …을 할 수 있는
n. capability

adj. able to do something

Five hundred grams of coal is **capable** of generating one kilowatt-hour of energy in a thermoelectric plant.

syn. competent   *ant.* incapable

---

alloy 인간이 만든 최초의 합금인 청동은 구리와 주석의 합성물이다.   **alternative** 점점 더 많은 지역사회들이 바람과 물 같은 대체 에너지원에 의존하기 시작하고 있다.   **average** 일반인은 자신이 매일 사용하는 전기가 어떻게 발생되는지 전혀 알지 못한다. / 2020년도의 미국 평균 전기료는 킬로와트시당 대략 10.66 센트였다.   **biomass** 목재는 전 세계적으로 가장 널리 사용되는 바이오매스이지만, 보다 효율적인 물질들이 개발되고 있다.   **blackout** 에너지 공급 업체들은 이례적으로 수요가 많은 시기에 때때로 단기적이고 계획적인 정전을 이용한다.   **capable** 화력 발전소에서 500 그램의 석탄은 1 킬로와트시의 에너지를 생산할 수 있다.

combustible
[kəmbʌ́stəbl]
ⓐ 불이 잘 붙는, 가연성인

n. combustion

adj. able to catch fire and burn easily

Natural gas, which is both colorless and odorless, becomes **combustible** when it is mixed with air.

syn. flammable

---

conflagration
[kὰnfləgréiʃən]
ⓝ 큰불, 대화재

n. a large fire that causes a lot of damage

Even the smallest fire at an oil refinery can quickly grow into an extremely dangerous **conflagration**.

syn. inferno

---

crude
[kru:d]
ⓐ 원래 그대로의, 미가공의

adj. in its natural state

Crude oil, sometimes called petroleum, is a liquid substance found in underground geological formations.

syn. unrefined　*ant.* refined

Useful Tips

crude가 사람 또는 사람의 행동을 묘사할 경우, '버릇 없는, 무례한'의 의미로 사용된다.

---

customary
[kʌ́stəmèri]
ⓐ 관례적인, 습관적인

n. custom

adj. usually done in certain situations

It is **customary** to refer to any piece of machinery that creates electricity as a generator.

syn. traditional　*ant.* abnormal

---

depletion
[diplí:ʃən]
ⓝ 감소, 고갈, 소모

v. deplete

n. the act of reducing the amount of something

The **depletion** of natural resources has accelerated in recent years and shows no signs of slowing down.

syn. reduction

---

drone
[droun]
ⓝ 드론(무인 비행기)

n. an unmanned aircraft

Drones have been used by the power industry to inspect the blades of turbines at wind farms.

---

combustible 무색무취인 천연가스는 공기와 섞이면 가연성이 된다.　**conflagration** 정유 공장에서는 가장 작은 불꽃조차 극도로 위험한 대화재로 빠르게 번질 수 있다.　**crude** 때때로 석유로 불리는 (미가공) 원유는 지하의 지층에서 발견되는 액체 물질이다.　**customary** 전기를 발생시키는 모든 기계는 발전기라고 부르는 것이 관례이다.　**depletion** 최근 몇 년간 천연자원의 고갈이 가속화되어 왔으며, 둔화될 기미가 보이지 않는다.　**drone** 드론(무인 비행기)은 전력 업계가 풍력 발전소의 터빈 날을 검사하는 데 사용되어 왔다.

ART & DESIGN

SOCIAL SCIENCE

NATURAL SCIENCE

HUMANITIES

EARTH & SPACE

SOCIAL ISSUES

★★★ **fuel**
[fjúːəl]
[명] 연료

n. something that is burned to provide heat or create power

Fossil **fuels** are carbon-rich substances that were formed from the decomposition of organic matter.

★★ **geothermal**
[dʒìːouθə́ːrməl]
[형] 지열의

adj. relating to heat beneath the surface of the Earth

The country of Iceland acquires approximately two thirds of its energy from **geothermal** sources.

★★ **harness**
[háːrnis]
[동] …을 (제어하여) 이용하다

v. to control something in order to use it

Early attempts to **harness** the power of nuclear energy began in the first half of the 20th century.

Useful Tips
harness가 명사로 사용되면, 말(horse)에 채우는 가죽끈인 '마구'를 의미한다.

★ **kindle**
[kíndl]
[동] (불을) 붙이다

v. to light material on fire in order to create a larger fire

One of the first known uses of solar power was to **kindle** fires by concentrating the sun's rays.

syn. ignite *ant.* extinguish

★ **markedly**
[máːrkidli]
[부] 현저하게, 두드러지게

adv. to a noticeable degree

The available amounts of some natural resources have **markedly** decreased since the beginnings of industrialization.

syn. noticeably

★★ **maximize**
[mǽksəmàiz]
[동] 극대화하다
n., adj. maximum

v. to make something as big or powerful as it can be

Attempts to **maximize** profits have led some energy companies to cause serious harm to the environment.

ant. minimize

fuel 화석 연료는 유기물의 분해로 형성된 탄소가 풍부한 물질이다. **geothermal** 아이슬란드는 자국 에너지의 약 2/3를 지열원에서 얻는다. **harness** 핵 에너지의 동력을 이용하려는 초기의 시도들은 20세기 전반기에 시작되었다. **kindle** 최초로 알려진 태양 에너지의 활용 중 하나는 태양광을 집중시켜 불을 붙이는 것이었다. **markedly** 일부 천연자원의 가용량은 산업화가 시작된 이래로 현저히 감소했다. **maximize** 일부 에너지 회사들의 이윤을 극대화하려는 시도들이 환경에 심각한 해를 끼쳤다.

★★

mine

[main]

[동] (광석·석탄 등을) 채굴하다

v. to dig for valuable minerals

Countries that **mine** for coal have had to deal with many serious safety issues over the years.

syn. extract

★★

parallel

[pǽrəlèl]

[형] 평행한

adj. side by side at an equal distance throughout

The wires used to transmit electricity are sometimes arranged in **parallel** lines atop tall poles.

ant. intersecting

★★★

persistent

[pərsístənt]

[형] 1. 끈질긴, 집요한
2. 끊임없이 지속되는

v. persist

adj. 1 continuing to do something despite difficulties *syn.* steadfast
2 continuing to happen over a long period *syn.* enduring

1. Despite the **persistent** efforts of environmentalists, the oil industry was given permission to drill in the nature reserve.
2. The **persistent** rain could have a negative effect on businesses that rely on the generation of solar energy.

★★

promising

[prɑ́misiŋ]

[형] 유망한, 전망이 좋은, 장래성이 있는

n., v. promise

adj. having the potential to be good

Biogas, which is created through the breakdown of organic matter, is considered a **promising** new energy source.

★

reclamation

[rèkləméiʃən]

[명] 교정, 개간

v. reclaim

n. the act of transforming something useless into something useful

The **reclamation** of land that has been used for mining can be a long and difficult process.

★★

renewable

[rinjúːəbl]

[형] 재생 가능한, 회복할 수 있는

v. renew

adj. capable of replacing what is used through natural processes

Along with sunlight and wind, **renewable** sources of energy include the ocean's tides and organic materials.

mine 석탄을 채굴하는 국가들은 수년 동안 많은 심각한 안전 문제들을 처리해야만 했다. **parallel** 전기를 보내는 데 쓰이는 전선들은 때때로 높은 기둥 꼭대기에 평행한 선으로 배열된다. **persistent** 1. 환경 운동가들의 끈질긴 노력에도 불구하고, 석유 업계는 자연 보호 구역에서의 석유 시추를 허가받았다. 2. 지속되는 비는 태양 에너지 발전에 의존하는 기업들에게 부정적인 영향을 줄 수 있다. **promising** 유기물의 분해를 통해 생성되는 바이오가스는 유망한 새로운 에너지원으로 여겨진다. **reclamation** 채굴에 사용되어 온 땅의 개간은 길고 어려운 과정이 될 수 있다. **renewable** 재생 가능한 에너지원은 햇빛, 바람과 더불어, 바다의 조수 간만과 유기재를 포함한다.

★★ **replenish**
[riplénɪʃ]
[동] 다시 채우다, 보충하다

v. to fill something back up after it has been used

The sustainability of a natural resource is directly linked to how quickly it can be **replenished**.

syn. refill *ant.* deplete

★★ **sparse**
[spɑːrs]
[형] 드문, 희박한

adj. small in amount or widely spaced

Most of the nation's uranium mines are located in rural areas that have a **sparse** population.

syn. meager *ant.* lush

★★★ **supply**
[səplái]
[명] 비축(양)
[동] 공급하다

n. an amount of something kept for later use *syn.* stock

Canada's **supply** of natural gas is believed to be large enough to meet the country's needs for many years.

v. to provide something *ant.* take away

The OPEC nations, which include Saudi Arabia and Venezuela, **supply** the world with about one third of its oil.

★★★ **surpass**
[sərpǽs]
[동] 능가하다, 뛰어넘다

v. to be better or more than something else

Hydropower is widely used today, but it is expected to be **surpassed** by wind power in the near future.

syn. exceed *ant.* fall short

★★★ **ultimately**
[ʌ́ltəmətli]
[부] 궁극적으로, 결국

adv. in the end

Ultimately, countries must weigh the need for precious metals against the damage caused by obtaining them.

★★ **venture**
[véntʃər]
[명] (사업상의) 모험
[동] 위험을 무릅쓰고 하다, 모험하다

n. a risky project or activity *syn.* endeavor

The company's **venture** to find and secure oil reserves beneath the ocean floor was a failure.

v. to go somewhere or do something risky

Although they were resistant at first, oil companies are beginning to **venture** into renewable energy markets.

---

replenish 천연자원의 지속 가능성은 그 천연자원이 얼마나 빨리 보충될 수 있는지와 직결된다. **sparse** 그 나라 우라늄 광산의 대부분은 인구가 희박한 농촌 지역에 위치하고 있다. **supply** 캐나다의 천연가스 비축량은 여러 해 동안 자국의 수요를 충분히 충족시킬 수 있을 만큼 많다고 여겨진다. / 사우디아라비아와 베네수엘라를 포함하는 OPEC 국가들은 전 세계 석유량의 약 1/3을 공급한다. **surpass** 오늘날 수력은 널리 이용되지만, 머지않아 풍력이 수력을 능가할 것으로 예상된다. **ultimately** 궁극적으로, 국가들은 귀금속의 필요성과 그것을 획득함으로써 야기되는 피해를 따져 봐야 한다. **venture** 해저면 아래의 석유 매장량을 알아내서 확보하려는 그 기업의 모험은 실패했다. / 비록 석유 회사들이 처음에는 저항했지만, 재생 에너지 시장에 위험을 무릅쓰고 뛰어들기 시작하고 있다.

EXERCISES

ART & DESIGN

SOCIAL SCIENCE

NATURAL SCIENCE

HUMANITIES

EARTH & SPACE

SOCIAL ISSUES

A Match each definition with the correct word.

1 relating to heat beneath the surface of the Earth   ⓐ promising

2 in the end   ⓑ geothermal

3 having the potential to be good   ⓒ drone

4 to control something in order to use it   ⓓ fuel

5 an unmanned aircraft   ⓔ harness

6 a combination of two or more metals   ⓕ alloy

7 something that is burned to provide heat or create power   ⓖ ultimately

8 the act of transforming something useless into something   ⓗ reclamation
   useful

B Choose the word that is closest in meaning to each underlined word.

1 Crude ore removed from the ground must be crushed before it can be processed.
   ⓐ massive   ⓑ precious   ⓒ burdensome   ⓓ unrefined

2 Excessive use of water for farmland irrigation has led to the severe depletion of many lakes.
   ⓐ relocation   ⓑ reduction   ⓒ corruption   ⓓ purification

3 The project is a collaborative venture between NASA and the European Space Agency.
   ⓐ rivalry   ⓑ miscalculation   ⓒ proposition   ⓓ endeavor

4 There was a time when people believed the ocean's supply of fish was inexhaustible.
   ⓐ expanse   ⓑ stock   ⓒ range   ⓓ lack

5 Some governments are already making plans to mine precious metals on the Moon.
   ⓐ transmit   ⓑ detect   ⓒ extract   ⓓ classify

6 The industry's customary methods of dealing with toxic waste are no longer acceptable.
   ⓐ traditional   ⓑ favorable   ⓒ costly   ⓓ antiquated

7 This year's total rainfall is expected to surpass that of last year before the end of October.
   ⓐ approach   ⓑ underwhelm   ⓒ emulate   ⓓ exceed

345

Lesson 47

> 고생물학

Paleontology

★★★

controversial

[kàntrəvə́ːrʃəl]

[형] 논란이 많은

n. controversy

adj. causing a lot of disagreement or disapproval

Paleontologists seek to prove or disprove **controversial** beliefs about the appearance of dinosaurs.

syn. contentious

★★★

decay

[dikéi]

[동] 부패하다

v. to break down due to natural processes

Because soft tissues **decay** quickly, few internal organs of ancient creatures have ever been discovered.

syn. decompose

★

denote

[dinóut]

[동] 나타내다, 의미하다

v. to be a sign of something

Imprints of shells can be found in the rock, which **denotes** the existence of an ancient inland sea.

syn. signify

★★

detach

[ditǽtʃ]

[동] 분리되다

v. to remove from a larger whole

Smaller bones are sometimes lost when they **detach** from the main skeleton, leaving it incomplete.

ant. attach

★★

eon

[íːən]

[명] 누대(지질학에서 100억 년)

n. an extremely long period of geologic time

The first **eon**, known as the Hadean, began with the formation of the Earth and lasted about 600 million years.

Useful Tips

천문학에서 eon은 우주의 한 시대인 10억 년을 의미한다.

★★

fauna

[fɔ́ːnə]

[명] (한 지역·시대의) 동물군

n. the animals that live in a particular area

Most of the **fauna** of this region was much larger during prehistoric times, although no one is sure why.

syn. wildlife

controversial 고생물학자들은 공룡의 출현에 대한 논란이 많은 믿음들을 증명하거나 그것들이 틀렸음을 증명하려고 한다. **decay** 연조직들은 빨리 부패하므로, 고대 생물들의 내장은 발견된 것이 거의 없다. **denote** 바위에서 조개 자국들이 발견될 수 있는데, 그것은 고대 내해의 존재를 나타낸다. **detach** 자잘한 뼈들이 주된 뼈대에서 분리되면서 때때로 유실되어, 주된 뼈대가 불완전한 상태로 남게 된다. **eon** 명왕누대로 알려진 최초의 누대는 지구가 형성되면서 시작해 약 6억 년 동안 지속되었다. **fauna** 아무도 그 이유를 확실히 모르지만, 이 지역 동물군의 대부분은 선사 시대에 몸집이 훨씬 더 컸다.

ART & DESIGN

SOCIAL SCIENCE

NATURAL SCIENCE

HUMANITIES

EARTH & SPACE

SOCIAL ISSUES

fossil
[fásəl]

ⓝ 화석

adj. fossilized

n. part of a plant or animal that has been preserved in rock

A **fossil** of a whale brain, which a woman had mistaken for coral, may be worth millions of dollars.

---

hominid
[hámənid]

ⓝ 인류, 인류의 조상

n. a member of the primate family that includes humans and human ancestors

"Lucy," an ancient **hominid** discovered in 1974, is thought to have lived more than three million years ago.

---

identify
[aidéntəfài]

ⓥ 식별하다, …임을 알다

n. identity

v. to establish what something or who someone is

Once a fragment of a fossilized creature has been **identified**, it is tagged and placed in storage.

---

implausible
[implɔ́:zəbl]

ⓐ 믿기 어려운

adj. unlikely to be true

During the Victorian era, many people found the idea that giant reptiles once walked the earth **implausible**.

syn. improbable   *ant.* plausible

---

implement
[ímpləmənt]

ⓥ 시행하다
ⓝ 도구

v. to begin something that has been planned   *syn.* carry out

Once the new system has been **implemented**, it will be easier to transport dinosaur bones internationally.

n. a device used for a particular purpose   *syn.* tool

Paleontologists use a sharp **implement** known as a chisel to separate fossils from sandstone.

---

infer
[infə́:r]

ⓥ 추론하다

n. inference

v. to conclude something based on indirect information

From the size and shape of an ancient creature's teeth, scientists can **infer** what its diet may have been.

syn. deduce

---

fossil 한 여성이 산호로 착각했던 고래의 뇌 화석은 수백만 달러의 가치가 있을 수 있다. **hominid** 1974년에 발견된 고대 인류인 'Lucy'는 3백만 년보다 더 오래 전에 살았던 것으로 생각된다. **identify** 일단 화석화된 생물의 조각이 식별되면, 꼬리표를 달아 보관한다. **implausible** 빅토리아 시대 동안, 많은 사람들은 과거에 거대한 파충류가 지구상에 존재했었다는 발상을 믿기 어려워했다. **implement** 일단 그 새로운 체제가 시행되면, 공룡 뼈들을 국제적으로 운반하는 것이 더 쉬워질 것이다. / 고생물학자들은 화석들을 사암에서 분리하기 위해 끌이라는 도구를 사용한다. **infer** 과학자들은 고대 생물 이빨의 크기와 모양을 보고, 그 생물의 식습관이 어땠을지 추론할 수 있다.

★
insight
[ínsàit]
[명] 통찰력, 식견
adj. insightful

n. a deeper understanding of something

Examining ancient organisms can bring about **insights** into what primordial Earth may have been like.

★★
invaluable
[invǽljuəbl]
[형] 매우 유용한, 귀중한

adj. very useful

Radiometric dating is an **invaluable** technique for determining the approximate age of a fossil.

syn. indispensable *ant.* useless

★★
journey
[dʒə́:rni]
[명] 여정, 여행
[동] 여행하다, 이동하다

n. a long trip

During their long **journey** from Mongolia to California, several of the dinosaur bones were damaged.

v. to travel to a distant place

In 1931, Louis Leakey **journeyed** to Africa's Olduvai Gorge to search for ancient stone tools.

★★★
legacy
[légəsi]
[명] 유산, 흔적

n. something passed down from the past

The large numbers of fossils in this cave may be the **legacy** of an ancient predator that dragged its prey here.

★★★
mammal
[mǽməl]
[명] 포유동물

n. a type of animal that gives birth to live young and nurses them

The giant ground sloth was an enormous **mammal** that went extinct about 12,000 years ago.

★★
meticulous
[mətíkjuləs]
[형] 세심한, 꼼꼼한

adj. extremely careful and precise

Extracting a fossil from the surrounding rock without damaging it is a **meticulous** and time-consuming process.

syn. fastidious *ant.* sloppy

---

insight 고대 생물들을 조사하면 원시 지구가 어땠을지에 대한 식견을 얻을 수 있다. **invaluable** 방사능 연대 측정은 화석의 대략적 연대를 결정하는 데 매우 유용한 기술이다. **journey** 몽골에서 캘리포니아까지의 긴 여정 동안, 그 공룡 뼈들 중 몇 개가 손상되었다. / 1931년에 Louis Leakey는 고대 석기 도구들을 찾아 아프리카의 올두바이 협곡으로 여행했다. **legacy** 이 동굴 안의 수많은 화석들은 먹이를 이곳으로 끌고 온 고대 포식자의 흔적일 수 있다. **mammal** 땅나무늘보는 약 만 2천 년 전에 멸종된 거대한 포유동물이었다. **meticulous** 화석을 손상시키지 않고 그것을 감싸고 있는 암석에서 떼어내는 것은 세심하고 시간이 걸리는 과정이다.

★ **minute**
[mainjúːt, mi-]
[형] 미세한

adj. very small

Why **minute** organisms evolved into large, complex creatures is one of the great questions of paleontology.

syn. tiny *ant.* huge

★★ **peculiar**
[pikjúːljər]
[형] 특이한

adj. strange or unusual

Whenever a **peculiar** fossil turns up, local experts are called in to see if they can identify it.

syn. odd *ant.* normal

★ **periphery**
[pərífəri]
[명] 주변
adj. peripheral

n. the edges or outer part of something

A pair of hikers discovered a trove of plant fossils in a small cave located at the **periphery** of the city.

syn. perimeter *ant.* center

★ **pervasive**
[pərvéisiv]
[형] 만연하는
v. pervade

adj. found or felt throughout something

There is a **pervasive** but erroneous belief among the public that all dinosaurs were large and stupid.

syn. ubiquitous *ant.* rare

★★ **petrified**
[pétrəfàid]
[형] 석화된
v. petrify

adj. hardened to a rock-like state over time

Petrified trees are formed underground, often when wood is buried in volcanic ash in a moist environment.

Useful Tips
공포를 느끼면 몸이 돌로 변한 듯 경직되기 때문에, '극도로 겁에 질린'이라는 뜻으로 petrified가 사용되기도 한다.

★ **query**
[kwíəri]
[명] 질문, 문의
[동] 조회하다, 질문하다

n. a question asked to verify information *syn.* inquiry

The paleontologist responded to a **query** from a museum curator who had acquired the skull of an ancient cave bear.

v. to inquire into something to verify information

By **querying** an online database, researchers were able to find a match for the femur they had discovered.

minute 미세한 유기체들이 왜 크고 복잡한 생물들로 진화했는지가 고생물학에서 중요한 의문점들 중 하나이다. **peculiar** 특이한 화석이 나타날 때마다, 그 정체를 알아낼 수 있는지 보려고 현지 전문가들이 소환된다. **periphery** 도보 여행자 두 명이 그 도시 주변에 있는 작은 동굴 안에서 식물 화석 수집물을 발견했다. **pervasive** 일반인들 사이에는 모든 공룡이 크고 둔했다는 만연하지만 잘못된 믿음이 있다. **petrified** 흔히 습한 환경에서 나무류가 화산재에 파묻힐 때, 석화된 나무들이 지하에 형성된다. **query** 그 고생물학자는 고대 동굴 곰의 두개골을 인수했던 한 박물관 큐레이터의 질문에 답했다. / 연구원들은 온라인 데이터베이스를 조회해, 그들이 발견했던 대퇴골과 일치하는 것을 찾을 수 있었다.

★
★ **retrieve**

[ritríːv]

ⓥ 회수하다, 되찾아오다

v. to get something and bring it back

The paleontologists returned to the site to **retrieve** the small bone fragments they had left behind.

syn. fetch

★
★ **significant**
★

[signífikənt]

ⓐ 중요한

adj. having importance

Thanks to technological advances, the study of prehistoric microbes has become a **significant** part of paleontology.

★
★ **span**
★

[spæn]

ⓝ 길이, 기간, 범위
ⓥ …에 걸치다

n. a length of distance or time between two points

Over a **span** of about 250 million years, trilobites were one of the dominant life forms on Earth.

v. to stretch out between two points   *syn.* traverse

The Gobi Desert, which **spans** nearly 1.3 million square kilometers, has been the site of many important fossil discoveries.

★
★ **unearth**

[ʌnə́ːrθ]

ⓥ 발굴하다, 파내다

v. to dig up something that was hidden

A rare nest of fossilized dinosaur eggs was **unearthed** by a Chinese boy playing near a lake.

syn. excavate   *ant.* bury

★
 viscous

[vískəs]

ⓐ 끈적거리는, 점성이 있는

adj. having a consistency halfway between a solid and a liquid

Some insects were enveloped by a **viscous** liquid called amber, which hardened and perfectly preserved them.

syn. gummy

★
★ **yield**

[jiːld]

ⓥ (수익·결과 등을) 내다, 산출하다

v. to produce something desirable

The Zhucheng fossil site, located in eastern China, has **yielded** more than 7,500 fossils.

syn. generate

Useful Tips

도로 표지판에 쓰인 yield 표시는 '다른 차들이 먼저 가게 양보하시오'라는 뜻으로 사용된다.

---

retrieve 그 고생물학자들은 남겨뒀던 작은 뼈 조각들을 회수하려고 그 유적지로 돌아갔다.   **significant** 과학 기술의 발전 덕분에, 선사 시대 미생물에 대한 연구가 고생물학의 중요한 부분이 되었다.   **span** 약 2억 5천만 년의 기간에 걸쳐, 삼엽충들은 지구상의 지배적인 생물 형태들 중 하나였다. / 거의 130만 평방 킬로미터에 걸친 고비 사막은 많은 중요한 화석 발견의 현장이 되어 왔다.   **unearth** 화석화된 공룡 알이 담긴 희귀한 둥지가 호수 근처에서 놀고 있던 한 중국 소년에 의해 발굴되었다.   **viscous** 몇몇 곤충들이 호박이라는 끈적거리는 액체에 뒤덮였는데, 그것이 굳어서 그 곤충들을 완벽하게 보존했다.   **yield** 중국 동부에 위치한 주정의 화석 현장에서 7,500개 이상의 화석들이 나왔다.

EXERCISES

ART & DESIGN

SOCIAL SCIENCE

NATURAL SCIENCE

HUMANITIES

EARTH & SPACE

SOCIAL ISSUES

A Match each definition with the correct word.

1 to remove from a larger whole   ⓐ legacy

2 a length of distance or time between two points   ⓑ detach

3 part of a plant or animal that has been preserved in rock   ⓒ identify

4 a deeper understanding of something   ⓓ fossil

5 having a consistency halfway between a solid and a liquid   ⓔ eon

6 an extremely long period of geologic time   ⓕ insight

7 to establish what something or who someone is   ⓖ viscous

8 something passed down from the past   ⓗ span

B Choose the word that is closest in meaning to each underlined word.

1 The astronomer Tycho Brahe took meticulous notes describing his observations.
   ⓐ tedious   ⓑ fallacious   ⓒ fastidious   ⓓ illegible

2 It may sound implausible, but solar flares can disrupt transmissions from GPS satellites.
   ⓐ unconditional   ⓑ disrespectful   ⓒ improbable   ⓓ irresistible

3 When a dead whale begins to decay, it becomes a source of nutrients to smaller organisms.
   ⓐ contract   ⓑ solidify   ⓒ reanimate   ⓓ decompose

4 Feldspar is the most pervasive mineral found in the Earth's crust.
   ⓐ precious   ⓑ ubiquitous   ⓒ noxious   ⓓ obscure

5 The company announced it will implement its planned installation of solar panels next month.
   ⓐ carry out   ⓑ tone down   ⓒ give up   ⓓ decide on

6 Attempts to artificially influence the weather are controversial, as their effects are unknown.
   ⓐ ambitious   ⓑ lucrative   ⓒ contentious   ⓓ infectious

7 Wilderness areas located on the periphery of the farmlands are being affected by the use of pesticides.
   ⓐ midsection   ⓑ floodplain   ⓒ sphere   ⓓ perimeter

Natural Phenomena

★
blaze
[bleiz]

ⓝ (대형) 화재
ⓥ 활활 타다

n. a large fire   *syn.* conflagration

During the **blaze**, a fire whirl rose up from the flames, causing onlookers to gasp in surprise.

v. to burn brightly

The green and yellow lights of the aurora borealis **blazed** across the sky for a few minutes before fading away.

★
★
blizzard
[blízərd]

ⓝ 눈보라

n. a large snowstorm with heavy winds

The **blizzard** shut down schools and highways, leaving the city buried under three feet of snow.

★
★
★
captivate
[kǽptəvèit]

ⓥ …의 마음을 사로잡다, 매혹하다

adj. captivating

v. to capture and hold someone's attention

Beachgoers were **captivated** by the double rainbow that formed over the ocean after the rain shower.

syn. enchant   *ant.* repel

★
★
condensation
[kàndenséiʃən]

ⓝ (기체의) 응축, 액화

n. the process of changing from a gas to a liquid

The sparkling dew drops covering the foliage were caused by the **condensation** of moisture in the air.

★
elusive
[ilúːsiv]

ⓐ 붙잡기[파악하기·달성하기] 어려운

v. elude

adj. difficult to catch, understand, or achieve

Tourists gather at the waterfall every evening during the full moon, hoping for a glimpse of an **elusive** moonbow.

syn. evasive

★
★
formidable
[fɔ́ːrmidəbl]

ⓐ 무서운, 경외심이 일게 하는

adj. causing fear or respect due to being very large or powerful

The waterspout was a **formidable** sight, but it spun harmlessly for a few minutes before dissipating.

syn. imposing

---

blaze 대형 화재가 나는 동안, 화염에서 불 회오리가 올라왔는데, 지켜보던 사람들이 숨이 턱 막힐 정도로 놀랐다. / 북극광의 초록색과 노란색 불빛은 사라지기 전 몇 분 동안 하늘에서 활활 타올랐다.   **blizzard** 눈보라로 학교들과 고속도로가 폐쇄되었고, 도시는 3 피트의 눈 속에 파묻혔다.   **captivate** 해수욕을 하던 사람들은 소나기가 그친 후 바다 위에 생긴 쌍무지개에 매료되었다.   **condensation** 나뭇잎을 뒤덮은 그 반짝이는 이슬방울들은 공기 중 수분의 액화로 생겼다. **elusive** 관광객들은 보름달이 뜨는 동안 매일 저녁 폭포 앞에 모여, 포착하기 어려운 문보우(달빛의 굴절로 생기는 무지개)를 보기 희망한다.   **formidable** 용오름은 무서운 광경이었지만, 몇 분 동안 아무런 피해를 입히지 않고 회전하다가 소멸되었다.

★★

gale

[geil]

[명] 강풍, 돌풍

n. a very strong wind

Blown by a **gale**, the small sailboat was able to sail across the wide bay at record speed.

★

hailstorm

[héilstɔ̀ːrm]

[명] 우박을 동반한 폭풍

n. a storm during which ice pellets fall as precipitation

Fans and players alike scurried for shelter when a sudden **hailstorm** hit the soccer stadium.

★

harbinger

[hɑ́ːrbindʒər]

[명] 조짐

n. a sign that something is coming or going to happen

In the past, some ancient civilizations considered lunar eclipses to be **harbingers** of bad things to come.

syn. portent

★★

hemisphere

[hémisfìər]

[명] 반구

n. half of a sphere or similarly shaped object

In 1816, atmospheric dust from a volcanic eruption wreaked havoc with weather across the northern **hemisphere**.

Useful Tips

hemisphere는 보통 지구나 뇌의 절반을 지칭하는 데 사용된다.

★★

hollow

[hɑ́lou]

[형] (속이) 빈
[명] (땅 속으로) 움푹 꺼진 곳

adj. empty inside *ant.* solid

Snow rollers are **hollow**, cylindrical snowballs that form naturally as they roll down mountainsides.

n. a depression in the ground

A low mist sometimes forms early in the morning, filling the region's **hollows** as if they were ponds.

★★★

incident

[ínsədənt]

[명] 일, 사건

n. something that happens

An unfortunate **incident** occurred when a bolt of lightning struck a tree, causing it to topple onto a car.

syn. occurrence

---

gale 그 작은 돛단배는 강풍에 밀려서, 기록적인 속도로 넓은 만을 가로질러 항해할 수 있었다. **hailstorm** 축구 경기장에 갑자기 우박을 동반한 폭풍이 들이치자, 팬들과 선수들 모두 대피소를 찾아 황급히 달려갔다. **harbinger** 과거에 일부 고대 문명들은 월식을 나쁜 일이 생길 징조로 여겼다. **hemisphere** 1816년에 화산 분출로 생긴 대기 먼지는 북반구 전역의 기상에 큰 문제를 초래했다. **hollow** 두루마리 눈은 산비탈을 굴러 내려오면서 자연스럽게 형성되는, 속인 빈 원통형의 눈덩이이다. / 자욱한 안개는 때때로 이른 아침에 형성되는데, 마치 연못인 것처럼 그 지역의 움푹 꺼진 곳들을 채운다. **incident** 나무에 번개가 쳐서 그 나무가 차 위로 쓰러진 안타까운 사건이 일어났다.

★★★

intersect
[ìntərsékt]

[동] 교차하다

n. intersection

v. to cross over each other

The worst of the destruction took place at the spot where the paths of the two tornadoes **intersected**.

★

iridescent
[ìrədésnt]

[형] 보는 각도에 따라 색깔이 변하는, 무지갯빛의

n. iridescence

adj. having colors that constantly seem to change

When tiny ice crystals scatter sunlight, it can cause the surface of a cloud to appear **iridescent**.

★★

kinetic
[kinétik]

[형] 운동의, 운동에 의해 생기는

adj. relating to motion

Diffusion is a natural process that occurs when gaseous particles experience an increase in **kinetic** energy.

★

manifold
[mǽnəfòuld]

[형] (수가) 많은, 여러 가지의

adj. many and of various kinds

There are **manifold** theories concerning the origins of crop circles, but many experts believe they are a hoax.

syn. assorted

★★

monsoon
[mɑnsúːn]

[명] (동남아시아 여름철의) 우기, 장마

n. the rainy season in South Asia

Monsoons in the Indian subcontinent generally begin sometime in June and last until September.

Useful Tips

monsoon은 원래 우기를 맞이하는 바람을 지칭하지만, 보통은 우기[장마철] 전체나 그 비 자체를 의미한다.

★★

outright
[áutràit]

[형] 완전한

[부] 완전히, 즉석으로

adj. complete *syn.* absolute

The scientist couldn't offer an **outright** explanation of the strange ice formations, but she had a convincing theory.

adv. completely or instantaneously

The ancient trees were destroyed **outright** by the freak windstorm, which tore them up by their roots.

---

intersect 두 개의 토네이도가 교차하는 지점에서 최악의 파괴가 일어났다. **iridescent** 미세한 눈 결정들이 햇빛을 산란시킬 때, 그것은 구름의 표면을 무지갯빛으로 보이게 할 수 있다. **kinetic** 확산 작용은 기체 입자들의 운동 에너지가 증가할 때 발생하는 자연스러운 과정이다. **manifold** 크롭 서클(곡물 밭에 나타나는 원인 불명의 원형 무늬)의 기원에 관한 여러 가지 이론들이 있지만, 많은 전문가들은 그것들이 조작된 것이라 믿는다. **monsoon** 인도 아대륙의 우기는 일반적으로 6월 중에 시작되어 9월까지 지속된다. **outright** 그 과학자는 기이한 얼음 형성에 대해 완벽하게 설명할 수 없었지만, 설득력 있는 이론은 가지고 있었다. / 유별난 폭풍이 고목 숲을 완전히 파괴했고, 그로 인해 나무들이 뿌리째 뽑혔다.

rapid

★★★

[rǽpid]

혱 빠른

adj. happening or moving very quickly

Lightning causes a **rapid** increase in air temperature, which is what creates the sound of thunder.

syn. swift   *ant.* slow

sleet

★★

[sli:t]

혱 진눈깨비

n. freezing rain

Sleet is said to form either when raindrops begin to freeze or when snowflakes begin to melt.

solar

★★★

[sóulər]

혱 태양의

adj. relating to the sun

Sunspots, a type of **solar** phenomenon, are dark patches that appear when there are changes in the sun's magnetic field.

ant. lunar

sporadic

★★

[spərǽdik]

혱 산발적인, 이따금 발생하는

adv. sporadically

adj. happening at irregular intervals

The **sporadic** shooting stars that appear in the sky are actually meteors that have entered the Earth's atmosphere.

syn. intermittent   *ant.* steady

squall

★★

[skwɔːl]

혱 스콜(때로 눈·비를 동반하는 돌풍)

n. a sudden storm or wind

The sailors rushed to get below deck when they unexpectedly encountered a violent **squall**.

surreal

★★

[sərí:əl]

혱 아주 이상한, 초현실적인

n. surrealism

adj. having qualities that are strange and seem unreal

Light pillars, caused by ice crystals in the air above street lamps, create an unforgettably **surreal** sight.

syn. bizarre

---

rapid 번개는 빠른 기온 상승을 일으키는데, 그것이 천둥소리를 낸다.   **sleet** 진눈깨비는 빗방울이 얼기 시작하거나 눈송이가 녹기 시작할 때 형성된다고 한다.
solar 태양 현상의 일종인 흑점은 태양의 자기장에 변화가 있을 때 나타나는 어두운 부분이다.   **sporadic** 하늘에 산발적으로 나타나는 별똥별은 사실 지구의
대기에 진입한 유성들이다.   **squall** 선원들은 뜻밖의 맹렬한 스콜을 만나자, 서둘러 갑판 아래로 갔다.   **surreal** 가로등 위 공기 중의 얼음 결정에 의해 생기는
빛기둥들은 잊을 수 없는 초현실적인 광경을 만들어 낸다.

temporary
[témpərèri]
③ 일시적인

adj. lasting for only a limited period of time

Algae will sometimes bring about a **temporary** change in the color of fallen snow, turning it a shade of pink.

ant. permanent

translucent
[trænslúːsnt]
③ 반투명한

n. translucence

adj. not clear, but allowing light to pass through

When light enters **translucent** material, subsurface scattering occurs, causing it to exit at random points.

> **Useful Tips**
> '투명한'을 의미하는 단어는 transparent, '불투명한'을 의미하는 단어는 opaque이다.

tremor
[trémər]
③ 약한 지진, 진동

n. a small earthquake

Some **tremors** in polar regions are the result of collapsing glaciers rather than tectonic activity.

tsunami
[sunάːmi]
③ 쓰나미(지진 등에 의한 엄청난 해일)

n. a large, destructive wave caused by an earthquake

Although **tsunamis** are sometimes mistakenly referred to as tidal waves, they are two different phenomena.

twilight
[twáilàit]
③ 황혼, 해 질 녘

n. the time of day just before the sun goes down

A flash of green light can sometimes be observed just above the sun at either **twilight** or dawn.

syn. dusk

ultraviolet
[λltrəváiəlit]
③ 자외선의

adj. having a wavelength beyond violet on the color spectrum

It is the **ultraviolet** light of the sun's rays that causes skin damage such as sunburn and premature aging.

---

temporary 때때로 조류는 내린 눈의 색을 일시적으로 변화시켜 분홍빛이 되게 할 것이다. **translucent** 빛이 반투명한 물체로 들어가면 표면하 산란이 일어나, 임의 지점에서 빛이 빠져나가게 된다. **tremor** 극지방의 일부 약한 지진은 지각 활동이라기보다는 빙하가 붕괴한 결과이다. **tsunami** 쓰나미는 때때로 tidal wave(해일)로 잘못 불리지만, 이 둘은 각기 다른 현상이다. **twilight** 때때로 해 질 녘이나 새벽에 태양 바로 위에서 초록빛의 섬광을 목격할 수 있다. **ultraviolet** 피부가 햇빛에 타는 것과 조기 노화 같은 피부 손상을 초래하는 것은 태양 광선의 자외선이다.

EXERCISES

ART & DESIGN

SOCIAL SCIENCE

NATURAL SCIENCE

HUMANITIES

EARTH & SPACE

SOCIAL ISSUES

A Match each definition with the correct word.

1 half of a sphere or similarly shaped object   ⓐ solar

2 a small earthquake   ⓑ kinetic

3 a large snowstorm with heavy winds   ⓒ condensation

4 having a wavelength beyond violet on the color spectrum   ⓓ ultraviolet

5 the process of changing from a gas to a liquid   ⓔ tremor

6 relating to motion   ⓕ hemisphere

7 relating to the sun   ⓖ blizzard

8 lasting for only a limited period of time   ⓗ temporary

B Choose the word that is closest in meaning to each underlined word.

1 Just after <u>twilight</u>, the temperature began to drop and the light rain turned into snow flurries.
   ⓐ dusk   ⓑ daybreak   ⓒ noon   ⓓ midday

2 Few ships are able to navigate the <u>formidable</u> currents of the strait, so it is generally avoided.
   ⓐ erratic   ⓑ unforeseen   ⓒ imposing   ⓓ favorable

3 <u>Rapid</u> changes rarely take place in geology—they occur over long periods of time.
   ⓐ diverse   ⓑ subtle   ⓒ gradual   ⓓ swift

4 Environmentalists fear that the current die-off of bees is a <u>harbinger</u> of a mass extinction.
   ⓐ determent   ⓑ consequence   ⓒ replica   ⓓ portent

5 Researchers continue to search for the <u>elusive</u> energy source that is clean and efficient.
   ⓐ evasive   ⓑ commonplace   ⓒ universal   ⓓ counterproductive

6 <u>Sporadic</u> radio signals from outer space have been detected, but they seem to have no pattern.
   ⓐ enigmatic   ⓑ astonishing   ⓒ intermittent   ⓓ proverbial

7 The man's claim of having found a "missing link" between humans and apes was an <u>outright</u> lie.
   ⓐ uncertain   ⓑ well-meaning   ⓒ absolute   ⓓ amusing

천문학

Lesson 49 Astronomy

★★

aerial

[έəriəl]

[형] 공중의, 대기의

adj. in or from the air

Unmanned **aerial** vehicles, commonly known as drones, are used for the maintenance of large telescopes.

Useful Tips

명사 aerial은 영국에서 전파를 송수신하는 antenna의 뜻으로 사용된다.

★

aggregate

[ǽgrigət]

[명] 혼합체, 집합체

n. something composed of several different things

Some of the moon rocks brought back to Earth by the Apollo missions are **aggregates** known as breccias.

★★

ascend

[əsénd]

[동] 올라가다, 오르다

n. ascent

v. to rise or go up

As a rocket **ascends** through the atmosphere, the burning of fuel leaves behind a trail of smoke.

syn. climb *ant.* descend

★★

asteroid

[ǽstərɔ̀id]

[명] 소행성

n. a minor planet circling around the sun

Most of the solar system's **asteroids** are found in the broad area between Mars and Jupiter.

syn. planetoid

★

axis

[ǽksis]

[명] 축, 축선

n. an imaginary line running through the center of a shape or object

The **axis** of Uranus leans at a 98 degree angle, making the planet appear to be spinning on its side.

★★★

celestial

[səléstʃəl]

[형] 천체의, 천상의

adj. relating to the heavens, sky, or space

Icarus, a star located five billion light-years away, may be the farthest **celestial** body visible from Earth.

syn. heavenly *ant.* terrestrial

---

aerial 보통 드론으로 알려진 무인 비행 물체들은 대형 망원경들을 관리하는 데 사용된다. **aggregate** 아폴로 미션들이 지구로 가져온 몇몇 월석은 각력암이라는 혼합체이다. **ascend** 로켓이 대기를 뚫고 올라갈 때, 연료가 연소되면서 긴 연기를 남긴다. **asteroid** 태양계 소행성들의 대부분은 화성과 목성 사이의 광활한 구역에서 발견된다. **axis** 천왕성의 축은 98도로 기울어져 있어, 모로 누워 회전하는 것처럼 보인다. **celestial** 50억 광년 떨어진 곳에 있는 항성 이카루스는 지구에서 보이는 가장 먼 천체일 것이다.

★★ **clash**
[klæʃ]
[동] 충돌하다

v. to collide violently

Astronomers believe that the Milky Way may **clash** with Andromeda in about five billion years.

★★★ **comet**
[kámit]
[명] 혜성

n. an object composed of ice and dust that revolves around the Sun

A **comet**'s tail usually points away from the Sun, so it cannot be used as an indicator of direction.

★★ **constellation**
[kànstəléiʃən]
[명] 별자리

n. a group of stars that form a pattern when viewed from Earth

The Big Dipper, one of the most recognizable **constellations**, is made up of seven bright stars.

★★ **core**
[kɔːr]
[명] 중심부

n. the center of a spherical object

Scientists now believe that Mars has a relatively large **core** that is made up primarily of liquid iron.

★★ **corona**
[kəróunə]
[명] 1. (태양·달 주위의) 광환
2. 광관

n. 1 a circle of light around the Sun or Moon *syn.* halo
2 the outer atmosphere of the Sun

1. The **corona** that sometimes appears to form around the Moon can be caused by ice crystals in clouds.
2. The variability in the size and shape of the **corona** is caused by changes in the Sun's magnetic field.

★★ **crater**
[kréitər]
[명] 분화구

n. a hole in the surface of a planet caused by an eruption or impact

The South Pole–Aitken basin, the Moon's largest **crater**, is about 2,500 kilometers in diameter.

clash 천문학자들은 약 50억 년 후에 우리은하가 안드로메다 은하와 충돌할 수 있다고 믿는다. **comet** 혜성의 꼬리는 보통 태양의 반대쪽을 가리켜서, 방향의 지표로 사용될 수 없다. **constellation** 가장 쉽게 알아 볼 수 있는 별자리들 중 하나인 북두칠성은 7개의 밝은 항성들로 이루어져 있다. **core** 현재 과학자들은 화성이 주로 액체 상태의 철로 된 비교적 큰 중심부를 지니고 있다고 믿는다. **corona** 1. 때때로 달 주위에 형성되는 것으로 보이는 광환은 구름 안의 빙정들 때문에 생길 수 있다. 2. 광관의 크기와 형태의 가변성은 태양의 자기장 변화에 의해 야기된다. **crater** 달의 가장 큰 분화구인 남극 에이트켄 분지는 지름이 약 2,500 킬로미터이다.

dwarf

[dwɔːrf]

웽 특별히 작은, 왜소한

adj. smaller than others of its kind

Dwarf stars, which are classified by color, are generally dimmer and smaller in size than other stars.

eclipse

[iklíps]

웽 (해·달의) 식(蝕)

n. an instance when the view of the Moon or Sun is wholly or partially blocked

A solar **eclipse** occurs when part of the Earth is covered in the shadow that is cast by the Moon.

elaborate

[ilǽbərèit]

통 자세히 설명하다

[ilǽbərət]

웽 정교한

v. to explain in further detail

Due to a lack of information, the scientists were unable to **elaborate** on the problem with the Mars rover.

adj. very detailed or complicated   *syn.* intricate   *ant.* plain

An astrolabe is an **elaborate** device used by ancient astronomers to perform a variety of calculations.

equinox

[íːkwənàks]

웽 주야 평분시, 분점

n. one of the two times a year when the day and night are of equal length

The autumn **equinox** marks the end of astronomical summer in the northern hemisphere.

explode

[iksplóud]

통 폭발하다

n. explosion

v. to violently burst into pieces

Even after a star **explodes**, its core may remain intact and become what is called a neutron star.

syn. blow up

extraterrestrial

[èkstrətəréstriəl]

웽 지구 밖의, 외계의

adj. coming from somewhere outside of Earth

Some SETI projects are designed to detect any signals that may be coming from an **extraterrestrial** source.

syn. alien

---

dwarf 색으로 분류되는 왜성들은 일반적으로 다른 항성들보다 더 흐리고 크기가 더 작다.   **eclipse** 일식은 지구의 일부가 달이 드리운 그림자에 가려질 때 발생한다.   **elaborate** 그 과학자들은 정보가 부족해서, 그 화성 탐사 로봇의 문제점에 대해 자세히 설명할 수 없었다. / 아스트롤라베는 고대 천문학자들이 다양한 측정에 사용했던 정교한 기구이다.   **equinox** 북반구에서 추분은 천문학상 여름의 끝을 나타낸다.   **explode** 항성이 폭발한 후에도, 그 중심부는 손상되지 않고 남아 소위 중성자성이 될 수 있다.   **extraterrestrial** 몇몇 외계 지적 생명 탐사 프로젝트들은 지구 밖 어디에선가 올 수 있는 신호들을 감지하도록 설계되어 있다.

fascinate
[fǽsənèit]
ⓥ 매혹하다

n. fascination

v. to attract and hold someone's attention in a positive way

The stars have **fascinated** humans since ancient times, but we still have much to learn about them.

syn. captivate   *ant.* repel

flare
[flɛər]
ⓝ 플레어(태양·별 등이 순간적으로 밝아지는 것)

n. a brief burst of bright light

A solar **flare** is a bright burst of electromagnetic energy coming from the surface of the Sun.

galaxy
[gǽləksi]
ⓝ 은하계

n. a large system of stars

Our **galaxy** is shaped like a spiral and may contain as many as 400 billion stars.

Useful Tips
우리의 solar system이 속해 있는 galaxy는 Milky Way이다.

gravity
[grǽvəti]
ⓝ 중력

adj. gravitational

n. the force that attracts objects to one another

Earth's **gravity** is the force that keeps the Moon from breaking free and drifting away into space.

heliocentric
[hìːliouséntrik]
ⓐ 태양 중심의

adj. having the Sun at its center

The idea that our solar system is **heliocentric** was first proposed by Nicolaus Copernicus in the 16th century.

launch
[lɔːntʃ]
ⓥ (우주선 등을) 발사하다
ⓝ 발사

v. to send something into the air or space

The Soviet Union **launched** Sputnik 1 into space in 1957, followed by Sputnik 2 one month later.

n. the act of sending something into the air or space

NASA's initial space shuttle **launch** took place at the Kennedy Space Center in April of 1981.

fascinate 별들은 고대부터 사람들을 매혹해 왔지만, 우리는 아직 그것들에 대해 배울 것이 많다.   **flare** 태양 플레어는 태양 표면에서 나오는 전자기 에너지가 갑자기 빛을 내며 방출되는 것이다.   **galaxy** 우리의 은하계는 나선형이며, 무려 4천억 개의 별들을 가지고 있을 수 있다.   **gravity** 지구의 중력은 달이 궤도에서 벗어나 우주로 표류해 가지 않도록 해 주는 힘이다.   **heliocentric** 우리 태양계가 태양 중심이라는 개념은 16세기에 Nicolaus Copernicus에 의해 처음으로 제시되었다.   **launch** 소비에트 연방은 1957년에 스푸트니크 1호를 우주로 발사했고, 한 달 후 스푸트니크 2호가 발사되었다. / NASA의 첫 우주 왕복선 발사는 1981년 4월에 케네디 우주 센터에서 이루어졌다.

lodestar
[lóudstà:r]
ⓝ 길잡이가 되는 별

n. a star used for navigation in the past

Polaris, also known as the Pole Star, served as a **lodestar** for both sailors and astronomers.

luminous
[lú:mənəs]
ⓐ 빛을 내는, 빛나는

adj. full of or emitting bright light

Although the Moon may appear to be **luminous**, it is merely reflecting the light of the Sun.

syn. radiant   *ant.* dark

lunar
[lú:nər]
ⓐ 달의

adj. relating to the Moon

The **lunar** surface is covered with impact craters and dark splotches formed by ancient lava flows.

ant. solar

meteor
[mí:tiər]
ⓝ 유성

n. an object from space that enters Earth's atmosphere

After a **meteor** crashes into the Earth, the part that remains becomes known as a meteorite.

nebula
[nébjulə]
ⓝ 성운

adj. nebulous

n. a large cloud of dust and gas in space

In some **nebulae**, matter begins to clump together, eventually forming stars, planets, and other celestial objects.

orbit
[ɔ́:rbit]
ⓥ …의 주위를 궤도를 그리며 돌다
ⓝ 궤도

v. to circle around a large body in space

To date, astronomers have identified 79 moons **orbiting** Jupiter, 53 of which have been named.

n. the path of an object circling around a large body in space

Pluto's **orbit** around the Sun differs from those of the planets in that it is far more elliptical.

---

lodestar 북극성으로도 알려진 폴라리스는 선원들과 천문학자들에게 길잡이가 되는 별 역할을 했다.   **luminous** 달이 빛나는 것처럼 보일 수 있지만, 단지 태양의 빛을 반사하고 있을 뿐이다.   **lunar** 달 표면은 충돌 분화구들과 아주 오래된 용암류에 의해 형성된 짙은 반점들로 뒤덮여 있다.   **meteor** 유성이 지구에 추락한 후, 남은 부분은 운석으로 알려지게 된다.   **nebula** 몇몇 성운들 안에서, 물질이 덩어리지기 시작해 결국 항성과 행성, 그리고 다른 천체들을 형성한다.   **orbit** 지금까지 천문학자들은 목성 주위를 궤도를 그리며 도는 79개의 위성들을 찾았는데, 그 중 53개에 이름이 붙여졌다. / 태양 주위를 도는 명왕성의 궤도는 훨씬 더 타원형이라는 점에서 행성들의 궤도와 다르다.

★

proliferate

[prəlífərèit]

[동] 급증하다

n. proliferation

v. to quickly grow in number

The use of bright lights to illuminate cities is **proliferating**, which is making it harder for astronomers to observe space.

syn. multiply

★★★

satellite

[sǽtəlàit]

[명] 위성

n. an object that circles around a large body in space

There are thousands of artificial **satellites** circling around the Earth, many of which are no longer functional.

★★

shimmer

[ʃímər]

[동] 희미하게 빛나다, 일렁이다

v. to glow with an unsteady light

Stars seem to **shimmer**, but planets don't, which is due to the fact that planets are much closer.

syn. glimmer

★★

singularity

[sìŋgjulǽrəti]

[명] 특이점(밀도가 무한대로 됨)

n. a point of zero volume and infinite mass density in space

In theory, **singularities** should form at the center of black holes, but this has never been proven to be true.

★★

solstice

[sɑ́lstis]

[명] (태양의) 지점

n. the day of either the longest or shortest night of the year

During a **solstice**, the Sun appears to reach either its highest or lowest point in the sky.

Useful Tips

solstice에는 summer solstice(하지)와 winter solstice(동지)가 있다.

★★

spectacular

[spektǽkjulər]

[형] 굉장한, 극적인

adj. amazing or impressive

NASA's Juno space probe has taken **spectacular** photographs of Jupiter while orbiting the planet.

syn. striking

proliferate 도시들을 밝히는 밝은 조명의 사용이 급증하고 있어서, 천문학자들이 우주를 관측하는 것이 더 어려워지고 있다. **satellite** 지구 주위를 도는 수천 개의 인공위성이 있는데, 그 중 많은 수가 더 이상 정상 가동되지 않고 있다. **shimmer** 항성들은 희미하게 빛나는 것처럼 보이지만 행성들은 그렇게 보이지 않는데, 그것은 행성들이 훨씬 더 가까이 있다는 사실 때문이다. **singularity** 이론상으로 특이점들은 블랙홀들의 중심에서 형성되어야 하지만, 이것이 사실로 증명된 적은 없다. **solstice** 지점 동안에는, 태양이 하늘의 가장 높은 지점이나 가장 낮은 지점에 나타난다. **spectacular** NASA의 주노 우주탐사선은 목성 주위를 궤도를 그리며 돌면서 굉장한 목성 사진들을 찍었다.

★★ **stagger**

[stǽgər]

[동] (진행되는 일에) 시차를 두다, 엇갈리게 배치하다

v. to arrange objects or events so they do not collide or overlap

Space agencies tend to **stagger** their launches in order to be able to focus their resources on each mission.

★★ **supernova**

[sù:pərnóuvə]

[명] 초신성

n. an exploding star

The Crab Nebula is believed to have been created by a **supernova** that was observed in the year 1054.

★★ **tilt**

[tilt]

[동] 기울다

v. to lean to one side

With the exception of Mercury, all of the planets in the solar system **tilt** on their axis to varying degrees.

syn. slant

★★★ **vacuum**

[vǽkjuəm]

[명] 진공, 공백

n. an area containing no matter

Although there is very little matter in space, it cannot be considered a perfect **vacuum**.

syn. void

★★ **wary**

[wέəri]

[형] 신중한

n. wariness

adj. cautious due to potential problems or danger

After the Challenger disaster of 1986, NASA became **wary** of sending more civilians into space.

syn. leery

★ **zenith**

[zí:niθ]

[명] 천정(天頂)

n. the highest point of an object in space

From our observation point on Earth, the Sun reaches its **zenith** at exactly noon of each day.

syn. apex *ant.* nadir

---

stagger 항공 우주국들은 각 미션에 자원을 집중시킬 수 있도록 시차를 두고 발사하는 경향이 있다. **supernova** 게 성운은 1054년에 관측되었던 초신성에 의해 형성되었다고 여겨진다. **tilt** 수성을 제외하고, 태양계의 모든 행성들은 축이 다양한 각도로 기울어져 있다. **vacuum** 우주에는 물질이 거의 없지만, 완전한 진공으로 간주될 수는 없다. **wary** 1986년의 챌린저호 참사 이후, NASA는 더 많은 민간인을 우주로 보내는 것에 신중해졌다. **zenith** 지구에서 관측하면, 태양은 매일 정확히 정오에 천정에 도달한다.

EXERCISES

A Match each definition with the correct word.

1 to circle around a large body in space   ⓐ lunar

2 to send something into the air or space   ⓑ launch

3 a brief burst of bright light   ⓒ dwarf

4 relating to the Moon   ⓓ core

5 the center of a spherical object   ⓔ flare

6 smaller than others of its kind   ⓕ satellite

7 coming from somewhere outside of Earth   ⓖ orbit

8 an object that circles around a large body in space   ⓗ extraterrestrial

B Choose the word that is closest in meaning to each underlined word.

1 Dinosaurs <u>fascinate</u> children, so they can be used to introduce young learners to science.
     ⓐ intimidate   ⓑ captivate   ⓒ perplex   ⓓ mimic

2 As warm, wet air <u>ascends</u> and cools, its moisture condenses and begins to form clouds.
     ⓐ swirls   ⓑ accelerates   ⓒ freezes   ⓓ climbs

3 Experts are <u>wary</u> of claims that corn is an efficient source of ethanol, as it has drawbacks.
     ⓐ enthusiastic   ⓑ gratified   ⓒ outraged   ⓓ leery

4 The frozen bubbles in the lake are full of methane, so they will <u>explode</u> if exposed to fire.
     ⓐ break down   ⓑ blow up   ⓒ spin around   ⓓ spread out

5 When the sun reaches its <u>zenith</u>, the temperature is expected to soar into the high 30s.
     ⓐ slope   ⓑ midpoint   ⓒ apex   ⓓ boundary

6 The Grand Canyon is a <u>spectacular</u> example of the effects that water erosion can have.
     ⓐ disputed   ⓑ striking   ⓒ monotonous   ⓓ ambiguous

7 A <u>luminous</u> phenomenon called the milky sea effect is caused by bacteria that glow.
     ⓐ radiant   ⓑ mediocre   ⓒ peculiar   ⓓ contemporary

[환경]

Lesson 50 Environment

★ **additive**
[ǽdətiv]
[명] 첨가물, 첨가제

n. something added in small amounts to improve or preserve a substance

Metal **additives** in plastics may be contaminating the environment and poisoning wildlife.

★★★ **anxious**
[ǽŋkʃəs]
[형] 걱정하는, 염려하는

adj. worried about something that has not yet happened

Many young people are **anxious** about the effects of climate change they may face in the future.

syn. apprehensive

★ **biodegradable**
[bàioudigréidəbl]
[형] 생분해[자연분해]성의

adj. capable of decomposing naturally

The use of **biodegradable** plastics could reduce greenhouse gas emissions and improve landfill issues.

★★ **blast**
[blæst]
[명] 폭발, 폭약
[동] 폭파하다, 폭발시키다

n. a large explosion

When miners use controlled **blasts** to break up rock, it releases dangerous dust into the air.

v. to damage something with an explosion or a powerful impact

To end the damage it was causing to the area, authorities **blasted** a hole in the aging dam.

★ **bleak**
[bli:k]
[형] 황량한, 음산한

adj. cold, empty, and unwelcoming

In the **bleak** Arctic landscape surrounding the oil wells, many small species are experiencing negative effects.

syn. barren

★ **carcinogenic**
[kɑ:*r*sənədʒénik]
[형] 발암성의
n. carcinogen

adj. capable of causing cancer

Not only do **carcinogenic** substances affect human health, they also have a negative impact on ecosystems.

---

additive 플라스틱의 금속 첨가제는 환경을 오염시키며 야생 동물들을 중독시키고 있을지도 모른다. **anxious** 많은 젊은이들이 미래에 닥칠지도 모르는 기후 변화의 영향에 대해 염려한다. **biodegradable** 생분해성 플라스틱의 사용은 온실가스 배출을 줄이고, 쓰레기 매립지 문제를 개선할 수 있다. **blast** 광부들이 암석을 부수기 위해 세심히 제어된 폭발을 사용할 때, 그로 인해 위험한 먼지가 공기 중으로 방출된다. / 당국은 노후화된 댐으로 그 지역에 생기는 피해를 끝내기 위해, 그 댐을 폭파하여 구멍을 뚫었다. **bleak** 유정(油井)을 둘러싼 황량한 북극 지형에서 많은 작은 종들이 부정적인 영향을 받고 있다. **carcinogenic** 발암 물질은 인간 건강에 영향을 줄 뿐만 아니라, 생태계에도 부정적인 영향을 미친다.

ART & DESIGN

SOCIAL SCIENCE

NATURAL SCIENCE

HUMANITIES

EARTH & SPACE

SOCIAL ISSUES

catastrophic
[kæ̀təstráfik]

(형) 큰 재앙의, 파멸의

n. catastrophe

adj. causing great destruction or suffering

The **catastrophic** effects of the Fukushima Daiichi accident will be felt for generations to come.

syn. cataclysmic

caution
[kɔ́ːʃən]

(명) 조심, 신중

adj. cautious

n. great care taken to avoid something negative

New technologies have the potential to lessen environmental problems, but we must proceed with **caution**.

syn. prudence   *ant.* carelessness

complicated
[kámpləkèitid]

(형) 복잡한

v. complicate

adj. difficult to do or understand because it contains many details

Ecosystems are **complicated** networks of relationships that humans should not tinker with.

syn. intricate   *ant.* simple

conserve
[kənsɔ́ːrv]

(동) 보호하다, 아끼다

n. conservation

v. to protect or save something

The government needs to take action to **conserve** the nation's wetlands before they're all gone.

syn. preserve   *ant.* squander

corrosion
[kəróuʒən]

(명) 부식 (작용)

v. corrode

n. gradual damage caused by a chemical reaction

The **corrosion** of man-made materials can create airborne particles that pollute the air we breathe.

disaster
[dizǽstər]

(명) 재해, 재난, 참사

adj. disastrous

n. a tragic event causing great damage or loss of life

In response to the Deepwater Horizon **disaster**, new safety regulations for offshore drilling were created.

syn. calamity

---

catastrophic 후쿠시마 제 1 원전 사고의 재앙적 결과는 미래 세대들에게도 영향을 미칠 것이다.   **caution** 신기술들은 환경 문제들을 줄일 가능성이 있지만, 우리는 신중히 진행해야만 한다.   **complicated** 생태계는 인간이 어설프게 손대면 안 되는 복잡한 관계의 네트워크이다.   **conserve** 정부는 그 나라의 습지가 모두 소실되기 전에 그것들을 보존하기 위한 조치를 취할 필요가 있다.   **corrosion** 인공 물질의 부식은 우리가 숨쉬는 공기를 오염시키는, 진애(공기 중에 떠다니는 작은 고체 입자)를 만들어낼 수 있다.   **disaster** 미국 멕시코만 원유 유출 사고에 대응하여, 해상 시추에 대한 새로운 안전 규정들이 생겼다.

dispose of

[dispóuz əv]

ⓥ …을 처리하다, 처분하다, 치우다

n. disposal

v. to get rid of

People need to think carefully before they **dispose of** items that can be reused or repurposed.

syn. discard

---

disrupt

[disrʌ́pt]

ⓥ 방해하다, 지장을 주다

n. disruption

v. to interrupt something and temporarily prevent it from continuing

Underwater noise pollution generated by human activity can **disrupt** communication between whales.

---

emigrate

[émigrèit]

ⓥ 이민을 가다, (다른 나라로) 이주하다

n. emigration

v. to leave your country to live in a new one

As climate change worsens in certain parts of the world, people may begin to **emigrate** en masse.

ant. immigrate

---

endangered

[indéindʒərd]

ⓐ 멸종 위기에 처한

n. endangerment

adj. facing the prospect of extinction

Habitat loss due to overdevelopment is one of the main problems faced by **endangered** species.

syn. threatened

---

fertilizer

[fə́ːrtəlàizər]

ⓝ 비료

v. fertilize

n. a substance used to promote the growth of plants

Runoff from **fertilizer** applied to lawns and gardens can result in the contamination of coastal zones.

---

heedless

[híːdlis]

ⓐ …에 부주의한, 경솔한

v. heed

adj. acting in a careless way

Heedless industrialization is turning pristine wilderness areas into wastelands in some countries.

syn. reckless   *ant.* cautious

---

dispose of 사람들은 재사용할 수 있거나 용도 변경할 수 있는 물건들을 처분하기 전에 신중하게 생각할 필요가 있다.   **disrupt** 인간 활동에 의해 발생된 수중 소음 공해는 고래들 간의 의사소통을 방해할 수 있다.   **emigrate** 세계의 특정 지역에서의 기후 변화가 악화되면서, 사람들이 집단으로 이주하기 시작할 수도 있다. **endangered** 과잉 개발로 인한 서식지의 소실은 멸종 위기 종들이 직면한 주요 문제들 중의 하나이다.   **fertilizer** 잔디와 정원에 뿌려진 비료에서 나온 유출액은 해안 지역의 오염을 초래할 수 있다.   **heedless** 부주의한 산업화가 일부 국가에서 자연 그대로의 원생 지역을 황무지로 변화시키고 있다.

imbalance

[imbǽləns]

ⓝ 불균형

n. a lack of proper proportion or distribution

Even the slightest **imbalance** in nature can have ripple effects that cause lasting problems.

ant. balance

imminent

[ímənənt]

ⓐ 금방이라도 닥칠 듯한, 임박한

adj. likely to happen very soon

Some experts believe a global environmental disaster is **imminent**, while others have a more optimistic view.

syn. impending

landfill

[lǽndfìl]

ⓝ 쓰레기 매립지

n. a place where trash or waste is buried

As **landfills** continue to fill up, more and more people are demanding new ways of dealing with waste.

litter

[lítər]

ⓥ (쓰레기 등을) 버리다
ⓝ (버려진) 쓰레기

v. to throw trash on the ground

Hikers who casually **litter** are destroying the very environment that brings them pleasure.

n. trash that has been thrown on the ground   *syn.* rubbish

Some concerned students decided to take action by cleaning up the **litter** along the river's banks.

penalty

[pénəlti]

ⓝ 처벌, 형벌

v. penalize

n. a punishment for doing something wrong

Greedy companies that dump toxic waste face **penalties**, but this does little to stop them.

ant. reward

pollutant

[pəlúːtənt]

ⓝ 오염 물질, 오염원

v. pollute

n. a substance that harms the environment

Pollutants in the air can have an especially strong impact on trees, weakening their natural defense systems.

syn. contaminant

---

imbalance 자연에서의 가장 사소한 불균형조차도 지속적인 문제를 일으키는 파급 효과를 낳을 수 있다.   **imminent** 일부 전문가들은 지구 환경 재앙이 임박했다고 믿는 반면, 다른 전문가들은 좀 더 낙관적인 견해를 가지고 있다.   **landfill** 쓰레기 매립지가 계속 가득 차면서, 점점 더 많은 사람들이 쓰레기를 처리하는 새로운 방법들을 요구하고 있다.   **litter** 쓰레기를 무심코 버리는 등산객들은 그들에게 즐거움을 주는 바로 그 환경을 파괴하고 있다. / 염려가 된 몇몇 학생들은 강둑을 따라 쓰레기를 치우는 조치를 취하기로 결정했다.   **penalty** 유독성 폐기물을 버리는 탐욕스러운 회사들은 처벌을 받게 되지만, 이것은 그들을 막는 데 거의 도움이 되지 않는다.   **pollutant** 공기 중의 오염 물질은 특히 나무에 강한 영향을 미쳐서, 나무의 자연 방어 체계를 약화시킨다.

★★★
produce
[prədjú:s]
⑤ 생산하다

n. production

v. to create something

The majority of carbon dioxide **produced** by humans comes from the burning of fossil fuels.

syn. generate　*ant.* consume

★★★
prohibit
[prouhíbit]
⑤ (특히 법으로) 금지하다

n. prohibition

v. to officially stop people from doing or having something

Many countries **prohibit** residents from importing non-native plants that could become invasive.

syn. ban　*ant.* allow

Useful **Tips**

미국인들이 Prohibition을 한정사 없이 사용할 경우, 이는 1920-1933년 사이의 금주법 시행 시대를 의미한다.

★★★
recycle
[rì:sáikl]
⑤ 재활용하다

n. recycling

v. to process waste in order to make it usable again

In 2020, Norway **recycled** 97% of its plastic bottles, the highest percentage in the European Union.

★★
regulation
[règjuléiʃən]
⑨ 규정

v. regulate

n. an official rule about how something must be done

There is a **regulation** that requires people to obtain a permit before burning waste that will create air pollution.

syn. requirement

★★
rescue
[réskju:]
⑤ (위험에서) 구하다, 구조하다

v. to save someone or something in danger

Injured animals that are **rescued** from wildfires are cared for and then returned to the wild.

★★★
restore
[ristɔ́:r]
⑤ 회복시키다, 복원하다

n. restoration

v. to return something to its proper state

It may be impossible to **restore** the damaged land, but we can make significant improvements to it.

---

produce 인간이 만들어내는 이산화탄소의 대부분은 화석 연료의 연소로 생긴다.　**prohibit** 많은 나라들은 주민들이 침습성이 될 수 있는 외래 식물을 수입하는 것을 금지한다.　**recycle** 2020년에 노르웨이는 97%의 플라스틱 병을 재활용했는데, 이는 유럽연합에서 가장 높은 비율이었다.　**regulation** 사람들이 대기 오염을 유발하는 폐기물을 소각하기 전에 허가를 받아야 하는 규정이 있다.　**rescue** 산불에서 구조된 다친 동물들은 보살핌을 받은 후, 야생으로 돌려보내진다.
restore 훼손된 토지를 복구하는 것은 불가능할지 모르지만, 상당히 개선할 수는 있다.

★
★★★
rot
[rɑt]
ⓥ 썩다, 부패하다

adj. rotten

v. to gradually soften and fall apart

When organic materials begin to **rot**, their nutrients are gradually returned to the soil.

syn. decay

Useful Tips

rot은 부정적인 뜻이 내포되어 있는 반면, 같은 의미의 단어인 decay는 중립적인 의미를 가진다.

★
★★
roughly
[rʌ́fli]
ⓐ 대략

adj. rough

adv. more or less

Nations across the globe have established **roughly** 200,000 nature preserves for the protection of plants and animals.

syn. approximately   *ant.* precisely

★
★★
scatter
[skǽtər]
ⓥ (흩)뿌리다, 흩어지다

v. to move away or cause to move away in many different directions

If plants are prevented from properly **scattering** their seeds, their populations will gradually decrease.

syn. disperse   *ant.* gather

★
sewage
[súːidʒ]
ⓝ 하수, 오물

n. human waste that is removed via pipes

Sadly, releasing untreated **sewage** into oceans and rivers because of flooding is a common occurrence.

★
solitary
[sálətèri]
ⓐ (다른 사람 없이) 혼자 하는

n. solitude

adj. without any others

After becoming the **solitary** nation to leave the Paris Climate Agreement, the USA rejoined it in 2021.

syn. lone

★
★★
spill
[spil]
ⓝ 유출
ⓥ 유출하다, 쏟다

n. an instance of something accidentally coming out of its container

Scientists have been experimenting with oil-eating microbes that could be used to clean up **spills**.

v. to accidentally cause something to come out of its container

After a damaged tanker **spilled** its cargo into the sea, these beaches were covered in oil.

---

rot 유기 물질들이 썩기 시작하면, 그 영양소는 서서히 토양으로 돌아간다.   **roughly** 전 세계의 국가들은 동식물의 보호를 위해 대략 20만 개의 자연 보호 구역을 세웠다.   **scatter** 만약 식물이 씨를 적절히 뿌리지 못하게 되면, 그 개체수가 점차 줄어들 것이다.   **sewage** 안타깝게도, 홍수로 인해 처리되지 않은 하수를 바다와 강에 방출하는 것은 흔한 일이다.   **solitary** 미국은 파리 기후 협약을 홀로 탈퇴한 후, 2021년에 재가입했다.   **spill** 과학자들은 (기름) 유출을 치우는 데 사용될 수 있는 기름 먹는 미생물들을 실험해 오고 있다. / 손상된 유조선이 석유를 바다에 유출한 후, 이 해변들은 기름으로 덮여 버렸다.

★★ **spur**
[spəːr]
[동] 박차를 가하다, 자극하다

v. to encourage something or cause it to happen sooner

The government hopes that its new carbon tax will **spur** businesses to find ways to reduce emissions.

syn. incite *ant.* discourage

★ **stench**
[stentʃ]
[명] 악취

n. an extremely unpleasant smell

The smoke from the factory pollutes the air we breathe and creates a **stench** that sickens local residents.

★★★ **survive**
[sərváiv]
[동] 살아남다, 생존하다
n. survival

v. to remain alive despite difficulties

It is estimated that 60% of fish species would be unable to **survive** if the oceans were to become five degrees warmer.

★★ **timber**
[tímbər]
[명] 목재

n. wood used for construction

The ever-increasing global demand for **timber** is driving companies to cut down more and more trees.

★ **topsoil**
[tάpsɔ̀il]
[명] 표토(표면 또는 상층부의 흙)

n. the upper layer of the ground

Agricultural practices are causing an acceleration in the erosion of **topsoil** in many parts of the world.

★★★ **transport**
[trænspɔ́ːrt]
[동] …을 수송하다, 옮기다, 나르다

v. to move something from one place to another

When fruit and vegetables are **transported** long distances, they end up being harmful to the environment.

spur 정부는 새로운 탄소세가 기업들이 (탄소) 배출을 줄이는 방법들을 찾도록 자극할 것으로 기대한다. **stench** 공장에서 나오는 연기는 우리가 숨쉬는 공기를 오염시키고, 지역 주민들을 역겹게 하는 악취를 낸다. **survive** 해양 온도가 5도 올라가면, 어종의 60%가 살아남지 못할 것으로 추정된다. **timber** 계속 증가하는 전 세계 목재 수요 때문에 기업들이 점점 더 많은 나무들을 베고 있다. **topsoil** 농경 활동들이 전 세계의 많은 지역에서 표토 침식의 가속화를 초래하고 있다. **transport** 과일과 채소가 장거리 운송되면, 그것들은 결국 환경에 해가 된다.

EXERCISES

ART & DESIGN

SOCIAL SCIENCE

NATURAL SCIENCE

HUMANITIES

EARTH & SPACE

SOCIAL ISSUES

A Match each definition with the correct word.

1 an extremely unpleasant smell   ⓐ disrupt

2 to protect or save something   ⓑ corrosion

3 to return something to its proper state   ⓒ stench

4 a place where trash or waste is buried   ⓓ spill

5 gradual damage caused by a chemical reaction   ⓔ landfill

6 a substance used to promote the growth of plants   ⓕ conserve

7 to accidentally cause something to come out of its container   ⓖ restore

8 to interrupt something and temporarily prevent it from continuing   ⓗ fertilizer

B Choose the word that is closest in meaning to each underlined word.

1 People once considered the ocean the perfect place to <u>dispose of</u> waste.
   ⓐ observe   ⓑ purify   ⓒ arrange   ⓓ discard

2 <u>Heedless</u> storm chasers sometimes seek out tornadoes and try to get close to them.
   ⓐ courageous   ⓑ professional   ⓒ reckless   ⓓ subtle

3 A 2017 study found plastic <u>pollutants</u> in 83% of tap water samples taken internationally.
   ⓐ additives   ⓑ fabrications   ⓒ contaminants   ⓓ determinants

4 Although it is certainly not an <u>imminent</u> event, the Sun will eventually run out of fuel and die.
   ⓐ impending   ⓑ imperative   ⓒ unconventional   ⓓ perpetual

5 Worries about our dwindling supply of oil have <u>spurred</u> the development of solar power.
   ⓐ hindered   ⓑ incited   ⓒ defined   ⓓ divided

6 It is believed that the <u>blast</u> from the impact of a huge asteroid is what killed off the dinosaurs.
   ⓐ inferno   ⓑ flood   ⓒ aftermath   ⓓ explosion

7 A volcano called Krakatoa erupted in 1883, causing <u>catastrophic</u> effects that were felt globally.
   ⓐ secondary   ⓑ cataclysmic   ⓒ mundane   ⓓ successive

A Choose the correct words.

1 The word average has the same meaning as

ⓐ vengeful   ⓑ standard   ⓒ excessive   ⓓ uncertain

2 The word peculiar has the same meaning as

ⓐ potent   ⓑ major   ⓒ ideal   ⓓ odd

3 The word proliferate has the same meaning as

ⓐ advocate   ⓑ grapple   ⓒ reject   ⓓ multiply

4 The word disaster has the same meaning as

ⓐ calamity   ⓑ debut   ⓒ depiction   ⓓ scrutiny

5 The word surreal has the same meaning as

ⓐ serene   ⓑ bizarre   ⓒ rational   ⓓ startled

6 The word vacuum has the same meaning as

ⓐ void   ⓑ base   ⓒ reserve   ⓓ maze

7 The word prohibit has the same meaning as

ⓐ impress   ⓑ confirm   ⓒ ban   ⓓ disintegrate

8 The word fauna has the same meaning as

ⓐ newborn   ⓑ wildlife   ⓒ victor   ⓓ glitch

B Fill in the blanks with the best words from the box.

1 During a long _____, an electric car's battery may need to be recharged several times.

2 In this _____ landscape where little grows, scientists have discovered a dinosaur skeleton.

3 This _____ photo taken from an airplane shows the deforestation of the Amazon rainforest.

4 The deadly blizzard was accompanied by a(n) _____ that blew the falling snow horizontally.

5 Many more turbines are required to _____ the potential of the region's wind power.

6 Many astronomers noticed the change in the star, as it had become _____ dimmer.

aerial	journey	maximize	bleak	gale	markedly

C Read the following passages.

ART & DESIGN

SOCIAL SCIENCE

NATURAL SCIENCE

HUMANITIES

EARTH & SPACE

SOCIAL ISSUES

[1-2]   **1** Choose one word that fits both blanks.

> The telescope remains an essential _____ for astronomers. The Hubble Space
> Telescope is the most important telescope in use today, but it is more than 30 years
> old. A replacement was scheduled to be launched in 2007, but NASA has not yet
> been able to _____ that plan.

ⓐ supply   ⓑ measure   ⓒ span   ⓓ implement

2 Choose the appropriate pair of words to fill in the blanks.

> Geysers and hot springs are popular tourist attractions in many places, but there
> have been numerous _____ in which people have been seriously injured.
> _____ by the amazing natural phenomena, they fail to observe safety
> guidelines and end up with life-threatening burns.

ⓐ insights — Overwhelmed   ⓑ incidents — Captivated
ⓒ ventures — Surpassed   ⓓ regulations — Disrupted

[3-4]

> Rangers recently reintroduced bighorn sheep into a national park. The sheep scattered
> in different directions as soon as they were released. The rangers grew anxious,
> wondering if the sheep could survive on their own. However, they soon gathered
> back together on a nearby mountainside.

3 In the context of the passage, scattered means _____.
ⓐ gazed   ⓑ rotated   ⓒ dispersed   ⓓ originated

4 The word anxious in the passage could best be replaced by
ⓐ elated   ⓑ offended   ⓒ inquisitive   ⓓ apprehensive

[5-6]

> Researchers have long been searching for a practical replacement for plastic bags.
> Their persistent efforts may finally have paid off, but the solution is not some newly
> developed material. Instead, it is jute, a common plant fiber that has been used for
> thousands of years. Jute is inexpensive, 100% biodegradable, and easy to grow,
> making it the perfect _____ material for bags.

5 The word persistent in the passage is closest in meaning to
ⓐ steadfast   ⓑ frantic   ⓒ fruitful   ⓓ reciprocal

6 Choose the word that is most suitable for the blank.
ⓐ geothermal   ⓑ temporary   ⓒ alternative   ⓓ carcinogenic

그리스어 어근
Greek Roots

그리스어 접두사처럼, 그리스어 어근을 포함한 영어 단어들이 의학, 과학, 정치학 등과 같은 전문 분야에서 많이 사용된다. Chapter 5에서 배운 asteroid, recycle, geothermal은 그리스어 어근인 aster/astro, cycl, therm(o)을 포함한 단어들이다. 주요 그리스어 어근들의 고유 의미를 살펴보고, 그 어근이 사용된 단어들도 함께 숙지해 보자.

ROOTS	EXAMPLES
aster/astro *star*	asterisk 별표 asteroid 소행성 astrology 점성술 astronaut 우주 비행사 astronomer 천문학자 astrophysics 천체물리학
chron(o) *time*	anachronism 시대착오 chronic 만성적인 chronograph 스톱워치 chronological 연대순의 synchronous 동시 발생하는
cycl *circle*	cyclist 자전거 타는 사람 cyclone 인도양의 열대성 폭풍 motorcycle 오토바이 recycle 재활용하다 tricycle 세발자전거 unicycle 외바퀴 자전거
dem(o) *people*	democracy 민주주의 demographic (특정) 인구 집단 demotic 일반 대중의 endemic 풍토병 epidemic 유행병
gen(e) *birth, kind, origin, race*	gene 유전자 genealogy 가계도[족보] genesis 기원 genetics 유전학 homogeneous 동종의 oxygen 산소
gram/graph *letter, something written*	cryptogram 암호 diagram 도표 grammar 문법 graphic 그래픽(의) telegram 전보 typography 활판술[조판]
log *speech, word, discourse*	logic 논리 monologue 독백 analogy 유사, 비슷함 apologize 사과하다 catalogue 카탈로그 epilogue 끝맺는 말
meter/metr *measure*	barometer 기압계 centimeter 센티미터 chronometer (항해용) 정밀 시계 metric 미터법의 speedometer 속도계 thermometer 온도계
scope *to see, examine, observe*	endoscope 내시경 horoscope 별점, 점성술 microscope 현미경 periscope 잠망경 stethoscope 청진기 telescope 망원경
therm(o) *heat*	exothermic 발열성의 geothermal 지열의 thermal 열의 thermography 온도 기록 thermosphere (대기권 중) 열권

CHAPTER

6

SOCIAL ISSUES

Lesson **51**

공중 보건과 위생

Public Health & Hygiene

★★★

addiction

[ədíkʃən]

[명] 중독

adj. addicted

n. a severe mental or physical dependence on a substance or activity

There are many people who struggle with **addiction** to prescription painkillers after being hospitalized.

★

airborne

[ɛ́ərbɔ̀ːrn]

[형] 공기로 전염[운반]되는

adj. transmitted through the air

Airborne diseases spread when people talk, cough, or sneeze in crowded areas with poor ventilation.

Useful Tips

수인성 질병은 waterborne diseases라고 한다.

★★

allergic

[ələ́ːrdʒik]

[형] 알레르기가 있는

n. allergy

adj. having a severe physical reaction to a normally harmless substance

Many children are **allergic** to nuts, making it vital that foods containing them are clearly labeled.

★★

chronic

[kránik]

[형] 만성적인

adj. lasting for a long time

Pollutants in the air may be the cause if you experience a **chronic** cough that lasts for several weeks.

syn. protracted

★

clot

[klɑt]

[명] (피 등의) 엉긴 덩어리, 응혈

n. a thick mass that forms in a liquid

People who travel long distances by air may be at risk of developing blood **clots** in their legs.

syn. clump

★★★

contagious

[kəntéidʒəs]

[형] 전염성의

n. contagion

adj. capable of being spread from organism to organism

Rubella is a **contagious** disease that is sometimes referred to as the German measles.

syn. communicable

---

addiction 병원 입원 후 처방된 진통제에 중독되어 힘들어하는 사람들이 많다. **airborne** 공기로 전염되는 질병들은 환기가 잘 되지 않는 밀집된 구역에서 사람들이 말하고 기침하거나 재채기를 할 때 확산된다. **allergic** 많은 아이들이 견과류에 알레르기가 있어서, 견과류가 포함된 식품들에 정보가 명백하게 표기된 라벨을 붙이는 것이 필수적이다. **chronic** 만성 기침이 몇 주 동안 계속된다면, 공기 중의 오염 물질이 그 원인일 수 있다. **clot** 비행기로 장거리 여행을 하는 사람들은 다리에 응혈이 생기는 위험에 처할 수 있다. **contagious** 풍진은 때로 독일 홍역으로 지칭되기도 하는 전염병이다.

ART & DESIGN

SOCIAL SCIENCE

NATURAL SCIENCE

HUMANITIES

EARTH & SPACE

SOCIAL ISSUES

cramped
[kræmpt]
ⓐ 비좁은

adj. having too little space

Living in **cramped** areas without running water leaves people susceptible to a variety of illnesses.

syn. crowded   *ant.* spacious

germ
[dʒəːrm]
ⓝ 세균, 미생물

n. a microorganism that causes disease

Germs are disease-causing organisms that can be spread through both direct and indirect contact.

syn. microbe

Useful Tips

germs의 대표적인 두 유형은 viruses와 bacteria이다.

ignore
[ignɔ́ːr]
ⓥ 무시하다

v. to pay no attention to someone or something

Individuals who **ignore** the symptoms of an illness could be putting the people around them at risk.

syn. disregard   *ant.* focus on

immune
[imjúːn]
ⓐ 면역성이 있는
n. immunity

adj. protected from a disease by antibodies

People who suffer from measles at some point in their life subsequently become **immune** to the disease.

ant. susceptible

incinerate
[insínərèit]
ⓥ 소각하다
n. incinerator

v. to burn something to ashes

Traditionally, medical waste that has the potential to put the public at risk has been **incinerated** on-site.

infect
[infékt]
ⓥ 감염시키다
n. infection

v. to cause someone to contract a disease

Animals with rabies become erratic and aggressive, and they can **infect** humans by biting them.

---

cramped 사람들이 수돗물 없이 비좁은 지역에서 생활하면 다양한 병에 걸리기 쉽다.   **germ** 세균은 직접·간접적 접촉 모두를 통해 퍼질 수 있는 질병을 일으키는 유기체이다.   **ignore** 병의 증상들을 무시하는 개인들은 주위 사람들을 위험에 빠뜨리고 있을 수 있다.   **immune** 인생의 어느 한 시점에서 홍역을 앓은 사람들은 그 후 그 병에 면역성이 생긴다.   **incinerate** 전통적으로, 일반인들을 위험에 처하게 만들 가능성이 있는 의료 폐기물은 현장에서 소각되어 왔다.
infect 광견병에 걸린 동물들은 변덕스럽고 공격적이며, 사람들을 물어 감염시킬 수 있다.

lethargic
[ləθáːrdʒik]
ⓐ 무기력한

n. lethargy

adj. having little energy

People generally feel **lethargic** due to lack of sleep, but it could also be the symptom of an illness.

syn. sluggish *ant.* energetic

outbreak
[áutbrèik]
ⓝ (질병·전쟁 등의) 발생, 발발

n. a sudden occurrence of a disease in an area

An **outbreak** of Ebola in Western Africa in 2013 led to more than 11,000 deaths, with a 40% mortality rate.

pandemic
[pændémik]
ⓝ 전국[전 세계]적인 유행병

n. a disease that affects a large area

The **pandemic** began in the winter and had soon spread across the entire globe.

pathology
[pəθálədʒi]
ⓝ 병리학

n. the study of the causes and effects of diseases

Pathology experts are retained by hospitals to interpret the results of laboratory tests administered to patients.

pharmaceutical
[fàːrməsúːtikəl]
ⓐ 약학의, 제약의

n. pharmacy

adj. relating to the production and sale of medicinal drugs

Large **pharmaceutical** companies have been criticized for doing too little to develop innovative products.

precarious
[prikέəriəs]
ⓐ 불안정한, 위태로운

adj. likely to change in a negative way

Experts warn that public health is **precarious** and can be threatened by disease at anytime.

syn. unstable *ant.* stable

---

lethargic 사람들은 보통 수면이 부족하면 무기력하게 느끼지만, 그것은 어떤 병의 증상일 수도 있다. **outbreak** 2013년 아프리카 서부의 에볼라 바이러스 발생으로 11,000명 이상이 사망해, 40%의 사망률을 보였다. **pandemic** 그 전 세계적인 유행병은 겨울에 시작되어 곧 전 세계로 퍼졌다. **pathology** 병원에는 환자들에게 시행된 실험실 테스트들의 결과를 해석하는 병리학 전문가들이 있다. **pharmaceutical** 대형 제약 회사들은 혁신적인 제품을 개발하려는 노력을 거의 기울이지 않는다는 비판을 받아 왔다. **precarious** 전문가들은 공중 보건이 위태로우며 언제라도 질병의 위협을 받을 수 있다고 경고한다.

ART & DESIGN

SOCIAL SCIENCE

NATURAL SCIENCE

HUMANITIES

EARTH & SPACE

SOCIAL ISSUES

proper
[prápər]

⑩ 적절한, 올바른

adj. correct, suitable, or expected

This video will teach young children the **proper** way to wash their hands after they have been outside.

syn. appropriate   *ant.* improper

protocol
[próutəkɔ̀ːl]

⑩ 프로토콜(환자 치료 실행을 위한 계획)

n. a set of rules to be followed in a certain situation

The government has established **protocols** that will be activated in the case of a public health emergency.

quarantine
[kwɔ́ːrəntìːn]

⑩ 격리
ⓥ 격리하다

n. the act of isolating someone to prevent the spread of disease

During your **quarantine**, you are required to report any possible symptoms you may experience.

v. to isolate someone to prevent the spread of disease

After arriving in the country, the family was required to **quarantine** at their hotel for two weeks.

recur
[rikə́ːr]

ⓥ 반복되다, 재발하다

n. recurrence

v. to happen more than once

The contamination of the village's tap water has **recurred** several times over the past decade.

syn. reappear

rehabilitate
[rìːhəbílətèit]

ⓥ 회복시키다, 갱생시키다

n. rehabilitation

v. to restore a person to good health or a normal lifestyle

The doctors and nurses work hard to **rehabilitate** patients who have recently had major surgery.

sanitary
[sǽnətèri]

⑩ 위생적인, 청결한

n. sanitation

adj. relating to being clean and free of contaminants

If you are unsure about the **sanitary** conditions of a local eatery, you should dine at another place.

syn. hygienic   *ant.* unsanitary

---

proper 이 영상은 어린아이들에게 외부에 있다 온 후 손을 씻는 올바른 방법을 가르쳐 줄 것이다.   **protocol** 정부는 공중 보건 응급 상황의 경우 작동시킬 프로토콜을 설정했다.   **quarantine** 격리 중에는, 당신이 겪을 수 있는 어떤 증상도 보고해야 한다. / 그 가족은 그 나라에 도착한 후, 호텔에서 2주 동안 격리해야 했다.   **recur** 지난 10년 동안 그 마을의 수돗물 오염이 몇 차례 반복되었다.   **rehabilitate** 그 의사와 간호사들은 최근 큰 수술을 받은 환자들을 회복시키기 위해 많은 노력을 기울인다.   **sanitary** 어떤 현지 식당의 위생 상태가 의심스러우면, 다른 곳에서 식사를 해야 한다.

★★ **severe**
[səvíər]
[형] 심각한
n. severity

adj. extreme in degree

Eating unwashed fruit or vegetables can lead to **severe** stomach illnesses due to pesticides or bacteria.

syn. acute *ant.* mild

★ **suffice**
[səfáis]
[동] 충분하다
adj. sufficient

v. to be adequate

Some people insist on using hand sanitizers, but washing with soap and warm water will usually **suffice**.

Useful Tips
Suffice (it) to say...는 '(더 많은 말을 할 수 있지만) …라고만 해도 충분할 것이다'라는 뜻으로 쓰인다.

★★★ **toxic**
[tάksik]
[형] 독성의, 유독한
n. toxin

adj. containing poison

The park will remain closed indefinitely, as authorities have found **toxic** materials in the soil.

syn. poisonous *ant.* nontoxic

★★★ **treat**
[triːt]
[동] 치료하다
n. treatment

v. to use medicine or a medical procedure on a sick person

Humidifiers are good for dry skin, and they can also be used to **treat** sinus infections or allergies.

★★ **vaccinate**
[vǽksənèit]
[동] 백신 주사를 놓다
n. vaccination

v. to inject someone with a substance to protect them from a disease

The government announced that it had begun **vaccinating** people at a rate of nearly one million a day.

syn. inoculate

★★ **welfare**
[wélfὲər]
[명] 안녕, 복지, 후생

n. a person's health and happiness

Volunteer medical workers visit the town's elderly residents once a week to check on their **welfare**.

syn. well-being

severe 씻지 않은 과일이나 채소를 먹는 것은 농약이나 박테리아로 인한 심각한 위장병을 발생시킬 수 있다. **suffice** 어떤 사람들은 손 살균제를 사용해야 한다고 주장하지만, 보통은 비누와 따뜻한 물로 씻으면 충분할 것이다. **toxic** 당국이 그 토양에서 독성 물질을 발견했기 때문에, 그 공원은 무기한 폐쇄될 것이다. **treat** 가습기는 건조한 피부에 좋고, 축농증이나 알레르기를 치료하는 데 사용될 수도 있다. **vaccinate** 정부는 하루에 거의 백만 명의 속도로 사람들에게 백신 주사를 놓기 시작했다고 발표했다. **welfare** 자원 봉사 의료진들은 그 도시 노령층 거주자들의 안녕을 확인하려고 일주일에 한 번 그들을 방문한다.

EXERCISES

A Match each definition with the correct word.

1 the study of the causes and effects of diseases   ⓐ quarantine

2 to cause someone to contract a disease   ⓑ pathology

3 protected from a disease by antibodies   ⓒ outbreak

4 to be adequate   ⓓ immune

5 a sudden occurrence of a disease in an area   ⓔ suffice

6 to restore a person to good health or a normal lifestyle   ⓕ incinerate

7 to burn something to ashes   ⓖ infect

8 the act of isolating someone to prevent the spread of disease   ⓗ rehabilitate

B Choose the word that is closest in meaning to each underlined word.

1 The nutritionist explained that individuals who fail to eat a balanced diet may become lethargic.
    ⓐ aggressive   ⓑ nauseous   ⓒ sluggish   ⓓ obese

2 Due to the country's precarious political situation, tourists are advised against traveling there.
    ⓐ cautious   ⓑ unstable   ⓒ primitive   ⓓ outlandish

3 Having easy access to affordable and nutritious food is essential to the welfare of families.
    ⓐ affluence   ⓑ relocation   ⓒ dignity   ⓓ well-being

4 Children living in cramped environments require opportunities to run around in open spaces.
    ⓐ urban   ⓑ unclean   ⓒ crowded   ⓓ traditional

5 Although the symptoms of the illness are not severe, they often last for an extended period.
    ⓐ persistent   ⓑ apparent   ⓒ erratic   ⓓ acute

6 Bad behavior is usually a phase for toddlers, but it may recur during their development.
    ⓐ cease   ⓑ vanish   ⓒ reappear   ⓓ alter

7 People who ignore nonverbal cues during a conversation are likely to be labeled "socially awkward."
    ⓐ disregard   ⓑ circulate   ⓒ reconsider   ⓓ intercept

Food & Nutrition

---

antioxidant
[æ̀ntiɑ́ksədənt, -tai-]

ⓝ 항산화 물질, (비타민 C·E 등의) 산화 방지제

n. a substance that slows the damaging effects of oxidation

Foods high in **antioxidants**, such as blueberries, are believed to offer a wide range of health benefits.

---

appetite
[ǽpətàit]

ⓝ 식욕

adj. appetizing

n. a desire to eat

Stress sometimes makes people lose their **appetite**, which can cause them to physically weaken.

syn. hunger

---

artificial
[ɑ̀ːrtəfíʃəl]

ⓐ 인공의, 인위적인

adj. made by people

Artificial coloring added to processed foods is unnecessary, and it may even present health risks.

syn. synthetic   *ant.* natural

---

balanced
[bǽlənst]

ⓐ 균형 잡힌

n., v. balance

adj. having the proper proportion or distribution

A **balanced** diet should contain representatives from each of the major food groups.

ant. imbalanced

---

condiment
[kɑ́ndəmənt]

ⓝ 양념, 조미료

n. a substance people add to their food to improve its taste

Condiments are available by request from the cashier at the time you pick up your order.

---

consume
[kənsúːm]

ⓥ 먹다, 마시다

n. consumption

v. to eat or drink something

The more calories you **consume** during the day, the harder you will need to exercise to burn them off.

syn. ingest

---

antioxidant 블루베리와 같이 항산화 물질의 함유량이 높은 음식들은 다양한 건강상의 이점을 제공하는 것으로 알려져 있다.   **appetite** 사람들은 때때로 스트레스 때문에 식욕을 잃는데, 이로 인해 신체적으로 약해질 수 있다.   **artificial** 가공식품에 첨가된 인공 색소는 불필요하며, 이는 건강상의 위험까지 야기할 수도 있다.   **balanced** 균형 잡힌 식단은 각 주요 식품군의 대표적인 음식들을 포함해야 한다.   **condiment** 조미료는 주문한 음식을 찾을 때 계산대 직원에게 요청하면 받을 수 있다.   **consume** 하루 동안 더 많은 칼로리를 섭취할수록, 그 칼로리를 모두 소진하기 위해 더 열심히 운동해야 할 것이다.

ART & DESIGN

SOCIAL SCIENCE

NATURAL SCIENCE

HUMANITIES

EARTH & SPACE

SOCIAL ISSUES

crave
[kreiv]
ⓥ 갈망하다, 열망하다

n. craving

v. to have a strong desire for something

People often **crave** sweet or salty foods, but they must be careful to eat them in moderation.

culinary
[kʌ́lənèri]
ⓐ 요리의, 주방의

adj. relating to cooking or kitchens

The impressive **culinary** skills of the young chef caught the eye of the owner of the restaurant.

dairy
[dɛ́əri]
ⓐ 유제품의

adj. relating to milk or foods made from milk

Dairy products such as butter and cheese can cause digestion issues for people who are lactose intolerant.

debilitating
[dibílətèitiŋ]
ⓐ (심신을) 쇠약하게 만드는

v. debilitate

adj. making someone weak or unable to function properly

Chronic irritable bowel syndrome is a **debilitating** digestive disorder that affects many people.

syn. crippling

deficiency
[difíʃənsi]
ⓝ 결핍, 부족

adj. deficient

n. a lack of something

In the past, sailors often suffered from a condition called scurvy, which is caused by a vitamin C **deficiency**.

syn. shortage   *ant.* abundance

diabetes
[dàiəbíːtis]
ⓝ 당뇨병

n., adj. diabetic

n. a disease that prevents the body from regulating blood sugar levels

Type 2 **diabetes** is partially genetic, but it can also result from unhealthy eating habits.

Useful **Tips**

diabetes는 -s로 끝나지만, 복수형이 아닌 불가산 명사이다.

---

crave 사람들은 종종 달거나 짠 음식을 갈망하지만, 적당히 먹도록 주의해야 한다.   **culinary** 그 젊은 주방장의 인상적인 요리 솜씨가 식당 주인의 눈을 사로잡았다.
dairy 버터와 치즈 같은 유제품은 젖당 불내성을 가진 사람들에게 소화 장애를 일으킬 수 있다.   **debilitating** 만성 과민성 대장 증후군은 심신을 쇠약하게 만드는 소화기 질환으로, 많은 사람들에게 영향을 끼친다.   **deficiency** 과거에 항해사들은 종종 괴혈병이라는 병을 앓았는데, 이것은 비타민 C의 부족으로 생긴다.
diabetes 2형 당뇨병은 일부 유전적이지만, 건강하지 않은 식습관에 의해 야기될 수도 있다.

digest

★★★

[didʒést, dai-]

ⓥ (음식을) 소화하다, 소화시키다

n. digestion

v. to break down food in the body

It takes a lot of energy for the body to **digest** food, which is why we feel sleepy after a big meal.

edible

★★★

[édəbl]

ⓐ 먹을 수 있는, 먹어도 되는

adj. capable of being eaten

Some mushrooms are **edible**, but there are many varieties that are poisonous to human beings.

ant. inedible

essential

★★★

[isénʃəl]

ⓐ 필수적인, 매우 중요한

adj. necessary or very important

To keep your body healthy, it is **essential** to include green leafy vegetables in your diet.

syn. vital   *ant.* unimportant

examine

★★★

[igzǽmin]

ⓥ 조사[검토]하다, 검사[진찰]하다

n. examination

v. to look over carefully

A professional dietician will **examine** your daily eating habits and make suggestions for improvements.

syn. inspect

fiber

★★

[fáibər]

ⓝ 섬유질

n. material in food that cannot be digested

Beans and other foods that are high in **fiber** keep your digestive system running smoothly.

flavor

★★

[fléivər]

ⓝ (독특한) 풍미, 맛

adj. flavorful

n. the way something tastes

While **flavor** is sensed mostly by the taste buds, our senses of smell and touch are also involved.

---

digest 음식을 소화하기 위해서는 많은 에너지가 필요한데, 이것이 우리가 많이 먹은 후에 졸음을 느끼는 이유이다.   **edible** 일부 버섯들은 식용 가능하지만, 인간에게 유독한 품종들이 많다.   **essential** 몸을 건강하게 유지하기 위해 식단에 푸른 잎줄기 채소를 포함시키는 것이 매우 중요하다.   **examine** 전문 영양사가 일상 식습관을 검토하고, 개선을 위한 제안을 해 줄 것이다.   **fiber** 콩과 섬유질이 많은 다른 음식들은 소화기관을 원활하게 유지시켜 준다.   **flavor** 맛은 대부분 미뢰에 의해 감지되지만, 우리의 후각과 촉각 또한 관련되어 있다.

ART & DESIGN

SOCIAL SCIENCE

NATURAL SCIENCE

HUMANITIES

EARTH & SPACE

SOCIAL ISSUES

genetically modified
[dʒənétikəli mádəfàid]
ⓐ 유전자 조작[변형]의

adj. having had its genetic structure altered artificially

Genetically modified organisms, also known as GMOs, can be found in many of the foods we eat.

gourmet
[guərméi]
ⓐ 미식가의, 미식가를 위한 요리용의
ⓝ 미식가, 식도락가

adj. relating to high-quality food

This market sells **gourmet** products, but its prices are too high for most of the local residents.

n. someone who enjoys high-quality food   *syn.* epicurean

As she considers herself a **gourmet**, the woman can be highly critical of food that doesn't meet her standards.

indulge
[indʌ́ldʒ]
ⓥ 마음껏 하다, 즐기다, 탐닉하다

adj. indulgent

v. to do something pleasurable that you don't normally do

It is okay to **indulge** in sweets now and again, but too much sugar can have adverse effects on the body.

ingredient
[ingríːdiənt]
ⓝ 재료, 성분

n. one of the foods used to make a specific dish

Flour, eggs, and milk are three of the main **ingredients** found in most baked goods.

intake
[íntèik]
ⓝ 섭취(량)

n. the amount of something that someone ingests

The doctor advised her patient to reduce his salt **intake** in order to lower his blood pressure.

syn. consumption

malnutrition
[mælnjuːtríʃən]
ⓝ 영양실조

n. a medical condition caused by a lack of healthy food

Children who suffer from **malnutrition** are more likely to experience stunted growth and developmental delays.

---

genetically modified GMO로도 알려진 유전자 조작 생물은 우리가 먹는 많은 음식에서 발견될 수 있다.   **gourmet** 이 시장에서는 미식 용품을 팔지만, 그 가격이 대부분의 지역 거주자들에게는 너무 비싸다. / 그 여자는 자신을 미식가라고 여기기 때문에, 자신의 기준에 맞지 않는 음식에 매우 비판적일 수 있다.
indulge 가끔 단 것을 마음껏 먹는 것은 괜찮지만, 과도한 설탕은 몸에 악영향을 미칠 수 있다.   **ingredient** 밀가루, 달걀, 그리고 우유는 대부분의 제과에 들어있는 세 가지 주재료이다.   **intake** 그 의사는 자신의 환자에게 혈압을 낮추기 위해 소금 섭취를 줄이라고 권고했다.   **malnutrition** 영양실조로 고통받는 아이들은 왜소 생장과 발육 지연을 겪을 가능성이 더 높다.

marinade
[mærənéid]
명 (고기·생선 등을 재는) 양념장
v. marinate

n. a sauce used to flavor food before cooking it

The chef allows the chicken to sit in his signature **marinade** for three hours before barbecuing it.

nourish
[nə́ːriʃ]
통 영양분을 공급하다
n. nourishment

v. to provide with healthy food

Food **nourishes** the body, but it also provides the brain with a pleasurable experience.

nutritious
[njuːtríʃəs]
형 영양분이 많은, 영양가가 높은
n. nutrition

adj. containing healthy elements that the body requires

Children should get in the habit of eating **nutritious** snacks rather than chips or candy.

syn. nourishing

obese
[oubíːs]
형 비만인, 뚱뚱한
n. obesity

adj. severely overweight

Obese individuals face an increased risk of suffering from a variety of diseases and health conditions.

syn. corpulent   *ant.* emaciated

organic
[ɔːrgǽnik]
형 유기농의, 화학비료를 쓰지 않는
adv. organically

adj. grown without the use of chemicals

The vendor claims that all of his vegetables are **organic**, but it is impossible for shoppers to know for sure.

palatable
[pǽlətəbl]
형 맛있는, 맛이 좋은
n. palate

adj. having a pleasant taste

Some people find blue cheese quite **palatable**, while others are driven away by its strong smell.

syn. tasty   *ant.* unpalatable

---

marinade 그 주방장은 닭을 굽기 전에 3시간 동안 그의 특제 양념장에 재워 둔다.   **nourish** 음식은 신체에 영양분을 공급하지만, 뇌에 즐거운 경험을 제공하기도 한다.   **nutritious** 아이들은 과자나 사탕보다는 영양가가 높은 간식을 먹는 습관을 들여야 한다.   **obese** 비만인 사람들은 다양한 질병과 건강 문제를 겪을 위험이 높아진다.   **organic** 그 상인은 자신의 모든 채소가 유기농이라고 주장하지만, 소비자들이 확실히 알기는 불가능하다.   **palatable** 일부 사람들은 블루치즈가 꽤 맛있다고 생각하지만, 다른 이들은 강한 냄새 때문에 기피한다.

★★ **poultry**
[póultri]
[명] 가금(식용 사육 조류)

n. domestic fowls used for meat or eggs

Poultry must be cooked thoroughly in order to kill off any harmful bacteria that may be present.

★★ **protein**
[próutiːn]
[명] 단백질

n. a substance found in food such as meat, eggs, and beans

Some doctors suggest that we should not eat red meat more than once or twice a week, even though it is a good source of **protein**.

★★★ **pure**
[pjuər]
[형] 순수한

adj. containing no additives or contaminants

This jar contains **pure** honey, but water and sugar have been added to the honey in that jar.

syn. unadulterated *ant.* contaminated

★ **ravenous**
[rǽvənəs]
[형] 배가 고파 죽을 지경인

adj. extremely hungry

The children were **ravenous** after the long hike, eating two hamburgers apiece and then clamoring for more.

syn. voracious

★★★ **recommend**
[rèkəménd]
[동] 추천하다, 권하다
n. recommendation

v. to advise someone to do or try something

Nutritionists **recommend** that adult women consume between 1,600 and 2,400 calories per day.

syn. suggest

★ **relish**
[réliʃ]
[동] 즐기다, 맛있게 먹다
[명] 렐리시(소스의 한 종류)

v. to enjoy something immensely *syn.* savor *ant.* detest

Due to health issues, the elderly man rarely eats dessert anymore, but he **relishes** it when he does.

n. a type of sauce added to food to enhance it

Along with mustard, many Americans commonly put **relish** or sauerkraut atop their hot dogs.

poultry 가금류는 존재할지도 모르는 모든 해로운 박테리아를 없애기 위해서 완전히 요리되어야 한다. **protein** 일부 의사들은 붉은 육류가 훌륭한 단백질 공급원임에도 불구하고, 우리에게 일주일에 한두 번 이상 먹지 말라고 권한다. **pure** 이 단지에는 순수한(자연산) 꿀이 담겨 있지만, 저 단지의 꿀에는 물과 설탕이 가미되었다. **ravenous** 아이들은 긴 하이킹 후에 배가 고파 죽을 지경이었는데, 각자 햄버거 두 개씩을 먹고도 더 달라고 아우성쳤다. **recommend** 영양학자들은 성인 여성이 하루에 1,600-2,400 칼로리를 섭취할 것을 권한다. **relish** 건강 문제 때문에 그 노인은 더 이상 디저트를 잘 먹지 않지만, 먹을 때는 맛있게 먹는다. / 겨자와 더불어, 많은 미국인들이 보통 렐리시나 사우어크라우트(독일식 김치)를 핫도그 위에 얹는다.

★

savory

[séivəri]

[형] 1. 짭짤한, 자극적인 맛이 나는
2. 맛 좋은, 냄새가 좋은

adj. **1 having a taste that is salty or spicy**
2 having a pleasing taste or smell *syn.* appetizing

1. Some of the bakery's pastries are sweet, but others have been stuffed with **savory** fillings.
2. The **savory** smell of roast turkey wafted from the kitchen, making everyone even hungrier.

★★★

strengthen

[stréŋkθən]

[동] 강화하다, 튼튼하게 하다

n. strength

v. **to make or become tougher or more powerful**

Calcium is important for many reasons, but primarily because it **strengthens** our teeth and bones.

syn. bolster *ant.* weaken

★

succulent

[sʌ́kjulənt]

[형] (과일·고기 등이) 즙이 많은

adj. **juicy and delicious**

To ensure that the meat remains **succulent**, it should be cooked at a medium temperature.

ant. dry

Useful Tips

succulent가 명사로 쓰이면 알로에와 선인장 같이 줄기나 잎에 물을 많이 머금은 '다육 식물'을 의미한다.

★★

swallow

[swálou]

[동] (음식 등을) 삼키다

v. **to move something down through the throat**

It is recommended that people chew their food about 30 times before they **swallow** it.

★

unflavored

[ʌnfléivərd]

[형] 맛을 내지 않은, 가미를 하지 않은

adj. **having no added taste**

Unflavored yogurt is generally the healthiest option, as it doesn't contain any added sugar.

syn. plain *ant.* flavored

★★★

vegetarian

[vèdʒətéəriən]

[형] 채식주의(자)의
[명] 채식주의자

n. vegetable

adj. **made only from plants** *syn.* herbivorous *ant.* carnivorous

When making **vegetarian** dishes, mushrooms can be an appealing substitute for meat.

n. **someone who eats only plants** *syn.* herbivore *ant.* carnivore

The woman claims to have much more energy since she became a **vegetarian** last year.

---

savory 1. 그 빵집의 일부 페이스트리는 달콤하지만, 다른 것들은 짭짤한[감칠맛 나는] 소로 채워져 있다 2. 주방에서 맛있는 칠면조 구이의 냄새가 풍겨 모두를 더 배고프게 만들었다. **strengthen** 칼슘이 중요한 이유는 여러 가지가 있지만, 우리의 이와 뼈를 튼튼하게 해 준다는 점이 주된 이유이다. **succulent** 고기의 육즙을 유지하기 위해서는 중간 온도로 요리해야 한다. **swallow** 사람들에게 음식을 삼키기 전 30번 정도 씹도록 권장된다. **unflavored** 가미되지 않은 요구르트는 첨가당이 들어있지 않기 때문에 일반적으로 가장 건강에 좋은 선택이다. **vegetarian** 채식 요리를 만들 때, 버섯은 고기의 매력적인 대체재가 될 수 있다. / 그 여자는 작년에 채식주의자가 된 이후로 훨씬 더 기운이 생겼다고 주장한다.

EXERCISES

ART & DESIGN

SOCIAL SCIENCE

NATURAL SCIENCE

HUMANITIES

EARTH & SPACE

SOCIAL ISSUES

A Match each definition with the correct word.

1 grown without the use of chemicals

2 to have a strong desire for something

3 a medical condition caused by a lack of healthy food

4 domestic fowls used for meat or eggs

5 relating to high-quality food

6 to provide with healthy food

7 relating to milk or foods made from milk

8 juicy and delicious

ⓐ poultry

ⓑ organic

ⓒ nourish

ⓓ dairy

ⓔ crave

ⓕ succulent

ⓖ malnutrition

ⓗ gourmet

B Choose the word that is closest in meaning to each underlined word.

1 Speaking politely to your coworkers will <u>strengthen</u> your position in the office hierarchy.
ⓐ enumerate   ⓑ resolve   ⓒ bolster   ⓓ sabotage

2 The woman's job involves developing affordable <u>artificial</u> limbs for people in poor countries.
ⓐ synthetic   ⓑ intricate   ⓒ superfluous   ⓓ durable

3 This ingenious device allows people to keep track of their caloric <u>intake</u> with little effort.
ⓐ stipulation   ⓑ consumption   ⓒ differential   ⓓ status

4 Children <u>relish</u> the chance to show off newly acquired skills in front of their parents.
ⓐ dread   ⓑ savor   ⓒ evoke   ⓓ bypass

5 Because he now suffers from <u>debilitating</u> back pain, the man can no longer travel on his own.
ⓐ reoccurring   ⓑ shifting   ⓒ crippling   ⓓ abating

6 It is <u>essential</u> to report crimes immediately, or the police may not be able to help you.
ⓐ disastrous   ⓑ arduous   ⓒ habitual   ⓓ vital

7 The water of this stream was once <u>pure</u>, but it is now undrinkable due to pollution.
ⓐ inevitable   ⓑ unadulterated   ⓒ dissolved   ⓓ nondescript

[>] 레저와 여행

Lesson 53 Leisure & Travel

★★
amenity
[əménəti]
[명] 편의[오락] 시설

n. a feature or facility that is desirable

The hotel offers its guests many **amenities**, from a deluxe sauna to a 24-hour airport shuttle service.

★
ample
[ǽmpl]
[형] 충분한

adj. more than enough

When scheduling a vacation, make sure to leave yourself **ample** time for rest and relaxation.

syn. plentiful *ant.* meager

★★
breathtaking
[bréθtèikiŋ]
[형] 놀라운, 숨막히는

adj. extremely impressive

The **breathtaking** views from atop the mountain make the long trek to the top worth the effort.

syn. awesome

★★★
cancel
[kǽnsəl]
[동] 취소하다

n. cancellation

v. to stop something from taking place

As long as you **cancel** more than 24 hours before your arrival date, you will receive a full refund.

syn. call off

★
carousel
[kæ̀rəsél]
[명] 1. (공항의) 수화물 컨베이어
2. 회전목마

n. 1 a device that conveys baggage in an airport *syn.* conveyor
2 a children's ride that slowly spins in a circle

1. If your bags fail to appear on the **carousel**, please alert an airline representative.
2. The amusement park features an antique **carousel** that is a favorite of both kids and adults.

★★
complimentary
[kàmpləméntəri]
[형] 무료의

v., n. compliment

adj. provided free of charge

Some airlines provide passengers with **complimentary** ear plugs and sleep masks on overnight flights.

syn. free

---

amenity 그 호텔은 고급 사우나에서 24시간 공항 셔틀 서비스에 이르는 많은 편의 시설을 투숙객들에게 제공한다. **ample** 휴가를 계획할 때, 휴식을 취하고 긴장을 풀 수 있는 충분한 시간을 꼭 남겨 두시오. **breathtaking** 산꼭대기에서 보는 놀라운 광경은 정상까지 가는 장시간의 트레킹을 보람 있게 해 준다. **cancel** 도착일 전 24시간 이전에만 취소하면, 전액을 환불받을 것이다. **carousel** 1. 가방이 수화물 컨베이어 위로 나타나지 않으면, 항공사 직원에게 알리시오. 2. 그 놀이공원에는 아이들과 어른들 모두가 좋아하는 오래된 회전목마가 있다. **complimentary** 어떤 항공사들은 야간 비행을 하는 승객들에게 무료 귀마개와 수면 마스크를 제공한다.

ART & DESIGN

SOCIAL SCIENCE

NATURAL SCIENCE

HUMANITIES

EARTH & SPACE

SOCIAL ISSUES

★★★
delay
[diléi]
ⓝ 지연, 연기
ⓥ 미루다, 연기하다

n. a situation in which something begins later than planned

Several of the passengers missed their connecting flights due to the unexpected **delay**.

v. to cause something to begin later than planned *syn.* put off

Because of the unseasonably cold weather, the couple decided to **delay** their vacation plans.

★★★
destination
[dèstənéiʃən]
ⓝ 목적지

n. the place where someone or something is going

The train's final **destination** is Istanbul, but it makes numerous stops along the way.

★★
disembark
[dìsimbáːrk]
ⓥ 내리다

n. disembarkation

v. to leave a ship or airplane

The cruise passengers lined up to **disembark** the ship as it slowly approached the port.

syn. get off *ant.* board

★
excursion
[ikskɔ́ːrʒən]
ⓝ 여행

n. a short trip taken for pleasure

A weekend **excursion** to the beach or mountains can be an effective stress reliever.

syn. jaunt

★
fare
[fɛər]
ⓝ 요금, 운임

n. the cost of riding public transportation

Please pay the correct **fare** as you board the bus or show the driver your transportation pass.

syn. fee

★★★
forbid
[fərbíd]
ⓥ 금지하다

adj. forbidden

v. to order people not to do something

The hotel **forbids** children under the age of 12 from entering the pool area without an adult.

syn. prohibit *ant.* allow

---

delay 뜻밖의 지연으로 몇몇 승객들이 연결 항공편을 놓쳤다. / 때아닌 추운 날씨로 인해, 그 부부는 휴가 계획을 미루기로 결정했다. **destination** 그 기차의 최종 목적지는 이스탄불이지만, 가는 도중에 수차례 정차한다. **disembark** 그 유람선이 서서히 항구에 다가가자, 승객들은 배에서 내리려고 줄을 섰다.
excursion 해변이나 산으로 떠나는 주말 여행은 효과적인 스트레스 완화 장치가 될 수 있다. **fare** 버스에 탑승하면서 정확한 요금을 내거나 운전사에게 대중교통 이용권을 보여 주시오. **forbid** 그 호텔은 12세 미만의 아동이 어른과 동행하지 않고 수영장 구역에 입장하는 것을 금지하고 있다.

haphazard
[hæphǽzərd]
ⓐ 무계획적인, 되는 대로의

adj. lacking organization or a plan

Traveling from place to place in a **haphazard** manner could leave you without a room for the night.

syn. random   *ant.* organized

indefatigable
[ìndifǽtigəbl]
ⓐ 지칠 줄 모르는, 끈기 있는

n. fatigue

adj. having endless energy

Even the most **indefatigable** vacationers need to schedule some downtime during their trips.

syn. tireless

insurance
[inʃúərəns]
ⓝ 보험

adj. insured

n. an arrangement in which a person pays a company to receive compensation in the event of an accident, crime, or injury

Travel **insurance** is available for tourists who worry about cancellations or other unforeseen difficulties.

intrepid
[intrépid]
ⓐ 두려움을 모르는, 대담한

adj. showing little or no fear

The **intrepid** couple spends their weekends pursuing extreme activities such as paragliding and rock climbing.

syn. fearless   *ant.* cowardly

itinerary
[aitínərèri]
ⓝ 여행 일정표

n. a detailed plan of a trip

Needing to make unexpected changes to her **itinerary**, the woman phoned her travel agent.

jet lag
[dʒét læg]
ⓝ 시차증

n. sleep disruption caused by traveling between time zones

While some degree of **jet lag** may be unavoidable, there are many things you can do to minimize it.

Useful Tips

jet lag은 표준 시간대가 다른 장소 사이를 오가는 장거리 비행 여행시 발생하는 피로, 신경 과민 등의 증상이다.

---

haphazard 무계획적으로 이리저리 여행을 하면, 밤을 지낼 방을 구하지 못하게 될 수도 있다.   **indefatigable** 가장 지칠 줄 모르는 피서객들도 여행 중에 한가한 시간을 일정에 넣어야 한다.   **insurance** 여행 보험은 취소나 다른 예상치 못한 곤경들을 우려하는 여행자들이 이용할 수 있다.   **intrepid** 두려움을 모르는 그 부부는 패러글라이딩과 암벽 등반 같은 극한 활동들을 하면서 주말을 보낸다.   **itinerary** 그 여자는 여행 일정표를 갑자기 변경해야 해서, 여행사 직원에게 전화를 했다.   **jet lag** 어느 정도의 시차증은 피할 수 없겠지만, 그것을 최소화하기 위해 할 수 있는 일은 많다.

★★★ **luggage**
[lʌ́gidʒ]
[명] (여행용) 짐, 수화물

n. suitcases and bags used for traveling

Bringing too much **luggage** on a trip can end up being both inconvenient and costly.

syn. baggage

★★ **mishap**
[míshæp]
[명] (경미한) 사고, 불행

n. an unintended event with minor negative consequences

Due to a **mishap** at the station, the man missed his train and had to wait for the next one.

syn. blunder

★★★ **navigate**
[nǽvəgèit]
[동] 길을 찾다
n. navigation

v. to travel along a planned course

It can be difficult to **navigate** a strange city, so it may be worth the money to hire a guide.

★ **perishable**
[périʃəbl]
[형] 부패하기 쉬운, 잘 상하는
v. perish

adj. susceptible to decay

It is a good idea to pack **perishable** goods in your carry-on bags rather than in checked luggage.

★★ **personnel**
[pə̀:rsənél]
[명] 인력

n. the people employed by a business

The airline did not have enough **personnel** due to a strike, so it had to cancel several flights.

syn. staff

★★ **priority**
[praiɔ́:rəti]
[명] 우선, 우선권
v. prioritize

n. the state of being more urgent or important than other things

Many people give **priority** to work over pleasure, which can lead to stress over time.

syn. preference

luggage 여행길에 너무 많은 짐을 가져오면 결국 불편하고 비용도 많이 들게 될 수 있다. **mishap** 그 역에서 일어난 사고로, 그 남자는 기차를 놓치고 다음 기차를 기다려야 했다. **navigate** 낯선 도시에서 길을 찾는 것은 어려울 수 있으므로, 가이드 고용 비용을 낼 만한 가치가 있을 수 있다. **perishable** 부패하기 쉬운 물품은 부치는 짐보다는 휴대용 가방 안에 꾸리는 것이 좋다. **personnel** 그 항공사는 파업 때문에 인력이 부족해서, 항공기 몇 편을 취소해야 했다. **priority** 많은 사람들이 즐거움보다 일을 우선으로 하는데, 그것은 시간이 지나면서 스트레스로 이어질 수 있다.

★★ **prolong**
[prəlɔ́:ŋ]
[동] 연장하다
adj. prolonged

v. to make something last longer

The family decided to **prolong** their stay in the seaside cottage by two extra days.

syn. extend *ant.* shorten

★★★ **purpose**
[pə́:rpəs]
[명] 목적, 의도
adj. purposeful

n. the reason something exists or is done

The **purpose** of leisure activities is to provide maximum enjoyment with a minimum of stress.

syn. intention

★★ **reminisce**
[rèmənís]
[동] 추억하다, 회상에 잠기다
n. reminiscence

v. to look back on enjoyable times from the past

My grandparents enjoy **reminiscing** about the trips they took together when they were young.

syn. recollect

★★★ **reservation**
[rèzərvéiʃən]
[명] 예약
v. reserve

n. the arrangement of having booked something for future use

Unless you make a **reservation** in advance, you are not guaranteed a seat on the ferry.

syn. booking

★★ **roam**
[roum]
[동] 돌아다니다, 배회하다

v. to move about without a fixed purpose

The rural area offers visitors fresh food, clean air, and plenty of open fields to **roam** through.

syn. wander

★★ **route**
[ru:t, raut]
[명] 길, 경로

n. the course taken to get from one place to another

The scenic **route** to the village takes twice as long, but it features spectacular views along the way.

syn. path

prolong 그 가족은 해변의 작은 별장에서 머무는 것을 이틀 더 연장하기로 결정했다. **purpose** 여가 활동의 목적은 최소의 스트레스를 받으면서 최대의 즐거움을 제공하는 것이다. **reminisce** 우리 조부모님은 젊었을 때 함께 갔던 여행들을 추억하는 것을 즐기신다. **reservation** 미리 예약하지 않으면, 그 연락선의 좌석을 확보한다는 보장은 없다. **roam** 그 시골 지역은 방문객들에게 신선한 음식과 깨끗한 공기, 그리고 돌아다니기에 충분한 공한지를 제공한다. **route** 그 마을로 가는 경치 좋은 길은 시간이 2배나 걸리지만, 가는 도중에 훌륭한 광경이 펼쳐진다.

★
secluded
[siklú:did]
ⓐ 외딴, 격리된

n. seclusion

adj. far away from other people

Spending a few days alone in a **secluded** cabin is a great way to refresh your overworked brain.

syn. isolated

★
★
★
sightseeing
[sáitsì:iŋ]
ⓝ 관광

n. the act of visiting tourist attractions

Sightseeing is an important part of any trip, but it can prove to be difficult and time-consuming.

★
★
sojourn
[sóudʒə:rn]
ⓝ 체류

n. a short stay somewhere

During their **sojourn** in the foreign city, the teens tried many foods they had never heard of before.

syn. visit

★
★
soothe
[su:ð]
ⓥ 달래다, 진정시키다

v. to cause someone to become calm or relaxed

Some say the sound of crashing waves at night **soothes** them, but others find it irritating.

syn. comfort   *ant.* rile

★
★
★
souvenir
[sù:vəníər]
ⓝ 기념품

n. an item purchased in order to remember a place or event

It is a good idea to avoid gift shops that sell cheap, generic **souvenirs** at inflated prices.

syn. keepsake

★
★
spot
[spɑt]
ⓝ 장소

n. a specific place

The father and son searched for a quiet **spot** next to the river where they could camp and fish.

syn. location

---

secluded 외딴 오두막에서 혼자 며칠을 보내는 것은 혹사당한 뇌에 생기를 되찾아 주는 훌륭한 방법이다.   **sightseeing** 관광은 어떤 여행에서도 중요한 부분이지만, 힘들고 시간이 걸리는 것으로 판명될 수 있다.   **sojourn** 그 외국 도시에서 체류하는 동안, 그 십 대들은 전에 한번도 들어 보지 못했던 많은 음식들을 먹어 보았다.   **soothe** 어떤 사람들은 밤에 부서지는 파도 소리가 그들을 달래 준다고 말하지만, 다른 사람들은 그 소리를 거슬려 한다.   **souvenir** 싸고 일반적인 기념품들을 고가에 판매하는 기념품 가게들은 피하는 것이 좋다.   **spot** 그 아버지와 아들은 야영과 낚시를 할 수 있는 강가의 조용한 장소를 물색했다.

★
sumptuous
[sʌ́mptʃuəs]
[형] 호화로운, 사치스러운

adj. luxurious and impressive

Guests can choose from a wide array of **sumptuous** dishes at the resort's international buffet.

syn. lavish

★★
tranquil
[trǽŋkwil]
[형] 고요한

n. tranquility

adj. calm and peaceful

Walking down the **tranquil** country path, the tourists stopped to take a picture of some sheep.

syn. serene *ant.* chaotic

★★
transit
[trǽnsit, -zit]
[명] 환승, 통과

n. the act of traveling from one place to another

International passengers who are in **transit** may not leave the airport without a visa.

★★
turbulence
[tə́ːrbjuləns]
[명] 난기류, 난류

adj. turbulent

n. violent motion of the air or water

Due to **turbulence**, the flight attendants were unable to serve lunch at the scheduled time.

★★★
voyage
[vɔ́iidʒ]
[명] 여행, 항해
[동] 여행하다, 항해하다

n. a long trip *syn.* journey

These days, a **voyage** across the Atlantic takes about seven hours by air or seven days by sea.

v. to take a long trip *syn.* journey

The tour group **voyaged** across Russia by train before arriving in Vladivostok a week later.

★
wanderlust
[wɑ́ndərlʌ̀st]
[명] 방랑벽

n. a strong desire to travel

If you find yourself suffering from **wanderlust**, simply planning a trip may make you feel a bit better.

---

sumptuous 투숙객들은 그 리조트의 국제적 뷔페에서 다양한 종류의 호화로운 요리들 중 선택할 수 있다. **tranquil** 그 관광객들은 고요한 시골길을 걸어 내려가다가, 양 몇 마리의 사진을 찍으려고 멈췄다. **transit** 국제 환승객들은 비자를 소지하지 않고 공항을 떠나면 안된다. **turbulence** 난기류 때문에, 승무원들은 예정된 시간에 점심을 제공할 수 없었다. **voyage** 요즘, 대서양을 건너는 여행은 항공편으로 약 7시간 또는 배편으로 7일이 걸린다. / 그 단체 여행객들은 일주일 뒤 블라디보스톡에 도착하기 전에 기차로 러시아 전역을 여행했다. **wanderlust** 방랑벽으로 힘들다면, 단지 여행 계획을 세우는 것만으로도 기분이 좀 나아질 수 있다.

EXERCISES

A Match each definition with the correct word.

1 a feature or facility that is desirable   ⓐ itinerary

2 violent motion of the air or water   ⓑ carousel

3 a device that conveys baggage in an airport   ⓒ turbulence

4 to travel along a planned course   ⓓ wanderlust

5 a strong desire to travel   ⓔ destination

6 the act of visiting tourist attractions   ⓕ navigate

7 a detailed plan of a trip   ⓖ amenity

8 the place where someone or something is going   ⓗ sightseeing

B Choose the word that is closest in meaning to each underlined word.

1 Some professions involve facing serious risks and therefore require an intrepid attitude.
ⓐ naive   ⓑ reckless   ⓒ fearless   ⓓ practical

2 The thieves selected homes built in secluded areas so they could break into them unnoticed.
ⓐ affluent   ⓑ isolated   ⓒ venerable   ⓓ adjacent

3 Even when we're out on an excursion in the mountains, our phones connect us to the office.
ⓐ mission   ⓑ conference   ⓒ jaunt   ⓓ observance

4 Although the company had ample opportunities to hire minority candidates, it failed to do so.
ⓐ plentiful   ⓑ fortuitous   ⓒ noteworthy   ⓓ sporadic

5 The mere sound of their mother's voice is enough to soothe babies who have become upset.
ⓐ awaken   ⓑ identify   ⓒ alarm   ⓓ comfort

6 While a sumptuous dinner may be more enjoyable, a simple meal can be equally nutritious.
ⓐ communal   ⓑ lavish   ⓒ robust   ⓓ premature

7 Animals of all sorts used to roam this plain before the river was polluted by uranium mining.
ⓐ wander   ⓑ circumvent   ⓒ scrutinize   ⓓ stalk

> 의사소통
Communication

★★ **abound**
[əbáund]
ⓥ 아주 많다, 풍부하다

v. to exist in large numbers or amounts

Friendships **abound** when people choose to speak to one another in an open and honest manner.

★ **abridge**
[əbrídʒ]
ⓥ (책·희곡 등을) 요약[축약]하다
adj. abridged

v. to shorten a long piece of writing

The publishing company decided to **abridge** the novel to make it more accessible to readers.

syn. condense   *ant.* extend

★★★ **absolute**
[ǽbsəlùːt]
ⓐ 완전한, 완벽한

adj. total or complete

People rarely tell the **absolute** truth—white lies and other minor deceptions are inevitable.

syn. outright

★ **bicker**
[bíkər]
ⓥ (사소한 일로) 언쟁하다, 다투다

v. to argue about a trivial matter

The couple spent so much time **bickering** that they were unable to enjoy their vacation.

syn. squabble

★★ **communicative**
[kəmjúːnəkèitiv, -kə-]
ⓐ 이야기하기를 좋아하는, 속을 잘 털어놓는
v. communicate

adj. sharing ideas, feelings, and information often and easily

Without **communicative** employees, even the best-managed office will fail to run smoothly.

syn. talkative   *ant.* taciturn

★★ **companion**
[kəmpǽnjən]
ⓝ 동반자, 동행

n. a person who spends time with you in a friendly way

The elderly woman spent most of the train ride chatting happily with her two **companions**.

---

abound 사람들이 서로에게 개방적이고 정직한 태도로 말하기로 할 때, 우정은 두터워진다.　**abridge** 그 출판사는 독자들이 더 쉽게 읽을 수 있도록 그 소설을 요약하기로 결정했다.　**absolute** 사람들은 완벽한 진실을 말하는 경우가 드물다. 선의의 거짓말과 그 밖의 사소한 속임수는 피할 수 없다.　**bicker** 그 부부는 너무 많은 시간 동안 다투느라 휴가를 즐길 수 없었다.　**communicative** 가장 관리가 잘 되는 사무실조차도 직원들이 서로 소통하지 않으면, 원활하게 운영될 수 없을 것이다.　**companion** 그 노부인은 기차 여행의 대부분을 그녀의 두 동행인과 행복하게 이야기하며 보냈다.

ART & DESIGN

SOCIAL SCIENCE

NATURAL SCIENCE

HUMANITIES

EARTH & SPACE

SOCIAL ISSUES

conciliatory
[kənsíliətɔ̀ːri]

ⓐ 달래는, 회유적인

adj. seeking to make amends or end a disagreement

By sending a **conciliatory** message, the man was able to patch things up with his relative.

syn. appeasing　*ant.* antagonistic

consequence
[kánsəkwèns]

ⓝ 결과

adv. consequentially

n. a negative result of an action

One of the **consequences** of remaining silent is that others may perceive you as being standoffish.

syn. repercussion

convenient
[kənvíːnjənt]

ⓐ 편리한

n. convenience

adj. easy to access, do, or use

While digital communication may be **convenient**, it does little to strengthen interpersonal relationships.

ant. inconvenient

criterion
[kraitíəriən]

ⓝ (판단이나 결정을 위한) 기준

n. a standard upon which something is judged

One **criterion** of the speech contest is the effective use of eye contact and body language.

Useful **Tips**

현대 영어에서는 criterion의 복수형인 criteria가 더 많이 사용된다.

direct
[dirékt, dai-]

ⓐ 직접적인, 단도직입적인

adj. honest and clear

The woman gave **direct** answers to all the questions, which made a good impression.

syn. blunt　*ant.* vague

divert
[divɔ́ːrt, dai-]

ⓥ 방향을 바꾸게 하다, 전환시키다

n. diversion

v. to change the course or direction of something

Uncomfortable in the spotlight, the scientist tried to **divert** some of the attention to his colleagues.

syn. redirect

---

conciliatory 그 남자는 회유하는 메시지를 보냄으로써, 그의 친척과 화해할 수 있었다.　**consequence** 침묵으로 일관해서 생기는 결과 중의 하나는 다른 이들이 당신을 냉정하다고 여길 수 있다는 점이다.　**convenient** 디지털 의사소통이 편리할지는 몰라도, 대인 관계의 강화에는 별 도움이 되지 않는다.
criterion 말하기 대회의 한 가지 기준은 눈을 마주치는 것과 몸짓을 효과적으로 사용하는 것이다.　**direct** 그 여자는 모든 질문에 대해 단도직입적인 대답을 했고, 이것은 좋은 인상을 남겼다.　**divert** 그 과학자는 주목을 받는 것이 불편해서, 일부 관심을 그의 동료들에게 돌리려 했다.

★

elucidate

[ilúːsədèit]

[동] (더 자세히) 설명하다

v. to explain more clearly and in greater detail

The student requested that her professor **elucidate** a point he had made in the previous class.

syn. clarify

★★★

generation

[dʒènəréiʃən]

[명] 세대

n. all of the people born in a particular time period

Each **generation** comes up with its own slang and unique way of speaking that sets it apart.

★★

impede

[impíːd]

[동] 방해하다, 지연시키다

n. impediment

v. to hinder the progress of something

Nervousness or fear can sometimes **impede** a person's ability to communicate clearly.

syn. obstruct *ant.* expedite

★★

incisive

[insáisiv]

[형] 예리한, 날카로운

adj. able to express ideas clearly and directly

After looking over my report, my coworker made some **incisive** comments that were quite helpful.

★

incite

[insáit]

[동] 선동하다, 조장하다

n. incitement

v. to encourage extreme negative feelings or behavior

The politician's fiery rhetoric **incited** his supporters to attack the headquarters of his rival.

syn. provoke

★★★

interact

[ìntərǽkt]

[동] 소통하다, 교류하다

n. interaction

v. to communicate or spend time with others

Smiling and making eye contact will signal to others that you're interested in **interacting** with them.

---

elucidate 그 학생은 그녀의 교수에게 지난 수업 시간에 그가 제기한 사항에 대해 더 자세히 설명해 달라고 요청했다. **generation** 각 세대는 고유의 은어와 그 은어를 돋보이게 하는 독특한 말투를 생각해 낸다. **impede** 초조함이나 공포는 때때로 한 개인이 명확하게 의사소통하는 능력을 방해할 수 있다. **incisive** 내 동료는 나의 보고서를 훑어본 후, 상당히 도움이 되는 예리한 논평을 해 주었다. **incite** 그 정치인의 맹렬한 언사가 지지자들로 하여금 그의 경쟁자의 본부를 공격하도록 선동했다. **interact** 다른 이들에게 미소 짓고 눈을 마주치는 것은 당신이 그들과 소통하고 싶다는 뜻을 전달할 것이다.

★★ **mingle**
[míŋgl]
[동] 어울리다

v. to socialize with others at a gathering

Some people find it difficult to make small talk when they **mingle** with strangers at events.

★★ **miscommunication**
[mìskəmjuːnəkéiʃən]
[명] 의사소통 오류

n. a failure to explain or understand something properly

Due to a **miscommunication**, several of the club's members missed last month's meeting.

★★★ **mutual**
[mjúːtʃuəl]
[형] 상호 간의, 서로의

adj. shared, felt, or experienced by both sides

The two roommates made the **mutual** decision to find separate apartments to live in.

★★ **nonverbal**
[nὰnvə́ːrbəl]
[형] 말을 쓰지 않는, 비언어적인

adj. not involving spoken language

During a conversation, people send and receive numerous **nonverbal** cues that are essential.

ant. verbal

★★★ **oral**
[ɔ́ːrəl]
[형] 구어의, 구두의

adj. relating to spoken language

Worried about his upcoming **oral** exam, the student practiced answering questions in the mirror.

syn. spoken

Useful Tips

oral은 주로 history, exam, report와 결합하여, 각각 oral history(구전 역사), oral exam(구술시험), oral report(구두 보고)로 사용된다.

★★ **stand for**
[stænd fɔːr]
[동] 나타내다, 상징하다

v. to represent, usually as a symbol or abbreviation

ASAP, which **stands for** "as soon as possible," is commonly used in written business English.

syn. mean

---

mingle 어떤 사람들은 행사에서 낯선 이들과 어울릴 때, 가벼운 대화를 나누는 것을 어려워한다. **miscommunication** 의사소통의 오류 때문에 그 클럽 회원들 중 몇 명이 지난달 회의에 불참했다. **mutual** 그 두 룸메이트는 각자 살 아파트를 구하기로 상호 간 결정을 내렸다. **nonverbal** 대화를 나누는 동안, 사람들은 필수적인 수많은 비언어적 신호들을 주고 받는다. **oral** 그 학생은 다가오는 구술시험이 걱정이 되어서, 거울을 보며 질문에 답변하는 연습을 했다. **stand for** '가능한 한 빨리'를 나타내는 ASAP는 보통 서면 비즈니스 영어에서 사용된다.

★

taunt
[tɔːnt]
[동] 놀리다, 비웃다, 조롱하다

v. to use words to anger or humiliate someone

The soccer player was penalized for using bad language to **taunt** his opponents after scoring a goal.

syn. insult

> **Useful Tips**
> taunt는 잔인한 의도를 가지고 있는 반면, tease는 그 의도가 나쁘지 않고 유머스러운 느낌이 있다.

★★

throughout
[θruːáut]
[전] 도처에, 내내

prep. in every part of something

There were long pauses **throughout** the president's speech, which gave it a somber tone.

★★

timid
[tímid]
[형] 소심한

adj. shy and nervous

Timid people have a hard time expressing their needs, so they sometimes require encouragement.

syn. meek *ant.* bold

★★

trespass
[tréspæs]
[동] 무단 침입[출입]하다
n. trespassing

v. to enter someone's property without permission

Unable to read the posted signs, the foreign tourists accidentally **trespassed** on private land.

> **Useful Tips**
> 영어권 국가에서 일반인들이 들어가면 안 되는 장소에는 'No trespassing'이라는 표지가 흔히 보인다.

★★

via
[váiə, víːə]
[전] 경유하여, 통하여

prep. by way of

Teenagers prefer communicating **via** text messages, but older people find it cumbersome.

syn. through

★

vile
[vail]
[형] 극도로 불쾌한[나쁜]

adj. unpleasant and offensive

Some musicians use **vile** language to shock listeners and draw attention to their songs.

syn. disgusting *ant.* pleasant

---

taunt 그 축구 선수는 골을 넣은 후, 상대편 선수들을 조롱하기 위해 욕을 해서 벌칙을 받았다. **throughout** 대통령의 연설 내내 긴 침묵들이 있었는데, 이 때문에 침울한 어조가 되었다. **timid** 소심한 사람들은 그들이 원하는 것을 표현하는 데 어려움을 겪기 때문에, 때때로 격려가 필요하다. **trespass** 그 외국인 관광객들은 게시된 표지판을 읽지 못해서, 뜻하지 않게 사유지에 무단 침입했다. **via** 십 대들은 문자 메시지로 의사소통하는 것을 선호하지만, 나이가 든 사람들은 그것을 귀찮게 여긴다. **vile** 일부 음악가들은 듣는 이들을 놀라게 하고 자신들의 노래에 관심을 끌기 위해 극도로 불쾌한 말을 사용한다.

EXERCISES

ART & DESIGN

SOCIAL SCIENCE

NATURAL SCIENCE

HUMANITIES

EARTH & SPACE

SOCIAL ISSUES

A Match each definition with the correct word.

1 shared, felt, or experienced by both sides
ⓐ generation

2 to enter someone's property without permission
ⓑ abound

3 a standard upon which something is judged
ⓒ criterion

4 to communicate or spend time with others
ⓓ trespass

5 all of the people born in a particular time period
ⓔ taunt

6 to exist in large numbers or amounts
ⓕ mutual

7 to use words to anger or humiliate someone
ⓖ interact

8 in every part of something
ⓗ throughout

B Choose the word that is closest in meaning to each underlined word.

1 The use of racial slurs will always <u>incite</u> an angry response from considerate individuals.
ⓐ thwart   ⓑ provoke   ⓒ indicate   ⓓ mimic

2 After finding <u>vile</u> conditions in the kitchen, the health inspectors closed the restaurant down.
ⓐ unrequired   ⓑ congested   ⓒ disgusting   ⓓ astounding

3 Young siblings often <u>bicker</u>, but they usually work out their differences if given some time.
ⓐ squabble   ⓑ frolic   ⓒ scheme   ⓓ coordinate

4 The woman's straightforward and <u>direct</u> manner shows she is focused on her work.
ⓐ blunt   ⓑ swift   ⓒ arrogant   ⓓ humble

5 As time passes, the <u>consequences</u> of the nuclear accident are becoming more and more clear.
ⓐ expectations ⓑ repercussions ⓒ antecedents   ⓓ resolutions

6 Some workplace technology ends up <u>impeding</u> workers rather than saving them time.
ⓐ empowering   ⓑ obstructing   ⓒ informing   ⓓ rearranging

7 Sensing the guest's frustration, the hotel manager tried a more <u>conciliatory</u> approach.
ⓐ demanding   ⓑ disturbing   ⓒ energizing   ⓓ appeasing

405

Lesson 55 — Child & Adolescent Development

아동 및 청소년 발달

acquiesce
[ǽkwiés]

ⓥ (수동적으로) 동의하다, 묵인하다

v. to accept or agree to something reluctantly

A parent who **acquiesces** to a child's every demand is doing more harm than good.

syn. give in

allay
[əléi]

ⓥ 가라앉다, 완화시키다

v. to lessen the intensity of something negative

Some bedtime stories are designed to **allay** fears of the unknown that kids might be experiencing.

syn. alleviate

assimilate
[əsíməlèit]

ⓥ (아이디어나 정보를) 자기 것으로 흡수하다

n. assimilation

v. to take in new ideas or information

Infants are constantly **assimilating** new ideas simply by observing the world around them.

attachment
[ətǽtʃmənt]

ⓝ 애착

v. attach

n. strong feelings of fondness for someone or something

If a child fails to form an **attachment** to one parent, it can lead to conflicts down the road.

syn. bond

attentive
[əténtiv]

ⓐ 주의 깊은

v. attend

adj. paying close attention to someone's needs

Attentive caregivers provide children with a psychological safety net while they learn and explore.

syn. considerate   *ant.* negligent

autonomous
[ɔːtánəməs]

ⓐ 자주적인, 자율적인

n. autonomy

adj. able to live or make decisions without outside interference

The process of becoming an **autonomous** adult may include a period of teenage rebellion.

syn. independent   *ant.* dependent

---

acquiesce 아이의 모든 요구에 동의해 주는 부모는 아이에게 도움이 된다기보다 해를 끼치고 있는 것이다.   **allay** 잠재울 때 들려주는 어떤 이야기들은 아이들이 느끼고 있을 수 있는 미지의 것에 대한 두려움을 완화시키도록 고안되어 있다.   **assimilate** 유아들은 단순히 자기 주위의 세계를 관찰함으로써 새로운 개념들을 끊임없이 자기 것으로 흡수하고 있다.   **attachment** 아이가 한쪽 부모에 대한 애착을 형성하지 못하면, 언젠가는 갈등을 유발할 수 있다.   **attentive** 주의 깊게 아이를 돌보는 사람들은 아이들이 배우고 탐사하는 동안 심리적인 안전망을 제공한다.   **autonomous** 자주적인 성인이 되는 과정에는 십 대의 반항 시기가 포함될 수도 있다.

★★ **babble**
[bǽbl]
[동] (어린아이 등이) 서투른 말로 지껄이다

v. to speak in a way that cannot be understood
When babies **babble**, they are taking the first step toward mastering verbal communication.
syn. prattle

★ **burgeoning**
[bə́ːrdʒəniŋ]
[형] 급성장하는
v. burgeon

adj. developing rapidly
Infants are eager to test out their **burgeoning** motor skills by rolling over and beginning to crawl.
syn. growing *ant.* shrinking

★★ **cognitive**
[kágnətiv]
[형] 인식의, 인지의
n. cognition

adj. relating to the process of thinking or learning
Cognitive development occurs hand in hand with physical development, and both are essential.

★★ **concrete**
[kánkriːt]
[형] 1. 구체적인, 유형의
2. 명확한

adj. 1 capable of being seen or touched *syn.* tangible *ant.* abstract
2 clear and detailed *syn.* precise *ant.* vague
1. An understanding of **concrete** objects occurs in the early stages of child development.
2. Moody teenagers may struggle to give **concrete** examples of what is frustrating them.

★★ **custody**
[kʌ́stədi]
[명] 양육권

n. the legal right to raise and care for a child
After the child's parents died in an accident, a court awarded **custody** to his maternal grandmother.
syn. guardianship

★★ **detrimental**
[dètrəméntl]
[형] 해로운
n. detriment

adj. having negative effects
Poor nutrition can be **detrimental** to a child's development, so parents should plan meals carefully.
syn. harmful *ant.* beneficial

babble 아기들이 서투르게 말할 때, 그들은 언어적 의사소통 숙달로 향하는 첫발을 내딛고 있는 것이다. **burgeoning** 유아들은 몸을 뒤집고 기기 시작함으로써 급성장하는 운동 기능들을 시험해 보고 싶어한다. **cognitive** 인지 발달은 신체 발달과 밀접히 연관되어 일어나며, 이 두 가지 발달 모두 필수적이다. **concrete** 1. 구체적 대상에 대한 이해는 아동 발달의 초기 단계들에서 일어난다. 2. 침울한 십 대들은 자신에게 좌절감을 주는 명확한 예들을 제시하는 것을 어려워할 수도 있다. **custody** 그 아이의 부모가 사고로 사망한 후, 법정은 아이의 외할머니에게 양육권을 주었다. **detrimental** 영양실조는 아이의 발달에 해로울 수 있으므로, 부모는 세심하게 식사 계획을 세워야 한다.

★
★ **dyslexia**
[disléksiə]
몡 난독증
adj. dyslexic

n. a disorder that makes reading and writing difficult
After being diagnosed with **dyslexia**, the teenager began receiving special help after school.

★
egocentric
[ìːgouséntrik]
몡 이기적인
n. ego

adj. overly focused on oneself
Egocentric behavior is undesirable in adults, but it is normal and healthy in developing children.
syn. selfish   *ant.* selfless

★
evince
[ivíns]
통 (감정 등을) 나타내다

v. to show signs of a feeling or trait
The adolescent **evinced** no signs of guilt about his bad behavior, which caused his parents to worry.
syn. reveal

★
★ **exude**
[igzúːd]
통 (자신·매력이) 넘치다,
스며 나오게 하다

v. to show great amounts of something
Some young children naturally **exude** confidence, while others are more hesitant to try new things.
syn. radiate

★
★
★ **foster**
[fɔ́ːstər]
통 1. 조성하다, 발전시키다
2. 위탁 양육하다

v. 1 to encourage something to develop   *syn.* promote
2 to raise a child that is not your own
1. The parents **fostered** their daughter's interest in art by buying her a small easel and a set of paints.
2. The elderly couple **fostered** many children over the years, all of whom eventually found permanent homes.

Useful Tips
아이를 위탁 받아 기르는 가정을 foster home, 수양부모를 foster parents라고 한다.

★
★
★ **fulfill**
[fulfíl]
통 달성하다, 실현하다
n. fulfillment

v. to complete or achieve
Knowing how to set realistic goals and then **fulfill** them is a useful life skill for young people.
syn. accomplish

---

dyslexia 그 십 대는 난독증 진단을 받은 후, 방과 후에 특별한 도움을 받기 시작했다.   **egocentric** 성인들의 경우 이기적인 행동은 바람직하지 않지만, 자라고 있는 아이들의 경우에는 정상적이며 건강한 것이다.   **evince** 그 청소년은 자신의 나쁜 행동에 대한 죄책감을 전혀 나타내지 않아서, 그의 부모를 걱정하게 만들었다.
exude 어떤 어린아이들은 본성적으로 자신감이 넘치는 반면, 다른 아이들은 새로운 일을 시도해 보는 것을 좀 더 망설인다.   **foster** 1. 그 부모는 딸에게 작은 이젤과 물감 세트를 사 주어, 아이가 미술에 대해 관심을 갖게 했다.   2. 그 노부부는 수년간 많은 아이들을 위탁 양육했는데, 결국 그들 모두 영구적인 가정을 찾았다.
fulfill 현실적인 목표들을 세운 다음 그것들을 달성하는 법을 아는 것은 청년들에게 유용한 생활 기술이다.

★★★ **grasp**
[græsp]
[동] 완전히 이해하다, 파악하다

v. to fully understand

Some children require a little extra assistance in order to **grasp** concepts that are difficult or unfamiliar.

syn. get

★ **hyperactivity**
[hàipəræktívəti]
[명] 활동항진증
adj. hyperactive

n. a condition that makes people excessively active

Hyperactivity can lead to bad behavior if a child isn't given a chance to burn off excess energy.

★ **impairment**
[impέərmənt]
[명] 장애, 손상
v. impair

n. something that prevents proper functioning

Hearing **impairments** in infants are sometimes misdiagnosed as serious learning disabilities.

★★ **inclined**
[inkláind]
[형] …하는 경향이 있는
n. inclination

adj. tending or likely to do something

Many teenagers are **inclined** to spend time alone in their rooms, but it is not something to worry about.

syn. apt

★★ **insolent**
[ínsələnt]
[형] 버릇없는, 무례한
n. insolence

adj. failing to show proper respect

Due to her **insolent** behavior, the young girl was constantly being scolded by her parents.

syn. disrespectful *ant.* polite

★★ **intellectual**
[ìntəléktʃuəl]
[형] 지적인
[명] 지성인

adj. relating to intelligence or an interest in learning *syn.* cerebral

The ability to understand abstract concepts occurs in the later stages of a child's **intellectual** development.

n. an intelligent person who has an interest in academics
syn. scholar

Not every child will grow up to be an **intellectual**, but many people believe success in the classroom is important for everyone.

grasp 어떤 아이들은 어렵거나 익숙하지 않은 개념들을 완전히 이해하기 위해 약간의 추가적인 도움을 필요로 한다. **hyperactivity** 아이에게 과잉 에너지를 소모시킬 기회가 주어지지 않으면, 활동항진증은 불량 행위를 유발할 수 있다. **impairment** 유아들의 청각 장애는 때때로 심각한 학습 장애로 오진된다. **inclined** 많은 십 대들이 자기 방에서 혼자 시간을 보내는 경향이 있지만, 그것은 우려할 일이 아니다. **insolent** 그 어린 소녀는 버릇없는 행동 때문에 부모에게 계속 야단을 맞았다. **intellectual** 추상적인 개념들을 이해하는 능력은 아동의 지적 발달 후기 단계에서 생긴다. / 모든 아이가 자라서 지성인이 되지는 않겠지만, 많은 사람이 학업에 있어서의 성공은 모두에게 중요하다고 여긴다.

★
★ **intervention**
[ìntərvénʃən]
ⓝ 개입, 조정, 중재

v. intervene

n. the act of getting involved in a situation to help solve it

Children benefit from being allowed to solve problems without the **intervention** of their parents.

★
★ **intimidate**
[intímədèit]
ⓥ 겁을 주다

n. intimidation

v. to scare someone into doing what you want

Some parents **intimidate** their children into doing what they're told by raising their voices.

★
★ **juvenile**
[dʒúːvənl]
ⓐ 1. 청소년의
　　2. 유치한

adj. 1 relating to people who are not yet adults
　　　2 acting in a childish way

1. **Juvenile** crime can often be traced back to unresolved problems in the home or classroom.
2. As children become teens, they should begin to understand when **juvenile** behavior is inappropriate.

★
★ **mature**
[mətʃúər]
ⓐ 성숙한

n. maturation

adj. fully grown

A **mature** adult is better able to handle high-pressure situations than a child or teenager.

ant. immature

★
★ **naive**
[nɑːíːv]
ⓐ 순진한

adj. easy to fool due to a lack of experience

Kids are naturally **naive**, but this will change over time as they acquire more knowledge and experience.

syn. credulous　*ant.* skeptical

★
★ **nurture**
[nɔ́ːrtʃər]
ⓥ 양육하다, 교육하다

v. to take care of or help develop

The role of parents is to **nurture** their children and help them develop into responsible adults.

syn. care for

---

intervention 부모의 개입 없이 문제들을 해결하도록 허용되는 것은 아이들에게 도움이 된다.　**intimidate** 어떤 부모는 언성을 높임으로써 자녀에게 겁을 주어 시킨 일을 하게 한다.　**juvenile** 1. 청소년 범죄의 원인은 흔히 가정이나 학급에서 해결되지 못한 문제들로 거슬러 올라갈 수 있다. 2. 아이들이 십 대가 되면, 유치한 행동이 부적절한 때가 언제인지를 이해하기 시작해야 한다.　**mature** 성숙한 어른은 스트레스가 많은 상황들을 아이나 십 대보다 더 잘 처리할 수 있다.
naive 아이들은 원래 순진하지만, 시간이 지나며 더 많은 지식과 경험을 얻게 되면서 이런 특성은 바뀔 것이다.　**nurture** 부모의 역할은 자녀를 양육하고 그들이 책임감 있는 성인으로 성장하게 돕는 것이다.

obey
[oubéi]
ⓥ 따르다, 복종하다
adj. obedient

v. to do what you are told to do
Patient explanations are sometimes required to help kids understand why they must **obey** rules.

syn. comply   *ant.* disobey

Useful Tips
또래나 동료 집단으로부터 받는 사회적 압력을 peer pressure라고 한다.

peer
[piər]
ⓝ 또래

n. someone in the same age group or profession
Only children need opportunities to interact with their **peers** in order to be socially successful.

puberty
[pjúːbərti]
ⓝ 사춘기

n. the time when children begin to physically become adults
A frank talk about **puberty** will make this difficult time easier for a child to deal with.

rear
[riər]
ⓥ (아이·가축을) 기르다

v. to bring up a child or animal
Reared in a rural area, the teenager was overwhelmed by the hustle and bustle of city life.

syn. raise

resilience
[rizíljəns]
ⓝ 복원력
adj. resilient

n. the quality of being able to recover from adversity
Adults often underestimate the **resilience** of children, who can overcome even serious trauma.

shelter
[ʃéltər]
ⓥ 보호하다
ⓝ 보호소, 주거지

v. to protect someone from danger
Parents who want to **shelter** their kids from the real world may end up hindering their development.

n. a place that protects people from danger   *syn.* sanctuary
Along with food, **shelter** and clothing, parents must provide their children with love and affection.

---

obey 규칙을 따라야 하는 이유를 아이들이 이해하도록 돕는 데에는 때로 인내심 있는 설명이 필요하다.   **peer** 외동이 사회적으로 성공하기 위해서는 또래들과 교류할 기회가 필요하다.   **puberty** 사춘기에 대한 솔직한 대화는 아이가 이 힘든 시기를 더 쉽게 헤쳐 나가게 해 줄 것이다.   **rear** 시골에서 자란 그 십 대는 도시 생활의 분주함에 압도당했다.   **resilience** 어른들은 종종 아이들의 복원력을 과소평가하지만, 아이들은 심각한 정신적 외상조차 극복할 수 있다.
shelter 자녀들을 현실 세계로부터 보호하고 싶어하는 부모는 결국 그들의 발달을 저해하게 될 수 있다. / 부모는 자녀들에게 음식, 주거지, 의복과 더불어 사랑과 애정을 주어야 한다.

★★★

stubborn

[stʌ́bərn]

[형] 고집 센

adj. unwilling to compromise or admit mistakes

When children reach the age of three, they often become **stubborn** and hard to deal with.

syn. obstinate *ant.* flexible

Useful Tips

아주 고집이 센 사람을 가리켜 as stubborn as a mule이라고 표현할 수 있다.

★★

stunt

[stʌnt]

[동] 방해하다, 저해하다

v. to hinder growth or development

Scientific research now supports the old adage that smoking can **stunt** a teenager's growth.

syn. inhibit *ant.* facilitate

★

subsequently

[sʌ́bsikwəntli]

[부] 나중에, 그 후에

adv. after something else has happened

The child went through a difficult period; **subsequently**, her grades began to drop.

syn. afterward *ant.* previously

★★

tantrum

[tǽntrəm]

[명] 성질, 짜증, 화

n. extreme bad behavior in response to not getting one's way

Children are far less likely to throw **tantrums** in public if they are well fed and well rested.

syn. outburst

★★

trigger

[trígər]

[동] 촉발하다

v. to cause something to happen

Physical changes in adolescents are **triggered** by the release of hormones into their bodies.

syn. provoke

★

wean

[wiːn]

[동] 이유시키다

v. to change a baby's diet from mother's milk to solid food

Parents who are ready to **wean** their children should be aware that it may be an extended process.

---

stubborn 아이들이 세 살이 되면, 흔히 고집이 세져 다루기가 힘들어진다. **stunt** 과학적 연구는 이제 흡연이 십 대의 성장을 저해할 수 있다는 옛 격언에 힘을 실어주고 있다. **subsequently** 그 아이는 힘든 시기를 겪었고, 그 후에 성적이 떨어지기 시작했다. **tantrum** 아이들이 잘 먹고 잘 쉬면, 공공장소에서 성질을 부릴 가능성이 훨씬 더 적다. **trigger** 청소년의 신체 변화들은 체내 호르몬 분비에 의해 촉발된다. **wean** 아이들을 이유시킬 준비가 된 부모는 그것이 장기간에 걸친 과정이 될 수 있다는 것을 알고 있어야 한다.

EXERCISES

A Match each definition with the correct word.

1 someone in the same age group or profession   ⓐ resilience

2 a condition that makes people excessively active   ⓑ impairment

3 to take in new ideas or information   ⓒ dyslexia

4 fully grown   ⓓ assimilate

5 something that prevents proper functioning   ⓔ peer

6 a disorder that makes reading and writing difficult   ⓕ mature

7 the quality of being able to recover from adversity   ⓖ wean

8 to change a baby's diet from mother's milk to solid food   ⓗ hyperactivity

B Choose the word that is closest in meaning to each underlined word.

1 The insolent courtroom behavior of the defendant caused the judge to grow angry.
    ⓐ disrespectful   ⓑ dazzling   ⓒ insincere   ⓓ unconventional

2 The tech company produces digital devices that help disabled people live autonomous lives.
    ⓐ complicated   ⓑ lengthy   ⓒ active   ⓓ independent

3 Contrary to the expectations of traditional gender roles, men are capable of nurturing children.
    ⓐ taking after   ⓑ calming down   ⓒ showing off   ⓓ caring for

4 Many parents are hesitant to take their kids on a plane, fearful that they'll throw a tantrum.
    ⓐ reaction   ⓑ refusal   ⓒ outburst   ⓓ hiatus

5 The government has instituted new public health rules, but many people are refusing to obey.
    ⓐ vacate   ⓑ comply   ⓒ testify   ⓓ diversify

6 Facial expressions sometimes evince emotions that people are too polite to express in words.
    ⓐ reveal   ⓑ alter   ⓒ redirect   ⓓ arrange

7 The company acquiesced to its employees' demands and agreed to hire additional workers.
    ⓐ kept on   ⓑ gave in   ⓒ held up   ⓓ shut down

A Choose the correct words.

1 The word chronic has the same meaning as

    ⓐ distasteful   ⓑ toxic   ⓒ protracted   ⓓ unstable

2 The word ravenous has the same meaning as

    ⓐ intangible   ⓑ lethargic   ⓒ cowardly   ⓓ voracious

3 The word haphazard has the same meaning as

    ⓐ fatal   ⓑ remote   ⓒ random   ⓓ exposed

4 The word attentive has the same meaning as

    ⓐ considerate   ⓑ present   ⓒ ubiquitous   ⓓ distracted

5 The word abridge has the same meaning as

    ⓐ traverse   ⓑ decimate   ⓒ insulate   ⓓ condense

6 The word mishap has the same meaning as

    ⓐ rally   ⓑ blunder   ⓒ reversal   ⓓ midsection

7 The word obese has the same meaning as

    ⓐ nutritious   ⓑ suitable   ⓒ corpulent   ⓓ eminent

8 The word proper has the same meaning as

    ⓐ appropriate   ⓑ arranged   ⓒ proficient   ⓓ prosperous

B Fill in the blanks with the best words from the box.

1 It generally takes from one to three days for the body to completely _____ a meal.

2 A(n) _____ with the baker resulted in the cake having the wrong name on it.

3 The family dog was the child's constant _____, following her everywhere she went.

4 It took the _____ of a flight attendant to stop the two passengers from fighting.

5 A developmental _____ has caused the boy to fall behind the rest of his classmates.

6 Nurses must follow a strict _____ when dealing with patients with infectious diseases.

> delay   miscommunication   protocol   companion   digest   intervention

C Read the following passages.

ART & DESIGN

SOCIAL SCIENCE

NATURAL SCIENCE

HUMANITIES

EARTH & SPACE

SOCIAL ISSUES

[1-2] **1** Choose one word that fits both blanks.

> The trekkers were deep in the wilderness when a powerful storm hit. Wanting to _____ themselves from the rain and wind, they ran to a small, rundown cottage. The elderly couple living there kindly offered them _____, and the trekkers happily shared their food with them.

ⓐ relish ⓑ voyage ⓒ shelter ⓓ quarantine

2 Choose the appropriate pair of words to fill in the blanks.

> For many years, frozen yogurt has been a popular alternative for people who want to _____ their craving for ice cream without all the calories. However, sugar is often added to enhance the yogurt's _____, so it may not be the healthy option many people believe it to be.

ⓐ stunt — criterion ⓑ indulge — flavor
ⓒ prolong — custody ⓓ taunt — wanderlust

[3-4]

> Members of an international organization are visiting a village in the mountains. Although it is tranquil now, the village was severely damaged in a recent war. They are there to repair its sewage system and restore running water. After admiring the breathtaking views, they got to work.

3 In the context of the passage, tranquil means _____.
ⓐ serene ⓑ impoverished ⓒ victorious ⓓ distant

4 The word breathtaking in the passage could best be replaced by
ⓐ risky ⓑ awesome ⓒ insufficient ⓓ bizarre

[5-6]

> Timid schoolchildren are far less likely to be proactive in establishing healthy social relationships than their peers. At organized school events where students from different classes are brought together, for example, they may stay close to familiar faces and refuse to _____ with others. It is up to teachers and other adults to gently nudge them into being more socially adventurous.

5 The word Timid in the passage is closest in meaning to
ⓐ infantile ⓑ adolescent ⓒ studious ⓓ meek

6 Choose the word that is most suitable for the blank.
ⓐ ignore ⓑ disembark ⓒ mingle ⓓ allay

415

★★
abolish
[əbáliʃ]
ⓥ (법률·제도·조직을) 폐지하다

v. to officially get rid of or put an end to something

The government **abolished** all of the laws that were designed to keep the races separate.

★
animosity
[æ̀nəmásəti]
ⓝ 반감, 적대감

n. strong feelings of dislike

Sadly, people often display **animosity** towards those they perceive to be strange or different.

syn. hostility　*ant.* friendliness

★★
compulsive
[kəmpʌ́lsiv]
ⓐ 강박적인, 조절이 힘든
n. compulsion

adj. caused by an irresistible desire

It turns out that gender has nothing to do with **compulsive** behavior, which is generally caused by obsessive thoughts.

★★
consensus
[kənsénsəs]
ⓝ 의견 일치, 합의

n. a general agreement among everyone involved

The current scientific **consensus** is that there is no biological basis for dividing human beings by race.

ant. disagreement

★
demographic
[dèməgræfik]
ⓝ (특정) 인구 집단

n. a specific part of the population

Young women make up the **demographic** that is most often targeted by advertisers.

★★
deport
[dipɔ́ːrt]
ⓥ 강제 추방하다
n. deportation

v. to force someone to leave a country they are not a citizen of

According to research, black immigrants in the USA face a greater risk of being **deported** than any other group.

syn. expel

---

abolish 정부는 인종들을 분리하기 위해 만들어진 모든 법들을 폐지했다.　**animosity** 슬프게도, 사람들은 낯설거나 다르다고 여기는 이들에게 종종 적대감을 드러낸다.　**compulsive** 강박적인 행동은 성별과 무관한 것으로 밝혀졌는데, 이는 일반적으로 강박적 사고에 의해 발생한다.　**consensus** 인간을 인종별로 나눌 생물학적인 근거가 없다는 것이 현재의 과학적 합의이다.　**demographic** 젊은 여성들은 광고주들이 가장 빈번하게 타깃으로 삼는 인구 집단이다.
deport 연구에 따르면, 미국의 흑인 이민자들은 다른 어떤 집단보다 추방당할 위험이 더 크다.

★
despise
[dispáiz]
ⓥ 경멸하다

v. to hate intensely

People who **despise** sexist behavior are working together to put an end to it.

syn. loathe *ant.* adore

★
discord
[dískɔːrd]
ⓝ 불화, 다툼

adj. discordant

n. a lack of agreement or harmony

Discord between the races is a centuries-old problem without any simple solutions.

syn. strife *ant.* unity

★★★
discriminate
[diskrímənèit]
ⓥ 차별하다

n. discrimination

v. to treat someone unfairly based on race, gender, ethnicity, etc.

Any company or business that **discriminates** against female job applicants is breaking the law.

★★★
exploit
[iksplɔ́it]
ⓥ (부당하게) 이용하다, 착취하다

n. exploitation

v. to take advantage of for personal gain

Some unethical politicians choose to **exploit** racial tensions in order to get more votes.

★★
flee
[fliː]
ⓥ (사람·장소 등에서) 달아나다, 도망치다

v. to escape from danger

The family decided to **flee** the country in order to avoid the racial abuse they had been facing.

syn. run away

★★
genocide
[dʒénəsàid]
ⓝ 집단 학살, 종족 학살

adj. genocidal

n. the murder of everyone from a specific nation, religion, race, or ethnic group

In order to prevent future **genocides**, humans must view themselves as members of a single race.

---

despise 성차별적인 행동을 경멸하는 사람들이 그것을 근절하기 위해 함께 노력하고 있다. **discord** 인종 간의 불화는 간단한 해결책이 없는 수백 년 된 문제이다.
discriminate 여성 구직자들을 차별하는 회사나 기업은 법을 어기고 있는 것이다. **exploit** 일부 비윤리적인 정치인들은 더 많은 표를 얻기 위해 인종 간의
갈등을 이용한다. **flee** 그 가족은 그들이 겪어 왔던 인종 학대를 피하기 위해 그 나라에서 도망치기로 결정했다. **genocide** 향후의 집단[종족] 학살을 방지하기
위해, 인간은 스스로를 단일 민족의 일원으로 여겨야 한다.

★★ **hospitality**
[hàspətǽləti]
[명] 환대, 후한 대접
adj. hospitable

n. **warm and friendly behavior towards visitors**
The Asian family's new neighbors welcomed them and showed them great **hospitality**.

★ **inconceivable**
[ìnkənsíːvəbl]
[형] 상상[생각]도 할 수 없는, 믿을 수 없는
v. conceive

adj. **hard to imagine or believe**
It is **inconceivable** to many youths that women didn't have the right to vote until relatively recently.
syn. unbelievable

★★★ **invade**
[invéid]
[동] 침략하다, 쳐들어가다
n. invasion

v. **to enter another country's land by force**
European armies **invaded** many African and Asian countries in order to colonialize them.

★★ **massacre**
[mǽsəkər]
[명] 대학살

n. **the murder of a large number of people**
A racial **massacre** that took place in Tulsa, Oklahoma, in 1921 was ignored by history books for decades.

★★★ **minority**
[minɔ́ːrəti, mai-]
[명] 1. 소수 집단
2. (절반이 못 되는) 소수

n. **1 a small group within a society that is different in some way**
2 less than half of the total *ant.* majority

1. Asians are currently the largest **minority** in Canada, making up nearly 18% of the total population.
2. A **minority** of Americans are male, as approximately 50.8% of the population is female.

★★★ **nomad**
[nóumæd]
[명] 유목민, 방랑자
adj. nomadic

n. **someone who moves from place to place with no fixed home**
Women played many powerful and important roles in the traditional culture of Central Asian **nomads**.

Useful Tips
현대 영어에서 digital nomad는 이곳저곳을 돌아다니면서 인터넷을 이용해 원격으로 일하는 사람들을 일컫는다.

hospitality 그 아시아계 가족의 새로운 이웃들은 그들을 환영했고, 큰 환대를 해 주었다. **inconceivable** 비교적 최근까지 여성들에게 투표할 권리가 없었다는 사실이 많은 젊은이들에게는 상상도 할 수 없는 일이다. **invade** 유럽의 군대들은 아프리카와 아시아의 많은 국가들을 식민지화하기 위해 침략했다. **massacre** 1921년에 오클라호마 주의 털사에서 일어난 인종 대학살은 수십 년 동안 역사책에서 무시되었다. **minority** 1. 아시아인들은 현재 캐나다에서 가장 큰 소수 민족 집단인데, 캐나다 전체 인구의 거의 18 퍼센트를 차지한다. 2. 미국 인구의 약 50.8 퍼센트가 여성이므로, 소수의 미국인은 남성이 된다. **nomad** 중앙아시아 유목민들의 전통 문화에서 여성들은 강력하고 중요한 역할들을 많이 했다.

★★ **norm**
[nɔːrm]
[명] 표준, 규범, 기준
adj. normal

n. **something that is considered standard and acceptable**
Traditional gender **norms** are constantly being challenged by younger members of societies.

★★★ **obstacle**
[ábstəkl]
[명] 장애(물)

n. **something that blocks or hinders progress**
Modern women have succeeded in overcoming many **obstacles** in the business world.
syn. obstruction

★★ **outnumber**
[àutnʌ́mbər]
[동] …보다 수가 더 많다, 수적으로 우세하다

v. **to exist in greater numbers than something else**
Black South Africans vastly **outnumbered** their white counterparts during the apartheid era.
syn. exceed

★ **patronizing**
[péitrənàiziŋ]
[형] 잘난 체하는, 거만한
v. patronize

adj. **speaking or behaving in a manner that suggests the other person is inferior**
The customer spoke to an Asian clerk at the local supermarket in a **patronizing** manner.
syn. condescending

★★★ **prejudice**
[prédʒudis]
[명] 편견

n. **a bias against a group of people based on preconceived notions**
People may not even be aware of some of the **prejudices** that influence the way they behave.
syn. intolerance

★★ **ridicule**
[rídikjùːl]
[명] 조롱, 조소
[동] 비웃다, 조롱하다
adj. ridiculous

n. **an instance of making fun of someone in a cruel way**
syn. mockery
Early civil rights activists who demanded respect and fair treatment had to endure terrible **ridicule**.

v. **to make fun of someone in a cruel way** *syn.* mock
Despite being **ridiculed** by her classmates, the young girl was proud of her diverse racial background.

norm 사회의 젊은 구성원들이 전통적인 성 규범에 끊임없이 이의를 제기하고 있다. **obstacle** 현대 여성들은 비즈니스 세계에서 많은 장애물들을 극복하는 데 성공했다. **outnumber** 아파르트헤이트[인종 차별 정책] 시대에는 남아프리카의 흑인들의 수가 백인들의 수보다 훨씬 더 많았다. **patronizing** 그 고객은 지역 슈퍼마켓의 아시아계 점원에게 거만한 태도로 말했다. **prejudice** 사람들은 그들이 행동하는 방식에 영향을 미치는 일부 편견들을 인식조차 못하고 있을 수도 있다. **ridicule** 존중과 평등한 대우를 요구한 초기 시민권 운동가들은 끔찍한 조롱을 견뎌야만 했다. / 그 어린 소녀는 급우들에게 비웃음을 당했음에도, 자신의 다양한 인종적 배경을 자랑스러워했다.

★★ **segregation**
[sègrigéiʃən]
[명] (인종·종교·성별에 따른) 분리[차별] (정책)
v. segregate

n. the practice of separating people based on race, religion, or sex

The policy of racial **segregation** in the United States was ended by the Civil Rights Act of 1964.

syn. separation *ant.* integration

★★★ **stereotype**
[stériətàip]
[명] 고정 관념
adj. stereotypical

n. a set idea about a type of person or thing

Even a positive **stereotype** about a group of people can have damaging effects on individuals.

★★ **sympathize**
[símpəθàiz]
[동] 동정하다, 측은히 여기다
n. sympathy

v. to show compassion toward someone who is suffering

Many people **sympathize** with victims of racial injustice, and more and more of them are taking action.

★★ **urge**
[əːrdʒ]
[명] 욕구, 충동
[동] 촉구하다, 요구하다

n. a strong feeling of wanting to do something *syn.* compulsion

Feeling the **urge** to get involved, the teens volunteered at an organization promoting racial harmony.

v. to strongly suggest that someone should do something *syn.* implore

Hundreds of people called the politician, **urging** her to vote for the bill banning racial profiling.

Useful Tips
urge는 때때로 on과 함께 쓰여 'The crowd urged the runners on.'에서처럼 '응원하다'라는 의미로 쓰이기도 한다.

★ **varied**
[vέərid]
[형] 다양한

adj. including a wide range of types

The **varied** racial backgrounds of the people of this neighborhood make it an exciting place to live.

syn. diverse *ant.* uniform

★★ **withstand**
[wiθstǽnd]
[동] 견뎌내다, 이겨내다

v. to endure something difficult or unpleasant

It takes courage and strength to **withstand** the taunts and insults of intolerant people.

syn. resist

segregation 미국의 인종 분리 정책은 1964년 민권법에 의해 종료되었다. **stereotype** 어떤 인종 집단에 대한 긍정적인 고정 관념조차도 개개인에게 해로운 영향을 끼칠 수 있다. **sympathize** 많은 사람들이 인종 차별의 피해자들을 동정하며, 그들 중 점점 더 많은 이들이 행동에 나서고 있다. **urge** 그 십 대들은 참여하고 싶은 욕구를 느껴서, 인종의 화합을 촉진하는 단체에서 자원봉사를 했다. / 수백 명의 사람들이 그 정치인에게 전화를 걸어 인종 프로파일링(피부색·인종에 기반하여 용의자를 찾는 수사 기법)을 금지하는 법안에 찬성할 것을 촉구했다. **varied** 이 마을 사람들의 다양한 인종적 배경은 이곳을 살기 흥미로운 곳으로 만든다. **withstand** 편협한 사람들의 조롱과 모욕을 견뎌내려면 용기와 힘이 필요하다.

EXERCISES

ART & DESIGN

SOCIAL SCIENCE

NATURAL SCIENCE

HUMANITIES

EARTH & SPACE

SOCIAL ISSUES

A Match each definition with the correct word.

1 a general agreement among everyone involved   ⓐ stereotype

2 something that is considered standard and acceptable   ⓑ invade

3 a set idea about a type of person or thing   ⓒ norm

4 warm and friendly behavior towards visitors   ⓓ hospitality

5 a specific part of the population   ⓔ demographic

6 someone who moves from place to place with no fixed home   ⓕ nomad

7 to officially get rid of or put an end to something   ⓖ abolish

8 to enter another country's land by force   ⓗ consensus

B Choose the word that is closest in meaning to each underlined word.

1 When it comes to preparing fresh meals at home, the pros greatly <u>outnumber</u> the cons.
     ⓐ resemble   ⓑ intersect   ⓒ enable   ⓓ exceed

2 Airplane windows are built to <u>withstand</u> the extreme pressure that exists at high altitudes.
     ⓐ reduce   ⓑ delay   ⓒ resist   ⓓ destroy

3 An unsupervised classroom full of young children will quickly fall into a state of <u>discord</u>.
     ⓐ discipline   ⓑ progression   ⓒ bliss   ⓓ strife

4 As the woman felt no <u>animosity</u> towards the thieves, she accepted their courtroom apology.
     ⓐ affinity   ⓑ hostility   ⓒ contrition   ⓓ gratitude

5 Fifty years ago, it was <u>inconceivable</u> that televisions could be thin enough to hang on a wall.
     ⓐ unbelievable   ⓑ disorganized   ⓒ desirable   ⓓ instructional

6 At an early age, most of us learn that the best way to deal with <u>ridicule</u> is to simply ignore it.
     ⓐ mockery   ⓑ failure   ⓒ dissent   ⓓ yearning

7 With an infectious disease spreading rapidly, residents began to <u>flee</u> to the countryside.
     ⓐ look into   ⓑ move around   ⓒ run away   ⓓ do over

Lesson 57 Technology

과학 기술

★★
algorithm
[ǽlgərìðm]
[명] 알고리즘, 연산 방식

n. a set of mathematical rules used to solve a problem

Search engines utilize complex **algorithms** to determine the relative significance of each web page.

★
apparatus
[æpərǽtəs]
[명] 기구, 장치, 기계

n. machinery or equipment used to do something

The team's laboratory is equipped with the most advanced scientific **apparatus** available.

syn. gear

★
bogus
[bóugəs]
[형] 가짜의, 위조의

adj. not real or proper

The **bogus** signal had seemed to come from space, but it was actually terrestrial in origin.

syn. fraudulent *ant.* genuine

★★
breach
[briːtʃ]
[명] 위반, 파기

n. an incident in which a rule, law, or security measure is broken

In an apparent **breach** of protocol, the hospital's gene editor was used on a human sample.

syn. transgression

★★★
breakthrough
[bréikθrùː]
[명] 돌파구, 비약적 발전

n. a sudden advancement or discovery

A recent **breakthrough** in rocket science will likely make it easier to send a manned craft to Mars.

★
cache
[kæʃ]
[동] 캐시(고속 기억 장치)에 저장하다
adj. cached

v. to save something in a computer's memory for easy access in the future

The operating system **caches** large amounts of information in order to speed up performance.

syn. store

---

algorithm 검색 엔진들은 각 웹 페이지의 상대적 중요도를 결정하기 위해 복잡한 알고리즘을 사용한다. **apparatus** 그 팀의 실험실은 이용할 수 있는 최첨단 과학 기구들을 갖추고 있다. **bogus** 그 가짜 신호는 우주에서 온 것처럼 보였지만, 사실 지상에서 발생한 것이었다. **breach** 그 병원의 유전자 편집기가 프로토콜을 명백히 위반하며, 인간 표본에 사용되었다. **breakthrough** 최근 로켓 과학의 비약적 발전으로 유인 우주선을 화성에 보내는 것이 더 쉬워질 것이다. **cache** 그 운영 체제는 처리 속도를 높이기 위해 많은 양의 정보를 캐시에 저장한다.

ART & DESIGN

SOCIAL SCIENCE

NATURAL SCIENCE

HUMANITIES

EARTH & SPACE

SOCIAL ISSUES

★★ **combat**
[kəmbǽt, kάmbæt]
ⓥ 방지하다, 싸우다
adj. combative

v. to fight against something
Modified drones are now being used to **combat** the seasonal wildfires that plague parts of the world.

★★★ **compatible**
[kəmpǽtəbl]
ⓐ 호환되는

adj. capable of being used by a certain device or system
Many people have accidentally downloaded an app that was not **compatible** with their device.

ant. incompatible

★★ **compress**
[kəmprés]
ⓥ 압축하다
n. compression

v. to reduce in size to facilitate easy storage
This program **compresses** music files, which tend to be large and take up too much space.

syn. condense   *ant.* enlarge

★★ **confirm**
[kənfə́ːrm]
ⓥ 확인하다
n. confirmation

v. to ensure or show that something is true or correct
The users' identities can be **confirmed** by scanning either their fingerprints or their retinas.

syn. validate

★★★ **cutting-edge**
[kʌ́tiŋèdʒ]
ⓐ 최첨단의

adj. representing or including the most recent technology
The teens attended the gaming convention in the hopes of trying out some **cutting-edge** game consoles.

★★ **decipher**
[disáifər]
ⓥ 판독하다, 해독하다
n. cipher

v. to figure out the hidden meaning of something
Archaeologists now use software that helps them **decipher** messages written in ancient alphabets.

syn. decode

---

combat 개조된 드론들이 현재 세계 일부 지역에 횡행하는 계절적 들불을 방지하기 위해 사용되고 있다.   **compatible** 많은 사람들이 그들의 기기와 호환되지 않는 애플리케이션을 실수로 다운로드해 왔다.   **compress** 이 프로그램은 크고 너무 많은 공간을 차지하는 음악 파일들을 압축한다.   **confirm** 그 이용자들의 신원은 그들의 지문이나 망막을 스캔해 확인될 수 있다.   **cutting-edge** 그 십 대들은 몇몇 최첨단 게임기들을 테스트해 볼 수 있을 거라는 희망을 가지고 그 게임 전시회에 참석했다.   **decipher** 고고학자들은 이제 고대 알파벳으로 쓰여진 메시지의 판독을 도와주는 소프트웨어를 사용한다.

★★★
devise
[diváiz]

동 고안하다, 발명하다

v. to come up with an idea for something

A team of researchers is trying to **devise** a garment that will make its wearer invisible to cameras.

syn. invent

★★
eliminate
[ilímənèit]

동 없애다, 제거하다

n. elimination

v. to get rid of completely

It is likely that new technology will **eliminate** the need for batteries sometime in the future.

syn. eradicate

★
encryption
[inkrípʃən]

명 암호화(정보를 암호나 약호로 바꾸기)

v. encrypt

n. the act of protecting information by making it unreadable to outsiders

High-tech criminals now use **encryption** to keep their communications hidden from the police.

Useful **Tips**

암호 작성술이나 해독술은 cryptography라 한다.

★
epitome
[ipítəmi]

명 전형

n. the clearest example of something

Smart glasses are the **epitome** of technology that was introduced before the public was ready for it.

syn. embodiment

★★
ethical
[éθikəl]

형 윤리의

n. ethics

adj. following or relating to moral principles

There are still many **ethical** questions related to driverless cars that remain unanswered today.

syn. moral   *ant.* unethical

★★
extant
[ékstənt]

형 현존하는

adj. currently existing

The **extant** blueprints of Babbage's Analytical Engine have been digitized by the British Science Museum.

ant. extinct

---

devise 한 연구팀이 착용자가 카메라에 보이지 않게 만드는 옷을 발명하려고 노력하고 있다.   **eliminate** 새로운 과학 기술이 언젠가 배터리의 필요성을 없앨 것으로 보인다.   **encryption** 첨단 기술을 이용하는 범죄자들은 이제 자신들의 연락 내용을 경찰로부터 숨기려고 암호화를 사용한다.   **epitome** 스마트 안경은 대중이 받아들일 준비가 되기 전에 선보여졌던 과학 기술의 전형이다.   **ethical** 무인 자동차와 관련해 현재 해결되지 않은 채로 남아 있는 윤리 문제들이 아직 많다.   **extant** 현존하는 배비지의 해석기관(기계적 범용 컴퓨터의 설계)의 청사진들은 영국 과학 박물관에 의해 디지털화되었다.

★
extravagant
[ikstrǽvigənt]
⒜ 터무니없이 비싼, 사치스러운

n. extravagance

adj. unnecessarily fancy and expensive

While some new technology may be **extravagant**, many innovations are practical and affordable.

syn. indulgent   *ant.* practical

★
★
gadget
[gǽdʒit]
⒜ (작고 유용한) 기기

n. a small tool or device with a specific purpose

One of the latest fads in electronics centers on wearable **gadgets** that monitor a person's health.

syn. implement

★
★
hazardous
[hǽzərdəs]
⒜ 위험한

adj. involving or causing risk

Portable digital devices can be **hazardous**, as they distract people from the world around them.

★
★
indispensable
[ìndispénsəbl]
⒜ 꼭 필요한, 필수적인

adj. too useful to do without

Once considered an **indispensable** tool, typewriters have been replaced by computers and printers.

syn. essential   *ant.* nonessential

★
★
ingenious
[indʒíːnjəs]
⒜ 독창적인

adj. extremely clever or innovative

Language translation earbuds are an **ingenious** innovation that may change the way we communicate.

syn. brilliant

★
★
★
install
[instɔ́ːl]
⒮ 설치하다

n. installation

v. to set something up so that it can be used

People in remote rural areas **install** satellite dishes on their roofs in order to watch television.

ant. uninstall

---

extravagant 어떤 새로운 과학 기술은 터무니없이 비싼 반면, 많은 획기적인 기술들은 실용적이고 비용도 감당할 만하다.   **gadget** 전자 공학의 최신 유행들 중 하나는 개인의 건강을 추적 관찰하는 착용 기기들에 중점을 두고 있다.   **hazardous** 휴대용 디지털 기기들은 사람들의 주의를 주변 환경에서 딴 데로 돌리기 때문에, 위험할 수 있다.   **indispensable** 한때 꼭 필요한 도구로 간주되었던 타자기는 컴퓨터와 프린터로 대체되었다.   **ingenious** 언어 번역용 초소형 헤드폰은 우리가 의사소통하는 방식을 바꿀 수 있는 독창적인 획기적 기술이다.   **install** 외딴 시골 지역의 사람들은 텔레비전을 시청하려고 지붕에 위성 방송 수신 안테나를 설치한다.

invention
[invénʃən]
★★★
ⓝ 발명품
v. invent

n. something that has been created or thought of for the first time

The steam engine is widely considered one of the most impactful **inventions** of its time.

syn. creation

---

malfunction
[mælfʌ́ŋkʃən]
★★
ⓝ 고장, 오작동
ⓥ 제대로 작동하지 않다

n. an instance of failing to work properly

Unless a user's data is backed up, a simple **malfunction** can cause it to disappear forever.

v. to fail to work properly

If your computer **malfunctions** again, call the IT department as soon as it happens.

---

miscellaneous
[mìsəléiniəs]
★
ⓐ 여러 종류의, 갖가지의

adj. belonging to a variety of types or categories

The inventor keeps a box full of **miscellaneous** mechanical parts that may someday be of use.

syn. various

---

momentum
[mouméntəm]
★★
ⓝ 기세, 추진력, 탄력

n. the force gained by moving in a particular direction

An economic recession would have an adverse effect on the **momentum** of the tech sector.

syn. impetus   *ant.* inertia

---

obsolete
[ὰbsəlíːt]
★
ⓐ 더 이상 쓸모 없게 된
n. obsolescence

adj. no longer needed or useful

Some museums are beginning to collect **obsolete** technology and preserve it for future generations.

syn. outdated

Useful Tips
새 제품 구매 유도를 위해 계획적으로 기존 제품이 곧 구식이 되게 하는 것을 planned obsolescence 라고 한다.

---

optical
[áptikəl]
★★
ⓐ 광학의
n. optics

adj. relating to light, vision, or the eyes

Optical fiber is a kind of thin wire made of glass or plastic that is used to transmit light pulses.

syn. visual

---

invention 증기 기관은 당대에 가장 영향력이 강한 발명품들 중 하나로 널리 알려져 있다.   **malfunction** 사용자의 데이터가 백업되어 있지 않으면, 단순한 오작동으로 그것이 영구히 사라질 수 있다. / 컴퓨터가 또다시 제대로 작동하지 않으면, 그런 일이 발생하자마자 IT 부서로 연락하시오.   **miscellaneous** 그 발명가는 언젠가 사용할 수도 있는 갖가지 기계 부품들로 가득한 상자를 가지고 있다.   **momentum** 경기 침체는 기술 분야의 기세에 악영향을 미칠 수 있다.   **obsolete** 몇몇 박물관들은 더 이상 쓸모 없게 된 기계를 수집해 차세대를 위해 보존하기 시작하고 있다.   **optical** 광섬유는 광 펄스 전달에 사용되는, 유리나 플라스틱으로 된 일종의 가는 섬유이다.

★★ **output**
[áutpùt]
[명] 출력, 출력한 데이터

n. **the amount of something that is produced by a person or process**

The researchers use the **output** from the computer program to test the validity of their theories.

ant. input

★★ **override**
[òuvəráid]
[동] 중단시키다, 무시하다

v. **to stop something and take control of it**

Although planes do have an autopilot function, the human pilot can **override** it at any time.

★ **painstaking**
[péinstèikiŋ]
[형] 힘이 드는, 공들인

adj. **done with great care and attention to detail**

Assembling a computer from scratch is a **painstaking** process, but some people find it enjoyable.

syn. meticulous *ant.* careless

★★★ **paradigm**
[pǽrədàim]
[명] 전형, 모범, 범례

n. **a model or example of something**

It is often said that old ways must be put aside so that new **paradigms** can take their place.

syn. archetype

★★ **patent**
[pǽtnt]
[명] 특허

n. **the legal right to exclusively produce or sell an invention**

The **patent** on the inventor's revolutionary device is set to expire in less than five years.

★★★ **progress**
[prάgres]
[명] 발전, 향상, 진보
[prərgrés]
[동] 발전하다, 진보하다

n. **movement toward a goal** *syn.* advancement

Not a lot of **progress** has been made in the field of robotics when compared to the field of computing.

v. **to get closer to a goal** *syn.* advance

As new technology improves and **progresses**, our lives change in order to accommodate it.

output 그 연구원들은 컴퓨터 프로그램이 출력한 데이터를 이용해 그들의 이론들이 타당한지 테스트한다. **override** 비행기에 자동 조종 장치 기능이 있기는 하지만, 인간 조종사가 언제든지 중단시킬 수 있다. **painstaking** 맨 처음부터 컴퓨터를 조립하는 것은 힘이 드는 과정이지만, 어떤 사람들은 그것을 즐긴다. **paradigm** 예전 방식들을 없애서 새로운 전형들이 그 자리를 차지할 수 있게 해야 한다고 흔히들 말한다. **patent** 그 발명가의 획기적인 장치에 대한 특허는 5년 안에 만료될 예정이다. **progress** 컴퓨터 사용 분야와 비교해 볼 때, 로봇 공학 분야에서는 많은 발전이 이루어지지 않았다. / 새로운 과학 기술이 향상되고 발전하면서, 그것을 수용하기 위해 우리의 삶이 변화한다.

propulsion

[prəpʌ́lʃən]

ⓝ 추진, 추진력

v. propel

n. the act of moving something forward through force

Most of the modern passenger jets in the skies today rely on turbine engines for **propulsion**.

radically

[rǽdikəli]

ⓐ 근본적으로, 철저히

adv. in a way that causes fundamental change

Genetic modification has the potential to **radically** change the way crops are grown.

syn. thoroughly

semiconductor

[sèmikəndʌ́ktər]

ⓝ 반도체

n. a material that allows more electricity to pass through it as its temperature rises

Semiconductors such as silicon are a vital component of laptops, scanners, and cell phones.

sophisticated

[səfístəkèitid]

ⓐ 정교한, 수준 높은

n. sophistication

adj. very advanced or complex

All-electric cars powered by a **sophisticated** motor can travel more than 300 kilometers on a single charge.

ant. basic

Useful **Tips**

패션, 예술, 사회 예절 등에 대해 잘 알고 있는 세련된 사람을 서술할 때에도 sophisticated를 사용할 수 있다.

ubiquitous

[juːbíkwətəs]

ⓐ 어디에나 있는, 아주 흔한

n. ubiquity

adj. seeming to exist everywhere

Cell phones may be **ubiquitous** today, but they were a seldom-seen luxury item just 30 years ago.

syn. pervasive   *ant.* rare

vulnerable

[vʌ́lnərəbl]

ⓐ 취약한

n. vulnerability

adj. susceptible to harm or damage

Experts are warning that many devices connected to the IoT may be **vulnerable** to hackers.

syn. defenseless   *ant.* impenetrable

---

propulsion 비행하는 현대 제트 여객기들의 대부분은 터빈 엔진에 의해 추진력을 얻는다.   **radically** 유전자 조작은 농작물 재배 방식을 근본적으로 바꿀 수 있는 잠재력을 지니고 있다.   **semiconductor** 실리콘 같은 반도체들은 노트북, 스캐너, 휴대폰의 필수 부품이다.   **sophisticated** 정교한 모터에 의해 완전히 전기만으로 작동하는 자동차들은 1회 충전으로 300 킬로미터 이상을 주행할 수 있다.   **ubiquitous** 휴대폰은 오늘날 아주 흔하지만, 30년 전만해도 좀처럼 보기 힘든 사치품이었다.   **vulnerable** 전문가들은 사물 인터넷에 연결된 많은 기기들이 해커들에게 취약할 수 있다고 경고하고 있다.

EXERCISES

ART & DESIGN

SOCIAL SCIENCE

NATURAL SCIENCE

HUMANITIES

EARTH & SPACE

SOCIAL ISSUES

A Match each definition with the correct word.

1 capable of being used by a certain device or system   ⓐ propulsion

2 the act of moving something forward through force   ⓑ override

3 no longer needed or useful   ⓒ malfunction

4 an instance of failing to work properly   ⓓ compatible

5 the legal right to exclusively produce or sell an invention   ⓔ obsolete

6 to stop something and take control of it   ⓕ ingenious

7 a sudden advancement or discovery   ⓖ patent

8 extremely clever or innovative   ⓗ breakthrough

B Choose the word that is closest in meaning to each underlined word.

1 In order to <u>combat</u> the spread of germs, individuals are advised to wash their hands often.
    ⓐ identify   ⓑ isolate   ⓒ fight   ⓓ remove

2 Suspecting that the email she had received was <u>bogus</u>, the woman phoned her bank directly.
    ⓐ insightful   ⓑ expedient   ⓒ eminent   ⓓ fraudulent

3 When travelers insert this <u>gadget</u> into a water bottle, it filters out dangerous impurities.
    ⓐ implement   ⓑ remedy   ⓒ disinfectant   ⓓ monitor

4 Fingerprints were once used to identify criminals, but more <u>sophisticated</u> methods are now available.
    ⓐ uncertain   ⓑ affordable   ⓒ timely   ⓓ advanced

5 If you often barbecue, a meat thermometer is an <u>indispensable</u> tool you should purchase.
    ⓐ unwieldy   ⓑ essential   ⓒ pricey   ⓓ simple

6 Making racist comments to coworkers is considered the <u>epitome</u> of bad workplace behavior.
    ⓐ aftermath   ⓑ punishment   ⓒ embodiment   ⓓ maneuver

7 It is a cashier's responsibility to <u>confirm</u> the amount of money in the till before finishing a shift.
    ⓐ document   ⓑ validate   ⓒ maximize   ⓓ distribute

Lesson 58 Work Life

★
affable
[ǽfəbl]
[형] 상냥한, 붙임성 있는

adj. friendly and easy to get along with

Thanks to her **affable** personality, the secretary was able to adapt well to her new job.

syn. amiable *ant.* disagreeable

★★
analyze
[ǽnəlàiz]
[동] …을 분석하다, …을 검토하다
n. analysis

v. to examine in order to gain information

After the sales numbers have been gathered, they will be **analyzed** and presented to the board.

syn. study

★★★
attitude
[ǽtitjù:d]
[명] 태도, 사고방식

n. the way a person thinks and feels about a situation

By maintaining a professional **attitude** during the crisis, the manager kept the clients calm.

syn. demeanor

★★
colleague
[káli:g]
[명] (직업상의) 동료

n. a person you work with

The attorney approached one of her **colleagues** for advice about an upcoming court case.

syn. associate

Useful Tips
colleague는 일반적으로 더 많이 사용되는 같은 의미의 단어인 coworker보다 조금 더 격식을 차린 단어로 볼 수 있다.

★★
compensate
[kámpənsèit]
[동] 보상하다
n. compensation

v. to pay someone to make up for the loss of something

The company's employees are treated well, but they are not **compensated** enough for their overtime work.

syn. reimburse

★
concoct
[kankákt]
[동] …을 섞어서 만들다, 조합[조제]하다
n. concoction

v. to create something complicated by mixing things together

Researchers in the company's lab are constantly **concocting** new beverages to be test-marketed.

syn. formulate

---

affable 그 비서는 상냥한 성격 덕분에, 새로운 직장에 잘 적응할 수 있었다. **analyze** 판매량이 수집된 후에, 분석되어 이사회에 보고될 것이다. **attitude** 그 관리자는 위기 가운데서 전문적인 태도를 유지함으로써, 고객들을 진정시켰다. **colleague** 그 변호사는 곧 다가오는 법정 사건에 대한 조언을 구하기 위해 자신의 동료 중 한 명에게 접촉했다. **compensate** 그 회사의 직원들은 좋은 대우를 받지만, 시간 외 근로에 대해서는 충분히 보상받지 못한다. **concoct** 그 회사 연구실의 연구원들은 시험 판매될 새로운 음료수들을 끊임없이 섞어 만들고 있다.

★★ cooperative
[kouápərətiv]

ⓐ 협력하는, 협동하는
ⓝ 협동조합

v. cooperate

adj. willing to assist or work with others   *syn.* helpful

A **cooperative** attitude is a must when working on an important project with a small staff.

n. an organization that is owned by its workers

This supermarket is a **cooperative**, so its profits are distributed among all of the employees.

Useful Tips
'협동조합'의 의미로 사용될 경우, 종종 약자인 co-op의 형태로도 쓰인다.

★ deputy
[dépjuti]

ⓝ (한 조직의 장 바로 다음 가는 직급인) 부, 대리인

v. deputize

n. a person who acts as second in command to a leader

As the CEO's **deputy**, Ms. Williams will be making all of the high-level decisions during his absence.

★★ eager
[íːgər]

ⓐ 열망하는

adj. excited about doing something

The recently hired employees are **eager** to meet their coworkers and get started in their new positions.

syn. enthusiastic   *ant.* disinterested

★★ employ
[implɔ́i]

ⓥ 고용하다

n. employee

v. to pay someone to do work on a regular basis

It is estimated that airlines **employ** more than three and a half million people across the globe.

★★ executive
[igzékjutiv]

ⓝ (기업이나 조직의) 경영 간부, 임원

n. a high-level manager in a company

The offices of the **executives** are located on the top the floor of the corporation's headquarters.

syn. administrator

★★ expertise
[èkspərtíːz]

ⓝ 전문 지식, 전문 기술

n. expert

n. knowledge and skills related to a task or profession

It takes many years of studying, training, and hands-on experience to acquire a high level of **expertise**.

syn. proficiency

---

cooperative 소수의 직원들과 함께 중요한 프로젝트를 진행할 때, 협동적인 태도는 필수이다. / 이 슈퍼마켓은 협동조합이어서 그 수익이 모든 직원들에게 분배된다.
deputy Williams 씨는 최고 경영자의 대리인으로서 그가 없는 동안 모든 고위급 결정들을 내릴 것이다.   **eager** 최근 고용된 직원들은 동료 직원들을 만나서, 자신들의 새로운 직책을 시작하기를 열망한다.   **employ** 항공사들이 전 세계에서 350만 명 이상의 사람들을 고용하고 있다고 추정된다.   **executive** 임원들의 사무실은 기업 본사의 가장 위층에 위치하고 있다.   **expertise** 높은 수준의 전문 지식을 익히기 위해서는 다년간의 학습, 교육 및 실무 경험이 필요하다.

★★ hustle
[hʌ́sl]

동 서두르다, 급히 하다

v. to move quickly to get things done

The convention center workers had to **hustle** in order to get the conference hall ready in time.

syn. hurry

★★ inspect
[inspékt]

동 점검하다, 검사하다

n. inspection

v. to look something over carefully to check its quality

It is the quality control department's job to **inspect** every garment before it is shipped off.

syn. examine

★★ labor
[léibər]

명 노동, 근로
동 (육체적인) 노동을 하다, 일을 하다

adj. laborious

n. difficult physical work

After four hours of **labor** in the hot sun, the farmworkers were given a 30-minute break for lunch.

v. to do difficult physical work   *syn.* toil

The architect **labored** over the model home for weeks, but he wasn't satisfied with the results.

> **Useful Tips**
>
> labor가 명사로 쓰일 때, '(산모의) 진통[분만]'이라는 의미로도 사용되는데, 보통 'The woman is in labor.'라고 표현한다.

★★ operate
[ápərèit]

동 1. (기계를) 가동[조작]하다
2. 수술하다

n. operation

v. 1 to control a device or machine
2 to perform surgery

1. These new workers are being trained to **operate** the cranes at the company's shipyard.

2. Surgeons sometimes have to spend hours **operating** on a patient without a break.

★★ pension
[pénʃən]

명 연금, 생활 보조금

n. money that people collect regularly after they stop working

Since leaving their jobs last year, the elderly couple has been getting by on their **pensions**.

★ pinnacle
[pínəkl]

명 정점, 절정

n. the most successful part of something

Being nominated for a Nobel Prize is considered the **pinnacle** of a scientific researcher's career.

syn. peak   *ant.* nadir

---

hustle 컨벤션 센터 직원들은 회의장이 제시간에 준비되게 하기 위해 서둘러야 했다.   **inspect** 발송 전에 모든 의류를 점검하는 것은 품질 관리 부서의 일이다.
labor 뜨거운 태양 아래서 4시간 동안 노동을 한 후, 농장 근로자들에게 30분의 점심 시간이 주어졌다. / 그 건축가는 모델 하우스를 만들기 위해 몇 주 동안 일했지만, 결과물에 만족하지 않았다.   **operate** 1. 이 새로운 근로자들은 회사의 조선소에서 크레인을 조작하는 교육을 받고 있다. 2. 외과 의사들은 때때로 몇 시간 동안 쉬지 않고 환자를 수술해야 한다.   **pension** 그 노부부는 작년에 일을 그만둔 후, 연금으로 그럭저럭 살아가고 있다.   **pinnacle** 노벨상 후보가 되는 것은 과학자 커리어의 정점이라고 여겨진다.

ART & DESIGN

SOCIAL SCIENCE

NATURAL SCIENCE

HUMANITIES

EARTH & SPACE

SOCIAL ISSUES

★★★★ **practice**
[præktis]

ⓥ 1. 연습하다
2. (의사·변호사 등의 전문직으로)
일하다, 종사하다

v. 1 to do something over and over to improve at it   *syn.* train
2 to do the work of a certain profession

1. The sales team **practiced** their presentation for hours, determined to make sure it went flawlessly.

2. One of the local doctors has been **practicing** medicine in this town since the late 1980s.

★ **referral**
[rifə́:rəl]

ⓝ (전문적인 도움을 받을 곳으로)
보내기, 소개, 위탁

v. refer

n. the act of sending someone to another professional to receive help

The legal aid organization provides callers with **referrals** to attorneys who specialize in certain areas.

★★★ **resign**
[rizáin]

ⓥ 사퇴[사임]하다, 물러나다

n. resignation

v. to formally announce that you are leaving a job

Tired of receiving little recognition for her work, the public relations supervisor **resigned** yesterday.

syn. quit

★★ **resourceful**
[risɔ́:rsfəl]

ⓐ 기지가 있는, 수완이 좋은

adj. able to find ways to deal with difficult situations

The company is looking for a **resourceful** salesperson who can work well without supervision.

syn. capable   *ant.* incompetent

★★★ **retire**
[ritáiər]

ⓥ 은퇴하다, 퇴직하다

n. retirement

v. to stop working upon reaching a certain age

In most countries, people are expected to **retire** from their jobs when they reach their mid-sixties.

★ **sabbatical**
[səbǽtikəl]

ⓝ 안식 기간, 장기 휴가

n. an extended period during which a person doesn't work but gets paid

During her **sabbatical**, the art professor traveled around Europe visiting famous museums.

syn. leave of absence

---

practice 1. 그 영업팀은 프레젠테이션이 완벽하게 진행되도록 하기 위해 몇 시간 동안 연습했다. 2. 이 지역 의사들 중 한 명은 1980년대 후반부터 이 도시에서 의료업에 종사해 왔다.   **referral** 그 법률 보조 기구는 전화한 사람들을 특정 분야의 전문 변호사들에게 소개해 준다.   **resign** 그 홍보 실장은 직장에서 인정을 거의 못 받는 것에 지쳐서, 어제 사임했다.   **resourceful** 그 회사는 감독 없이도 일을 잘 할 수 있는, 수완이 좋은 영업 사원을 찾고 있다.   **retire** 대부분의 나라에서, 사람들은 60대 중반이 되면 직장에서 은퇴할 것으로 예상된다.   **sabbatical** 안식년 동안, 그 미대 교수는 유명한 박물관들을 방문하며 유럽 여기저기를 여행했다.

shelve
[ʃelv]

동 (계획을) 보류하다

v. to put something on hold until a later date

The firm decided to **shelve** its plans to expand to Australia until the economic situation improves.

syn. defer

---

solicit
[səlísit]

동 요청하다, 얻으려고 하다

n. solicitation

v. to ask for something

The manager regularly **solicits** advice and opinions from the staff, which is good for morale.

syn. request

---

status
[stéitəs]

명 지위, 신분, 상태

n. a person or thing's rank, standing, or condition

Unsure of her **status** due to the upcoming merger, the woman asked to speak with her boss.

---

substitute
[sʌ́bstətjùːt]

명 대리인, 대체물
동 대신하다, 교체하다

n. substitution

n. someone or something that serves as a replacement
　　syn. surrogate

If a teacher is too ill to work, it is up to the school to find a **substitute** for the day.

v. to serve or make something serve as a replacement　*syn.* swap

By **substituting** cheap ingredients for more expensive ones, the company will save lots of money.

---

supplement
[sʌ́pləmənt]

명 보충(물)
동 보충하다, 추가하다

adj. supplementary

n. something that serves to enhance a larger thing

Management is distributing a list of rules that will serve as a **supplement** to the employee manual.

v. to enhance a larger thing　*syn.* augment

During the busy season, temporary workers are brought in to **supplement** the full-time staff.

---

volunteer
[vàləntíər]

동 자원하다, 자원 봉사로 하다

n. volunteerism

v. to offer to do something

Two personnel department employees **volunteered** to stay late and sort through the backlog of résumés.

---

shelve 그 회사는 경제 상황이 나아질 때까지 호주로 확장하는 계획을 보류하기로 결정했다.　**solicit** 그 관리자는 정기적으로 직원들의 조언과 의견을 구하는데, 이것은 사기를 올리는 데 도움이 된다.　**status** 다가오는 합병 때문에 자신의 지위에 대한 확신이 없었던 그 여자는 상사에게 면담을 요청했다.　**substitute** 만약 교사 한 명이 너무 아파서 일을 못하면, 그날 대신할 사람을 찾는 일은 학교의 몫이다. / 더 비싼 재료를 저렴한 재료로 대신함으로써, 그 회사는 많은 비용을 절약할 것이다.
supplement 경영진은 직원 안내서에 대한 보충 자료가 될 규칙 목록을 배포하고 있다. / 성수기 동안, 임시직 근로자들이 정규직 직원 인력을 보충하기 위해 투입된다.　**volunteer** 인사과 직원 두 명이 늦게까지 남아서 밀린 이력서들을 살펴보는 일에 자원했다.

EXERCISES

A Match each definition with the correct word.

1 to stop working upon reaching a certain age

ⓐ employ

2 money that people collect regularly after they stop working

ⓑ deputy

3 to pay someone to do work on a regular basis

ⓒ operate

4 to offer to do something

ⓓ pension

5 a person or thing's rank, standing, or condition

ⓔ volunteer

6 to control a device or machine

ⓕ status

7 to put something on hold until a later date

ⓖ retire

8 a person who acts as second in command to a leader

ⓗ shelve

B Choose the word that is closest in meaning to each underlined word.

1 The criminal was extremely <u>resourceful</u>, always figuring out clever ways to evade the police.

ⓐ notorious   ⓑ relentless   ⓒ capable   ⓓ regretful

2 When children feel valued and respected, they are usually <u>cooperative</u> rather than disobedient.

ⓐ helpful   ⓑ confused   ⓒ proud   ⓓ insightful

3 The tour bus driver's <u>affable</u> commentary over the PA system put the passengers at ease.

ⓐ humorous   ⓑ amiable   ⓒ brisk   ⓓ instructive

4 The factory will be <u>inspected</u> to ensure that it is not releasing excessive pollution.

ⓐ abandoned   ⓑ lauded   ⓒ examined   ⓓ relocated

5 At the <u>pinnacle</u> of her career, the software designer was considered the best in the business.

ⓐ peak   ⓑ conclusion   ⓒ reevaluation   ⓓ prospect

6 After his department's failure to prevent an outbreak, the public health director <u>resigned</u>.

ⓐ apologized   ⓑ quit   ⓒ explained   ⓓ returned

7 The company hires workers based on their <u>expertise</u>, with no regard for gender or race.

ⓐ affluence   ⓑ cordiality   ⓒ maturity   ⓓ proficiency

Lesson 59 | ▶범죄 Crime

accomplice
[əkámplis]
ⓝ 공범

n. a person who helps someone break the law

The criminal mastermind escaped, but the police managed to arrest two of his **accomplices**.

syn. collaborator

allegedly
[əlédʒidli]
ⓟ 전해진 바에 의하면, 이른바

v. allege

adv. according to reports that have not yet been proven true

The woman was arrested for **allegedly** stealing several valuable items from a parked car.

syn. purportedly

arson
[áːrsn]
ⓝ 방화

n. the crime of purposely starting a destructive fire

The police don't believe the warehouse fire was a case of **arson**, but some people find it suspicious.

atone
[ətóun]
ⓥ 속죄하다

n. atonement

v. to make amends or show regret for wrongdoing

The man tried to **atone** for his past crimes by volunteering at a nonprofit that helps young offenders.

atrocity
[ətrásəti]
ⓝ 잔혹 행위, 악행

n. a horrific act of violence

Police officers who deal with **atrocities** on a regular basis may need to seek professional counselling.

bail
[beil]
ⓝ 보석금

n. money used to keep someone out of jail until their trial

Unable to pay her **bail**, the woman had to spend a week in jail waiting for her trial.

> **Useful Tips**
>
> bail out은 상황에 따라 '…에 대한 보석금을 내다', '배에서 물을 퍼내다', '낙하산으로 비행기에서 탈출하다'라는 뜻으로 사용된다.

---

accomplice 그 범죄의 배후 조종자는 달아났지만, 경찰은 그의 공범 둘을 가까스로 체포했다.   **allegedly** 전해진 바에 의하면, 그 여자는 주차되어 있던 차에서 몇 가지 귀중품을 훔친 혐의로 체포되었다고 한다.   **arson** 경찰은 그 창고의 화재가 방화 사건이었다고 믿지 않지만, 몇몇 사람들은 그 화재에 의혹을 갖고 있다.   **atone** 그 남자는 소년범들을 돕는 비영리 단체에서 자원봉사를 함으로써 자신이 과거에 저지른 죄를 속죄하려 했다.   **atrocity** 정기적으로 잔혹 행위(범죄)를 다루는 경찰관들은 전문적인 상담을 받아야 할 수도 있다.   **bail** 그 여자는 보석금을 내지 못해서, 재판을 기다리며 일주일 동안 수감되어 있어야 했다.

★★
blackmail
[blǽkmèil]
[명] 갈취, 협박

n. the crime of demanding money to keep something secret

The lawyer became a victim of **blackmail** after some embarrassing photos were stolen from his phone.

★★
bribery
[bráibəri]
[명] 뇌물 수수
v., n. bribe

n. the crime of offering money to an official in return for a favor

Bribery is the most common form of a corruption, taking place on a daily basis in some places.

★★★
casualty
[kǽʒuəlti]
[명] 사상자, 부상자

n. a death or injury caused by an event

The shootout during the bank robbery caused several **casualties**, but luckily no one was killed.

★★★
charge
[tʃɑːrdʒ]
[동] 기소하다, 고발하다
[명] 기소, 고발

v. to officially accuse someone of a crime

The accountant was **charged** with stealing money from his clients over a period of several years.

n. an official accusation of a crime

The **charges** against the man include assault, disorderly conduct, and resisting arrest.

★★★
commit
[kəmít]
[동] 저지르다, 범하다

v. to do something illegal or wrong

Although the woman **committed** a crime, the judge decided against sending her to prison.

syn. perpetrate

★★★
culprit
[kʌ́lprit]
[명] 범인
adj. culpable

n. the person responsible for a crime or other wrongdoing

Security camera footage clearly shows the **culprits** breaking into the business through a window.

syn. offender

---

blackmail 그 변호사는 자신의 전화기에서 곤혹스러운 사진들을 도난당한 후, 협박을 받게 되었다. **bribery** 뇌물 수수는 가장 흔한 부패의 형태이며, 어떤 곳에서는 매일 일어나고 있다. **casualty** 그 은행 강도 사건 도중 벌어진 총격전으로 부상자가 몇 명 발생했지만, 다행히 사망자는 나오지 않았다. **charge** 그 회계사는 몇 년 동안에 걸쳐 자신의 고객들로부터 돈을 가로챈 혐의로 기소되었다. / 그 남자에 대한 기소들에는 폭행, 풍기 문란 행위, 체포 불응이 포함되어 있다. **commit** 그 여자가 죄를 짓기는 했지만, 판사는 그녀를 수감시키지 않기로 결정했다. **culprit** 보안 카메라 영상은 그 범인들이 창문을 통해 그 사업장에 잠입하고 있는 것을 분명히 보여 준다.

embezzlement
[imbézlmənt]

ⓝ 횡령, 착복

v. embezzle

n. the crime of altering financial records to steal money from an employer

The company accused an employee of **embezzlement** after noticing some unexpected losses.

espionage
[éspiənà:ʒ]

ⓝ 스파이 행위

n. the crime of spying on a country or business

Corporate **espionage** is becoming more common as tech companies struggle for a competitive edge.

syn. spying

exonerate
[igzánərèit]

ⓥ …의 결백[무죄]을 입증하다

v. to prove someone innocent

The woman accused of the robbery claimed to have video evidence that would **exonerate** her.

syn. absolve

felony
[féləni]

ⓝ 중죄(살인·방화·무장 강도 등의 흉악 범죄)

n. a serious crime

Identity theft is a **felony** in some countries, punishable by multiple years in prison.

fine
[fain]

ⓝ 벌금
ⓥ 벌금을 과하다

n. an amount of money that must be paid for breaking a rule or law

The man responsible for the damage avoided prison time, but he had to pay a large **fine**.

v. to make someone pay money for breaking a rule or law

If you are caught dumping trash on public land, you will likely be arrested and **fined**.

forensic
[fərénsik]

ⓝ 법의학적인

n. forensics

adj. relating to the use of scientific methods to solve crimes

Several items from the crime scene were brought to the police station for **forensic** analysis.

---

embezzlement 그 회사는 예상치 못한 손실을 알아챈 후, 직원 한 명을 횡령으로 고소했다.　**espionage** 기술 업체들이 경쟁 우위를 차지하려고 다투면서, 산업 스파이 행위가 점점 더 흔해지고 있다.　**exonerate** 강도 혐의로 기소된 그 여자는 자신의 무죄를 입증해 줄 영상 증거물을 가지고 있다고 주장했다.　**felony** 몇몇 국가에서 신원 도용은 중죄이며, 수년간의 징역형에 처해질 수 있다.　**fine** 손해를 입힌 그 남자는 수감되는 것은 피했지만, 막대한 벌금을 내야 했다. / 공유지에 쓰레기를 버리다가 잡히면, 체포되어 벌금형을 받을 것이다.　**forensic** 그 범죄 현장의 물품 몇 점이 법의학적 분석을 위해 경찰서로 옮겨졌다.

★★★

harassment

[hərǽsmənt]

[명] 괴롭힘, 희롱

v. harass

n. the act of treating someone in an unpleasant or unacceptable way

It was the woman's continual **harassment** of her neighbors that eventually led to her arrest.

★

hijacking

[háidʒæ̀kiŋ]

[명] 공중[해상] 납치

n. the act of taking control of a vehicle through force or threats

To prevent **hijacking**, the door to the cockpit of a passenger jet is kept locked at all times.

Useful Tips

차량 탈취는 carjacking, 차량이나 비행기 탈취범은 hijacker라 한다.

★★

hostage

[hástidʒ]

[명] 인질

n. a person held captive and threatened with harm unless demands are met

The police stormed the bank, arresting several people and freeing all of the **hostages**.

syn. captive

★★

imprison

[imprízn]

[동] 수감하다, 구속하다

n. imprisonment

v. to keep someone in a place against their will

The man's lawyers claim he was **imprisoned** for nearly 20 years for a crime that he didn't commit.

syn. incarcerate *ant.* release

★★★

investigate

[invéstəgèit]

[동] 수사하다, 조사하다

n. investigation

v. to look into a situation to find information

The police were called in to **investigate** reports of strange noises coming from an abandoned building.

syn. inspect

★★

lead

[li:d]

[명] 단서, 실마리

n. a piece of information that may help solve a crime

The detective thought she had found a **lead**, but it turned out to be useless information.

syn. clue

harassment 그 여자가 결국 체포된 것은 바로 이웃들을 지속적으로 괴롭혔기 때문이었다. **hijacking** 공중 납치를 방지하기 위해, 여객기 조종석의 문은 항상 잠겨 있다. **hostage** 경찰이 그 은행을 기습해, 몇 명의 사람들을 체포하고 인질을 모두 풀어 주었다. **imprison** 그 남자의 변호사들은 그가 자신이 저지르지 않은 죄 때문에 20년 가까이 수감되어 있었다고 주장한다. **investigate** 방치된 건물에서 이상한 소리가 난다는 신고들을 수사하기 위해 경찰이 출동했다. **lead** 그 탐정은 자신이 단서를 찾았다고 생각했지만, 그것은 결국 쓸모 없는 정보로 밝혀졌다.

★

misdemeanor
[mìsdimí:nər]

[명] 경범죄, 비행

n. a minor crime

Juveniles who are convicted of a **misdemeanor** may be sentenced to community service.

ant. felony

★

mug
[mʌg]

[동] (공공장소에서) 강도짓을 하다

v. to take someone's money or valuables by force in a public place

An elderly woman was **mugged** by a group of teens, who pushed her down and took her purse.

syn. rob

★★★

murder
[mə́:rdər]

[명] 살인
[동] 살인하다

n. the act of deliberately killing another human being *syn.* homicide

Although the man was originally accused of **murder**, the charge was later reduced to manslaughter.

v. to deliberately kill another human being

After he **murdered** a pair of police officers, the criminal was sentenced to life in prison.

★★

notorious
[noutɔ́:riəs]

[형] 악명 높은

adj. well known or famous for negative reasons

The **notorious** drug lord has been wanted by the police for years, but he remains at large.

syn. infamous

★★

parole
[pəróul]

[명] 가석방

n. a conditional release from prison before the person's sentence is over

The woman was released on **parole** after serving just seven years of her 12-year sentence.

★★

perjury
[pə́:rdʒəri]

[명] 위증, 위증죄

n. the act of lying in court while under oath

Perjury should not be taken lightly, as it can lead to prison terms of up to five years.

---

misdemeanor 경범죄 선고를 받은 청소년들은 사회봉사 명령을 받을 수 있다. **mug** 어떤 할머니가 한 무리의 십 대들에게 강도를 당했는데, 그들은 할머니를 밀어 넘어뜨린 후 그녀의 지갑을 탈취했다. **murder** 그 남자는 원래 살인죄로 기소됐으나, 그 기소는 후에 과실치사로 낮춰졌다. / 그 범인은 경찰관 두 명을 살해한 후, 무기징역을 선고받았다. **notorious** 악명 높은 그 마약 카르텔 보스는 오랫동안 경찰의 수배를 받아 왔지만, 아직 잡히지 않았다. **parole** 그 여자는 12년 형 중 7년만 복역한 후 가석방되었다. **perjury** 위증은 5년에 이르는 징역형까지 받을 수 있으므로, 가볍게 생각해서는 안 된다.

ART & DESIGN

SOCIAL SCIENCE

NATURAL SCIENCE

HUMANITIES

EARTH & SPACE

SOCIAL ISSUES

pickpocket
[píkpàkit]
몡 소매치기

n. someone who steals money or valuables from a person's pocket

When riding on crowded trains or buses, you should always be on the lookout for **pickpockets**.

premeditated
[pri:médətèitid]
옝 계획적인, 의도적인

n. premeditation

adj. planned in advance

The shooter claims that his crimes weren't **premeditated**, but evidence suggests otherwise.

syn. calculated   *ant.* spontaneous

ransom
[rǽnsəm]
몡 몸값, 배상금

n. money that is paid for the release of a captive

The family was asked to pay a $50,000 **ransom** for the return of their kidnapped daughter.

shoplifter
[ʃáplìftər]
몡 가게 좀도둑

n. someone who steals items from a store while pretending to shop

It is estimated that American businesses lose billions of dollars each year due to **shoplifters**.

smuggle
[smʌ́gl]
옝 밀수하다

v. to illegally bring items into a country

Some gangs are believed to use small submarines to **smuggle** drugs into other countries.

Useful **Tips**

밀수품은 smuggled goods, 밀수범은 smuggler라고 한다.

suspect
[səspékt]
몡 용의자, 피의자

n. someone who is believed to have committed a crime

The police have identified a **suspect** and are asking for the public's help in locating him.

---

pickpocket 붐비는 열차나 버스를 타고 갈 때, 항상 소매치기를 경계해야 한다.   **premeditated** 그 저격범은 자신이 저지른 죄가 계획적인 것이 아니었다고 주장하지만, 증거에 의하면 그렇지 않다.   **ransom** 그 가족은 납치된 딸을 돌려주는 조건으로 5만 달러의 몸값을 지불하라는 요구를 받았다.   **shoplifter** 미국의 업체들이 가게 좀도둑들 때문에 연간 수십억 달러를 손해보는 것으로 추정된다.   **smuggle** 몇몇 갱단들이 다른 나라들로 마약을 밀수하는 데 소형 잠수함들을 이용한다고 여겨진다.   **suspect** 경찰은 용의자 한 명의 신원을 파악했으며, 그의 소재를 파악하기 위해 사람들에게 도움을 요청하고 있다.

★

theft

[θeft]

[명] 절도, 훔침

n. the act of taking something that doesn't belong to you

The **theft** of the *Mona Lisa* from the Louvre by an Italian artist was front-page news in 1911.

syn. stealing

★★

vandalize

[vǽndəlàiz]

[동] (문화·공공시설 등을) 파손하다

n. vandal

v. to willfully damage public or private property

Troublemakers tried to **vandalize** the abandoned school, but a security guard chased them away.

syn. deface

★★★

victim

[víktim]

[명] 희생자, 피해자

v. victimize

n. someone who has been negatively affected by a crime or accident

The **victim** of the crime has been released from the hospital and is expected to fully recover.

★★★

violent

[váiələnt]

[형] 난폭한, 폭력적인

n. violence

adj. likely to hurt or kill

The police are warning residents that a **violent** criminal has escaped from the local prison.

ant. peaceful

★★

warrant

[wɔ́:rənt]

[명] 영장

n. an official document allowing the police to make an arrest or search a home

The police were unable to search the suspect's home because they didn't have a **warrant**.

★★

witness

[wítnis]

[명] 목격자

[동] (사건·사고를) 목격하다

n. someone who sees a crime or accident take place *syn.* observer

According to **witnesses**, the robber jumped into a waiting car, which then sped away.

v. to see a crime or accident take place *syn.* observe

Anyone who **witnessed** the terrible crime can call the police hotline anonymously.

---

theft 1911년에 한 이탈리아 화가가 루브르 박물관에서 *모나리자*를 훔친 사건은 톱뉴스였다. **vandalize** 말썽꾼들이 그 폐교를 파손하려 했지만, 한 경비원이 그들을 쫓아냈다. **victim** 그 범죄의 피해자는 퇴원해 완전히 회복할 것으로 예상된다. **violent** 경찰은 주민들에게 난폭한 범죄자가 현지 감옥에서 탈옥했다고 경고하고 있다. **warrant** 경찰은 영장이 없어서 그 용의자의 집을 수색할 수 없었다. **witness** 목격자들에 따르면, 그 강도가 대기 중인 차에 뛰어 올라타자 그 차는 쏜살같이 가버렸다. / 그 끔찍한 범죄를 목격한 사람은 누구든지 경찰의 긴급 직통 전화에 익명으로 연락할 수 있다.

EXERCISES

A Match each definition with the correct word.

1	likely to hurt or kill	ⓐ parole
2	relating to the use of scientific methods to solve crimes	ⓑ hijacking
3	the act of taking control of a vehicle through force or threats	ⓒ casualty
4	to officially accuse someone of a crime	ⓓ ransom
5	to make amends or show regret for wrongdoing	ⓔ violent
6	a death or injury caused by an event	ⓕ atone
7	money that is paid for the release of a captive	ⓖ forensic
8	a conditional release from prison before the person's sentence is over	ⓗ charge

B Choose the word that is closest in meaning to each underlined word.

1 A factory <u>allegedly</u> dumped toxic waste into the river to save money on waste disposal fees.
   ⓐ stealthily   ⓑ purportedly   ⓒ deliberately   ⓓ sporadically

2 The government is worried that the tiny video recorders may be used for <u>espionage</u>.
   ⓐ broadcasting   ⓑ cheating   ⓒ sabotaging   ⓓ spying

3 The counterfeiter's three <u>accomplices</u> helped him print and distribute the fake $100 bills.
   ⓐ adversaries   ⓑ mentors   ⓒ collaborators   ⓓ accusers

4 The police are investigating the <u>murder</u> to decide whether or not it was a hate crime.
   ⓐ hoax   ⓑ homicide   ⓒ litigation   ⓓ offence

5 The troubled child who <u>vandalized</u> a mural in the schoolyard was sent to speak to a counselor.
   ⓐ defaced   ⓑ chastised   ⓒ swindled   ⓓ composed

6 A rebel group seized the travelers, keeping them as <u>hostages</u> for several months.
   ⓐ detractors   ⓑ chaperons   ⓒ captives   ⓓ lodgers

7 This fast-food restaurant is <u>notorious</u> for creating menu items that contain lots of salt and fat.
   ⓐ revered   ⓑ cryptic   ⓒ averse   ⓓ infamous

★★
accumulate
[əkjú:mjulèit]
ⓥ 모이다, 축적되다

n. accumulation

v. to gather over an extended period of time

Over the years, a lot of plastic waste has **accumulated** in the middle of the Pacific Ocean.

syn. accrue   *ant.* disperse

★★
aftermath
[ǽftərmæθ]
ⓝ 여파

n. the consequences of a negative event

In the **aftermath** of the oil spill, beaches up and down the shoreline were closed indefinitely.

★★
alert
[əlɔ́:rt]
ⓝ 경계 경보
ⓐ (문제·위험 등을) 경계하는

n. a notification about potential danger   *syn.* warning

The weather center has issued an air quality **alert**, warning residents to remain indoors if possible.

adj. aware of or ready to deal with potential danger   *syn.* vigilant

We must remain **alert** for new threats to the environment and be prepared to deal with them.

★★★
available
[əvéiləbl]
ⓐ 구할 수 있는, 이용할 수 있는

adj. accessible or ready for use

Federal assistance is **available** for towns and villages making plans to clean up public land.

ant. unavailable

★★★
ban
[bæn]
ⓥ 금지하다

v. to make a law or rule against possessing or doing something

The activists are asking the government to **ban** the use of microplastics in cosmetics.

syn. prohibit   *ant.* allow

★★★
climate
[kláimit]
ⓝ 기후

n. the long-term weather trends of a region

As our local **climate** continues to change, we need to find ways to reduce greenhouse gas emissions.

---

accumulate 수년간, 많은 플라스틱 폐기물이 태평양 한가운데에 축적되었다.　**aftermath** 석유 유출의 여파로, 해안선 이곳저곳에 위치한 해수욕장들이 무기한 폐쇄되었다.　**alert** 기상청은 대기질 경계 경보를 발령하며, 주민들에게 가능한 한 실내에 머물라고 경고했다. / 우리는 환경에 대한 새로운 위협들을 경계해야 하고, 그것들에 대처할 준비가 되어있어야 한다.　**available** 도시와 마을들은 공유지를 정화하려는 계획을 세우는 데 연방 지원을 받을 수 있다.　**ban** (환경) 운동가들은 화장품에 미세 플라스틱 사용을 금지할 것을 정부에 요구하고 있다.　**climate** 우리 지역의 기후가 계속해서 변화함에 따라, 우리는 온실가스 배출을 줄일 방법을 찾아야만 한다.

ART & DESIGN

SOCIAL SCIENCE

NATURAL SCIENCE

HUMANITIES

EARTH & SPACE

SOCIAL ISSUES

clog
[klɑg]
ⓝ 방해물, 막는 것
ⓥ …을 막다, 막히게 하다

adj. clogged

n. something that stops a flow   *syn.* blockage

Products used to remove **clogs** from drains contain chemicals that can pollute the water supply.

v. to stop a flow   *syn.* block

Large deposits of fat, oil, and grease, sometimes called "fatbergs," are **clogging** urban sewer systems.

contaminate
[kəntǽmənèit]
ⓥ 오염시키다

n. contamination

v. to add something impure or harmful to a substance

Residents fear that a new manufacturing plant built next to the river will **contaminate** the water.

syn. taint   *ant.* purify

countermeasure
[káuntərmèʒər]
ⓝ 대책, 대응책

n. action taken in response to something negative that occurs

The government commission is tasked with finding effective **countermeasures** to the rise in air pollution.

deforestation
[diːfɔ̀ːristéiʃən]
ⓝ 삼림 벌채

n. the act of cutting down large portions of a forest

Not only does **deforestation** destroy natural habitats, it also increases carbon dioxide levels.

syn. clear-cutting

detergent
[ditə́ːrdʒənt]
ⓝ 세제

n. soap used for cleaning dishes or clothes

Consumers are being encouraged to seek out environmentally friendly laundry **detergents**.

syn. cleaner

devastating
[dévəstèitiŋ]
ⓐ 대단히 파괴적인, 엄청난 손상을 가하는

v. devastate

adj. causing great harm

The use of pesticides has taken a **devastating** toll on many bird species, including the bald eagle.

syn. disastrous

---

clog 배수구에 막힌 것들을 제거하는 데 쓰이는 제품들은 상수도를 오염시킬 수 있는 화학 물질들을 함유하고 있다. / 때때로 '팻 버그(하수구에서 발견되는 빙산같이 생긴 기름 덩어리)'라고 불리는 대량의 지방, 기름, 윤활유의 침전물은 도시 하수도를 막히게 하고 있다.   **contaminate** 주민들은 강 옆에 새로 생긴 제조 공장이 물을 오염시킬까 봐 우려한다.   **countermeasure** 정부 위원회는 대기 오염 증가에 대한 효과적인 대책을 마련하는 임무를 맡고 있다.   **deforestation** 삼림 벌채는 자연 서식지들을 파괴할 뿐 아니라, 이산화탄소의 수치도 증가시킨다.   **detergent** 소비자들은 친환경 세탁 세제를 찾도록 권장되고 있다.
devastating 살충제의 사용은 대머리 독수리를 포함한 많은 조류 종들에게 엄청난 피해를 입혔다.

★
★ **diffuse**
[difjúːz]
ⓥ 퍼지다, 번지다, 확산하다
n. diffusion

v. to distribute across a wide area

Due to the strong winds, the toxic smoke from the warehouse fire **diffused** across the city.

syn. spread out

★
★ **discharge**
[distʃáːrdʒ]
ⓥ 방출하다

v. to release a confined substance

These iron pipes were once used to **discharge** factory wastewater into a nearby canal.

syn. emit

★
★ **drawback**
[drɔ́ːbæ̀k]
ⓝ 결점, 문제점

n. a negative aspect of something

One of the major **drawbacks** of communications technology is the amount of e-waste it produces.

syn. flaw

> **Useful Tips**
> effluent를 철자가 비슷한 affluent(부유한)와 혼동하지 않도록 주의한다.

★ **effluent**
[éfluənt]
ⓝ 폐수, 오수

n. liquid waste that has been released

The large amounts of **effluent** entering the river have led to a dangerous imbalance in bacteria populations.

★
★ **evaluate**
[ivǽljuèit]
ⓥ 평가하다, 감정하다
n. evaluation

v. to consider something in order to make an assessment

The company has pledged to **evaluate** all of its packaging materials to ensure they are safe.

syn. assess

★
★ **exhaust**
[igzɔ́ːst]
ⓝ 배기가스
ⓥ 고갈시키다, 다 써버리다

n. gas that is released as waste

Vehicle **exhaust** emissions are a major source of smog and air pollution in many urban areas.

v. to use something up completely   *syn.* deplete   *ant.* replenish

After local coal deposits had been **exhausted**, the region switched to cleaner forms of energy.

---

diffuse 강한 바람 때문에, 창고 화재로 생긴 유독성 연기가 도시 전체로 번졌다.   **discharge** 이 철제 파이프들은 한때 공장 폐수를 인근 운하로 방출하는 데 사용되었다.   **drawback** 통신 기술의 큰 문제점 중 하나는 그것이 만들어내는 전자 폐기물의 양이다.   **effluent** 강으로 유입되는 엄청난 양의 폐수는 박테리아 개체수의 위태로운 불균형을 초래했다.   **evaluate** 그 회사는 자사의 모든 포장 자재들이 안전한지를 감정하겠다고 약속했다.   **exhaust** 차량의 배기가스 배출은 많은 도시 지역의 스모그와 대기 오염의 주요 원인이다. / 지역 석탄 매장량이 고갈된 후, 그 지역은 청정에너지로 전환했다.

★
★ **fatal**
[féitl]
ⓐ 죽음을 초래하는, 치명적인

n. fatality

adj. causing death

Exposure to the toxin is unlikely to be **fatal**, but it can cause long-term health issues.

★
★ **inevitably**
[inévətəbli]
ⓐ 필연적으로, 불가피하게

adj. inevitable

adv. in a way that cannot be avoided

Serial polluters **inevitably** seek out ways to circumvent any new environmental regulations.

syn. unavoidably

★
★ **inhale**
[inhéil]
ⓥ (숨을) 들이 마시다

n. inhalation

v. to take into the lungs

New studies indicate that human beings **inhale** thousands of microplastic particles every year.

syn. breathe in   *ant.* exhale

★ **instigate**
[ínstəgèit]
ⓥ 선동하다, 부추기다,
   실시하게 하다

v. to cause an action or process to begin

A sharp increase in pollution-related illnesses **instigated** the passage of the new clean-air law.

syn. initiate   *ant.* conclude

★
★ **nuclear**
[njú:kliər]
ⓐ 핵의, 원자력의

adj. relating to the production of energy through the splitting of an atom's nucleus

Although **nuclear** power doesn't create air pollution, it does produce large amounts of radioactive waste.

★ **nuisance**
[njú:sns]
ⓝ 성가심, 골칫거리

n. a source of annoyance

Burning fallen leaves is more than just a **nuisance**—it is a dangerous source of air pollution.

syn. irritation

---

fatal 그 독소에 대한 노출이 치명적인 것 같지 않지만, 장기적인 건강 문제를 일으킬 수 있다.   **inevitably** 상습적인 공해 유발 기업들은 필연적으로 새로운 환경 규제를 피하기 위한 방법을 모색하기 마련이다.   **inhale** 새로운 연구들에 따르면, 인간은 매년 수천 개의 미세 플라스틱 입자를 들이마신다고 한다.
instigate 오염 관련 질병들의 급격한 증가는 새로운 청정 대기법의 통과를 촉진시켰다.   **nuclear** 원자력은 대기 오염을 발생시키지 않지만, 많은 양의 방사성 폐기물은 만들어낸다.   **nuisance** 낙엽을 소각하는 것은 단순한 골칫거리 그 이상이다. 그것은 대기 오염의 위험한 원인이다.

★★★

poisonous

[pɔ́izənəs]

[형] 유독한, 독이 있는

n. poison

adj. capable of causing death or illness when ingested

Due to years and years of industrial pollution, most of the soil in this area is **poisonous**.

★

procrastinate

[proukrǽstənèit]

[동] 미루다, 질질 끌다

n. procrastination

v. to repeatedly put off doing something

While disinterested politicians **procrastinate**, our air quality issues are getting worse and worse.

★

sludge

[slʌdʒ]

[명] 침전물, (강바닥의) 연한 진흙, 앙금

n. a thick liquid

A layer of **sludge** at the bottom of the river was found to contain high levels of toxins.

syn. muck

★★

subsist

[səbsíst]

[동] 근근이 살아가다, 존속하다

n. subsistence

v. to manage to survive

Few forms of life are able to **subsist** in these waters, due to a heavy concentration of pollutants.

★★

suffocate

[sʌ́fəkèit]

[동] 질식사하다[시키다]

n. suffocation

v. to die or make someone die from a lack of oxygen

If the heavy smog continues to worsen, pedestrians may begin to feel like they're **suffocating**.

syn. asphyxiate

Useful Tips

suffocate는 'My work here never ends, even after I go home. It's suffocating me.'에서와 같이 실생활에서 은유적인 표현으로도 자주 사용된다.

★

tarnish

[tá:rniʃ]

[동] (금속 등이 광택을 잃고) 흐리게 하다, …을 변색시키다

v. to cause a material to lose its shine

People have noticed that the industrial pollution in the air is **tarnishing** their silver jewelry.

ant. polish

poisonous 수년간의 산업공해 때문에, 이 지역 대부분의 토양에는 독성이 있다. **procrastinate** 무관심한 정치인들이 늑장을 부리는 동안, 우리의 대기질 문제는 점점 악화되고 있다. **sludge** 그 강바닥의 침전물 층이 높은 수준의 독소를 함유하고 있다는 것이 밝혀졌다. **subsist** 고농도 오염 물질 때문에, 이 수역에서 살아갈 수 있는 생명체들은 거의 없다. **suffocate** 만약 짙은 스모그가 계속 악화되면, 보행자들은 숨이 막히는 듯한 느낌을 받기 시작할 수도 있다. **tarnish** 사람들은 대기의 산업공해가 그들의 은으로 된 장신구를 변색시키고 있다는 것을 알아차렸다.

EXERCISES

ART & DESIGN

SOCIAL SCIENCE

NATURAL SCIENCE

HUMANITIES

EARTH & SPACE

SOCIAL ISSUES

A Match each definition with the correct word.

1 action taken in response to something negative that occurs   ⓐ fatal

2 to manage to survive   ⓑ discharge

3 causing death   ⓒ tarnish

4 the consequences of a negative event   ⓓ countermeasure

5 to release a confined substance   ⓔ ban

6 to cause a material to lose its shine   ⓕ subsist

7 accessible or ready for use   ⓖ available

8 to make a law or rule against possessing or doing something   ⓗ aftermath

B Choose the word that is closest in meaning to each underlined word.

1 Bacteria can easily <u>contaminate</u> unrefrigerated food and cause people who eat it to fall ill.

   ⓐ preserve   ⓑ cultivate   ⓒ taint   ⓓ expand

2 A child who <u>instigates</u> fights needs to learn how to resolve conflicts peacefully.

   ⓐ initiates   ⓑ perceives   ⓒ circumvents   ⓓ denounces

3 Judging people based on their race can have <u>devastating</u> effects on their self-esteem.

   ⓐ disastrous   ⓑ secondary   ⓒ transitory   ⓓ poisonous

4 The practice of using <u>sludge</u> from sewage treatment plants as fertilizer is a public health risk.

   ⓐ merchandise   ⓑ muck   ⓒ gear   ⓓ literature

5 Discussing politics in the workplace will <u>inevitably</u> cause conflicts that adversely affect morale.

   ⓐ auspiciously   ⓑ intentionally   ⓒ periodically   ⓓ unavoidably

6 A poor diet and lack of exercise will likely result in body fat <u>accumulating</u> around the abdomen.

   ⓐ accruing   ⓑ exuding   ⓒ solidifying   ⓓ withdrawing

7 Sending out text <u>alerts</u> is an effective way of informing the public of danger.

   ⓐ apologies   ⓑ introductions   ⓒ warnings   ⓓ emblems

A Choose the correct words.

1 The word patronizing has the same meaning as
ⓐ intimidating   ⓑ condescending   ⓒ everlasting   ⓓ entertaining

2 The word eliminate has the same meaning as
ⓐ cultivate   ⓑ refrigerate   ⓒ eradicate   ⓓ abbreviate

3 The word solicit has the same meaning as
ⓐ deny   ⓑ request   ⓒ exchange   ⓓ purchase

4 The word culprit has the same meaning as
ⓐ pioneer   ⓑ savior   ⓒ impostor   ⓓ offender

5 The word diffuse has the same meaning as
ⓐ dispose of   ⓑ spread out   ⓒ raise up   ⓓ slow down

6 The word imprison has the same meaning as
ⓐ elevate   ⓑ diagnose   ⓒ slacken   ⓓ incarcerate

7 The word extravagant has the same meaning as
ⓐ hysterical   ⓑ inadequate   ⓒ obscure   ⓓ indulgent

8 The word varied has the same meaning as
ⓐ intense   ⓑ diverse   ⓒ contrite   ⓓ frugal

B Fill in the blanks with the best words from the box.

1 Workers who habitually _____ are seldom able to finish their work on time.

2 Educating people is perhaps the best way to _____ societal racism and sexism.

3 The police talked to a(n) _____ who saw the men dumping trash into the ravine.

4 Some big companies _____ foreign factory workers by severely underpaying them.

5 It is hoped that robots will someday perform hard _____ instead of human beings.

6 The _____ stole a businessman's wallet and then ran off down the street.

| pickpocket | combat | exploit | procrastinate | witness | labor |

C Read the following passages.

ART & DESIGN

SOCIAL SCIENCE

NATURAL SCIENCE

HUMANITIES

EARTH & SPACE

SOCIAL ISSUES

[1-2]   **1** Choose one word that fits both blanks.

> Paul and Gloria are Canadian law students living in Toronto. They often get together with their classmates and professors to _____ legal techniques and study important cases. After they graduate, they want to get married and _____ law at a firm in the Vancouver area.

ⓐ charge   ⓑ practice   ⓒ progress   ⓓ urge

2 Choose the appropriate pair of words to fill in the blanks.

> Although this city has traditionally had a moderate _____, summers have been growing hotter and hotter. Unfortunately, this has worsened the quality of the city's air. Hot air tends to be stagnant, so it traps pollutants and keeps them low to the ground where people can _____ them.

ⓐ norm — withstand   ⓑ pension — substitute

ⓒ climate — inhale   ⓓ nuisance — suffocate

[3-4]

> There are some individuals who despise people who are different from them, as they are fearful of things they don't understand. Besides being hurtful to others, this kind of attitude can be an obstacle to achieving happiness in their own lives, preventing them from ever feeling fulfilled.

3 In the context of the passage, despise means _____.

ⓐ covet   ⓑ allocate   ⓒ query   ⓓ loathe

4 The word obstacle in the passage could best be replaced by

ⓐ obstruction   ⓑ upgrade   ⓒ repercussion   ⓓ precursor

[5-6]

> Home security systems are more popular than ever before, due in part to technological advances. In the past, these systems were difficult to install, usually requiring a team of expensive professionals. These days, however, homeowners can do it themselves. Far from being a _____ process, getting a security system up and running requires no more than an hour or two of your time.

5 The word install in the passage is closest in meaning to

ⓐ take after   ⓑ set up   ⓒ check out   ⓓ look over

6 Choose the word that is most suitable for the blank.

ⓐ painstaking   ⓑ premeditated   ⓒ resourceful   ⓓ compulsive

451

접미사
Suffixes

접미사란 파생어를 만드는 접사로, 주로 어근이나 단어의 뒤에 붙어서 새로운 단어가 되게 하는 말이다. 어떤 접미사가 붙느냐에 따라 단어의 의미뿐만 아니라 품사도 바뀌게 되는데, 영어에서 많이 쓰이는 대표 접미사들을 살펴보고, 그 접미사들이 사용된 단어들도 함께 숙지해 보자.

NOUN SUFFIXES	EXAMPLES
-er, -or, -ee, -ant, -ist, -ian *one who*	employer 고용주 spectator 관중 nominee 후보 descendant 자손 publicist 홍보 담당자 vegetarian 채식주의자
-tion, -ment, -ness, -cy, -ity, -ety, -ance *state of being*	addiction 중독 impediment 장애 fitness 건강, 적합함 deficiency 결핍 hospitality 환대 anxiety 걱정 insurance 보험
-ism *doctrine, belief*	altruism 이타주의 feudalism 봉건 제도 imperialism 제국주의

VERB SUFFIXES	EXAMPLES
-ate, -ish, -(i)fy, -ize, -en *to make or become*	navigate 길을 찾다 relish 즐기다 identify 식별하다 sympathize 동정하다 strengthen 강화하다
-ed/-ing *past tense/present participle*	discriminated 차별했다 obeyed 따랐다 accumulating 축적하는 committing 저지르는 nourishing 영양분을 공급하는

ADJECTIVE SUFFIXES	EXAMPLES
-able, -ible *capable of being*	available 구할 수 있는 conceivable 상상할 수 있는 vulnerable 취약한 compatible 호환되는 edible 먹을 수 있는 tangible 유형의
-al, -ic, -ial, -ant, -ine, -ive *pertaining to*	optical 광학의 allergic 알레르기가 있는 artificial 인공의 extravagant 사치스러운 divine 신의 cognitive 인지의
-(i)ous, -ful *full of*	hazardous 위험한 poisonous 유독한 ubiquitous 어디에나 있는 resourceful 수완이 좋은 skillful 숙련된 thoughtful 사려 깊은

ADVERB SUFFIXES	EXAMPLES
-ly *how something is (done)*	anonymously 익명으로 inevitably 필연적으로 previously 미리 radically 근본적으로 strictly 엄격히 subsequently 나중에
-ward *direction*	backward 뒤로 forward 앞으로 toward …쪽으로
-wise *in a manner of*	clockwise 시계 방향으로 likewise 똑같이 otherwise …와는 다르게

INDEX & FINAL CHECKUP

J

K

Q

각종 영어능력 시험에 빈도 높게 출제되는 주제별 어휘 엄선

최근 시험에 출제된 다양한 어휘 문제 유형 제시

어휘력과 독해력을 한 번에 잡을 수 있는 아카데믹한 예문과 지문 수록

영어능력 시험 대비 필수어휘 학습서

ACTIVATOR
VOCA

Answer Keys

TOEFL

TOEIC

TEPS

SAT

IELTS

G-TELP

공무원

편입

특목고

YBM

Chapter 1 | ART & DESIGN

Lesson 01 EXERCISES p.19

A Match each definition with the correct word.

1 ⓔ 2 ⓖ 3 ⓒ 4 ⓐ
5 ⓑ 6 ⓗ 7 ⓕ 8 ⓓ

B Choose the word that is closest in meaning to each underlined word.

1 ⓑ 그 빈티지 화병은 입구 주변에 금박 문양이 있어서, 그 가치가 훨씬 더 높아졌다.

2 ⓓ 그 목각사는 더 정교한 질감을 내기 위해 가면을 계속 수정했다.

3 ⓒ 나무 액자를 만들 때, 모서리에 바른 풀이 마를 수 있는 충분한 시간을 주어야 한다.

4 ⓐ 그 여배우는 자신을 좋아하는 관객들에게 매끄러운 구연 공연을 선보였다.

5 ⓒ 그래픽 디자인 분야에서 남을 능가하려면, 인상 깊은 온라인 포트폴리오를 개발해야 한다.

6 ⓓ 그 건축가는 그 고객에게 선보일 축소 모형 몇 점을 만들도록 인턴들에게 지시했다.

7 ⓑ Sophie는 자신의 미술 프로젝트를 위한 영감을 찾을 수 있을까 해서 방안을 훑어보았다.

Lesson 02 EXERCISES p.27

A Match each definition with the correct word.

1 ⓖ 2 ⓒ 3 ⓐ 4 ⓗ
5 ⓔ 6 ⓑ 7 ⓓ 8 ⓕ

B Choose the word that is closest in meaning to each underlined word.

1 ⓒ 그 예술가는 단순한 선들을 그려 자신의 생각을 표현하는 것에 능숙하다.

2 ⓑ 그 그림에 쓰인 어두운 색들은 비통하고 슬픈 분위기를 증폭시킨다.

3 ⓒ 실험 미술의 일시적인 유행은 새로운 양식의 사실주의로 대체되었다.

4 ⓐ 그 무용수들은 우아한 움직임과 통일된 점프로 관객들을 사로잡는다.

5 ⓒ 자신의 작품에 대한 그 감독의 통명스러운 설명은 영화제에서 팬들을 실망시켰다.

6 ⓐ 그 콘서트 홀은 표 가격을 낮춰서 콘서트 팬들을

끌어들이기로 결정했다.

7 ⓓ 그 오페라 가수는 긴 시간 동안 어려운 음들을 지속하는 능력으로 유명하다.

Lesson 03 EXERCISES p.33

A Match each definition with the correct word.

1 ⓔ 2 ⓐ 3 ⓒ 4 ⓗ
5 ⓖ 6 ⓓ 7 ⓕ 8 ⓑ

B Choose the word that is closest in meaning to each underlined word.

1 ⓒ 그 여자는 날카로운 도구를 사용해 그 뮤직 박스의 금속 면에 자기 이름의 첫 글자들을 새겨 넣었다.

2 ⓓ 그 세트장 디자이너들은 무대를 도시의 버스 정류장처럼 보이도록 바꿔 놓았다.

3 ⓑ 그 무용수들이 입은 의상의 선명한 분홍색과 노란색이 회색 배경과 대조되어 두드러져 보였다.

4 ⓒ 이 누비 이불들은 그것을 만든 사람 자신의 옷에서 뜯은 작은 천 조각들로 장식되어 있다.

5 ⓐ 토스카처럼 이태리어로 쓰인 훌륭한 오페라들이 많다.

6 ⓑ 그 가수의 공연은 그녀가 그 아리아의 제일 끝 부분에서 음을 하나 놓칠 때까지는 흠 잡을 데가 없었다.

7 ⓓ 그 극작가는 주인공을 모든 것에 대해 걱정하는 불안한 십 대로 묘사한다.

Lesson 04 EXERCISES p.39

A Match each definition with the correct word.

1 ⓕ 2 ⓒ 3 ⓑ 4 ⓔ
5 ⓖ 6 ⓗ 7 ⓓ 8 ⓐ

B Choose the word that is closest in meaning to each underlined word.

1 ⓐ 그 베테랑 배우는 자신의 새로운 시트콤이 전반적으로 호평을 받아 기뻤다.

2 ⓐ 만약 사진작가의 손이 떨리면, 사진들은 흐릿해지기 쉽다.

3 ⓒ 친환경적인 건물들과 집들이 그 건축가의 포트폴리오의 대부분을 이룬다.

4 ⓒ 그 16세기 화가의 뛰어난 색과 빛의 사용은 비평가들로부터 극찬 받는다.

5 ⓐ 그 오케스트라의 지휘자는 연주가들에게 더 열정적으로 연주할 것을 종용했다.

6 ⓒ Michelangelo가 르네상스 예술에 미친 영향의 정도는 아무리 강조해도 지나치지 않다.

7 ⓑ 그 새 뮤지컬은 많은 역동적인 노래와 춤이 특징이다.

Lesson **05**　**EXERCISES**　p.45

A **Match each definition with the correct word.**

1 ⓑ	2 ⓐ	3 ⓓ	4 ⓖ
5 ⓕ	6 ⓗ	7 ⓒ	8 ⓔ

B **Choose the word that is closest in meaning to each underlined word.**

1 ⓒ 바이올린은 숙달하기 힘든 악기여서, 자주 규칙적으로 연습하는 것이 아주 중요하다.

2 ⓐ Rodin은 그의 조각 작품들이 사실적이어서 호평을 받았고, 그런 사실성 때문에 그것들이 강렬한 예술 작품이 되었다.

3 ⓓ 그 발레리나는 이전 공연에서 발목을 삐어서, 오늘 밤에 공연하지 않을 것이다.

4 ⓒ 그 젊은 예술가의 창의적인 이미지 사용은 그의 그림들을 흥미롭고 독특하게 만든다.

5 ⓑ 그 장인은 명성을 얻은 적은 없지만, 작품을 통해 막대한 돈을 벌기는 했다.

6 ⓑ 그 피아니스트와 오페라 가수는 자선 기금 마련을 위해 노래 한 곡을 합작할 것이다.

7 ⓓ 한 무리의 힙합 댄서들이 다가오는 경연 대회에 대해 의논하려고 스튜디오에 모였다.

REVIEW TEST Lessons 01-05　pp.46-47

A **Choose the correct words.**

1 ⓓ	2 ⓑ	3 ⓓ	4 ⓒ
5 ⓐ	6 ⓒ	7 ⓐ	8 ⓑ

B **Fill in the blanks with the best words from the box.**

1 repertoire
그 배우의 레퍼토리는 1960년대 인기 있던 미국 뮤지컬의 노래들과 춤곡들을 많이 포함하고 있다.

2 carve
그 북미 원주민 예술가는 단순한 나무 토막을 전통적인 예술 작품으로 조각해 내는 재능이 있다.

3 choreography
그 여배우는 대단원의 안무를 외우는 데 어려움을 겪어서,

그녀를 도울 무용 강사가 고용되었다.

4 apprentice
그 위대한 조각가의 예전 견습생은 예술적인 능력과 호평 면에서 계속해서 그를 능가했다.

5 premiere
그 발레의 초연은 주연 무용수들 중 한 명의 부상으로 일주일 연기될 수 밖에 없었다.

6 improvise
연극 배우들은 공연 도중 자기 대사를 갑자기 잊어버린 것을 알게 되면 즉흥 연기를 하도록 배운다.

C **Read the following passages.**

1 ⓑ
Beethoven은 그의 교향곡들 중 한 곡에 대해 지휘자와 언쟁을 벌인 후 마음을 가다듬어야 했다. 그는 차를 한 잔 타서 발코니에 앉았다. 그는 충분히 마음을 진정시킨 후, 피아노로 걸어가서 새로운 곡을 작곡하기 시작했다.

2 ⓓ
텔레비전에서 마술을 공연하는 것은 현장 청중들 앞에서 하는 것보다 훨씬 더 쉽다. TV 속의 마술사가 난데없이 거대한 동물을 불러내는 듯이 보이는 것은, 단순히 녹화를 멈추고 무대 위로 그 동물을 데려온 다음 녹화를 다시 시작함으로써 만들어지는 환영일 수 있다.

3 ⓒ　　4 ⓓ
공연 제작에서 가장 중요한 부분 중 하나는 커튼이 처음으로 올라가 세심하게 설치한 무대 장치가 공개되는 순간이다. 만약 그 무대가 특별히 인상적이거나 사실적이면, 공연이 시작하기도 전에 박수 갈채를 유도해 낼 수 있다.

5 ⓑ　　6 ⓓ
금세공은 천에 금실을 짜 넣는 예술로, 보통 우아한 의상을 만드는 데 사용된다. 그 실은 단지 장식용일 뿐인데, 그것이 천의 견고성이나 내구성을 높이지는 못하기 때문이다. 하지만 평범한 의상을 별처럼 빛나게 해 줄 수 있다는 면에서 높이 평가된다.

Lesson **06**　**EXERCISES**　p.55

A **Match each definition with the correct word.**

1 ⓗ	2 ⓐ	3 ⓖ	4 ⓔ
5 ⓕ	6 ⓒ	7 ⓑ	8 ⓓ

B **Choose the word that is closest in meaning to each underlined word.**

1 ⓐ 그 작가는 형편없이 번역된 글을 논리 정연하게 바꾸는 능력이 있다.

2 ⓒ 그 영화 포스터에 묘사된 흥미진진한 장면들은 십 대들의

3

관심을 끌도록 만들어졌다.

3 ⓐ 그 민속 음악가들이 잔잔한 곡을 연주하자, 관객들은 눈을 감고 미소 지었다.

4 ⓒ 그 영화는 다른 사람들과 공감하는 것의 중요성에 대한 미묘한 메시지를 담고 있다.

5 ⓑ 그 직조공은 때때로 다른 이들에게 깊은 인상을 남기려고 자신의 작업 속도를 과장하곤 한다.

6 ⓒ 오늘날의 모델들에 비해서, 초창기의 필름 카메라들은 거대하고 들고 다니기 어려웠다.

7 ⓑ 역사적인 건축물들의 상태가 악화되기 시작하면, 복원을 위해 건축가들이 소환된다.

Lesson 07 **EXERCISES** p.61

A **Match each definition with the correct word.**

| 1 ⓔ | 2 ⓑ | 3 ⓗ | 4 ⓐ |
| 5 ⓓ | 6 ⓖ | 7 ⓒ | 8 ⓕ |

B **Choose the word that is closest in meaning to each underlined word.**

1 ⓓ 오페라 안경은 한때 무대 위의 공연자들을 확대하기 위해 흔히 사용됐다.

2 ⓗ 도시 계획 입안자들은 새로운 교통 신호등을 설치하기 전에 복잡한 교통 패턴을 분석해야 한다.

3 ⓒ 그 감독은 외계인을 연기하는 배우의 모습을 증강시키기 위해 CGI를 사용하기로 결정했다.

4 ⓐ 그 건축가들은 천장에 대형 채광창들을 설치하면 생길 수 있는 단점들을 고려했다.

5 ⓑ 아름다운 풍경에 영감을 받은 그 화가는 이젤과 가장 가까이 있는 깨끗한 캔버스를 잡았다.

6 ⓓ 그 인형 제작자는 자신의 작품들을 위한 시장이 있는지 보려고 조사를 좀 했다.

7 ⓑ 그 뮤지컬의 가장 인상적인 장면에서, 여주인공이 자기 이웃 사람을 사랑한다고 고백한다.

Lesson 08 **EXERCISES** p.69

A **Match each definition with the correct word.**

| 1 ⓐ | 2 ⓗ | 3 ⓓ | 4 ⓔ |
| 5 ⓑ | 6 ⓕ | 7 ⓒ | 8 ⓖ |

B **Choose the word that is closest in meaning to each underlined word.**

1 ⓐ 태양의 서커스 공연에 적합한 극장을 찾는 것은 어렵다.

2 ⓒ 그 바이올리니스트는 그의 큰 손에 더 잘 맞도록 악기를 주문 제작했다.

3 ⓓ 그 건축가는 벽에 난 금을 발견한 후, 인부들에게 건설 작업을 중단하라고 지시했다.

4 ⓒ 장인들이 다른 나라로 이주하면, 그곳에서 사용 가능한 재료들에 적응해야 한다.

5 ⓑ 그 배우들은 빈 무대에서 공연하기 때문에, 관객들이 배경을 마음속에 떠올려봐야 한다.

6 ⓓ 나무로 된 이젤은 풍경화가들에게 거추장스러워서, 그들은 더 가벼운 이젤들을 선호한다.

7 ⓓ 그 인기 있는 영화는 세 개의 각기 다른 스크린에서 동시에 상영되고 있다.

Lesson 09 **EXERCISES** p.75

A **Match each definition with the correct word.**

| 1 ⓗ | 2 ⓒ | 3 ⓐ | 4 ⓕ |
| 5 ⓓ | 6 ⓖ | 7 ⓑ | 8 ⓔ |

B **Choose the word that is closest in meaning to each underlined word.**

1 ⓑ 그 유화는 맛있는 음식이 담긴 접시들로 뒤덮인 식탁들이 놓인 호화로운 연회를 보여 준다.

2 ⓒ 그 연극의 등장인물은 가난하게 설정되어서, 그 배우는 누더기를 걸치고 있다.

3 ⓒ 그 도시와 인접 도시를 잇는 새로운 4차선 고속도로를 현재 구상 중이다.

4 ⓓ 오페라는 클래식 음악과 연극의 요소들을 모두 아우르기 때문에 인기가 있다.

5 ⓐ 우연히 캔버스가 못에 뚫린 그 그림은 복원 중이다.

6 ⓓ 한 도시의 교외 인구가 너무 밀집되기 시작하면, 그 교외 지역들이 시골 지역까지 확장되는 경향이 있다.

7 ⓐ 그 무용수들은 안무에 대해 불평했지만, 결국 감독이 이겼다.

Lesson 10 **EXERCISES** p.81

A **Match each definition with the correct word.**

| 1 ⓓ | 2 ⓑ | 3 ⓕ | 4 ⓔ |
| 5 ⓖ | 6 ⓗ | 7 ⓐ | 8 ⓒ |

B **Choose the word that is closest in meaning to each underlined word.**

1 ⓐ 사진작가들은 특별한 순간들을 평생 남을 이미지들로 담아내기 위해 노력한다.

2 ⓒ 그 밴드의 야외 공연이 끝나고 나서, 공원 직원들이 무대를 해체했다.

3 ⓓ 영화제 기간 동안 다수의 극장 상영시간들을 조정하는
것은 힘든 일이다.

4 ⓑ 그 발레리나는 아픈 무릎 때문에 부담이 적은 역할로만
제한되었다.

5 ⓐ 그 도시가 예술가의 허가를 받으면, 그 새로운 동상이 내일
공개될 것이다.

6 ⓐ 건축가와 건설 관리자 외에는 그 누구에게도 미완성된
건물 내부 출입이 허가되지 않는다.

7 ⓒ 직조와 조각을 결합한 그 장인의 독특한 작품이 전시되고
있다.

REVIEW TEST Lessons 06-10 pp. 82-83

A Choose the correct words.

| 1 ⓒ | 2 ⓓ | 3 ⓑ | 4 ⓐ |
| 5 ⓐ | 6 ⓒ | 7 ⓒ | 8 ⓑ |

B Fill in the blanks with the best words from the box.

1 symmetry
1960년대에 입구 왼쪽에 있는 세 개의 기둥 중 하나가
무너졌을 때, 그 고대 건축물의 완벽한 대칭이 망가졌다.

2 conscious
어떤 그림을 그릴지 모른 채 빈 캔버스 앞에 서는 예술가들은
거의 없는데, 위대한 예술 작품을 만들어 내기 위해서는
의식적인 계획이 필요하기 때문이다.

3 meander
계획 도시의 도로들은 대개 구불구불하지 않다. 그 도로들은
직각으로 서로 교차하는 직선들인 경향이 있다.

4 flaunt
그 황제는 도시 중심에 도금된 본인의 조각상을 세워 자신의
엄청난 부와 권력을 과시하기로 결심했다.

5 impetus
사고 후 병원에 입원한 동안, 자신을 표현하려는 Frida Kahlo의
욕구가 어린 시절 취미였던 그림 그리기로 돌아가도록 자극을
주었다.

6 candid
그 사진은 자연스러운 모습을 찍은 것이지만, 대부분의
사람들이 카메라를 똑바로 바라보고 있다는 사실이 자세를
잡고 찍은 것처럼 보이게 한다.

C Read the following passages.

1 ⓐ
전쟁 중에, 어떤 마을의 교회 근처에 폭탄이 떨어져서 그
교회의 목조부가 약간 손상을 입었다. 한 현지 여성이
무상으로 그것을 보수해 주겠다고 제안했다. 뛰어난 솜씨를
보인 그녀는 목세공인으로서 경력을 유지할 정도로 충분한
일감을 받았다.

2 ⓓ
대부분의 감독들은 편집이 영화 제작에서 매우 중요한
부분이라는 것에 동의하며, 어떤 감독들은 그것이 제작
과정에서 가장 중요한 단계라고 주장하기까지 한다. 장면들의
길이와 그것들이 스크린 상에 나오는 순서는 관객들이 그
사건을 어떻게 인식하는지에 직접적으로 영향을 미칠 수 있다.

3 ⓒ   4 ⓑ
패션 분야는 대부분의 다른 분야들보다는 반항아들에 더
관용적인데, 주로 그 분야가 앞을 향해 나아가게 하는
지속적인 혁신에 의존하기 때문이다. 최고급 브랜드들의 최고
경영자들은 거친 바느질이나 다른 엉성한 작업에 대해 불만을
표할 수는 있지만, 만약 그 디자인이 흥미로운 방식으로
원칙을 깨는 것이라면 그것을 눈감아 줄 것이다.

5 ⓒ   6 ⓐ
건축가가 새로운 건물들을 상상하고 디자인해서 건축하는 것이
쉽지 않지만, 역사적인 건축물들을 보수하는 것은 훨씬 더
어렵다. 벽돌들의 색조 같은 가장 작은 세부 사항들도 주의
깊게 살펴야 한다. 벽돌들이 수년간 햇빛에 바랬다면, 복원
부분이 두드러지지 않도록 새 벽돌들을 그것들과 똑같이
맞춰야 한다.

Chapter 2 | SOCIAL SCIENCE

Lesson 11 EXERCISES
p.91

A Match each definition with the correct word.
1 ⓑ   2 ⓐ   3 ⓕ   4 ⓖ
5 ⓒ   6 ⓔ   7 ⓗ   8 ⓓ

B Choose the word that is closest in meaning to each underlined word.
1 ⓓ 많은 국가들에서 공직에 출마하려면 상당한 돈이 필요하다.
2 ⓓ 그 고고학자들은 현장에서 가치 있는 것을 전혀 발견하지 못하자 장비를 챙겨 떠났다.
3 ⓒ 그 남자는 3년간 법대에서 공부해 변호사가 되겠다는 목표를 이루었다.
4 ⓒ 심리학 실험 보고서에는, 실험의 각 단계를 서술해야 한다.
5 ⓑ 윤리적인 사업 전략은 직원들과 고객들의 권리를 모두 존중한다.
6 ⓐ 그 식품 회사의 끈질긴 광고 캠페인은 회사의 평판을 개선하는 데 도움이 되었다.
7 ⓑ 한 나라의 국내 총생산이 떨어지기 시작하면, 그것을 신속히 안정시키기 위한 결정적 조치들을 취해야 한다.

Lesson 12 EXERCISES
p.99

A Match each definition with the correct word.
1 ⓒ   2 ⓗ   3 ⓔ   4 ⓐ
5 ⓕ   6 ⓖ   7 ⓓ   8 ⓑ

B Choose the word that is closest in meaning to each underlined word.
1 ⓐ 경제 침체의 예상 원인은 급작스러운 부도 증가였다.
2 ⓐ 그 정유 회사는 석유를 찾기 위한 미개척 지역으로의 원정을 후원했다.
3 ⓓ 그 화살은 과녁을 관통하는 데 실패하고, 튀어 나와 땅에 떨어졌다.
4 ⓑ 그 선생님은 학생들에게 그 고대 유물이 무엇에 쓰였을지 추측해 보라고 했다.
5 ⓒ 그 변호사는 자신의 의뢰인의 후회가 진짜라고 주장했지만, 그녀를 믿는 사람들은 거의 없었다.
6 ⓐ 그 광고는 시골 지역에 살며 가축들을 소유한 사람들을 대상으로 한다.
7 ⓑ 그 사업체는 존재했다는 흔적만을 남긴 채, 폐업하고 나갔다.

Lesson 13 EXERCISES
p.105

A Match each definition with the correct word.
1 ⓗ   2 ⓐ   3 ⓓ   4 ⓒ
5 ⓔ   6 ⓑ   7 ⓕ   8 ⓖ

B Choose the word that is closest in meaning to each underlined word.
1 ⓒ 저소득층 의뢰인들을 기꺼이 변호할, 자격 있는 변호사들이 꼭 필요하다.
2 ⓓ 보안 문제 때문에 기자들이 그 유적지에 들어가는 것이 거부되었다.
3 ⓐ 윤리학 논쟁들이 지루해 보일 수 있지만, 인간 본성을 이해하려면 그런 논쟁들이 필요하다.
4 ⓓ 직업 상담원들은 자신의 미래에 대한 확신이 없는 사람들에게 조언을 해 준다.
5 ⓐ 광범위한 부정 행위 때문에, 현재 많은 스포츠 행사들에서 약물 검사가 필수이다.
6 ⓑ 그 기업은 직원들이 그들의 기술을 발전시켜 줄 수업들에 등록하는 것을 권장했다.
7 ⓒ 그 정치인은 자신의 학문적 성취들을 자랑했지만, 유권자들은 그의 정책들에 대해 듣고 싶어했다.

Lesson 14 EXERCISES
p.113

A Match each definition with the correct word.
1 ⓑ   2 ⓕ   3 ⓗ   4 ⓖ
5 ⓒ   6 ⓔ   7 ⓓ   8 ⓐ

B Choose the word that is closest in meaning to each underlined word.
1 ⓑ 문제가 생겨 힘들어하는 초보자들은 좀 더 경험이 풍부한 동료들에게 조언을 구할 수 있다.
2 ⓐ 유권자들은 부도덕한 정치인들의 거짓말에 신물이 나서, 그들이 믿을 수 있는 사람을 간절히 원한다.
3 ⓑ 쇼핑몰에 현금을 지급하는 기계를 설치하는 것은 쇼핑객들이 더 지출하도록 부추긴다.
4 ⓒ 어떤 산업에 보조금을 줄지 결정하는 것은 어떤 정부에게나 어려울 수 있다.
5 ⓓ 그 코치는 자신의 모든 지식과 경험을 책 한 권에 통합시키기로 결심했다.
6 ⓒ 그 고고학자들은 자신들이 옳은 장소에 있다고 단호한

태도를 보였지만, 아무것도 발견하지 못했다.

7 ⓒ 좋은 광고는 제품과 그것의 특징들에 대한 정확한 설명을 제공할 것이다.

Lesson 15 EXERCISES p.121

A Match each definition with the correct word.

1 ⓑ   2 ⓔ   3 ⓕ   4 ⓗ

5 ⓒ   6 ⓖ   7 ⓓ   8 ⓐ

B Choose the word that is closest in meaning to each underlined word.

1 ⓐ 광고 캠페인 후에, 십 대들에게 그 기술 회사의 인기가 급등하기 시작했다.

2 ⓓ 그 학교 재학생들은 졸업 후 재계에서 번창하는 경향이 있다.

3 ⓒ 다른 쪽으로는 유능한 사람들도 대중 앞에서 말하게 되면 두려움에 얼어버린다.

4 ⓒ 우유부단한 사람들은 자신의 판단에 의문을 가지는 것 같은 인상을 준다.

5 ⓑ 싱가포르의 법은 세계에서 가장 엄중한 편이어서, 범죄율이 낮다.

6 ⓓ 셔츠가 남아도는 사태에 직면한 그 회사는 빈국들에 그 제품들을 기부하기로 결정했다.

7 ⓒ 그 농구 경기는 심판이 두 득점판 간의 불일치를 알아 차렸을 때 중단되었다.

REVIEW TEST Lessons 11-15 pp.122-123

A Choose the correct words.

1 ⓓ   2 ⓓ   3 ⓑ   4 ⓒ

5 ⓐ   6 ⓓ   7 ⓑ   8 ⓒ

B Fill in the blanks with the best words from the box.

1 shard

지금껏 단 한개의 도자기 조각만 발견됐다는 사실에도 불구하고, 그 고고학자들은 결국에는 고대 화병 전체를 찾을 수 있을 거라고 기대한다.

2 aspire

그 십 대 세 명은 언젠가 프로 농구 경기에서 뛰기를 열망하기 때문에, 동네 체육관에서 운동하고 기량을 다듬으며 많은 시간을 함께 보낸다.

3 shaman

그 현대 주술사가 거행하는 의식들은 수천 년 동안 이어져

왔다고 여겨지는 그 종족의 자연 치유 전통에 바탕을 둔다.

4 redundant

그 공장 직원은 회사의 제조 과정 발전으로 정리해고되었다는 것을 알게 된 즉시 새로운 일자리를 찾기 시작했다.

5 endure

자국이 독립과 민족 주체성을 유지할 수 있다면, 수년 간의 경제적 고난을 견딜 의향이 있는 국민들이 많았다.

6 Frugal

검소한 교사들은 전문적으로 보이는 교육 자료들을 가게나 인터넷 사이트에서 구매하기보다 스스로 만드는 방법을 찾는 데 능숙하다.

C Read the following passages.

1 ⓒ

일부 어린 학생들은 스스로 앉아 긴 이야기를 조용히 읽을 만한 절제력이 없다. 교사들은 이러한 무능력 때문에 그들을 벌 주어서는 안된다. 대신에, 그들은 학생들이 문장들을 돌아가며 크게 읽게 하는 것처럼 교재를 다루는 다른 방법들을 찾아야 한다.

2 ⓐ

그 직원들은 발표를 위해 값비싼 용품들을 구매한 후, 회사가 그것들을 배상해 주지 않는 것에 놀랐다. 그들은 소란스럽게 불평하면 상사가 좋지 않은 반응을 보일 것을 알고, 대신 그 상황을 설명하는 공식적인 서신을 썼다.

3 ⓐ   4 ⓒ

초기 인류는 유목민이었다. 마침내 정착하기 시작했을 때, 그들은 후손들이 한두 세대 정도 그곳에서 살고 떠날 것이라 생각했다. 그들은 후손들이 수천 년 동안 그곳에 남아 번영할 것임을 거의 알지 못했다.

5 ⓐ   6 ⓑ

전국 대회에 출전하지 못하게 된 것을 알게 되었을 때, 그 팀은 충격을 받고 속이 상했다. 다음 연습 때, 코치는 그들의 사기가 아주 낮다는 것을 알아차리고 조치를 취하기로 결심했다. 그는 선수들을 불러 모아 절대 포기하지 않는 것의 중요성에 대한 고무적인 연설을 했다.

Lesson 16 EXERCISES p.129

A Match each definition with the correct word.

1 ⓒ   2 ⓗ   3 ⓐ   4 ⓓ

5 ⓕ   6 ⓑ   7 ⓔ   8 ⓖ

B Choose the word that is closest in meaning to each underlined word.

1 ⓑ 변호사들은 예비 배심원들이 완전한 객관성을 가지고 경청할 것인지 확인하기 위해 면접을 본다.

2 ⓒ 위기 상황 동안 의사 결정하는 것은 힘든데, 예상치 못한 윤리적 문제들이 발생할 수 있기 때문이다.

3 ⓑ 프로 스포츠 팀들은 높은 (운영) 비용을 감당하는 데 도움이 되도록 다양한 상품에 의존한다.

4 ⓓ 집에서 자녀들을 가르치려는 부모들은 전문가들과 먼저 상담해야 한다.

5 ⓐ 그 축구 코치는 팀이 새로운 전술을 사용하기 원할 때, 팔을 흔든다.

6 ⓑ 그 젊은 정치인의 첫 번째 연설은 실수와 어색한 침묵으로 가득한 대실패였다.

7 ⓑ 박물관 방문객들은 고대 그리스 조각품들의 아름다움에 놀랐다.

Lesson 17 EXERCISES p.137

A Match each definition with the correct word.

1 ⓑ   2 ⓓ   3 ⓐ   4 ⓖ

5 ⓔ   6 ⓗ   7 ⓕ   8 ⓒ

B Choose the word that is closest in meaning to each underlined word.

1 ⓒ 그 정치인은 광고에서 상대 후보를 비방해 비난 받았음에도 불구하고, 선거에서 낙승했다.

2 ⓑ 그 학생들은 철학 공부가 인생의 도덕적 갈등들을 더 쉽게 다룰 수 있게 해 준다고 말한다.

3 ⓒ 법정의 편안한 분위기를 조성한 것은 바로 그 판사의 정감 있는 성격이었다.

4 ⓓ 그 스타 하키 선수는 자녀 학대 혐의로 체포된 후, 팀에서 퇴출되었다.

5 ⓒ 화가 난 그 의장은 손으로 탁자를 세게 쳐서 모두를 움찔하게 했다.

6 ⓑ 그 회사의 새 제품들은 대중의 갑작스러운 청결에 대한 강박 관념에 맞아 떨어진다.

7 ⓐ 그 인류학자들은 그 부족의 전통들에 대한 주장을 미심쩍어하면서도, 그것들을 조사하기로 했다.

Lesson 18 EXERCISES p.143

A Match each definition with the correct word.

1 ⓔ   2 ⓗ   3 ⓐ   4 ⓒ

5 ⓓ   6 ⓖ   7 ⓕ   8 ⓑ

B Choose the word that is closest in meaning to each underlined word.

1 ⓐ 경제학자들은 한 주요 은행의 붕괴가 경제 전체를 위험에

빠트릴 수도 있다고 경고했다.

2 ⓓ 경쟁사들에게 사기로 고발당한 그 회사는 이미지를 개선하기 위한 시도를 했다.

3 ⓑ 축구 경기가 표준화되기 전에, 축구 규칙들은 모호하고 일관성이 없었다.

4 ⓓ 그 십 대의 고고학에 대한 흥미는 한 박물관을 방문하면서 생겼다.

5 ⓒ 이타심으로 칭송받는 그 억만장자는 현재 대선 출마를 고려 중이다.

6 ⓐ 탐욕이 사회적으로 용인되지 않는다는 것을 아이들에게 이해시키는 것은 학교들의 몫이다.

7 ⓓ 그 남자가 범인일 것이라는 추측에도 불구하고, 그는 자신의 결백을 주장했다.

Lesson 19 EXERCISES p.149

A Match each definition with the correct word.

1 ⓑ   2 ⓖ   3 ⓒ   4 ⓗ

5 ⓓ   6 ⓔ   7 ⓕ   8 ⓐ

B Choose the word that is closest in meaning to each underlined word.

1 ⓒ 그 경제학자의 복잡한 이론들을 이해하기 쉽게 해 주는 것은 바로 그의 명료한 문체이다.

2 ⓑ 그 정치가는 그 사업체를 폐업시키겠다고 협박했지만, 그에게는 그럴 권한이 없다.

3 ⓓ 즉각적인 비디오 판독은 그 심판이 그 경기에서 반칙을 선언한 것이 정당했음을 입증했다.

4 ⓓ 그 심리학자는 문제가 많은 그 소년이 가족을 경멸하는 이유를 알아내려 애썼다.

5 ⓐ 새 연구는 잃어버린 도시 아틀란티스를 발견했다는 그 탐험가의 주장을 반박했다.

6 ⓑ 그 단체는 아이들 대상 프로그램 도중 나오는 광고들에 대한 더 엄격한 규제를 지지한다.

7 ⓒ 그 법안은 1987년에 제정된 이후, 캘리포니아에서 플라스틱 병의 재활용률을 높이는 데 일조했다.

Lesson 20 EXERCISES p.157

A Match each definition with the correct word.

1 ⓐ   2 ⓓ   3 ⓑ   4 ⓗ

5 ⓕ   6 ⓖ   7 ⓔ   8 ⓒ

B Choose the word that is closest in meaning to each underlined word.

1 ⓑ 그 제품의 대담한 포장은 그것이 신제품이고 개선되었음을
나타낸다.

2 ⓓ 이 보고서에서 보이는 암울한 경제 수치는 정부의 밝은
선전과 상충된다.

3 ⓐ 강의가 더욱 어려워지면서, 학생들의 초기 열정이
약해지기 시작했다.

4 ⓒ 화학 회사 연합이 제초제의 안전성에 대한 연구에 자금을
댔다.

5 ⓑ 고집스러운 사람을 대할 때는, 무력보다는 외교술이 더
유용하다.

6 ⓐ 어떤 믿음에 대한 광적인 지지는 개인이 비윤리적인
방식으로 행동하도록 만들 수 있다.

7 ⓓ 전 세계의 몇몇 나라에서, 사형은 반역죄에 합당한
벌이라고 여겨진다.

REVIEW TEST Lessons 16-20 pp.158-159

A Choose the correct words.

1 ⓐ   2 ⓒ   3 ⓓ   4 ⓐ

5 ⓑ   6 ⓑ   7 ⓒ   8 ⓒ

B Fill in the blanks with the best words from the box.

1 offset

우리의 잘못된 행동으로 인한 죄책감을, 사회적으로 용인되는
활동들에 의해 생기는 긍정적인 감정들로 상쇄하려는 것은
인간의 본성이다.

2 faction

의회 내부에, 특정 규칙에 대한 항의의 형태로 일상적인
활동들을 방해하기로 선택한 상원 의원들의 계파가 있다.

3 enforce

모종의 처벌과 함께 기꺼이 집행할 준비가 되어 있지 않은
어떠한 규칙도 만들어서는 안된다는 것이 리더십의 기본
원칙이다.

4 exempt

그 긴장한 남자는 재판에서 피고에게 불리한 증언을 하기로
동의하면 체포에서 면제될 것을 보장받았다.

5 confidential

그 환자는 모든 것이 기밀로 부쳐진다는 것을 알게 되자,
수년간 간직했던 비밀들을 심리학자에게 말하기 시작했다.

6 reputation

그 회사는 소비자들에게 아주 훌륭한 평판을 받아왔는데, 주로
그 회사의 제품들이 내구성에 중점을 두고 제작된다는 점
때문이다.

C Read the following passages.

1 ⓒ

현대 사회에서, 점잖은 사람들은 다른 이들을 불쾌하게 하거나
불편하게 할 방식으로 말하거나 행동하길 거부한다. 누군가가
사회적 갈등을 피하기 위해 충분히 노력하는 한, 다른 이들과
잘 지내는 것이 쉬워진다.

2 ⓒ

변호사들은 종종 자신들이 법정에서 격한 언쟁에 휘말린다는
것을 알게 된다. 하지만 일단 재판이 끝나면, 그들은 실제로
어떻게 느끼든, 만날 때마다 서로에게 따뜻하게 대할 것으로
기대된다. 그럼에도 불구하고, 이것은 그들 관계에 부담을 줄
수 있다.

3 ⓑ   4 ⓓ

자신이 옳다는 것을 아는 경우에도 사람들이 상사에게 맞서는
것은 결코 쉽지 않다. 이것은 정치에서 특히 더 그러하다. 예를
들어, 만약 독재자가 나라에 해가 되는 정책을 지지한다 해도
정부 내에서 기꺼이 무언가를 말하려고 하는 사람은 거의 없을
것이다.

5 ⓐ   6 ⓒ

경제가 일정하지 않게 상승하고 하락해 오면서, 대통령은 최고
경제학자들에게 그것을 안정시킬 방법을 찾게 했다. 그들은
다수의 가능한 방안들을 논의한 후, 정부 자금을 즉시
사용해서, 그것을 다시 경제로 환원할 중산층 가족들에게 나눠
주는 방법을 찾을 것을 조언했다.

A Match each definition with the correct word.

1 ⓓ   2 ⓔ   3 ⓕ   4 ⓖ
5 ⓒ   6 ⓐ   7 ⓗ   8 ⓑ

B Choose the word that is closest in meaning to each underlined word.

1 ⓐ 만약 식물의 뿌리가 불침투성이라면, 토양에서 수분을 얻지 못할 것이다.

2 ⓓ 각각의 개미는 죽은 메뚜기의 사체 조각을 보금자리로 날랐다.

3 ⓑ 일반적으로 사냥 집단의 지배적인 동물이 첫 번째로 먹이를 먹게 될 것이다.

4 ⓓ 연못의 수위가 충분히 높지 않으면, 어떤 어류도 그 연못에서 살 수 없을 것이다.

5 ⓒ 게와 다른 갑각류들은 정기적으로 딱딱한 외피를 벗고 새 외피를 만든다.

6 ⓑ 신장의 주요 역할은 독소와 노폐물을 제거해 혈액을 정화하는 것이다.

7 ⓒ 악성 종양 내의 세포들은 걷잡을 수 없이 증식하면서, 그 과정에서 다른 조직들을 파괴할 것이다.

A Match each definition with the correct word.

1 ⓓ   2 ⓐ   3 ⓑ   4 ⓖ
5 ⓗ   6 ⓔ   7 ⓒ   8 ⓕ

B Choose the word that is closest in meaning to each underlined word.

1 ⓒ 포식동물들의 개체수가 줄어들기 시작하면서, 그것들의 피식자 개체수가 늘어나고 있다.

2 ⓑ 물체의 표면에 반사되지 않는 빛은 흡수되어 열로 전환된다.

3 ⓑ 만약 신체의 근육들이 오랫동안 사용되지 않거나 충분히 사용되지 않으면, 약해지기 시작할 수 있다.

4 ⓓ 향수를 만들기 위해, 향기로운 화학 혼합물들을 함께 조합한 후, 알코올과 섞는다.

5 ⓐ 심각한 홍수 기간 동안, 어떤 개미 종들은 함께 모여 살아 있는 뗏목을 형성한다.

6 ⓓ 과학자들은 단단한 물질에 곧게 구멍을 뚫을 수 있는 레이저빔을 만들어 냈다.

7 ⓐ 인간의 눈이 너무 많은 수분을 생성하면, 그것은 눈물의 형태로 배출된다.

A Match each definition with the correct word.

1 ⓔ   2 ⓕ   3 ⓐ   4 ⓒ
5 ⓗ   6 ⓖ   7 ⓓ   8 ⓑ

B Choose the word that is closest in meaning to each underlined word.

1 ⓒ 어떤 곤충들은 눈에 띄지 않으려고 그들이 사는 식물의 잎처럼 위장한다.

2 ⓑ 인간은 자신들이 직접 효과를 느끼지 못하는 약물을 불신하는 경향이 있다.

3 ⓒ 격렬하게 흔들면 화합물들이 함께 섞여서 화학 반응 속도가 빨라진다.

4 ⓐ 아마존 열대 우림의 나무들은 1,200종이 넘는 새들에게 안식처를 제공한다.

5 ⓓ 모기들은 아주 빨리 알을 낳아서, 그 다음 세대는 살충제에 대한 저항력을 빨리 갖게 된다.

6 ⓑ 대부분의 사람들은 무시무시한 동물을 보면, 아드레날린 분출을 경험할 것이다.

7 ⓓ 물리학자들은 다양한 입자들을 좀 더 쉽게 구별하게 해 줄 배율이 더 높은 현미경을 개발하려고 노력 중이다.

A Match each definition with the correct word.

1 ⓕ   2 ⓔ   3 ⓐ   4 ⓑ
5 ⓗ   6 ⓓ   7 ⓒ   8 ⓖ

B Choose the word that is closest in meaning to each underlined word.

1 ⓓ 적혈구는 유연한 막을 지니고 있어, 모세 혈관들을 비집고 들어갈 수 있다.

2 ⓐ 꽃들의 밝은 색과 향기로운 냄새는 곤충들뿐만 아니라 인간도 끌어들인다.

3 ⓑ 어떤 약물들은 신경 자극들을 차단하여 신체 일부를 일시적으로 마비시킬 수 있다.

4 ⓑ 동물들은 포식자가 드물고 먹이가 풍부한 장소를 끊임없이 찾는다.

5 ⓒ 어떤 플라스틱은 내구성이 강하고 투명하여, 유리를 대체할 가능성이 있다.

6 ⓓ 범죄자들이 신분을 숨기려고 할 때, 이제 경찰들은 유전자 검사에 의지한다.

7 ⓒ 흉곽은 신체의 약한 내장들을 감싸고 보호하도록 되어 있다.

Lesson 25   EXERCISES   p.195

A Match each definition with the correct word.

1 ⓕ   2 ⓒ   3 ⓑ   4 ⓐ

5 ⓗ   6 ⓖ   7 ⓓ   8 ⓔ

B Choose the word that is closest in meaning to each underlined word.

1 ⓑ 과학자들은 소위 무작위 돌연변이라고 불리는 것의 이면에 복잡한 양식이 있을 것이라고 추측한다.

2 ⓐ 특정 종류의 도마뱀붙이들은 공격하는 포식자를 혼란시키려고 때때로 자신들의 꼬리를 떼어 버릴 것이다.

3 ⓒ 인간이 생태계를 교란시키면, 생태계의 균형을 되찾는 것은 인간의 책임이다.

4 ⓐ 인간 게놈 지도는 유전학에 대한 이해를 용이하게 하기 위해 만들어졌다.

5 ⓒ 화학 반응 도중 입자들이 충돌할 때, 그것들은 결합을 깨기 위해 에너지를 필요로 한다.

6 ⓓ 눈이 녹기 시작하고 얼어붙었던 토양이 부드러워지면, 일찍 개화하는 꽃들이 나타난다.

7 ⓓ 인간이 억지로 장시간 동안 정지 상태로 있게 된다면, 근육이 위축되기 시작할 것이다.

REVIEW TEST   Lessons 21-25   pp.196-197

A Choose the correct words.

1 ⓑ   2 ⓓ   3 ⓑ   4 ⓒ

5 ⓓ   6 ⓓ   7 ⓐ   8 ⓐ

B Fill in the blanks with the best words from the box.

1 thorns

기린은 먹이를 먹을 때 아카시아 나무의 가시를 피할 수 있는 길고 조종 가능한 혀를 가지고 있다.

2 territorial

식물들은 주변 경쟁 식물들로부터 물과 같은 자원을 보호해야 하므로, 영역 중심적이 될 수 있다.

3 Aquatic

잠자리와 같은 수생곤충들은 삶의 초반을 수중에서 보낸다.

4 rotate

원심 분리기는 물질의 성분들을 분리하기 위해 엄청나게 빠른 속도로 회전한다.

5 swarm

어류는 포식자들로부터 자신들을 보호하기 위해 떼를 지어 다니는데, 포식자들은 그 무리의 움직임에 혼란스러워 한다.

6 organisms

아주 다양한 종류의 미세 유기체들이 있는데, 인간 피부에 기생하는 균류와 진드기가 이에 속한다.

C Read the following passages.

1 ⓑ

원예사와 정원사들에게 인기가 많은 장식용 배나무는 보통 이른 봄에 개화한다. 그것은 매우 아름답지만, 각각의 흰색 꽃은 향기가 거의 없다. 사실, 몇몇 종들은 약간 불쾌한 냄새가 난다고 한다.

2 ⓑ

과학자들은 다리 6개의 유무처럼 특정한 기준에 맞지 않으면, 곤충처럼 생긴 생물들을 참 곤충으로 분류할 수 없다. 또 다른 기준은 그 몸체가 세 부분으로 뚜렷하게 구분되어 있어야 한다는 것이다. 첫 번째 부분은 머리, 두 번째 부분은 가슴, 그리고 마지막 부분은 배이다.

3 ⓓ   4 ⓓ

흰쥐는 종종 실험에 쓰인다. 이에는 두 가지 주요한 이유가 있다. 첫 번째는 그것들의 많은 유전적·행동적 특징들이 인간과 비슷하다는 것이다. 두 번째는 빨리 번식한다는 것이다. 이로 인해 과학자들은 여러 세대의 연구 표본을 얻을 수 있다.

5 ⓐ   6 ⓑ

원자는 만물의 구성 요소라고들 한다. 그리고 모든 원자의 가장 중심부에서 핵을 발견할 수 있을 것이다. 핵은 원자 크기의 미세한 부분만을 차지한다는 사실에도 불구하고, 원자의 거의 모든 질량을 차지한다. 왜냐하면 그것은 양성자와 중성자들로 빽빽하게 차 있어, 밀도가 아주 조밀하기 때문이다.

Lesson 26   EXERCISES   p.203

A Match each definition with the correct word.

1 ⓖ   2 ⓗ   3 ⓐ   4 ⓕ

5 ⓔ   6 ⓒ   7 ⓑ   8 ⓓ

B Choose the word that is closest in meaning to each underlined word.

1 ⓐ 소뇌는 운동 기능을 담당하는 인간 뇌의 일부분이다.

2 ⓓ 나뭇잎들이 말라 갈색으로 변한 후에도, 때때로 나무에는 잎이 남아있을 것이다.

3 ⓑ 인화성이 높은 플라스틱은 건축물에 적합하지 않다고 여겨진다.

4 ⓔ 오렌지는 구연산을 함유하고 있는데, 그것은 탄소, 산소, 그리고 수소 원자들의 화합물이다.

5 ⓒ 스컹크는 위협을 느끼면, 자기 방어를 위해 악취가 나는 물질을 내뿜을 것이다.

6 ⓖ 그 약물들은 혈장 안의 단백질과 결합하는데, 이는 그 약물들이 신체 전반에 퍼지게 돕는다.

7 ⓑ 벌은 '벌떡'이라고 불리는 것을 생산하는데, 이것은 화분과 화밀의 혼합물이다.

Lesson 27　EXERCISES　p.209

A Match each definition with the correct word.

1 ⓒ　　2 ⓐ　　3 ⓑ　　4 ⓔ
5 ⓕ　　6 ⓗ　　7 ⓓ　　8 ⓖ

B Choose the word that is closest in meaning to each underlined word.

1 ⓐ 세포 융합은 두 개 이상의 세포들이 하나의 다핵 세포를 형성하기 위해 합쳐지는 과정이다.

2 ⓓ 백신은 질병의 어떤 증상도 일으키지 않고 면역 반응을 개시한다.

3 ⓑ 혈액이 더 효과적으로 응고하는 데 도움이 되도록 사람들이 복용할 수 있는 몇몇 약물들이 있다.

4 ⓖ Albert Einstein은 빛의 속도가 일정하고 그 속도를 추월할 수 없다고 주장했다.

5 ⓒ 모든 생물은 유전자를 다음 세대에 전달하기 위해 번식한다.

6 ⓔ 사랑니는 불필요한 것으로 여겨져서, 흔히 치과 의사들에 의해 발치된다.

7 ⓓ 식물의 근본적인 특징들 중 하나는 광합성을 통해 햇빛을 양분으로 만드는 능력이다.

Lesson 28　EXERCISES　p.215

A Match each definition with the correct word.

1 ⓑ　　2 ⓕ　　3 ⓔ　　4 ⓗ
5 ⓐ　　6 ⓖ　　7 ⓒ　　8 ⓓ

B Choose the word that is closest in meaning to each underlined word.

1 ⓒ 세계적인 규모로 유전 정보를 모으려는 시도는 불신으로 저해되었다.

2 ⓓ 실험실에서 오염의 위험은 안전 절차를 따름으로써 경감될 수 있다.

3 ⓒ 고대 그리스인들은 오레가노가 다양한 위장병의 치료제라고 믿었다.

4 ⓒ 근육의 피로는 보통 운동 때문에 일어나지만, 다른 원인이 있을 수도 있다.

5 ⓑ 많은 곤충들은 자기 방어를 위해 독을 주입하는 데 쓰일 수 있는 침을 지니고 있다.

6 ⓒ 동물원의 동물들은 건강 진단을 받기 전에 진정제를 투여받아야 한다.

7 ⓐ 의도치 않은 화학 반응이 공장 안에 유독한 연기 구름을 방출했다.

Lesson 29　EXERCISES　p.221

A Match each definition with the correct word.

1 ⓔ　　2 ⓒ　　3 ⓗ　　4 ⓖ
5 ⓑ　　6 ⓐ　　7 ⓓ　　8 ⓕ

B Choose the word that is closest in meaning to each underlined word.

1 ⓒ 그 원예사는 현관에 놓인 화분에서 자라는 해바라기들을 정원에 옮겨 심을 것이다.

2 ⓑ 버너의 주된 용도는 화학 물질들을 적절한 온도로 가열하는 것이다.

3 ⓐ 한 실험에서, 과학자들은 원숭이들의 뇌에 특수한 컴퓨터 칩들을 심었다.

4 ⓑ 화학자들은 가장 강한 화학 결합조차 잘라내는 방법들을 찾아냈다.

5 ⓒ 모기에 물린 곳에 마늘로 만든 연고를 바르면 가려움이 줄어들 것이다.

6 ⓓ 해파리의 독은 피부에 경미한 염증을 일으킬 수 있지만, 그 통증은 심할 수 있다.

7 ⓐ 그 약은 기운을 확 떨어뜨려, 가장 원기 왕성한 환자들도 무력감을 느낄 것이다.

Lesson 30　EXERCISES　p.229

A Match each definition with the correct word.

1 ⓒ　　2 ⓖ　　3 ⓕ　　4 ⓔ
5 ⓐ　　6 ⓓ　　7 ⓑ　　8 ⓗ

B Choose the word that is closest in meaning to each underlined word.

1 ⓒ 햇빛에 장기적으로 노출되는 것은 피부를 어둡게 만들어서 그 모습을 변화시킬 것이다.

2 ⓑ 만약 기능이 각기 다른 알약들이 똑같이 생겼다면, 위험할 수 있다.

3 ⓓ 건기에 물이 부족해지면, 동물들은 물웅덩이 주변으로 모인다.

4 ⓑ 시간을 들일 가치가 없다는 의견들로 인해 그 실험이 취소되었다.

5 ⓐ 화학 반응이 시작되기 전에 존재했던 물질들은 변화를 겪을 것이다.

6 ⓒ 항체들은 신체를 보호하지만, 신체가 질병의 영향을 받지 않게 하지는 못한다.

7 ⓓ 비둘기라고 더 잘 알려져 있는 양(洋) 비둘기들은 도시화된 지역들에 널리 퍼져있다.

REVIEW TEST Lessons 26-30 pp. 230-231

A Choose the correct words.

1 ⓑ	2 ⓒ	3 ⓑ	4 ⓓ
5 ⓒ	6 ⓐ	7 ⓓ	8 ⓐ

B Fill in the blanks with the best words from the box.

1 transmits
중추 신경계는 뇌에서 나오는 메시지를 몸 전체로 전달한다.

2 inorganic
과학자들은 그 물고기들이 미세 플라스틱과 같은 무기물질을 먹어서 죽었을지도 모른다고 믿는다.

3 symptoms
그 환자는 어떤 증상도 보이지 않았지만, 그 병에 대해 양성 반응을 보였다.

4 spines
코알라의 척추는 굽어 있어서, 나뭇가지에서 살기가 더 쉽다.

5 derived
작은 곤충들의 몸에서 나온 카민산으로 만들어진 붉은 염료들이 있다.

6 tremendous
엄청난 수의 흰개미들이 하나의 개미굴에서 살 수 있으며, 몇 백만 마리나 될 것으로 추정된다.

C Read the following passages.

1 ⓐ
폐의 기능은 필수적인 산소를 얻기 위해 몸 안에 공기를 유입하는 것이다. 충분한 산소가 공급되지 않으면, 몸은 제대로 작동할 수 없어서 곧 죽음으로 이어진다. 그러므로, 건강한 폐는 생존에 필수적이다.

2 ⓑ
빠른 조치를 하는 것은 의학적 응급 상황에서 대단히 중요하다. 일단 환자가 병원에 오면, 의사들은 가능한 한 빨리 그 환자의 상태를 진단해야 한다. 이를 통해 의사들이 적절한 치료나 약물을 결정할 수 있으며, 그 후 이를 신속하게 투여할 수 있을 것이다.

3 ⓓ   4 ⓒ
세계 여러 곳에서, 곤충들이 미래에 주요 식량원으로써 소를 대체할 것이라고 예상된다. 곤충 사육의 중요한 이점은 그것들을 방목할 땅이 필요하지 않다는 것이다. 소의 수를 줄임으로써, 사람들은 손상된 생태계에 회복할 기회를 줄 수 있을 것이다.

5 ⓓ   6 ⓐ
방사선은 의술에서부터 에너지 생산에 이르기까지 다양한 분야에서 유용하게 응용된다. 하지만, 그것은 심각한 단점을 가지고 있는데, 바로 이러한 활동으로 인해 남겨진 원치 않은 방사성 물질들의 잔재이다. 이 폐기물은 오랫동안 치명적인 상태로 남아 있을 수 있기 때문에, 누출 가능성을 최소화 하도록 만들어진 특수 저장 시설에 폐기되어야 한다.

Lesson 31 EXERCISES p.239

A Match each definition with the correct word.

1 ⓔ   2 ⓖ   3 ⓓ   4 ⓒ
5 ⓕ   6 ⓐ   7 ⓗ   8 ⓑ

B Choose the word that is closest in meaning to each underlined word.

1 ⓑ 소설 *돈키호테*는 역사상 가장 영향력 있는 책들 중 하나로 간주된다.

2 ⓐ 이 모음집에 있는 고전 신화들은 아동에게 적합하도록 편집되었다.

3 ⓓ 이 책은 오류들 때문에, 더 이상 믿을만한 정보 출처로 여겨지지 않는다.

4 ⓐ Aristotle과 Socrates 같은 철학자들(의 말)은 현대에도 여전히 자주 인용된다.

5 ⓒ 미디어가 중요한 사건들을 보도하는 동안, 감정적 반응을 일으키는 단어들이 사용된다.

6 ⓓ 민속품을 만든 이가 미상일 때, 그것의 진품 여부를 확인하기 힘들다.

7 ⓑ 비평가들은 그 시장의 자서전에 실린 그의 정적들에 대한 서술에 선입견이 깔려 있다고 평했다.

Lesson 32 EXERCISES p.245

A Match each definition with the correct word.

1 ⓔ   2 ⓐ   3 ⓕ   4 ⓖ
5 ⓗ   6 ⓒ   7 ⓓ   8 ⓑ

B Choose the word that is closest in meaning to each underlined word.

1 ⓒ 현대 철학자들은 자신들의 생각을 일반 사람들이 쉽게 접할 수 있게 하려고 노력한다.

2 ⓑ 몇몇 종교적인 가르침들은 사람들이 더 나은 이웃이 되도록 고무하기 위해 만들어졌다.

3 ⓑ 열정적인 여행가들은 관광객에게 인기가 많은 지역들을 피하고, 그 대신 그곳의 진정한 문화를 찾아 나선다.

4 ⓓ 민속 예술의 지역적인 성향 때문에, 그것의 국가적인 특성들은 거의 일관되지 않는다.

5 ⓓ 비평가들은 그 소설가가 Hemingway를 표절했다고 비난했지만, 그는 자신의 책이 경의를 표한 것이라고 말했다.

6 ⓐ 신화에 나오는 허구적인 영웅들 중 몇몇은 역사적 인물들에 기반했을 수 있다.

7 ⓒ 역사가 우리에게 가르쳐 준 가장 중요한 교훈들은 수세기가 넘은 지금까지도 여전히 의미가 있다.

Lesson 33 EXERCISES p.251

A Match each definition with the correct word.

1 ⓒ   2 ⓓ   3 ⓕ   4 ⓔ
5 ⓗ   6 ⓐ   7 ⓖ   8 ⓑ

B Choose the word that is closest in meaning to each underlined word.

1 ⓓ 성경은 젊은이들이 더 다가가기 쉽도록 현대 영어로 옮겨졌다.

2 ⓐ 많은 훌륭한 신화적 영웅들은 그들의 용기와 미덕이 특징이었다.

3 ⓓ 수세기 동안, 철학자들은 우리를 인간답게 만드는 것이 무엇인가라는 질문을 열심히 탐구해 왔다.

4 ⓑ 이 전통 의상들은 좀처럼 착용되지는 않지만, 문화적 자부심을 불러 일으킨다.

5 ⓒ Ovid는 황제 본인에 의해 멀리 떨어진 지방으로 추방된 로마의 시인이었다.

6 ⓓ 한 기자가 그 화학 공장 폭발의 원인들에 대한 심층 기사를 썼다.

7 ⓒ 어떤 이들은 우리가 사용하는 격식어의 대부분이 가식일 뿐이라고 생각한다.

Lesson 34 EXERCISES p.259

A Match each definition with the correct word.

1 ⓓ   2 ⓔ   3 ⓖ   4 ⓕ
5 ⓐ   6 ⓒ   7 ⓑ   8 ⓗ

B Choose the word that is closest in meaning to each underlined word.

1 ⓓ 그 민속 예술가는 기술을 무시하고 대신 구식 기법을 쓰는 것으로 알려져 있다.

2 ⓐ *몬테 크리스토 백작*은 자신의 복수를 위해 수년을 기다린 한 남자에 관한 소설이다.

3 ⓑ 로마 제국은 한때 무적으로 보였으나, 결국 무너졌다.

4 ⓑ 그 기자의 끈기는 중요 정보를 알아내게 해 주었다.

5 ⓓ 1931년에 있었던 중국 홍수는 끔찍한 재앙이었으며, 많은 이들의 목숨을 앗아갔다.

6 ⓐ 많은 철학자들은 우리가 자멸을 향해 간다는 불길한 견해를 공유한다.

7 ⓓ 그 사람들은 강대국에 정복당한 후에도 자신들의 전통을 지키려고 노력했다.

Lesson 35　EXERCISES　p. 265

A Match each definition with the correct word.

1 ⓔ　　2 ⓒ　　3 ⓐ　　4 ⓗ

5 ⓓ　　6 ⓕ　　7 ⓑ　　8 ⓖ

B Choose the word that is closest in meaning to each underlined word.

1 ⓒ 신화에서 초인적인 힘을 얻은 등장인물들은 종종 그것을 어리석은 방식으로 사용한다.

2 ⓓ 때때로 기자들은 헤드라인이 해당 페이지에 맞도록 단어들을 줄여 써야 한다.

3 ⓐ 읽기 어려운 원고는 가치가 전혀 없어서, 과거에는 정갈한 서체가 필수적이었다.

4 ⓓ 외국어에 능한 사람들은 국제적으로 여행하는 것이 더 용이하다.

5 ⓑ 의미가 모호한 경전들은 다양한 시기 동안 각기 다르게 이해되어 왔다.

6 ⓒ 그 등장인물들은 작가의 공식적인 스타일과는 다른 구어체 영어를 쓴다.

7 ⓑ 유사 이래, 사람들은 먼 곳에 대해 비현실적으로 인식해 왔다.

REVIEW TEST Lessons 31-35　pp. 266-267

A Choose the correct words.

1 ⓓ　　2 ⓑ　　3 ⓑ　　4 ⓒ

5 ⓓ　　6 ⓐ　　7 ⓒ　　8 ⓑ

B Fill in the blanks with the best words from the box.

1 dystopian

고전 소설인 *1984*에서, 한 남자가 사람들이 끊임없이 감시 받는 반이상향적인 사회에서 산다.

2 mainstream

대부분의 민속 예술은 주류에서 벗어난 것으로 간주되어, 큰 관심을 받지 못한다.

3 shallow

철학은 우리가 얄팍한 생각에서 벗어나게 인도하고, 깊이 있는 사색가가 되는 법을 알려 준다.

4 ratings

뉴스 프로그램은 시청자에게 중요한 정보를 전달하지만, 높은 시청률을 얻는 데도 초점을 둔다.

5 rectify

현대 정부들은 때때로 과거에 국가가 저지른 심각한 실수들을 바로잡으려고 한다.

6 labyrinth

그 소설에서, 한 무리의 아이들이 상을 타기 위해 미로에서 빠져 나오는 길을 찾아야 한다.

C Read the following passages.

1 ⓓ

Bob Woodward는 현재 *워싱턴포스트*에서 일하는 유명한 미국 기자이다. 1970년대 초에, 그는 동료인 Carl Bernstein과 함께 Richard Nixon을 임기보다 빨리 대통령직에서 물러나게 한 워터게이트 사건에서 중요한 역할을 했다.

2 ⓒ

문학적 풍자는 수 세기 동안 어리석은 태도와 불공평한 사회 관습들을 조롱하는 데 쓰여 왔다. 이러한 글 중 일부는 더 이상 존재하지 않는 문제들을 다루고 있기 때문에, 현대 독자들은 그것을 이해하는 데 어려움을 겪는다. 하지만 그것이 인간 본성에 대해 다룰 때는, 변치 않는 특징을 갖는다.

3 ⓐ　　4 ⓓ

음성 언어는 인간의 가장 주된 의사소통 방식이다. 불행히도, 어떤 이들, 특히 어린아이들은 말더듬증과 같은 언어 능력 문제를 겪는다. 이것은 의사소통을 더 어렵게 만들 뿐만 아니라, 사회적인 관계 확립에 장애물이 될 수도 있다.

5 ⓑ　　6 ⓒ

*위대한 개츠비*는 1925년에 F. Scott Fitzgerald에 의해 쓰였다. 그 소설은 처음 출간되었을 때 엇갈린 비평을 받았지만, 현재에는 20세기의 가장 뛰어난 문학 작품들 중 하나로 간주된다. 그 소설의 주된 주제는 돈이다. 그것은 최근에 부자가 됐지만 부유한 집안에서 태어난 사람들로부터 사회적으로 수용 받지 못하는 한 남자의 이야기를 다룬다.

Lesson 36　EXERCISES　p. 273

A Match each definition with the correct word.

1 ⓒ　　2 ⓖ　　3 ⓑ　　4 ⓐ

5 ⓗ　　6 ⓕ　　7 ⓓ　　8 ⓔ

B Choose the word that is closest in meaning to each underlined word.

1 ⓓ 러시아 정교회 대성당들의 화려한 돔들은 독특한 외관을 부여한다.

2 ⓑ 그리스 신화의 매력 중 일부는 전적으로 선하거나 악한 인물이 거의 없다는 것이다.

3 ⓒ 그 대학교에는 세계에서 가장 명망 있는 철학과 중 한 곳이 있다.

4 ⓓ 대부분의 문화권에서 전통 약품은 토종 약초와 뿌리의 사용에 기반을 두고 있다.

5 ⓐ 그 작가의 데뷔 소설은 베스트셀러였지만, 그녀는 자신의 성공을 되풀이하지 못했다.

6 ⓐ 그 수집가는 자신이 진품 고래수염 조각을 구매했다고 생각했지만, 그것은 가짜였다.

7 ⓓ 아프리카의 코이산어들은 딸깍하는 소리를 내는 복잡한 체계를 사용한다.

Lesson 37 EXERCISES p.279

A Match each definition with the correct word.

1 ⑨ 2 ⓕ 3 ⓓ 4 ⓑ
5 ⓔ 6 ⓗ 7 ⓒ 8 ⓐ

B Choose the word that is closest in meaning to each underlined word.

1 ⓒ 각기 다른 몇몇 주요 종교들은 그들의 의식에 분향을 포함한다.

2 ⓐ 많은 미국 원주민 언어들이 사라졌지만, 살아남은 언어들도 있다.

3 ⓓ 몇몇 프리랜서 기자들은 잡지와 신문 모두에 기사를 기고한다.

4 ⓑ 민속 예술은 세련된 사교계에서는 주목을 받지 못하지만, 그래도 상당한 가치가 있다.

5 ⓒ 메두사는 고립된 채 살아야 했는데, 사람들이 그녀의 얼굴을 보면 돌로 변했기 때문이다.

6 ⓑ 작가인 Ernest Hemingway는 많은 사람들에게 전통적인 남성성을 구현시켰다.

7 ⓑ 그 도서관이 화재로 소실되어, 그곳의 어떤 필사본도 무사하지 못하다는 것은 사실이 아니다.

Lesson 38 EXERCISES p.285

A Match each definition with the correct word.

1 ⓐ 2 ⑨ 3 ⓒ 4 ⓗ
5 ⓕ 6 ⓔ 7 ⓓ 8 ⓑ

B Choose the word that is closest in meaning to each underlined word.

1 ⓓ 그가 목격한 끔찍한 장면들에도 불구하고, 그 그리스의 영웅은 침착함과 극기심을 유지했다.

2 ⓐ Attila 왕은 페르시아를 침공하는 것을 고려했지만, 그 대신에 동로마제국을 공격했다.

3 ⓒ 작은 마을들은 다른 어떤 곳에서도 발견되지 않는 특이한 민속 예술을 찾아내기에 이상적인 장소이다.

4 ⓑ 어떤 종교들은 신도들에게 물질적인 목표보다는 영적인 목표를 추구하도록 장려한다.

5 ⓓ 우리가 당연시 여기는 문화적인 전통들이 방문자들에게는 당혹스러워 보일 수도 있다.

6 ⓒ 사람들이 뉴스에서 읽는 것에 대해 회의적으로 변하는 것은 걱정스러운 일이다.

7 ⓐ Edith Wharton은 자신을 소설 쓰는 것에 국한시키지 않았다. 그녀는 단편 소설도 썼다.

Lesson 39 EXERCISES p.293

A Match each definition with the correct word.

1 ⓓ 2 ⓔ 3 ⑨ 4 ⓗ
5 ⓕ 6 ⓒ 7 ⓐ 8 ⓑ

B Choose the word that is closest in meaning to each underlined word.

1 ⓑ 그리스 신화에서, 확실한 죽음에 직면한 영웅들은 종종 신의 중재로 목숨을 구한다.

2 ⓑ 전사(戰史)의 열렬한 팬들은 때때로 모여 유명한 전투들을 재현한다.

3 ⓒ 한 교수가 쓴 논란의 여지가 있는 기사가 철학 분야에 분열을 일으켰다.

4 ⓓ 월든은 Thoreau가 숲에서 고립되어 사는 동안 은둔자로 생활한 것을 쓴 것이다.

5 ⓒ 그 기자는 박해 받고 있는 민족의 지도자들을 인터뷰했다.

6 ⓒ 그 고전 소설의 주제는 '인생의 의미는 무엇인가?'라는 불변의 질문이다.

7 ⓐ 라마단 기간에 이슬람 국가를 방문한다면, 공공장소에서의 음식 섭취를 자제해야 한다.

Lesson 40 EXERCISES p.301

A Match each definition with the correct word.

1 ⓒ 2 ⓗ 3 ⓔ 4 ⓐ
5 ⓕ 6 ⑨ 7 ⓓ 8 ⓑ

B Choose the word that is closest in meaning to each underlined word.

1 ⓒ 그 소설은 1968년 프라하의 봄(체코슬로바키아의 자유화 운동)의 혼란기를 배경으로 한다.

2 ⓒ 새로운 이슬람 사원 건설에 대한 분쟁은 종교적인 긴장 상태를 야기했다.

3 ⓐ Mark Twain의 예리한 재치 덕분에 그의 풍자적인 소설들이 100년이 넘도록 인기를 끌어 왔다.

4 ⓓ 한 미국 원주민 신화에 따르면, 달은 매일 밤 적대적인 한 부족에 의해 포획된다.

5 ⓑ 다른 사람들을 가족 구성원으로 칭하는 것은 일부 언어에서 연대감을 형성한다.

6 ⓓ 고소를 피하기 위해, 그 신문은 그릇된 정보를 실었던 것에 대한 사과문을 게재했다.

7 ⓓ 젊은 사람들이 전통에 등을 돌릴 때 조차도, 나이 든 사람들은 전통을 포기하기를 거부한다.

REVIEW TEST Lessons 36-40 pp.302-303

A Choose the correct words.

1 ⓑ   2 ⓒ   3 ⓓ   4 ⓒ

5 ⓒ   6 ⓑ   7 ⓐ   8 ⓓ

B Fill in the blanks with the best words from the box.

1 preserved

그 외딴 지역의 독특한 전통들은 후대가 누릴 수 있도록 보존되어 왔다.

2 demonstrated

방문 학생들은 현지 예술가들의 기량을 보여 주는 아름다운 퀼트 작품을 면밀히 살펴보았다.

3 ignorant

다른 문화권에서 온 사람들은 무지해 보일 수 있지만, 그들은 단지 다른 지식을 갖고 있을 뿐이다.

4 missionary

그 선교사는 그 지역 사람들에게 성경 이야기를 읽어 주고, 그들이 자신의 교회를 방문하도록 초대했다.

5 tyranny

그 잔인한 왕의 폭정은 국민들이 반란을 일으키면서 마침내 종식되었다.

6 extensive

방대한 어휘를 알고 있는 것은 생각과 의견을 더 생생하게 표현할 수 있게 해 준다.

C Read the following passages.

1 ⓑ

알자스로렌은 프랑스와 독일 제국 사이에 분쟁을 야기한 지역이었다. 프랑스가 프로이센 프랑스 전쟁에서 패했을 때, 독일 제국이 그 지역의 소유권을 주장했다. 프랑스는 후에 그곳을 되찾았지만, 어떤 사람들은 오늘날에도 그 지역의 국경에 대해 이의를 제기한다.

2 ⓑ

인생의 의미를 생각하는 것과 무엇이 옳고 그른지 구분 짓기 위해 노력하는 것은 철학자의 의무이다. 그들이 어떤 것을 근본적인 진리라고 표명할 때, 사실 그들은 우리에게 그들이 말한 것에 대해 생각해 보고, 우리 스스로 결론을 지어보게끔 하는 것이다.

3 ⓓ   4 ⓒ

결혼 약속을 둘러싼 다양한 전통들이 많이 있다. 대부분의 교양 있는 사회에서, 약혼하는 것은 그저 형식적인 일일 뿐이다. 그것은 법적 구속력이 있는 약속으로 간주되지 않는다. 하지만 다른 곳에서는, 집행 가능한 계약에 서명하는 것을 포함할 수 있다.

5 ⓐ   6 ⓒ

평범한 민속 예술은 보통 실용적이고 예측 가능하다고 여겨지는데, 그것이 수 세기 동안 존재했던 규범과 방식들을 면밀히 따르기 때문이다. 하지만, 새로운 세대의 민속 예술가들은 이 인식을 바꾸고 있다. 그들의 예술 작품은 밝은 색들과 예상할 수 없는 동시에 매력적인 현대적 형상들을 혼합하여, 화려하고 독특하다.

A Match each definition with the correct word.

1 ⓔ   2 ⓐ   3 ⓖ   4 ⓓ

5 ⓗ   6 ⓕ   7 ⓑ   8 ⓒ

B Choose the word that is closest in meaning to each underlined word.

1 ⓒ 허리케인이 그 해변 도시를 강타한 후, 도로들은 잔해로 어지러웠다.

2 ⓒ 그 고생물학자는 지면에 튀어나온 화석화된 공룡 뼈를 보고 깜짝 놀랐다.

3 ⓐ 동면에서 깨어나와 굶주린 곰들은 때때로 나무 껍질을 벗겨 낸다.

4 ⓑ 이상 눈보라 때문에 많은 가정에서 배관이 얼어붙어 파열했다.

5 ⓒ 우주에는 2천억 개의 은하계가 있는 것으로 추정되는데, 그것들은 수많은 별들을 포함한다.

6 ⓓ 지하에 매장된 석유에 접근하기 위해 거대한 천공기가 전통적으로 쓰인다.

7 ⓓ 보석을 찾는 사람들이 만든 작은 광산들은 현지 환경에 심각한 위협이 된다.

A Match each definition with the correct word.

1 ⓒ   2 ⓖ   3 ⓕ   4 ⓓ

5 ⓑ   6 ⓗ   7 ⓔ   8 ⓐ

B Choose the word that is closest in meaning to each underlined word.

1 ⓑ 모래는 파도가 암석과 조개 껍데기들을 장기간에 걸쳐 침식시킬 때 생긴다.

2 ⓒ 우주는 계속해서 확장되어, 다른 은하계들이 우리 은하계로부터 멀어지게 만들고 있다.

3 ⓒ 그 북극광은 잠시 후 소멸되기 전에 밤 하늘을 밝혔다.

4 ⓐ 대륙붕은 해안가로부터 바깥쪽으로 뻗어나가 갑자기 나타나는 경사지에서 끝난다.

5 ⓐ 거대한 빙산이 빙하에서 갈라져 나와 해류를 타고 떠내려갔다.

6 ⓓ 반도는 대륙에서 돌출되어 있고, 3면이 바다로 둘러싸여 있다.

7 ⓑ 그곳은 황량한 지역이지만, 지하 수원지역의 발견이 이를 변화시킬지도 모른다.

A Match each definition with the correct word.

1 ⓔ   2 ⓒ   3 ⓑ   4 ⓖ

5 ⓐ   6 ⓗ   7 ⓓ   8 ⓕ

B Choose the word that is closest in meaning to each underlined word.

1 ⓒ 지방 당국은 어제 발생했던 쓰나미가 입힌 피해 범위를 아직 가늠하지 못했다.

2 ⓐ 해저 운송 수단이 발전하면서, 해양학자들은 새로운 종의 발견을 기대한다.

3 ⓑ 옥수수 에탄올은 화석 연료보다 아주 약간 더 환경 친화적일 뿐이다.

4 ⓓ 사소한 발전들이 있었지만, 현대의 자동차들은 여전히 공해를 유발하는 주요 요인이다.

5 ⓐ 그 고생물학자는 해변에서 가져온 화석의 염분을 빼기 위해 그것을 담수에 담갔다.

6 ⓒ 이 해변은 이미 오염되었는데, 최근에 발생했던 석유 유출이 상황을 악화시켰다.

7 ⓓ 도시의 인공광 때문에 별들이 희미하게 반짝이는 빛 정도로만 보인다.

A Match each definition with the correct word.

1 ⓗ   2 ⓑ   3 ⓒ   4 ⓕ

5 ⓐ   6 ⓖ   7 ⓔ   8 ⓓ

B Choose the word that is closest in meaning to each underlined word.

1 ⓒ 시리우스 A의 동반성인 시리우스 B는 너무 어두워서 거의 보이지 않는다.

2 ⓑ 무성 전광은 많은 사람들이 목격한, 하늘의 기이한 불빛의 원천이다.

3 ⓐ 그 지역의 연간 강설량은 무시해도 될 정도로 아주 적지만, 가끔 눈보라가 일기도 한다.

4 ⓒ 그 지역은 평온한 외관에도 불구하고, 지하의 화산 활동이

활발하다.
5 ⓓ Amy는 빙산들이 녹아 깨끗한 물을 공급할 건조 지역으로
그 빙산들을 끌고 가길 원한다.
6 ⓓ 그 암석의 거대한 균열들은 물이 암석에 스며들어 얼어서
만들어졌다.
7 ⓑ 그 화석의 발견은 그 도시를 관광명소로 탈바꿈시키는
즉각적인 효과를 낳았다.

Lesson 45 EXERCISES
p.337

A Match each definition with the correct word.
1 ⓑ	2 ⓗ	3 ⓐ	4 ⓓ
5 ⓖ	6 ⓕ	7 ⓒ	8 ⓔ

B Choose the word that is closest in meaning to each underlined word.
1 ⓒ 도시의 불빛이 물에 침투해 들어가면, 그것은 유기체들의
삶의 과정들을 방해한다.
2 ⓑ 축축한 환경에서 일해야 하는 지질학자들은 미끄러져
넘어지지 않도록 주의해야 한다.
3 ⓒ 기업들이 기후 변화에 대처하는 방식에 대해 낙관적인
환경 운동가들은 거의 없다.
4 ⓒ 그 여행가들은 사막의 신기루가 진짜라는 생각에 사로
잡혀, 신기루가 있는 곳으로 가려고 했다.
5 ⓐ 화석화된 뼈대를 성급하게 뜯어내려 결과적으로 그것을
훼손할 수도 있다.
6 ⓓ 토네이도 경보로 인해, 모든 사람들에게 안전한 장소로
이동하라는 권고가 내려지고 있다.
7 ⓑ 그 공장들은 그것들이 발생시키는 오염을 개의치 않고,
화석 연료를 계속 태울 것이다.

REVIEW TEST Lessons 41-45
pp.338-339

A Choose the correct words.
1 ⓐ	2 ⓑ	3 ⓒ	4 ⓒ
5 ⓑ	6 ⓐ	7 ⓓ	8 ⓓ

B Fill in the blanks with the best words from the box.
1 vast
우리의 따뜻하고 온화한 기후와 남극 대륙의 기후 사이에는
막대한 차이가 있다.
2 strictly
그 공원 관리원들은 새들이 둥지를 트는 구역에 접근할 수
없다는 규칙을 엄격하게 시행한다.

3 relocate
그 마을 사람들은 인근 화산이 우르릉거리고 연기를 뿜어내기
시작하자, 이주하기로 결정했다.
4 diameter
그 지질학자는 암석의 지름을 재다가, 그것이 평균치보다 더
크다는 것을 발견했다.
5 vent
비가 너무 많이 내려서 교실 벽에 있는 환기구 사이로 빗물이
새기 시작했다.
6 onset
겨울이 시작되면, 그 지역의 많은 새들은 남쪽 해안으로
이동하기 시작한다.

C Read the following passages.
1 ⓒ
이번 주 현지 기온의 예상치 못한 급상승은 산설(山雪)이 녹는
속도를 가속시켰다. 그 결과, 현지 관리들은 이번 주말에 현지
강들의 수위가 높아져 도시 남쪽의 저지대가 침수될 수도
있다고 경고하고 있다.

2 ⓐ
천연가스를 배출시키려고 암석에 유동액을 주입하는 것을
수반하는 수압 파쇄법은 이미 심각한 우리 지역의 지하수
문제를 악화시킬지도 모른다. 그 공정은 지하수를 화학 물질로
오염시킬 수 있다고 한다. 천연가스가 필요하더라도, 우리는
현지 상수도를 보호해야 한다.

3 ⓓ   4 ⓒ
지난 달, 지진으로 산악 지대에 대규모 낙석이 발생했다. 몇몇
현지 금채굴광들이 금덩이를 찾아 그 잔해를 뒤지기 시작했다.
암석들 사이에서 금이 발견되지는 않았지만, 그들은 수천
달러의 가치가 있는 것으로 여겨지는 진귀한 보석을 발견했다.

5 ⓐ   6 ⓑ
우리 나라의 농업 지역들 중 한 곳에서, 농장주들과 들소들
사이에 팽팽한 교착 상태가 벌어졌다. 그 들소들은 인근
국립공원 안에서 법적으로 보호받으며 살고 있다. 하지만
들소들은 공원의 가장자리 근처에 있는 농지에서 풀을 뜯기
시작했다. 수확물의 상당한 양을 잃는 데 신물이 난
농장주들은 공원을 벗어나는 들소들을 총으로 쏠 수 있는
허가를 받길 원한다.

Lesson 46 EXERCISES
p.345

A Match each definition with the correct word.
1 ⓑ	2 ⓖ	3 ⓐ	4 ⓔ
5 ⓒ	6 ⓕ	7 ⓓ	8 ⓗ

B Choose the word that is closest in meaning to each underlined word.

1 ⓓ 땅에서 채굴된 원광은 가공되기 전에 분쇄되어야 한다.
2 ⓑ 농경지 관개를 위한 물의 과도한 사용은 많은 호수들의 심각한 고갈로 이어졌다.
3 ⓓ 그 프로젝트는 NASA와 유럽 우주 기관 간의 모험적인 공동 사업이다.
4 ⓑ 사람들이 바다의 어류 공급이 무궁무진하다고 믿었던 시절이 있었다.
5 ⓒ 몇몇 정부들은 벌써 달에서 귀금속을 채굴할 계획을 세우고 있다.
6 ⓐ 그 산업이 유독성 폐기물을 처리하는 관습적인 방법들은 더 이상 용인되지 않는다.
7 ⓓ 올해 총 강수량은 10월 말이 되기 전에 작년 총 강수량을 뛰어넘을 것으로 예상된다.

Lesson **47** **EXERCISES** p.351

A Match each definition with the correct word.

| 1 ⓑ | 2 ⓗ | 3 ⓓ | 4 ⓕ |
| 5 ⓖ | 6 ⓔ | 7 ⓒ | 8 ⓐ |

B Choose the word that is closest in meaning to each underlined word.

1 ⓒ 천문학자인 Tycho Brahe는 그가 관측한 것들을 서술한 세심한 기록을 남겼다.
2 ⓒ 믿기 어렵게 들리지만, 태양 표면 폭발은 GPS 위성들의 전송을 방해할 수 있다.
3 ⓓ 죽은 고래가 부패하기 시작하면, 더 작은 생물들을 위한 영양원이 된다.
4 ⓑ 장석(長石)은 지각에서 발견되는 가장 흔한 광물이다.
5 ⓐ 그 회사는 계획된 태양 전지판 설치를 다음 달에 시행할 것이라고 발표했다.
6 ⓒ 인공적으로 날씨에 영향을 주는 시도들은 그 결과를 알 수 없기 때문에 논란의 여지가 있다.
7 ⓓ 농경지 주변에 있는 황야 지역이 농약 사용으로 영향을 받고 있다.

Lesson **48** **EXERCISES** p.357

A Match each definition with the correct word.

| 1 ⓕ | 2 ⓔ | 3 ⓖ | 4 ⓓ |
| 5 ⓒ | 6 ⓑ | 7 ⓐ | 8 ⓗ |

B Choose the word that is closest in meaning to each underlined word.

1 ⓐ 황혼 직후, 기온이 떨어지기 시작했고, 이슬비가 눈보라로 변했다.
2 ⓒ 그 해협의 무시무시한 해류를 항해할 수 있는 선박은 거의 없기 때문에, 그것은 보통 지양된다.
3 ⓓ 지질학에서 급진적인 변화들은 좀처럼 일어나지 않는다. 그 변화들은 장기간에 걸쳐 일어난다.
4 ⓓ 환경론자들은 현재 벌들의 급격한 자연 소멸이 집단 멸종의 전조일까봐 두려워한다.
5 ⓐ 연구원들은 깨끗하고 효율적인, 찾기 어려운 에너지원을 계속해서 찾고 있다.
6 ⓒ 우주로부터 온 산발적인 전파 신호들이 감지되었지만, 패턴은 없어 보인다.
7 ⓒ 인간과 유인원 간의 '잃어버린 연결 고리'를 찾았다는 그 남자의 주장은 완전한 거짓이었다.

Lesson **49** **EXERCISES** p.365

A Match each definition with the correct word.

| 1 ⓖ | 2 ⓑ | 3 ⓔ | 4 ⓐ |
| 5 ⓓ | 6 ⓒ | 7 ⓗ | 8 ⓕ |

B Choose the word that is closest in meaning to each underlined word.

1 ⓑ 공룡들은 아이들을 매혹시키기 때문에, 어린 학습자들이 과학을 접하게 하는 데 사용될 수 있다.
2 ⓓ 따뜻하고 촉촉한 공기가 상승해 차가워지면서, 수분이 응결되어 구름을 형성하기 시작한다.
3 ⓓ 전문가들은 옥수수가 효과적인 에탄올 원이라는 주장에 신중한 입장을 취하는데, 그것이 결점을 갖고 있기 때문이다.
4 ⓑ 그 호수의 얼어붙은 포말들은 메탄으로 가득 차 있어서, 불에 노출되면 폭발할 것이다.
5 ⓒ 태양이 정점에 달하면, 기온이 30도 이상으로 치솟을 것으로 보인다.
6 ⓑ 그랜드 캐니언은 물에 의한 침식이 줄 수 있는 영향을 보여 주는 굉장한 예이다.
7 ⓐ milky sea 효과라는 야광 현상은 빛을 내는 박테리아에 의해 일어난다.

Lesson **50** **EXERCISES** p.373

A Match each definition with the correct word.

| 1 ⓒ | 2 ⓕ | 3 ⓖ | 4 ⓔ |
| 5 ⓑ | 6 ⓗ | 7 ⓓ | 8 ⓐ |

B Choose the word that is closest in meaning to each underlined word.

1 ⓓ 한때 사람들은 바다가 쓰레기를 처리하기에 완벽한 장소라고 여겼다.

2 ⓒ 부주의한 스톰체이서(폭풍 추격자)들은 때때로 토네이도를 찾아 그것에 가까이 가려고 애쓴다.

3 ⓒ 2017년의 한 연구는 전 세계에서 수집된 수돗물 샘플의 83%에서 플라스틱 오염 물질을 발견했다.

4 ⓐ 금방 닥칠 일은 확실히 아니지만, 태양은 결국 에너지원이 고갈되어 소멸될 것이다.

5 ⓑ 우리의 감소하는 석유 공급량에 대한 우려가 태양열 발전의 개발에 박차를 가했다.

6 ⓓ 거대한 소행성의 충돌로 생긴 폭발이 공룡들을 멸종시켰다고 간주된다.

7 ⓑ 크라카타우라는 화산은 1883년에 분출하여, 전 세계적으로 감지되었던 재앙적 결과를 초래했다.

REVIEW TEST Lessons 46-50 pp. 374-375

A Choose the correct words.

1 ⓑ	2 ⓓ	3 ⓓ	4 ⓐ
5 ⓑ	6 ⓐ	7 ⓒ	8 ⓑ

B Fill in the blanks with the best words from the box.

1 journey
긴 여행 동안, 전기차의 배터리는 여러 번 충전되어야 할 수도 있다.

2 bleak
생명체가 거의 자라지 않는 이 황량한 지형에서, 과학자들은 공룡 뼈를 발견했다.

3 aerial
비행기에서 찍은 이 항공 사진은 아마존 우림의 삼림 파괴를 보여 준다.

4 gale
그 맹렬한 눈보라는 내리는 눈을 가로로 날리는 강풍을 동반했다.

5 maximize
그 지역 풍력 발전의 잠재력을 극대화하기 위해서는 더 많은 터빈이 필요하다.

6 markedly
많은 천문학자들은 그 별에 일어난 변화를 감지했는데, 그것이 현저하게 희미해졌기 때문이다.

C Read the following passages.

1 ⓓ
망원경은 여전히 천문학자들에게 필수적인 도구이다. 허블 우주 망원경은 오늘날 사용되는 가장 중요한 망원경이지만, 그것은 30년도 더 되었다. 2007년에 대체용 망원경이 발사될 예정이었으나, NASA는 아직도 그 계획을 실행하지 못하고 있다.

2 ⓑ
간헐천과 온천은 많은 곳에서 인기 있는 관광지이지만, 사람들이 심각하게 다치는 사고가 많이 있었다. 사람들은 놀라운 자연 현상에 매료되어, 안전 지침들을 지키지 못하고 생명을 위협하는 화상을 입게 된다.

3 ⓒ 4 ⓓ
공원 관리인들은 최근 국립공원에 큰뿔야생양을 다시 들여왔다. 그 양들은 방사된 순간 각기 다른 방향들로 뿔뿔이 흩어졌다. 공원 관리인들은 그 양들이 자력으로 생존할 수 있을지 우려하게 되었다. 하지만, 양들은 곧 근처 산중턱에 다시 모였다.

5 ⓐ 6 ⓒ
연구원들은 비닐 봉지의 실용적인 대체재를 오랫동안 찾아 왔다. 그들의 끈질긴 노력이 마침내 결실을 맺었을지 모르지만, 그 해결책은 새로 개발된 어떤 물질이 아니다. 대신 그것은 수천 년 동안 사용되어 온 흔한 식물 섬유인 황마이다. 황마는 저렴하고, 100% 생분해성이며, 재배하기 쉬워 (비닐) 봉지의 완벽한 대체 물질이 된다.

Chapter 6 | SOCIAL ISSUES

Lesson 51 EXERCISES

p.383

A Match each definition with the correct word.

1 ⓑ   2 ⓖ   3 ⓓ   4 ⓔ

5 ⓒ   6 ⓗ   7 ⓕ   8 ⓐ

B Choose the word that is closest in meaning to each underlined word.

1 ⓒ 그 영양사는 균형 잡힌 식단을 섭취하지 못한 사람들이 무기력해질 수 있다고 설명했다.

2 ⓑ 그 나라의 불안정한 정치적 상황 때문에, 여행객들은 그곳을 여행하지 말라는 권고를 받는다.

3 ⓓ 적정가의 영양 있는 음식을 쉽게 접할 수 있는 것은 가정의 복지에 매우 중요하다.

4 ⓒ 비좁은 환경에서 생활하는 아이들에게는 탁 트인 공간에서 뛰어다닐 수 있는 기회가 주어져야 한다.

5 ⓓ 그 병의 증상들이 심각하지는 않지만, 종종 장기간 지속된다.

6 ⓒ 나쁜 행동은 보통 유아들이 거치는 한 시기이지만, 그들이 발달하는 동안 재차 나타날 수 있다.

7 ⓐ 대화하면서 비언어적 신호들을 무시하는 사람들은 '사회 부적응자'라는 꼬리표가 붙을 수 있다.

Lesson 52 EXERCISES

p.391

A Match each definition with the correct word.

1 ⓑ   2 ⓔ   3 ⓖ   4 ⓐ

5 ⓗ   6 ⓒ   7 ⓓ   8 ⓕ

B Choose the word that is closest in meaning to each underlined word.

1 ⓒ 동료들에게 정중하게 말하는 것은 사내 서열에서 당신의 위치를 강화시켜 줄 것이다.

2 ⓐ 그 여자의 직업은 빈국의 사람들을 위해 저렴한 인공 수족(의수·의족)을 개발하는 것을 포함한다.

3 ⓑ 그 기발한 장치는 사람들이 거의 힘들이지 않고 자신들의 칼로리 섭취량을 추적할 수 있게 해 준다.

4 ⓑ 아이들은 부모 앞에서 새로 습득한 솜씨를 자랑하는 기회를 맘껏 즐긴다.

5 ⓒ 그 남자는 현재 심신을 쇠약하게 만드는 요통을 겪고 있어, 더 이상 혼자 여행할 수 없다.

6 ⓓ 경찰에 즉시 범죄를 신고하는 것이 중요한데, 그렇지

않으면 경찰이 당신을 도와줄 수 없을지도 모른다.

7 ⓑ 한때 이 개울의 물은 깨끗했으나, 현재는 오염 때문에 마실 수 없다.

Lesson 53 EXERCISES

p.399

A Match each definition with the correct word.

1 ⓖ   2 ⓒ   3 ⓑ   4 ⓕ

5 ⓓ   6 ⓗ   7 ⓐ   8 ⓔ

B Choose the word that is closest in meaning to each underlined word.

1 ⓒ 어떤 직업들은 심각한 위험들에 직면할 수 있기 때문에 용기 있는 태도를 필요로 한다.

2 ⓑ 그 도둑들은 들키지 않고 침입할 수 있도록 외딴 지역에 지어진 집들을 골랐다.

3 ⓒ 우리가 산악 지역에 소풍을 나가 있을 때도, 휴대폰은 우리와 사무실을 이어 준다.

4 ⓐ 그 회사는 소수 민족 출신 지원자들을 채용할 충분한 기회가 있었지만, 그렇게 하지 못했다.

5 ⓓ 단지 엄마의 목소리만으로도 성이 난 아기들을 달래는 데 충분하다.

6 ⓑ 호화로운 저녁 식사가 더 즐거울 수는 있지만, 소박한 식사도 영양가는 동일할 수 있다.

7 ⓐ 우라늄 채굴 때문에 그 강이 오염되기 전까지는, 각종 동물들이 이 평원을 돌아다녔다.

Lesson 54 EXERCISES

p.405

A Match each definition with the correct word.

1 ⓕ   2 ⓓ   3 ⓒ   4 ⓖ

5 ⓐ   6 ⓑ   7 ⓔ   8 ⓗ

B Choose the word that is closest in meaning to each underlined word.

1 ⓑ 인종적인 비방의 사용은 항상 사려 깊은 사람들로부터 노여운 반응을 불러일으킬 것이다.

2 ⓒ 그 주방의 매우 나쁜 상태를 발견한 후, 그 위생 검사관은 그 식당의 문을 닫게 했다.

3 ⓐ 어린 형제자매들은 종종 다투지만, 보통 시간이 좀 주어지면 서로의 의견 차이를 해결한다.

4 ⓐ 그 여자의 솔직하고 직선적인 태도는 그녀가 자신의 일에 집중하고 있다는 것을 보여 준다.

5 ⓑ 시간이 지날수록, 그 원전 사고의 결과는 점점 더 분명해지고 있다.

6 ⓑ 일부 업무 현장 기술은 근로자들이 시간을 절약하도록 해 주기 보다는 결국 방해하는 것이 된다.

7 ⓓ 그 호텔 지배인은 투숙객의 불만을 감지하고, 좀 더 회유적인 접근을 시도했다.

Lesson 55 EXERCISES
p.413

A Match each definition with the correct word.

1 ⓔ　　2 ⓗ　　3 ⓓ　　4 ⓕ

5 ⓑ　　6 ⓒ　　7 ⓐ　　8 ⓖ

B Choose the word that is closest in meaning to each underlined word.

1 ⓐ 그 피고가 법정에서 보인 무례한 행동은 판사를 화나게 만들었다.

2 ⓓ 그 기술업체는 장애인이 자율적인 삶을 살 수 있게 도와 주는 디지털 기기를 만든다.

3 ⓓ 전통적인 성 역할에 대한 기대와는 달리, 남자들은 아이들을 양육할 수 있다.

4 ⓒ 많은 부모들은 자기 아이들이 짜증 낼까 봐, 비행기에 태우는 것을 주저한다.

5 ⓑ 정부는 새로운 공중 위생 수칙을 도입했지만, 많은 사람들은 따르기를 거부하고 있다.

6 ⓐ 얼굴 표정은 때때로 사람들이 예의상 말로 표현하지 못하는 감정들을 드러낸다.

7 ⓑ 그 회사는 고용인들의 요구를 받아들여 추가 직원을 채용하는 데 동의했다.

REVIEW TEST Lessons 51-55 pp.414-415

A Choose the correct words.

1 ⓒ　　2 ⓓ　　3 ⓒ　　4 ⓐ

5 ⓓ　　6 ⓑ　　7 ⓒ　　8 ⓐ

B Fill in the blanks with the best words from the box.

1 digest
　신체가 한끼 식사를 완전히 소화시키는 데는 보통 1일에서 3일 정도 걸린다.

2 miscommunication
　제빵사와의 의사소통 오류로 그 케이크에 잘못된 이름이
쓰여졌다.

3 companion
　그 애완견은 그 아이의 충실한 동반자여서, 아이가 가는 곳은 어디든 따라다녔다.

4 intervention
　두 승객의 싸움을 중지시키는 데 그 승무원의 중재가 필요했다.

5 delay
　발육 지체 때문에 그 소년은 다른 급우들보다 뒤처지게 되었다.

6 protocol
　간호사들은 전염병 환자들을 상대할 때 엄격한 프로토콜을 지켜야 한다.

C Read the following passages.

1 ⓒ
　그 트래커들은 강력한 폭풍이 몰아칠 때 황무지 깊은 곳에 있었다. 그들은 비바람을 피하려고, 작고 낡은 오두막으로 뛰어갔다. 그곳에 사는 노부부가 친절히 그들에게 쉴 곳을 제공했고, 트래커들은 그들의 식량을 기꺼이 노부부와 함께 나눠 먹었다.

2 ⓑ
　오랫동안, 냉동 요구르트는 많은 칼로리를 섭취하지 않고 아이스크림을 즐기고 싶어하는 사람들에게 인기 있는 대체재였다. 하지만 요구르트의 맛을 더 좋게 하려고 설탕이 종종 첨가되므로, 그것은 많은 사람들이 믿고 있는 것만큼 건강한 선택이 아닐 수 있다.

3 ⓐ　　4 ⓑ
　국제 기구의 회원들이 산악 지대의 한 마을을 방문 중이다. 그 마을은 현재는 평온하지만, 최근 전쟁으로 심각한 피해를 입었다. 그 회원들은 그곳의 하수도를 수리하고 수돗물을 복원시키기 위해 그곳에 있다. 그들은 멋진 경치를 감상한 후, 작업에 착수했다.

5 ⓓ　　6 ⓒ
　소심한 학생들은 건강한 사회관계를 맺는 데 또래 아이들보다 훨씬 덜 주도적일 수 있다. 예를 들면, 각기 다른 학급의 학생들이 함께 모이는 조직적인 학교 행사에서, 그들은 익숙한 사람들과 붙어 있으며 다른 이들과 어울리는 것을 거부할 수 있다. 그들이 좀 더 사회적으로 용기를 내도록 부드럽게 유도하는 것은 선생님들과 다른 어른들의 몫이다.

Lesson 56 EXERCISES
p.421

A Match each definition with the correct word.

1 ⓗ　　2 ⓒ　　3 ⓐ　　4 ⓓ

5 ⓔ　　6 ⓕ　　7 ⓖ　　8 ⓑ

B Choose the word that is closest in meaning to each underlined word.

1 ⓓ 가정에서 신선한 식단을 준비하는 것에 대해서라면, 장점이 단점보다 훨씬 많다.

2 ⓒ 비행기 창문은 높은 고도에 존재하는 극도로 높은 기압을 견디도록 제작된다.

3 ⓓ 감독자 없이 어린 학생들로 가득 찬 교실은 이내 불화의 상태로 빠질 것이다.

4 ⓑ 그 여자는 도둑들에게 어떠한 반감도 없었기 때문에, 그들이 법정에서 한 사과를 받아들였다.

5 ⓐ 50년 전에는 텔레비전이 벽에 걸 수 있을 만큼 얇아질 것이라는 것을 상상도 할 수 없었다.

6 ⓐ 우리는 대부분 조롱에 대처하는 가장 좋은 방법이 그저 그것을 무시하는 것이라는 것을 어린 나이에 알게 된다.

7 ⓒ 전염병이 급속도로 퍼지면서, 주민들은 시골 지역으로 도망치기 시작했다.

Lesson 57 EXERCISES
p.429

A Match each definition with the correct word.

| 1 ⓓ | 2 ⓐ | 3 ⓔ | 4 ⓒ |
| 5 ⓖ | 6 ⓑ | 7 ⓗ | 8 ⓕ |

B Choose the word that is closest in meaning to each underlined word.

1 ⓒ 병균의 확산을 막기 위해, 사람들은 손을 자주 씻으라는 권고를 받는다.

2 ⓓ 그 여자는 자신이 받은 이메일이 위조됐을 것이라는 의심이 들어, 즉시 은행에 전화했다.

3 ⓐ 여행자들이 이 기기를 물병에 넣으면, 위험한 이물질들을 걸러 준다.

4 ⓓ 한때 범죄자들의 신원을 파악하는 데 지문이 쓰였지만, 지금은 더 수준 높은 방법들을 사용할 수 있다.

5 ⓑ 바비큐를 자주 해 먹는다면, 육류용 온도계는 꼭 구매해야 하는 필수 도구이다.

6 ⓒ 동료에게 인종차별적인 발언을 하는 것은 업무 현장에서 옳지 않은 행동의 전형으로 간주된다.

7 ⓑ 교대 근무를 끝내기 전에 계산대 서랍에 있는 돈의 액수를 확인하는 것이 계산원의 책임이다.

Lesson 58 EXERCISES
p.435

A Match each definition with the correct word.

| 1 ⓖ | 2 ⓓ | 3 ⓐ | 4 ⓔ |
| 5 ⓕ | 6 ⓒ | 7 ⓗ | 8 ⓑ |

B Choose the word that is closest in meaning to each underlined word.

1 ⓒ 그 범인은 아주 수완이 뛰어나, 경찰을 피하는 교묘한 방법을 항상 생각해 냈다.

2 ⓐ 아이들이 소중하게 여겨지고 존중 받는다고 느끼면, 대개 반항적이기보다는 협조적이 된다.

3 ⓑ 차내 방송 설비를 통한 그 관광버스 운전자의 상냥한 설명은 승객들을 편안하게 했다.

4 ⓒ 그 공장은 과도한 오염 물질을 배출하고 있지 않은지 확인하기 위한 점검을 받을 것이다.

5 ⓐ 그 소프트웨어 디자이너는 경력의 정점 시기에 업계 최고라고 여겨졌다.

6 ⓑ 공중 보건국장은 그의 부서가 발병을 막는 데 실패하자, 사임했다.

7 ⓓ 그 회사는 성별이나 인종에 관계 없이, 전문 지식만 보고 직원들을 고용한다.

Lesson 59 EXERCISES
p.443

A Match each definition with the correct word.

| 1 ⓔ | 2 ⓖ | 3 ⓑ | 4 ⓗ |
| 5 ⓕ | 6 ⓒ | 7 ⓓ | 8 ⓐ |

B Choose the word that is closest in meaning to each underlined word.

1 ⓑ 전해진 바에 의하면, 한 공장이 폐기물 처리 비용을 아끼기 위해 유독성 폐기물을 강에 폐기했다고 한다.

2 ⓓ 정부는 그 소형 비디오 녹화 장치가 스파이 행위에 사용될까 봐 우려한다.

3 ⓒ 그 위조범의 공범 셋이 그가 100달러짜리 위조 지폐들을 찍어 내어 퍼뜨리는 것을 도왔다.

4 ⓑ 경찰은 그 살인 사건이 증오 범죄였는지의 여부를 알아 내기 위해 수사 중이다.

5 ⓐ 학교 운동장에 있는 벽화를 훼손한 그 문제아는 상담을 위해 상담 전문가에게 보내졌다.

6 ⓒ 한 반군 단체가 여행객들을 붙잡아 몇 개월 동안 인질로 삼았다.

7 ⓓ 이 패스트푸드 음식점은 다량의 염분과 지방을 포함한 메뉴 항목들을 구성하는 것으로 악명이 높다.

Lesson 60 EXERCISES
p.449

A Match each definition with the correct word.

| 1 ⓓ | 2 ⓕ | 3 ⓐ | 4 ⓗ |
| 5 ⓑ | 6 ⓒ | 7 ⓖ | 8 ⓔ |

B Choose the word that is closest in meaning to each underlined word.

1 ⓒ 박테리아는 냉장되지 않은 음식을 쉽게 오염시켜 그것을 먹은 사람들이 병에 걸리게 한다.

2 ⓐ 다툼을 시작하는 아이는 갈등을 평화적으로 해결하는 방법을 배워야 한다.

3 ⓐ 인종에 따라 사람들을 판단하는 것은 그들의 자존감을 엄청나게 손상시키는 영향을 줄 수 있다.

4 ⓑ 하수 처리장의 침전물을 비료로 쓰는 관행은 공중 위생에 위험 요소가 된다.

5 ⓓ 직장에서 정치를 논하는 것은 반드시 사기에 부정적인 영향을 주는 충돌을 야기할 것이다.

6 ⓐ 좋지 않은 식습관과 운동 부족은 복부 주위에 체지방이 축적되는 결과를 초래할 수 있다.

7 ⓒ 경보 문자를 보내는 것은 대중에게 위험을 알리는 데 효과적인 방법이다.

REVIEW TEST Lessons 56-60 pp.450-451

A Choose the correct words.

1 ⓑ	2 ⓒ	3 ⓑ	4 ⓓ
5 ⓑ	6 ⓓ	7 ⓓ	8 ⓑ

B Fill in the blanks with the best words from the box.

1 procrastinate
습관적으로 일을 미루는 근로자들은 좀처럼 제시간에 일을 끝내지 못한다.

2 combat
사람들을 교육하는 것이 사회적인 인종 차별과 성 차별을 방지하는 가장 좋은 방법일 것이다.

3 witness
경찰은 산골짜기에 쓰레기를 버리는 남자들을 목격한 증인과 이야기를 나누었다.

4 exploit
몇몇 대기업들은 외국인 공장 노동자들에게 극도로 낮은 임금을 지불하며 그들을 착취한다.

5 labor
언젠가 로봇들이 인간들을 대신하여 중노동을 할 것이라 기대된다.

6 pickpocket
그 소매치기는 한 사업가의 지갑을 훔쳐 거리를 따라 달아났다.

C Read the following passages.

1 ⓑ
Paul과 Gloria는 토론토에 사는 캐나다인 법대생들이다. 그들은 종종 동기들, 교수들과 모여 법률 기술을 연습하고 중요한 판례들을 연구한다. 그들은 졸업 후 결혼해, 밴쿠버 지역의 법률 사무소에서 변호사로 일하고 싶어 한다.

2 ⓒ
이 도시는 전통적으로 기후가 온화하지만, 여름이 점점 더 뜨거워지고 있다. 불행히도, 이 때문에 도시의 대기질이 악화되었다. 뜨거운 공기는 정체되기 쉬운데, 이는 오염 물질들을 가두어 사람들이 들이 마실 수 있는 지면까지 낮게 깔리게 한다.

3 ⓓ   4 ⓐ
어떤 사람들은 자신들이 이해할 수 없는 것들이 두려워 자신과 다른 이들을 경멸한다. 이와 같은 태도는 다른 이들에게 상처가 될 뿐만 아니라, 그들 자신의 인생에서 행복을 성취하는 데 방해물이 될 수 있는데, 그 태도로 인해 절대 충만함을 느끼지 못하기 때문이다.

5 ⓑ   6 ⓐ
주택 보안 시스템은 부분적으로는 과학 기술의 발전 때문에 그 어느 때보다 인기 있다. 과거에는 이러한 시스템 설치가 어려워, 보통 돈이 많이 드는 전문 팀이 필요했다. 하지만 오늘날에는 주택 소유주가 스스로 설치할 수 있다. 보안 시스템을 작동시키는 것은 전혀 힘든 절차가 아니며, 한두 시간 이상 소요되지 않는다.

영어능력 시험 대비 필수어휘 학습서
ACTIVATOR VOCA

영어능력 시험 대비 필수어휘 학습서

ACTIVATOR
VOCA